The Empire's New Cloth

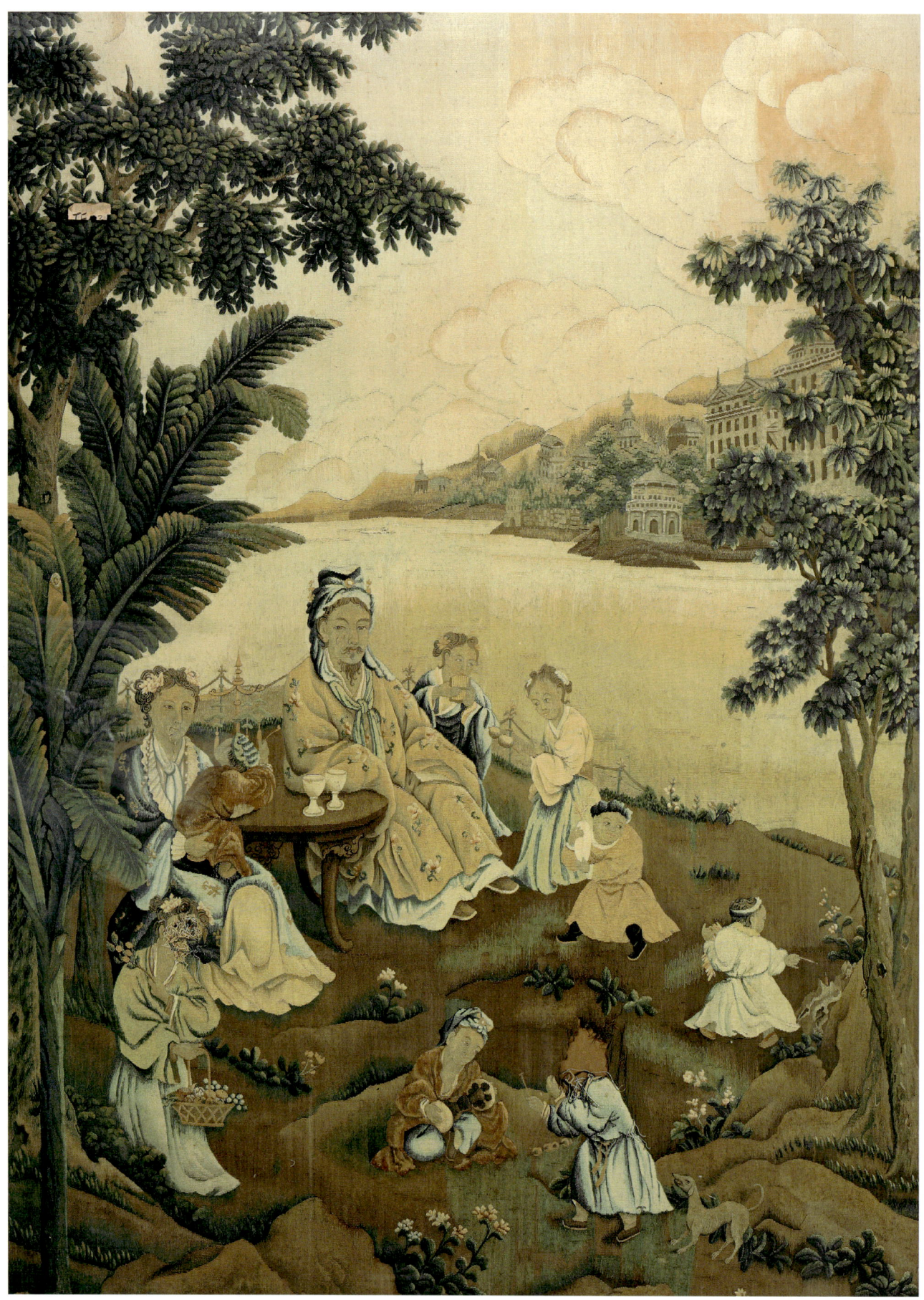

The Empire's New Cloth

CROSS-CULTURAL TEXTILES
AT THE QING COURT

Mei Mei Rado

Yale University Press   New Haven and London

Published with assistance from the Annie Burr Lewis Fund.

Copyright © 2025 by Mei Mei Rado.
All rights reserved.
This book may not be reproduced, in whole or in part, including illustrations, in any form (beyond that copying permitted by Sections 107 and 108 of the U.S. Copyright Law and except by reviewers for the public press), without written permission from the publishers.

yalebooks.com/art

Designed by Leslie Fitch; Tina Henderson, Miko McGinty, Inc.
Cover designed by Rita Jules, Miko McGinty, Inc.
Set in Crimson, Source Sans Pro, and Cronos Pro type by Tina Henderson, Miko McGinty, Inc.
Printed in Malaysia for Imago Group

Library of Congress Control Number: 2024942629
ISBN 978-0-300-27514-8

A catalogue record for this book is available from the British Library.

This paper meets the requirements of ANSI/NISO Z39.48-1992 (Permanence of Paper).

10 9 8 7 6 5 4 3 2 1

Jacket illustrations: (*front*) Detail of fig. 2; (*back*) detail of fig. 94.
Frontispiece: Detail of fig. 99.
Page 156: Detail of fig. 65.
Page 159: Detail of fig. 75.
Page 162: Detail of fig. 94.
Page 166: Detail of fig. 82.
Page 176: Detail of fig. 77.
Page 186: Detail of fig. 102.

To my parents,
Lai Qiurong and Mei Yunzhu

Contents

viii Acknowledgments

1 Introduction: Cross-Cultural Textiles and the Qing Empire

11 Chapter 1. Foreign Splendor: European Silks at the Qing Court

39 Chapter 2. "For His Majesty's Use": Western Silks and Manchu Rulership

75 Chapter 3. Encoding Global Aspirations: European Tapestries for the Qing Emperor

105 Chapter 4. Staging Imperial Narratives: The Qing Western Tapestries

147 Conclusion

157 Textile Terminology and Measurement Systems

163 Chinese Glossary

167 List of Abbreviations

167 Notes

177 Bibliography

185 Image Credits

187 Index

Acknowledgments

I could not have completed this book without generous support from many people and institutions. I consider myself extremely fortunate to have studied and now to work as a faculty member at Bard Graduate Center, an open and stimulating academic environment where I have the freedom to pursue interdisciplinary and transcultural research. I am deeply indebted to the members of my dissertation committee. François Louis, my adviser, exemplifies the ideal scholar who possesses solid knowledge and an unassuming manner. Michele Majer taught me everything about European textiles and introduced me to a splendid new field. Not only did Jeffrey Collins offer incisive comments and edits on various versions of this manuscript, but his mentorship has gone beyond this project and guided me in many other ways. I am also grateful to my former teachers at the University of Chicago—Judith Zeitlin and Wu Hung—whose intellectual inspirations have a continuing influence on me.

Many thanks are due to the fellowship programs of the Bei Shan Tang Foundation, the American Council of Learned Societies, the Institut national d'histoire de l'art, and the Metropolitan Museum of Art for enabling the research and writing of this book. I owe a great deal to colleagues around the world. At the Palace Museum, Beijing, Wen Ming, Yan Yong, Guo Fuxiang, Zhang Shuxian, Zhang Xin, Ruan Weiping, Qiu Taige, Liang Ke, Fang Hongjun, Zhang Qiong, Wang Zilin, Rui Qian, Fu Chao, Wan Xiufeng, Liu Guoliang, and Liu Zhenghong were instrumental in helping me access the key materials for this book. At the National Palace Museum, Taipei, I particularly thank Yu Pei-chin for her warm support. John Finlay showed me how to navigate the complex archives in Paris and inspired me with his groundbreaking work on Sino-French exchanges. Pascal-François Bertrand, Charissa Bremer-David, Gerlinde Klatte, and Elizabeth Cleland kindly shared their expertise on tapestries, while Melinda Watt, Anna Jolly, and Lesley Miller offered invaluable insights on silks. At the Met, the former and current team members at the Ratti Textile Center, including Melinda Watt, Amelia Peck, Giovanna Fiorino-Iannace, Eva Labson, Eva DeAngelis-Glasser, Elena Kanagy-Loux, Frantz Armand, and Heidi Hilker, have always graciously accommodated my requests for study appointments. Ken Soehner and many librarians at the Watson Library have made research particularly easy and pleasant. I equally benefited from the generosity and expertise of the textile conservators Marlene Eidelheit, Valerie Soll, Margaret O'Neil, Sarah Scaturro, and Robin Hanson.

Many other colleagues have provided research assistance, resources, or platforms to present various stages of this project. Although I cannot possibly name them all, I especially wish to thank Zhao Feng, Xu Zheng, Dong Jianzhong, Petra ten-Doesschate Chu, Philippe Sénéchal, Pierre-Yves Machault, Kristel Smentek, Anna Grasskamp, Ma Ya-chen, Heidi Strobel, Amanda Wunder, Meredith Martin, Wendy Bellion, Daniela Bleichmar, Lu Hui-wen, Jan Stuart, Grace Chuang, Kee Il Choi, Shi-yee Liu, Louise Mackie, Clarissa von Spee, Deidre Vodanoff, Anna Jackson, Lynn Hulse, Lisa Skogh, Matthew Winterbottom, Elaine Uttley, Alexandra Palmer, Deborah Metsger, Kristina Haugland, Jennifer Swope, Alan Kennedy, Bruno Ythier, Mariachiara Gasparini, Tatiana Lekhovich, Yu Ying, Joyce Yusi Zhou, and Natasha Coleman.

Over the years, tremendous moral and intellectual support has come from close academic friends. I am extremely thankful to Li Yuhang, Lai Yu-chih, Shih Ching-fei, Wang Cheng-hua, Wang Ching-ling, Wang Lianming, Yan Zinan, Lin Chi-Lynn, Lu Pengliang, Mia Liu, Xu Tingting, Tao Jin, Anne Feng, and Thomas Kelly. Constant encouragement from Young Yang Chung and Sally Yu Leung, tireless and ageless scholars of East Asian textiles, has deeply motivated me. My heartfelt gratitude also goes to two late textile scholars, Susan Miller and Terry Milhaupt, for their friendship, their belief in this project when it was still in an early stage, and their pioneering cross-cultural work.

Generous grants from the Annie Burr Lewis Fund at Yale University Press, Bard Graduate Center, and the Pasold Research Fund were indispensable for the image permissions and production of this book. I wish to thank Anne Louis-McGannon and Ann Twombly for their thoughtful and thorough copyediting of the manuscript. Amy Canonico, my editor at Yale University Press, is the best editor any author could have dreamed of working with—always patient, professional, and reassuring. Amy and her outstanding team, including Rachel Faulise, Alison Hagge, Tina Henderson, Rob Hill, Rita Jules, Kristy Leonard, Elizabeth Searcy, Owen Silverman, and Enid Zafran, have made this publishing process a pleasant journey.

This book could not have been possible without the support of my family. I cannot express enough gratitude to my parents, Lai Qiurong and Mei Yunzhu, and my husband, Andrei, for their unconditional love and unwavering faith in me.

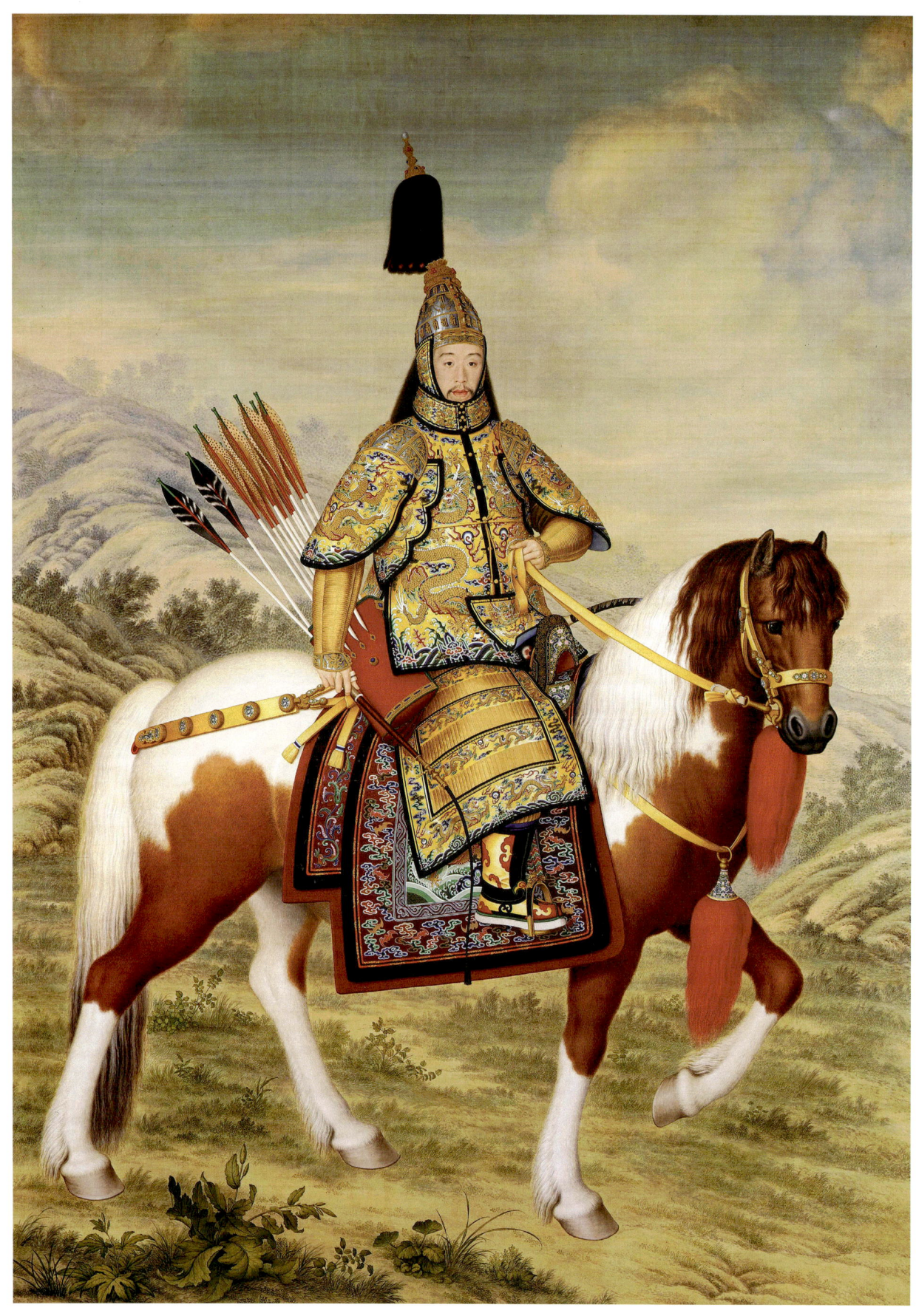

FIG. 1 Giuseppe Castiglione, *The Qianlong Emperor in the Grand Military Review*, 1739. Hanging scroll, ink and color on silk, 10 ft. 7 in. × 7 ft. 7⅜ in. (322.5 × 232 cm). Palace Museum, Beijing (gu8761).

Introduction

Cross-Cultural Textiles and the Qing Empire

The Qianlong emperor (r. 1736–95) reigned at the apogee of the Qing Empire's economic, political, and cultural achievements. He significantly expanded the Qing territories to Inner Asia through military campaigns, established the ideology of universal monarchy that legitimized his rulership of a multiethnic empire, and sponsored ambitious projects to promote both the Manchu and Chinese cultural heritages.[1] As the historian Pamela Crossley remarks on this powerful Manchu emperor, "A single person, in a single era, embodied magisterial bureaucratic government, universal dominion inherited from the Mongolian great khans, and the sagely kingship of the Chinese community."[2] To this we should add that Qianlong was also a sophisticated and imaginative patron who nurtured an eclectic European style into a defining feature of eighteenth-century Qing imperial arts.[3] Creatively assimilating European forms, motifs, and techniques into Chinese and Manchu traditions, this new style played an indispensable role in constructing the Qing Empire's multicultural identity.

Two monumental equestrian portraits of the Qianlong emperor in full ceremonial attire painted by Giuseppe Castiglione (1688–1766), the Italian Jesuit artist serving in the Qing Imperial Painting Academy, idealize this image of a multicultural empire ruled at its apex by a universal monarch (fig. 1). Drawing simultaneously from Chinese, Manchu, and European iconographic traditions, the portraits display manifold symbolic layers. Buddhist texts in Tibetan scripts, engraved on the emperor's helmet, identify him as the personification of the empire's protectorate religion; the dragon motifs on his armor assert his status as the Son of Heaven; and the implied skills of riding and shooting glorify his martial Manchu ancestry. Qianlong's emperorship is further manifested through references to European art. His equestrian pose astride a prancing horse—derived from Roman imperial statuary and associated with portraits of European monarchs since the Renaissance—reinforces a heroic image of a mighty ruler. Qianlong commissioned these paintings for the occasions of two major Grand Reviews (*dayue*) held during his reign, in 1739 and 1758. A state military ritual of the highest importance, the Grand Review enabled the emperor to inspect the regiments of the imperial army. The event aimed at showcasing Manchu military heritage and Qing political strength, and the emperor's portrait, displayed at the receptions on these occasions, was both symbolic and propagandistic in nature, representing him as a divine ruler of centralized power commanding absolute worship.[4]

The composition and iconography of the two paintings share many similarities, but there is one intriguing difference that easily escapes attention. Whereas the 1739 portrait depicts a plain leather quiver and a saddle blanket featuring dragon and cloud motifs, the 1758 portrait shows these trappings made of European silks with shining metallic grounds and large floral patterns—traits that correspond to the naturalistic style popular in European dress silks between 1733 and 1740 (fig. 2). This change hints at the increasing importance of European textiles in Qianlong's ritual regalia and propagandistic images over the course of his reign. Such a detail sheds light on the fascinating transformations of early modern luxury objects as they moved across cultures and contexts.

Following this clue, I have uncovered a range of neglected materials, comprising both European textiles that entered the Qing palaces and Qing court products inspired by European examples, at the Palace Museum, Beijing, where the majority of the former Qing imperial collections reside.[5] Qing court documents refer to both the European originals and the Chinese imitations indistinctively as "*xiyáng*" (Western), a term that this book adopts to describe the textiles in question and that will be further defined later in this introduction. As archival sources and extant objects reveal, the Western textiles present at the Qing court were mostly eighteenth-century luxury pieces in two categories: polychrome silks with complex weave structures bearing fanciful floral patterns and metal threads, and large woolen tapestries devised as wall hangings and featuring intricate pictorial designs. Treasured by the Qianlong emperor, these textiles figured prominently in imperial rituals and palace interiors at the high point of his reign. They represent one of the most innovative phases in eighteenth-century Qing imperial arts and epitomize a splendid episode in the artistic and cultural exchanges between the Qing court and Europe. Now kept in the Palace Museum's storerooms or long lost, they have left virtually no trace in the current interiors of the Forbidden City or in the copious scholarship on Qing visual and material culture.

This book reconstructs the forgotten history of these objects through an investigation of three principal sources: a core group of previously unknown silks and tapestries at the Palace Museum, obscure or misidentified objects scattered in European and American collections, and unpublished archives in Chinese and European languages. The written records, however, are scant and fragmentary. It is the extant textiles themselves that form my primary documents and evidence. This study is thus grounded in close examinations of their visual and material features, their history within and outside the Qing court, as well as their connections to relevant objects, images, and architectural spaces in China and Europe. These analyses allow me to parse the visions that drove intercultural exchanges and to reconstruct the meanings they imparted in specific historical contexts, messages that were rarely spelled out in the textual sources.

As this book makes clear, the Qing court's Western textiles were so culturally significant and complex because they lay at the intersection of two historical trajectories. First, both figured silks and tapestries were deeply anchored in the Chinese textile tradition, and by the eighteenth century, Qing imperial textiles of these types were being produced with ever more sophisticated techniques, elaborate design repertoires, and clearly defined usages. The small number of European pieces that reached the Qing palaces, counterparts of the finest Chinese works, introduced unfamiliar and appealing visual vocabularies, material compositions, weaving methods, and modes of display. When the two traditions came into contact at the Qing court, European textiles were recontextualized and reworked, while at the same time stimulating Chinese textile production to develop new stylistic and technical features. The distinct differences in both the styles and material qualities of these Western textiles made them particularly effective for conveying Qing imperial political ideologies. Second, figured silks and woolen tapestries were among the most precious diplomatic gifts and trade goods connecting the early modern world. China's role as a center for exporting silks to Europe is widely recognized, but much less is known about the reciprocal circulation of European textiles to China and their subsequent influence on court aesthetics and local production. Investigating the Western textiles at the Qing court thus adds nuance and complexity to current academic understandings of eighteenth-century global exchanges. It also foregrounds the indirect communications, circular transmissions, and unforeseeable outcomes that imbued objects with fluid meanings.

Structured by these intersecting historical frameworks that highlight issues of negotiation, transformation, and reinvention, this book traces Qing imperial encounters with European textiles that entered the Qing palaces through the global network of trade and diplomacy, and it

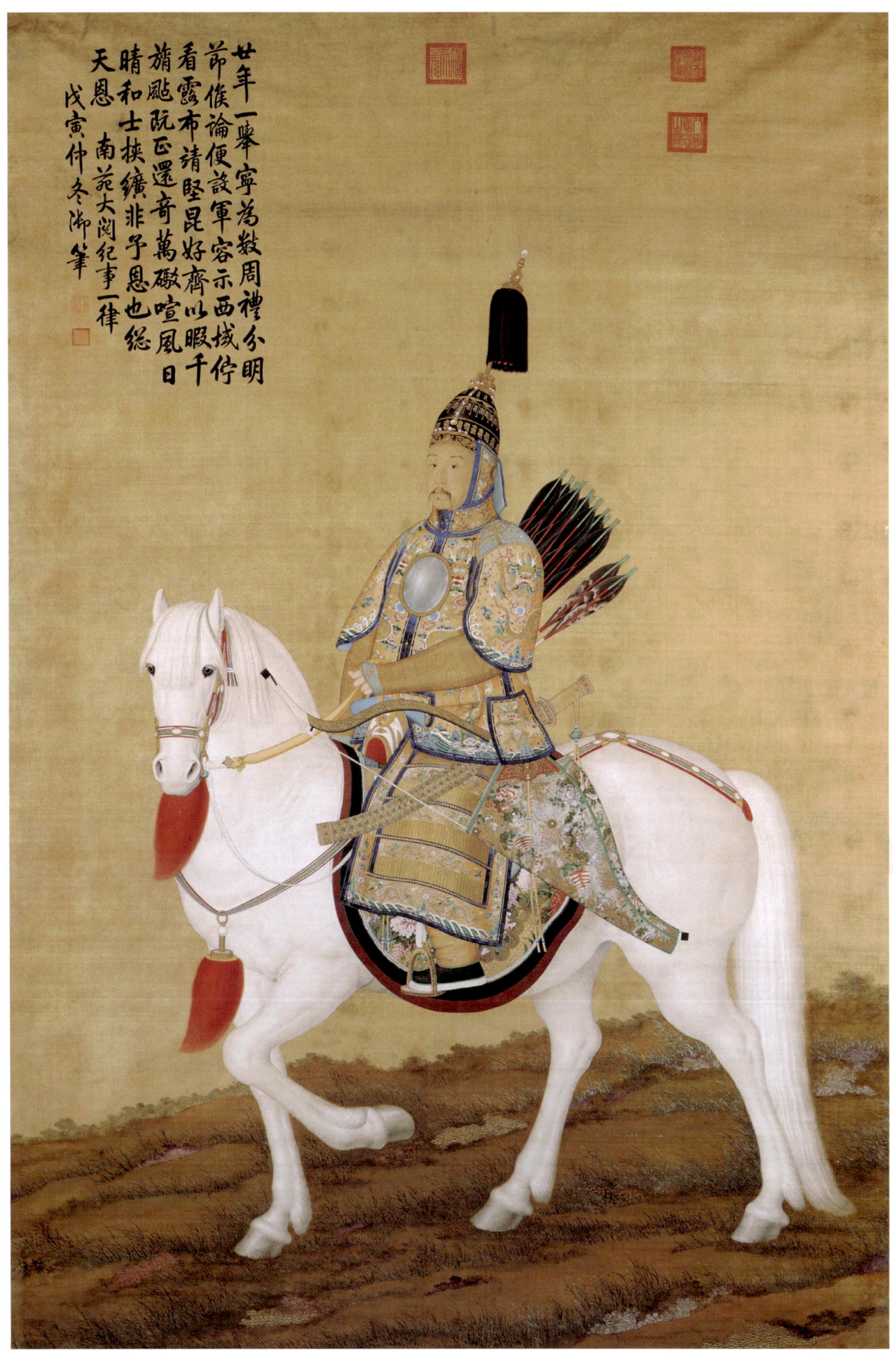

FIG. 2 Giuseppe Castiglione, *The Qianlong Emperor in the Grand Military Review*, 1758. Originally probably an affixed painting (*tieluo*), remounted as a hanging scroll, ink and color on silk, 14 ft. 1¼ in. × 9 ft. 5½ in. (430 × 288 cm). Palace Museum, Beijing (gu6488).

investigates how the court workshops, at the direct behest of the emperor, adapted their designs and techniques for new weavings. It also examines the specific roles and messages of Western textiles (both foreign and Chinese products) that were displayed on various Qing imperial occasions. Situating these textiles in their original ritual and architectural contexts at the Qing court, I suggest that the semiotic opacity of the foreign floral patterns made Western figured silks a symbolically malleable surface on which Manchu martial identity and religious vision could be projected. I also show how the visual devices and embedded spatial concept in European woolen tapestries offered the Qianlong emperor a novel means to reenact auspicious narratives that were directly pertinent to his emperorship. Together, Western silks and tapestries at the Qing court illustrate a unique pattern of imperial engagement with global flows of art and objects: European forms, styles, and related modes of seeing were internalized to refresh conventional Chinese imagery, and at the same time they created new ways to reframe and reinforce time-honored messages. These textiles were transcultural objects par excellence: they crossed and linked two geographies, and the culture of origin they evoked, however fragmentary, imprecise, or imaginary, came to play a powerful part in shaping their functions and meanings as perceived by the new audiences in the new contexts.

A GLOBAL PERSPECTIVE

In approaching the Qing court's Western textiles as transcultural objects, this book engages with issues central to the burgeoning field of global art history. The recent global turn in the discipline of art history—"global" in the sense of transcultural without necessarily implying globalization predicated on the geopolitics of nation-states—has thrown into relief long-distance networks and the fundamental interconnectedness of the early modern world. A transcultural approach focuses simultaneously on the mobility of things, the transmission of knowledge, the specific nature of contact zones, cross-cultural encounters and exchanges, the production of meanings through cultural negotiations, and the dynamism of both agents and practices.[6]

Global art history, however, does not seek to produce an overarching narrative or subscribe to a unified methodology. Various subfields have identified a multitude of special cases, each contributing a unique understanding to the complexity of the transcultural paradigm and helping shape the field as a whole. As the art historians Anna Grasskamp and Monica Juneja suggest, global art history is essentially about "finding the precise language" to describe the "processes of interaction" and "reinscription," which may involve "domestication, multiplication, reproduction, recasting, conversion, adaptation, partial assimilation," as well as "translation," "reconfiguration," and "refusal or resistance."[7] The host of possibilities shed light on the nuances of artistic practices and products enabled by global flows and transcultural exchanges, moving art history beyond its traditional fixation on cultural characteristics and notions of authenticity bound to one specific territory.

In the past decade, studies of Sino-European exchanges during the long eighteenth century and on High Qing imperial arts during the reigns of three emperors—Kangxi (r. 1662–1722), Yongzheng (r. 1723–35), and Qianlong—have yielded fruitful results that foreground the global perspective. One train of inquiry, focusing on the Chinese and French courts, has stressed the commensurability of the two equally civilized and powerful empires as the foundation for intercultural exchanges and mutual appreciation.[8] This comparative model, buttressed by a sensitive analysis of objects and primary evidence, disrupts Edward Said's theory of Orientalism, which presumes a simplistic binary consisting of "Western self" and "Eastern other" and inscribes a rigid, essentialized power imbalance into acts of cross-cultural imagination, representation, and simulation. As this book shows, eighteenth-century Sino-European exchanges were far more nuanced, dynamic, and multidimensional than the pattern of Orientalism. Communication, albeit often indirect, occurred through various channels, while curiosity about and admiration for others served as productive catalysts for revitalizing or transforming one's own culture.

The mutual appreciation between the Qing Empire and Europe gave rise to divergent rather than matching ways of engaging with each other. A group of French elites, most notably the prominent sinophile and statesman Henri-Léonard Bertin (1720–1792), viewed the Chinese system of governing as an ideal model for improving French politics and sought to expand commerce with China in order to promote cultural and intellectual exchanges.[9] By contrast, the Qing emperors' fascination with Europe hardly concerned the latter's political arena. Instead, they embraced European styles and technologies as new modes to express Qing ruling ideologies and imperial orders.[10] Notwithstanding these different agendas and perspectives, the two civilizations became deeply entangled in their search for resources and knowledge of each other and developed a keen sense of competition for cultural achievements.[11] Objects—particularly fine textiles—were at the center of these currents, whether they were new artistic productions spurred by political or economic interactions, or imported pieces acquiring new functions and values in a transcultural frame.

The recent wave of scholarship on Qing imperial arts assimilating European styles has made a major contribution to a global vision of art history. By reasserting the role of the Qing Empire as an integral, active player in the connected world of the eighteenth century, the body of work has helped revise a Eurocentric view of early modern history.[12] A series of in-depth studies focusing on specific media or genres—ranging from architecture, landscape design, porcelain, and paintings to prints and illustrated manuals—has demonstrated that European images and objects constituted a visible and essential part of Qing imperial visual and material culture, while European styles and techniques penetrated almost every type of Qing court art. Several new categories, including illusionistic painting in architectural settings, painted enamel, glass production, and clock making, were developed thanks entirely to the application of European pictorial modes, craftsmanship, or technologies.[13] This copious scholarship has elucidated an important pattern in Qing imperial engagement with Europe through which European elements enriched the traditional repertoire and rhetoric for representing the heavenly mandate of the ruling regime and for glorifying the Qing Empire.[14] As the art historian Cheng-hua Wang summarizes, European technologies and styles "lie at the core of the emperor's political agenda for visualizing his territory and empire."[15] The art historian Lai Yu-chih's research on Qing imperial tribute scrolls (pictures of foreign people and ethnic minorities in China) and albums of animals and birds fleshes out particularly well this ambitious program during the Qianlong period.[16]

By contrast, although European and European-style textiles figured prominently among the Qing court's Western objects, they have remained largely unstudied. This oversight reflects the inaccessibility or misidentification of primary materials, coupled with the marginalized status of textiles in studies of Chinese art and in the field of art history in general.[17] To an extent, the Qing court's adoption, adaptation, and manufacture of Western textiles shared features that characterized its mastery over other Western arts already thoroughly examined, namely, the emperor's absolute agency in forging aesthetics and controlling production as well as an underlying political aspiration to showcase the empire's strength. My discovery and contextualization of Western textiles at the Qing court, however, do not simply fill a gap in our knowledge of Qing imperial engagement with European styles. Unlike other art forms and technologies, such as perspectival painting, enameling, or clock making, which were novel to the Qing court's visual and material culture, figured silks and pictorial tapestries were rooted in a fully developed Chinese tradition that shaped the ways the Western counterparts were understood and used. The resulting dynamic offers a unique case and a nuanced account of how indigenous and foreign traditions were intermingled in a strategic way to serve Qing imperial ideologies. Western textiles were also distinctive from other media in their intimate interactions with the monarchical body, whether as Qianlong's personal accessories (figured silks) or surrounding backdrops (woolen tapestries). These new Western textiles thus offered the emperor unprecedented ways to physically animate visual programs incorporating Western elements and to act out intended political messages.

The global approach proves particularly productive for studying textiles—among the most mobile material objects in the early modern world—in trade and diplomatic exchanges. The landmark exhibition "Interwoven Globe: The Worldwide Textile Trade, 1500–1800," organized by the Metropolitan Museum of Art in 2013, offered an overview of the deeply intertwined and widely penetrating commercial network for silks and cottons.[18] Constant transactions involving textiles contributed to the widespread dissemination of certain designs and techniques while helping shape global knowledge and outlooks across continents. Existing scholarship on Sino-European textile exchanges, however, is predominately one-directional, centering on Europe and focusing either on Chinese export silks produced for European markets or on European designs featuring Chinese motifs and an imagined Chinese style (often categorized as "chinoiserie").[19] The reverse path of transmission and reception of European textiles in China has yet to be studied. Large woolen tapestries with pictorial representations—specialties of the weaving centers in Flanders and France—fell mostly under the category of official diplomatic gifts, valued for their extraordinary artistry and exorbitant cost. Extensive publications on tapestries have illuminated their movements among European courts and their roles in propagandizing power and spreading fashionable artistic styles.[20] Only recently have scholars begun to pay attention to two Gobelins and Beauvais cycles that reached China during the eighteenth century. Relying mainly on documents in European languages, these studies recount only half the story and have left the Chinese engagement with the tapestry medium largely unexamined.[21]

By reconstituting these missing links, this book offers a fuller view of the reciprocity and dynamism in early modern textile exchanges between China and Europe. It questions how works in textiles aligned with a Chinese specialty (polychrome figured silks) and featuring Chinese imagery (French tapestries with chinoiserie designs) in particular came to embody European messages for China and mediate the Qing imagination of Europe. In doing so, it aims to shift the narrative lens between the local and the global, and to unpack the multiple directions and strata in the process of transmission and assimilation. By putting China and Europe back in conversation, this study draws a more complete picture of how images, styles, and forms traveled a full circle replete with cultural imbrications and reinvented meanings.

THE QING IMPERIAL CONCEPT OF *XIYÁNG* (WESTERN)

This book adopts the historical concept of *xiyáng*, or Western, used in Qing court documents as the descriptive and analytical term for the materials in focus. Literally translated as "Western Ocean," *xiyáng* during the Ming dynasty (1368–1644) referred to the region from the South China Sea to the Indian Ocean. In the early Qing period, its connotation shifted to Europe, but it could also designate European colonies in South Asia.[22] In Qing imperial records, both original European objects and works made by the Qing court following a European model were classified as *xiyáng* without a clear differentiation, which suggests that these two groups of objects were perceived as belonging to the same category and were displayed as such. *Xiyáng* in the Qing court context simultaneously referred to three interconnected aspects: a homogeneous geographical area roughly encompassing Western Europe but without an exact boundary; a knowledge field comprising primarily scientific subjects—mathematics, astronomy, horology, cartography, hydraulics, and so on—introduced by European Jesuit missionaries who were themselves classified as *xiyáng ren* (people from the West Ocean) at the Qing court; and a set of motifs and themes as well as stylistic and technical attributes discernable in European images and objects, notably the pictorial modes of perspective and three-dimensional modeling. For the sake of conciseness, I use the short English translation "Western" for *xiyáng*, which keeps the term's original wording and its capacious meanings.

To an extent, the Qing court's *xiyáng* aesthetic came close to the notion of chinoiserie, a nineteenth-century term that has retroactively come to describe European enthusiasm for and imitations of objects and styles imported from East Asia, which had flourished earlier, especially from the late seventeenth through the eighteenth century.[23] Art historians have proposed various equivalent phrases—"Euroiserie," "Occidenterie," and "Européenerie"—in an attempt to name and theorize about Western-style objects at the Qing court, yet these terms do not sufficiently convey the ambiguity and fluidity embedded in the concept of *xiyáng*.[24] The most basic drawback is that they exclude original European pieces, which also carried the "Western" label at the Qing court. In addition, these newly coined expressions seem to imply that *xiyáng* was a historical counterpart of European chinoiserie. In reality, the two were very different. Whereas chinoiserie was popular across much of Europe and among various social classes, the Chinese enthusiasm for Western style was primarily a Qing imperial pursuit centering on the emperor. This fascination was echoed and extended throughout the network of elite officials and merchants in Canton, Suzhou, Yangzhou, and Beijing—all of them major commercial or manufacturing centers that supplied luxury goods to the court through commissions and the internal tribute system.[25] Also contrary to the contemporaneous European craze for China, which was frequently motivated by a strong desire to collect information on a distant, mysterious land and to represent its customs and culture, the Qing imperial passion for displaying and creating Western works exhibited little interest in developing systematic knowledge about the West or even playfully imagining European culture. The objects and activities simply employed foreign styles and techniques to reinforce traditional narratives essential to the Qing sovereignty. Likewise, another new term—"EurAsian artifacts"—which has recently emerged to conceptualize transcultural objects across China and Europe does not align with the Qing imperial vision of Western objects.[26] Indeed, the very ideas of "Asia" and "Europe" that are encoded in all these new terms, bound up as they are with the European Renaissance and early modern notions of four continents and continental geopolitics, remained vague to Qing rulers and courtiers.[27]

Although an influential stream of global art history has called for a rejection of territorial boundaries and a de-emphasis of localized cultures, the objects and documents scrutinized in this book contradict this revisionist stance and suggest that a strong desire to assert territory indeed motivated and guided Qianlong's projects involving Western textiles.[28] This focused political agenda also governed other imperial programs engaging with Western objects, styles, and techniques, such as mapmaking, panoramic scrolls documenting the land and inspection tours, and paintings of tributary people and exotic flora and fauna, all of which demonstrate the emperor's "consciousness of the vast territory under his reign and how this consciousness was reified and constructed through different types and levels of visual representations."[29] Equally important to reconstructing the territorial vision that pervaded Qianlong's Western projects is a historically rooted understanding of the Qing Empire's perceived status vis-à-vis all other countries. The Manchu Empire positioned itself as central and superior in the order of the world and viewed Western countries as an indispensable, albeit subordinate, part of the universe within its reach. From the Qing imperial perspective, access to the most luxurious and rare things from faraway lands and the process of subsuming them within its own physical or symbolic terrain reinforced the empire's centrality, domination, and glory. Acknowledging the Qing imperial sense of territory and its localized culture as an ideological filter for recontextualizing foreign ideas and objects is thus key to understanding its Western projects and products.

The New Qing History, which has gained prominence since the 1990s, provides a meaningful historical framework for interpreting the role of European elements in shaping Manchu ethnic identity and Qing rulership. Historians of this school postulate that the ideologies created by the Manchu leaders drew on both Han Chinese and non-Han sources, and that the Qing Empire's success essentially depended on the cultural links forged by the Manchu rulers with the non-Han peoples of Inner Asia.[30] The Qing emperor himself united diverse regions, which, in the imperial imagination and self-representations, included the geographical and cultural space of xiyáng, the West. The equestrian portraits of Qianlong that open this book perfectly visualize the image of a multicultural monarch. As the following chapters will detail, Western luxury textiles at the Qing court were almost exclusively associated with politically charged ceremonies rooted in Manchu and Central Asian traditions. The New Qing History framework helps illuminate the indispensable role of these textiles in embodying the universal Qing rulership.

The silks and tapestries discussed in this book reveal that the Western repertoire at the Qing court consisted of a range of carefully selected themes, styles, materials, and techniques, which reflected a perceived hierarchy of Chinese and European elements and operated in accordance with an overarching imperial rhetoric. This process was predicated on a mechanism that can be described as "deliberate hybridity"—that is, the conscious selection and combination of materials and signifiers from multiple cultural traditions, with the aim of making the end product both legible and meaningful to the intended audience as part of a new, synthesized whole. The concept of deliberate hybridity is employed here with neither the burden of postcolonial theory nor the assumption of the implicit "purity" of either hybridizing culture, and it is akin to what Anna Grasskamp and Monica Juneja have described as the "simultaneous staging and disavowal of difference."[31] As the following chapters will argue, this deliberate hybridity in stylistic and technical arrangements orchestrated by the Qianlong emperor mirrored the Qing Empire's universal and simultaneously hierarchical political-cultural map.

In addition to investigating the origin and nature of the Qing court's hybrid style, the chapters on tapestries explore how European chinoiserie, itself a hybrid of Chinese export imagery and European iconography, became in Qing imperial eyes a source of Western motifs and styles. This intriguing and seemingly paradoxical transformation demonstrates how circular transmissions and entangled appropriations shaped the reception of the distinct visual repertoire generally known as chinoiserie. It also suggests how this artistic mode, traditionally regarded as a uniquely Western phenomenon, developed capacious, even contradictory significations over the course of its movement across the globe. Recent scholarship on chinoiserie has considered how Chinese and European artists and merchants, through the network of trade, collaboratively produced the exotic visual vocabulary that became the foundation of the chinoiserie style. It has also begun to examine the chinoiserie imagery that made its way to China.[32] This book further destabilizes chinoiserie studies, a field that has so far predominately dealt with European contexts and points of view, by contributing the

Chinese side of the story, looking specifically at the reception, connotations, and adaptations of chinoiserie motifs at the Qing court. From this vantage point, I propose that chinoiserie is, in fact, a shared, fluid global style floating back and forth between China and Europe, evoking in each place something foreign and exotic while also adapting to local cultural desires and expectations.

REPOSITIONING TEXTILES IN ART HISTORY

This book harbors another major goal: to recenter textiles in art history, and in the history of Chinese art in particular. Previous publications on textiles in China have focused primarily on economic history, technological development, and stylistic evolution.[33] Textiles from a given period are either analyzed as a vector of socioeconomic progress or presented as a series of masterpieces that illustrate aesthetic changes and technical innovations. The horizon has only recently begun to expand, as exemplified by new scholarship that adopts interdisciplinary approaches, focuses on specific periods, and deals with issues such as identity, commercial networks, and cross-cultural exchanges.[34] Still overlooked are the complex meanings and visual experiences derived from the formats, designs, and materials of textiles in specific contexts. This book thus seeks new art-historical methodologies that better address textiles' multivalent roles as a synthesis of artistic medium, image-bearing surface, pictorial device, symbol, and structural and performative components. To this end, I investigate key pieces not merely as stand-alone woven fabrics but as constituent elements in a coherent visual program, and I pay close attention to their relationships to images and architectural space. For example, I examine how Western silks depicted in Qianlong's portraits functioned as a constructed display, and how the emperor's wool tapestries animated their architectural settings to stage a multilayered visual program. This approach, I believe, can productively deepen our understanding of both the function of Western textiles at the Qing court and the new tendencies in Qing imperial pictorial and architectural experimentations.

The two types of textiles examined in these pages—one silk and ornamental, the other wool and pictorial—open up a rich array of art-historical questions concerning surface, material, tactility, representation, iconography, and space. Three key aspects link these issues together and anchor my analyses throughout the book: materiality, visual experience, and performance. Materiality has long been an important dimension of art-historical inquiries, but the term itself is often taken for granted and used without a clear definition.[35] I employ this word to refer to the capacity of a textile's material components (and related aspects of scale, weight, and sheen) to shape meanings and to mediate human cognitive and sensory experience, apart from any pattern, ornament, or representative content. For instance, in discussing the metal threads of silks and the wool fiber of tapestries, I not only analyze the inherent significance of these materials in Qing imperial perceptions, but also explore how they elicited certain sensory experiences in a given context to produce meaning. Moreover, in looking at the interrelations between textiles, images of textiles, and images in textiles, I contemplate the role of visual representations in evoking or re-creating ephemeral, contingent experiences of textile surfaces, while also interrogating the tensions between the intrinsic material quality of fabrics and their perceived reality as mediated through period-bound modes of seeing and sensing.

The second dimension, visual experience, explores how textile designs (often in dialogue with their material properties) induced an aesthetic and cultural response that was situated in historical time and space. Over the past few decades, critical inquiries on period modes of seeing have proved effective for understanding historical productions and the roles of images, objects, and sites.[36] Neither textiles in China nor Qing imperial arts, however, have been subjected to in-depth scrutiny within this framework. Positioning the Qing court's Western textiles in their original contexts wherever possible, this book explores how they would have solicited viewers' attention, how this visual experience differed from that associated with traditional Chinese textiles in the palaces, and how it served to construct the imperial identity. The visual experience offered by these textiles was contingent on their spectators, an audience that shifted, depending on the occasion, from the emperor himself to those conquered and controlled by him, and at times even to fictional beings that the monarch devised. Investigating these aspects enables us to fully comprehend Qianlong's intentions in creating and displaying his preferred Western textiles.

The final lens, performance, moves from Qianlong's manipulation of vision to his corporeal and sensory engagement with the textiles' patterns, motifs, and materials in reenacting political messages. In her study on eighteenth-century French domestic interiors, the art historian Mimi Hellman has examined how the structures and contents of furniture, decorative objects, and tapestries engaged the body, allowing a kind of joint performance of both person and thing that actively shaped subjectivities and social personae.[37] Although Qianlong's deployment of Western textiles and his concerns differed significantly from those of contemporaneous French elites, Hellman's methodology is still useful in that it highlights the interaction between objects and the human body in space as an effective means to convey identity. Both Qianlong's equestrian regalia depicted in a monumental portrait and his newly woven Western tapestry displayed in a private room staged a politically charged message or narrative. In the latter case, I show how he fully explored the image-body-space relationship embedded in the tapestry's scale and design to act out his imperial identity and ruling ideology. The Western textiles provided the Qing monarch with innovative visual and material forms to devise and perform his emperorship.

ORGANIZATION OF THE BOOK

As an object-driven study, this book is structured around two types of textiles: the first two chapters focus on figured silks, and the last two on woolen tapestries with pictorial designs. This arrangement allows for a narrative centered on surviving objects as well as a full analysis of the technical aspects, material qualities, and visual repertoires unique to each textile category. Only on this foundation can we understand the very different functions and receptions of the two types of textiles at the Qing court, while detecting ways that they parallel each other in terms of the Qing imperial conceptions of and engagement with Western objects.

Chapter 1 surveys the channels of circulation, categories, and features of European silks at the Qing court. Through a comparative study of European and traditional Chinese repertoires of silk patterns and design concepts during the eighteenth century, it foregrounds the new aesthetic vocabularies, decorative schemes, and weaving methods that the former introduced to Qing imperial production. In particular, this chapter examines how, for the Qianlong emperor, gold and silver threads stood out as the major trait of luxury European silks, imbued with special significance. Chapter 2 reconstructs the history of the Qing court's production of European-style silks and investigates the functions and meanings of Western silks (of both European and Chinese origins) in Qing imperial contexts. The chapter begins by positioning the Qing court's experimentations with Western-style patterns and weaving in the global network of textile consumption and transmission of designs. It then delves into the two major contexts for displaying Western silks—imperial martial ceremonies and court-sponsored Tibetan Buddhist sites—both of which were essential for demonstrating the Qing ruling ideology and Manchu heritage. The magnificent surfaces and fantastical patterns of silks rendered them the ideal objects for fabricating the Qing imperial identity rooted in the Manchu tradition.

Chapter 3 establishes the history of the Qing court's encounters with European tapestries. A brief review of the traditions of tapestry design, making, and use in both China and Europe illuminates the significant difference between the two in terms of material components, visual styles, and embedded concepts of space. The chapter then recounts the itineraries of three identifiable sets of French tapestries made in the Beauvais and Gobelins manufactories that entered the Qing court. Their trajectories highlight the uncertain, contingent nature of early modern diplomatic and cultural encounters as well as the autonomy of objects in motion. Chapter 4 examines Qing imperial production and displays of Western tapestries triggered by Qianlong's fascination with European pieces. It first discusses the cultural significance of woolen material in the Manchu ethnic tradition and then investigates how Qianlong inventively adopted the new tapestry medium to create pictorial spaces for enacting auspicious narratives essential to Qing emperorship. The new tapestries were commissioned predominantly for private palace rooms and featured themes of familial bliss and dynastic prosperity. Two case studies—one portraying a Western family and the other depicting a Chinese New Year celebration—throw into relief the deliberately hybrid nature of the Qing court's Western tapestries. The former opens a window into the Qing court's assimilation and transformation of European chinoiserie imagery, while the latter, placed in its original context in the Hall of Mental Cultivation (*Yangxin dian*), reveals how Qianlong manipulated the architectonic and pictorial features of the new tapestry medium for performing emperorship.

Overall, this book reinscribes the Qing court's Western textiles in the history of Sino-European exchanges in the eighteenth century, offering a new and special angle on cross-cultural interactions and Qing imperial engagement with Western objects and ideas. In doing so, this study celebrates what neglected, isolated objects can tell us about dynamic intercultural connections and multiple historical perspectives, and it also sheds fresh light on textiles as a potent and versatile actor carrying complex meanings in the early modern transcultural network.

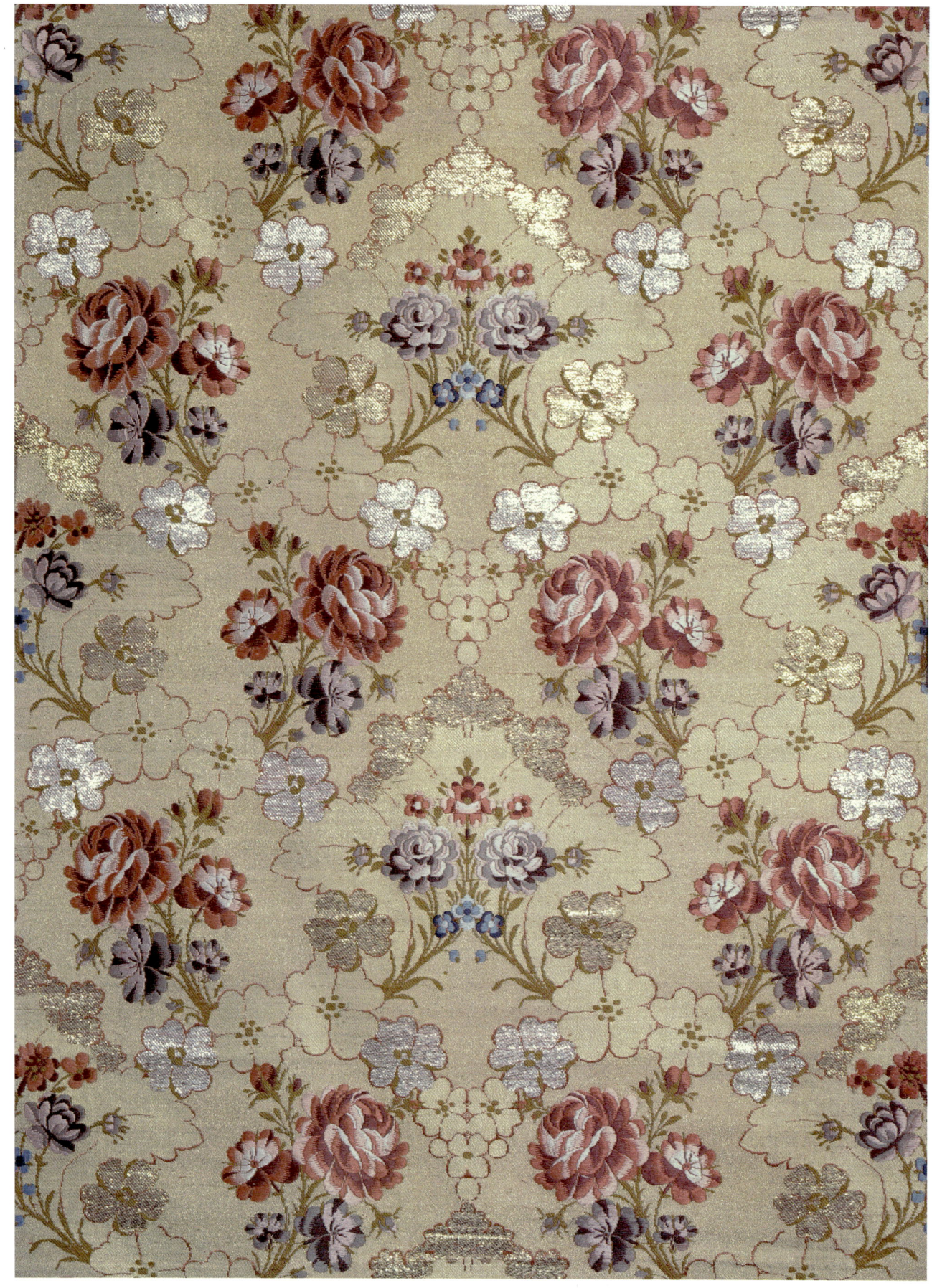

1 Foreign Splendor

European Silks at the Qing Court

By the eighteenth century, silk was a major commodity in the global trade network, and both China and Europe had developed a splendid silk-weaving tradition. Though we may know silks as imports from China to Europe, the 1758 portrait of the Qianlong emperor depicting luxury European silks reveals that fine silks moved eastward as well (see fig. 2). At the Qing palaces, a domain already suffused with opulent and refined Chinese textiles, European silks with their fanciful patterns and rich metal threads introduced compelling visual, tactile, and cognitive experiences that were quite different from those offered by their Chinese counterparts. These foreign pieces not only inspired the Qing imperial manufactories to weave imitative works; they also furnished new means for the Qing emperor to convey political messages or religious beliefs. This chapter examines the stylistic features and material properties of the extant European silks at the Palace Museum in Beijing, contextualizing them in both the Chinese and European traditions of silk design and weaving, and addressing the respective cultural concepts associated with textile patterns. This close focus on the objects illuminates what fascinated the Qing monarch about these Western textiles and lays the foundation for the discussions in the next chapter on how their foreign designs and materiality enabled Western silks to serve as visual surrogates of the Qing imperial body and to project political power in state rituals.

THE MANUFACTURING AND PATTERNING SYSTEMS OF QING IMPERIAL SILKS

As the predominant material used for imperial clothing, furnishings, and ritual displays, silk was ubiquitous at the Qing palaces. The three official textile manufactories (*zhizao*), located more than a thousand kilometers south of Beijing in the traditional silk centers of Jiangning (present-day Nanjing), Suzhou, and Hangzhou—the region known as Jiangnan—produced nearly all the silks for the court.[1] Administrated by Manchu bondservants appointed by the Imperial Household Department (*Neiwu fu*), these manufactories received orders from the Imperial Workshops (*Zaoban chu*) at court and organized the weaving work accordingly. All three establishments could weave common types of silks, ranging from simple tabby, gauze, and satin to more complex figured damasks, brocaded works, and lampas. In addition, each place specialized in certain categories of fabrics destined for specific occasions or applications. The Jiangning manufactory supplied silks used in imperial rituals and ceremonies; these comprised "divine silks" for Grand Sacrifices, imperial proclamations—essentially woven texts—for bestowing on government officials, and a special type of polychrome ribbon for decorating the ceremonial costumes of the imperial guards. The Hangzhou manufactory also wove ceremonial textiles, but its finest products were soft monochrome silks, including twill damask (*ling*), plain silk, gauze, and crepe. The Suzhou manufactory, the most versatile of the three, excelled in the production of velvet as well as *jin*, a range of polychrome silks with complex weave structures.[2] According to the *Archives of the Imperial Workshops under the Imperial Household Department* (*Neiwu fu zaoban chu gezuo chengzuo huoji qingdang;* hereafter HJD, standing for its short title, *Huoji dang*), ateliers under the Suzhou bureau also produced the majority of the silk tapestries (*kesi*) and embroideries for the imperial household. In addition, Suzhou created all the theater costumes for the Qing court and a large percentage of the textiles for dragon robes. Most of the Qing imperial commissions of European-style silks and tapestries discussed in this book were made in Suzhou.

Each manufactory followed a different production system. In Suzhou, for instance, the officials distributed imperial orders and budgets to weaving agents, who in turn organized individual weavers and craftsmen to complete the assignments in government-run ateliers.[3] The standard procedure for new commissions, as recorded in the HJD, ran as follows: the court workshops of the Imperial Household Department drafted designs based on the emperor's ideas and requirements and, upon his approval, dispatched these drawings and instructions to the supervisor of the appropriate silk manufactory. The finished works would then be sent to the emperor for his review. Those that failed to meet his expectations would be returned to the manufactory for remaking. In addition to their primary responsibility of producing silk, the three manufactories functioned as administrative bureaus and purveyors of non-textile products for the court. The emperor frequently ordered the supervisors to arrange for the purchase or manufacture of regional specialties and luxury goods. For example, the production of jade and lacquerworks for the court was organized by the Suzhou bureau.

Of all the patterned silks woven at the imperial manufactories, the two most sumptuous and technically demanding types were brocaded satin (*zhuanghua duan*) and *jin*, both of which featured intricate polychrome designs. To brocade is to weave a pattern employing supplementary, discontinuous wefts confined to the width of the motifs they create.[4] The name *zhuanghua duan* denotes

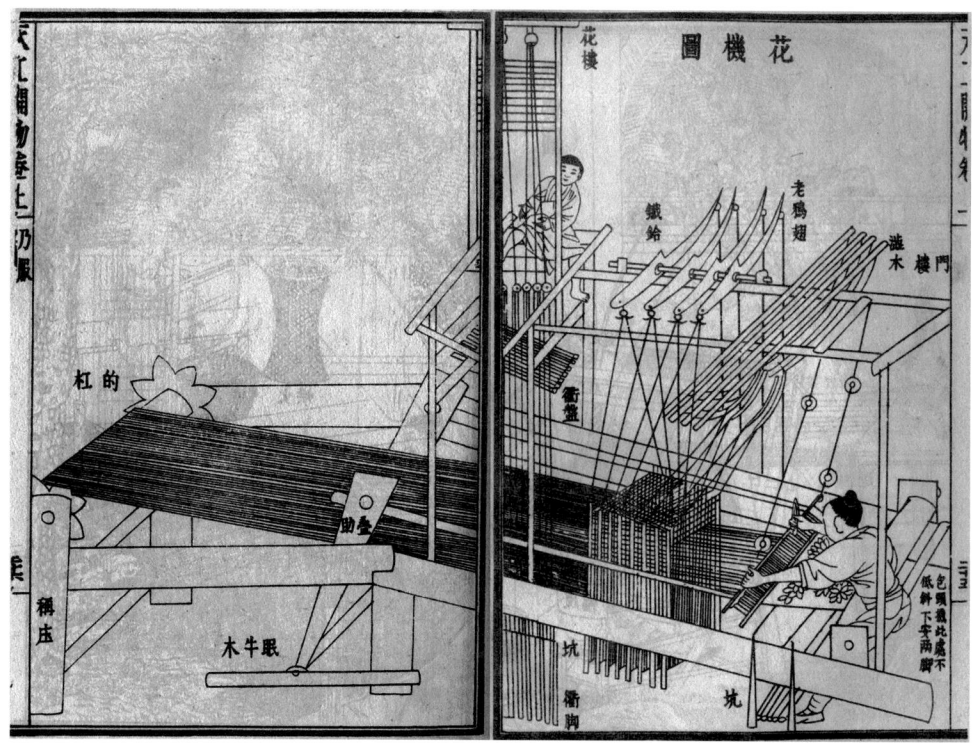

FIG. 3 Illustration of a drawloom. From Song Yingxing, *The Exploitation of the Works of Nature* (*Tiangong kaiwu*), 1637.

silk featuring brocaded patterns on a satin (*duan*) ground. The Chinese category *jǐn* does not have a single equivalent in English and has been frequently mistranslated as "brocade." Throughout the three-thousand-year history of Chinese silk weaving, the name *jǐn* has been applied to fabrics that exhibit three general technical variations: compound weaves (including both warp-faced and weft-faced weaves), double cloth, and lampas weave.[5] Lampas weave is characterized by one or more sets of supplementary warps that bind supplementary wefts to create the pattern, in addition to a ground formed by a main warp and ground weft. Lampas weave first became popular in China during the Yuan dynasty (1279–1368) and flourished in the Ming (1368–1644) and Qing periods.[6] By the eighteenth century, warp- and weft-faced compound weaves had faded from Chinese silk repertoires, and all the Qing court's polychrome *jǐn* silks of Chinese and European origins discussed in this book have a lampas weave. For the sake of concision and clarity, this book refers to them as *jǐn-lampas*. Apart from supplementary warps, the finest *jǐn-lampas* of the Qing period often combined two weft-patterning techniques—brocading and *lancé*—to compose intricate designs. Lancé wefts run across the fabric width and surface only on the front side in designated areas to form the pattern or enrich the ground. In a floral silk, the main motifs such as flower heads were typically brocaded, while the secondary patterns such as branches, leaves, and gold borders on flowers were rendered in lancé.[7] One design could feature as many as twenty or more colors, which resulted in a thick and stiff fabric.

Figured, polychrome silks with brocaded and lampas weaves were woven on a drawloom (*hualou ji*)—a large frame loom equipped with a figure tower rising in the middle. By the Ming dynasty, the technical sophistication of the drawloom had reached its height, as described in the 1637 illustrated encyclopedia of technology *The Exploitation of the Works of Nature* (*Tiangong kaiwu*) (fig. 3). Variations of the same loom type continued to be used during the Qing dynasty, and the loom structure was expanded to accommodate the weaving of larger and more complex patterns. In preparing for weaving, the textile design was first transferred to a cord system called *huaben*, which stored the pattern information. On the drawloom, this cord system was connected to a figure harness, which controlled all or part of the warp threads. The huaben and the harness cords were suspended from the figure tower. The drawloom allowed two systems in coordination to weave the design: the weaver operated the standard shafts, or the ground harness, using foot treadles to raise warp threads needed for developing a plain and simple ground weave, while the figure harness, controlled by an assistant sitting on the figure tower, executed the complex motifs. This assistant activated the preprogrammed draw mechanism by pulling the drawcords, which lifted selected warp threads in sequences to allow the weaver to pass the patterning weft threads.[8]

For Qing imperial silks, the three manufactories both fulfilled regular orders for established repertoires and wove new designs according to imperial commissions. No surviving documents from the local bureaus reveal how individual artisans were trained or how they worked, nor are there extant technical drawings or huaben cord units dated to the eighteenth century that would offer insights into specific weaving projects.[9] We must therefore rely on Qing imperial textiles themselves to understand their design repertoires and technical achievements and look to imperial documents for information about the Qing court's commissions and demands. Numerous entries in the HJD files show that artists working in the Painting Academy (*Ruyi guan*) at the court in Beijing drew patterns in the intended size of the finished textiles or on a smaller scale. These were then given to the supervisors of the three weaving centers in the south. The Chinese term for these drawings, *yàng* (literally, "model"), semantically suggests transferability, repetition, and a regenerative potential. Supervisors of the silk manufactories traveled to Beijing regularly and acted as mediators between the court and local weaving facilities. Court artists in Beijing did not communicate directly with regional workshops, whose employees were responsible for transferring the initial design to the huaben cord system and conducting the weaving. Nor is there evidence that the court painters responsible for creating the design patterns had any knowledge of how looms worked or took into consideration the various weaving techniques. In other words, skilled weaving masters assumed great responsibilities in interpreting patterns aesthetically and technically to fulfill the commissions.

Qing imperial silks featured motifs largely inherited from the Ming-dynasty repertoires, but their styles tended to be more ornate and meticulous than those of the earlier era. Despite the many varieties of silks, the majority of the nonpictorial designs used for court dress and furnishings fell into three categories. The first were imperial symbols

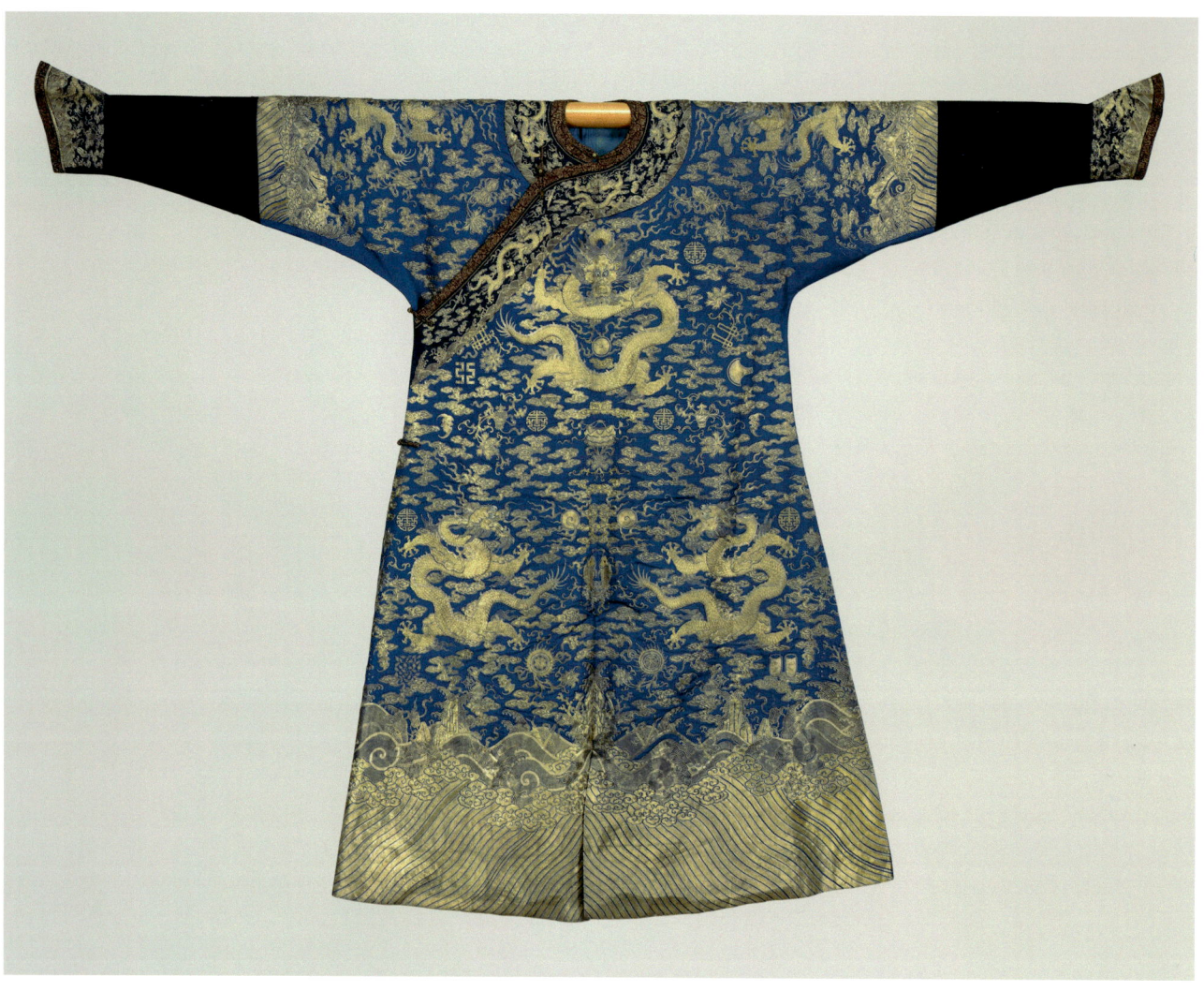

FIG. 4 Emperor's twelve-symbol ceremonial robe (*jifu*), 1736–95. Made by the Qing Imperial Silk Manufactory. Silk and gold and silver thread embroideries on silk twill, 56⅝ × 63½ in. (143.8 × 161.3 cm). Metropolitan Museum of Art, New York, gift of Lewis Einstein (54.14.2).

and hierarchical emblems institutionalized and controlled by the ruling house, consisting of celestial bodies, cosmological elements, natural and mythical creatures, and special plants and objects. They denoted the wearer's political status within the court hierarchy while imbuing a cosmic, divine order into this state infrastructure. The motifs meant for the exclusive use of the emperor included the five-clawed dragon (*long*)—the embodiment of the Son of Heaven—and the so-called twelve symbols, which originated in the Confucian classic the *Book of Documents* (*Shangshu*) and epitomized the universe and superior virtues. The composition of the motifs varied according to the garment type and the occasion for which it was to be worn, and the patterns could be both woven and embroidered. The latter is exemplified by a semiformal ceremonial robe (*jifu*) for the emperor (fig. 4). The empress, empress dowager, and crown prince as well as high-ranking princes and imperial consorts were entitled to wear and display the five-clawed python (*mang*) motif; all other members of the imperial family as well as officials and their spouses had access only to the four-clawed python.[10] The dragons and pythons in Qing imperial silks were highly formulaic: they could be depicted either in full frontal view or in profile, free-floating on the textile background or framed within a roundel. Additional devices of clouds and fire pearls provided a cosmological framework for the mythical creatures, and the sea waves and cliffs symbolized dynastic stability and longevity. Besides clothing, images of dragons and pythons appeared on imperial furnishing textiles and decorative objects.

The second category of Qing imperial textile patterns comprised representations of ordinary animals, plants, and objects with well-established auspicious meanings in Chinese visual culture. Popular motifs included plum blossoms, orchids, peonies, bamboo, lotus flowers, peaches, butterflies, and bats (*fu,* a pun for good luck). Rather than realistically depicting nature or still lifes, these motifs lent themselves as puns, allusions, or metaphors, conveying time-honored values and virtues such as longevity, prosperity, happiness, and purity. In other words, they subscribed to an overarching semiotic system expressing earthly fulfillment ensured by spiritual righteousness. Two or more symbols often appeared in tandem, as seen in a brocaded satin woven in the Jiangning manufactory for imperial ladies' informal robes (fig. 5). In this silk, butterflies, citrus fruits called "Buddha's hands," and flowers of four seasons signify a profusion of good wishes. Felicitous messages were also expressed through stylized variations of the character *shou* (longevity) and assorted antique objects. Woven patterns rarely depicted human figures, except for the images of young boys at play, a motif wishing for abundant descendants. Many silks used at the Qing court for informal garments and furnishings belonged to this category. Auspicious symbols, however, were not exclusive to the imperial and elite circles; indeed, they pervaded many types of objects and images and were embraced by all social classes.

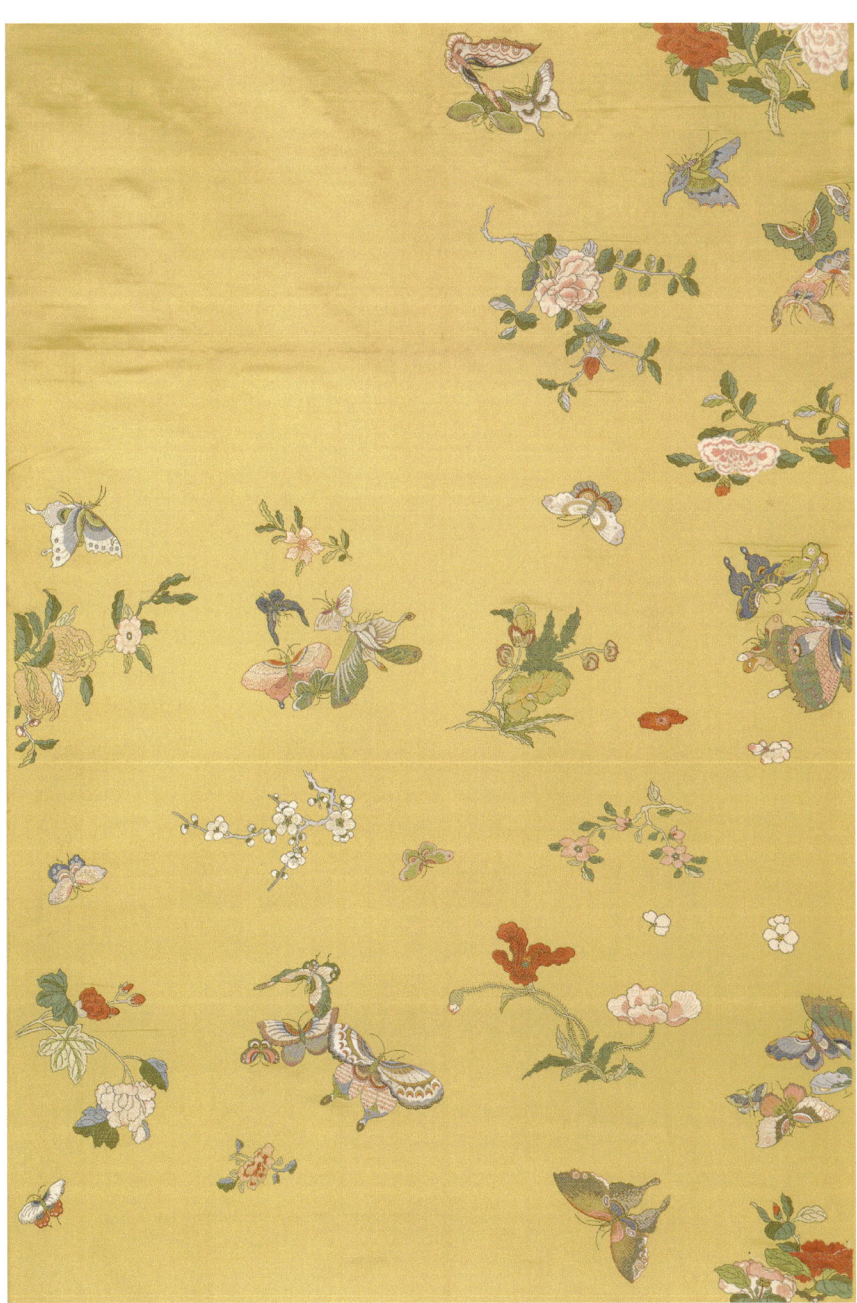

FIG. 5 Textile length (detail), 1736–95. Made by the Qing Imperial Silk Manufactory in Jiangning. Silk satin brocaded with silk threads, width 30 ¾ in. (78 cm). Palace Museum, Beijing (gu23293).

A great quantity of woven silks and embroideries at the Qing court featured these two pattern systems of authority symbols and auspicious themes, although embroideries and tapestries with pictorial designs had more diverse repertoires, a topic that is beyond the focus of this chapter.[11] The third, and special, type of woven silk, called *songjin* (literally, Song dynasty-style *jin*-lampas), was characterized by elaborate designs of interlocking geometric shapes and a complex lampas weave comprising multiple sets of lancé patterning wefts. A wrapper for the Qing court handscroll painting *Empress Supervising the Rites of Sericulture* (*Qincan tu*) exemplifies the finest kind of *songjin* made during the Qianlong period: here, large, stylized floral medallions edged by cloud-shaped *ruyi* (a pun for "as you wish") punctuate an interlinked structure, the interstices being filled by lotus flowers and overlapping coins (fig. 6). A Suzhou specialty, *songjin* emerged in the Ming dynasty, and its unique geometric patterns recalled the architectural decorations represented in the 1103 building manual *Treatise on Architectural Methods* (*Yingzao fashi*) of the Northern Song dynasty (960–1127).[12] At the Qing court, *songjin* served primarily as mounting materials for paintings, exterior fabric covers for stationery boxes and books, and borders for screens; they were not fashioned into garments or soft furnishings. Their functions and physical placement suggest a secondary, auxiliary role in the hierarchy of imperial silks, but their intricate patterns and the technical virtuosity in their weaving nonetheless conveyed a sense of luxury and refinement.

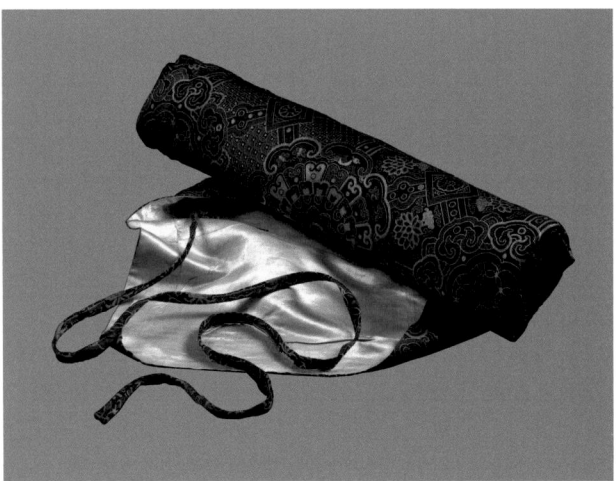

FIG. 6 Wrapper for the scroll painting *Empress Supervising the Rites of Sericulture* (*Qincan tu*), 1736–95. Made by the Qing Imperial Silk Manufactory. Silk lampas. National Palace Museum, Taipei (guhua920).

All three pattern design categories for Qing imperial silks foreground a decorative logic that operated through the language of symbolism. Drawing on the hieroglyphic link between the Chinese character *wen*, for "pattern," and the word *wen*, for "civility," "refinement," and "learning," the art historian Jonathan Hay points out that patterns in Chinese culture were essentially perceived as "external manifestation of some 'substance' or 'natural principle.'" Patterning was "deeply meaningful as a revelation of cosmic order," and the presence of such order in the domestic environment affirmed "human participation in that order."[13] The perception of textile patterns as a symbolic system beyond mere surface ornament was deeply entrenched in the cultural imagination and collective consciousness of Chinese viewers. As manifested in the visual domain, throughout the Chinese dynasties, depictions of clothing persistently rendered textile patterns as autonomous images superimposed onto the body and space, disregarding the material properties of the fabric such as folds and seams. When the European naturalistic style, introduced to the Qing court by Jesuit painters, challenged this cultural concept of transcendental and autonomous patterns, Qing imperial painting would negotiate the limits of the new representational style in order to maintain the familiar visual mode. In a 1736 portrait of Qianlong by Castiglione employing European perspective and three-dimensional modeling, the Italian artist kept the folds of the emperor's formal court robe (*chaofu*) to a minimum, strategically placing them on the margins or around relatively insignificant motifs (fig. 7). He also rendered the shading on the garment nearly imperceptible, restricting it to the yellow satin ground so that the dragons could fully extend without appearing broken or encroached on.

An understanding of this distinctive and enduring perception of textile patterns enables us to see the ubiquitous silks at the Qing palaces not simply as luxury decorations, but as a vast web of meaningful symbols that defined the identities of the members of the imperial household while prescribing their spaces and movements. Take, for example, the emperor's robes and surroundings. The elaborately executed motifs on the garments he wore for state rituals and ceremonial events did not necessarily require an audience: one dragon situated on the proper right underside of a ceremonial robe was completely hidden by the overlapping flap, and a ceremonial robe was usually worn beneath a slate-blue formal

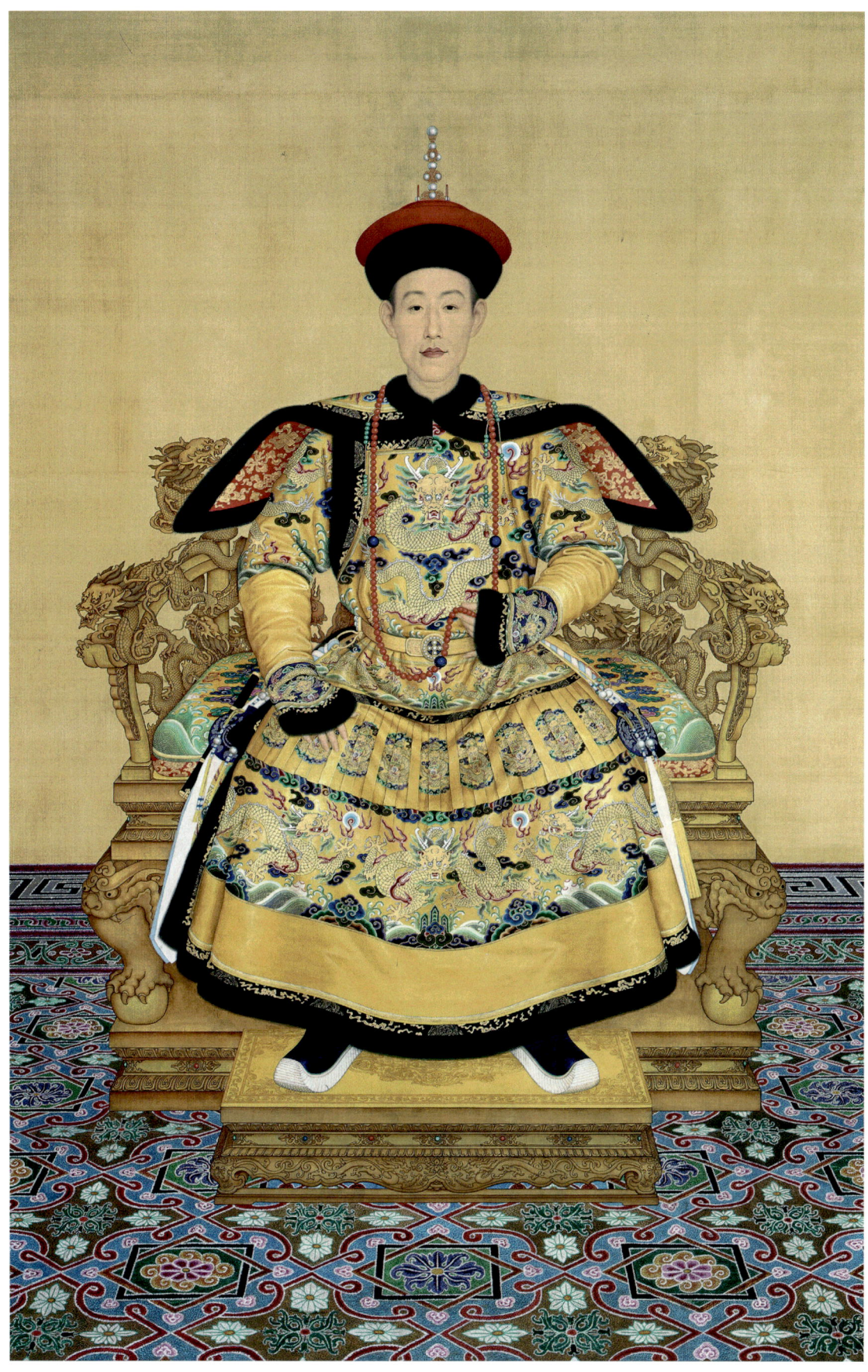

FIG. 7 Giuseppe Castiglione, *Portrait of the Qianlong Emperor*, 1736. Hanging scroll, ink and color on silk, 95¼ × 70½ in. (242 × 179 cm). Palace Museum, Beijing (gu6464).

overcoat that covered the dragons entirely and exposed only the water stripes on the bottom. The patterns signaled the emperor's identity as the embodiment of the cosmic order and the intermediary between Heaven and Earth. These manifestations operated on a supernatural level far beyond the visible spectacle intended for human admiration. From the altars of state sacrifices and the audience hall to his private studies and bedrooms, the spaces that the emperor regularly occupied were replete with silks bearing imperial symbols and auspicious motifs: they floated on screens, adorned cushions, embellished bed curtains, and much more. Reaffirming the imperial order as well as perfect, perpetual bliss, these obsessive reprises existed as superimposed visual dimensions in the palace spaces. To an extent, objects in other media, such as porcelain and lacquer, shared with textiles the same repertoire of symbolic patterns. In a Qing court environment saturated with prestigious and auspicious symbols, silks were unique in their proximity to the imperial body, for they were used in both the emperor's clothing and his personal furnishings. Therefore, visually and psychologically, the textile medium enabled the symbols to appear as though they were emanating from the monarch himself.

The three categories of silk patterns outlined above—hierarchical and cosmological symbols, auspicious motifs, and geometric designs—had an enduring presence in late imperial China. Despite aesthetic and stylistic shifts over time, the design principle and decorative grammars for nonnarrative woven textiles remained virtually unchanged until the very end of the Qing dynasty. A fashion cycle did not exist for these textiles, and, in any case, an infrastructure for disseminating new styles did not center at the court. Although new trends, especially from the wealthy southern region where the silk manufactories were located, sometimes found their way into the informal wear of imperial consorts, there was no audience to appreciate these innovations since imperial women neither appeared outside the palaces nor exhibited their portraits in public until the very end of the Qing dynasty.[14]

As this book demonstrates, in this well-established visual system of woven textile patterns, fresh modes of patterning and cognition emerged primarily in response to European silks. The eighteenth century witnessed the first wave of Qing imperial fascination with European silks, which, although representing only a small percentage of Qing court textiles, played a significant role in introducing innovative design vocabularies and imparting a new visual mode for conveying imperial magnificence.[15]

CONTEXTUALIZING THE QING COURT'S EUROPEAN SILKS

Today we have only sporadic evidence attesting to the presence of European silks in China before the Qing dynasty. Velvet was the only known type, which possibly came to the Ming Empire as tributary gifts from Southeast Asian countries and later as Portuguese trade goods.[16] More varieties of European silks were mentioned in High Qing records, which reflects the significant development of the European silk industry since the late seventeenth century as well as the expansion of Catholic missions, diplomatic liaisons, and commercial ties between China and Europe. Although archival documents indicate that European embassies presented textiles to the Qing court as early as the second half of the seventeenth century, no examples from this era have survived.[17] Most of the European silks collected in the Palace Museum are high-end eighteenth-century products. A brief overview of the silk industry in Europe, especially in the weaving center, Lyon, helps contextualize the manufacture and designs of these pieces.

In the 1660s, with the support of Louis XIV (r. 1643–1715), Jean-Baptiste Colbert (1619–1683), the powerful Comptroller General of Finance (*Contrôleur general des finances*), began reforming the French silk industry, initially by imitating Italian styles in order to protect the French market from domination by Italian imports.[18] By the early years of the eighteenth century, French silk had gained a pan-European reputation for its fashionable style and sophisticated weaving.[19] Lyon rose as the undisputed center of European silk weaving, leading the continent in stylistic innovations, loom technology, and merchandising. Lyonnais products ranged from plain taffetas to velvet, but it was the elaborately figured silks (*grands façonnés*) that defined the state of the art. Like their Chinese counterparts, European silks with a complex weave structure were produced on a drawloom. Illustrations in the *Encyclopédie* (1751–72) make clear that the basic construction of the drawloom (*métier à la grande tire*) was the same as that of the Chinese type (fig. 8). It consisted of two independent systems for raising the warp threads to develop the design: the ground harness, moved by foot treadles operated by the weaver, created a simple ground weave, while the figure harness, controlled by cords manipulated by a drawboy, produced complicated patterns.[20]

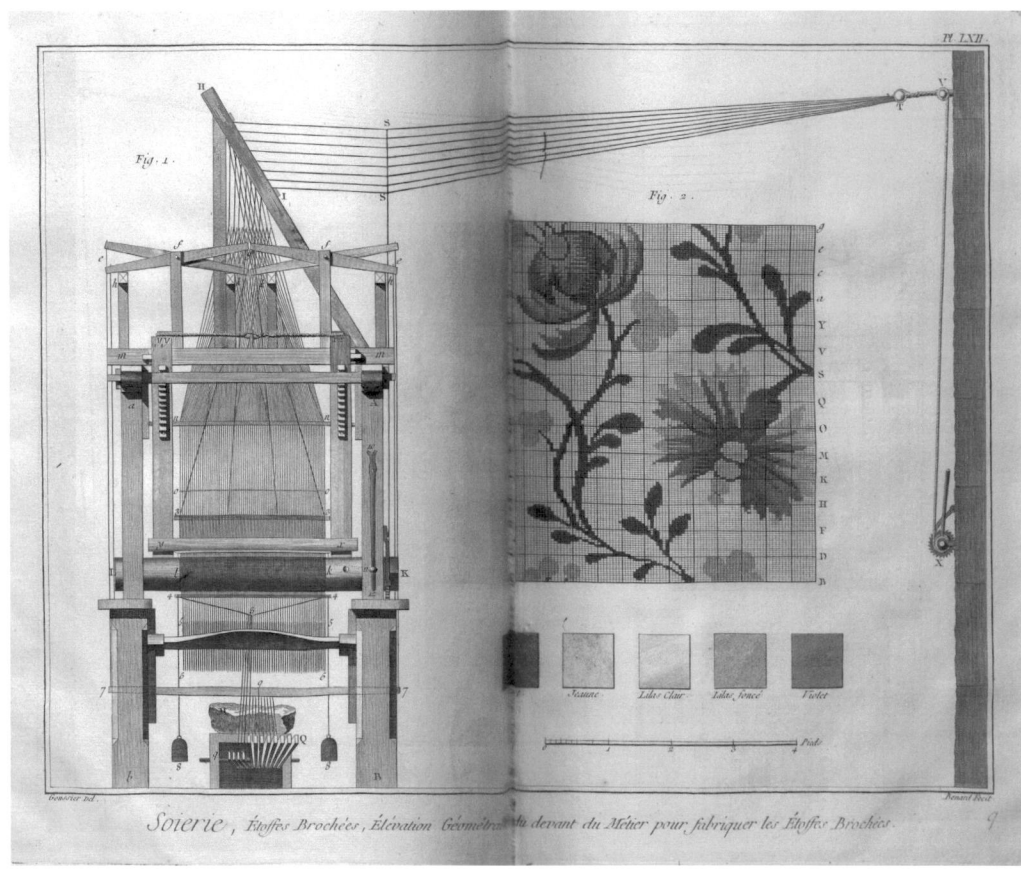

FIG. 8 Illustration of a drawloom (*métier à la grande tire*) and point paper (*mise-en-carte*). From "Soierie," pl. LXII, in Denis Diderot and Jean-Baptiste le Rond d'Alembert, *Encyclopédie*, vol. 28 (Paris: Le Breton, 1772).

Other European cities that produced high-quality silks during this century included Tours, Venice, Genoa, Valencia, Spitalfields (in east London), Amsterdam, Haarlem, Krefeld (Germany), and Moscow. The silk industries in England and Holland grew especially rapidly at the end of the seventeenth century, benefiting from the migration of skillful Huguenot (French Protestant) artisans to these two countries following the revocation of the Edict of Nantes by Louis XIV in 1685.[21] French silk designs were avidly emulated in old and new weaving centers throughout Europe. Yet despite the sweeping influence of French style, each city maintained its own specialty and market. Genoa, for example, specialized in *jardinière* velvet, a preferred choice for furnishings in the grand style in many European countries, whereas Venice excelled at traditional types of damask, which continued to appeal to the Ottoman Empire.[22] Spitalfields was most renowned for its naturalistic botanical designs on an open ground; these dominated the fashionable taste in the first half of the 1740s.[23] Amsterdam developed a special repertoire of chinoiserie designs woven in an extra-wide size (about 30 in. [78 cm]) during the first half of the eighteenth century in response to popular demand for Chinese silks, whose import had been officially banned in France and England.[24]

The well-studied Lyonnais silk industry provides a useful model for understanding the most successful system in eighteenth-century Europe in which silk fabric was designed, produced, and circulated. As the textile historian Lesley Miller has elucidated, the organization of silk manufacturing in Lyon created a collective, corporate identity for the city's products. The Grande Fabrique, a professional guild, governed private weaving establishments with individual specializations and oversaw regulations for training, workshop management, and quality control.[25] Merchant manufacturers (*marchands fabricants*)—entrepreneurs at the top of the guild structure—controlled the capital and distributed the raw materials to the weavers.[26] Silk designers (*dessinateurs*) played a visible and pivotal role in the industry, often serving as partners in weaving firms. According to the silk designer Antoine Nicolas Joubert de l'Hiberderie (1715–1770), a good designer was expected to master the following: a technical understanding of the loom gained through actual weaving practice; excellent skills in drawing human figures and botanical specimens; knowledge of how to make point paper

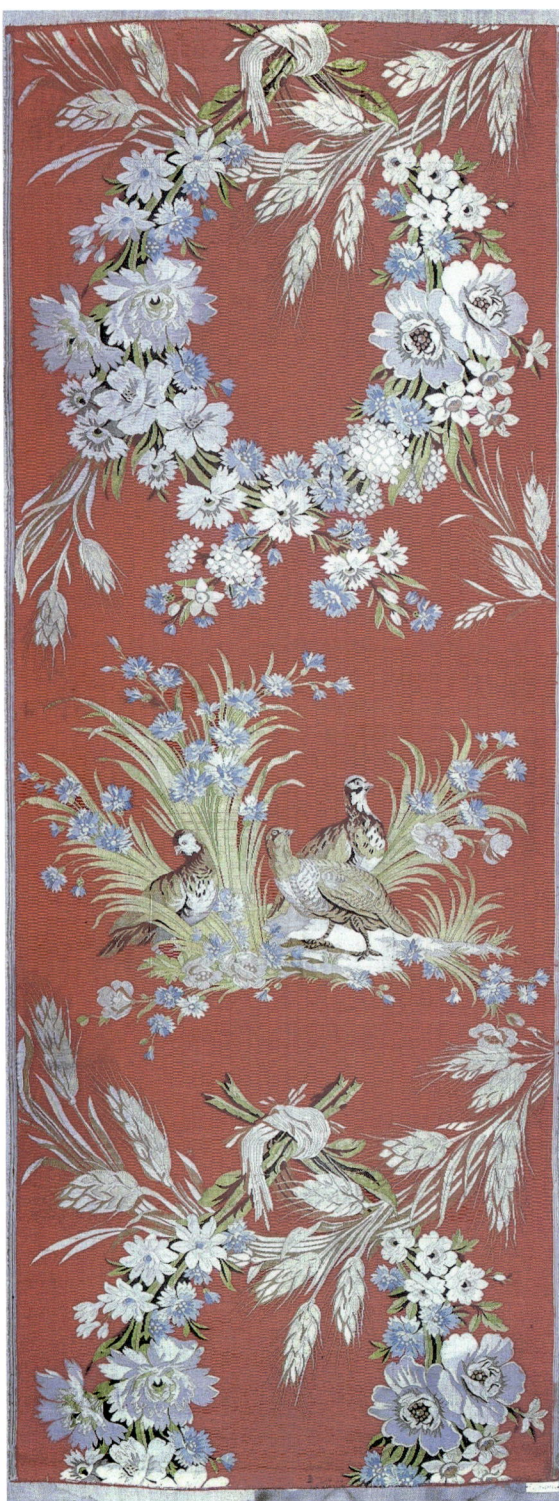

FIG. 9 *The Partridges* (*Les Perdrix*), textile panel, c. 1770. Designed by Philippe de Lasalle, woven in Lyon. Brocaded silk, 55 × 22 in. (139.7 × 55.9 cm). Victoria and Albert Museum, London (T.187–1931).

(*mise-en-carte*)—squared paper on which the design was translated into a grid system as a guide for setting up the loom (see fig. 8); and expertise in the design of a particular type of fabric or weave.[27] Until the establishment of the public school of drawing in Lyon in 1756 to train silk designers, those pursuing such a career had to come from well-to-do families or secure sponsorship in order to complete the long and costly education needed to prepare them for this work. A prospective designer learned drawing in a fine art school in Paris or in a workshop of one of the painters working for the royal tapestry manufactory at Gobelins, and preferably his education also involved contacts with Parisian tastemakers.[28] A weaving apprenticeship in a silk manufactory enabled a designer to gain technical knowledge of the loom, and through this channel or by marriage, he could enter a partnership with a merchant manufacturer or became a power broker in his own right. To gain a good knowledge of the market, research changing Parisian tastes, and maintain an elite cultural network, designer-partners sojourned in Paris at least once a year. Designers played a direct role in innovating silk patterns and techniques, crossing the boundary between silk manufacturing and fine art practice. Lesley Miller has compared their status to that of the Painters of the King (*peintres du roi*), "who provided models of tapestries and porcelains for the royal manufactories."[29]

The customers of Lyonnais silks consisted of members of the royal family, the nobility, the higher clergy, and the upper echelons of the bourgeoisie and merchant class, but serving the French court had always been the principal goal of this industry. As articulated in a 1731 petition by the Lyonnais manufacturer Barnier, the French court set the trend for novelty and fashionable taste, which was in turn imitated in Paris, in the provinces, and at foreign courts.[30] The economic historian Carlo Poni has discussed how the strategies of Lyonnais silk merchants helped shape the fashion system from the late seventeenth through the eighteenth centuries.[31] Lyonnais firms established a business model of introducing new fabrics annually with a short fashionable lifespan. This in turn injected an unprecedented dynamism into production and consumption practices, increased demand for diversified designs, and triggered the restructuring of the international silk market.[32] From the early eighteenth century through the mid-1770s, the overall silhouettes and basic components of men's and women's clothing remained largely the same, and it was primarily fast-changing textiles that defined fashion. Poni observes that this fashion system was predicated on "flexible production, monopolistic competition, and barriers to entry." According to him, the phenomenon of "Paris fashions made in Lyon" had taken shape around 1685.[33] By the 1720s, Lyonnais silk merchants were sending out quarterly previews of seasonal collections to potential clients before going into full production.[34]

Studies of extant eighteenth-century European silks show that each distinct style for fashion fabrics lasted approximately ten to fifteen years.[35] Floral and foliate motifs remained the mainstay through the 1770s, but the visual vocabularies, decorative modes, and compositional schema changed dramatically in every phase, and the design aesthetics shifted from flamboyant fantasies and outright exoticism to naturalism and abstraction. Within this longer organic cycle, annual or quarterly novelties programmed by Lyonnais manufacturers featured subtler variations, often through strategic altering of small details or colorways in existing designs.[36] Legislation passed in 1787 stipulated that a manufacturer's designs for dress silk were protected by copyright for six years, but those for furnishing and church silks were protected for fifteen years—strong indicators of the industry's view on the life expectancy of designs for each textile category.[37]

Aside from fashionable dress fabrics, specially commissioned silks intended for use in royal ceremonies and palace furnishings constituted a major part of the orders coming from the French court. Documented works by Barnier, Bron et Ringuet, Philippe de Lasalle, Pernon, and other Lyonnais manufacturers demonstrate that sumptuous silks for such purposes did not necessarily align with the fashion cycle of dress fabrics, although some characteristic contemporaneous styles could underlie such pieces.[38] The much-celebrated works by the designer-manufacturer Philippe de Lasalle (1723–1804) provide a case in point. One example, "The Partridges" (*Les Perdrix*; fig. 9), rendered alternating motifs of garlands and partridges in a large pattern repeat and a vivid, naturalistic style, features that disassociated it from contemporary fashion, which was increasingly dominated by small flowers and striped composition. The design was commissioned in the early 1770s to decorate a salon in the Palais Bourbon in Paris, and it appealed to the Russian empress Catherine the Great (1729–1796), who in the early 1780s ordered a version on a blue ground for furnishing her Peterhof Palace.[39] Likewise, silks for liturgical functions enjoyed a longer lifespan beyond the timeline of fashion.

Indeed, many ecclesiastical textiles began life as luxury fabrics for fashion; having become outdated, they were later donated to religious institutions. Newly woven silks for churches could feature conventionalized designs that were preserved for decades or even centuries.[40]

Interestingly, furnishing silks in the grand style made in Lyon or other European weaving centers have not been found in the Palace Museum, though we cannot rule out the possibility that some existed at the Qing court but were subsequently looted, destroyed, or lost during the many upheavals between 1860, when English and French armies invaded Beijing, and 1924, when the abdicated last emperor was finally evicted from the Forbidden City. With the exception of a particular floral design associated with church silks, which will be discussed below, the small number of European silks at the Palace Museum were all fashion fabrics representing every stylistic phase from circa 1700 to circa 1765. Placing them in the European silk design chronology sheds light on their original contexts of production.

The earliest extant piece is an extraordinary brown silk in the "bizarre" style datable to the first decade of the eighteenth century (figs. 10A, 10B). The bizarre style in silk, a modern term coined by the textile scholar Vilhelm Slomann in 1953, refers to a unique repertoire popular around 1700 to 1712 that featured exuberant, fantastic motifs.[41] Bizarre silks exhibit a mixture of exotic details loosely drawn from Chinese, Japanese, Indian, and Ottoman sources as well as from medieval and Renaissance silks; these are coupled with imaginative motifs and indeterminate, seemingly molten shapes.[42] The patterns appear to be undergoing a metamorphosis, penetrating each other and defying representation, while the composition favors an elongated arrangement (the repeat can be as long as about 27½ in. [70 cm]) and diagonal movement. Lavish use of gold and silver threads also characterizes bizarre silks. The birthplace of the bizarre silk remains a mystery to scholars, but major silk centers in France, England, and Italy all embraced this trend.

The Palace Museum fragment does not contain a full vertical repeat of the pattern, but the remaining part suffices to show the ingenuity and dynamism of the design. On the brown satin ground unfold fantastic, densely composed patterns woven with gold and silver threads, with only a touch of red, cream, and light-brown silk for small details and outlines. The central motif features a single enormous eye clinging to a sharply

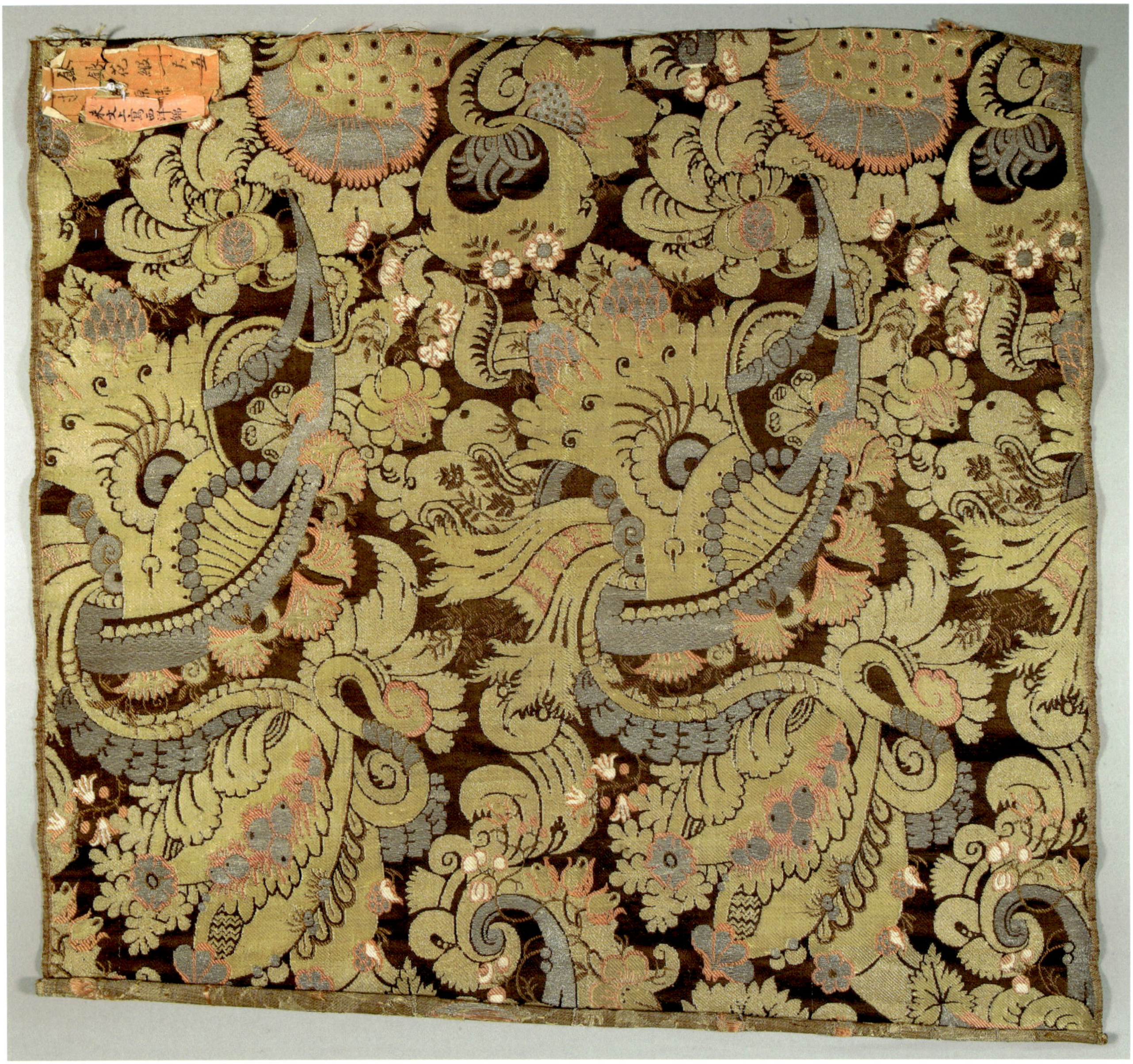

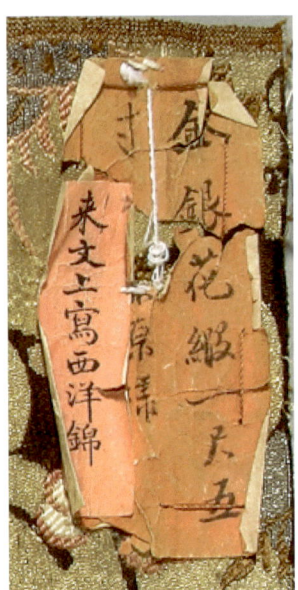
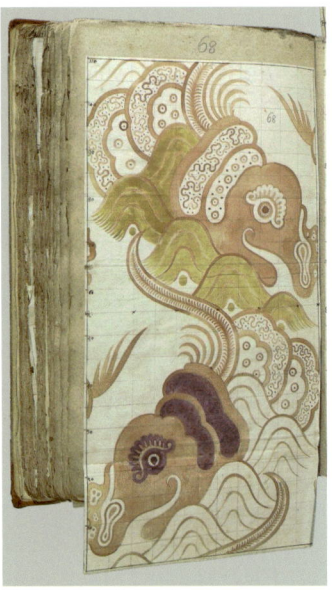

FIG. 10A (ABOVE) A fragment of silk in the "bizarre" style, c. 1710, probably Lyon. Silk lampas with metal threads, width 21⅛ in. (53.5 cm). Palace Museum, Beijing (gu17838).

FIG. 10B (FAR LEFT) Detail of the labels attached to the corner of fig. 10A.

FIG. 11 (LEFT) James Leman, design for silk, dated May 11, 1710, Spitalfields, London. Pencil, pen and ink, and watercolor on laid paper, 20¼ × 10½ in. (51.4 × 26.7 cm). Victoria and Albert Museum, London (E.1861:77–1991).

upturned, paisley-shaped structure, which transforms into a swollen, serpentine cluster below, evoking a bird's body. From this hybrid form emanate whimsical flowers, sprigs, feathers, and exotic fruits that punctuate the wild structure of twists and curves. This design is highly unusual, even among all the known examples of bizarre silks to date, and no comparable fabric has been found so far. Only a drawing dated 1710 by the English silk designer James Leman (1688–1745) bears some resemblance to this piece (fig. 11). Leman's work depicts a similar single-eyed, hybrid creature surrounded by an amorphous mass in dynamic motion, but its overall composition is much simpler. The loom width of the Palace Museum fragment, about 21 in. (53.5 cm), complies with the regulated width of French silks, and the superior quality of its weaving further suggests it is a Lyonnais product.[43]

Silk designs made around 1713 to 1719 retained some earlier bizarre elements, but their patterns and compositions had become tamer and shifted to luxuriant plants. A blue silk with floral and fruit motifs in red and yellow in the Palace Museum attests to this stylistic transition. The blue damask self-pattern on the ground, which shadows the main motif, and the whimsical scrolling ornaments bear witness to the lingering bizarre vocabulary (fig. 12).

The period from 1720 to 1732 saw the new fashion of lace-patterned silks (called "persiennes" at that time), which were characterized by a symmetrical structure with stylized flowers and foliage framed by lacelike bands or diapered interstices.[44] Large in scale, one complete motif extended across the entire width of the fabric, and the mirror repeat and strong vertical emphasis imparted an air of formality. Like bizarre silks, lace-patterned silks often contained a generous amount of gold and silver threads. In the Palace Museum, an early 1720s example dazzles with abundant metal weft threads composed in three layers: a set of light-toned silver threads in lancé render the main motifs; another set of brocaded silver threads in a darker shade fill the visual background and mesh interstices; and additional gold threads, also brocaded, create rhythmic highlights (fig. 13). The dark red ground wefts only peep out as thin outlines around the motifs. Such a rendering of gold and silver motifs on a silver background is unknown in the Chinese silk-weaving tradition. Moreover, the relationship between the supplementary metal threads that serve as the optical background and the actual red ground fabric reverses the familiar mode of Chinese weaving of jin-lampas, in which

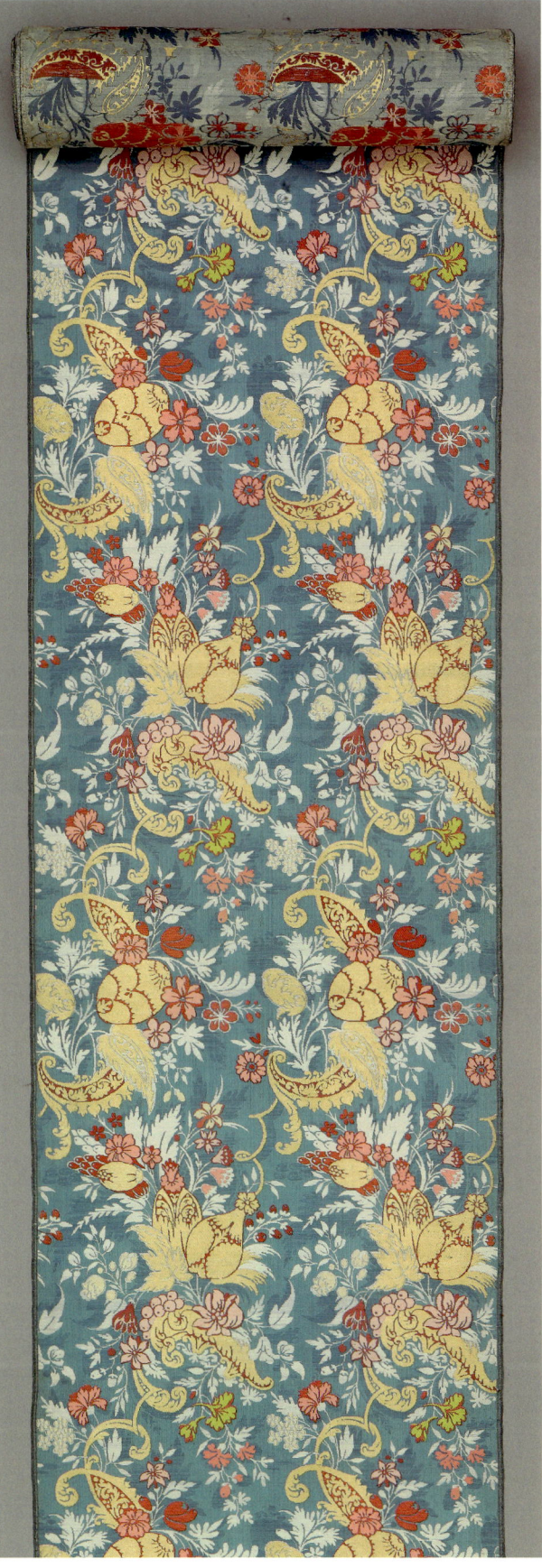

FIG. 12 Bolt of textile (detail), c. 1715, European. Silk lampas with metal threads. Palace Museum, Beijing (gu17763).

Foreign Splendor 23

gold threads are often woven in lancé and surface only on the front side of the fabric as the thin edges of the primary motif. In both material composition and technical treatment, this lace-patterned silk would have stood out as a striking novelty. In the silk patterns of the second half of the 1720s, the lace scrolls grew wider and more articulated, whereas flowers diminished into small heads, garlands, and sprigs. This stylistic phrase is represented by a silk in the Palace Museum featuring a bright yellow ground and silver lace patterns, which has survived both as an uncut piece and in a set of bow-and-arrow cases (fig. 14, see also fig. 62).

In the early 1730s, the ornamental mode gave way to a naturalistic style emphasizing three-dimensional forms that was in full bloom from 1733 to 1742.[45] The Lyonnais silk designer Justin Courtois (1692–1738) was the first to successfully explore the technique to render shading, but it was the famed designer-manufacturer Jean Revel (1684–1751) who both perfected and popularized this new weaving technique and the style it made possible.[46] The new naturalistic designs featured large flowers and fruits, and at times architectural devices, in massive, self-contained units against a blank ground on which secondary decorative patterns were sometimes rendered in monochrome. A remarkable floral silk made into two saddle blankets in the Palace Museum exemplifies the naturalistic style in its full glory around 1733 (figs. 15, 16). The textile's exquisite design and superb weaving unmistakably indicate a Lyonnais

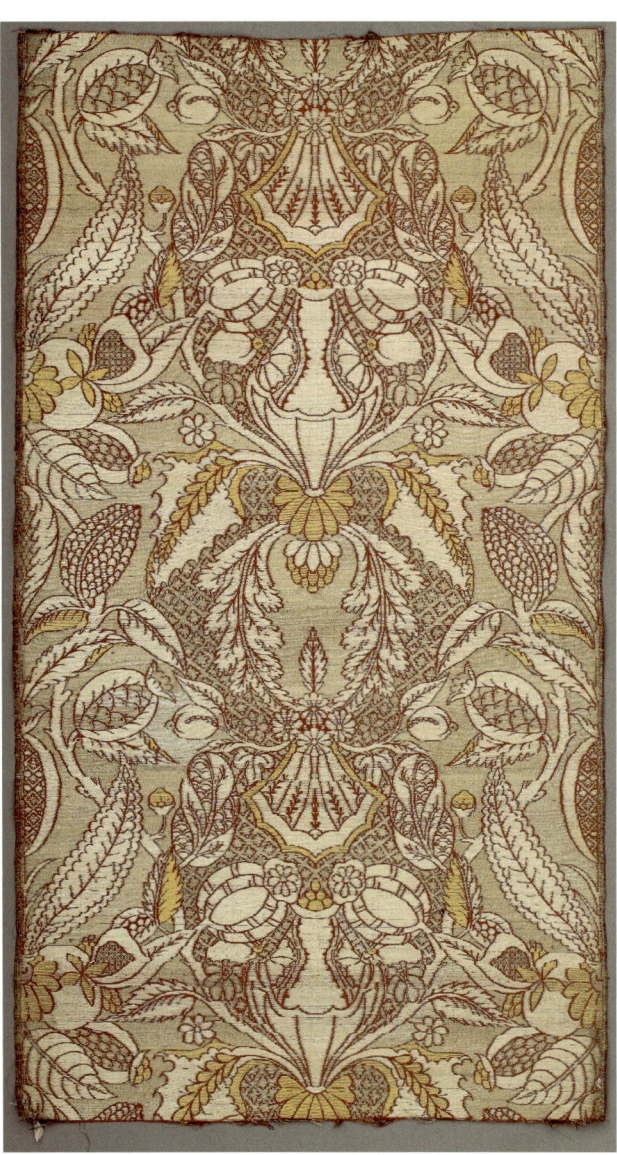

FIG. 13 Textile length, 1720–25, European. Silk lampas with metal threads, 37¾ × 21¼ in. (96 × 54 cm). Palace Museum, Beijing (gu17837).

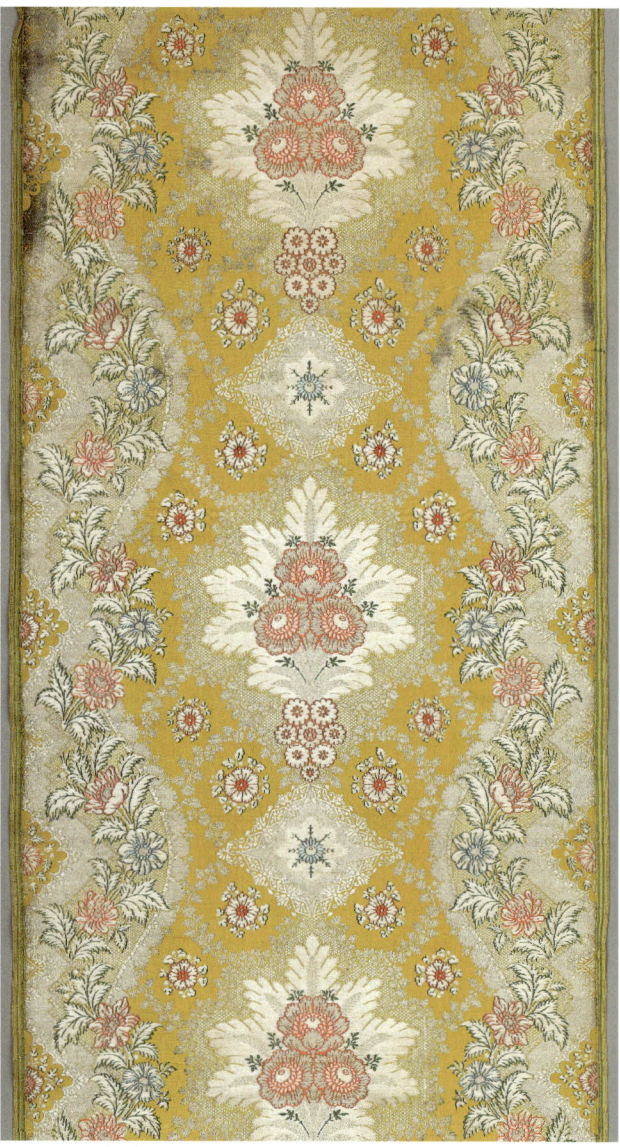

FIG. 14 Textile length (detail), 1725–30, European. Silk lampas with metal threads, width 21⅞ in. (55.5 cm). Palace Museum, Beijing (gu17946).

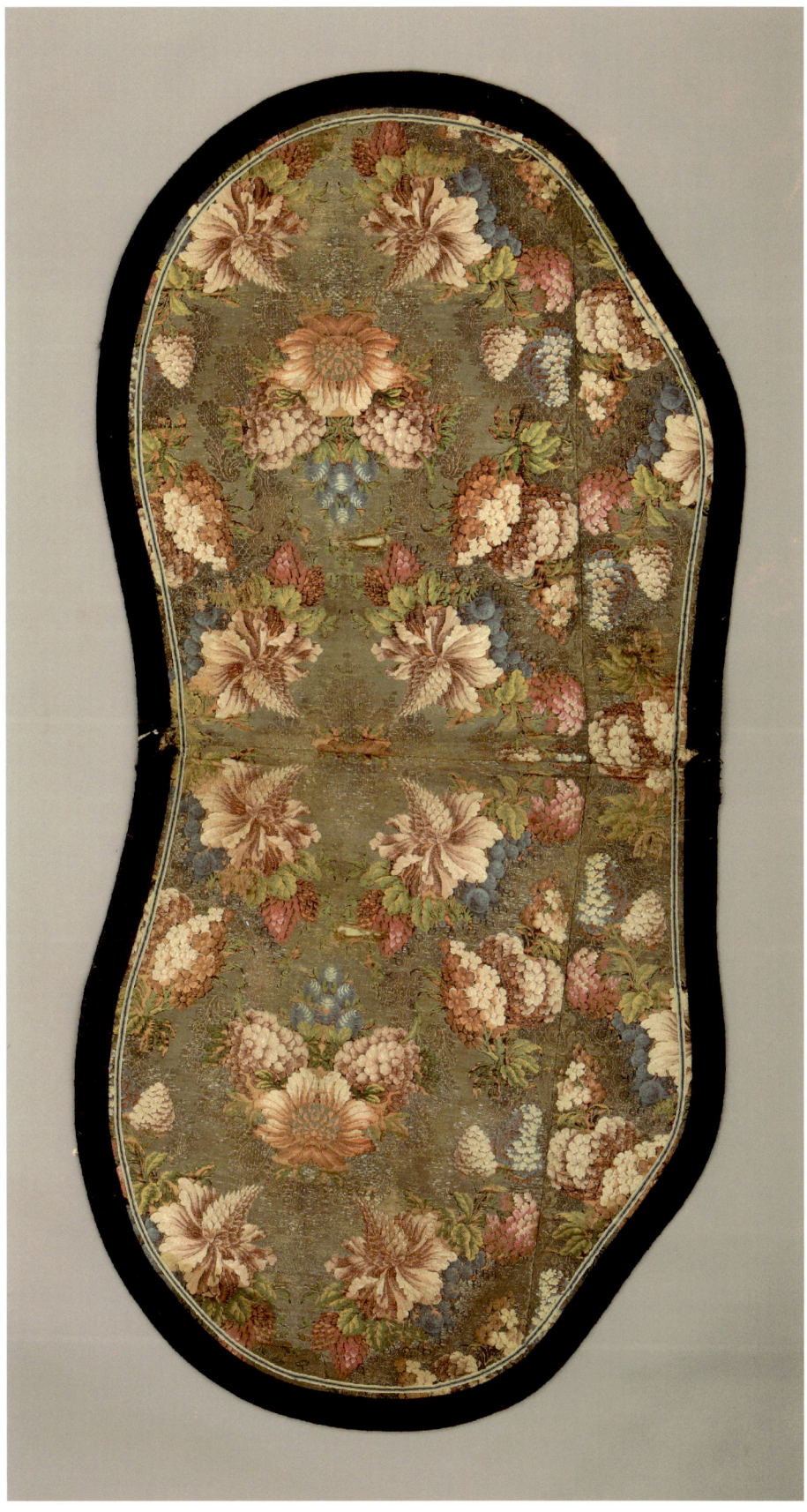

FIG. 15 Saddle blanket, made by the Qing Imperial Workshops, c. 1750s. Textile, c. 1733, Lyon. Silk lampas with metal threads, 58 ⅝ × 28 ⅜ in. (149 × 72 cm). Palace Museum, Beijing (gu212410).

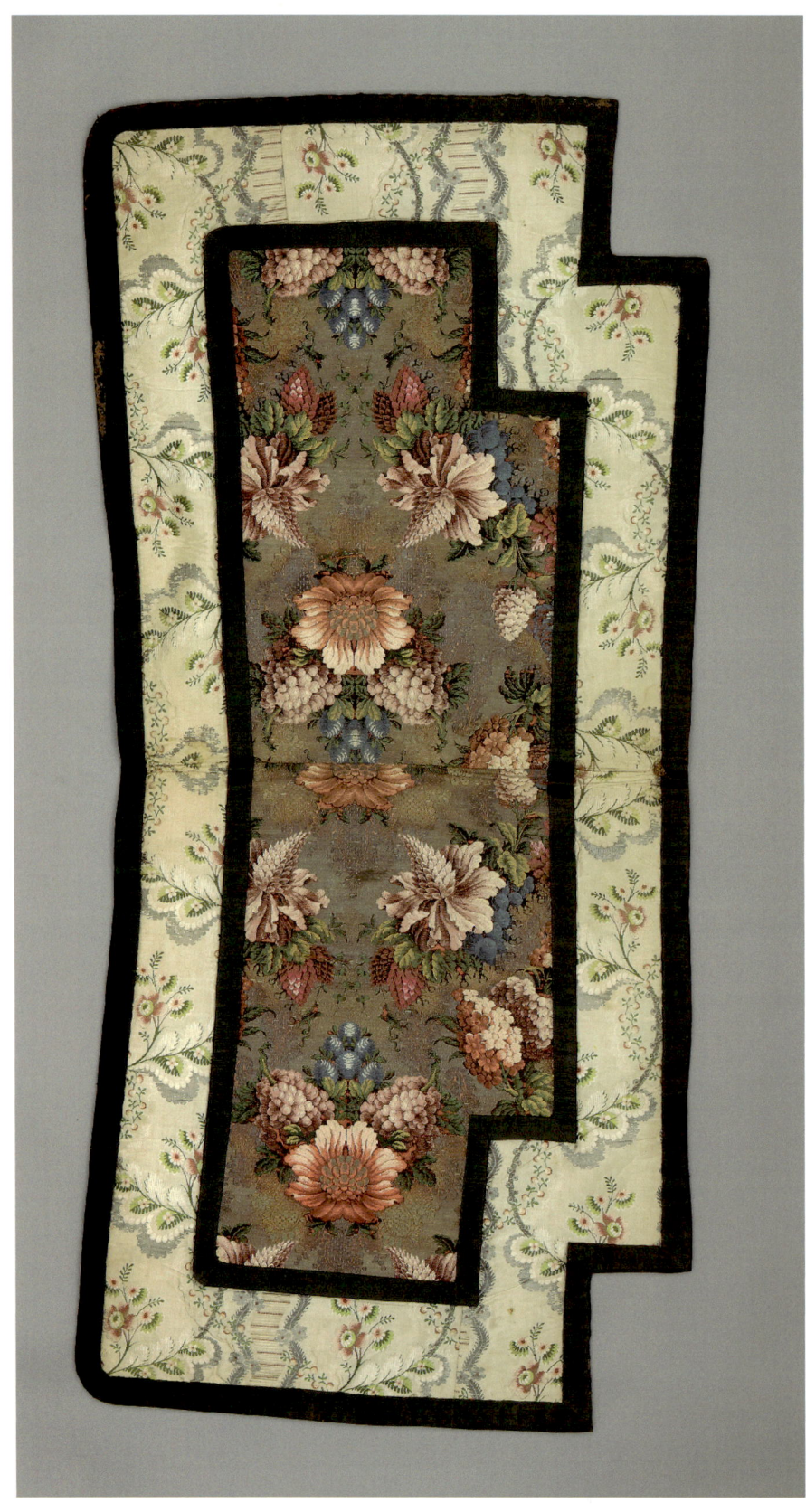

FIG. 16 Saddle blanket, made by the Qing Imperial Workshops, c. 1750s. Central textile panel, c. 1733, Lyon. Silk lampas with metal threads, 57½ × 25⅝ in. (146 × 65 cm). Palace Museum, Beijing (gu212439).

product of the finest caliber. In this silk, the light-pink satin ground is barely visible beneath the dense layers of silver and gold threads that constitute the background and the ornamental structures surrounding the main motifs—robust, tantalizing flowers and fruits such as guelder roses and grapes.[47] A striking, three-dimensional effect is achieved through the trademark *points rentrés* (or *berclé*) technique, a Lyon innovation: wefts of different colors intersect with each other to create the optical effect of a halftone that reads as shading (fig. 17). This vivid painterly effect and technical wonder would no doubt have been refreshing and stimulating to Qing imperial viewers.

A newer naturalistic style emerged around 1739. Its lighter and airier compositions favored asymmetrical trailing branches in graceful curves on an open ground, elements that embodied the prevailing rococo taste. In this period, English and French styles diverged. Spitalfields silks designed by Anna Maria Garthwaite (1688–1763) typified the high English style, which was marked by accurate renditions of botanical details and a sense of spontaneity in design. The English taste preferred a light-colored ground, especially in white, ivory, or other pale shades. French patterns of this period, although similar in scale and arrangement, tended to be more stylized and less realistic in their depictions of flowers.[48] The points rentrés technique continued to be employed. Around 1747, the scale of the flower sprays shrank further and their distribution on textiles became more scattered. Characteristic Spitalfields silks from the 1740s have not been found in the Palace Museum, but several Chinese copies in the museum's collections, which will be examined in detail in chapter 2,

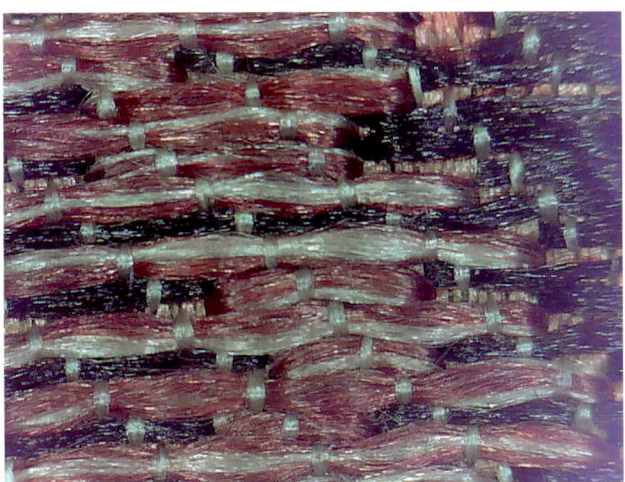

FIG. 17 The *points rentrés* (or *berclé*) technique; microscopic view of the weave structure of fig. 15.

corroborate the Qing imperial exposure to this distinct style (see figs. 38–40).

From the mid-1750s through the 1760s, floral patterns gradually moved away from naturalism, and French taste dominated the fashion in Europe once again. The points rentrés technique became simpler and more stylized or was abandoned altogether. In this period, the *liseré* technique—in which part of the ground weft threads float intermittently on the surface of the textiles to form small patterns—enjoyed increasing popularity as a means to render background designs and textured effects. The meandering composition stood out as a major characteristic of silk design. Vertically disposed serpentine decorative bands or garlands were interspersed with small bouquets of stylized roses, carnations, or tulips. During the first half of the 1760s, woven motifs took inspiration from fashionable trims such as lace, ribbons, feathers, and ermines.

A number of silks in the Palace Museum share similar floral patterns in the style popular circa 1755 to 1765, exemplified by a yellow piece and two gold lengths. They all feature a symmetrical design and a meandering trellis framework interspersed with small rose bouquets. Silks of this category have survived in the largest numbers among the Palace Museum's European silks, which indicates their special appeal to the Qing imperial patrons. In terms of the weaving technique, these silks can be divided into two groups: fabrics in the first one have a colored ground with monochrome diaper or foliage self-patterns executed in liseré (figs. 18, 19); and those in the second group bear a full gold background woven in lancé and patterns accentuated with brocaded gold and silver thread (figs. 20, 21). Overall, this floral design scheme exhibits the stylistic traits of French dress silks fashionable in the mid-1750s. French silks in that period, however, rarely featured a full gold composition, and by the 1760s French fashion silks had also abandoned such mirror repeat, although symmetrical designs continued to be woven and used for liturgical vestments in France and elsewhere. Indeed, this floral design was particularly associated with church textiles in Europe and enjoyed a prolonged life in production and use for ecclesiastical functions well into the nineteenth century.[49]

The rose-patterned silks in the Palace Museum strongly resemble a group of Russian silks manufactured from the 1760s to the 1790s and may well have been Russian imports. Russia lacked a silk-weaving tradition,

Foreign Splendor 27

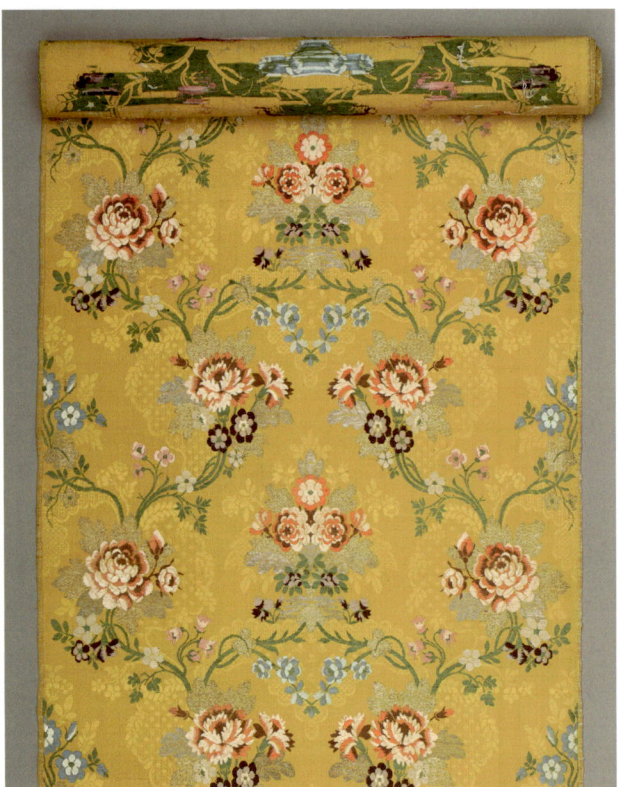

and despite repeated efforts to establish a silk industry during the seventeenth century and the first half of the eighteenth, significant advancements came about only during the second half of the eighteenth century. Private manufactories owned by merchants and nobles and located near Moscow largely followed the French lead.[50] For example, in the 1780s and 1790s, the Lazarev Manufactory in Fryanovo copied French designs, including those by Philippe de Lasalle, and produced silks whose quality rivaled that of the best Lyonnais products.[51] The group of silks in the Palace Museum with a liseré ground pattern and a relatively stiff tripartite arrangement of rose heads linked by thin vines (see fig. 18) are very similar to a green silk dated to the 1760s in the State Historical Museum in Moscow (fig. 22). Another closely related version with a pale blue ground in the State Hermitage Museum in St. Petersburg bears the maker mark of the Lazarev Manufactory and dates to circa 1768–94.[52] The gold lengths in the Palace Museum (see figs. 20, 21) show strong affinities to a Moscow silk made into a phelonion

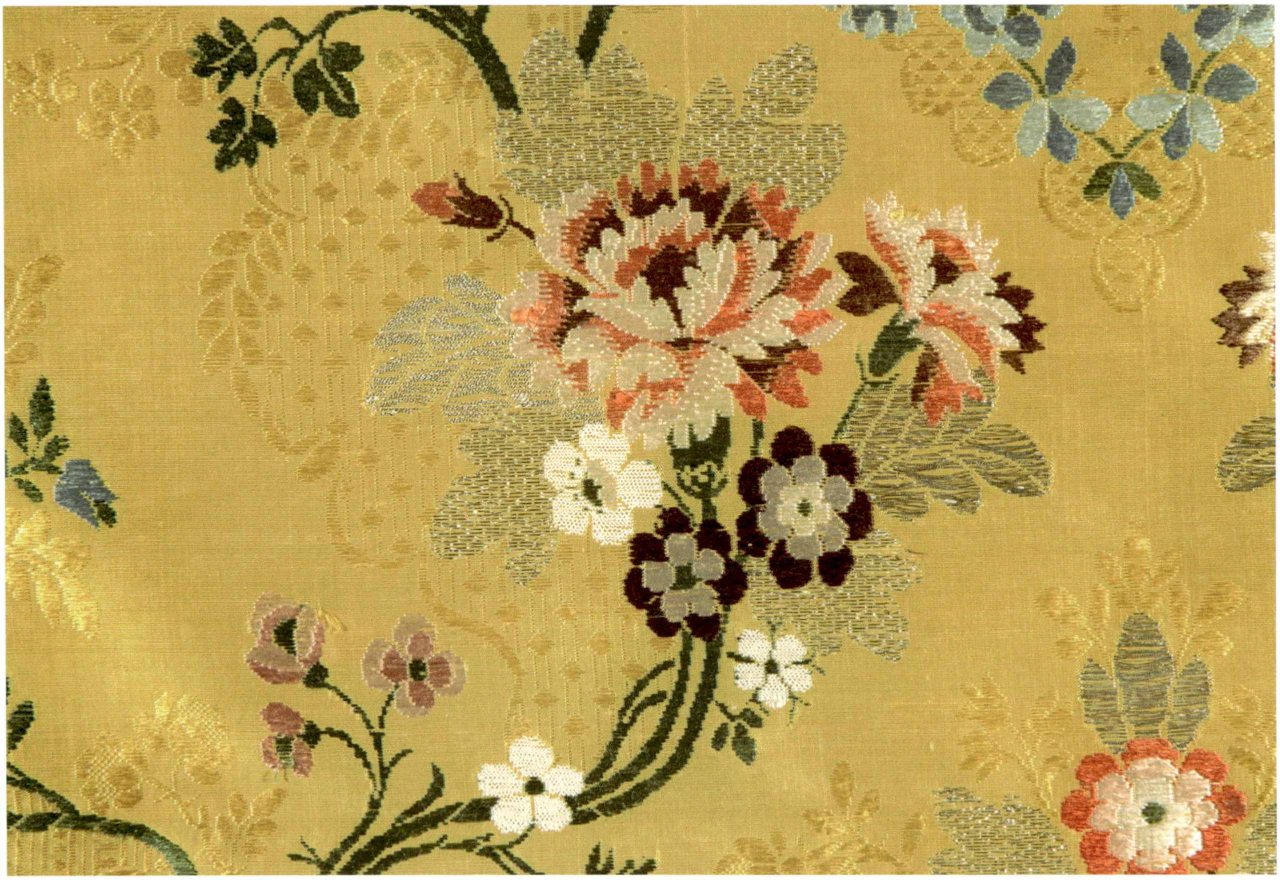

FIG. 18 (TOP) Bolt of textile (detail), second half of the eighteenth century, probably Russian. Silk and metal threads. Palace Museum, Beijing (gu25483).

FIG. 19 (ABOVE) Detail of fig. 18.

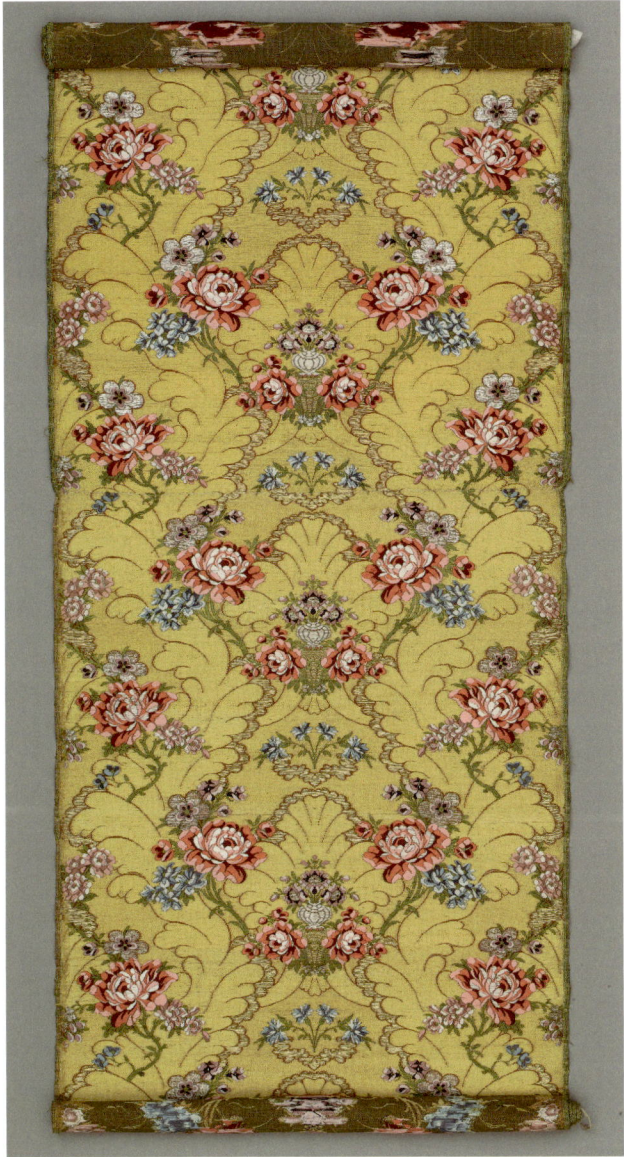
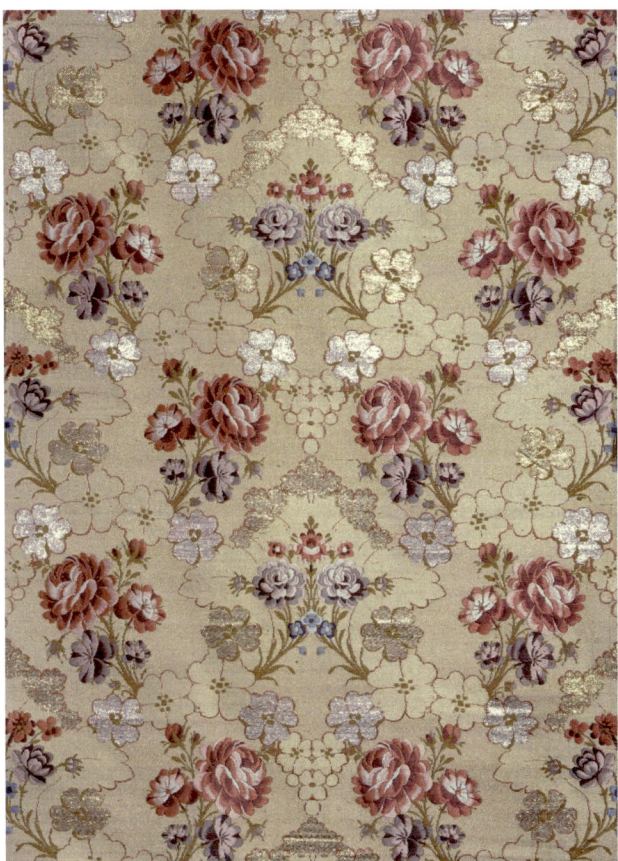

FIG. 21 Bolt of textile (detail), second half of the eighteenth century, probably Russian. Silk lampas with metal threads, 24 ft. 8 in. × 24 ⅜ in. (752 × 62 cm). Palace Museum, Beijing (gu17830).

FIG. 20 Bolt of textile (detail), second half of the eighteenth century, probably Russian. Silk lampas with metal threads, 79 ⅞ × 21 ¼ in. (203 × 54 cm). Palace Museum, Beijing (gu17831).

(priest's vestment; fig. 23). One silk (see fig. 20) featuring a vase motif and billowing, featherlike foils with scalloped edges especially resembles this Russian example.

From the mid-1760s onward, increasingly smaller and more abstract floral patterns proliferated in dress silks, and stripes gradually replaced the curvilinear clusters in response to the sweeping neoclassical trend in art and fashion that gave preference to straight lines and simplified designs. This tendency grew more radical during the 1770s, and by the 1780s, patterns for dress silks had completely dissolved into plain stripes and dots with sporadic tiny flowers. These fabric types are completely absent from the collections of the Palace Museum, which suggests the Qianlong emperor's lack of interest in such modest designs.

This survey of the Qing court's eighteenth-century European silks brings into relief their status as luxury products of the highest weaving quality for fashion and religious purposes. Some were probably manufactured in Lyon and Moscow, but others cannot be clearly attributed to a country of origin (as is the case with many silks once they were cut off from the loom and dispersed). The fanciful, magnificent designs of these silks, their lavish use of precious metal threads, and their weaving methods—all of which differed from the Chinese norms—would have sparked aesthetic excitement and curiosity among Qing imperial viewers. Thanks to the multiple elements and sinuous movement of their compositions, the European silks introduced a new dynamism to the Qing court, whose own imperial textiles gravitated toward formulaic frameworks such as roundels and staggered horizontal rows. In terms of technique, the two methods of points rentrés, used to achieve a three-dimensional effect, and liseré, employed for self-patterning on the ground, did not exist in traditional Chinese weaving. The treatment of adding brocaded metal thread highlights on a full metal lancé background—characteristic of several Russian silks—presented yet another fresh visual concept and technical manipulation.[53]

The overall design logic of these European silks formed a sharp contrast to that of the Qing imperial textiles and thus posed an interpretive challenge, as symbolism, so prevalent in the latter, was hardly an underlying design principle in the former. In contrast to the Qing system, a floral or decorative motif in European dress silks rarely contained a coded message arising from an established semiotic system of ideologies and values. These patterns were surface ornaments and changed according to the whims of fashion, reverberating with contemporary tastes and artistic trends. The Qing imperial patrons, however, were probably unaware of the silks' original visual contexts and stylistic timeline. Some pieces

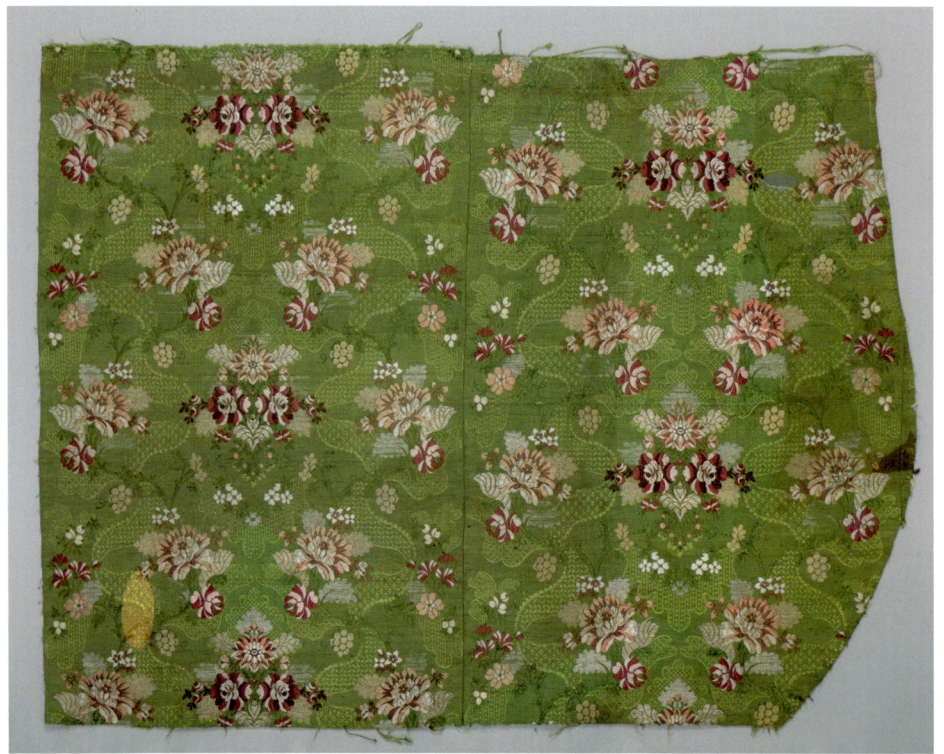

FIG. 22 Textile panel, c. 1760s, Moscow. Silk and metal threads, 31½ × 41¾ in. (80 × 106 cm). State Historical Museum, Moscow (78142/160 A-36043).

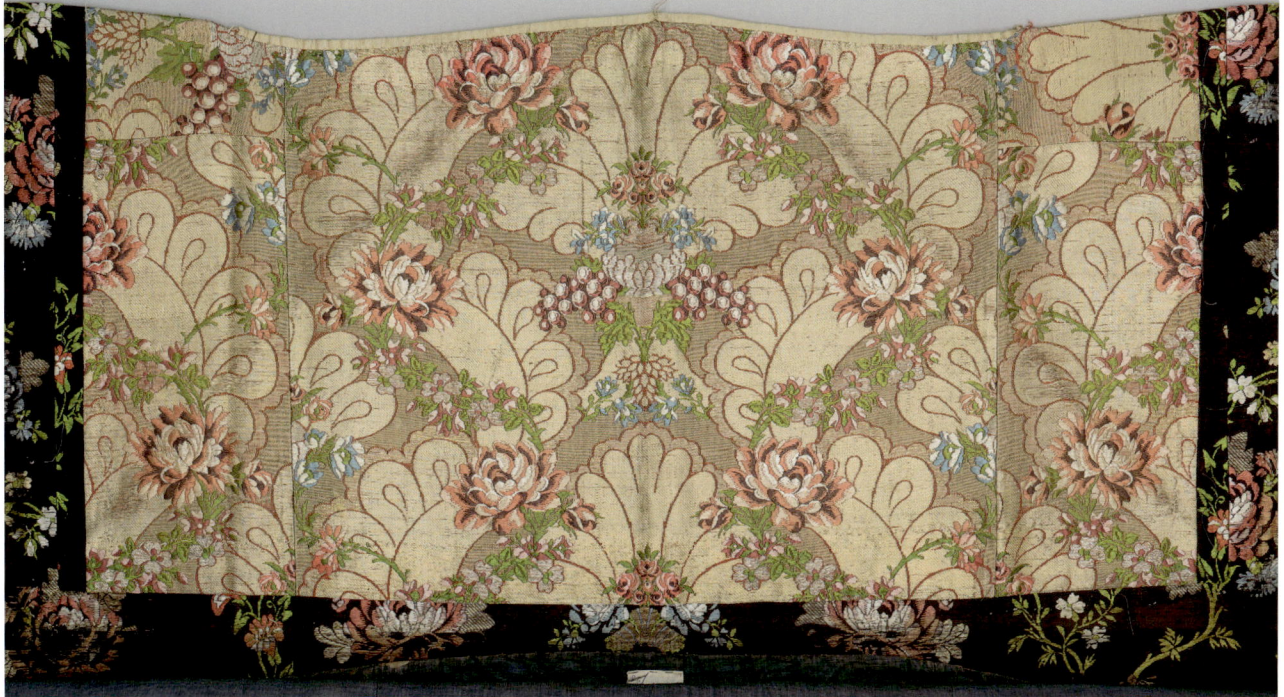

FIG. 23 Phelonion (priest's vestment), second half of the eighteenth century, Moscow. Central textile panel: (ground weave) silk and cotton threads; (pattern) silk and metal threads, 58 ¼ × 68 ⅞ in. (148 × 175 cm). State Historical Museum, Moscow (78142/28 RB-3806).

remained in the imperial storage for decades before being put to use. Annual inventory documents show that, for instance, in 1735, a bolt of "Western grand gold [figured] satin" (*xiyáng da jīnduan*) entered the storerooms, where it remained untouched until 1759.[54] To be sure, symbolism certainly factored in European designs for specially commissioned furnishing and ceremonial silks, and individual motifs in typical dress fabrics could evoke specific meanings in certain circumstances. Yet any significance these motifs might have conjured in European contexts would have been completely opaque to Qing imperial viewers. When the Qing emperor encountered European silks, the aesthetic or semiotic dissonance would have elicited an entirely new visual experience, which in turn became the departure point for these textiles to develop new functions and meanings in the Qing imperial context.

THE QING IMPERIAL PERSPECTIVE ON EUROPEAN SILKS

No documents have yet been discovered that reveal how and when the individual European silks now in the Palace Museum entered the Qing court, but Qing official records of "tributary objects" (*gongwu*) and occasional entries on purchased textiles offer general clues that point to these silks as diplomatic gifts and trade goods. Given such roles, they presumably arrived in China within a few years of their manufacturing dates. The concept of "tributary objects" reveals that the Qing Empire viewed itself as a supreme entity at the center of the universe. "Tributary objects" subsumed everything presented by neighboring states with which Qing had close political and economic ties, including Korea, Vietnam, Siam, Ryukyu, and others, and by European countries engaging in maritime trade with China and granted regular embassy visits, such as Portugal and Holland. The category of "tributary objects" also applied to items that European countries sent to the Qing court not through formal emissaries but through the Jesuit missionaries.

Silks were frequently featured among the diplomatic gifts that European embassies presented to the Qing court. The Dutch East India Company (Verenigde Oost-Indische Compagnie, hereafter VOC) began to send delegations as early as in 1656, soon after the Qing dynasty was established. In 1686, shortly after the Kangxi emperor lifted the prohibition on maritime trade and opened the port of Canton, Holland changed the "tribute period" from every eight years to every five.[55] As Qing imperial records show, the silks offered by the Dutch embassies in 1667 ranged from "grand figured satin" (*dahuaduan*) and "Dutch grand polychrome figured satin" (*Helan wuse dahuaduan*) to "grand purple and gold [figured] satin" (*da zise jīnduan*) and

Foreign Splendor 31

"red and silver [figured] satin" (*hong yinduan*); those offered in 1686 included "figured satin woven with gold" (*zhijīn huaduan*) and "Dutch figured satin" (*Helan huaduan*).[56] In 1727, on behalf of the Portuguese king João V (r. 1706–50), the embassy of Alexandre Metelo de Sousa e Meneses (1687–1766) presented the Yongzheng emperor with "[figured] satin with gold threads" (*jīnsi duan*), "[figured] satin with gold and silver threads" (*jīnyinsi duan*), and "figured satin with gold" (*jīnhuaduan*).[57] The term *satin* (*duan*) used in Qing court documents should not be taken literally: written by non-textile specialists, it could refer to an actual satin ground as part of a complex weave structure, or it could be used loosely to include tabby, twill, or damask, all of which could serve as the typical ground weave for an elaborate silk fabric.

From the perspective of the European countries seeking to develop trade with China, carefully selected diplomatic gifts projected their self-image as ever-expanding maritime powers, aiming to win the favor of the Qing emperor in order to achieve commercial and political goals. An assessment of the gift records from Holland and Portugal reveals that these countries did not limit their items to domestic specialties. For instance, the 1667 Dutch gifts included Southeast Asian spices, African ivories, and "small, white cow from the Grand West," whereas the 1752 Portuguese gifts featured mostly French and English goods, which pleased Qianlong deeply.[58] Such diplomatic offerings celebrated the geographical reach of Holland and Portugal, the vast material resources they could access and mobilize, and the active role the two countries played in the global trade linking Asia, Europe, Africa, and the New World. The various silks presented by these two embassies were presumably not only their own national products but also the best pieces they had acquired from major weaving centers in Italy, France, and possibly England.

European silks also appeared among the offerings to the Qing court from South and Southeast Asian regimes. For example, the 1720 gifts from Siam contained "Western gold [figured] satin" (*xiyáng jīnduan*) and "Grand Western wide songjin [lampas]" (*da xiyáng kuo songjīn*).[59] It is not clear what type of silk the latter referred to, but the Chinese term *songjīn*, as discussed earlier, suggests some dense and intricate abstract patterns. The Siamese king probably acquired these silks as precious European trade goods or official gifts, and he probably chose them to showcase the cosmopolitanism and resourcefulness of his kingdom while glorifying the Qing Empire and seeking a smooth political relationship. In a similar spirit, the Siamese embassy to Versailles in 1686 presented Louis XIV with 1,500 pieces of Chinese and Japanese porcelain and Japanese gold vases, among other treasures from China and Japan that made up the majority of the gifts.[60] Before entering the Qing court, the Western silks that traveled from European countries to Southeast Asian kingdoms already embodied mobility in global exchanges, and the geographical distances and cultural boundaries they traversed imbued them with additional assets beyond their material value. For the Qing emperor, the novelties gathered from all over the world reinforced the centrality of the Manchu Empire, as in the discourse on imperial tribute, only his supremacy and benign rulership could entail such endeavors and devotion. Regardless of their original purposes, all European luxury silks catalogued as "tributary objects" became material symbols celebrating the power and prestige of the Qing monarch.

Among the European silks that reached the Qing court, those received as diplomatic gifts were supposedly the most opulent and expensive, and it was these high-end pieces that evidently shaped the Qing emperor's overall impression of European silks. Other pieces acquired through the trade network probably varied in quality. European commercial ships trading in Canton brought different kinds of silks, the best of which were acquired by local government officials on behalf of the Qing court or as their annual or seasonal tributary gifts for the emperor. The well-developed internal tribute system required regional officials to offer gifts to the emperor regularly; these consisted of local specialties and valuable goods they had acquired through domestic and foreign channels.[61] The published tax regulations for the port of Canton list several types of taxable European silks as regular imports, including "velvet" (*tian'e rong*), "red satin woven with flowers" (*zhihua hongduan*), and "foreign gold [figured] satin" (*yáng jīnduan*).[62] European silks, like other foreign novelties, appeared frequently among the gifts presented by Canton officials to the emperor.[63] For example, in August 1771 Li Shiyao (d. 1788), then Governor General of Guangdong and Guangxi Provinces (*Liangguang zongdu*), presented nine kinds of imported treasures, including "twenty bolts of foreign jīn-lampas and satin" (*yáng jīnduan*).[64] European silks also figured as gifts from government officials stationed in other regions, who competed with each other in gathering rare and valuable objects to flatter the emperor. Gao Heng (1717–1768), the wealthy and powerful Salt Commissioner of the Huai Region (*Lianghuai yanzheng*), presented "a hundred pieces of foreign figured satin" (*yáng huaduan*) to the Qianlong emperor in 1762.[65]

In addition to obtaining European silks as gifts, Qianlong sought to acquire them through the Canton maritime trade. In spring 1761 he ordered the supervisor of the Canton Customs Bureau (*Yue haiguan*) to purchase some "[figured] satins with gold threads and those with silver threads" (*jīnxian duan, yinxian duan*).[66] The difficulty and long process involved in such a special procurement, however, is revealed by another document in which Qianlong impatiently reprimanded the Canton official because his previous order had still not been fulfilled in the summer of 1762.[67] The challenge may be also due to the fact that by this time silks woven with lavish metal threads were falling out of fashion in western Europe, and this situation could be the direct trigger for the Qing court to turn to Russian products.

Trade with Russia opened another channel for the Qing court to acquire European silks. The Treaty of Nerchinsk of 1689, which established trade relations between China and Russia, permitted Russian merchants to conduct business in Beijing. Nearly four decades later, the Treaty of Kyakhta of 1727 moved the trading center to the eponymous city on the border between the two countries.[68] Records of Qing imperial acquisitions of Russian silks can be found in the documents of the Grand Council (*Junji chu*) and the *Registers Attached to Financial Reports* (*Zouxiao dang*), compiled for the emperor's approval and overseen by the Imperial Household Department. From 1762 to 1774, for example, the Russian trade brought in four major types of silks: "[figured] satin with gold threads" (*jīnsi duan*), "[figured] satin with silver threads" (*yinsi duan*), "figured satin with gold" (*jīnhuaduan*), and "Russian [figured] satin" (*Eluosi duan*).[69] The HJD documents also contain information on Russian silk: an entry dated December 1762 mentions "purchased figured satin with gold from Russia" (*suomai Eluosi jīnhuaduan*).[70] The special commerce with Russia and recurrent product types help explain the prominent presence of Russian silks with consistent floral designs and featuring a generous amount of metal threads in the Palace Museum (see figs. 18, 20, 21). It is also possible that not all these silks sold to China were locally manufactured in Russia; some may have come from other European countries. The same holds true for woolen textiles that Russia traded to China, some of which were reexported wools from Prussia and England of better quality than Russia's own products.[71]

The various records cited above show that the names for European silks in Qing imperial gift records are short and imprecise. As a result, matching an extant piece to a description is practically impossible. A similar tendency exists in the HJD entries referring to European silks and to those made by the Qing imperial manufactories imitating European styles. These textiles shared the same overarching designation of "Western" (*xiyáng*) and were not necessarily distinguished in their classification. The nomenclature used relied on both sensorial experiences and conceptual notions of such textiles rooted in a cultural tradition. The often awkward and ambiguous names for European silks in Qing court documents reveal what imperial patrons regarded as the salient features of these pieces as well as how their cognitive understanding of textile patterns limited their ability to accommodate new visual impressions.

The art historian Craig Clunas has noticed a precise, detailed way of naming objects in Ming dynasty texts ranging from literati treatises on taste to state inventories of confiscated treasures. Evocative names for material objects capture the color, form, decoration, and texture so vividly that they enable instant visualization, even several centuries later.[72] For instance, *A Record of the Water of Heaven and the Iceberg* (*Tianshui bingshan lu*), an inventory of the properties seized from the corrupt minister Yan Song (1480–1565), lists various textiles. Translated in the original word sequence, examples include "blue/woven with gold/phoenix passing through flowers/songjīn-lampas" (*qing zhijīn chuanhuafeng songjīn*) and "pure red/woven with gold/brocaded *qilin* [a mythical beast]/chest square/gauze" (*dahong zhijīn zhuanghua qilin bu luo*).[73] This mode of textile nomenclature packs rich information in concise but expressive words, typically structured in the following sequence: ground color, metal threads (if any), weave structure forming the pattern, main motif, placement of the pattern on the textile (in the case of a nonrepeated design), and ground weave (which also indicates the material). Sometimes one or more categories are omitted.

Scribes of the Qing dynasty continued to qualify Chinese textiles in this way, as shown in countless examples across different genres, from official documents to pawnshop records and popular literature. This deeply anchored knowledge system and visual sensibility, however, encountered limitations with regard to Western-style silks. For instance, a 1723 HJD inventory of textiles in the imperial storage lists various European silks, including some "light yellow/silver threads/foreign/jǐn-lampas" (*ehuang yinxian yángjǐn*) and "white ground/polychrome flowers/foreign/jǐn-lampas /satin [ground]" (*baidi wucai-hua yáng jǐnduan*).[74] Likewise, another 1723 HJD document detailing European silks sent by the Qing court workshops to the three imperial silk manufacturers in the south for replication lists several items, such as "yellow ground/gold threads/Western barbarian flowers and birds/jǐn-lampas" (*huangdi jīnxian xifan huaniao jin*) and "blue ground/gold threads/Western barbarian flowers and fruits/jǐn-lampas" (*landi jīnxian xifan huaguo jin*).[75] Even though these terms carefully maintain the conventional descriptive structure, the words fall short when it comes to describing the patterns. Unlike the well-composed, and at times poetic, phrases for Chinese textiles—which not only identify the motifs but also address the movement and relationship between the patterns—the phrases for Western patterns simply combine the broad geographic term for the West with generic categories of plants and birds. The imprecise names disclose the Qing imperial impression of foreign patterns as somewhat strange and unclassifiable.

The inclusion of a geographic word for the West—*xifan* (Western barbarian), *xiyáng* (Western ocean), or simply *yáng* (ocean)—is a major indicator that an object was European or European-style. The word *fan*, "barbarian," had long referred to non-Han ethnic groups and foreign countries and was traditionally imbued with a pejorative sense. After the Yongzheng period, the more neutral expressions *yáng* and *xiyáng* largely replaced *fan* in Qing court texts to identify foreignness in ornaments and styles.[76] *Xiyáng* clearly refers to Europe when indicating a silk's origin and style, and so does *yáng* in most cases.[77] Whereas the silk descriptions in the 1723 files cited above still strive to include information on color, motif, and stylistic origin, in many cases Qing imperial documents mention Western silks in very sketchy terms that do not specify their foreign association but simply highlight their material components. Many entries reading "figured satin with gold/silver threads" (variously phrased as *jīnsi duan*, *yinsi duan*, *jīnyinsi duan*, or *jīnyin huaduan*) in fact refer to Western silks. Two Qianlong-period imperial labels still attached to the brown bizarre-style silk discussed earlier identify the piece as a "Western jǐn-lampas" (*xiyáng jǐn*) and a "figured satin with gold and silver" (*jīnyin huaduan*), providing concrete evidence of the interchangeability of these two terms (see fig. 10 detail). Although numerous Qing imperial silks with Chinese designs also contain abundant gold threads, the nuanced wording of their names clearly distinguishes them from Western ones. The two major types of gold fabrics that the imperial textile manufactories regularly supplied to the court bore the conventional names "[figured] satin woven with gold" (*zhijīn duan*) or "imperial storeroom gold [fabric]" (*kujīn*), and their Chinese motifs were normally described. By contrast, the general descriptor "gold/silver threads" and the unspecific *hua* (meaning both "flower" and "patterned/figured") were associated only with Western silks probably owing to the lack of a proper glossary for the unfamiliar designs. Silver threads, it should be noted, were rarely used in Chinese silks and conspicuously absent from the regular repertoire of Qing imperial silks. Therefore, those pieces mentioned in the Qing imperial archives as having silver threads were undoubtedly either European silks or specially commissioned Qing imitations.

The nomenclature system reveals that two features of European silks especially captivated the Qing imperial patrons: their unnamable patterns and their abundance of metal threads. The Palace Museum examples surveyed in this chapter certainly merit this overall impression. The metal threads in European silks fascinated the Qianlong emperor not only as components of opulent textiles but as materials in their own right, and he frequently sought to acquire such threads from abroad. For example, in 1750, in accordance with the emperor's instructions, the supervisor of the Imperial Workshops drafted a list of "useful Western things" to be procured overseas through the Canton Customs Bureau, including "gold and silver threads."[78] A year later, the emperor again urged Tang Ying (1682–1756), then Supervisor (*Jiandu*) of the Canton Customs Bureau, to purchase "Western gold and silver threads" and warned him not to deliberately economize on these items.[79] As the HJD makes clear, the repeated orders for European metal threads sent by the court to Canton suggest Qianlong's regular consumption of these materials. Gold threads also figured among the Russian trade goods that the Qing imperial officials procured for the emperor.[80]

Gold threads were not new to Qianlong, as sumptuous Chinese silks featured a profuse amount of such thread of the domestic kind, but European metal threads clearly exuded a special appeal. Silver threads, rare in Chinese textiles but present in almost all the European silks at the Qing court, would have been perceived as particularly novel. The prestige of silver threads is testified to by an imperial regulation from 1765 that permitted only the emperor himself to use archery accessories made of Western "[figured] satin with silver threads" (*yinsi duan*)—no gold is mentioned—in the Grand Review (see fig. 57).[81]

Chinese gold threads also differed significantly from European ones in terms of composition, color, and texture. High-quality Chinese gold threads have a warm yellow tone and radiate a soft glow, a result of the high percentage of pure gold they contain.[82] During the late imperial period, Chinese gold threads used in the southern silk centers were fabricated by attaching hand-beaten gold foil to paper substrate with reddish lacquer adhesive, and the gilt paper was then cut into thin, flat strips. These strips, called "flat gold" (*pianjīn*), were ready for weaving (fig. 24). Winding the flat strips around a silk core produced "rounded gold" (*yuanjīn*), another type of gold thread commonly used for weaving and embroidery (fig. 25).[83]

By contrast, European gold threads in the early modern period were typically gilt silver or gilt alloy rather than pure gold. No paper base was used. Lead was often added to melted gold to add resilience, and other ingredients included pounded glass and alkaline salts with wax. To correct the yellow color, the metal was often greased with verdigris and sal ammoniac distempered with urine and vinegar. Silver was treated by being boiled in water with crushed yellow sulphur.[84] As in China, the first step in making gold threads was to hammer a piece of metal alloy into a flat bar. Then, through the process of wire-drawing, the heated metal was passed through the ever-smaller holes of a winch so that it gradually diminished in size until it became a long, thin wire. This was then beaten flatter and thinner in a few successive stages before being cut into strips.[85] This process changed little from the sixteenth through the eighteenth centuries.[86] The resultant flat strip, called a *lame* (lamella), could be used directly for weaving, but the more common types were threads prepared by spinning the lame around a silk or linen yarn. There were two types of composite threads—the *filé*, or rounded thread with a smooth silk core, and the *frisé*, or crinkled thread, featuring a spiral core (figs. 26, 27). Compared to Chinese gilt-paper threads, the European counterparts have colder and brighter tones. While the lame and filé threads resembled Chinese "flat gold" and

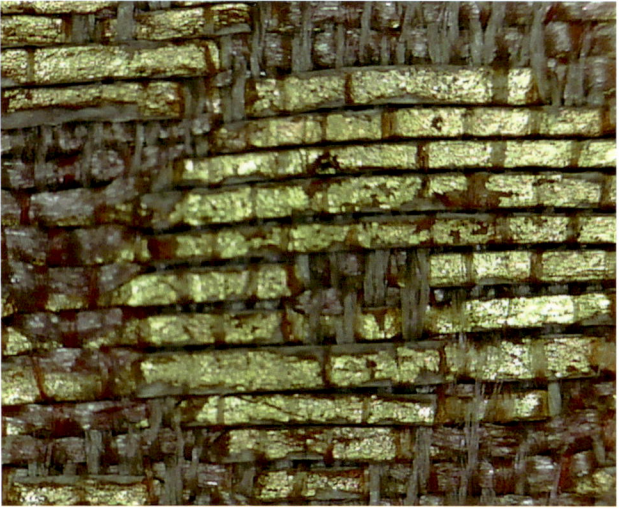

FIG. 24 Chinese flat gold thread (*pianjīn*); microscopic view of a mid-eighteenth-century silk.

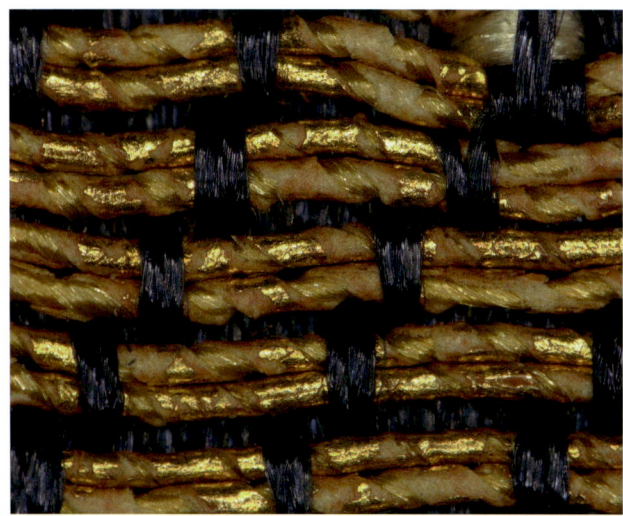

FIG. 25 Chinese rounded gold thread (*yuanjīn*); microscopic view of a mid-eighteenth-century silk.

"rounded gold," respectively, in form, frisé was a novelty to Qing audience.

Each of these three types of European metal thread—lame, filé, and frisé—gleams differently when interplaying with light, especially the flickering candlelight that was ubiquitous in both Europe and China during the eighteenth century. The lame is the crispest and most brittle, having an immediate eye-catching effect; the full-bodied filé appears duller and moist, as if retreating to the background when juxtaposed with lame; and the undulating frisé sparkles dramatically. All three types have been identified in the extant European silks at the Palace Museum and, as in other luxury eighteenth-century silks,

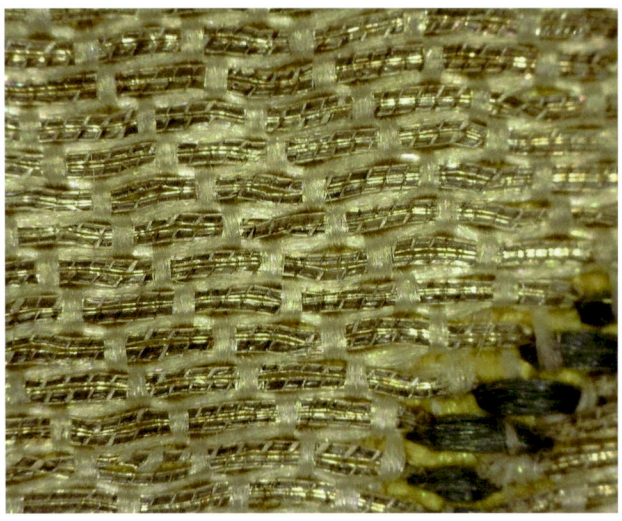

FIG. 26 European silver *filé* thread; microscopic view of a c. 1730s silk.

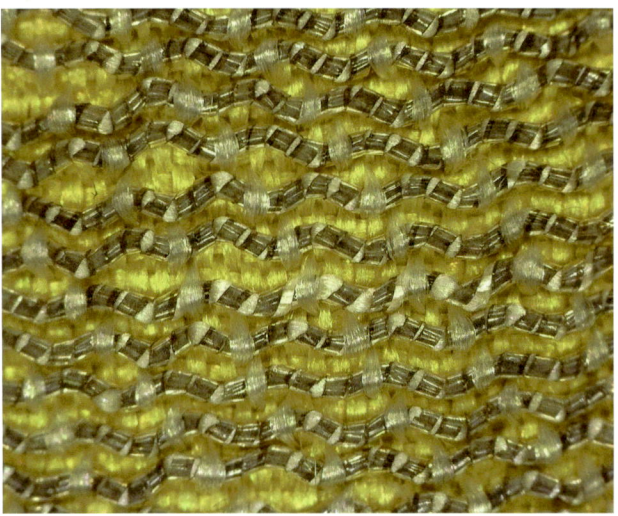

FIG. 27 European silver *frisé* thread; microscopic view of a c. 1730s silk.

often coexist in a single textile to create an exuberant surface with dynamic visual effects. In a detail of the yellow floral silk, for example, the silver foil surrounding the bouquet juxtaposes filé (right), frisé (left), and lame (top and bottom) (see fig. 19). In another Russian length, gold filé threads fill the ground, while gold and silver lames highlight some parts of the interstitial garlands (see fig. 21). One can imagine how these metal threads, rhythmically distributed according to the design, scintillated in flowing, ever-changing pulses when exposed to shifting sources of light.

The unfamiliar appearance of the European metal threads and their dynamic play of light evidently interested the Qianlong emperor, for he eagerly incorporated them into his imperial silks of special significance. The HJD records show that, as treasured and controlled properties, European metal threads were used primarily for embroidery on three types of garments: a unique style of dragon robe for the emperor, the emperor's dragon armor, and clothes for religious icons. For each commission sent to the Suzhou manufactory, the Imperial Workshops at the court allocated an estimated quantity of metal threads from the palace storage and demanded that unused materials be returned in full. For instance, in December 1748, Qianlong ordered Suzhou to make a blue dragon robe with flowers executed in silver threads and nine dragon bodies in gold threads. The Imperial Workshops then dispensed 48 *liang* (about 4 lbs. [1,790 g]) of "Western silver threads" (*xiyáng yinxian*) and 86.5 *liang* (about 7 lbs. [3,227 g]) of "Western gold threads" (*xiyáng jīnxian*) for the project.[87] This type of dragon robe, embroidered solely in metal threads using couching stitches, was a Qianlong-period innovation and epitomized the emperor's uninhibited taste for the spectacular and the extravagant. A few surviving robes of this kind are remarkably similar. In the example in the Metropolitan Museum, the main body of the garment features embroidered designs executed entirely in European gold and silver threads on a contrasting deep blue ground, which beautifully sets off the metallic shine (see fig. 4).[88] Here, gold filé threads were used to render the dragons' bodies and most parts of the waves, clouds, and other symbolic motifs, while silver filé threads accentuate the dragons' teeth, manes, and claws and highlight the secondary motifs. In addition to the cool brilliance of the silver threads, the tone of the gold filé varies from pale yellow (threads with a white silk core) to a more saturated yellow (threads with a yellow silk core) (fig. 28). The different metallic shades create a subtly fluid sheen. Although no records reveal exactly for which occasions this type of robe was intended, the rareness of the European metal threads and the sheer amount of these costly materials consumed for just one garment indicate its association with a high-status event.

The HJD records that in 1759, "foreign gold threads [stored] at the inner court" (*neiting yáng jīnxian*) were sent to Suzhou for embroidering the emperor's armor featuring gold dragons on a yellow satin ground.[89] On another occasion, in January 1764, displeased by the quality of the Chinese gold threads used to embroider the *shou* (longevity) characters on a statue robe for the Daoist icon Laozi, Qianlong ordered the work to be redone with European gold threads. Accordingly, the Imperial Workshops allocated 1.8 *liang* (about ⅛ lb. [67.1 g]) of "extremely fine foreign gold threads [stored] at the inner court."[90] These uses affirm that it was primarily the visual and material qualities of the European metal threads, rather than their cultural evocation of the West, that made these foreign materials most desirable to the Qing emperor. As components of embroideries, they were fully integrated into the symbolic and auspicious Qing motifs and served to reinforce the magnificence of the imperial textiles.

Although the European silks that survive in the Palace Museum represent nearly all the major stages of eighteenth-century silk design, they did not enter the Qing court systematically. Those that arrived during the first half of the eighteenth century did so serendipitously, and the circumstances and decisions by foreign embassies that presented them are now impossible to trace. Nevertheless, their complex, fanciful patterns and brilliant, dynamic metal threads shaped Qing imperial notions about Western silks and led the Qianlong emperor to pursue that same level of quality in his later acquisitions. His aesthetic preferences during the latter half of the eighteenth century can be deduced from the salient presence of one consistent design related to the 1760s French style but filtered through the Russian taste: floral bouquets arranged in a sinuous trellis framework in mirror repeat, which was normally rendered with abundant metal threads.

Once at the Qing palaces, the European silks lost their original temporality and came to represent a homogeneous, timeless "Western" textile style in imperial eyes. They introduced a rich array of novel designs, material compositions, and weaving techniques. Because their motifs lacked any symbolic significance for the Qing imperial audience, the magnificent designs of the European silks would have challenged the deeply rooted understanding of the role of pattern in Chinese textiles and elicited a whole new visual and psychological experience based solely on the surface splendor of the fabric. As we will see in the next chapter, European silks at the Qing court inspired the production of "Western" silks through close copies and interpretive adaptations. Offering visually saturated but semantically opaque surfaces, these Western silks—both original European pieces and Qing court imitations—opened up new possibilities to construct and convey meanings related to Qing imperial ideologies and beliefs.

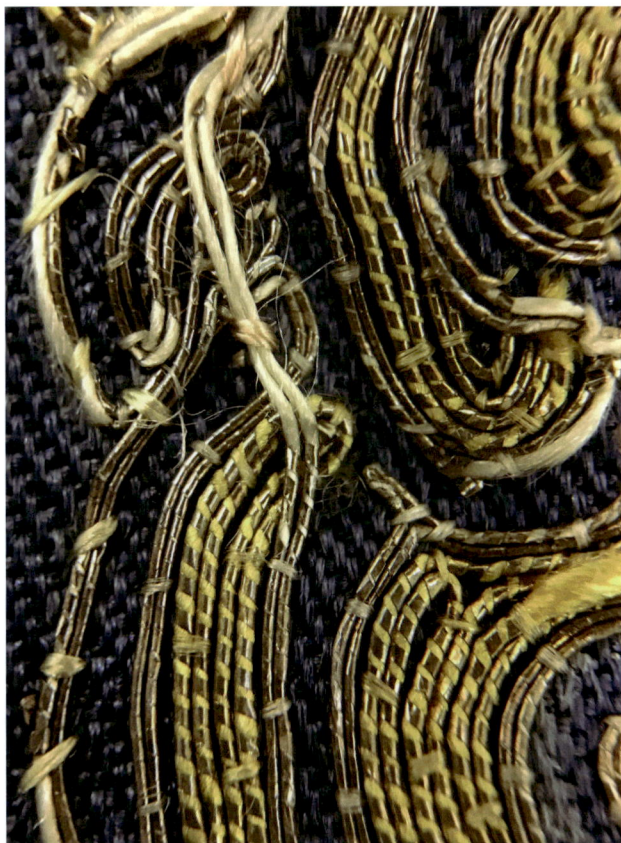

FIG. 28 Detail of fig. 4: European gold and silver *filé* threads used for embroidery in a Qing imperial dragon robe. Photo by Antonio Ratti Textile Center and Reference Library, Metropolitan Museum of Art, New York.

Foreign Splendor 37

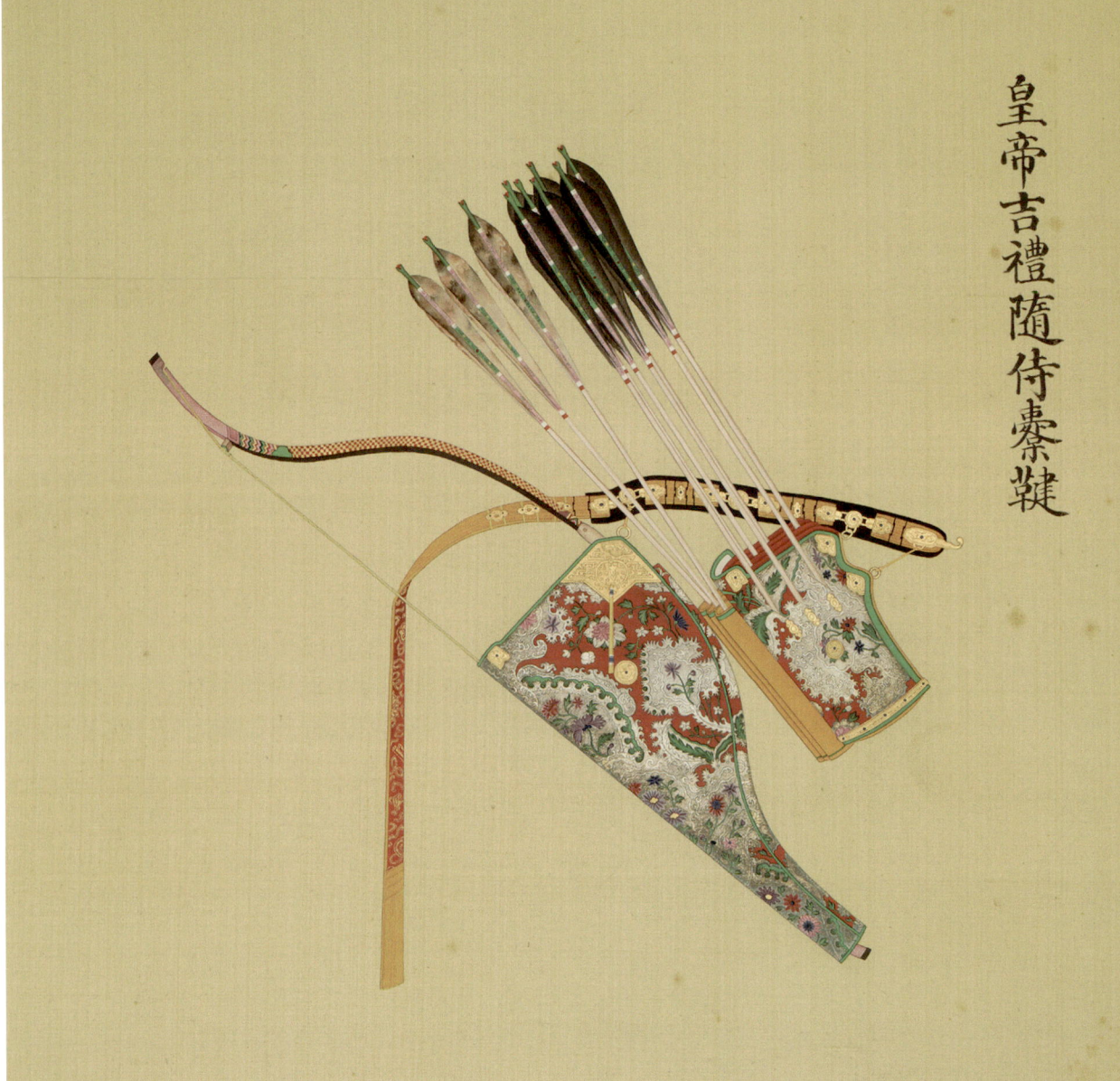

皇帝吉禮隨侍櫜鞬

2 "For His Majesty's Use"

Western Silks and Manchu Rulership

The Qing imperial fascination with European silks led to ardent experimentations in manufacturing so-called Western textiles, which included both close copies of the originals and new designs that assimilated European styles and techniques. At the Qing court, those Chinese-produced Western silks were not distinguished from the European originals in their terminology and uses. Beginning in the Yongzheng reign, the imperial silk manufactories carried out a series of weaving projects under the emperor's instructions; such projects multiplied during the Qianlong period. In Qing court documents, all Western silks, whether imported European ones or Chinese imitative works, merited the same classification of "superb jin-lampas for His Majesty's use" (*shàngyong haojǐn*), which suggests their elevated status in the hierarchy of imperial textiles and their exclusive association with the Qing monarch.[1] Combing through archives and extant objects, this chapter first stitches together the fragmented history of the Qing court's production of Western silks. Much like contemporary endeavors at the Qing court to decode, imitate, and develop the techniques used in other European and Japanese arts and crafts, such as glassmaking, clock making, enamel painting, and lacquer decorated with sprinkled pictures (*maki-e*), this effort to weave luxury Western silks reflected a larger ambition to demonstrate imperial power through advanced mastery of the art and technology of other cultures.

Moving from production to function, this chapter then contextualizes two major uses of Western silks at the Qing court: to fabricate the emperor's regalia for imperial military ceremonies and to adorn Tibetan Buddhist spaces in the palaces. These two domains, one political, the other spiritual, were essential in sustaining the Manchu ethnic traditions and ruling mandate. Magnificent Western silks deployed for these purposes came to channel new sets of messages and serve as a potent vehicle for conveying the Manchu identity and ideology, both of which were pivotal to Qing sovereignty.

WEAVING WESTERN SILKS IN THE QING EMPIRE

The Yongzheng emperor began to commission copies of European silks in 1723, the first year of his reign. A document entitled *Records of the Jin-Lampas Submitted by the Three Silk Manufactories* (*Sanchu zhizao laijin dang*) indicates that in August of that year, Prince Yi (Yi Qinwang, 1686–1730), then in charge of the Imperial Workshops, selected twenty-seven of the finest jīn-lampas from storage and ordered the three silk manufactories in Suzhou, Hangzhou, and Jiangning to replicate five bolts of each sample provided. Seven of the selections were distinguished by name as Western silks, bearing "Western barbarian" (*xifan*) patterns of flowers, birds, or fruits and gold threads. Before this year, the Imperial Workshops had never commissioned replicas of European silks, so it is unquestionable that the Western silks distributed as samples were all original European fabrics. The three weaving bureaus delivered their works between 1724 and 1726.[2] This project probably aimed to test the capacity of the manufactories to produce luxury silks with complex designs, but no evaluation of the products has been discovered in court records. Later, as seen in the archives from the Qianlong period, only Suzhou was commissioned to weave Western silks, which suggests that it had proved itself to be the best qualified to perform this specific task.

Reserved for the exclusive use of the emperor, these cherished jīn-lampas textiles could either serve his personal needs or fulfill a major political function: many were used "for imperial bequests" (*shǎngyong*)—that is, as gifts that the emperor bestowed on prominent officials and spiritual leaders of Tibetan Buddhism. For example, in 1725 Yongzheng honored the powerful Grand General Nian Gengyao (1679–1726) with two bolts of each of the seven newly woven Western floral silks.[3] Such textiles lent themselves as a material token of imperial favor and recognition, while solidifying a special bond between the monarch and his loyal subordinate.

In addition to ordering replicas, Prince Yi, on behalf of the Yongzheng emperor, also commissioned new designs of European-style motifs to be woven in silk. In May 1723 he instructed the Imperial Workshops to copy eight different designs on sheets of "Western stationery paper with gold flowers" (*xiyáng jīnhuajian*) and "send [the drawings] to the silk manufactories to be woven into jīn-lampas."[4] The earliest record of Western decorated paper at the Qing court dates to 1720, and it was among the birthday gifts presented to the Kangxi emperor by the Italian Lazarist friar Teodorico Pedrini (1671–1746).[5] Western floral paper was also mentioned several times in Yongzheng-period HJD files and in the registers of gifts offered by Canton officials.[6] No such paper has been discovered in the two Palace Museums in Beijing and Taipei, but the art historian Michèle Pirazzoli-t'Serstevens identifies it as *dominoterie* (or *Buntpapier*), a type of colored paper with drawn, painted, stenciled, or woodblock-printed motifs. Popular in Europe since the late sixteenth century, it was used there for bookbindings, box linings, wrapping paper, playing cards, wall coverings, and so on. The finest paper of this kind was crafted in southern Germany, especially in Augsburg and Nuremberg; its embossed gold designs imitating printed textiles earned it the name *Brokatpapier* (brocade paper).[7] Some of the floral paper present at the Qing court probably resembled the Augsburg examples, such as a signed sheet with an ornamental pattern in gold varnish by the German engraver and publisher Jacob Enderlin (fig. 29). Qing imperial silks featuring patterns taken from European decorated paper have not survived.

The Qianlong emperor continued this passion for commissioning Western silks and expanded the practice to a grander level, but he was less interested in exploring new designs with cross-media motifs than in pursuing high-quality copies. In addition to sending orders to the imperial manufactory in Suzhou, he occasionally entrusted the supervisor of the Canton Customs Bureau with the same tasks. In May 1761, for instance, the court sent the Canton supervisor five samples of foreign jīn-lampas in purple, green, yellow, white, and pink and instructed him to see to the manufacture of two bolts of each model.[8] Canton had convenient access to European trade silks and a production network for supplying Chinese export textiles. No record reveals how the Canton official organized the weaving to fulfill this assignment, but he may have contracted the work out to private weaving establishments.

A string of informative entries from 1762 in the HJD sheds light on the competitive and experimental weaving activities organized by the Qing court as well as on the quality and cost of Western silks produced by the Suzhou manufactory. In June 1762, in response to an order from Qianlong, the Imperial Workshops sent a Russian "figured satin with gold" (*jīnhuaduan*) purchased from the market and a "Western jīn-lampas" (xiyáng jīn) to You Anning (c. 1700–1762), then supervisor of the Suzhou manufactory, and asked him to replicate each in the length of one *chi* (14 in. [35.6 cm]) using European gold and silver threads allocated by the court. The Imperial Workshops also instructed Anning to forward the original samples to his brother You Bashi (fl. mid-1700s), at the time in charge of the Canton Customs Bureau, who was likewise to produce a copy of each in the same length. There is no further information regarding the Canton products, but Suzhou delivered its works in December of that

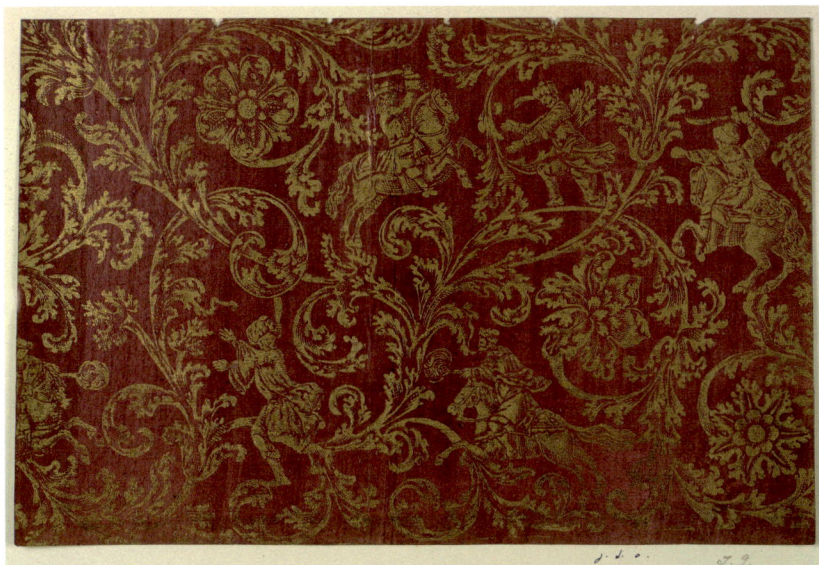

FIG. 29 Bronze and gold varnish paper, late seventeenth century, Augsburg. Signed by Jacob Enderlin. Olga Hirsch Collection of Decorated Papers, British Library, London (Hirsch J. 9).

year.[9] After comparing the commissioned pieces with the Russian samples, Qianlong concluded that the Suzhou products were of better quality. He ordered the officials of the Imperial Household Department to investigate the cost. A thorough report was submitted, which explained that "the purchased figured satin with gold from Russia costs 0.75174 *liang* [of silver tael] per *cun* [3.56 cm], while the figured satin with gold [threads] and Western *jin*-lampas received from Suzhou cost 1.673 *liang* and 0.8753 *liang* per *cun*, respectively. We compared them carefully [and observed that] the pieces made in Suzhou are thick and dense and exquisitely woven, but they seem to have consumed more materials and labor." The report ends with a stipulation: "[With regard to] the figured satin with gold [threads] woven in Suzhou: in the areas with no gold on the front side, there is still full gold floating on the back.... We demand that when the patterns show no gold on the front side, there should be no gold on the back side either. Please report whether this is feasible."[10] This text clearly shows that silk weavers in Suzhou employed the selvedge-to-selvedge lancé technique instead of brocading (as in the Russian sample) for weaving the gold patterning wefts, a practice consistent with the conventional Chinese manner of weaving luxury patterned silks with gold threads during the Ming and Qing periods. The two major types of Chinese gold textiles that the imperial manufactories regularly supplied to the Qing court handled gold threads in this way.[11] Evidently, in the test weaving process, the Suzhou weavers had turned to the familiar technique rather than following exactly a foreign weaving method decoded directly from the textile samples. As the record from June 1762 reveals, in producing Western silks for the Qing court, Chinese weavers exercised a certain degree of liberty in interpreting and realizing the emperor's vision, drawing on their traditions, and, in negotiating with the court, taking measures to modify and adapt their normal techniques to meet imperial requirements.

The record also suggests that, by the early 1760s, Suzhou weavers had developed sophisticated skills in replicating European silks and achieved superb quality exceeding that of the originals. As early as the Kangxi reign, the Qing emperor and his courtiers had ascribed political significance to the mastery of foreign techniques. In 1703 Kangxi invited the revered minister Gao Shiqi (1645–1704) to view glassware made in the Imperial Workshops using European technology that was newly perfected under the supervision of Jesuit missionary artisans at the court. Echoing the emperor's stance, Gao exclaimed, "Although these are simply earthenware [*sic*], their success concerns political governing. These pieces made in China are far superior to those made in the West."[12] Driven by a similar political standpoint, in 1721 Kangxi sent diplomatic gifts consisting of glassware and enamelware—again made using a European technique recently mastered by the Qing Imperial Workshops—to Pope Clement XI (r. 1700–21) and King João V of Portugal.[13] These objects were carefully selected to pay homage to the European leaders while demonstrating to them the Qing Empire's ingeniousness. They embodied a keen sense of competition with regard to artistic and technological advancements, which, as Gao Shiqi made abundantly clear, ultimately reflected a country's political strength and power.

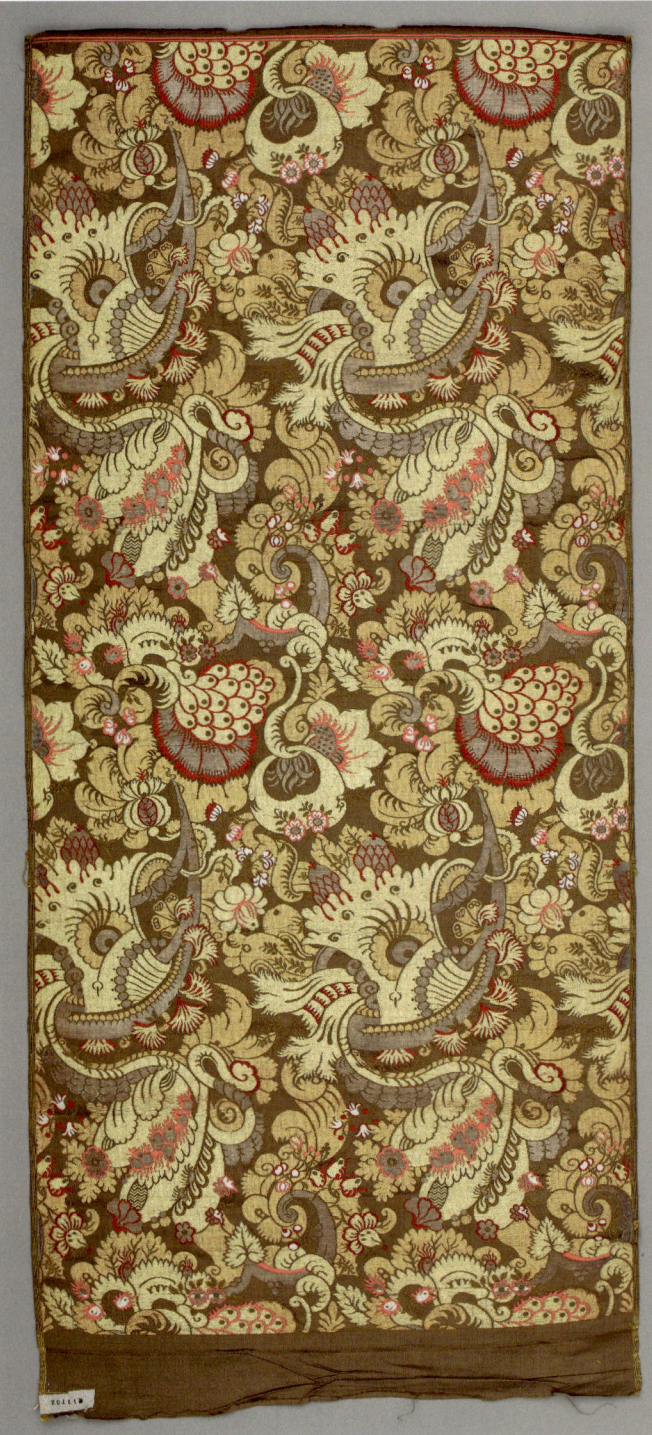

FIG. 30 Textile length, mid-eighteenth century. Made by the Qing Imperial Silk Manufactory, probably in Suzhou. Silk lampas with metal threads, width 21⅛ in. (53.5 cm). Palace Museum, Beijing (gu17782).

FIG. 31 Detail of fig. 30.

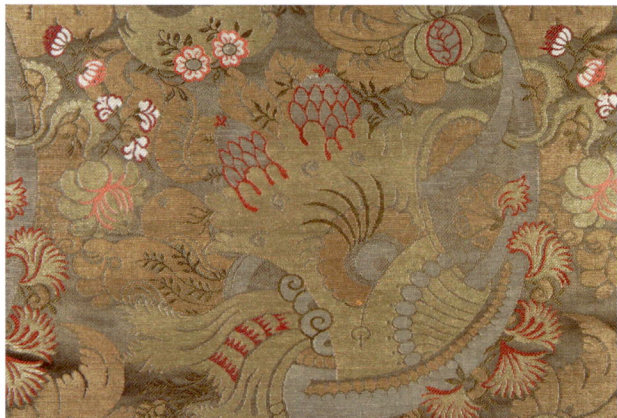

By the same token, although no written records indicate the specific political motivation for producing Western silks, we may speculate that this endeavor was equally propelled by an ambition to affirm the Qing Empire's eminence through the mastery of foreign craftsmanship. As the HJD reveals, Qianlong emphasized that he desired the Western silks made in Suzhou to be "of better quality than the [European] originals."[14] From his viewpoint, the Manchu Empire was the center of the world; hence, decoding the secrets of a foreign technique and excelling at it served to underscore the empire's all-encompassing power. What is more, re-creating these products was a symbolic act of taking possession of a faraway land.

Three related silks in the Palace Museum tell us much about the experiments involved in the Qing imperial projects of making Western silks. The first, a fragment of a French brown bizarre silk datable to circa 1710, introduced in chapter 1, has two imperial label strips still attached (see fig. 10). On one strip, the word "original model" (*yuanyàng*) indicates that this textile once served as a prototype for reproduction; on the other strip, the phrase "incoming document" (*laiwen*) probably refers to a written edict accompanying this silk during its transfer from the Imperial Workshops at the court to a textile manufactory in the south (probably Suzhou). The two other pieces are closely modeled after this fragment, both measuring 21 in. (53.5 cm) wide from selvedge to selvedge, the same as the French original. One length, with only two repeats of the pattern, seems to be the product of the first test weaving (fig. 30). It faithfully captures the pattern of the bizarre silk, rendering the dynamic rhythm of the design in a sophisticated manner. The gold filé threads are Chinese, confirmed by the red binder and paper base. The silver threads, now significantly tarnished, also have a paper foundation and could have been produced locally for this project. The gold threads are woven in lancé while the silver threads

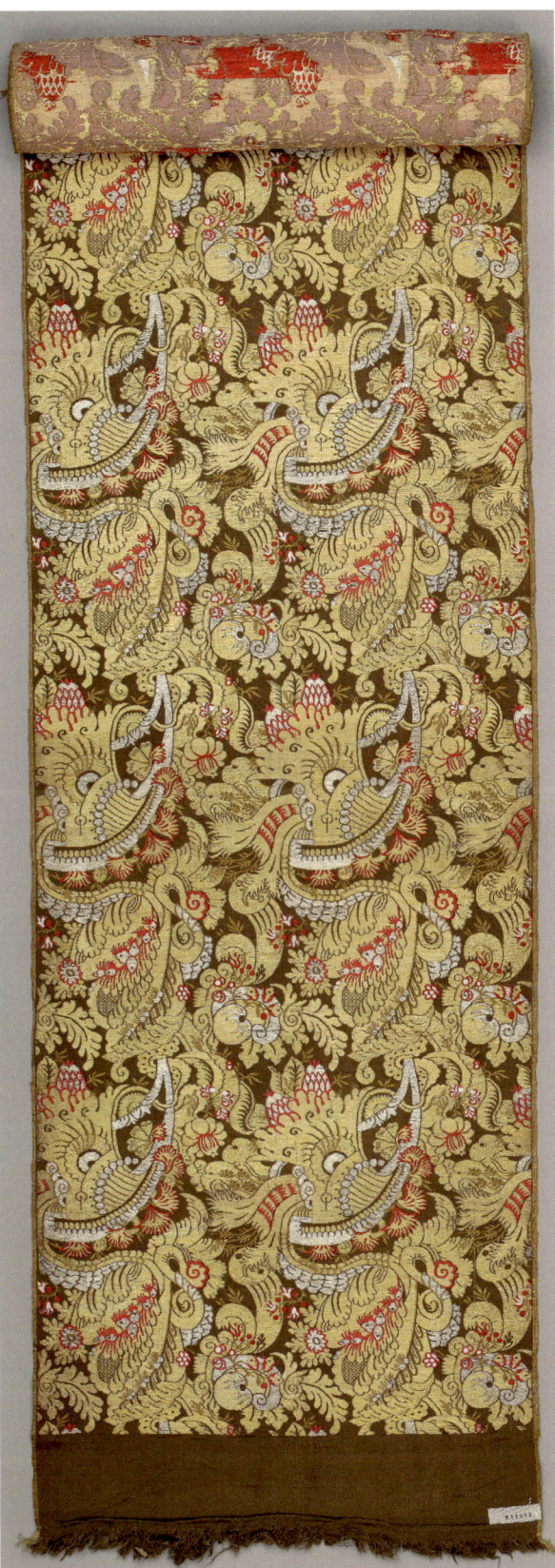

FIG. 32 Bolt of textile (detail), mid-eighteenth century. Made by the Qing Imperial Silk Manufactory, probably in Suzhou. Silk lampas with metal threads, width 21⅛ in. (53.5 cm). Palace Museum, Beijing (gu17782).

FIG. 33 Detail of fig. 32.

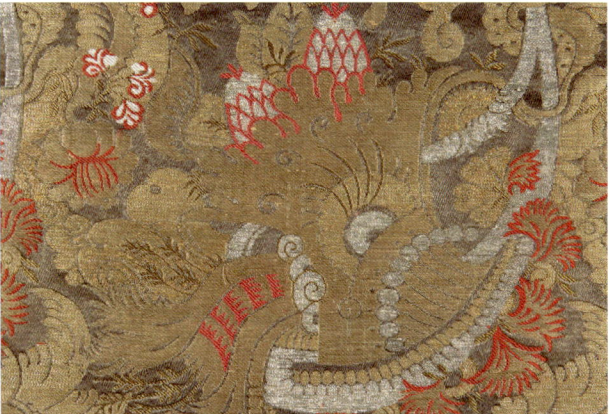

are brocaded. No metal frisé threads are employed, as they had been in the original piece (fig. 31). Although well executed, this test weaving apparently did not meet with the emperor's expectations, as another sample appears to be the approved version since it was woven into a full bolt (fig. 32). This version displays two important changes that reflect the Qianlong emperor's preferences as expressed in the 1762 HJD documents. Not only have European gold and silver threads replaced the Chinese ones, but the gold threads are now brocaded instead of crossing the entire width of the fabric on the back. Imported metal frisé threads are also featured throughout the fabric to enrich the surface texture (fig. 33). Interestingly, this weaving has significantly modified the original design, probably at Qianlong's request. The most conspicuous change concerns the omission of an entire horizontal section of swirling flowers and succulent fruit, which is simply transformed into a short, scalloped ribbon that carries the tip of the horn-shaped frame into the amorphous birdlike body.

While these two bizarre silks closely follow the original French design, several other Western silks in the Palace Museum show a stronger Chinese aesthetic in the rendering of the European motifs and compositions. These pieces resemble various Chinese-made silks with Western-style patterns found in European and American museums, where they are often classified ambiguously as "Chinese export silks." Today's scholarship generally assumes that they were too strange for Chinese taste and therefore not used in China.[15] The similar pieces found in the Palace Museum, however, provide evidence that such hybrid designs did not target the maritime trade alone. Indeed, they strongly appealed to the Qing imperial taste, and at the Qing court they were given the equally ambivalent name of "Western" silks. Despite the dearth of written records on the production of these silks and their circulation in China and abroad, a careful examination of extant

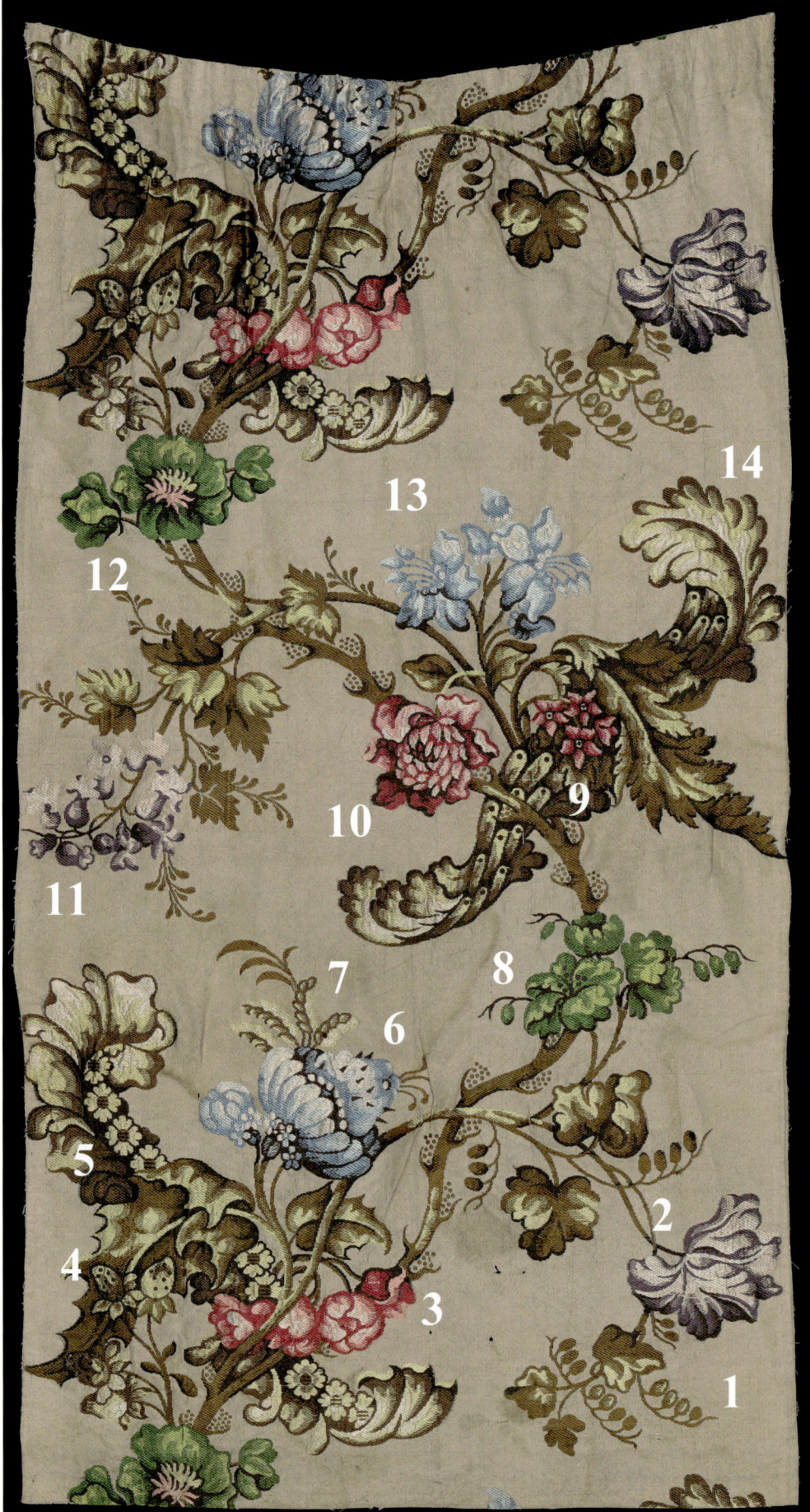

FIG. 34 Textile length, c. 1742, Spitalfields, London. Brocaded silk tabby, 38 × 20½ in. (96.5 × 52 cm). Museum of Fine Arts, Boston, gift of Gertrude Sturgis Eaton via her daughter Katharine Eaton Dreier (1992.244).

Plausible identifications of the floral motifs (by Deborah Metsger):

1. twining vine and flower buds
2. poppy
3. phlox
4. strawberry
5. wallflower
6. thistle or sweet sultan or teasel
7. lily of the valley
8. plum or cherry or quince flower
9. jasmine
10. double anemone
11. catchfly
12. camellia or rose
13. fraxinella
14. acanthus leaf

fabrics yields rich insights into their fluid trajectories and fascinating transformations.

Several versions of a circa 1742 English rococo botanical design offer an intriguing case study on how a silk pattern circulated globally and underwent multiple metamorphoses. Over twenty known silks bearing this pattern have survived in British, continental European, North American, and Chinese collections. They range from uncut lengths and fragments to whole garments. Although textile patterns often traveled far and wide, no other early modern examples have survived in such impressive numbers and variations, indicators of the design's immense popularity and adaptability across cultures.

The pattern is consistent in all the versions despite variations in the colors and a few details. In some pieces, the pattern appears mirror-reversed—a fact that indicates repeated copying and reweaving of the original design. Made in either England or China, the extant examples share a similar weave structure in which the motifs are brocaded with supplementary, discontinuous patterning weft threads and bound to the ground in twill. The patterning threads are significantly thicker than the ground warps and wefts, thus creating a slight relief effect. On the basis of different loom widths, color schemes, foundation weaves, and renditions of the motifs, we can divide the extant examples into three groups: made in England, made in China for export, and made in China for use in the Qing Empire.[16] Despite some exceptions, loom width, when considered in tandem with other stylistic and technical traits, is a crucial element in determining the manufacturing location of eighteenth-century silks. Eighteenth-century English dress silks varied from 19¼ to 21⅝ in. (49 to 55 cm) wide but did not reach the regulated half-ell width of 22½ in. (57 cm).[17] By contrast, Chinese silks, whether for export or domestic use, usually ranged from 22 to 30¾ in. (56 to 78 cm) wide. Other features, such as the choice of colors, the ground weaves, and nuances in the execution of the motifs, betray culturally specific tastes and visual sensitivities.

The first group of silks—those made in England—is exemplified by a skirt panel, now in the Museum of Fine Arts, Boston; it was originally part of an eighteenth-century dress (fig. 34).[18] This silk has a plain ground weave and measures about 20½ in. (52 cm) from selvedge to selvedge, consistent with the typical English loom width. The cream color reflects the English preference for light ground colors in dress textiles, and the motifs are finely rendered in the points rentrés technique, introduced from France in

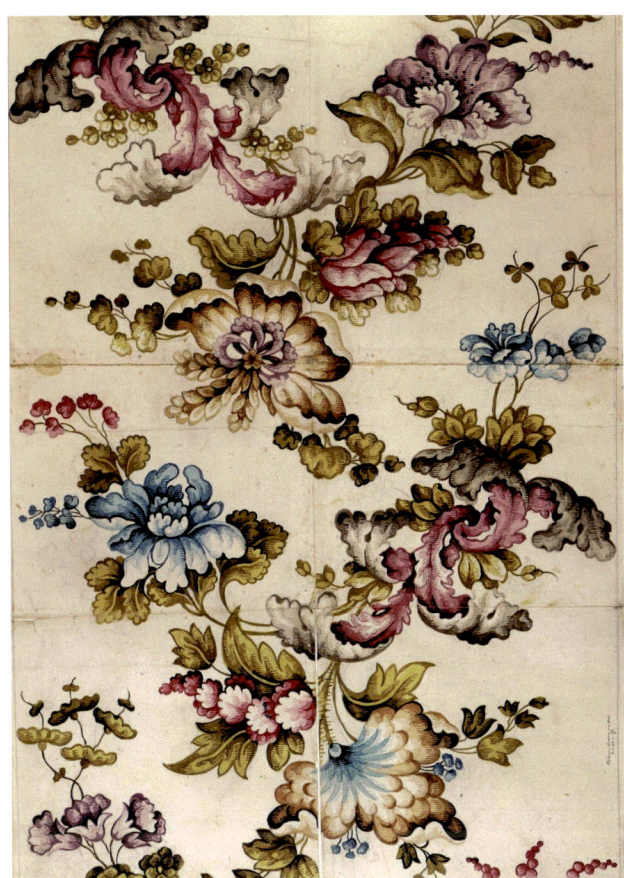

FIG. 35 Anna Maria Garthwaite, design drawing for silk, dated 1742, Spitalfields, London. Victoria and Albert Museum, London (5980:5).

the 1730s. In a large pattern repeat across the fabric's width and measuring 26 in. (66 cm) along the vertical axis, a sinuous stem carries alternating luxuriant floral branches and smaller tendrils. The imagery may be best described as a rococo botanical fantasy. Whether in full, three-quarter, or profile view, the flowers appear realistic and are reminiscent of species of garden plants common to the period. Large flowers resemble poppy, double anemone, phlox, camellia, thistle, fraxinella, jasmine, and so on. The oversized, curling branches are composed of rocaille-like ornaments, acanthus leaves, and irregularly serrated foliage. Smaller motifs, such as strawberries, lily of the valley, and generic flower buds, occupy the interstices or dangle from the branches.[19]

The pattern shows a close affinity with works created by the English silk designer Anna Maria Garthwaite in the early 1740s, especially one drawing that features the similar device of rocaille-style coiling leaves with a sculptured effect progressing in an alternating diagonal line and interspersed with large flower heads and sprouting buds (fig. 35). As scholars have pointed out, Garthwaite's silk designs often incorporated species newly imported to England, benefiting from the vibrant botanical culture in London sustained by the British Empire's colonial and trade systems.[20] In the early modern period, European empires, such as Britain's and Spain's, shared the same zeal for collecting, classifying, and documenting the plants of Asia, Africa, and the Americas. These endeavors did not merely constitute Enlightenment-era exercises in the study of natural history; they also fulfilled imperial ambitions to govern distant lands and thereby control their natural resources.[21] Garthwaite's silk designs reveal how fashionable textiles encapsulated the rising global interest in botany and exotic things. They turned scientific knowledge into quotidian visual and material culture while offering their wearers channels of imagination that transcended geographical boundaries.

Colonial North America was the most important market for Spitalfields silks outside London in the first sixty years of the eighteenth century, but costly floral silks woven on a drawloom made up just a small portion of exported English textiles, and even wealthy colonial elites possessed few of them.[22] The silk in the Museum of Fine Arts, Boston, came from the prominent local Sturgis family, several generations of which were powerful merchants of overseas trade during the eighteenth and nineteenth centuries. The family's mercantile wealth and maritime connections would have given them access to the finest English brocaded silks.

The majority of the extant examples bearing this rococo botanical design were made in China for export—our second group. They share similar soft, pastel colors and a plain ground weave. The light hues of the ground conformed to English taste, but these pieces differ from the first group in their larger loom widths, which range from 22⅞ to 25 in. (58 to 63.5 cm). An example is provided by a pink length made in China and now in the Philadelphia Museum of Art (fig. 36).[23] It deviates from the original English production in the colorway of the flowers and leaves. Notably, the large foliage is rendered in green to distinguish it from the brown rocaille motif that intertwines with it. This feature also characterizes all other Chinese versions for export as well as those used in the Qing Empire. The pink color, rather unusual for silks used in China, may have been an adaptation to the European taste. The points rentrés technique is used throughout this piece, but shading has become more decorative than descriptive, a sign that the pattern was probably copied

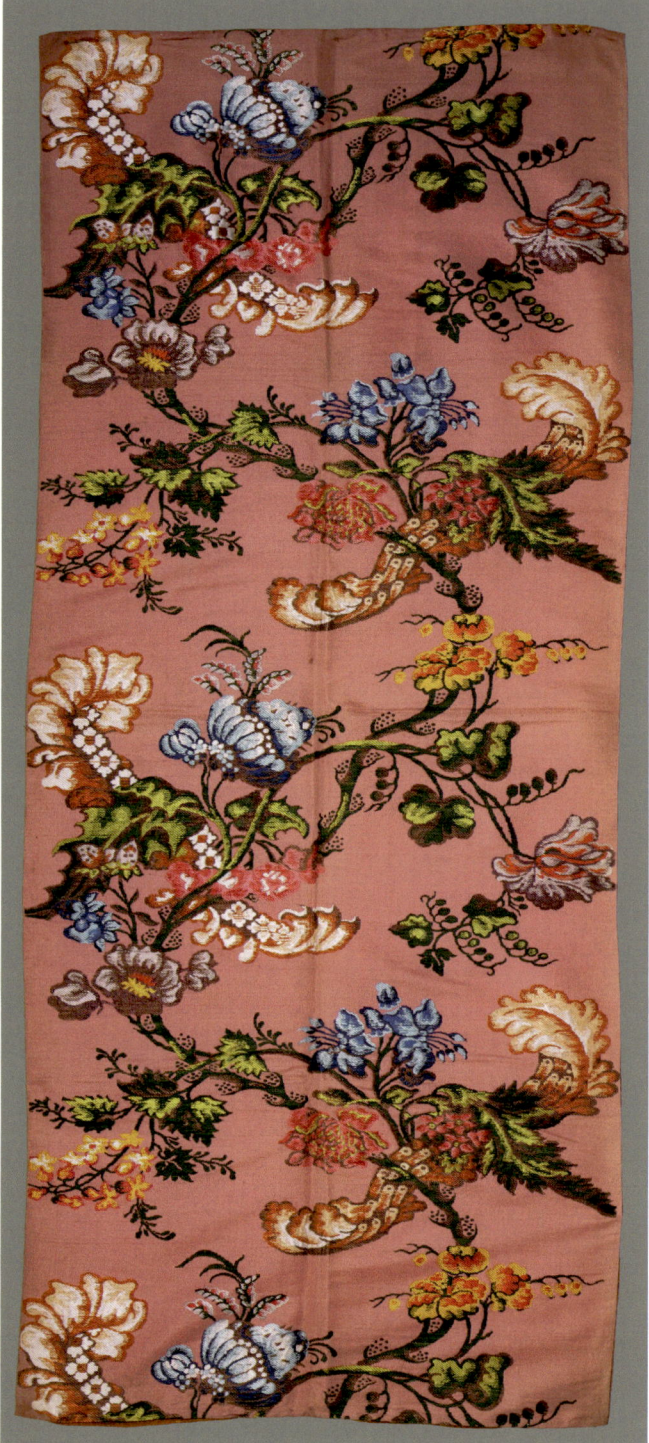

FIG. 36 Textile length, mid- to late eighteenth century, Chinese. Brocaded silk tabby, 55¾ × 25 in. (141.6 × 63.5 cm). Philadelphia Museum of Art, gift of Horace H. F. Jayne (1928–24–3).

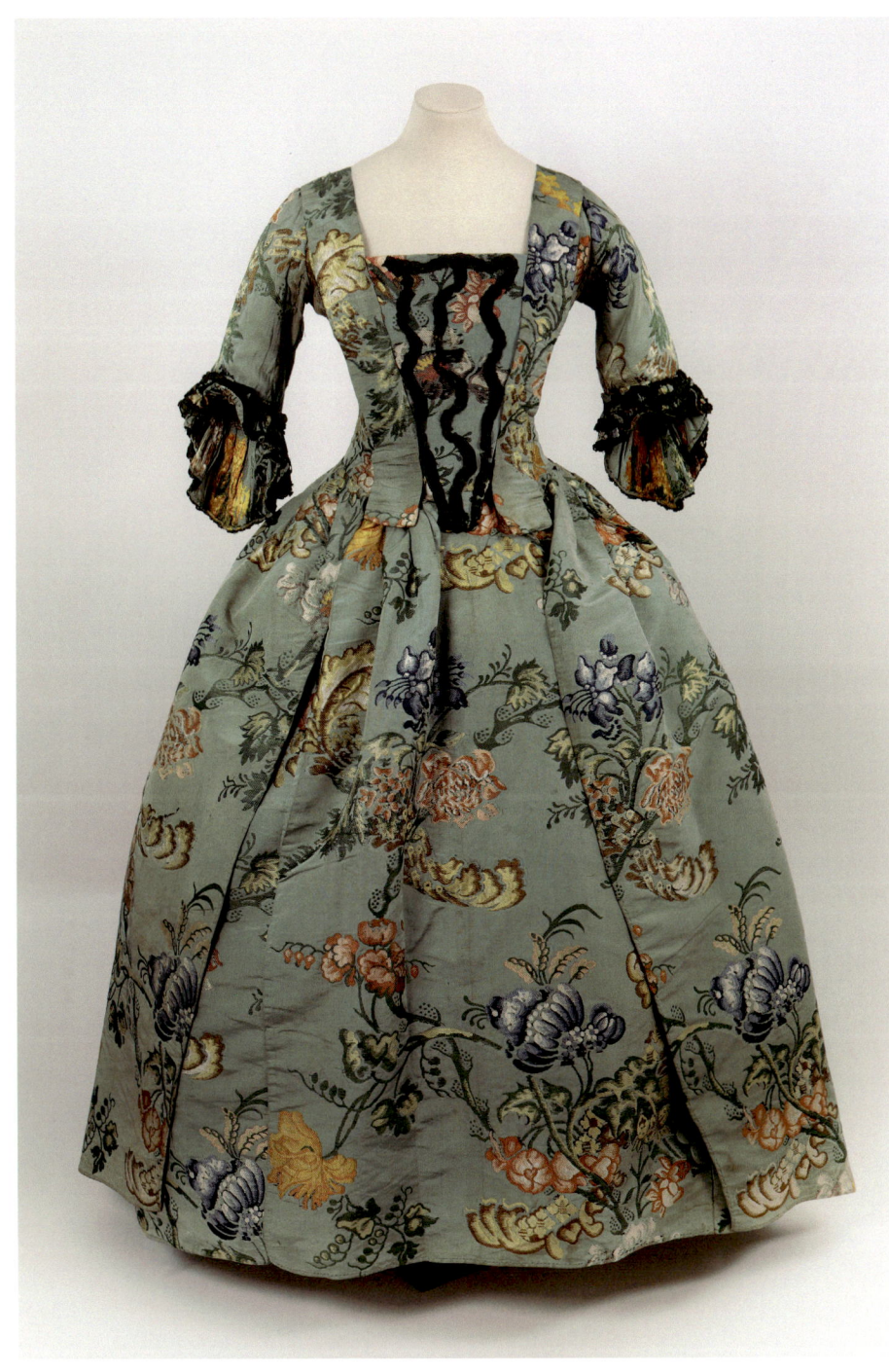

FIG. 37 Dress (*robe à l'anglaise*), remodeled c. 1760s, English. Textile: brocaded silk tabby, early 1740s, probably Chinese, Fashion Museum Bath (BATMCIII.09.1).

secondhand from a finished silk rather than developed from an original design drawing or point paper. In such processes, the intention of the initial design was often misinterpreted or even lost.

Like the English example in the first group, several silks in the second category served as dress textiles and have survived as refashioned garments. A pale blue version, now in the Fashion Museum, Bath, was made into a *robe à l'anglaise,* an open gown with a fitted bodice back (fig. 37). The current dress, dated to around the 1760s, was probably remodeled from an earlier *robe à la française* with loose back pleats. The silk measures 22⅞ in. (58 cm) wide and the pattern repeat extends to 27½ in. (70 cm) in the warp direction, in a larger scale compared to the English silk in the first group. Another example with a cream ground, in the Victoria and Albert Museum, now survives as a man's fancy-dress coat with a built-in waistcoat tailored around the late nineteenth century. The textile was probably first used for a woman's gown around the mid-eighteenth century, which was subsequently altered twice.

The silk has a pattern repeat estimated at 28 in. (71.5 cm) long in the warp direction, based on the visible parts, which suggests a loom width of approximately 22⅞ to 23⅝ in. (58 to 60 cm).[24] Chinese woven silks with elaborate patterns reached England in very small numbers. British navigation laws and prohibition acts required all silks brought back by the East India Company to be reexported to continental European cities, the West Indies, or the British colonies in North America.[25] Nevertheless, Chinese silks were still present in Britain as a result of smuggling and private purchases by East India Company crew members. Given their small quantity and luxury status, finely brocaded floral silks like the above-mentioned pieces, whether for reexport or as personal orders, were unlikely to be regular supplies from Chinese weaving houses. They were almost certainly made-to-order commissions that weavers produced after receiving fabric samples.

Silks featuring the same rococo botanical pattern, often tailored into garments, have been found in a number of other European collections, including those in Ireland, Scotland, Sweden, Norway, and France. They may be Spitalfields productions or Chinese export works. According to published sources, the ground colors vary from pink to blue to yellow. The Nordic countries were one of the main markets for silks from England, which possibly included Chinese silks reexported by the East India Company. In Sweden, Chinese silks were imported from Canton and overland through Russia.[26] The various silks featuring this design found in Britain, colonial North America, and continental Europe demonstrate how a widespread and deeply interconnected trading system created a synchronized network of fashion, engaging their widely dispersed wearers in the same global trends of botanical fascination and rococo taste. While facilitating the spread of this fashion in the West, Chinese silks bearing this particular pattern, initially ordered by foreign merchants for the markets outside China, embarked on a very different journey within the Qing Empire.

The Palace Museum has three eighteenth-century iterations of this botanical pattern. Two uncut lengths, both with a satin ground and a loom width of 23⅝ in. (60 cm), feature an overall color of dark blue and bright yellow, respectively (figs. 38, 39). The latter contains Chinese gold filé threads that highlight the shading of some of the flowers. The third example, a sky blue version with a plain weave ground, was made into a standard theatrical costume for a female role type as a married lady or

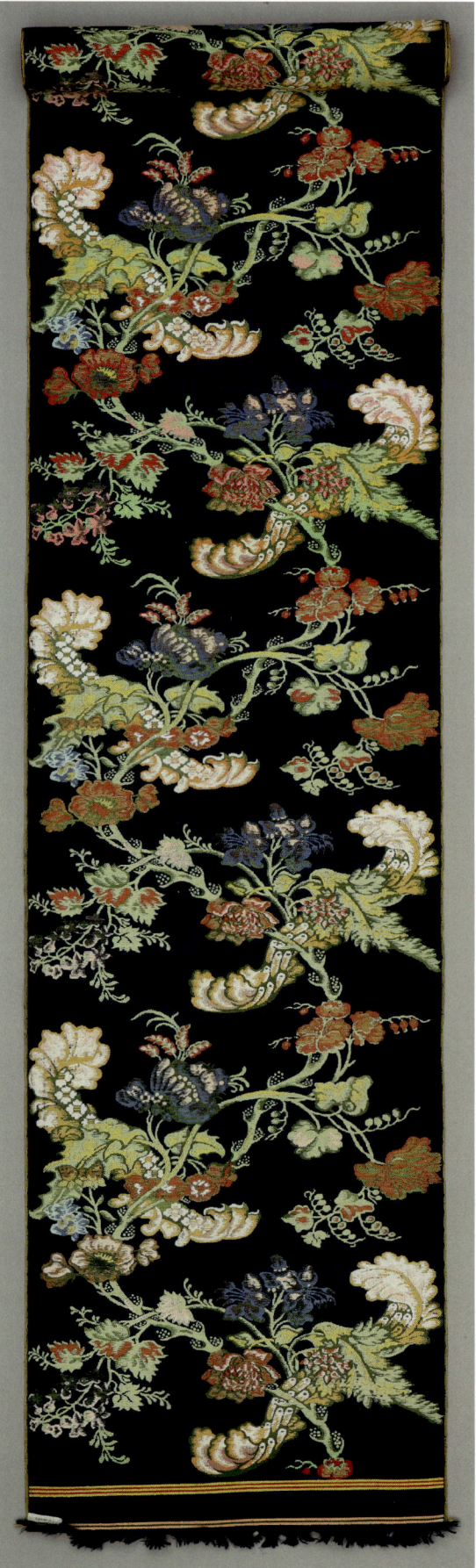

48   Chapter 2

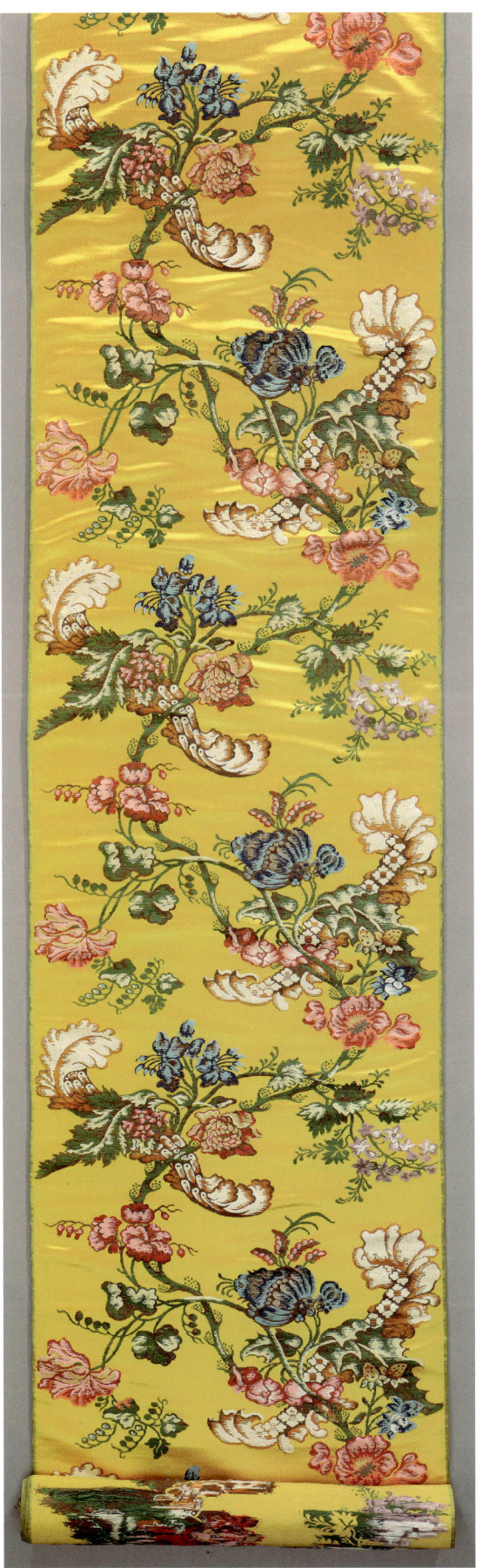

a young maiden (fig. 40). No records reveal the production or acquisition history of these silks, but their fine quality, consistent with that of other imperial silks, indicates that they may have been commissioned by the court and woven in one of the imperial manufactories.

In the Palace Museum pieces, the light ground colors popular in the English taste have given way to more saturated hues that echoed the palette of Qing imperial costume and furnishing textiles. Bright yellow (*minghuang*) was a restricted color, reserved exclusively for the emperor, empress, and high-ranking consorts, whereas dark blue and sky blue, termed *shiqing* (literally, slate blue) and *yuebai* (literally, moon white), respectively, in Qing documents, appeared often in both formal and informal court garments. These standard shades would have enabled the silks to be harmoniously integrated into the Qing court's visual environment. The satin weave, which brings out the maximum shine of the silk threads, was also the most common ground weave in Chinese silks in general. It is not seen in the English works or in the Chinese exports bearing this design; it appears only in those fabrics used in the Qing territories. Likewise, metal threads (the Chinese type made of gilt paper wrapped over a silk core), which are not present in the first two groups of silks bearing this botanical pattern, are found in these two pieces and several other examples made for the domestic Qing market. Gold and silver threads added an extra dimension of luxury and splendor. In the Qing imperial pieces, the shading effect rendered by the points rentrés technique has become even more abstract and decorative compared to the effects in the export versions.

The Qing court domesticated this English rococo botanical design, but the pattern remained markedly exotic. This silk's quasi-realistic depictions of foliage, flowers, and fruits—quite different from the fantastical styles of early eighteenth-century European silks at the Qing court—would have resonated with the Qianlong

FIG. 38 (OPPOSITE) Bolt of textile (detail), mid- to late eighteenth century. Made by the Qing Imperial Silk Manufactory. Silk satin brocaded with silk and metal threads, 28 ft. 9⅝ in. × 23⅝ in. (878 × 60 cm). Palace Museum, Beijing (gu25478).

FIG. 39 (LEFT) Bolt of textile (detail), mid- to late eighteenth century. Made by the Qing Imperial Silk Manufactory. Silk satin brocaded with silk and metal threads, width 23⅝ in. (60 cm). Palace Museum, Beijing (gu17952).

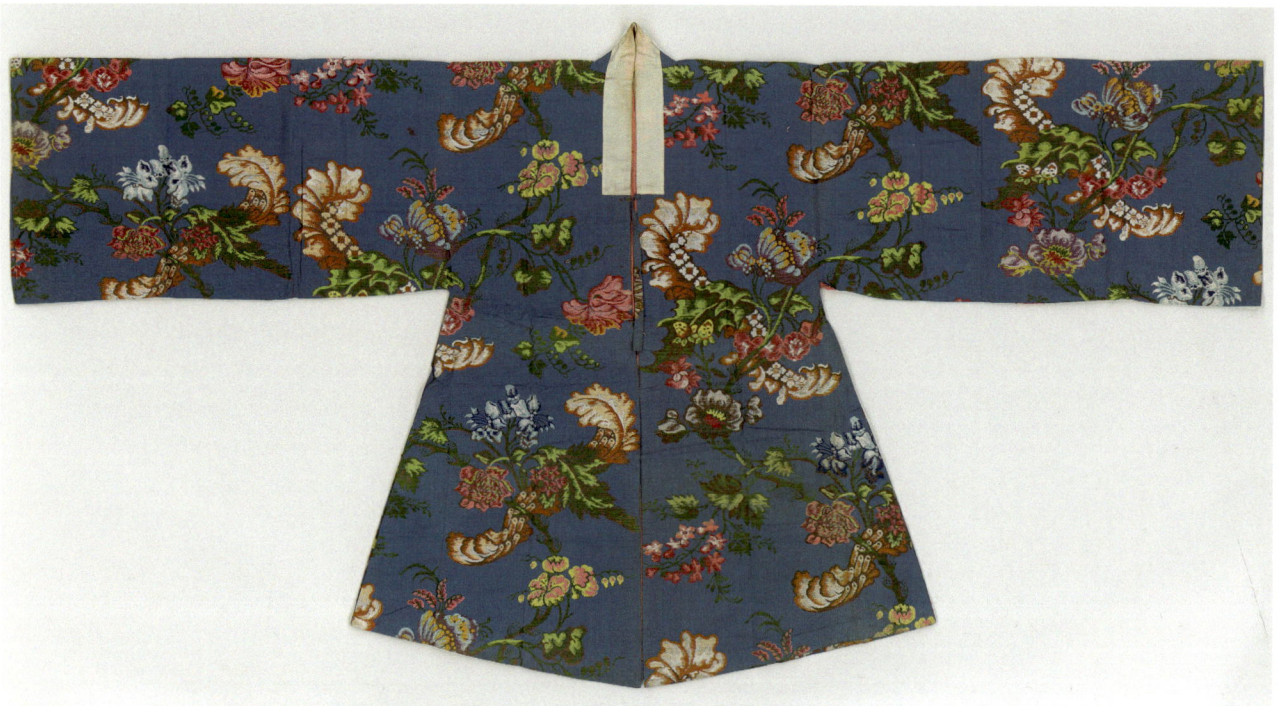

FIG. 40 Qing court theatrical costume for a female role, mid- to late eighteenth century. Textile made by the Qing Imperial Silk Manufactory. Silk tabby brocaded with silk threads, length 43¼ in. (110 cm). Palace Museum, Beijing (gu215980).

emperor's growing interest in European plants and botanical imagery. During the eighteenth century, the Qing court did not send out scientific expeditions or undertake taxonomic studies of plants on a grand scale, as did their European counterparts. Nevertheless, Qianlong engaged in parallel projects of cultivating and depicting foreign plants, in which Jesuit missionaries serving at the court were instrumental by introducing foreign species to the Qing imperial gardens and transmitting European botanical knowledge. The emperor was curious to learn about the Western flowers illustrated in European publications on botany housed in the Jesuit library in Beijing. He also appointed Father Pierre-Noël Le Chéron d'Incarville (1706–1757), a versatile French scientist with botanical training, to oversee the landscaping of the European Palaces in his Garden of Perfect Brightness (*Yuanming yuan*), an enormous imperial estate complex in the northwestern outskirts of Beijing. D'Incarville corresponded with well-known European botanists and agriculturalists, notably the French naturalist Bernard de Jussieu (1699–1777) of the Jardin du Roi. In 1742 he asked Jussieu to send him seeds from a range of popular Mediterranean and South American flower species that could potentially interest Qianlong and engage him in further discussions of botany. The list included huge poppies of different colors, tulips, ranunculus, anemones, small and large nasturtiums, bush basils, and lilies, among others. Many of the plants later bloomed in the gardens of the European Palaces and the Jesuit church.[27]

D'Incarville noted that the emperor was attracted primarily to the flowers' color variations and then to the fruits.[28] This preference with regard to live plants may equally explain Qianlong's fascination with this rococo botanical pattern in silk as well as the design in the circa 1733 French silk he used for his saddle blankets (see figs. 15, 16). Both textiles abound with colorful flora and succulent fruits with a striking, exotic appearance. These naturalistic silk patterns constituted a part of the Qing imperial visual project to assemble botanical images. Evolving from a long native Chinese tradition of realistic depictions of botanical subjects dating back to the "flowers and birds" genre in Song dynasty (960–1279) Academy painting, flower paintings continued to thrive in Qing court arts. The European pictorial techniques of perspective and three-dimensional modeling, introduced by Jesuit missionaries, especially Castiglione, injected a new, lifelike quality to this genre. Adapting Western techniques to suit Chinese visual conventions, which rejected dramatic shadows, Castiglione used the Chinese painting medium of ink and color on silk and invented a soft modeling style of highlights on a light surface. His undated album *Immortal Blossoms in an Everlasting Spring* (*Xian'e Changchun*), completed around 1723–35, showcases his novel style and virtuosic skill. The sixteen leaves represent flowers ranging from tree peony and peach blossom to cockscomb and tiger lily—all native Chinese species—and feature compositions and accurate botanical depictions quite different from traditional Chinese flower paintings.[29]

Castiglione's album dates to a period before the production of the English silk design discussed here, but the visual kinship between them may well explain the appeal of the latter to the Qing imperial taste. For example, the graceful stem of the tree peony in Castiglione's image bends at the same angle as the curvilinear vines in the silk (fig. 41). Some representations in other leaves, such as the dangling cluster of purple lilacs and the sensuous poppy with fringed petals, bear strong similarity to corresponding details in the silk design, even though the flower species may not be exactly the same (figs. 42–45). These circumstantial similarities, across two different media, from far-flung locales, and belonging to unrelated contexts, refracted the interest in botanical images that swept many parts of the world, cultural sectors, and artistic forms, linking unconnected patrons to a network of knowledge and imagery. This web in turn generated an epistemological and cognitive foundation for the Qing court to search for and adopt new botanical species and images. Traveling from England to Canton and to the Qing court, this English silk design stood as a valuable visual and material vestige of this network.

During the Qianlong reign, newly commissioned images of foreign flowers documented some of the exotic species cultivated in the palace gardens and confirmed the imperial interest in plants from beyond the Qing territories. The 1757 album *Assorted Flowers from the West Ocean* (*Haixi jihui*) by the court painter Yu Sheng (1692–1766?) provides a notable example. It depicts eight kinds of flowers with scientific explanations for each: buttercup, nasturtium, white and red anemones, red and yellow ranunculus, and white and purple bush basils (fig. 46). All but one of these appeared on d'Incarville's list for Jussieu in 1742.[30] Yu's paintings lack the vivid three-dimensionality and dynamic composition of Castiglione's album, but his depictions of the entire plant rather than just a close-up of the flower stressed empirical observation and functioned more as illustrated scientific samples than as aesthetic images.

As the Qing court's botanical images and Qianlong's own inscriptions reveal, the emperor valued foreign flowers, regarding them in a way as rare tributes from the far west. From the Qing imperial perspective, the movement and acquisition of these species glorified the Qing Empire's superiority and far-reaching power over all other regions.[31] The pictures of exotic plants complemented a contemporaneous Qing imperial effort to compile illustrated zoological manuals. Both *Manual of Birds* (*Niaopu*) and *Manual of Beasts* (*Shoupu*), which will be discussed in chapter 3, stood as part of a larger agenda of constructing the empire's universal power through encyclopedic images. Interestingly, Qianlong never commissioned plant images in the same large numbers that characterize the manuals of birds and beasts. It is tempting to argue that the Western silks displaying naturalistic flora at the Qing court partially fulfilled this purpose, since their botanical patterns present an array of novel and fanciful species. Porcelain and copper vessels made for the Qing court and bearing designs in overglaze enamel—itself a recently

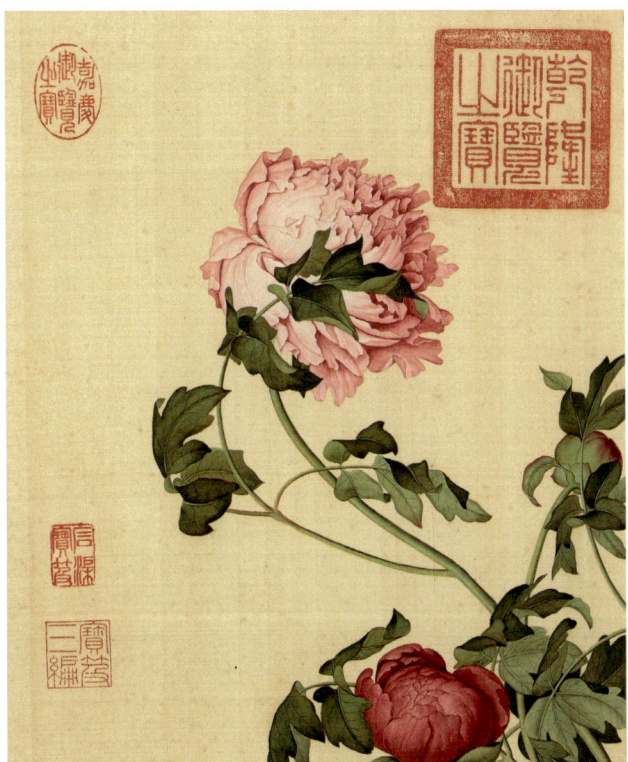

FIG. 41 Giuseppe Castiglione, "Tree Peony," in *Immortal Blossoms in an Everlasting Spring* (*Xian'e Changchun*), 1723–35. Album leaf, ink and color on silk, 13⅛ × 11 in. (33.3 × 27.8 cm). National Palace Museum, Taipei (guhua1222).

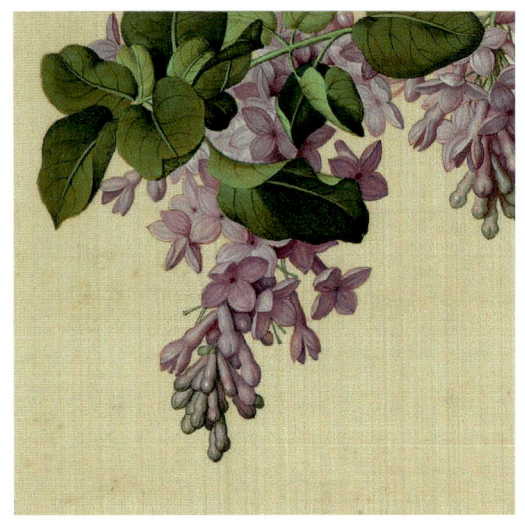
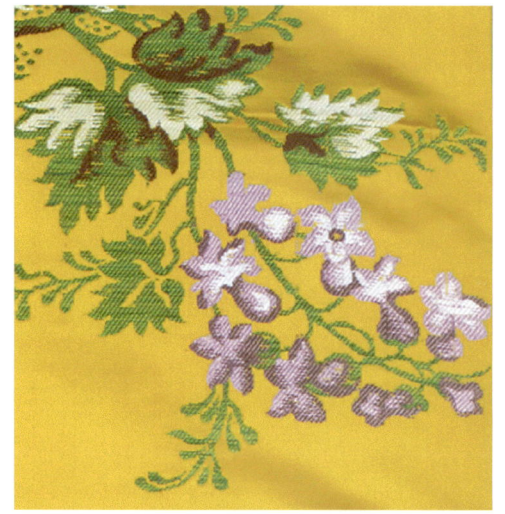

FIG. 42 (FAR LEFT) Giuseppe Castiglione, "Purple and White Lilacs" (detail), in *Immortal Blossoms in an Everlasting Spring* (*Xian'e Changchun*), 1723–35. Album leaf, ink and color on silk, 13⅛ × 11 in. (33.3 × 27.8 cm). National Palace Museum, Taipei (guhua1222).

FIG. 43 (LEFT) Detail of fig. 39, probably catchfly.

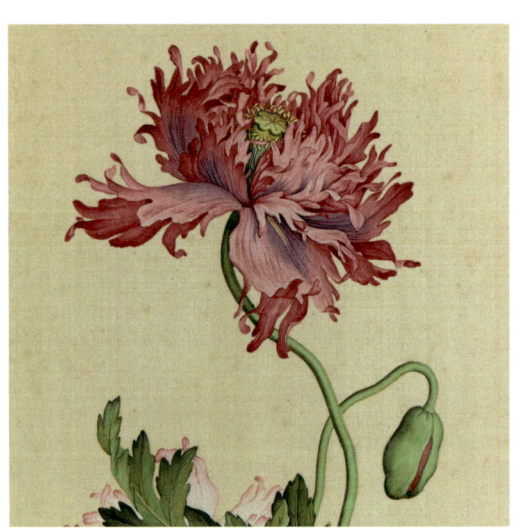

FIG. 44 (FAR LEFT) Giuseppe Castiglione, "Poppy" (detail), in *Immortal Blossoms in an Everlasting Spring* (*Xian'e Changchun*), 1723–35. Album leaf, ink and color on silk, 13⅛ × 11 in. (33.3 × 27.8 cm). National Palace Museum, Taipei (guhua1222).

FIG. 45 (LEFT) Detail of fig. 39, probably poppy.

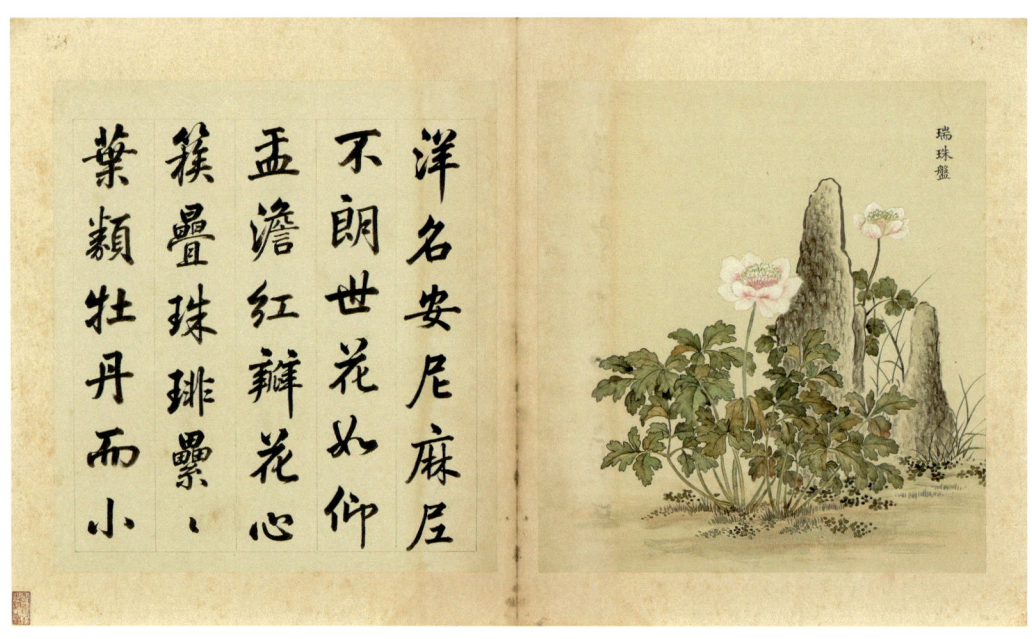

FIG. 46 Yu Sheng, "White Anemone," in *Assorted Flowers from the West Ocean* (*Haixi jihui*), 1757. Album leaf, ink and color on paper, each leaf 12¾ × 11⅞ in. (32.4 × 30.3 cm). National Palace Museum, Taipei (guhua 3379).

introduced Western technique—also depicted various foreign flowers newly grown in the imperial gardens. These vessels joined the textiles in creating a new imperial visual realm of botanical decoration charged with political meaning.[32]

This rococo botanical pattern moved farther in the Qing Empire and reached as far as its subjugated and governed lands. Two versions of silk preserved in the Abegg-Stiftung—both coming from the old storage of an unspecified Buddhist monastery in Tibet—reveal yet another context and function of textiles bearing this design. One of them, with a deep-red satin ground, contains Chinese gold threads and has four Chinese characters written in ink on the back, which are partially legible as "respect" (or "respectably") and "receive" (fig. 47).[33] Like the first version of the brown bizarre silk made by the Qing imperial workshops (see fig. 30), this piece was woven as only a short length with two repeats and complete top and bottom borders, which suggests a sample weaving. The other small fragment, with an orange satin ground, has a triangular folding mark, indicating that it was once part of a banner for a Buddhist hall.[34] Such banners are usually patchworks consisting of an assortment of small floral silks with the ends folded in a triangular shape. In East Asia, Buddhist vestments and furnishing textiles, including robes for priests, coverlets for statues and relics, and various textiles for adorning the temples, have long been made from assembled fabric fragments, recalling the practice of using rags collected at the burial ground and in the streets as specified in the *Vinaya Piṭaka*, a Buddhist scripture regulating monastic conduct and procedures.[35] Many precious silks were acquired by temples or donated by patrons in the late imperial period. The act of cutting them up and piecing together the fragments symbolized renouncing the worldly value of the original pieces.

The Abegg silks may well have come from the Qing court as an imperial offering; the red one was possibly a commissioned sample sent to Tibet for review. As the last section of this chapter will further elaborate, the practice of using Western floral silks to adorn Tibetan Buddhist spaces originated at the Qing court and spread to other court-sponsored monasteries through imperial gift giving and donations. Multiple entries in the HJD also record that the Qing emperor bestowed gifts on the spiritual leaders of Tibetan Buddhism—the Dalai Lama and the Panchen Lama—as well as on other Tibetan dignitaries.

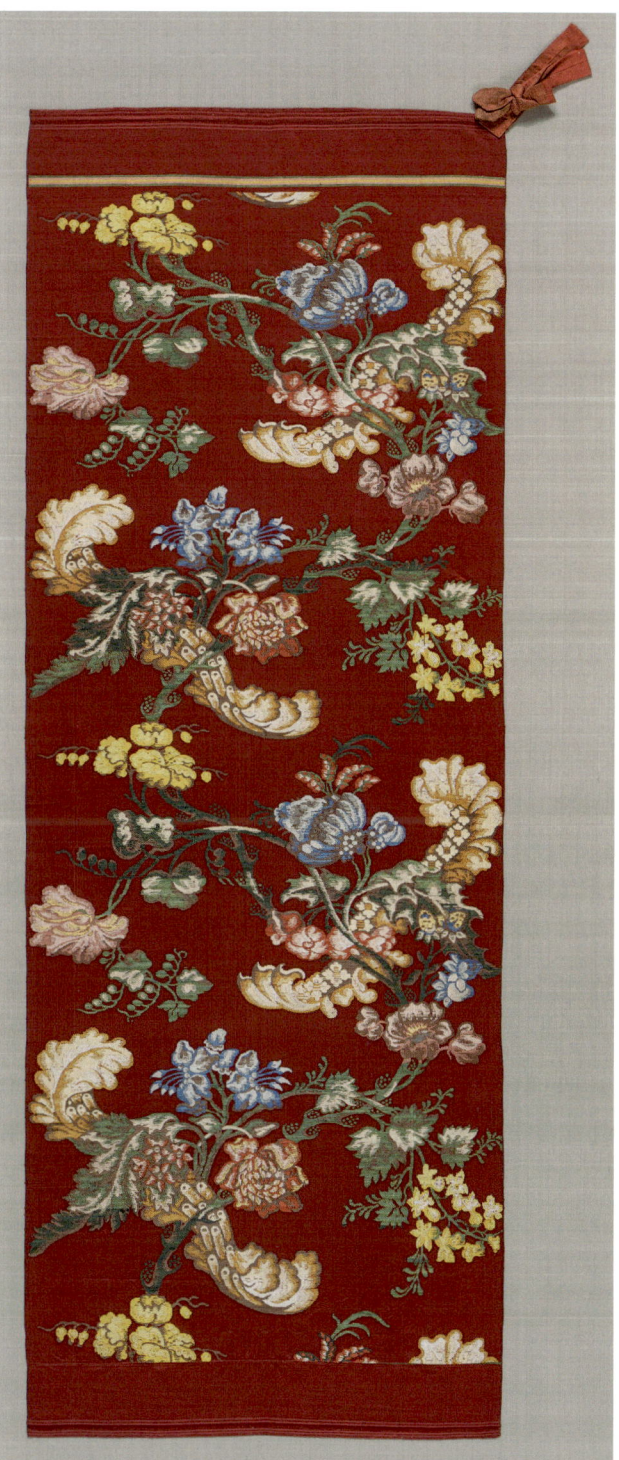

FIG. 47 Textile length, mid- to late eighteenth century, Chinese. Silk satin brocaded with silk and metal threads, width 22½ in. (57 cm). Abegg-Stiftung, CH-3132 Riggisberg (inv. no. 3995a).

Imperial textiles figured regularly among such gifts, which possibly included Western silks, given their special function as "imperial bequests."³⁶ This channel would probably have helped disseminate luxury Western fabrics to remote but prestigious temples in Tibet, where this English botanical design underwent yet another recontextualization and became integrated into a sacred environment.

This rococo floral pattern, and its many incarnations, was not only spread throughout vast regions; it also inhabited different times over a long period. During the nineteenth century, it continued to enjoy popularity in the Qing Empire, where it underwent further transformation into a fully sinicized decorative pattern. In one bright yellow length of silk in the Palace Museum, the composition, proportions, and color of the original design have been modified with great liberty: each bough is both compressed in width and elongated in order to fit into the new composition of two trails (rather than just one) across the fabric width of 30¾ in. (78 cm), and part of the alternating branch on the left side has been omitted. The points rentrés technique is absent, and the shading effect that characterizes other versions discussed above has been flattened into contrasting color blocks (fig. 48). Another example, a nineteenth-century polychrome velvet in the Nelson-Atkins Museum of Art, retains the original composition and the basic structure of the large foliage and rocaille motif, but the leaves and flowers have been significantly stylized (fig. 49). The naturalistic botanical representation that marked the English original and most Chinese copies has given way to a two-dimensional decorative pattern that reflects traditional Chinese aesthetics. In particular, all the tendrils have become formalized scrolls similar to those prevalent in late imperial Chinese textiles and porcelains.

From Europe and America to Canton, the Qing court, and Tibet, the movements of this long-lived, versatile design did not follow a straightforward or linear course. The pattern underwent a series of changes through aesthetic adaptations and technical reinterpretations, and at each turn it came to play a new role and convey new sets of values or messages. Its flexibility to inhabit and shape different cultural contexts defies the modern attempt to classify it as European or Chinese. As a visual and material agent in the global exchange of luxury goods and scientific knowledge, it engaged the imagination of users in different locales for various cultural, political, and religious purposes. Its metamorphoses in the Qing Empire,

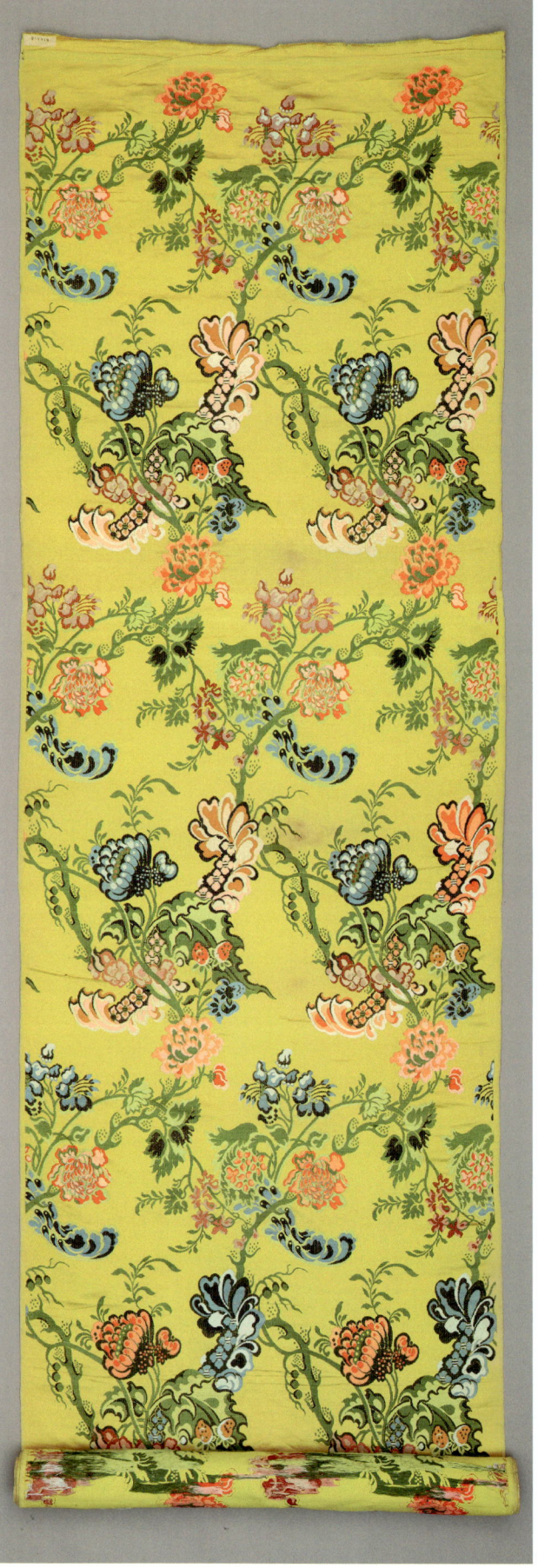

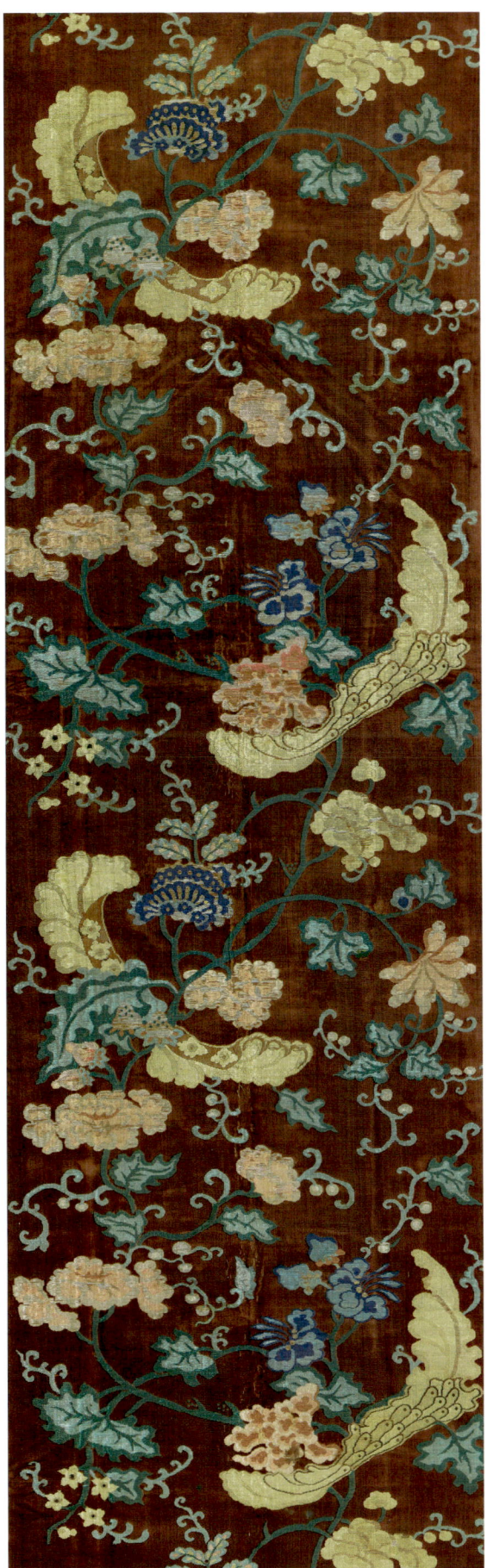

which deviated from original function as a fashion item, unfold a story of exoticizing and domesticating—themselves botanically related terms—that characterized early modern global encounters and exchanges.[37]

Beyond these variations of the English rococo botanical designs, several other eighteenth-century silks in the Palace Museum show Chinese interpretations of Western patterns. They strongly resemble some Chinese-made silks in the Western style that are now in European and American collections, where they are typically classified as "Chinese export." In one example featuring a symmetrical design of large floral heads on an open ivory damask ground, elements drawn from different stylistic periods of European silks converge (fig. 50). The pineapple-like central motif with sprouting leaves recalls the prototype of 1720s lace-patterned silks; the large lotus blossoms and peonies are flattened interpretations of three-dimensional flowers; and the diaper pattern on the ivory damask ground, rendered rather incoherently, is also borrowed from the decorative vocabulary of 1720s European silks. The color scheme, weave structure, and visual sensibility of this textile recall an eighteenth-century Chinese silk with an exotic floral pattern made into a Japanese *kesa* (Buddhist priest's cape), now in the Metropolitan Museum of Art (fig. 51). The latter has a similar ivory damask ground with stylized vegetal motifs. We do not know how or why this textile ended up in Japan, but a recent exhibition catalogue gave the dubious explanation that it was a Chinese export silk with "awkward" patterns that did not meet European expectations, so it did not make its way beyond Japan.[38]

Such an unfounded speculation exposes problems in the classification of textiles exhibiting transcultural styles that do not fit comfortably into conventionally defined categories bound to one specific culture. The presence of similar silks both at the Qing court and outside China propels us to rethink the categorization and definition of so-called Chinese export silks. Current scholarship and

FIG. 48 (OPPOSITE) Bolt of textile (detail), nineteenth century, Chinese. Silk satin brocaded with silk threads, 28 ft. × 30 ¾ in. (852 × 78 cm). Palace Museum, Beijing (gu18218).

FIG. 49 (LEFT) Textile panel (detail), nineteenth century, Chinese. Uncut and voided silk velvet brocaded with silk threads, 94 × 59 ½ in. (239 × 151 cm), for three panels sewn together. Nelson-Atkins Museum of Art, Kansas City; purchase, William Rockhill Nelson Trust (33–844).

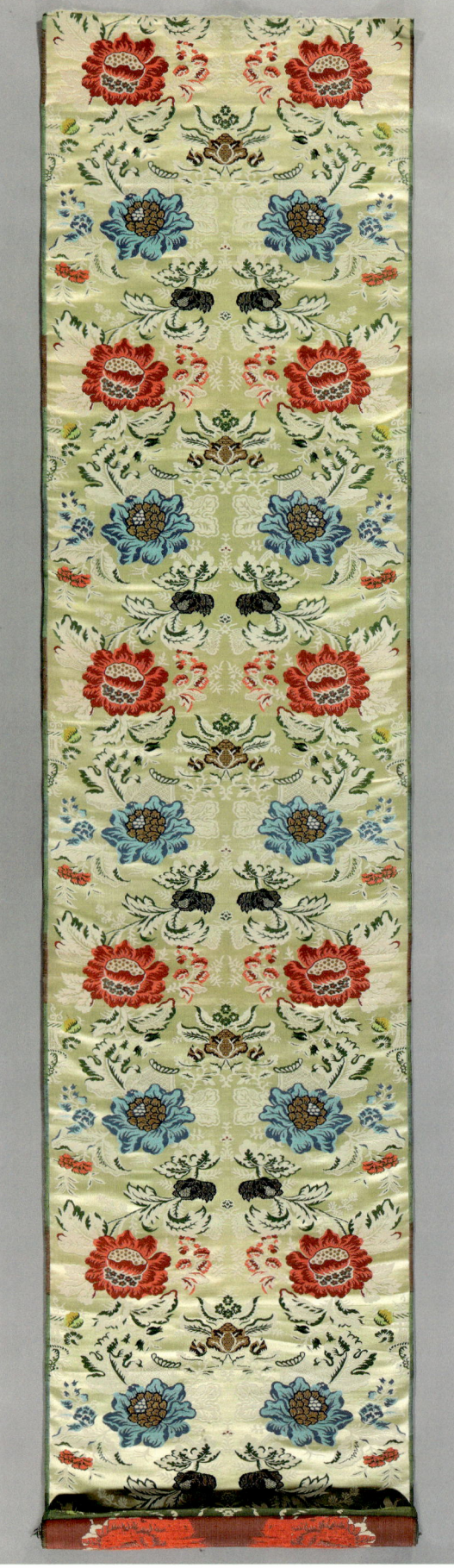

museum catalogues tend to label all textiles made in China in the European style as Chinese export works intended for Western markets, a view that implies the mutual exclusiveness of Chinese and European tastes. The consumption of these silks in China, especially at the imperial court, however, problematizes the arbitrary opposition of "export" versus the "domestic" market, while challenging the perception of the textile trade as a unidirectional movement from China to Europe. The perceived "awkwardness" of these textiles exactly reflects how a design negotiated between different cultural norms could evolve into a distinct new style.

Another group of silks at the Qing court further demonstrates how European patterns, compositions, and weaving techniques were integrated into Qing imperial textiles, which gave rise to some standardized designs for Chinese Western silks. Multiple pieces woven at the Qing imperial manufactories and dated to the second half of the eighteenth century or to the nineteenth century feature one particularly popular design derived from European models but unique among Qing court productions: here, small morning glories facing either upward or downward sprout from a symmetrical structure formed by ogival-shaped meandering scrolls, while peonies rendered in profile punctuate the central axis (figs. 52, 53). The overall

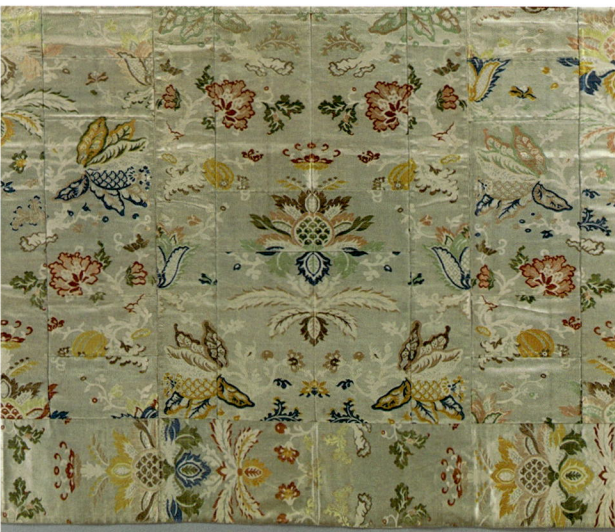

FIG. 50 (LEFT) Bolt of textile (detail), mid- to late eighteenth century, Chinese. Silk lampas with metal threads, 17 ft. × 23¼ in. (518 × 59 cm). Palace Museum, Beijing (gu17766).

FIG. 51 (ABOVE) Japanese Buddhist vestment (*kesa*) (detail), eighteenth century. Textile: mid- to late eighteenth century, Chinese. Silk lampas, 46 × 83 in. (116.8 × 210.8 cm). Metropolitan Museum of Art, New York; purchase, Joseph Pulitzer Bequest (19.93.111).

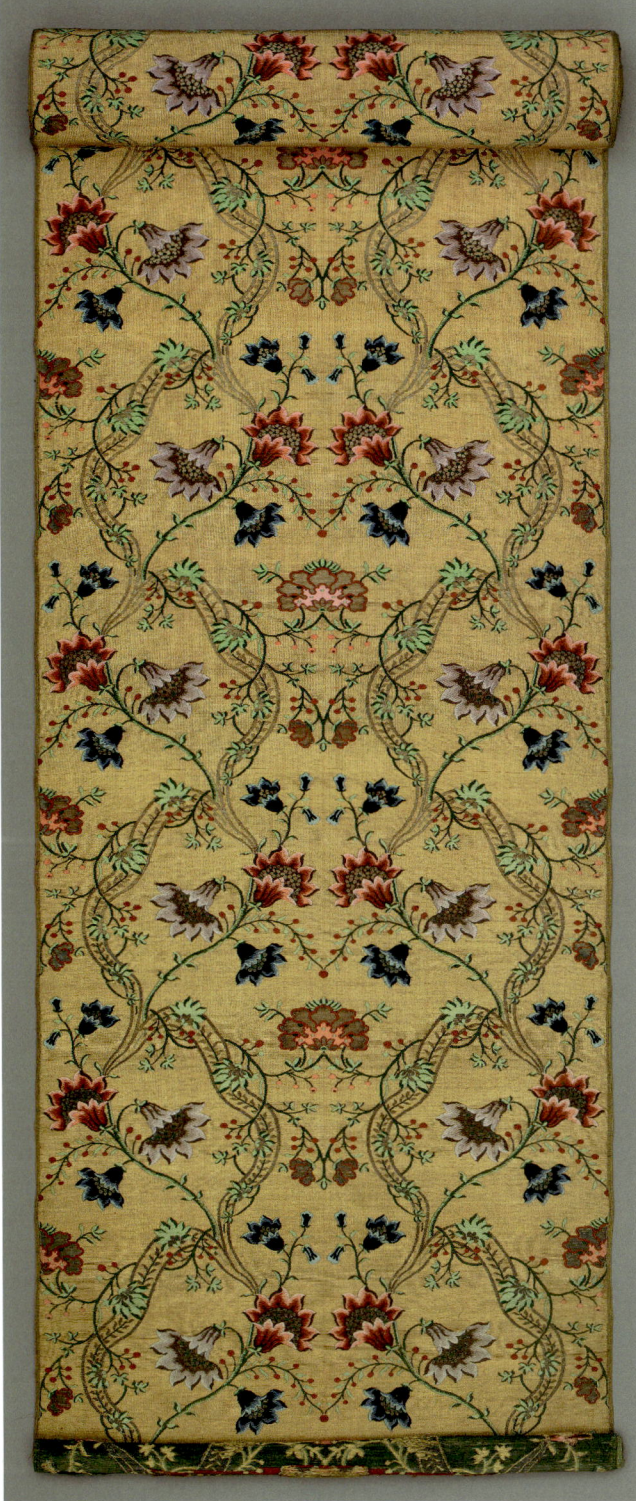

FIG. 52 Bolt of textile (detail), late eighteenth century or nineteenth century. Made by the Qing Imperial Silk Manufactory. Silk lampas with metal threads. Palace Museum, Beijing (gu25480).

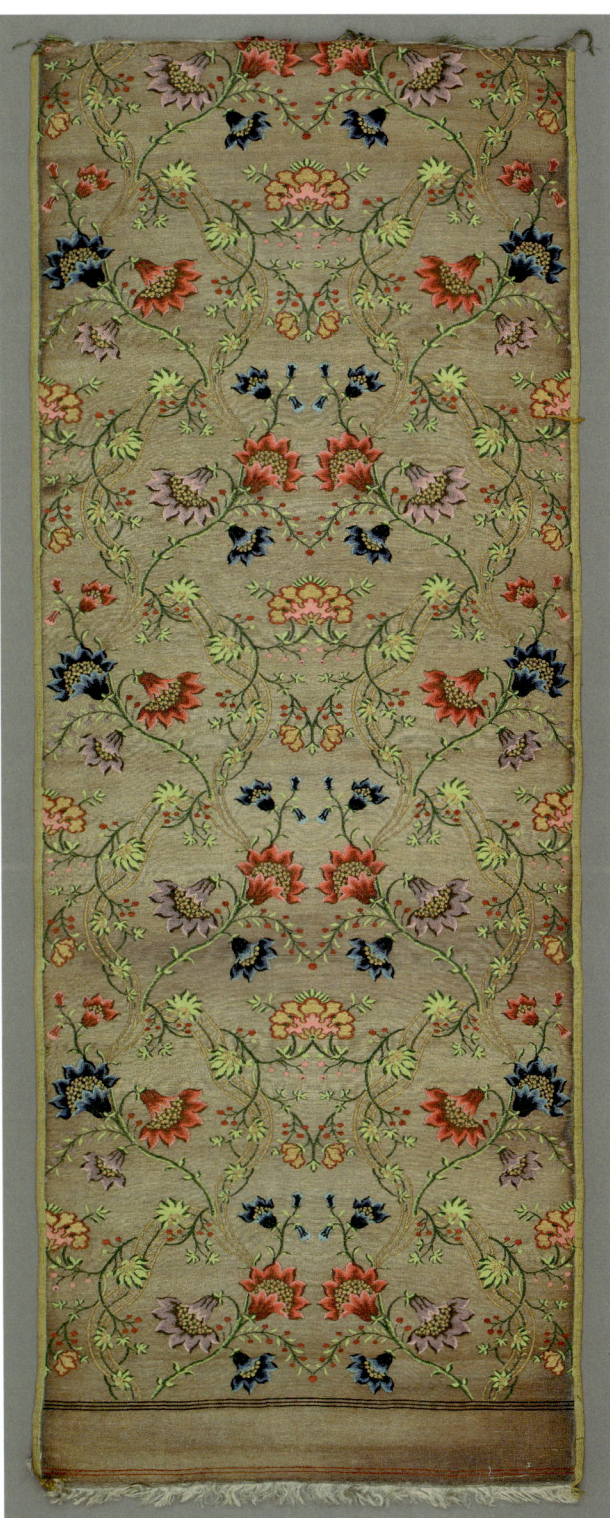

FIG. 53 Textile length, late eighteenth century or nineteenth century. Made by the Qing Imperial Silk Manufactory. Silk lampas with metal threads. Palace Museum, Beijing (gu17829).

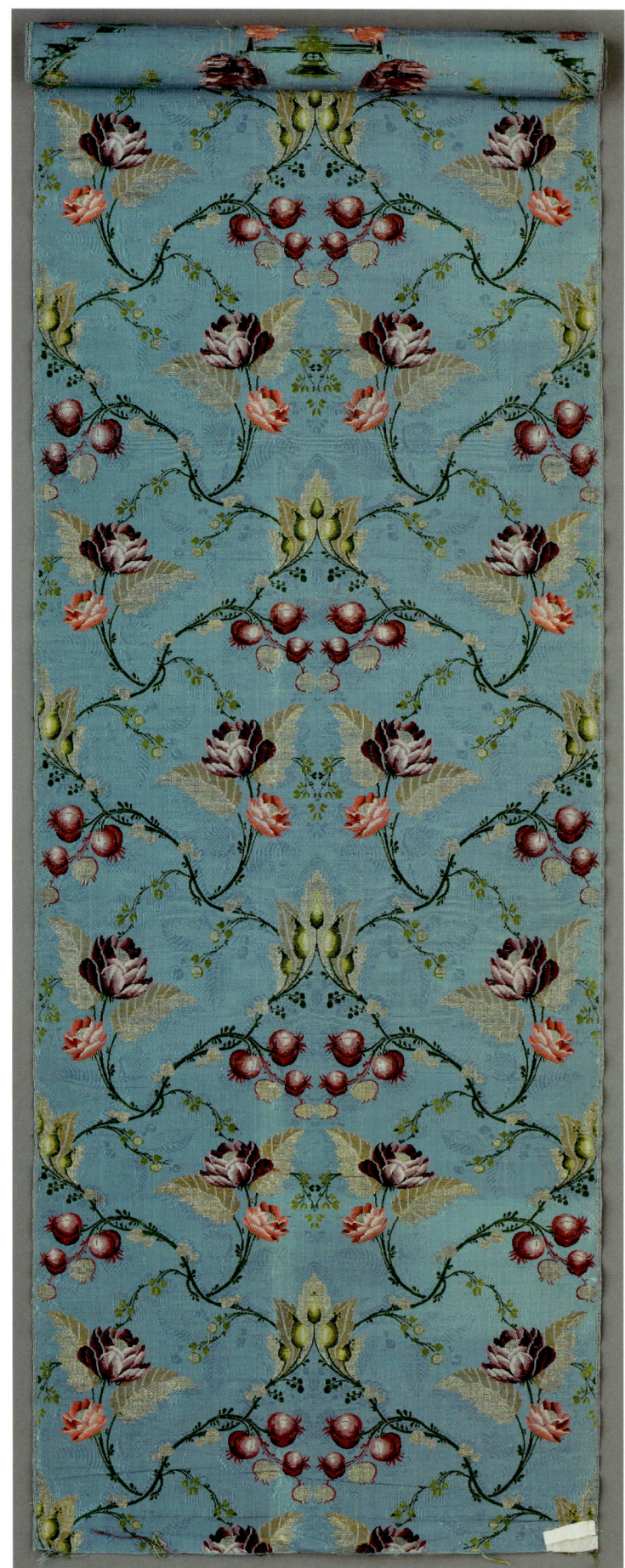

FIG. 54 Bolt of textile (detail), mid-eighteenth century, European. Silk and metal threads, 11 ft. 7 ⅜ in. × 21 ⅝ in. (354 × 55 cm). Palace Museum, Beijing (gu17815).

composition resembles that of mid-eighteenth-century French silks and Russian ones modeled after French prototypes, as exemplified by a circa 1750s blue silk in the Palace Museum (fig. 54). In the Qing pieces, the simplified but still pronounced shading effect of the morning glories shows an attempt to translate European naturalism, whereas the stylized, two-dimensional peonies display a conventional Chinese aesthetic. In terms of the technique, several versions in this group of silks have a full gold or full silver ground (see figs. 52, 53), executed in the same weave structure as an eighteenth-century Russian-style gold floral silk at the Qing court (see figs. 20, 21). The metal threads woven in lancé cover almost the entire background, and the silk ground is exposed only as the narrow, dark green vines. Additional brocading wefts create other parts of the patterns. The Russian prototype clearly informed the design and weaving method of this group of silks.

Overall, the various Qing pieces examined in this section share the same strong European flavor mediated through Chinese taste. They provide concrete examples of the numerous domestically made silks that were recorded in Qing court documents as "Western/foreign." Their uneven quality suggests different manufacturing locations and acquisition channels. Some may have been imperial commissions executed in the official weaving establishments in Suzhou, while others were probably woven in Canton or acquired on the market and came to the court as provincial gifts. Together, the pieces found in the Qing imperial collections challenge assumptions about Chinese "export" textiles in modern museology and scholarship by demonstrating that the same stylistic attributes were equally appealing to the Qing court, and that "Western" was a fluid stylistic concept and repertoire subsuming imitative or inventive Chinese works.

WESTERN SILKS FOR MANCHU MILITARY REGALIA

In Europe, luxurious silks were intended for use in fashionable dress, interior furnishings, and church decorations and vestments. Once they entered the Qing imperial precinct, or when their designs were copied and remade, their functions changed completely, and the cycle of fashion, so important in their original contexts, ceased to matter. Westerns silks were used only in a few isolated cases for court theater costumes, for which the choice of fabrics was at times whimsical. Extant examples include the above-mentioned robe for a female lead made from a blue floral silk in the Garthwaite style (see fig. 40) and two identical suits of armor for a warrior role, which feature panels cut from a circa 1725–30 lace-patterned silk woven with fuzzy chenille threads and silver threads (fig. 55).[39] There is no obvious connection between the textiles' designs and the role types. Apart from theatrical costumes, no Western silks were tailored as imperial garments, nor did they decorate palace domestic interiors. This absence is not surprising, given that their fanciful patterns lacked the symbolic meanings expected of textiles normally serving such purposes. Nonetheless, as this section will argue, it was exactly this semiotic opacity of Western silk designs, coupled with their material magnificence, that led them to play a unique role in Qing imperial military rituals. Extant objects, archival materials, and visual evidence together reveal that Western silks at the Qing court were primarily made into two kinds of objects—the emperor's martial regalia and the furnishings for his military lodgings. They were on prominent display on two politically significant occasions, namely, the annual Autumn Hunt (*mulan qiuxian*) and the Grand Military Review (*dayue*). Both were pivotal to maintaining the Manchu martial heritage and propagandizing Qing imperial power.

The Autumn Hunt and the Grand Review were institutionalized rituals that showcased the Manchu warrior tradition, and they held both practical and symbolic significance for the Qing rulers. Qing emperors had consistently stressed the importance of maintaining the "Manchu Way" through dress, language, organized physical drills, and other political and cultural measures. In evaluating the fall of the Jurchen Jin dynasty (1115–1234) as a consequence of slipping into the Han Chinese mode of decadent leisure, the founding emperor of Qing, Hong Taiji (1592–1643), warned his descendants of the danger of abandoning the Manchu language, replacing Manchu clothing with Chinese dress, and neglecting shooting and riding. Hong Taiji rejected wide, Chinese-style sleeves on the grounds that they hampered martial activities. Instead, the Manchus opted for narrow sleeves with cuffs shaped like a horse hoof, as well as front and side slits on the men's garments to accommodate riding.[40] The Qing rulers celebrated bravery and military prowess as the principal Manchu qualities that distinguished them from the Han Chinese. As essential manifestations of Manchu masculinity, archery skills and horsemanship not only defined Manchu ethnicity but also guaranteed dynastic security.

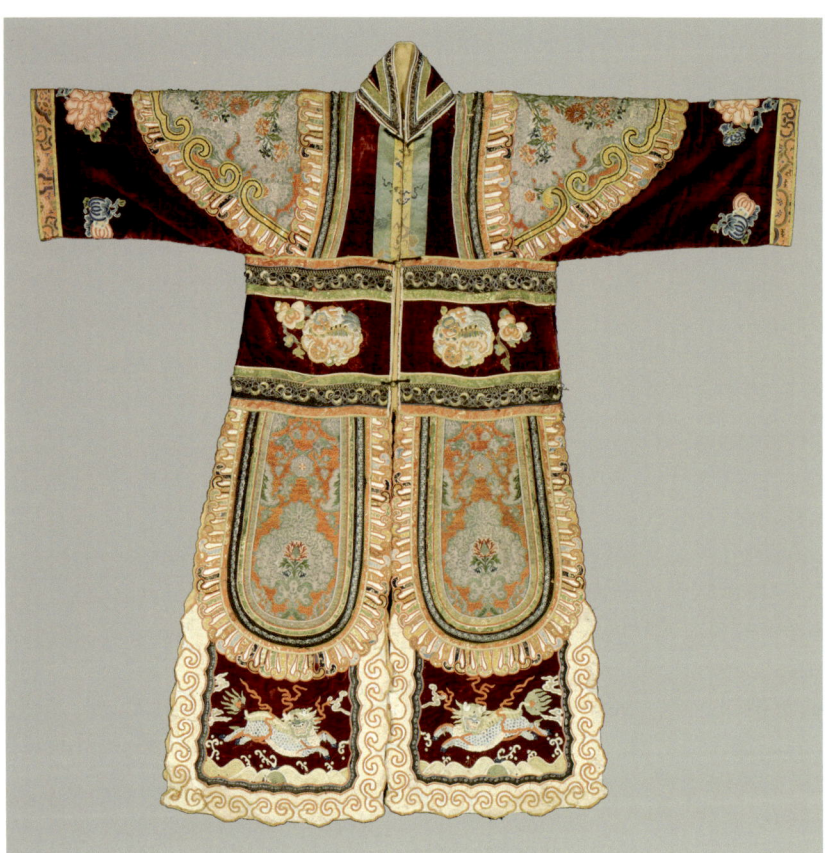

FIG. 55 Qing court theatrical costume for a warrior's role, 1736–95. Textile for the shoulder and knee panels: silk lampas with chenille threads and metal threads, c. 1725–30, European. Length 56 in. (142.2 cm). Minneapolis Institute of Art (41.74.4).

Hunting was practiced by garrison troops and the emperor alike. The historian Mark Elliott points out that, as a legacy of their Inner Asian origin, the Manchus regarded hunting as the most important paramilitary exercise and a hallmark of the Manchu way.[41] In 1683, soon after the nascent empire achieved political stability, the Kangxi emperor revived the seasonal hunts. The impetus was a trip in 1681 to an area north of the Great Wall belonging to Kharachin Mongols, where the emperor and his troops hunted with Mongol leaders. The Kharachin later presented this region—known in Chinese as Rehe (present-day Chengde)—to Kangxi, who turned this vast forest into an imperial hunting resort and named it "mulan preserve" (*mulan weichang*). *Mulan*, a phonetic transcription of the Manchu word *muran*, means "troating for deer" (*shaolu*), a hunting trick of luring deer into the shooting ground by mimicking their bleat.[42] From 1683 until his death in 1722, Kangxi made annual hunting trips to Rehe during the seventh and eighth months of the lunar calendar (typically around August and September), accompanied by Manchu soldiers and Mongol allies. Although the Yongzheng emperor also emphasized the importance of the hunt, he never set foot in the preserve during his short reign. The Qianlong emperor revived this annual ritual in 1741, and he reiterated the significance of the mulan hunt as an opportunity to "cultivate the Manchu way" (*jiaoyang Manzhou zhidao*).[43]

By the mid-eighteenth century, the annual Autumn Hunt was a highly regimented program, mobilizing over ten thousand persons and requiring extensive logistical support.[44] The hunt and the related banquets, sacrifices, acrobatics, and wrestling events took place as a series of elaborately staged spectacles showcasing Qing imperial prestige and strength. Apart from the practical military purpose of maintaining Manchu rigor, the hunt had several other symbolic and political dimensions. First, it was closely intertwined with the imperial rituals of ancestor worship. Every year, the hunting trip began with a sacrificial ritual at the Temple of Offering for the Ancestors (*Fengxian dian*) in Beijing and concluded with the same ceremony when the emperor and his entourage returned to the capital. During the hunt, the prey captured by the emperor himself was sent express to Beijing and offered at the temple. This ancestral sacrifice thus reinforced the link between the Autumn Hunt and the Manchu lineage; and it also elevated the hunt to the level of a divine mission. As the art historians Hou Chin-lang and Michèle Pirazzoli point out, the rite affirmed the Qing emperor's imperial legitimacy and political supremacy.[45]

Second, the hunt provided a major occasion for the emperor to observe the courage and intelligence of the young princes and to identify his future successor. It was during his last hunting trip, in 1722, that the aged emperor Kangxi symbolically nominated his twelve-year-old grandson Hongli, the future Qianlong emperor, on the hunting ground. Kangxi staged a scene for Hongli to kill a bear and a deer as a demonstration of the young prince's exceptional abilities. Likewise, in 1791, the Qianlong emperor arranged for his grandson Minning, the future Daoguang emperor (r. 1820–50), to kill a deer as an auspicious sign of his imperial legitimacy.[46] The Autumn Hunt provided a context for the symbolic crowning of an imperial heir and thereby the enacting of dynastic succession through a carefully planned performance extolling the Manchu heritage.

Third, in celebrating riding and shooting as martial arts rooted in nomadic traditions, the annual hunt helped strengthen the non-Han identity that Qing shared with Mongolian, Tibetan, and other Central Asian regimes, while providing an opportunity for the Manchu ruler to exercise domination over these regions. The participants in the hunt included primarily Qing imperial clans, Manchu and Mongol nobles, and bannermen soldiers. The banner, or *qi*, was the military organizational unit of Manchu society. No non-bannermen Han Chinese were admitted to the hunting ground, and there was a clearly defined hierarchy that placed Manchus—the sole supervisors responsible for hunting matters—over Mongols, who could serve only as assistants. In addition, Qianlong required Tibetan prelates, Kazakh chieftains, and lords of other conquered or surrendered Central Asian regimes to come to the Autumn Hunt to pay their respects.[47] Qianlong arranged for these regional leaders to observe Qing military prowess, which was displayed through orchestrated spectacles, and he hosted lavish banquets and offered largesse as a means of maintaining alliances with these regions and ensuring their subordinate status. The hunt thus functioned as an imperial institution to fortify the Manchus' Central Asian links. As Mark Elliott argues, "The staging ground for the Manchu hunts . . . became a microcosm of the Qing empire."[48] The fact that Han Chinese were generally excluded from the hunt suggests that the Manchu rulers viewed their martial identity as independent of and superior to Han Chinese culture. Systematized Manchu military rituals reinforced a stereotypical image of the Han Chinese as militarily weak, which in turn justified their inevitable conquest. By excluding the Chinese from the hunting ritual, the Qing emperors dismissed any potential military threat that Han armies posed, especially during the early decades of the Qing dynasty. The hunt thus served to emphasize the Manchus' military triumph and demonstrate their long-term control over the Chinese.

Like the Autumn Hunt, the Grand Review was a large-scale ceremony celebrating Manchu military achievement. At this event, the emperor inspected the imperial troops of bannerman soldiers, who paraded in full armor and wielded powerful weapons. The Shunzhi emperor (r. 1643–61) institutionalized the Grand Review in 1651. "Our dynasty was founded on military strength," he maintained. "Now the universe is unified, and we should not forget about military training during peacetime."[49] Although imperial regulations specified that the review should be held every three years, in reality this schedule was not followed. During the sixty years of the Qianlong reign, only six parades took place, in 1739, 1743, 1751, 1758, 1761, and 1763.[50]

From the Kangxi through the Qianlong period, a major goal of the Grand Review was to inspire awe in neighboring regimes, especially those in Central Asia, so as to retain their loyalty and keep them subordinated. For example, shortly after the Revolt of the Three Feudatories (*sanfan zhiluan*; 1673–81) was quelled, Kangxi held a Grand Review in 1685 and arranged for the leaders of Khalkha and Khoit-Oirat as well as delegates of Zunghar Khanate to watch the parade. According to *The Veritable Records of the Emperor Shengzu* [Kangxi] (*Shengzu Ren Huangdi shilu*), written from the Qing imperial perspective, these delegates were astounded by the powerful troops and armaments and came to realize that "the military strength of the divine Qing dynasty was unmatched anywhere in the universe."[51]

In 1758 Qianlong held the grandest review since the beginning of his reign. This ceremony took place after his conquest of Zunghar in 1755 and shortly before he launched a campaign against the rebellious Khojas of Kashgar, at a moment strategically critical for his military propaganda. The conquest of Zunghar was one of the most crucial military expansions of the Qing dynasty. The conflict had begun during the Kangxi reign as a series of battles against the Galdan Boshugtu Khan (1644–1697). In 1757, upon the death of the Oirat Khan Amursana (1723–1757), Qianlong was able to make great advances in incorporating Zunghar into the Qing Empire. After the campaigns concluded in 1761, the region was completely absorbed into the Qing territories and became known as Xinjiang (New Frontier).⁵²

The 1758 Grand Review celebrated the Qing court's military progress and announced the empire's resolution to continue its Central Asian campaigns. It had a specific agenda: to showcase the empire's strength and to welcome the Muslim lords of Kyrgyz and of Kazakh of the Senior Jüz, who had recently pledged allegiance to the Qing Empire.⁵³ Qianlong's self-annotated poem commemorating this event clearly spells out his intentions.

Imperially Composed Poem on the Event of the Great Review at Nanyuan in the Second Month of Winter, the Twenty-Third Year of the Qianlong Reign [1758]

After twenty years, I am organizing the military parade again. [From the 1739 review until now, it has been twenty years.]*

It is the appropriate time for such an event, as suggested by the Confucian rites.

The ambassadors of the Western Frontiers witness my military strength. [I have ordered ambassadors from the Muslim regions of Kazakh, Kyrgyz, Tashkent, etc., to watch the parade.]

I am waiting to read the report of victory from the campaign at Yenisei Kyrgyz. [I am looking forward to the joyful news from the generals at the frontier.]

My army is orderly and at ease, a thousand flags swaying;

My army is well-disciplined and marvelous, ten thousand cannons roaring.

On this clear, windy day, the soldiers forget the cold;

This is not my blessing but always the blessing of Heaven.⁵⁴

*The texts in brackets are Qianlong's original commentaries.

As the poem proudly proclaims, this long-awaited, strategically planned parade had a twofold mission: to intimidate the subjugated leaders and to uplift the morale of the Qing troops in anticipation of the final victory in the Kyrgyz campaign.

In these two military events, the annual Autumn Hunt and the Grand Review, colorful and brilliant Western silks forged conspicuous displays. The HJD files reveal two major functions of such silks: to decorate the interiors of imperial Mongolian yurts (*Menggu bao*) and to embellish the saddle blankets and archery sets used by the emperor and his immediate attendants. Mongolian yurts provided temporary lodgings and ceremonial spaces during Qing imperial hunts and other important martial events held outside the Forbidden City. Qing court paintings show that the imperial yurt, constructed in different sizes, was an elevated structure in a dome or square shape (fig. 56). The interior of the emperor's yurt was usually furnished with woolen carpets from Central Asia and the walls lined with Dutch printed felt. A detailed description of the furnishings for such a yurt used during the Grand Review is provided in *The Illustrated Regulations for Ceremonial Paraphernalia of the Imperial Dynasty* (*Huangchao liqi tushi*), an eighteen-volume manual on the forms and functions of all objects used in imperial rituals, compiled by the court from 1751 to 1772. As the entry specifies, "In the center [of the yurt] is placed a screen made of [figured] satin with gold threads [*jīnsi duan*] for the imperial throne."⁵⁵ Western silks had been used for such screens. For instance, in November 1739 Qianlong selected a length of "brown Western jǐn-lampas" (*zongse xiyáng jǐn*) to be mounted in the center of a screen that was placed inside

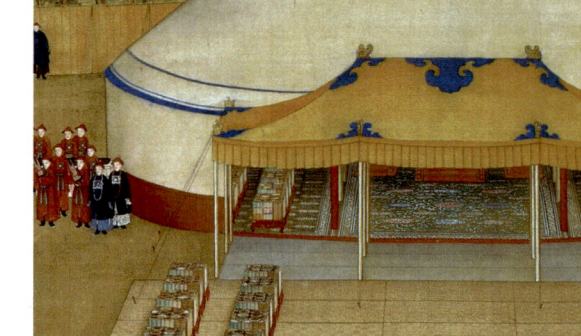

FIG. 56 Giuseppe Castiglione, Jean Denis Attiret, and others, *Imperial Banquet at the Garden of Ten Thousand Trees* (*Wanshu yuan ciyan tu*), detail, 1755. Affixed painting (*tieluo*), ink and color on silk, 87⅛ in. × 13 ft. 9⅛ in. (221.2 × 419.6 cm). Palace Museum, Beijing (gu6275).

62 Chapter 2

a large Mongolian yurt.⁵⁶ In May 1755 the emperor chose a "Western figured satin with gold" (*xiyáng jīnhuaduan*) to be made into "two screens in a Mongolian yurt used during excursions."⁵⁷

A small, square-shaped yurt sometimes referred to as a "Western house" (*xiyáng fang*) was often erected alongside the Mongolian yurts to provide a temporary living and resting space for the emperor.⁵⁸ The word *Western* in the name was derived from the European and European-style furnishing textiles used inside. One such Western house, recorded in an HJD entry from 1762, contained bed curtains made of "slate blue foreign figured satin" (*shiqing yáng huaduan*) and "purple foreign figured plain silk" (*zise yáng huachou*).⁵⁹ In both the ceremonial yurts and the emperor's traveling houses, Western silks created distinctive decorative surfaces around the emperor, physically demarcating his sphere while visually signaling his presence.

In addition to yurt furnishings, the emperor's archery cases (*tuojian*) often featured Western silks with intricate floral patterns. As depicted in *The Illustrated Regulations*, the quiver (*tuo*) was a small, rectangular container with an oval bottom, while the bow case (*jian*) was a flat, curved bag that fit snugly over the lower half of the bow (figs. 57, 58). A belt hooked to the quiver and the bow case completed the set. A number of HJD entries offer detailed information on the making of archery sets for the imperial hunt. These were constructed from either leather or a combination of leather, patterned silks, and velvets. Exotic materials and decorations of European and Central Asian origins were prominent in these archery sets. The leather ones, most of them in lambskin, often featured incised patterns and gilt floral ornaments in the European style. The fabric ones, in addition to using Western silks on the exterior, frequently contained superimposed gold openwork ornaments and precious stones, and the top corner at the wider end of the bow case was decorated with a contrasting textile, incised leather, or metal ornaments. A layer of leather or plain cut velvet served to line and reinforce the silk archery sets.⁶⁰

The regulations for the emperor's regalia worn during the Grand Review were officially established and written into *The Illustrated Regulations* in 1765, incorporating the system and practice that already existed.⁶¹ The manual describes the materials and construction of the emperor's archery accoutrement for the Grand Review: "The emperor's bow case is made of [figured] satin with silver threads [*yinsi duan*] and edged with green leather, and his quiver is made of leather covered with [figured] satin with silver threads" (see fig. 57). "During the ritual ceremonies, the emperor's personal guard uses archery sets made of [figured] satin with gold and silver threads [*jīnyinsi duan*]" (see fig. 58). All other members of the imperial family and court officials were assigned materials of lesser prestige.⁶² The regulation clearly reveals how hierarchy was encoded in the materials selected for the archery accoutrements; silks woven largely from silver threads represented the highest level. As I discussed in chapter 1, textile names such as "[figured] satin with silver/gold threads" referred to Western silks. The accompanying illustrations for the emperor and his guard's archery cases unmistakably depict those objects made of Western silks, and the images correspond to extant sets in the Palace Museum.

Despite the different colorations of the flowers and buds, the silk depicted in the illustration of the emperor's archery cases has the same pattern as that of the textile used for a set of arrow and bow cases; the latter has a label marking the storage date as 1778 (fig. 59). In this silk, on a full silver background, a wide meandering gold-toned band is intertwined with scattered flower heads and a large, gold-toned foliage accentuated by a budding central stem. The actual silk appears more colorful and elaborate than the representation; it boasts a textured silver ground with parallel wavy patterns, and its serrated foliage has a similar striped texture. The presence of gold components in the illustration and in the fabric seems at odds with the regulation text that clearly states "silver threads," but the regulation may have focused on an overall impression and the predominant material of the textile. The illustration of the imperial guard's quiver and bow case matches exactly a set made of a lace-patterned silk, datable to about 1725–30, which features dense silver motifs on a red background woven with chenille threads (fig. 60). A very similar textile was used for the theatrical costumes of armor suits (see fig. 55). Specified and reproduced in the manual, luxury Western silks were officially integrated into the Qing imperial rituals, becoming an indispensable element of the emperor's image and the Qing Empire's order.

Beyond these two examples, several other sets of archery accessories in the Palace Museum may have also been used by the emperor or his guard in ritual occasions. Among these objects, two sets are made of the brown bizarre silk introduced earlier, and one of them still bears a fragment of an imperial storage label written with Qianlong's posthumous honorary name, "Gaozong

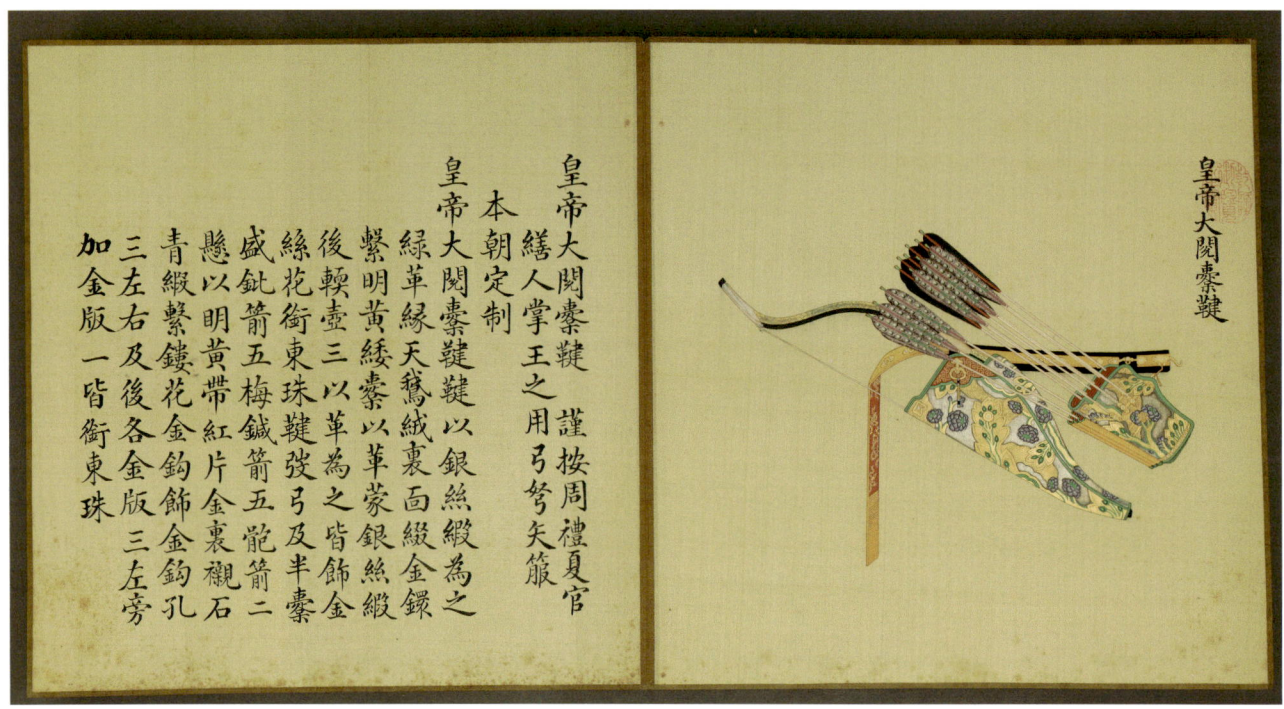

FIG. 57 "The Emperor's Arrow and Bow Cases during the Grand Review" (*Huangdi dayue tuojian*), in vol. *Armament* (*Wubei*), *The Illustrated Regulations for Ceremonial Paraphernalia of the Imperial Dynasty* (*Huangchao liqi tushi*), 1751–72. Album leaf, ink and color on paper, each leaf 16¼ × 15⅞ in. (41.3 × 40.3 cm). Palace Museum, Beijing (gu6116).

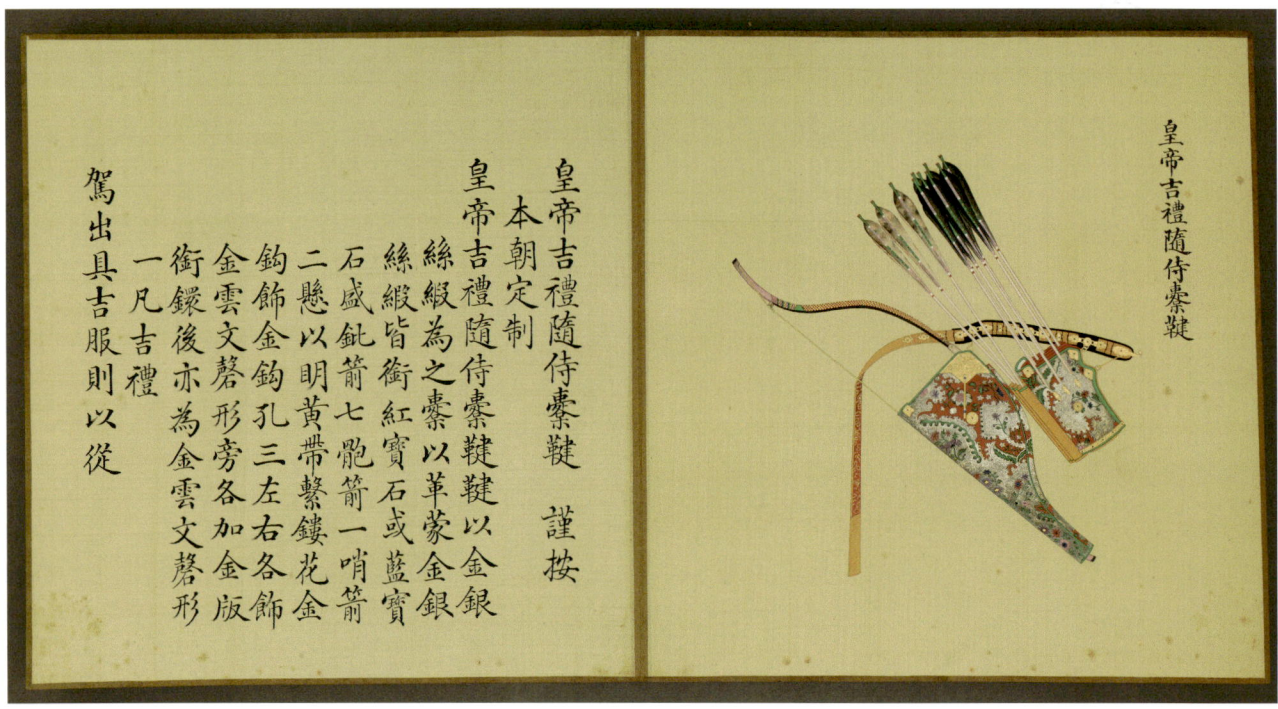

FIG. 58 "The Arrow and Bow Cases of the Emperor's Attendant during the Ritual Ceremonies" (*Huangdi jili suishi tuojian*), in vol. *Armament* (*Wubei*), *The Illustrated Regulations for Ceremonial Paraphernalia of the Imperial Dynasty* (*Huangchao liqi tushi*), 1751–72. Album leaf, ink and color on paper, each leaf 16¼ × 15⅞ in. (41.3 × 40.3 cm). Palace Museum, Beijing (gu6116).

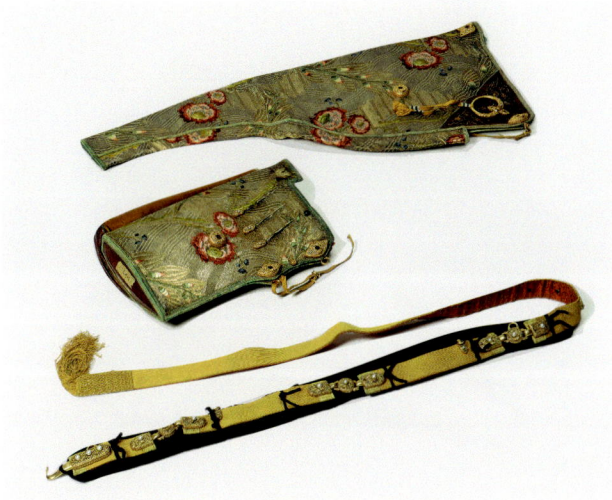

FIG. 59 Set of quiver and bow case (for the emperor), made by the Qing Imperial Workshops, before 1765. Textile: silk lampas with metal threads, mid-eighteenth century, European. Quiver: 14⅛ × 8¼ in. (36 × 21 cm); bow case: length 31⅛ in. (79 cm). Palace Museum, Beijing (gu222008).

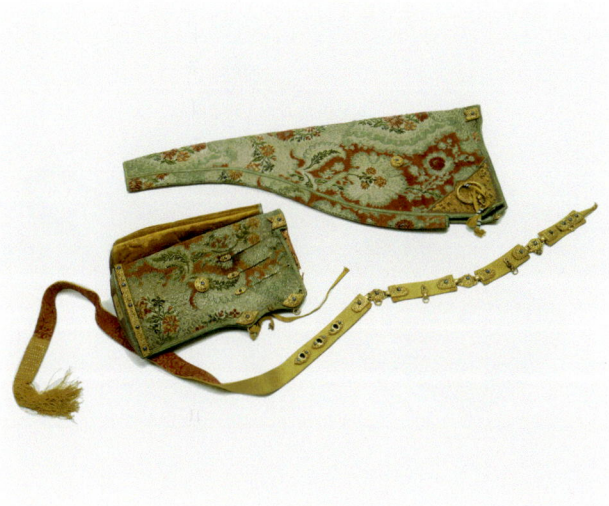

FIG. 60 Set of quiver and bow case (for the emperor's attendant), made by the Qing Imperial Workshops, before 1765. Textile: silk lampas with chenille threads and metal threads, c. 1725–30, European. Quiver: 14⅛ × 8¼ in. (36 × 21 cm); bow case: length 31⅞ in. (81 cm). Palace Museum, Beijing (gu222011).

Chun Huang[di]," indicating his ownership (fig. 61, also see fig. 10).[63] Another set is made of a yellow lace-patterned silk that is identical to a remaining uncut length (fig. 62; see also fig. 14).

The military regalia displayed by the emperor and his attendants during the imperial hunt and parade also included a saddle blanket draped across the horse's back. HJD entries show that the saddle blankets had two forms: the bean-shaped type with rounded ends and the straight type with notched borders (see figs. 15, 16). Both kinds featured narrow edges made of a plain satin, and the straight blanket usually included a wide border made from a different silk with a contrasting pattern.[64] The HJD records a number of occasions when Western silks were selected for the making of the saddle blankets.[65]

Qing court paintings commemorating the Autumn Hunt and the Grand Review offer ample visual evidence of Qing imperial military regalia made of Western silks, permitting further insights into the cultural and political contexts of their display. These paintings meticulously depict textiles that were actually used or imaginary trappings deemed appropriate for such occasions. For instance, the painting *Taking a Stag with a Mighty Bow* (*Weihu huolu tu;* inscription dated circa 1760) portrays Qianlong and a concubine dressed in a Uyghur outfit on horseback chasing a deer (fig. 63). They both ride on saddle blankets made of the same silk, which features intertwined flowers and rococo-style C and S scrolls. HJD entries describing saddles made for women attest to the participation of imperial ladies in the hunt.[66] The female figure has been interpreted as Qianlong's Uyghur consort Rong Fei, but it would have been inappropriate to depict an imperial lady in this manner. Hence, this painting probably represents a fictional scene and an idealized female companion.[67] The textile for the saddle blanket, probably an actual item or modeled on an existing pattern, was not a typical Chinese design, and its foreignness highlighted the consort's exotic, non-Han identity. A very similar fabric is depicted in the painting *Ten Thousand Countries Coming to Pay Tribute* (*Wanguo laichao tu;* inscription dated circa 1761) where it appears as the wrapping cloth for an enormous package carried by Siamese emissaries (fig. 64; see also B.2 in fig. 108). As Lai Yu-chih has argued, Qing court paintings of foreign tributes represent imagined events that transcended temporal and spatial reality while glorifying the Qing Empire as the center of the universe.[68] This time-honored imperial ideology of tribute was renewed by the insertion of contemporary details. As I noted in chapter 1, Siam had presented Western silks to the Qing court as tributary gifts. The exotic fabric wrapping the Siamese gifts, together with the ivory, elephants, and other fanciful objects, betray the

"For His Majesty's Use"

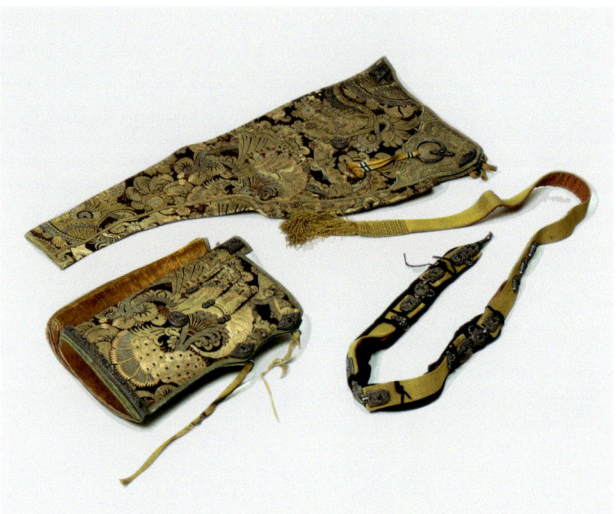

FIG. 61 Set of quiver and bow case (for the emperor), made by the Qing Imperial Workshops, mid-eighteenth century. Textile: silk lampas with metal threads, c. 1710, probably Lyon. Quiver: 14⅝ × 8⅝ in. (37 × 22 cm); bow case: length 31⅛ in. (79 cm). Palace Museum, Beijing (gu222013).

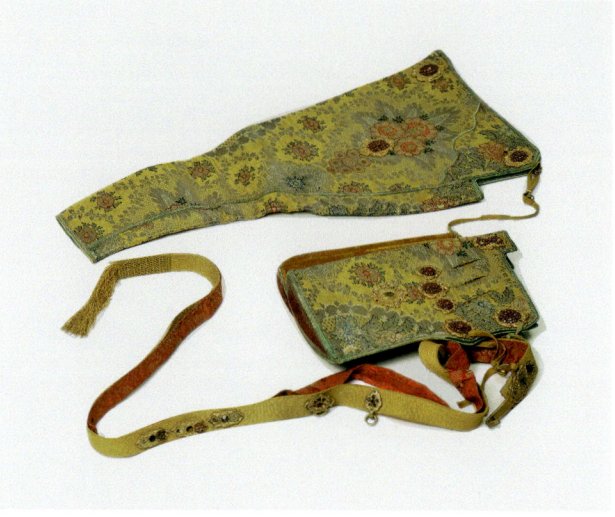

FIG. 62 Set of quiver and bow case, mid-eighteenth century. Textile: silk lampas with metal threads, c. 1725–30, European. Quiver: 13¾ × 7⅞ in. (35 × 20 cm); bow case: length 30⅜ in. (77 cm). Palace Museum, Beijing (gu171731).

stereotypical Qing impression of this kingdom refracted through their material objects.

The imperial hunt was a recurrent subject in Qing court paintings ranging from a series of long scrolls recording the entire procedure to various "snapshot" portraits of Qianlong shooting a stag, catching a tiger, or confronting a bear. As commemorative images, these paintings were imagined composites of historical events. Court artists strategically incorporated realistically depicted details sketched from life, such as visages, animals, costumes, and objects, into carefully controlled narrative structures, and the material objects often functioned as a symbolic, rhetorical display. The compositions and narratives of these paintings always accentuated the emperor's bravery and leadership, while the European naturalistic style and fleshed-out details, such as dress and textiles, created a vivid impression of a heroic, glorious moment as if observed firsthand. The European technique signaled the "documentary" aspect of this type of painting and clearly distinguished it from traditional Chinese genres such as ink landscape and figure painting, which emphasized brushwork and representational modes dictated by established canons.

The scroll *The Qianlong Emperor Hunting Hare* (*Qianlong Huangdi shetu tu*; inscription dated 1755), painted by Giuseppe Castiglione in collaboration with other court artists, depicts several saddle blankets made of Western textiles (fig. 65). Qianlong himself, wearing a blue jacket, rides on a rounded one made of a silk with scrolling floral branches on a white ground, and the attendant following him sits on a straight-sided blanket consisting of a pink center and a green border (probably printed textiles), both featuring sinuous flowers in the Western style. In the 1741 painting *Troating for Deer* (*Shaolu tu*) by Castiglione, which represents Qianlong and his entourage leading an imperial procession to the deer hunt in a mountain landscape, all the riders in the foreground use saddle blankets made of Western textiles (fig. 66). Two members of the royal retinue immediately behind Qianlong ride on saddle blankets made of a yellow-and-silver lace-patterned silk, which matches the fabric for an archery set and an uncut length (see figs. 14, 62). Like the Western textiles that furnished the emperor's travel lodgings, those made into military trappings came into intimate contact with the monarch and his attendants, who can be viewed as an extension of the emperor himself. Those precious and magnificent textiles functioned as a salient visual marker of imperial prestige and established a boundary that distinguished the emperor's inner circle from others on the hunting or parade ground.

Qianlong's portrait commissioned for the 1758 Grand Review best illustrates the preeminence of Western silks in imperial martial rituals (see fig. 2). At first glance, the naturalistic floral patterns on the saddle blanket and bow case seem to clash with the dragons and cosmological motifs that suffuse the emperor's armor. This visual

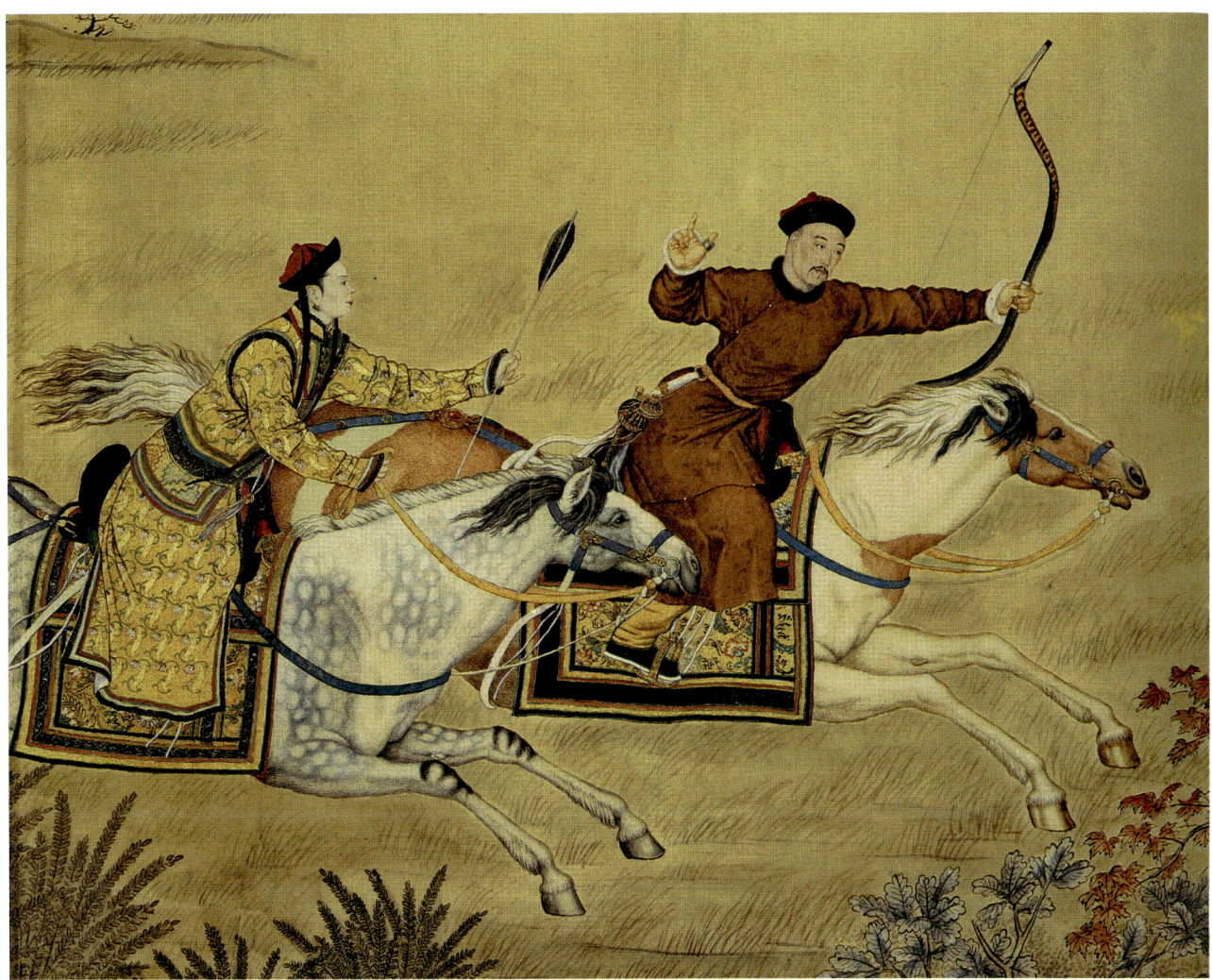

FIG. 63 Qing court artist(s), *Taking a Stag with a Mighty Bow* (*Weihu huolu tu*), detail, c. 1760. Handscroll, ink and color on paper, 14¾ × 77 in. (37.6 × 195.5 cm). Palace Museum, Beijing (gu9205).

tension derives as much from the different formal styles as from the contrasting decorative logic that underlies the textile trappings and the armor. Because their motifs did not adhere to the familiar symbolic visual syntax rooted in the Chinese tradition, Western silks would have precluded deeper associations habitually sought by Qing viewers. Instead, they would fixate beholders on their surfaces—the patterning, texture, hue, and tactility. Although no period testimony shows how Qianlong's Western silks were perceived, it is logical to postulate that their lack of a referential framework coupled with their elaborate surface features would at once impose a more immediate sense of magnificence and maintain an aura of mystery.

The visual experience associated with Western silks was also unique in comparison to other types of Western art at the Qing court. Sporadic written records have revealed how a viewer marveled at the deceptive power of illusionistic paintings or the refined techniques used to make glassware and enamelware.[69] None of these works, however, had absolute opacity in terms of its iconography or patterns. The trompe-l'oeil paintings in the imperial precincts depicted familiar architecture and Chinese figures, and the glass and enameled pieces often featured traditional Chinese motifs or vessel forms. By contrast, Western textiles presented a completely foreign visual realm offering no familiar cultural references. When interpretative challenges posed by this foreignness were paired with the extraordinary patterns and shine of the fabrics, especially when this experience centered on the emperor himself, Western silks could have evoked feelings of wonder and awe in the intended audience. This psychological experience of being overwhelmed by magnificence without full comprehension would have paralleled the impression projected by a dominant monarch commanding absolute worship.

At the Qing court, a visual environment suffused with symbolic motifs, Western silks with their foreign patterns and compelling material characteristics carved out a zone of ornament that operated in a potentially powerful way. As Jonathan Hay puts it, "Ornament *becomes* surface and is able to participate in the larger articulation of the adorned human body and the overall form of the artifacts."[70] In Qing imperial rituals, Western textiles fabricated the emperor's ornamental surface, both figuratively and in a more literal sense, thanks to their proximity to the monarchical body. In *The Mediation of Ornament,* the art historian Oleg Grabar proposes that ornament acts as an intermediary between object and viewer. These intermediaries "are included in the work of art even though they are not truly part of it. They are instead filters through which messages, signs, symbols, even probably representations are transmitted, consciously or not, in order to be most effectively communicated."[71] Grabar's argument helps illuminate the role of Western silks in Qianlong's martial ceremonies if we extend his discussion of "object" and "works of art" to include the sign-bearing subject—the emperor himself—in actual events and in commemorative images. Lacking identifiable motifs and thus semantically flexible, the textiles surrounding him mediated between the subject of power and his audience and served to transmit the emperor's glory.

The saddle blanket depicted in Qianlong's 1758 portrait displays the identical pattern seen on a blanket in the Palace Museum (see fig. 15). They must have been made from the same Lyonnais silk dated to about 1733, but the painted version appears to have overlaid metal decorations. The pronounced shading and chiaroscuro in this silk, created

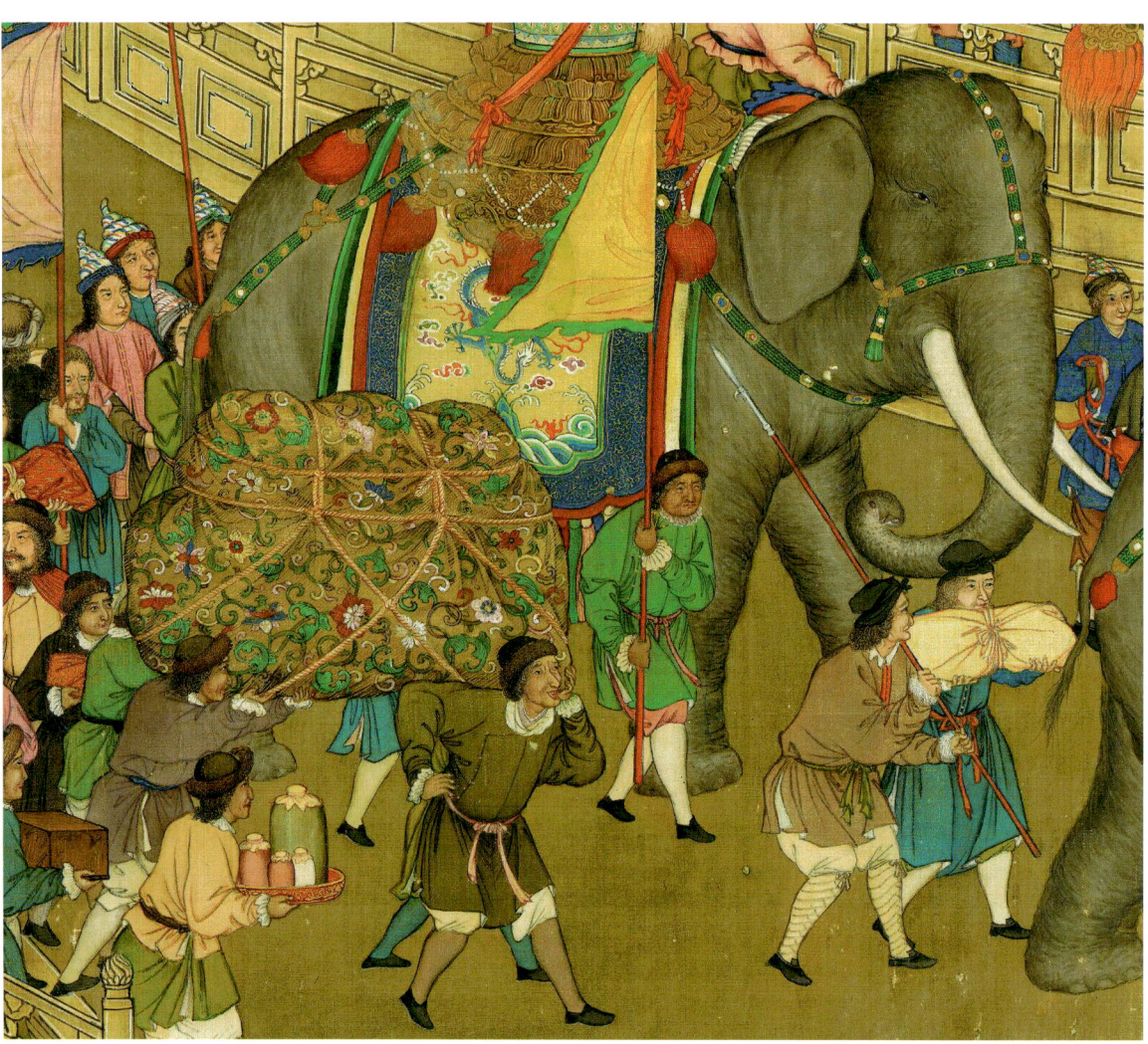

FIG. 64 Detail showing the textile wrapper for the Siamese embassy's gift, in Qing court artists, *Ten Thousand Countries Coming to Pay Tribute* (*Wanguo laichao tu*), inscription dated 1761. Originally an affixed painting (*tieluo*), remounted as a hanging scroll, ink and color on silk, 10 ft. 6 ¾ in. × 7 ft. 1 in. (322 × 216 cm). Palace Museum, Beijing (gu6274).

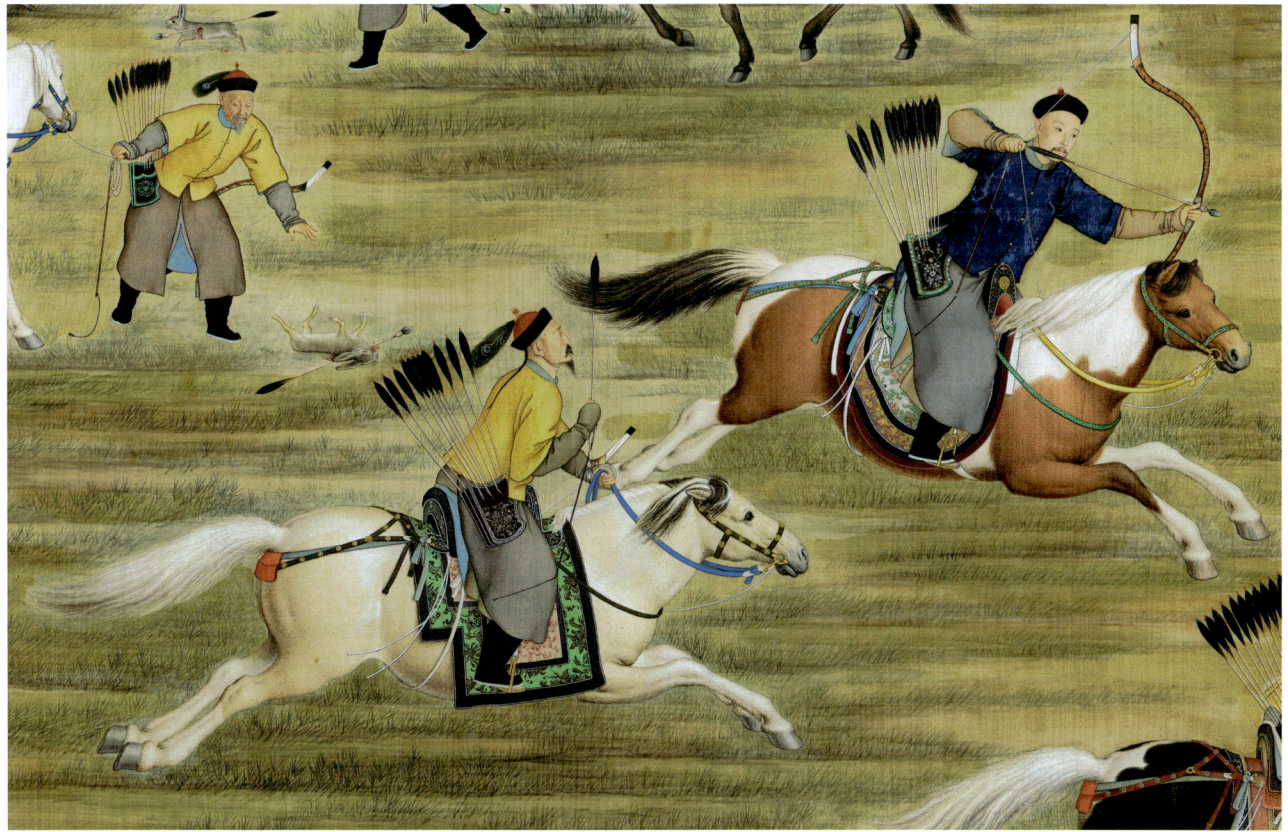

FIG. 65 Giuseppe Castiglione and others, *The Qianlong Emperor Hunting Hare* (*Qianlong Huangdi shetu tu*), detail, c. 1755. Hanging scroll, ink and color on silk, 45½ × 71⅜ in. (115.5 × 181.4 cm). Palace Museum, Beijing (gu5362).

by the points rentrés weaving technique, recall Qing court paintings executed in the European naturalistic style, by now firmly established as a Qing imperial style. Trompe-l'oeil mural paintings with illusionistic perspective were a particular favorite of Qianlong, who began to commission such works as early as 1736, the first year of his reign.[72] The pictorial modes of naturalism and illusionism displayed in this woven silk were therefore not new to the Qing court, but they were uncommon in the textile medium, which posed additional technical challenges. Such a silk would have imparted a heightened sense of rarity and prestige.

The silk's European metal threads, much admired by Qianlong, would have produced a dazzling effect: the reflected light seemingly emanated from the emperor himself, thereby visually augmenting his glory. The shine of gold and silver was also reminiscent of the sagacious reign of an ideal Confucian monarch, whose wisdom and fairness had long been described in Chinese as "luminous," or *ming*, the same word used to describe the radiance of a precious metal. In a symbolic sense and on a psychological level, the rich gold and silver in the Western silks conveyed the theme of wise and benevolent rulership.

According to the HJD, Qianlong's equestrian portrait was commissioned three weeks before the ceremony was to be held. On November 14, 1758, the emperor asked Castiglione to produce "a large painting [of himself] in the Grand Review on a white silk" for the rear golden wall of the Pleasure Boat Studio (*Huafang zhai*), located in the new mobile palace at Nanyuan, outside Beijing.[73] It was there that conquered and surrendered Central Asian leaders, together with Tibetan and Mongol allies, would pay their respects to Qianlong during the course of the Grand Review. Measuring more than 14 ft. (4.3 m) high, this monumental portrait depicted Qianlong larger than life size and elevated him high above the ground. On the parade field, the envoys would not have been able to see the emperor clearly, as he remained far from the audience. The portrait thus functioned as an overture, or even a stand-in, for the real encounter with the emperor in person. Depicted in a formidable equestrian pose, Qianlong was eternalized at a most powerful moment in the proceedings. Given his close involvement in commissioning this portrait, it is likely that the emperor carefully chose every detail, including the textiles, to advance his agenda of impressing and intimidating

"For His Majesty's Use"

the intended viewers. For the Central Asian, Tibetan, and Mongolian guests, who might not be familiar with the European painting style, the emperor's highly realistic face, armor, and accessories in the portrait would have been astonishing. When approaching the portrait, the viewers' first and most direct visual encounter would have been with the meticulously rendered Western silks of the bow case and saddle blanket, which were situated at eye level. Thanks to their lifelike representation, the beholders could experience their fanciful patterns and shine, aspects that would have been impossible to appreciate from a distance on the parade ground. The painted textiles invited scrutiny and admiration, while heightening the anticipation for the actual audience with the monarch. In other words, the painted image was able to command viewers' attention through its dimensions and the positioning of the Western silks, which the emperor animated as his personal surface to stage an encounter with his majesty, like a rehearsal of worshiping him in person.

Although a number of the saddle blankets and archery accoutrements depicted in Qianlong's hunting scrolls and ceremonial portraits find matches among the surviving objects, we should not simply view these images as pictorial records of the actual silks used in these events. The paintings were themselves constructed representations and formed part of the imperial propaganda program. The prominence of Western silks at state martial events and in politically charged images suggests that, in the Qing imperial imagination, they came to embody masculine vigor and military excellence. This is not to suggest, however, that Western textiles, or Western-style objects in general, were perceived by the Qing court as inherently masculine. Rather, in Qing imperial perceptions, the illegibility of the textiles' exotic patterns and their lack of specific cultural connotations made them particularly malleable for projecting new meanings.

In brief, Western silks used in military rituals acquired deep political significance anchored in the Qing imperial ideology. Neither their foreign designs nor their remote geographic origin infringed on the projection of Manchu identity. Indeed, their predominant use in hunting expeditions and martial parades, both rooted in the nomadic tradition, seems to suggest that their geographic association with the West essentially complemented or reasserted the non-Han character of these activities. Moreover, unlike the Han Chinese regions, Tibet, Mongolia, or Uyghur

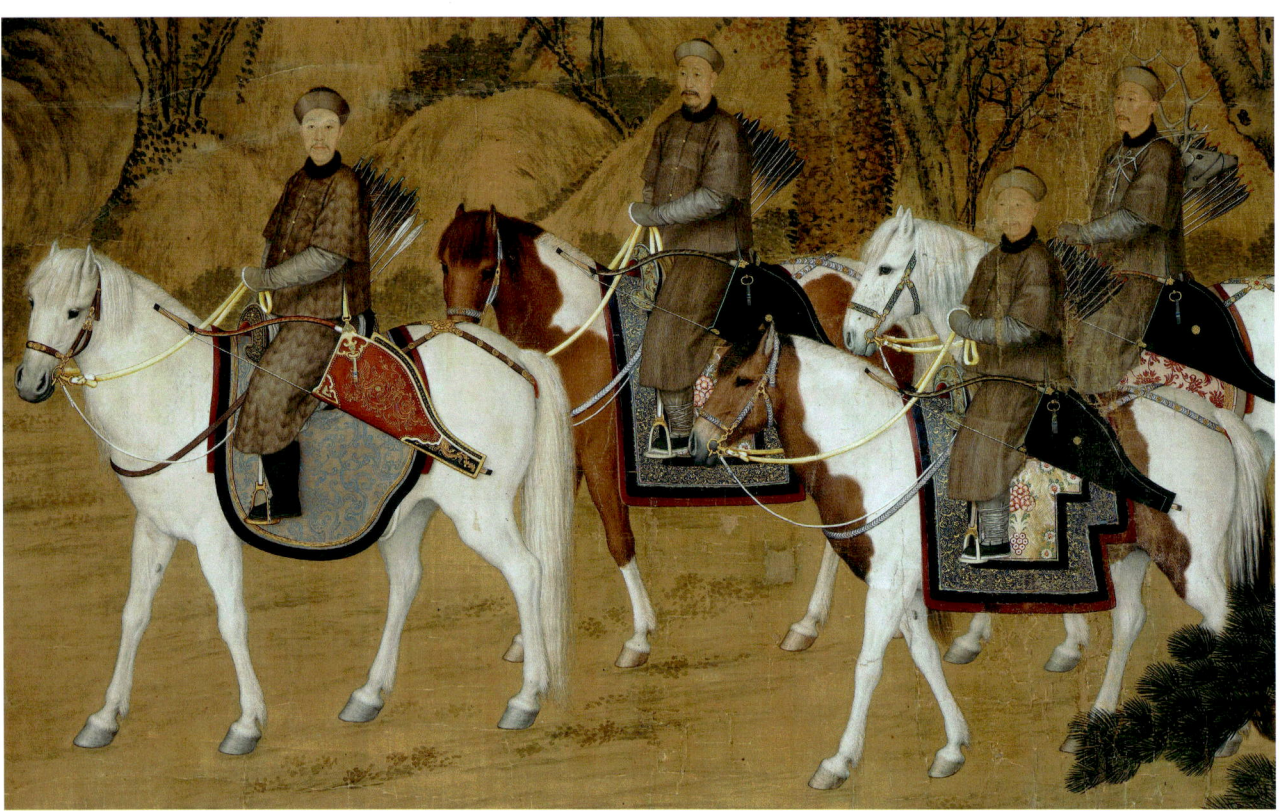

FIG. 66 Giuseppe Castiglione, *Troating for Deer* (*Shaolu tu*), detail, 1741. Hanging scroll, ink and color on silk, 8 ft. 9 ⅛ in. × 10 ft. 5 ⅝ in. (267 × 319 cm). Palace Museum, Beijing (gu5365).

Central Asia, the West in the Qing imperial perception essentially lay outside the territory of the Manchu Empire. Therefore, silks bearing Western patterns could be freely manipulated and recontextualized to express Manchu values and political legitimacy without posing an iconographical burden. Moreover, the fanciful, magnificent Western textiles constituted a material sector of all the things under the rulership of the Qing emperor. Rather than simply reflecting a whimsical taste for the exotic, possession of these precious foreign-looking textiles reinforced the universal order, wherein Qing was at the center of the world. Reserved for the highest imperial power at the very center of the parade—the emperor and his immediate attendants—Western silks came to signify the emperor's absolute domination over the expansive Qing Empire.

WESTERN FLOWERS IN TIBETAN BUDDHIST SPACES

According to HJD records, the other major use of Western silks during the Qianlong period was to adorn Tibetan Buddhist spaces (*fotang*) at the Qing court. Qing imperial patronage of Tibetan Buddhism began before 1621, and the Kangxi, Yongzheng, and Qianlong emperors renovated or constructed a total of thirty-two Lama temples in Beijing, in Rehe, and on Mount Wutai (*Wutai shan*).[74] During the Qianlong period, Tibetan Buddhism reached its height. In addition to devoutly practicing the religion under the guidance of National Preceptor Changkya Rölpé Dorjé (1717–1786), Qianlong systematically built monasteries, organized massive projects to translate and catalogue the Buddhist scriptures, and commissioned a series of Buddhist-themed paintings, including those portraying him as Bodhisattva Mañjuśrī, the Bodhisattva of Great Wisdom. Inside the Forbidden City, Qianlong established numerous Tibetan Buddhist structures that ranged from large temple compounds, such as the Pavilion of Raining Flowers (*Yuhua ge*)—a major Buddhist learning center and a vault for statues, mandalas, and *thangkas* (icon images)—to small meditation halls and alcove spaces scattered about the various palace buildings.[75]

Scholars of Qing history generally hold that Tibetan Buddhism played a major part in Qing imperial strategies to maintain control over the territories of Inner Asia, especially the regions populated by Mongols and Tibetans. They also agree that the concept of the Buddhist king *cakravartin*, a world conqueror and a universal ruler, together with the Tibetan Buddhist notion of reincarnate lineages, provided the Qing monarchs with a model of their own rulership and a framework of state building.[76] Although these arguments account for the Manchu emperors' devotion to Tibetan Buddhism, they do not fully explain the complexity and hybridity of the Qing court's Tibetan Buddhist art and material culture, which were not simply political by-products.

The use of Western silks in Qing imperial Tibetan Buddhist spaces constituted one aspect of this visual hybridity, but the reason for this choice is not clear. Archival materials show that Western silks were often made into valances for Buddhist altars and wall coverings for small prayer alcoves. For instance, an HJD entry dated November 1749 records that, to adorn "the alcove in the upper level of the Pavilion of Raining Flowers," Qianlong selected a "[figured] satin with gold threads and floral patterns" (*hua jīnxian duan*) for the center of the altar valance (*huanmen*), a "[figured] satin with gold threads" (*jīnxian duan*) for the borders, and a "silver [figured] satin with floral patterns" (*hua yinduan*) for the cloud-shaped corners.[77] A prayer alcove in the Qing palaces was typically a small, rectangular chamber formed by three walls lined with splendid silks and featuring one or two thangkas on the central wall. The emperor used such spaces for private meditation. An HJD entry dated November 1745 records an example embellished with Western floral silks: Qianlong chose a bolt of "foreign jin-lampas with large flowers" (*dahua yángjin*) to cover the three walls of an alcove in the Studio of Respect and Superiority (*Jingsheng zhai*). A thangka was integrated into the central textile panel.[78]

Despite the numerous records that indicate the use of Western floral silks in Buddhist spaces in the Qing palaces, virtually none has survived in situ except in the Buddhist hall on the upper level of the west wing of the Hall of Mental Cultivation (fig. 67). Here, in the two small chambers on the southeast and southwest corners, panels made of original eighteenth-century brocaded floral silks still cover their walls.[79] Each panel is composed of two different Western silks, now significantly faded: on the central field is a light blue silk featuring a symmetrical composition of roses and carnations on featherlike ornamental foils; the wide border is formed by a blue silk brocaded with small roses carried by meandering stems, which are echoed by monochrome liseré branches on the ground (fig. 68). The latter fabric is also used for the short valance that demarcates this alcove. Stylistically, these textiles belong to the Russian type that was modeled after French designs of the 1750s and 1760s. There is no corresponding record in the HJD on the making of these panels, but other entries give evidence to the uses of Western silks in the same upper-level Buddhist hall. In 1767, for instance, three wall coverings for an unspecified chamber in this space were made of a "slate blue figured satin with gold" (*shiqing jinhuaduan*) for the central panels and a "red figured satin with gold" (*hong jinhuaduan*) for the border.[80]

Modern silks in similar styles derived from eighteenth-century European prototypes continue to be a staple adornment in Tibetan Buddhist monasteries formerly patronized by the Qing court, such as the Potala Palace in Lhasa, temples on Mount Wutai, and the Yonghe Monastery (*Yonghe gong*) in Beijing (fig. 69). Their presence as banners, altar curtains, and clothing for Buddhist statues attests to a special and long-lasting connection between floral-patterned silks in the Russo-French style and Tibetan Buddhism. Western floral silks probably first reached Tibetan monasteries as Qing imperial gifts or donations, and they gradually became established as part of the visual vocabulary of Tibetan Buddhist ritual spaces. Since the mid-nineteenth century, the Indian city of Varanasi (formerly known as Benares) has been weaving this type of silk, which is called "Chinese brocade" by local weavers, for Tibetan Buddhist establishments. Many of these fabrics are modeled on old textiles provided by Tibetan monastic patrons. Textile designs for Buddhist temples have proved particularly persistent, and the same patterns have been woven repeatedly.[81]

Interestingly, as I discussed in chapter 1, this style of rose-bouquet pattern, which originated in mid-eighteenth-century French silk designs, has also become a fossilized staple for liturgical silks used in Catholic churches in Europe. Were these similar choices in China and Europe purely coincidental or mediated by Jesuits serving at the Qing court, who may have initially recommended such uses following the convention in their homelands? The flexible religious association of such designs is further testified to by their uses in Russian Orthodox liturgical vestments (see fig. 23).[82] Does the striking resemblance between the format of the Russian phelonion and that of the wall coverings for Qing imperial Buddhist alcoves, both consisting of a central panel and a border made of silks with similar floral patterns but contrasting colors, indicate that the former could be a potential source of inspiration? It is impossible to know the answers, but

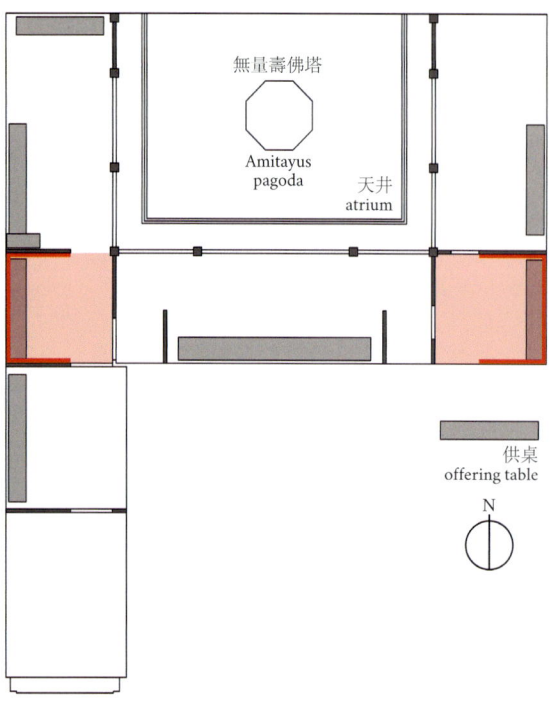

FIG. 67 Plan of the Buddhist hall on the upper level of the west wing of the Hall of Mental Cultivation in the Forbidden City. Diagram by Tao Jin.
Pink spaces: the southwest and southeast chambers
Red lines: walls hung with panels made of Western floral silks

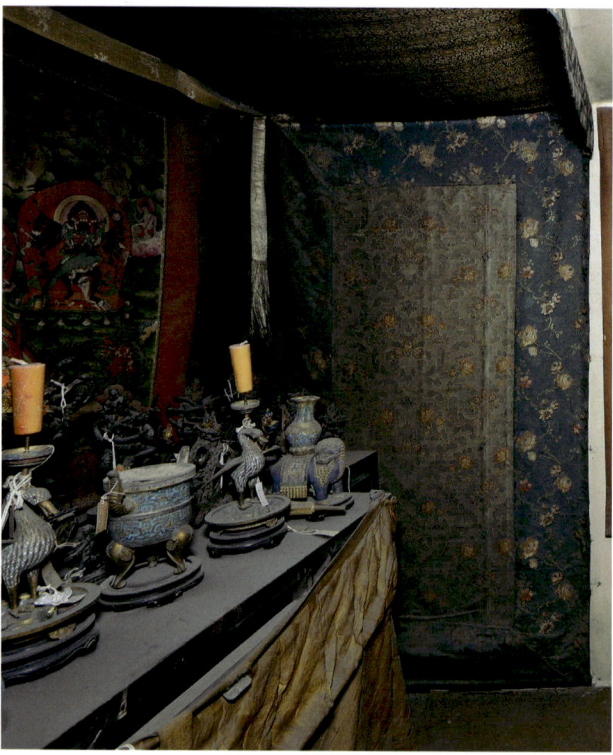

FIG. 68 Wall panel made of Western floral silks, mid- to late eighteenth century. View of the south wall of the southeast chamber, on the upper level of the west wing of the Hall of Mental Cultivation.

one thing is certain: the evocations of the flower bouquets in these silks are malleable and contingent on context. In Tibetan Buddhist halls and European Christian churches alike, the special visual power of this design for religious engagement is derived from the distinctive ornament rather than from any specific iconographic meaning.

In the Buddhist context, banners, valances, covers, and so on made of Western floral silks help convey the doctrinal concept of *zhuangyan,* the Chinese translation of the Sanskrit word *vyūha.*[83] Typically translated as "ornamentation" or "adornment," zhuangyan indicates "the beautiful, pleasant, and soteriologically effective objects that are found in a buddha's land . . . a realm where a buddha resides and in which a direct encounter with the buddha preaching the dharma will bring expedited enlightenment."[84] Splendid display in a Buddhist space functions as visual and material apparatus of transcendence. Beautiful flowers, painted on ceilings and beams or woven or embroidered in textiles, have long permeated Buddhist built environments to create zhuangyan and help worshippers visualize Buddha's sacred domain. One such flower, the lotus blossom, is a time-honored Buddhist symbol of purity, wisdom, and enlightenment; most other motifs, however, such as the stylized treasure medallion (*baoxiang hua*), do not possess any particular Buddhist symbolism and instead more generally create a blissful, divine atmosphere. In a similar vein, the inclusion of opulent Western silks in these spaces beginning in the eighteenth century was probably not predicated on the flowers' specific meanings for a Buddhist audience. As in the case of the imperial military trappings, decoration itself was the goal, to which Western silks contributed precisely because of their character as "pure" ornaments. In the eighteenth-century Qing contexts, exotic European flowers introduced a new dimension to the magnificent, miraculous sites of Tibetan Buddhist spaces. To an extent, their foreignness and identification with the geographic "Western Ocean" may have helped evoke the Western Paradise—the Western Pure Land of Amitābha, the celestial Buddha.

In her book *Empire of Emptiness,* the art historian Patricia Berger posits that the overall visual culture of the Qianlong period represented "a range of hybrids that maps out the world as the Manchus understood it, with all of its shaded, ambiguous zones of cultural interaction." Occupying a place in the "collaged," multilayered "visual world" of the vast, polyglot Manchu Empire, Qing

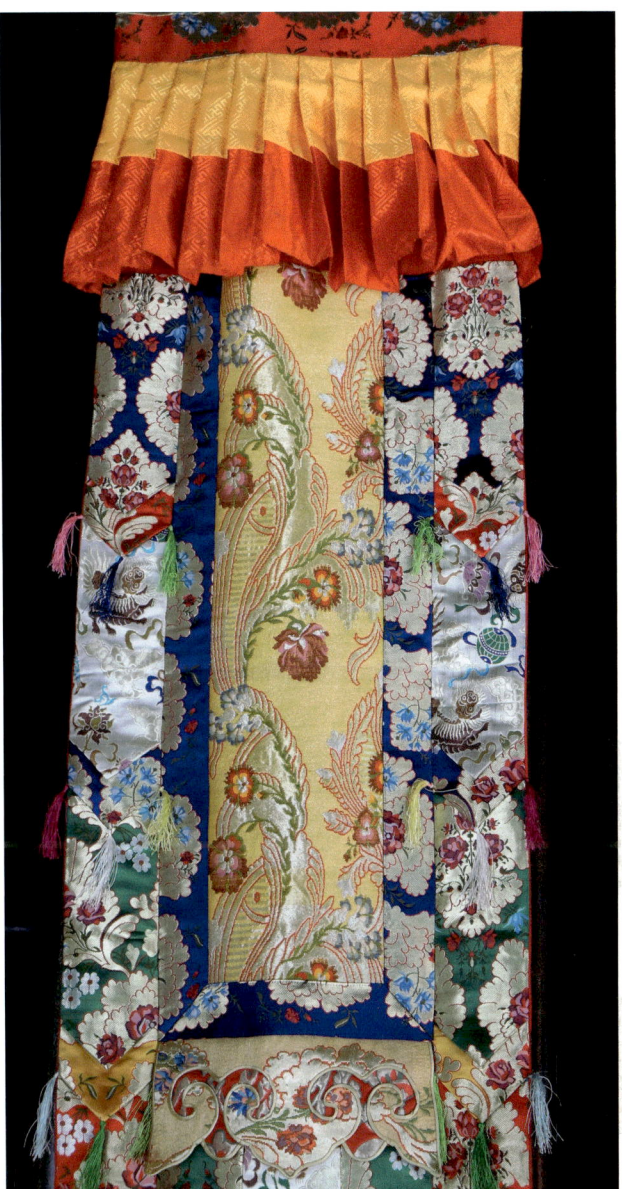

FIG. 69 Modern floral silks in the mid-eighteenth-century European style used for a banner in the Yonghe Monastery (*Yonghe gong*), Beijing, 2012. Textiles probably woven in Nanjing or Varanasi, India.

imperial Buddhist art integrated diverse visual modes, juxtaposing elements that had transparent meanings with those that were unfathomable. Berger argues that "impenetrability and the refusal to yield meaning" were essential attributes of Qing imperial Buddhist art.[85] Her observation provides a framework for understanding the Western silks used in the Qing court's Tibetan Buddhist spaces. Without a clear, legible meaning for the Manchu and Tibetan worshippers, these dazzling, exotic textiles fabricated a splendid surface that nonetheless conveyed the Qing imperial vision of the material environment of the Buddhist realm.

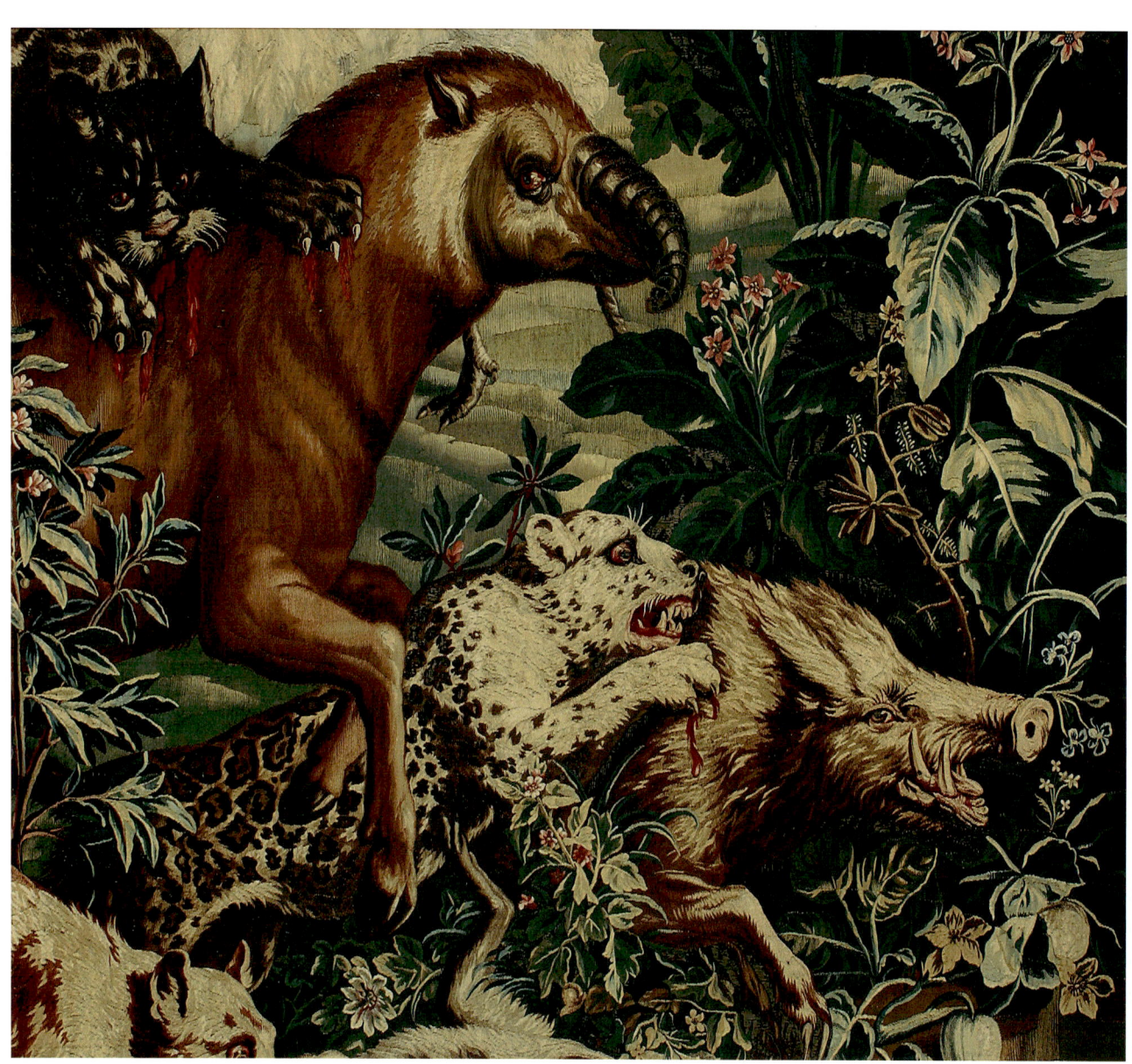

3 Encoding Global Aspirations

European Tapestries for the Qing Emperor

In early modern Europe, large-scale pictorial tapestries ranked among the most prestigious art forms, signified stately splendor and political power, and conspicuously decorated palaces, churches, and aristocratic residences. The circulation and function of tapestries at European courts during the seventeenth and eighteenth centuries have been well studied. Less well-known is their role in mediating diplomatic and cultural exchanges between China and Europe. This chapter uncovers the history of European tapestries that entered the Qing court. It focuses on three French sets whose presence there can be established by archival evidence: the first and second *Tentures chinoises* (Chinese Tapestries), woven by the Beauvais manufactory, and the *Tenture des Indes* (Tapestries of the Indies), made by the Gobelins manufactory. Reconstructing their stories from both European and Qing sources sheds light on the complex cross-cultural encounters that took the form not of direct dialogues and predictable missions, but of contingent trajectories fraught with unexpected turns. In this process, the themes of these tapestries, marked by idealized exoticism compressing distance and time, functioned as a kind of diplomatic lingua franca—one that was fluidly adaptable to expressing changing visions and intentions. When their inherent characteristics of monumentality and portability were combined with exotic designs, the European tapestries that traveled far and long to China came to embody and manifest the global aspirations of both cultures.

TAPESTRY AT THE CROSSROADS OF TWO TRADITIONS
Tapestry is a plain-weave textile formed by warps interwoven with discontinuous wefts of various colors, a weave structure that allows great freedom to compose intricate, nonrepeating designs with vivid pictorial effect.[1] China and Europe each has a long tradition of tapestry weaving, the former featuring silk fibers, the latter wool. By the eighteenth century, when the Qianlong emperor encountered European woolen tapestries and developed a strong interest in them, tapestry weaving had achieved a high level of sophistication in both cultures, but their products of this art form remained vastly different in terms of the formats, visual repertoires, and functions.

In China, silk tapestries had flourished since the eleventh century. Woolen tapestries, by contrast, were rare. Although fragments of Central Asian woolen tapestries have been found in tombs in northwestern China dated to as early as the first or second century, they were absent from Chinese culture during the subsequent dynasties until European examples entered the Qing court.[2] The Chinese word for silk tapestry, *kesi* (literally, "carving the silk") refers to the slit effect created by the disjoined weft threads that is distinctive of tapestry weaving.[3] During the Southern Song dynasty (1127–1279), the center for kesi was established in the southern cities of Suzhou and Songjiang (in today's Shanghai) and has remained there to the present day. Under the imperial patronage, a category of highly sophisticated, artistic kesi emerged and would have a long-lasting influence in the following centuries. Such works closely reproduced paintings and demonstrated technical virtuosity in capturing the compositions and color nuances of pictorial images.[4]

To weave kesi requires only a simple loom. Information about historical looms is scant, but presumably the looms did not change much over time, and those used in the late imperial period were probably similar to the modern horizontal ones operated in Suzhou today (fig. 70). The warp threads for Chinese kesi are undyed raw silk. In preparation for weaving, designs were sketched onto the strung warp threads with a brush and ink, and the weavers worked from the back of the textile. They employed small bobbins to interlace the weft threads of different colors with the warps and used a comb to pack the wefts tightly. The finished piece is weft-faced, as warps are not visible from the front side.[5]

Kesi reached its zenith during the Qianlong era, propelled by the emperor's patronage and enriched by the new significance he infused in this medium. Kesi at the Qing court consisted of three major categories: imperial garments and accessories; furnishing textiles such as cushion covers, chair slips, and bedspreads; and works reproducing paintings and calligraphies. The Qianlong emperor commissioned numerous kesi pieces after both ancient and contemporary paintings and calligraphies, ranging from religious icons and auspicious scenes to masterpieces from the past and present. Most remarkably, he ordered many kesi after his own works, including his copies of old masters' calligraphic pieces, his writings commemorating important political and personal events, his poems as transcribed by courtiers, and paintings that bear his inscriptions.

Throughout China's long history, the practice of copying famous paintings and calligraphies not only constituted an essential part of classical learning, but also was a way to continue the cultural heritage these works represented. Qianlong fully exploited the capability of the kesi medium to create faithful reproductions of painted and written works, turning it into an effective art form for asserting his cultural legitimacy and marking his imperial presence. By commissioning kesi copies of ancient and contemporary masterpieces, Qianlong followed in the footsteps of the Southern Song court and of Han Chinese literati from earlier dynasties; through these activities, he positioned himself as a cultivated ruler, linking his reign to the cultural lineage of ancient dynasties. The project of producing kesi copies played a part in his larger enterprise of collecting, creating, and displaying art of all categories and all media. As a Manchu—an "uncivilized barbarian" in Chinese eyes—Qianlong took great efforts to legitimize his rulership by engaging with the most refined Han Chinese art and culture.[6] The kesi medium offered him an aesthetic means of categorizing and preserving his art collections—politically charged acts that served to culturally validate his sovereignty.

Moreover, in turning his own calligraphy and texts into woven silks, Qianlong drew on the materiality of kesi to give his brushwork a permanent presence. To an extent,

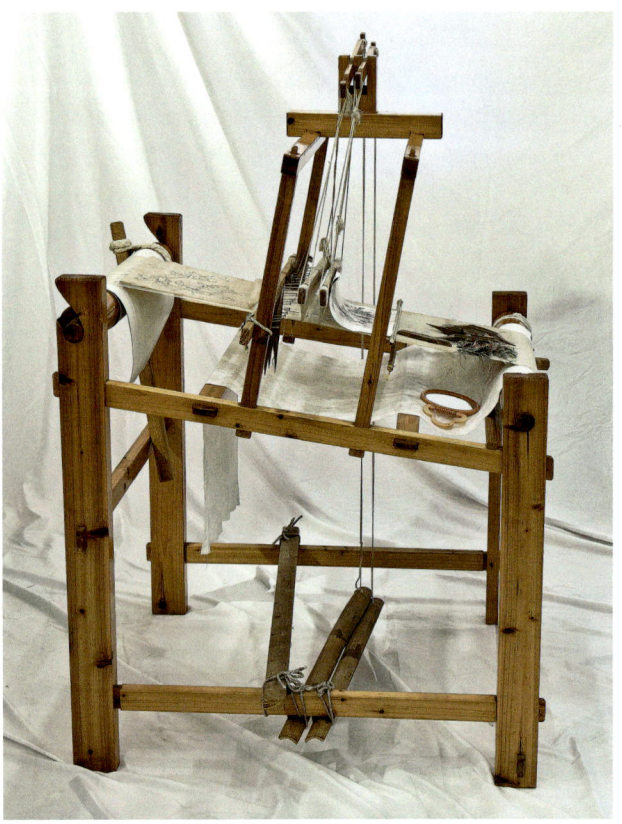

FIG. 70 Loom for weaving silk tapestry, Suzhou region, twenty-first century. Courtesy of Lü Gang.

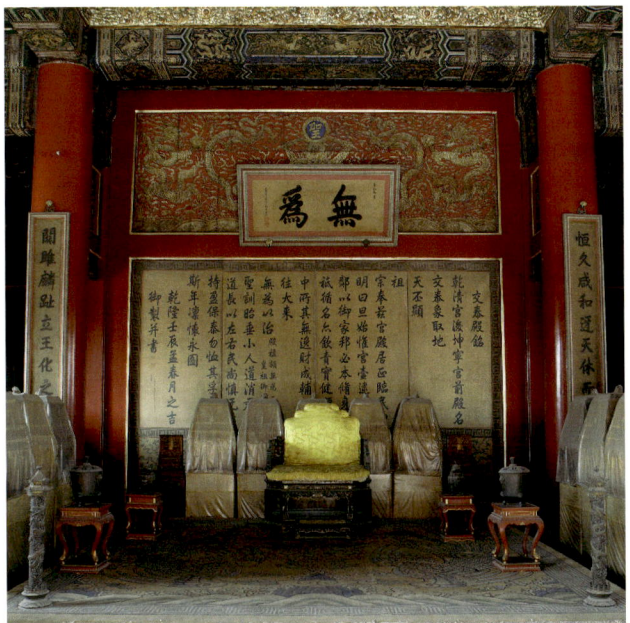

FIG. 71 Interior of the Hall of Unified Peace (Jiaotai dian), the Forbidden City.

the woven versions of the emperor's writings stood in for his own physical body. Throughout the Chinese dynasties, the imperial body and visage remained forbidden images and were strictly guarded from public display. When painted, they were reserved for a limited audience and exclusive occasions. In discussing the Kangxi emperor's calligraphy, Jonathan Hay posits that "the imperial presence . . . has principally been disseminated by means of calligraphy, on a model that owes nothing to mimesis and is more presentation than representation."[7] In a similar manner, Qianlong's own writings functioned as representations of the emperor's body and face in textual form, carrying the aura of divinity like the Son of the Heaven himself. For example, in the Hall of Unified Peace (Jiaotai dian), the official audience room inside the Forbidden City where the empress performed her birthday ceremony and other seasonal rituals, a screen, a couplet, and a placard reproducing Qianlong's texts and calligraphy in kesi conveyed instructions on the empress's duty and the significance of this space (fig. 71). Framing the empress's throne, these kesi asserted the ubiquitous presence and dominance of the emperor, even when he was physically absent. In another case—the multiple tapestry versions of the Southern Song painting *Baby Chicks Waiting to Be Nourished* (Jichu daisi tu) bearing Qianlong's inscription—the tapestry medium helped disseminate to the provinces the imperial message of a compassionate sovereign, which was alluded to by the classical image and Qianlong's commentary.[8]

Apart from reproducing preexisting paintings and texts, many pictorial kesi at the Qing court were woven from underdrawings. These image-bearing textiles were typically displayed in the palace interiors as hanging scrolls and screens. HJD shows that this type of kesi mainly represented auspicious themes expressing good wishes such as vignettes of allegories, popular religious figures (other than icons), and folk deities, as well as plants, birds, and animals signifying blessings or virtue. For example, images of the three gods Fortune, Prosperity, and Longevity appeared in multiple versions of kesi and embroideries (fig. 72). In a standard procedure, court artists prepared the underdrawings, which were submitted to the Qianlong emperor for his review, and, upon his approval, they were then sent to the imperial manufactory in Suzhou for weaving into kesi.

With their cultural links to a refined past and the sense of permanence embedded in their materiality, the pictorial and calligraphic silk tapestries widely visible in the Qing palaces provided Qianlong with a potent vehicle for multiplying and perpetuating his imperial presence. He avidly explored this art form for the service of his imperial enterprise, both as a cultural investment and as a means for propaganda. When the emperor encountered European tapestries, his intimate knowledge of the visual repertoires, material traits, and symbolic importance of kesi would have framed his perception of these foreign pictorial textiles, rendering them at once familiar and novel.

By the late seventeenth century, when European tapestries and related engravings reached the Qing court, tapestry weaving in Europe had developed a magnificent repertoire and refined techniques over the course of three centuries of progress. Wool was the primary material for the warps and wefts, while high-end productions also employed silk, and sometimes metal threads, in the weft direction for highlights.[9] Although tapestries in Europe varied in size and purpose, from small devotional pictures to upholstery textiles woven to fit the shape of seating furniture, it was large-scale wall hangings with complicated pictorial designs that represented the highest artistic achievement and prestige. Tapestries of the last type had much more imposing dimensions than Chinese kesi pieces. In eighteenth-century France, for example, such works could measure more than 13 ft. (4 m) in height and width. Their pictorial subjects ranged from figural

Encoding Global Aspirations 77

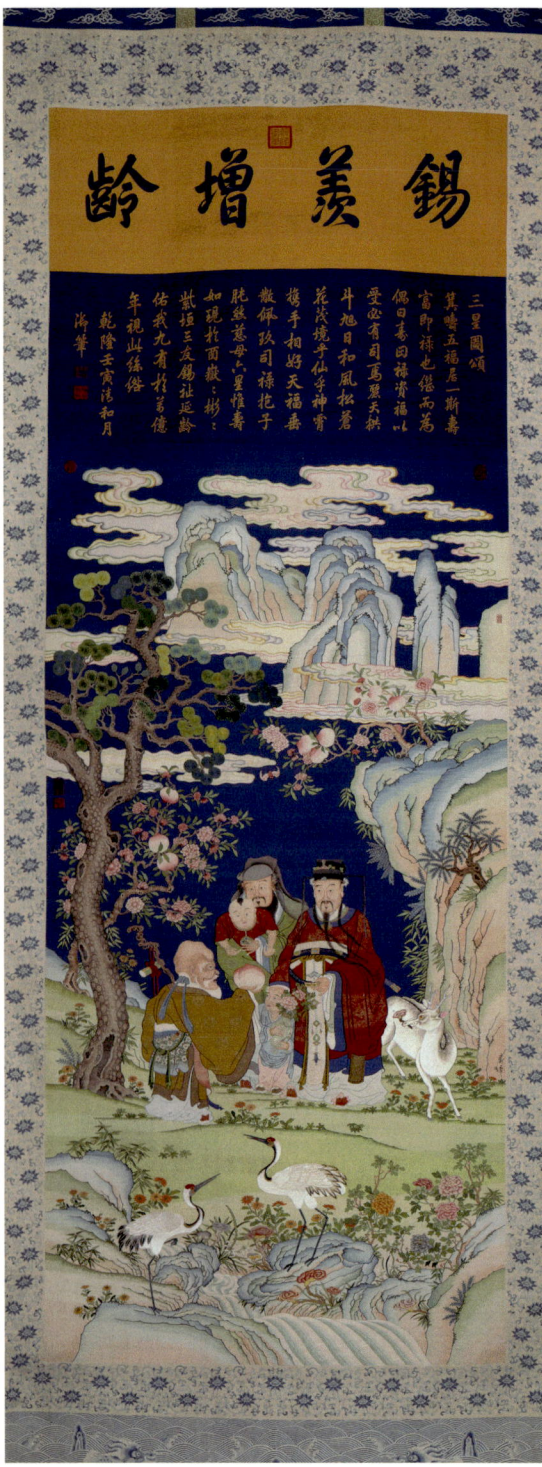

FIG. 72 *Three Gods*, mid-eighteenth century. Made by the Qing Imperial Silk Manufactory, probably in Suzhou. Hanging scroll, silk tapestry and embroidery, 13 ft. 6¼ in. × 53⅛ in. (412 × 135 cm). Palace Museum, Beijing (gu72711).

and narrative scenes drawn from the Bible, classical mythology, and allegories to images from ancient and contemporary history. Other popular designs included heraldic and plant motifs. From the sixteenth century onward, the finest European tapestries were often based on paintings supplied by leading artists of the day—including Raphael (1483–1520), Peter Paul Rubens (1577–1640), Charles Le Brun (1619–1690), and François Boucher (1703–1770), to name a few. The visual complexity, material splendor, monetary value, and symbolic weight of such tapestries reflected the sophistication and power of their patrons and rendered them ideal objects for diplomatic exchanges between European courts. It was this type of monumental, pictorial tapestry that traveled across the oceans to reach the Qing palaces, embodying the senders' political, diplomatic, or commercial ambitions.

As this chapter will demonstrate, the surviving evidence related to European tapestries at the Qing court points to a salient French connection, which corresponds to the country's leadership in European tapestry manufacture from the 1660s onward. Jean-Baptiste Colbert, the prominent French statesman, was a key figure in institutionalizing tapestry production in France and turning the medium into a conveyor of political propaganda. The 1660s marked the watershed of this industry. Between 1662 and 1664 Colbert, then Superintendent of the Bâtiments du Roi (the royal office in charge of buildings and public works), established the Manufacture royale de tapisseries des Gobelins by consolidating existing Parisian workshops and recruiting talented craftsmen; the following year he appointed Charles Le Brun, First Painter of the King (*premier peintre du Roi*), as director to oversee the designs and production. In 1664 Colbert founded the Manufacture royale de tapisseries de Beauvais as a private enterprise subsidized by royal funds.[10] Colbert mobilized the best resources, including funds, talent, and labor, to promote the tapestry medium as the ultimate expression of French royal splendor and courtly taste. The Gobelins and Beauvais manufactories produced tapestries of the highest quality and set the trend for this art form in Europe. The Gobelins served the French Crown exclusively, creating tapestries for the royal residences and state ceremonies, while Beauvais executed commissions for a private clientele comprising French and foreign royalty, the wealthy nobility and bourgeoisie, and religious orders.

Scholars have thoroughly studied the role of Gobelins tapestries as a highly politicized art form, whose iconography and style consistently aggrandized the French king.[11] The first five sets that were put to the loom in the 1660s—*The Four Elements, The Four Seasons, The Story of Alexander, The History of the King,* and *The Months of Royal Residences*—created a systematic visual scheme to celebrate Louis XIV's virtue, grandeur, and political achievements as embodied in ancient allegories, heroic prototypes, contemporary events, and royal residences and activities.[12] For ceremonial occasions, such as the coronation of Louis XV (r. 1715–74) on October 25, 1722, at Reims Cathedral, antique tapestries from the royal collections were displayed alongside newly woven Gobelins cycles to evoke a majestic atmosphere and manifest the monarch's sublimity.[13] Grand tapestries of the past and present unfolded the religious and historical narratives of the king's divine lineage and supreme power. From 1683 to 1691, during his term as Superintendent of the Bâtiments du Roi, the Marquis de Louvois (1641–1691) oversaw the weaving of a remarkable new cycle called the *Tenture des Indes*. Its depictions of Brazilian subjects were based on paintings presented to the court by Prince Johan Maurits van Nassau-Siegen (1604–1679), the former Governor General of the Dutch West Indies in Brazil.[14] This suite in particular embodied a vision of global exploration across continents.

In contrast to the "grand manner," "perfect paintings," and mighty political subjects in which Gobelins specialized, tapestries made by the Beauvais manufactory showed more diverse styles and themes. Exemplifying the fashionable taste of the day, they were intended primarily as display for private interiors. Beauvais tapestries closely echoed contemporary decorative trends, ranging from the revived grotesques and chinoiserie that emerged in the late seventeenth century to the rococo style prevalent in the first half of the eighteenth century.[15] Two Chinese series—the first *Tenture chinoise*, woven between 1688 and 1731, and the second *Tenture chinoise*, woven between 1743 and 1775—enjoyed tremendous success in France and other European countries. As milestones of the chinoiserie style, they contributed a great deal to the dissemination of this long-lasting fashion.[16] The second *Tenture chinoise*, which was based on original paintings by François Boucher, represented the apogee of French rococo art. By the mid-eighteenth century, interior decoration styles had changed. As the focus shifted from grand state rooms to more intimate private quarters, tapestries of smaller size increasingly replaced the larger ones favored in earlier decades. Over the course of the century, other forms of wall decoration such as wood paneling and wallpaper gained popularity, and the demand for tapestries substantially declined.[17]

French tapestries served as diplomatic gifts for foreign courts. Beauvais series and some later Gobelins sets were also ordered by prestigious patrons from other European countries. The circulation of French tapestries helped spread the taste of the French court and the image of its splendor. Louis XVI (r. 1774–92), for instance, presented the Gobelins set *Tenture de Boucher* to Joseph II of Austria, Holy Roman emperor, in 1777, to Grand Duke Paul Petrovich and Grand Duchess Maria Feodorovna of Russia in 1782, and to Prince Henry of Prussia in 1784. English aristocrats commissioned six sets of this design.[18] During the eighteenth century, notable patrons of Beauvais tapestries included the kings of Denmark and Sweden, as well as the French Ministry of Foreign Affairs, which ordered Beauvais suites as diplomatic gifts on behalf of the king.[19]

Two types of looms were used in French tapestry workshops during the seventeenth and eighteenth centuries: the high-warp loom (*métier de haute lisse*; fig. 73) and the low-warp loom (*métier de basse lisse*; fig. 74). Gobelins had ateliers of both types, whereas Beauvais specialized in low-warp weaving.[20] The large scale of European tapestries and their heavy wool fibers required a much larger loom with more complicated lifting and support mechanisms than the relatively small and simple loom for the Chinese kesi. Weavers operating either type of European loom worked from the back of the textile. In high-warp weaving, the cartoon (a full-scale painted model adapted from the initial design) was hung on the wall behind the weavers, and contour lines were sketched onto the warp threads as guides. The weavers would look through the warp threads at the cartoon's reflection in a mirror placed on the front side of the tapestry, though they relied largely on their visual memory and exercised individual artistic interpretations. The weavers used one hand to manipulate the alternating warp threads and the other to pass the bobbin carrying the patterning weft thread. In low-warp weaving, the cartoon was cut into strips and placed directly beneath the warp threads. Because weavers used foot pedals to control the warp threads, both hands were free to manipulate the patterning wefts, which resulted in a faster weaving process.[21] In the finished products, high-warp and low-warp weaving are indistinguishable. There

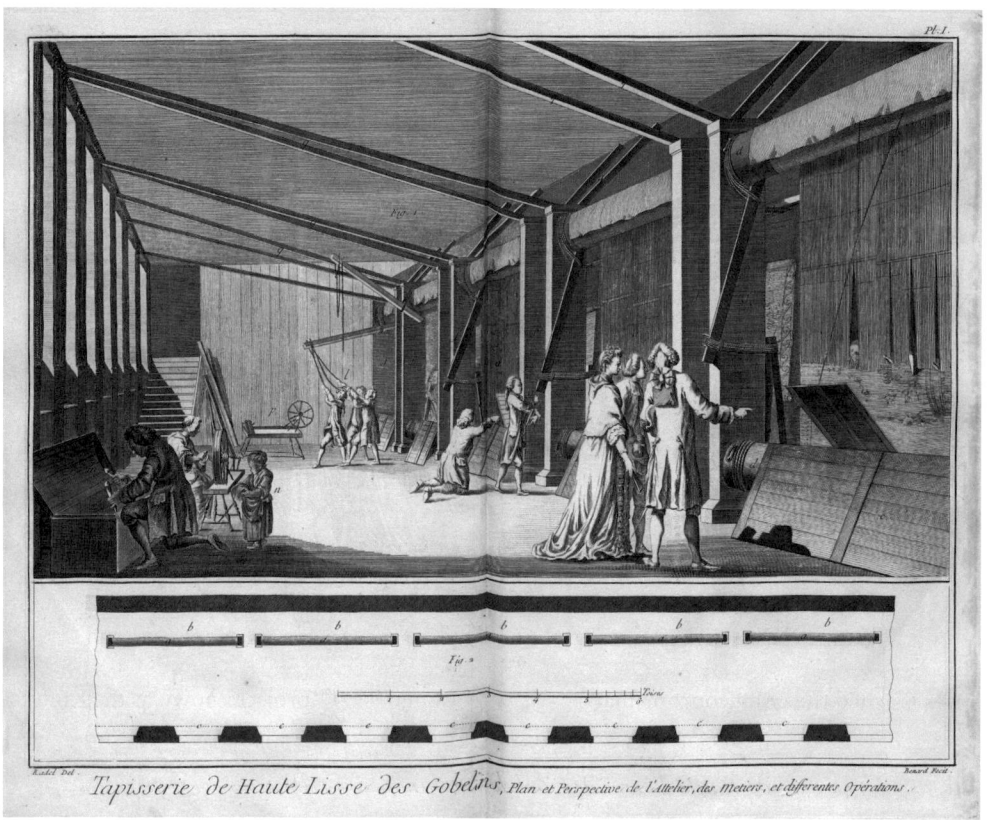

FIG. 73 Illustration of high-warp tapestry looms (*métier de haute lisse*). From "Tapisserie de haute lisse des Gobelins," pl. I, in Denis Diderot and Jean-Baptiste le Rond d'Alembert, *Encyclopédie*, vol. 26 (Paris: Le Breton, 1771).

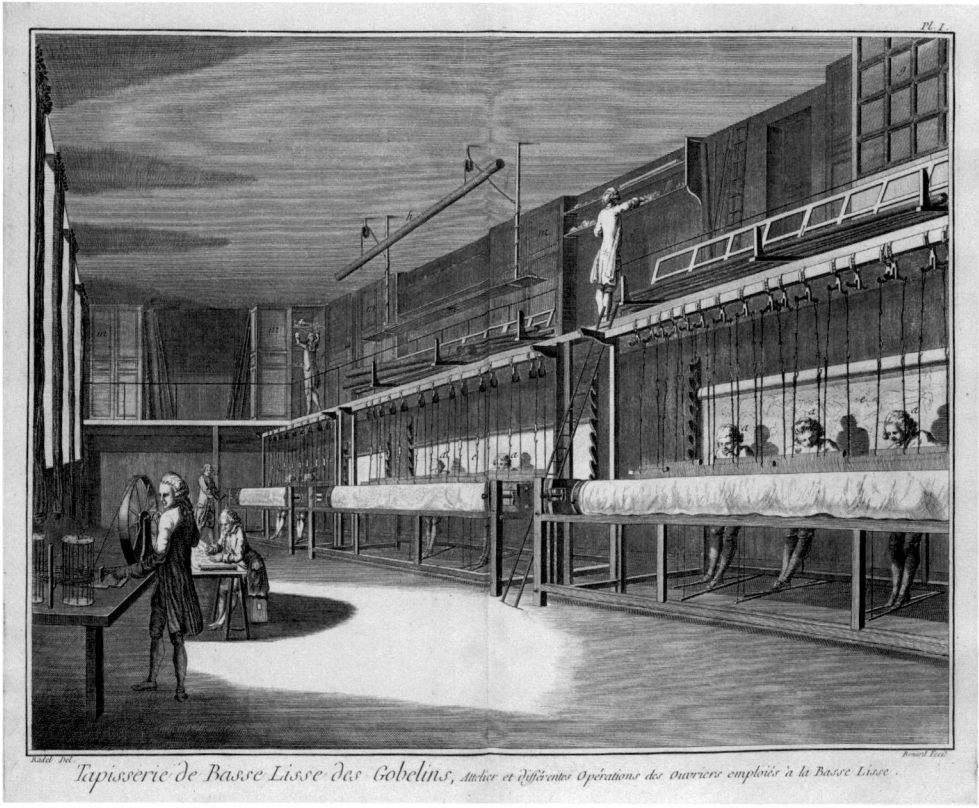

FIG. 74 Illustration of low-warp tapestry looms (*métier de basse lisse*). From "Tapisserie de basse lisse des Gobelins," pl. I, in Denis Diderot and Jean-Baptiste le Rond d'Alembert, *Encyclopédie*, vol. 26 (Paris: Le Breton, 1771).

is no record showing that tapestry weavers from France or other European regions had ever traveled to China during the seventeenth and eighteenth centuries, nor is there evidence indicating the direct transmission of tapestry looms or weaving techniques from Europe to China.

Despite many differences, Qing imperial kesi and French royal tapestries shared two fundamental characteristics: both were highly regarded art forms employing weaving techniques to achieve painterly effects in the textile medium, and both carried political connotations by glorifying the virtue, prestige, and cultural authority of the monarch. These common features provided the Qing emperor with an initial foundation to develop his knowledge and appreciation of the European tapestries presented to his court.

QING ENCOUNTERS WITH EUROPEAN TAPESTRIES

European tapestries reached the Qing court primarily as diplomatic gifts presented by foreign embassies. Soon after the Qing dynasty was established, items with ambiguous names that were presumably tapestries began appearing in the Qing court's gift registries of "tributary objects." The Dutch VOC embassy, for example, presented "patterned woolen textile[s]" (*huatan*) in 1656 and "polychrome woolen textile[s]" (*wuse maotan*) in 1667. In 1669 the gifts from the embassy of Manoel de Saldanha in the name of the Portuguese king Afonso VI (r. 1656–83) also featured "patterned woolen textile[s]" (*huazhan*).[22] The Chinese words *tan* and *zhan* simply mean large flat woolen textiles. Given that no extant seventeenth-century European tapestries with a Qing court provenance have been found to date, it is difficult to ascertain whether those recorded pieces referred to tapestries, carpets, or blankets. In the sixteenth and early seventeenth centuries, Portuguese and Dutch merchants presented Flemish tapestries to Japanese shoguns, nobles, and merchants to facilitate the trading relationship with Japan. Works that were later cut up and used in the Gion Festival in Kyoto show such themes as Greco-Roman history and biblical stories.[23] In light of their similar purpose for developing commerce with China, Portuguese and Dutch embassies may well have chosen similar tapestries as appropriate gifts for the Qing monarchs.

The French court did not send official embassies to China, but Louis XIV dispatched gifts regularly to French Jesuit missionaries in Beijing, and tapestries were among them. According to the chronicle of Catholicism in China compiled by the Chinese Jesuit priest Huang Bolu in 1876, some colorful tapestries (*caiji*) received from Louis XIV decorated Beitang (North Church), the church of the Catholic mission in Beijing that was completed in 1703.[24] The themes of these tapestries are unrecorded. We do not know if French Jesuits also presented tapestries to the Kangxi emperor, but in 1688 he received engravings reproducing famous Gobelins suites along with other gifts that had recently been sent by Louis XIV. A register of books and prints "delivered to Jesuit missionary fathers going to China, on the order of Monseigneur de Louvois," dated February 19, 1685, lists "three [copies] of the book of tapestries of *The Four Elements* and *The Four Seasons*" and "three [engravings] of each of the three tapestries *The Alliance with the Swiss, The Siege of Tournai,* and *The Defeat of Marsin.*"[25] The same register also lists another fifteen groups of various prints belonging to Louis XIV's vast publishing project known as the King's Cabinet (Cabinet du Roi).[26] The Jesuit missionaries mentioned in the texts, known as the five "mathematicians of the king," traveled to China under the auspices of Louis XIV. They arrived in Beijing in February 1688 and presented these gifts to the Kangxi emperor on March 21.[27] Two of the missionaries—Joachim Bouvet (1656–1730) and Jean François Gerbillon (1654–1707)—stayed on and served at the Qing court, instructing Kangxi in the Western sciences and other subjects.[28] The tapestry album listed in the register was probably the 1679 edition of *Tapisseries du Roy*.[29] A copy of this album from the same edition still existed in 1940 in the library of Beitang, which held books brought by European missionaries to China from the sixteenth century onward.[30] The three engravings from *The History of the King* series mentioned in the register may have been bound together and included at the end of the album, in the same format as other extant copies of the 1679 edition.

Tapisseries du Roy played a crucial part in Louis XIV's propaganda program. Published by the royal historian André Félibien (1619–1695) by order of the king's Petite Académie, the 1679 version was a reprint of the 1670 first edition, which consolidated and expanded Félibien's earlier publications on the iconography of the Gobelins sets *The Four Elements* and *The Four Seasons*.[31] In this deluxe, large-format album of engravings, each design from the two series is first printed in its entirety on a double-page spread, followed by long texts describing the scene and explaining the allegories, the Latin inscriptions, and the devices on the borders. As the texts elucidate, every image

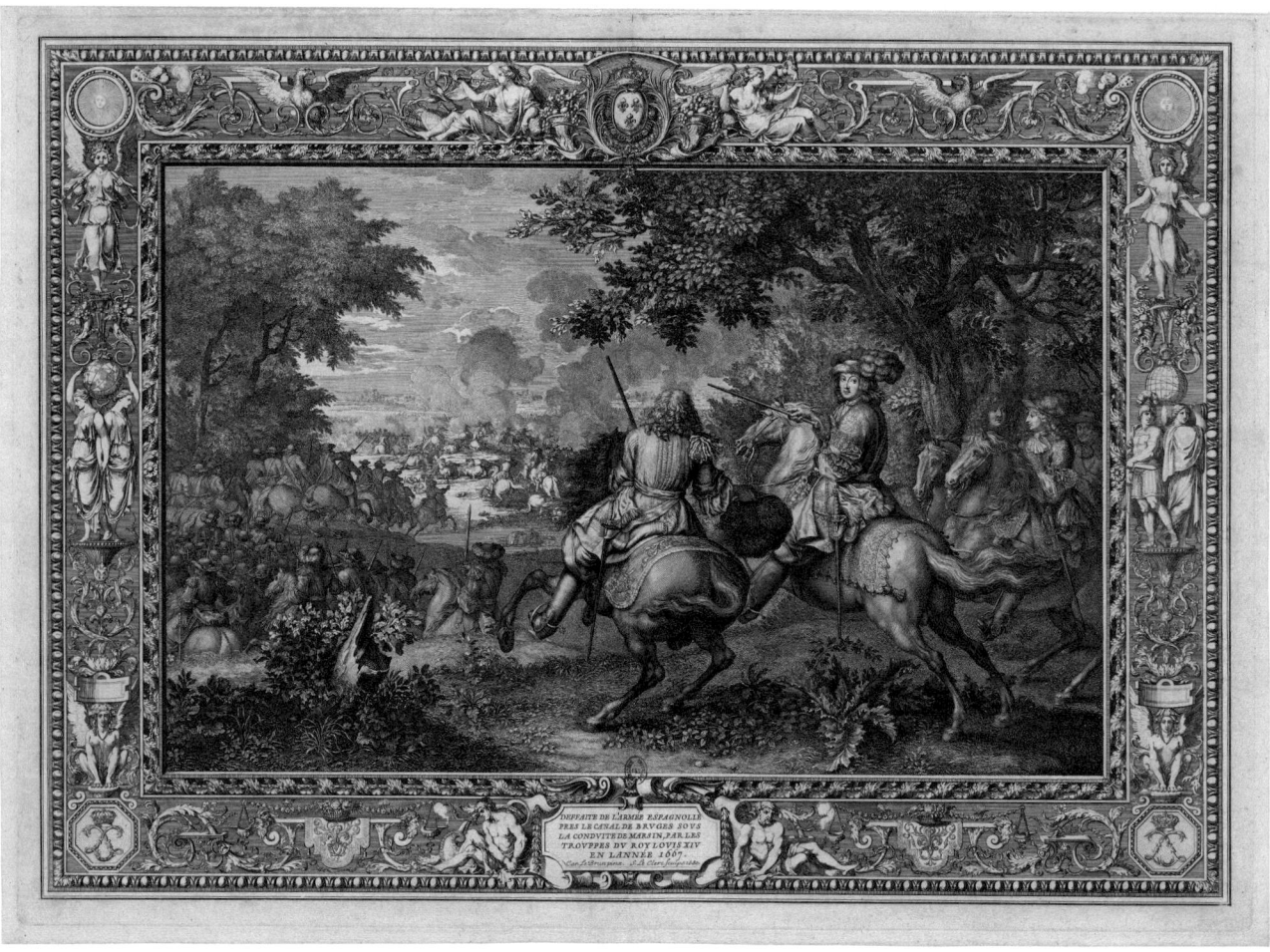

FIG. 75 Engraving of the tapestry *The Defeat of Marsin*, from the series *L'Histoire du Roi*, published in Félibien, *Tapisseries du Roy* (1679). After the tapestry designed by Charles Le Brun. Bibliothèque nationale de France, Paris, Réserve, QB-201 (170)-FT4.

and emblem on these tapestries represents Louis XIV's heroic actions, noble qualities, or virtues, which ultimately ensured the political order in France.

The three engravings from the Gobelins series *The History of the King—The Alliance with the Swiss, The Siege of Tournai,* and *The Defeat of Marsin*—are also double-page prints, as seen in the 1679 edition in the Bibliothèque nationale de France (hereafter BNF). The Flemish painter Adam Frans van der Meulen (1632–1690), who served as Ordinary Painter of the History of the King (*peintre ordinaire de l'Histoire du Roi*) at Louis XIV's court, created many oil studies that were adapted as cartoons for these tapestries.[32] The battle scenes in *The Siege of Tournai* and *The Defeat of Marsin* showcase van der Meulen's signature composition: a panoramic view of a battleground and small figures in dynamic action. *The Defeat of Marsin* portrays Louis XIV as a large figure in the foreground, commanding a rearing horse while turning his head toward the viewer (fig. 75).

Félibien's *Tapisseries du Roy* was reprinted in 1690 and 1727. From 1684 through 1701, numerous copies were presented as diplomatic gifts to European and Asian courts, reaching as far as Siam and spreading the image of French monarchical grandeur.[33] The three copies sent to China were part of this massive, systematic diplomatic project. During the seventeenth and eighteenth centuries, missionaries at the Qing court would have explained the illustrations and texts in the album to the Qing emperors, introducing tapestry as a magnificent medium for celebrating imperial glory. In the absence of specific evidence, it is difficult to estimate the effect of this album on the Qing monarchs' perception of European tapestry, and it is equally impossible to assess whether they indeed understood these engravings as diminutive representations of textiles or simply viewed them as stand-alone images. The influence of this album on Qing court arts, however, can be observed in the painting and print series that Qianlong commissioned in the 1760s to celebrate the success of his

East Turkestan Campaign. The motifs and compositional schemes in the latter clearly drew inspiration from the French prints.[34]

It took the Qing emperors several decades to gradually acquire knowledge about European tapestries. Interestingly, a 1727 Qing official record of gifts from the Portuguese king João V (r. 1706–50) to the Yongzheng emperor lists a "woven painting [or paintings] to be seen from a distance" (*zhicheng yuanshi hua*).[35] The wording suggests a large tapestry. Indeed, the images in monumental wool tapestries become clear and coherent only when viewed from a certain distance. This rather awkward nomenclature reveals that at the Qing court, European tapestries, like kesi, were essentially understood as pictorial images in a woven form. By 1745 it seems that Qianlong was still unfamiliar with European tapestries. An entry in HJD dated that year mentions that "the eunuch Yongtai brought a Western woolen textile [*tanzi*] and communicated the emperor's order to have it identified by a Westerner [*xiyáng ren*]."[36] The emperors frequently consulted the Westerners (referring to the Jesuit missionaries) at the court about the functions and meanings of unknown European objects. A large woolen textile that needed to be identified probably bore complex narrative images and thus was most likely a tapestry. Well-educated Jesuits would have been familiar with the magnificent tapestries displayed in European churches and palaces and equally well versed in their biblical, allegorical, and historical themes.

Qianlong's interest in European tapestries began to surge in the late 1740s. In 1749 he sent a special order to the Governor General of Guangdong and Guangxi Provinces, whose administrative responsibilities included overseeing the Canton port. The order stressed that foreign-style gifts presented to the court, including "clocks, Japanese lacquer utensils, [figured] satin with gold and silver threads, and large woolen textiles [*zhantan*]," "must be made abroad." In the same instructions, the emperor also attempted to reestablish a system in use during the Kangxi reign for commissioning European objects through the Canton Customs Bureau: Canton officials passed the orders from the imperial court to European merchants active there, who then had the works produced in their home countries and sold them to Canton officials on their next trip to China.[37] Qianlong eagerly sought to acquire tapestries from Europe through this trading system.

Correspondence sent by European Jesuit missionaries in China also reveal that Qianlong attempted to commission tapestries from Europe. A letter dated October 12, 1766, from Father Michel Benoist (1715–1774) to Henri-Léonard Bertin, then Louis XV's Minister and Secretary of State (*Ministre et secrétaire d'État*), mentions that Qianlong had not received the tapestries he ordered for his European Palaces in circa 1751 and for which he provided specific measurements.[38] The European Palaces, often referred to as "*palais d'été*" (summer palaces) or "*maisons de plaisance*" (pleasure houses) in French documents, occupied the northeast corner of the Yuanming yuan. The construction of the first group of buildings in the European Palaces began in 1747 and was completed in 1751.[39] Giuseppe Castiglione and Michel Benoist supervised the design and construction of the architecture and hydraulic works, drawing inspiration from European books available at the court and in the Jesuit library in Beijing. The resulting architecture and garden were hybrid in style, combining elements of Italian baroque villas, French royal palaces and landscapes, and Chinese palaces.[40]

Those tapestries that Qianlong commissioned around 1751 were intended to decorate the apartments in the newly built Palace of Harmonious Delight (*Xie qiqu*). HJD records from 1750 show that the emperor also planned to furnish the interiors of this new palace compound with European chairs, desks, and printed felt carpets.[41] Unfortunately, there is no further information regarding the subject matter and dimensions of the tapestries he ordered, and it seems that the officers of the French East India Company (*Compagnie française pour le commerce des Indes orientales*) in Canton failed to communicate this commission.[42] Nevertheless, the fragmentary information about this unfulfilled order reveals some clues about Qianlong's view of European tapestries: first, they should be woven in specific dimensions in accord with the intended spaces; and second, they should resonate with other European furniture and objects to create an interior in the European style. This perception clearly distinguished European tapestries from other familiar types of interior textiles in the Qing palaces.

By the early 1750s, the Qing court had developed better knowledge of European tapestries. The imperial record of gifts from the Portuguese embassy in 1752 in the name of King José I (r. 1750–77) lists "patterned tapestry [or tapestries] woven with figures" (*zhi renwu huatan*), attesting to a more precise identification.[43] A report on this event composed by Pierre-Antoine-Étienne Lacere, procurator of the Society of Foreign Missions of Paris (*Société des missions étrangères de Paris*) in Macao indicates that the items consisted of "nine pieces of Gobelins tapestries," and that the Qianlong emperor had them placed "in a new palace which was built in recent years in the European taste and which was called the little Versailles by the Jesuit fathers, who were its architects."[44] This "new palace" was the Palace of Harmonious Delight. Unfortunately, neither the Qing record nor the French document describes the themes of these tapestries. It remains unclear whether the nine pieces came from one set or were assembled from different series. Given that Beauvais tapestries were often called "Gobelins" without distinction in period documents written by nonspecialists, these diplomatic gifts from the Portuguese king were probably commercial Beauvais products.

Some European tapestries received as tributary gifts at the Qing court may have come from Southeast Asian countries. From the Kangxi period onward, "Dutch tapestries/carpets" (*Helan tan*) appeared regularly among Siamese gifts.[45] In 1781 the Siamese king Taksin (in Chinese, Zheng Zhao; r. 1767–82) presented three "Western tapestries/carpets" (*xiyáng tan*)—two for the Qianlong emperor and one for the empress—along with precious spices, incense, ivories, rhinoceros horns, and elephants.[46] These woolen textiles could have been European tapestries circulated to Siam as diplomatic gifts or trade goods. The 1781 occasion marked the official reestablishment of Siam's tributary status to the Qing Empire after the new king recovered Siam from Burmese invaders in 1768. By this time, the Qianlong emperor had developed substantial knowledge and a strong appreciation of European tapestries, and such gifts would have certainly pleased him. The inclusion of these items in the Siamese gifts for the Qing Empire attests to the global mobility and universal diplomatic currency of European tapestries, which traveled great distances from one court to another and encoded layered political messages.

Most European tapestries mentioned in Qing imperial documents have not survived, and their subjects remain unknown. By piecing together archival materials and other fragmentary evidence, we can identify three sets of French tapestries that entered the Qing court: the first and second *Tentures chinoises* from Beauvais and the *Tenture des Indes* from Gobelins. Charged with the senders' political and cultural ambitions, these pieces, once reaching the Qing palaces, acquired new meanings framed by the recipients' agendas and perspectives.

FRENCH TAPESTRIES FOR THE QING EMPERORS

The first *Tenture chinoise*, better known as *The Story of the Emperor of China*, was created in 1688 during a time of burgeoning interest at the French court in all things Chinese. In the last third of the seventeenth century, this interest in China swept Europe thanks largely to two immensely popular publications: *Het gezantschap der Neêrlandtsche Oost-Indische Compagnie* (*The Embassy of the Dutch East India Company;* Amsterdam, 1655) by Johan Nieuhof (1618–1672) and *China illustrata* (Amsterdam, 1667) by Athanasius Kircher (1602–1680), which were translated into several languages.[47] At the French court, two events that took place at Versailles directly contributed to the Chinese craze: the 1684 visit of a young Chinese Christian named Shen Fuzong (spelled Chin-fo-tsoung in French; d. 1691) accompanied by the Flemish Jesuit Father Philippe Couplet (1623–1693), and the reception of the Siamese embassy in 1686.[48] The latter brought many precious Chinese objects among the diplomatic gifts. The French alliance with Siam signified the potential for France to open a new trading center to have more access to Chinese porcelain, silk, and other luxury goods.[49]

Produced in this context, *The Story of the Emperor of China* represented a distant and mysterious land that the French perceived as prosperous and enlightened. Designed by Guy-Louis Vernansal (1648–1729), Jean-Baptiste Monnoyer (1636–1699), and Jean-Baptiste Belin de Fontenay (1653–1715), the complete set consisted of nine themes: *The Audience of the Emperor, The Emperor on a Journey, The Astronomers, The Collation, Harvesting Pineapples, The Return from the Hunt, The Emperor Sailing, The Empress Sailing,* and *The Empress's Tea*.[50] Typical orders normally specified six of the nine. The representations integrated historically based details, including the recognizable visages of the Shunzhi emperor, the Kangxi emperor, and European Jesuit astronomers stationed in the Qing palaces, with fairyland-like settings abundant with opulent objects, fanciful plants and animals, and exotic tents and pavilions. Illustrations from Nieuhof's and Kircher's publications were key sources for the tapestries' designs.

Fragmentary but credible clues suggest it is very likely that a set of *The Story of the Emperor of China* was in the Qing imperial collections. A 1964 auction catalogue from Sotheby's London lists a tapestry from this set, *The Emperor on a Journey,* which had been looted from the Yuanming yuan (fig. 76). According to the catalogue, "It

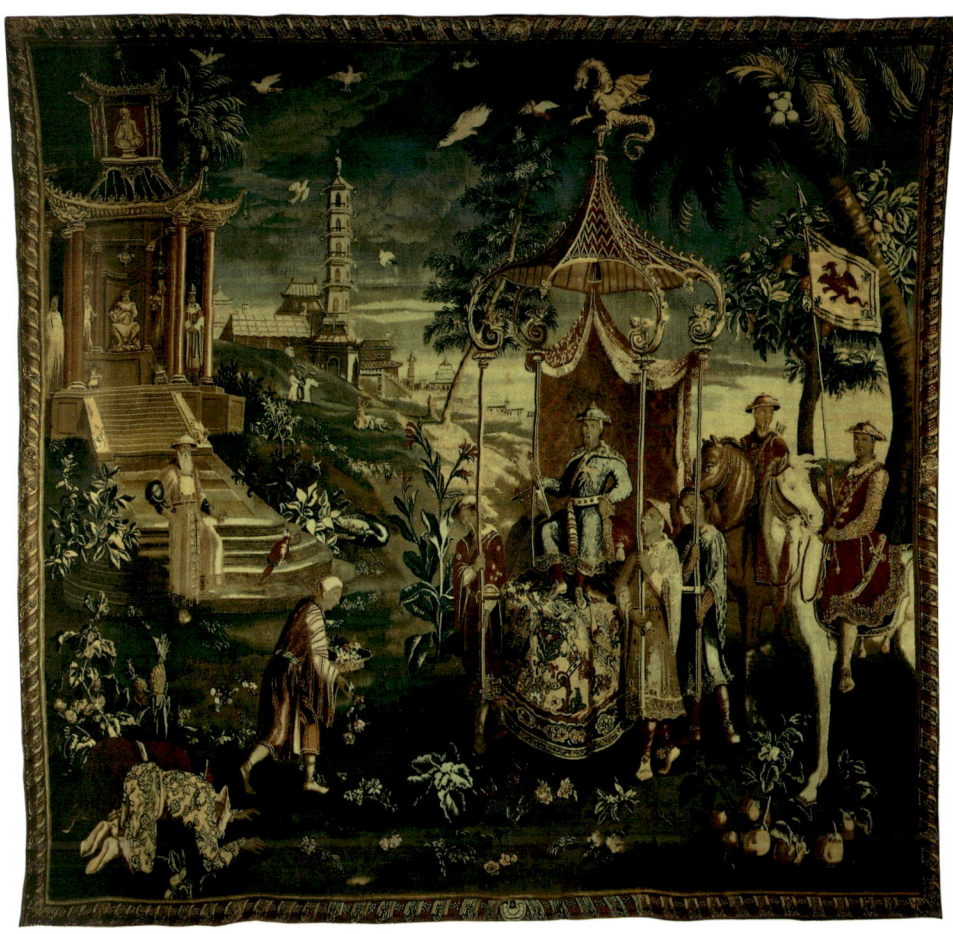

FIG. 76 *The Emperor on a Journey*, from the first *Tenture chinoise* series, early eighteenth century. Made by the Manufacture royale de Beauvais. Tapestry, wool and silk, 12 ft. 6⅜ in. × 11 ft. 4⅝ in. (382 × 347 cm). From Christie's London, *Highly Important French Furniture and Tapestries* (April 12, 1984), lot 3.

was presented to the Army & Navy Club in 1864 by Major Geoffrey Rhodes, who served as an unattached officer in the China Campaign of 1860. It is supposed to have come from the Emperor's Summer Palace at Pekin and have been bought by Major Rhodes at the auction of the loot ordered by General Sir Hope Grant for the benefit of the Army."[51] This account corresponds to actual historical events and appears reliable. Toward the end of the Second Opium War (1856–60), English and French troops plundered and burned down the Yuanming yuan in October 1860. As the historian James Hevia notes, the British loot was then distributed according to the British prize law, a legal code that ensured an equitable distribution of war spoils. On October 10, 1860, three days after the pillaging began, General Grant appointed a prize committee, gathered all the objects looted by the British army, and had them auctioned off to convert the plunder into private property in an orderly and hierarchical manner.[52]

The donation date of this tapestry, 1864—not long after the auction—sustains the credibility of its Qing imperial provenance. Unfortunately, there are no other textual records of its arrival at the Qing court or of its subsequent uses. Moreover, the documents at Beauvais dated before 1723 are incomplete, further preventing the precise identification of the commission and sale of each set of *The Story of the Emperor of China*.[53] Nevertheless, visual evidence found in Qing imperial tapestries produced after European models, a topic that will be discussed in detail in the next chapter, strongly supports the presence of this suite at the Qing court. The likely sender of the *Emperor of China* series was one of the Portuguese embassies, which, as this chapter noted earlier, presented at least one tapestry to the Qing court in 1727 and another nine French tapestries featuring figures in 1752. By 1752 Beauvais had long ceased weaving the first *Tenture chinoise* (the cartoons were in service until 1731), but the Portuguese could have presented a set acquired earlier. For a European mission, these magnificent tapestries glorifying the Chinese emperor expressed a timeless felicitous message and served as a reverent diplomatic gesture. Their imagery of an idyllic kingdom blessed with peace, material abundance, and a wise and benevolent ruler expressed Europe's admiration for China and would help communicate the intention to build a trading and diplomatic connection.

Encoding Global Aspirations

The second *Tenture chinoise* woven at the Beauvais Manufactory is the best-documented set of European tapestries that entered China. Bertin, France's Minister and Secretary of State, sent a complete suite to China in 1765 through his protégés, two Chinese Jesuit students—Aloys Ko (Gao Leisi, aka Louis Ko) and Étienne Yang (Yang Dewang)—who resided in France for over a decade.[54] The subject of several recent studies, this gift presentation offers a window into the role of tapestries in forging an unofficial diplomatic relationship between France and China and in demonstrating the commensurability of the two countries.[55] The scholarship to date has focused primarily on the French perspective. After briefly recounting this set's journey from France to China, I will turn to its reception at the Qing court and examine how this new context reshaped the meanings of these pieces. Chapter 4 will further explore how the second *Tenture chinoise* proved to be a rich source of decorative motifs and figural representations for the Qing court's designs. The suite indeed marked a turning point in the Qing court's creations of European-style woolen tapestries and depictions of Western people and life.

By 1731 the cartoons of the first *Tenture chinoise* had worn out. As the chinoiserie style continued to enjoy wide popularity in the 1730s and 1740s, Jean-Baptiste Oudry (1686–1755), director of the Beauvais Manufactory, engaged François Boucher to design a new cycle of Chinese tapestries. Boucher exhibited eight (of a total of ten) small oil painting *modelli* for the tapestries at the 1742 Salon at the Louvre, and six of them were later selected for tapestries. Jean-Joseph Dumons (1687–1779), the official royal painter at the tapestry workshops at Aubusson, enlarged these paintings into cartoons. Their subjects were *Chinese Feast, Chinese Dance, Chinese Fishing, Chinese Fair, Chinese Hunt,* and *Chinese Toilette* (aka *Chinese Garden*).[56]

Unlike the first *Tenture chinoise*, which depicted the splendor of the court and the emperor's activities, the second set represented imaginary scenes of vibrant daily life in China as well as the leisure pursuits of Chinese nobles and commoners (fig. 77). A variety of sources inspired the scenes in these tapestries, including illustrations in popular travelogues, descriptions of the Chinese court by Jesuits living there, decorative vignettes on Asian porcelains and other export objects, and earlier chinoiserie compositions by Antoine Watteau (1684–1721).[57] In mid-eighteenth century Europe, these repertoires summarized the best knowledge of China to that date, and they underscored a sincere admiration for and a serious interest in Chinese civilization. The second *Tenture chinoise* was woven twelve times between 1743 and 1775. The French king ordered at least five sets through the Department of Foreign Affairs as diplomatic gifts.[58] A 1763 document from the King's Household (Maison du Roy) indicates that Bertin ordered a complete set "for the King to be sent to China" for the price of 14,339 livres 1 sol. The largest pieces in this set measured around 18 to 22 ft. (5.5 to 6.6 m) wide.[59] Like other sets commissioned by the king, this cycle for China bore Louis XV's coat of arms on the upper border, which consisted of the impaled arms of France and Navarre topped by a crown.[60] Still, this set was not an official gift from the French king to the Qing emperor, but instead a material constituent of Bertin's ambitious project to advance Sino-French connections. One of the greatest Sinophiles in eighteenth-century Europe, Bertin admired China's political philosophy and governing system, and he avidly collected Chinese books, pictures, and objects. By presenting informal diplomatic gifts to the Qing emperor, he intended to open up channels for commercial and cultural exchanges between the two countries, an agenda motivated by his vision of the compatibility of the Chinese and French courts as civilized equals.[61]

In 1765 Bertin entrusted his Chinese protégés Ko and Yang, who had by then become Roman Catholic priests, to take the second *Tenture chinoise* (along with other precious objects from the French royal manufactories) to China on their return journey home. In Bertin's initial plan, these tapestries were not meant for the Qianlong emperor but rather for carefully chosen high officials and noblemen. He soon changed his mind, however, and in his subsequent instructions he specified that the French king intended these tapestries for the emperor of China, not as an official gift from the monarchy, but simply to gauge the Qing emperor's taste for luxury French products.[62]

Ko and Yang had arrived in France in 1752 as teenagers under the aegis of the French Jesuit mission in Beijing. They studied at the Jesuit colleges for their future proselytizing mission in China until 1762, when a decree by the Parliament of Paris against the Jesuits deprived them of sponsorship. Ko and Yang came to Bertin's attention in 1763, when he was briefly supervising the French East India Company, through which the pair were requesting free return passage to China.[63] Sensing an opportunity to build ties between China and France that he could control, Bertin envisioned turning the two Chinese priests

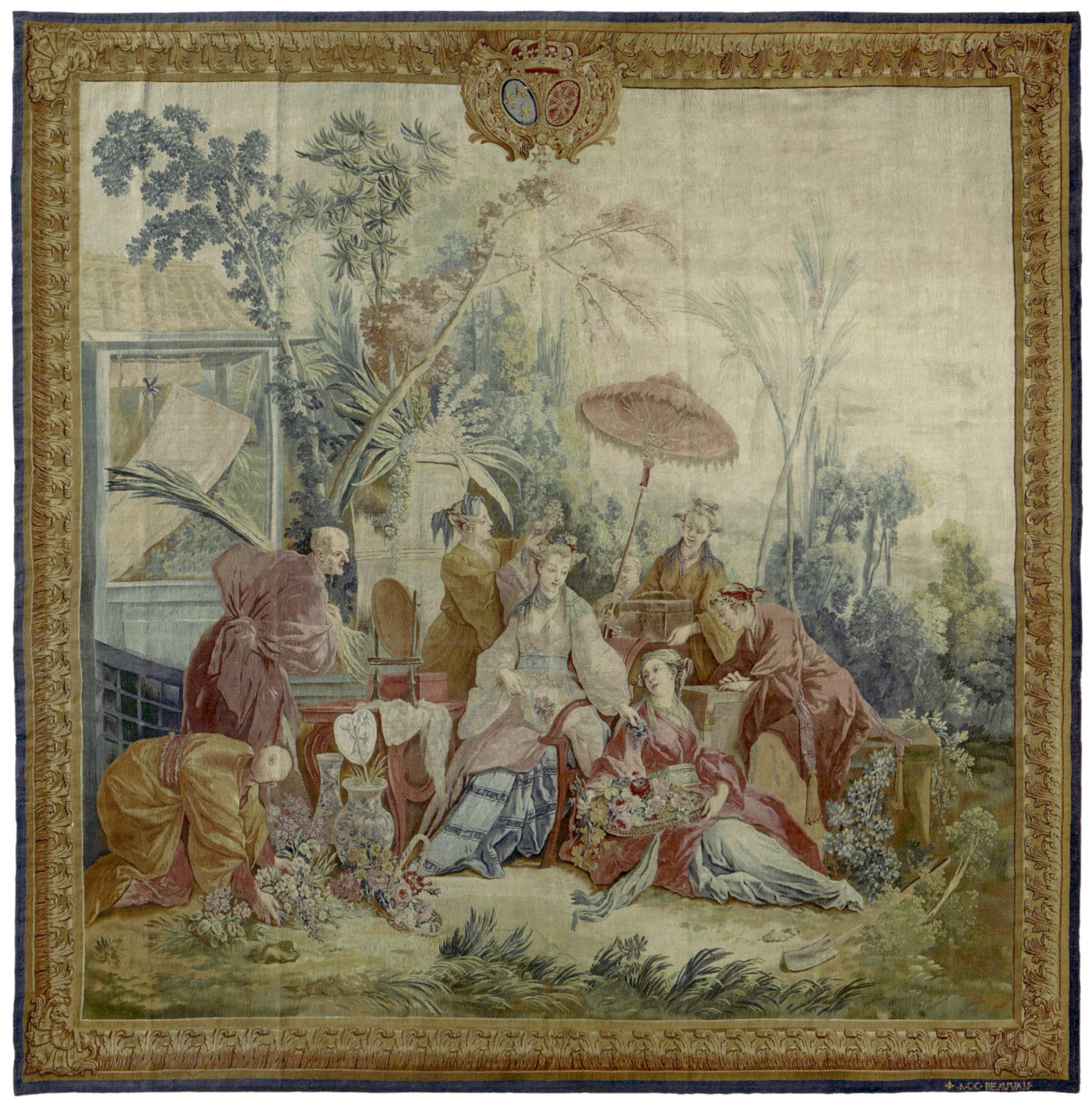

FIG. 77 *Chinese Toilette*, from the second *Tenture chinoise* series, c. 1758–60. Made by the Atelier André-Charlemagne Charron, the Manufacture royale de Beauvais. Tapestry, wool and silk, 11 ft. 9¾ in. × 11 ft. 3⅝ in. (360 × 345 cm). Galerie Armand Deroyan et Maison Pierre-Yves Machault, Paris.

into qualified agents so that upon their return they could propagandize French industrial products to the Chinese and at the same time collect information about Chinese manufactories for him. To provide Ko and Yang with the necessary knowledge and skills for their future tasks, Bertin arranged for them to study drawing and etching and organized trips to the French royal manufactories. They toured the ateliers at Sèvres (porcelains), Gobelins (tapestries), Savonnerie (carpets), and Lyon (silks). In addition, they were introduced to papermaking, enameling, pin production, printing, and the operation of electricity machinery. Bertin required Ko and Yang to submit lengthy study reports on the technologies they observed and on the differences between French and Chinese products.[64] On tapestry, they wrote:

> In China we make a type of tapestry with camel hair. It hardly deserves the name of tapestry. They are just variegated patterns without much taste or coordination [between patterns], and the Chinese only use them as some kind of foot carpet. Two or three tapestry hangings from this country [France] in the [Chinese] Emperor's palace would perhaps bring him more pleasure than all the magnificent thrones with which he adorns his court. He would be surprised by the éclat of the colors and the beauty of the pictures. Figures and flowers are preferable to all other representations, but the figures must be decent, because the Chinese are extremely sensitive about this matter.[65]

In another report on Savonnerie carpets, Ko and Yang commented: "The Chinese would better appreciate and be more inclined to purchase these velvety carpets than Gobelins tapestries. This is why it would be desirable for the Emperor of China to have some of these pieces that represent animals, flowers, and landscapes. The sight of such lively and animated representations could excite the desire of the lords at court to have similar ones."[66] Ko and Yang's accounts expose their unfamiliarity with Chinese silk tapestries and their ignorance of the basic features of the tapestry medium. Their humble social status would not have allowed them access to the Qing palaces or to the emperor himself, and therefore their pronouncements on the emperor's taste in tapestries were merely vague assumptions.[67] Lacking adequate knowledge of the Chinese foreign trade system and regulations, Ko and Yang offered an estimation of the Qing court's potential for acquiring French tapestries that was also unfoundedly optimistic. Nevertheless, Bertin believed that the pair hailed from literati families, and he relied heavily on their advice in projecting the commercial and cultural success of French tapestries at the Chinese court.[68]

On February 1, 1765, Ko and Yang finally embarked on their return journey to Canton carrying Bertin's gifts for the Qing emperor.[69] In addition to the six tapestries of the second *Tenture chinoise,* other items included "two portraits by [Louis] Vigée, with glass and frames," "a case of twelve mirrors measuring 30 by 24 inches [*pouces*]," "a group of Sèvres porcelains," "a portable printing machine," "a Brisson electrical apparatus" (Leyden jar), and various optical devices, booklets, and maps.[70] These objects represented the technological and artistic achievements of France, and Bertin's choices aligned with the common practice of the French Crown and its officials of showing such objects to foreign dignitaries as a matter of national pride. For example, the Siamese ambassadors were taken to the Saint-Gobain mirror manufactory in 1686, and the Ottoman ambassador Mehmed Efendi was given a tour of the Gobelins manufactory during his diplomatic visit from 1720 to 1721.[71] By selecting tapestries with Chinese scenes and Sèvres porcelains (a medium that originated in China), Bertin clearly wished to convey the French knowledge and appreciation of Chinese civilization and in so doing to facilitate a dialogue between the two countries.

Letters sent to Bertin by Ko, Yang, and Benoist from China contain detailed accounts of the vicissitudes of the *Tenture chinoise* after the suite arrived in Canton in November 1765. The tapestries were immediately confiscated by the Governor General of Guangdong and Guangxi Provinces (referred to in the letter as "Tsong-tou," the French spelling for *Zongdu*), who wished to acquire them himself.[72] The problematic status of these tapestries made them highly suspicious: neither were they official tributes, nor did they match the emperor's order from fifteen years earlier. After negotiating for nearly a year, the supervisors of the French East India Company in Canton, in consultation with Bertin and French missionaries in China, were able to persuade the Canton officials to release the tapestries.[73] The French Jesuits in Beijing finally presented the works to the Qianlong emperor on December 9, 1766, in their own name instead of that of Bertin or Louis XV. Neither Ko and Yang nor Benoist was admitted to this occasion, and the tapestries were presented through a "grand Mandarin of the palace."[74] A Qing court record in the *Register of Provincial Tributary Gifts*

(*Gongzhong jindan*) dated December 10, 1766, corresponding to this event notes that Yang Tingzhang (1689–1772), Governor General of Guangdong and Guangxi Provinces, and Fang Tiyu (b. 1735), Supervisor of the Canton Customs Bureau, presented "six tapestries" (*tanzi*) as "tributary objects" (*gongpin*) on behalf of unspecified "Westerners."[75]

Although they were not present at this occasion, the Jesuits described Qianlong's enthusiastic response in their letters to Bertin on the basis of reports from court officials. Yang's letter dated December 29, 1767, recounts, "The emperor, upon seeing these rare pieces, was so enchanted that he stood up and said, 'O beautiful things; there is nothing similar in my empire.' This was like a celebration day at the court."[76] Benoist's letter, drafted between September 10 and November 10, 1767, gave an even more vivid account of this event: "He [the grand Mandarin] came out from the Emperor's place and admitted to me that, upon seeing the six tapestry pieces, he [the Emperor] was seized with admiration. He recounted how His Majesty placed them at different viewing angles and admired them even more as he attentively examined the fineness of their workmanship."[77]

France's competition with other European countries in terms of industry, commerce, and political power clearly underlay Bertin's motivation for presenting the *Tenture chinoise*. Yang's letter to Bertin on December 29, 1767, reported: "These tapestries [the second *Tenture chinoise*] were compared to those presented to the emperor by the ambassador of Portugal. The ugliness of the latter uplifts even more the beauty of the former."[78] The ugly tapestries in question referred to the French ones presented by the Portuguese embassy in 1752, and Yang's emphasis on their inferiority should be understood as an unfounded exaggeration for the purpose of pleasing Bertin. Upon reading this note and without knowing that the Portuguese embassy indeed presented French tapestries, Bertin was anxious to find out more details about the Portuguese set. He asked whether their themes were figures or foliage (verdures), whether the Portuguese ambassador presented them as tribute on behalf of his king, and what reward the Chinese emperor granted for this present—questions Yang failed to answer.[79] The tapestries' subject matter and imagery lay at the center of Bertin's anxieties over the Portuguese rivalry with France in developing liaisons with China and over the delicate diplomatic matter of the French gifts being relegated as subordinate tribute.[80] As the Qing court's gift record shows, however, these tapestries were inevitably classified as tribute from Westerners.[81]

Although specific discussions of the tapestries' themes are not found in French or Chinese documents, it is logical to conjecture that Bertin would have thoroughly considered the matter and chosen the most suitable ones in order to accomplish his ambitious diplomatic goal. Boucher's chinoiserie designs, interpreted in the tapestry medium, represented the high style of French art at the time and demonstrated French knowledge of and admiration for China. In choosing these pieces, Bertin could not only showcase the highest achievement of French painting and tapestry weaving, but also glorify the Qing monarch.

In his letters, Bertin expressed high expectations that the *Tenture chinoise* would gain the favor of the Qing emperor for France and trigger a desire on the part of the sovereign and his court for French luxury goods. In a letter written before he learned of Qianlong's response to this gift, Bertin stated, "I also very much count on the Missionaries to use this occasion to turn the merit of this work to the advantage of the French nation and her commerce, and in this regard to gain the protection of the Emperor and above all make it distinguished from other European countries."[82] Thrilled to learn about Qianlong's admiration for the tapestries, Bertin wrote, "I read with a new satisfaction . . . that they [the tapestries] had just the effect on his imperial majesty's spirit that I had hoped for by giving him a high idea of the perfection that the arts in France have reached and to awaken his attention in favor of an industrious and learned nation, which for more than a century the missionaries have brought to his knowledge by advantageous means."[83]

As Bertin had anticipated, the second *Tenture chinoise* indeed fascinated Qianlong, and the emperor commissioned a new building with a ceiling high enough to accommodate these tapestries—the Observatory of the Distant Ocean (*Yuanying guan*; fig. 78).[84] In a French-Chinese bilingual map of the European Palaces sent from China by the Jesuit missionary François Bourgeois (1723–1792) and received in France in 1787, the caption for the observatory marks it as a "new European building, specially built for the Gobelins [Beauvais] tapestries."[85] Presumably, the full set of the second *Tenture chinoise*, or part of it, was still in the observatory when the English and French armies sacked the Yuanming yuan in October 1860. Upon the troops' return to Europe the following spring, many of the looted objects immediately went to

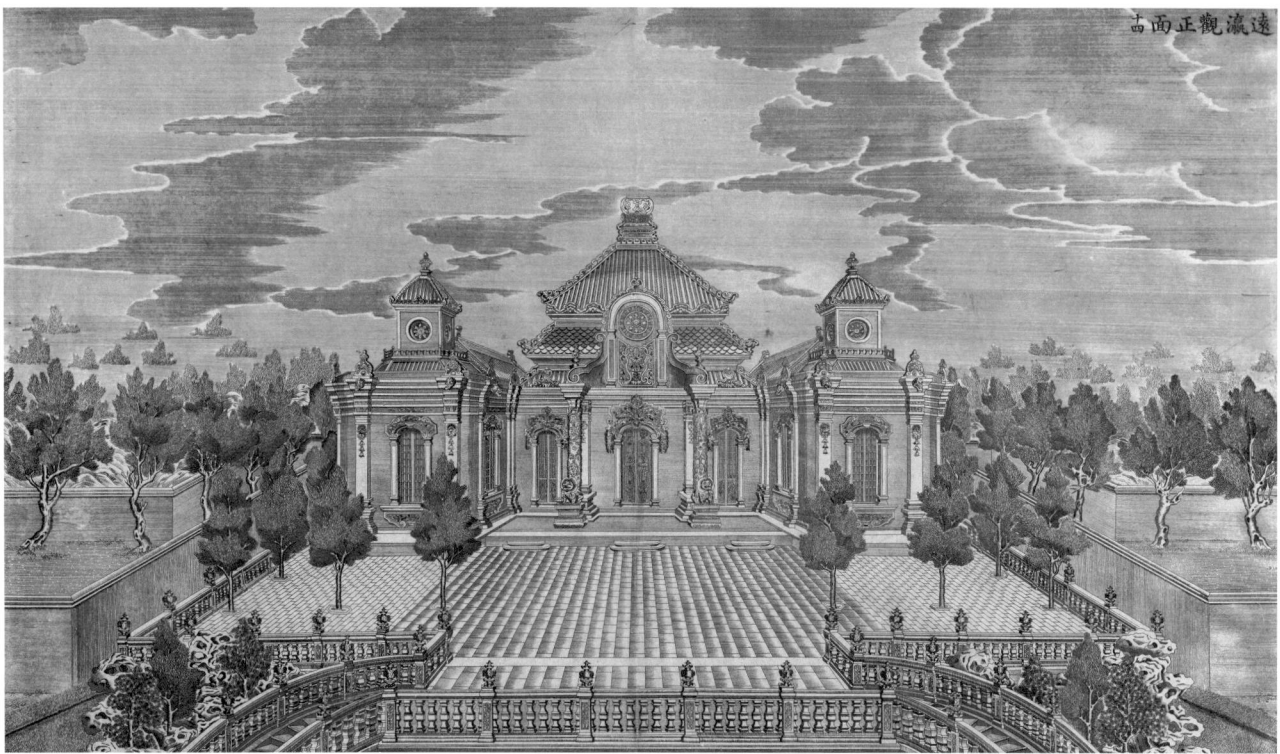

FIG. 78 Yi Lantai, *Front Side of the Observatory of the Distant Ocean*, 1783–86. Engraving, 19 ¾ × 34 ½ in. (50 × 87.5 cm). Getty Research Institute, Los Angeles (86-B26695).

auction. In July 1861 the French journal *L'Art pour tous* illustrated *Chinese Fair* from this set, which was being exhibited and auctioned, describing it as "returned from China following the latest expedition" (fig. 79).[86]

The subtlety of Bertin's message was inevitably lost when these tapestries were presented to Qianlong, whose view of foreign objects and of the place of the Qing Empire within the world order gave rise to very different meanings of these pieces. When classified as "tributary objects," the *Tenture chinoise* that came by way of the French Mission in Beijing simply glorified the superiority of his empire. In the Qing imperial ideology, only the emperor, with his dominant and centralized power, could mobilize people all over the world to show devotion and pay their respects. Thus, fanciful and precious "tributary goods" that traveled far to reach his court manifested the devotion of their presenters. Moreover, it is dubious that Qianlong would have understood Bertin's choice of Boucher's Chinese images as a sensible homage to his empire and civilization. In the absence of textual evidence about Qianlong's view of the themes depicted, it is questionable whether he or his courtiers even recognized Boucher's imagery as "Chinese." On the contrary, it is more likely that the shading on the figures' faces and clothing, their blond, curly hair, the fanciful chinoiserie motifs, and the rococo decorative borders would have registered as Western and exotic to Qianlong and therefore fascinated him as a fresh, foreign style. This conjecture is supported by the fact that the chinoiserie images and rococo ornaments in the tapestries soon found their way into the Qing court's own tapestries representing "Western" scenes, a topic that will be examined in chapter 4. Lastly, Qianlong might not have associated these tapestries with France and French culture at all. In the Qing documents, these tapestries, like other sets from Europe, were indistinguishably classified as Western.[87] Phrases such as "French tapestries" or "French goods" do not appear in the Qing archives for labeling categories of stylistic attribution or scientific knowledge, nor do we find the specific manufactory names Gobelins and Beauvais, which seem to have been unknown to the Qing court.[88] Instead of privileging France, the second *Tenture chinoise* served as a material and visual clue to a homogeneous, exotic land as imagined by the Qing Empire. This romanticized Western land, discussed in the introduction to this volume, played an indispensable role in Qing imperial understanding of the cultural-geographic universe, where it remained subordinated to the Qing Empire.

Bertin would not have been aware of Qianlong's true perception of the French tapestries, which defied his high expectations. A few years after the tapestries' presentation, in 1772, he persisted in asking Ko and Yang, "Have our Beauvais tapestries and our mirrors that were so successful not aroused any desire in the court and in the sovereign himself to have more?"[89] As provincial priests with no access to the court, Ko and Yang could not answer Bertin's question. Instead of resulting in more commissions of French tapestries, as Bertin had hoped, Qianlong's admiration of them would soon lead the Qing court to experiment with designing and weaving woolen tapestries in the European mode. Although Bertin's attempt to promote more direct communication and commerce between China and France in official channels through the tapestry gift ultimately failed, these magnificent textiles nonetheless benefited him on a personal level by sparking Qianlong's favor for the French Jesuits, who were then granted the special convenience of collecting Chinese materials for Bertin, including Qing imperial works. Bertin's fruitful pursuit of Chinese knowledge eventually resulted in an impressive collection that represents a milestone in eighteenth-century European sinology: it included the fifteen-volume *Mémoires concernant l'histoire, les sciences, les arts, les moeurs, les usages, &c. des Chinois, par les missionnaires de Pékin* (*Articles on the History, Science, Arts, Customs, Practices, etc. of the Chinese, by the Missionaries of Beijing;* Paris, 1776–91), compiled by Bertin; more than a dozen bound albums of pictures depicting Chinese themes (now in the BNF); and numerous Chinese objects that have since been dispersed.[90]

Different from the two suites of *Tenture chinoise*, which served as diplomatic gifts, the *Tenture des Indes*, woven by the Gobelins manufactory, was the only known cycle that was brought to China as commercial goods. This set entered the Qing Palace in 1771 and remained in the Yuanming yuan until 1860. One tapestry from the original Qing imperial series—*The Animals' Combat*—has survived and is now in the collection of the Ashmolean Museum at the University of Oxford (figs. 80, 81).[91] Recent scholarship has shed light on the political ideologies implied in the colonial conquest scenes of this suite as well as on how these tapestries served as a potent political agent in early modern diplomatic negotiations.[92] While those studies situate the designs and movements of the *Tenture des Indes* mainly in the context of the European courts, the following discussion traces the suite's journey to the Qing court and explores how its imagery resonated with Qianlong's political agenda and global vision.

The *Tenture des Indes* featured designs derived from sketches and paintings of Brazilian animals, fishes, plants, and indigenous inhabitants executed by the Dutch painters

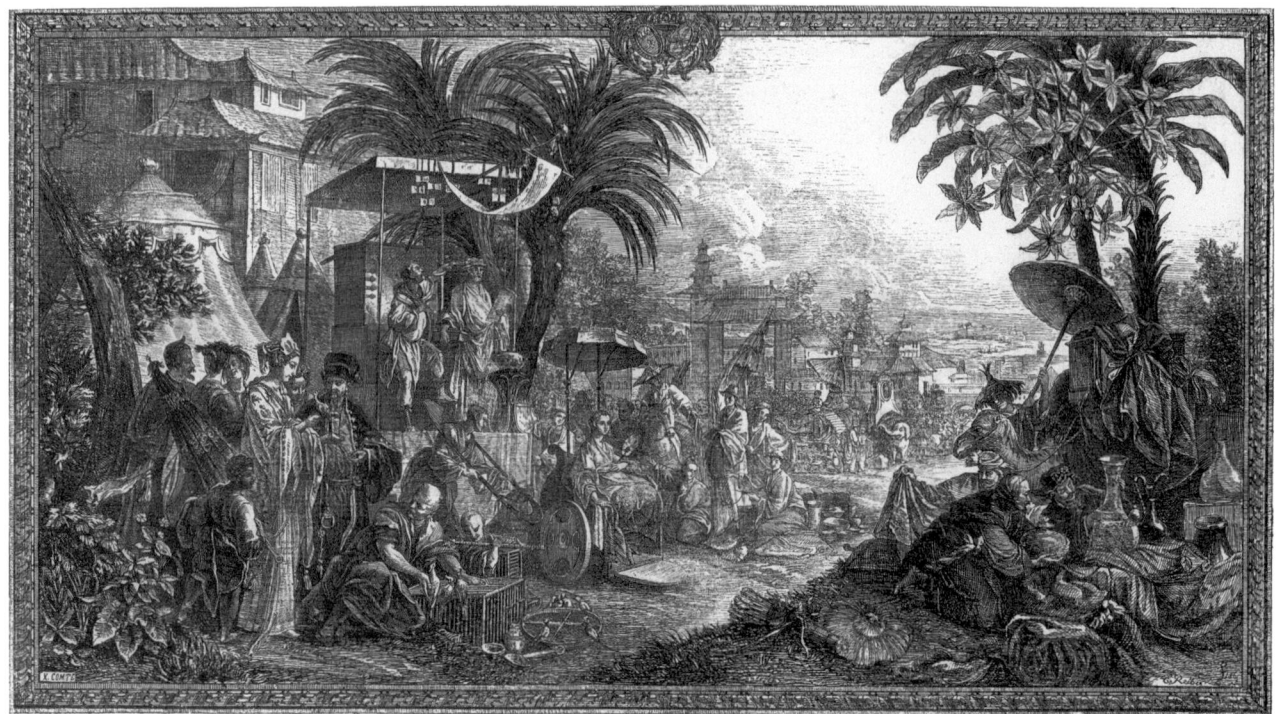

FIG. 79 Illustration of *Chinese Fair*, tapestry from the second *Tenture chinoise* series, looted from the Yuanming yuan in 1860. From *L'Art pour tous*, no. 16 (August 31, 1861): 63.

Encoding Global Aspirations   91

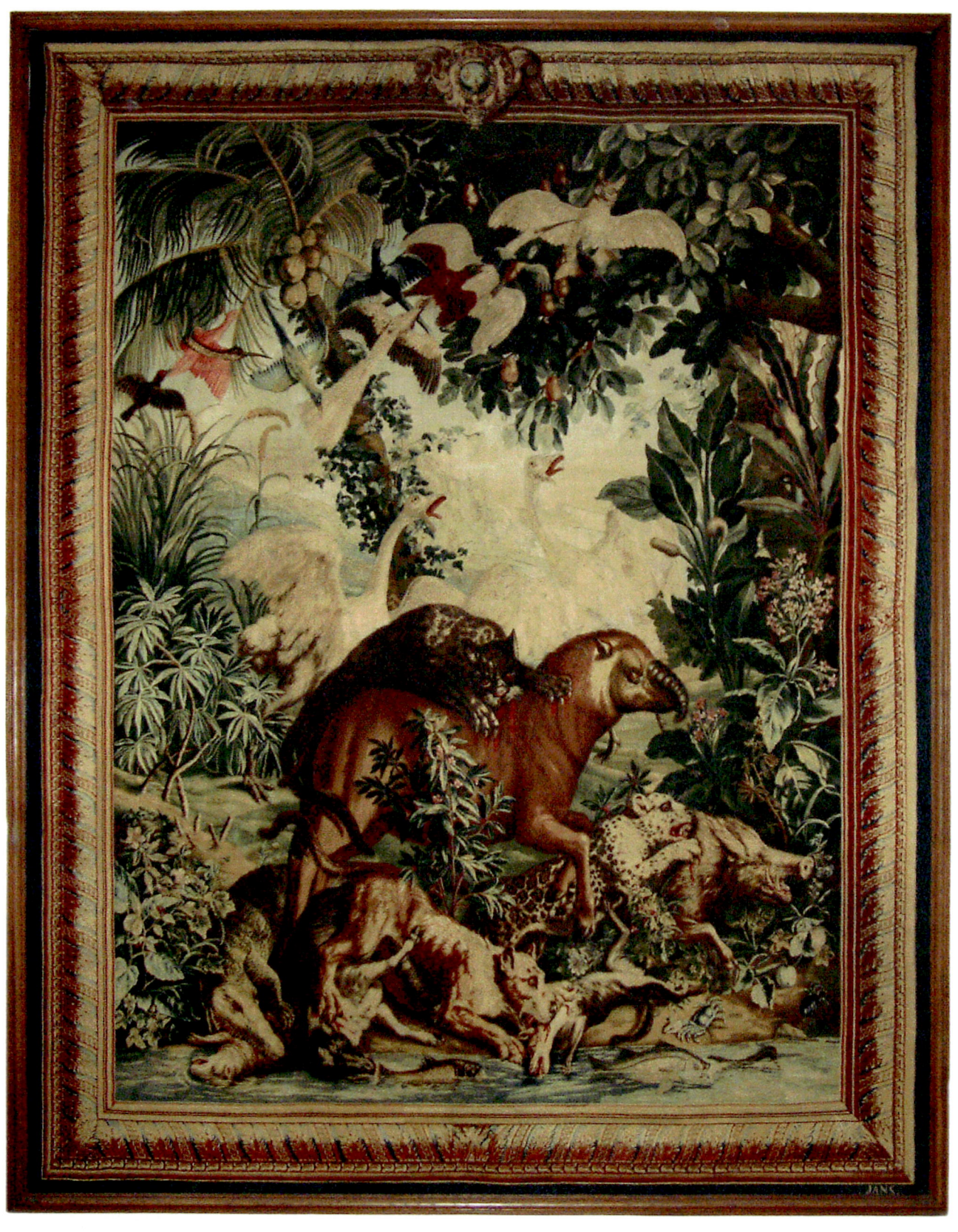

FIG. 80 *The Animals' Combat*, from the fifth set of the series *Anciennes Grandes Indes (Tenture des Indes)*, 1718–20. Made by the atelier of Jean Jans le fis, the Manufacture royale des Gobelins. Tapestry, wool and silk, 16 ft. × 12 ft. 8 in. (487.5 × 386 cm). Ashmolean Museum, University of Oxford (WA1901.1).

Albert Eckhout (c. 1610–1665) and Frans Post (1612–1680) during their expedition from 1637 to 1644 in the company of the Governor General of Dutch Brazil, Johan Maurits van Nassau-Siegen. In 1679 Maurits presented thirty-four of these paintings as gifts to Louis XIV, of which eight were prepared in a large size to be used as cartoons for tapestries.[93] Their subjects were *The Indian on Horseback, The King Carried by Two Moors, The Indian Hunter, The Striped Horse, The Fishermen, The Animals' Combat, The Two Bulls,* and *The Isabella Horse* (aka *The Elephant*).[94] From 1687 to 1730, the Gobelins Manufactory wove the complete set eight times. This group is typically referred to as the *Anciennes Indes* (*Old Indies*), to distinguish them from the later *Nouvelles Indes* (*New Indies*), which used modified designs and were woven between 1740 and 1800. Among the eight sets of *Anciennes Indes,* the first five measured four French *aunes* (15 ft. 7 in. [475 cm]) high, while the last three featured a reduced height of three and half French *aunes* (13 ft. 5⅜ in. [410 cm]). They are called the *Grandes Indes* and the *Petites Indes,* respectively.[95]

A letter dated November 21, 1769, from Jacques-Germain Soufflot (1713–1780), Director of the Manufactory of Gobelins, to the Marquis de Marigny (1727–1781), Director General of the Bâtiments du Roi, proposed the sale of a set of the old *Tenture des Indes* in the Gobelins that was "especially faded as it has been loaned on several occasions since it was made around 1720" at a reduced price of 16,000 livres instead of the original 28,470 livres.[96] The price corresponded to the dimensions of the tapestry suite in its used condition—107 square *aunes*—as remeasured in February 1768.[97] The letter states the major reason for this sale: the tapestries were of a considerable height that did not suit the French anymore.[98] By this time, French taste in interior decoration had changed, and smaller tapestries were preferred to monumental pieces.

Soufflot's letter also describes the buyer and his motivation for this purchase:

> The buyer is a merchant who is sometimes in Paris, sometimes in the Indies and in China. On his last journey, he learned that the emperor of China was enchanted by a set of tapestries, probably from Beauvais, that Mr. Bertin sent several years ago to see if these works might please China and lead to exchanges. . . . As a consequence, our merchant gambled on our set. . . . If his gamble succeeds, he will probably purchase several tapestry sets successively without fearing, as he does now, that he will incur too much risk on the price.[99]

The original price, the height, and the total dimensions of the tapestries indicated in Soufflot's letter clearly identify this suite to be sold to China as the fifth weaving, made between 1718 and 1720 on a high-warp loom by the ateliers of Jans and Lefebvre.[100] It was the last set of the *Grandes Indes.*

Marigny approved Soufflot's proposal on December 26, 1769, and the tapestries were presumably delivered immediately to Lorient, the headquarters of the French East India Company, to meet the sailing schedule of this merchant, who departed in January 1770 for Pondicherry, India.[101] Probably by late 1770 or early 1771, these tapestries had arrived in Canton. A letter dated September 8, 1771, from Ko to Bertin reports on a set of "Gobelins [tapestries] that were brought by Mr Le Chevalier Rothe," mentioning

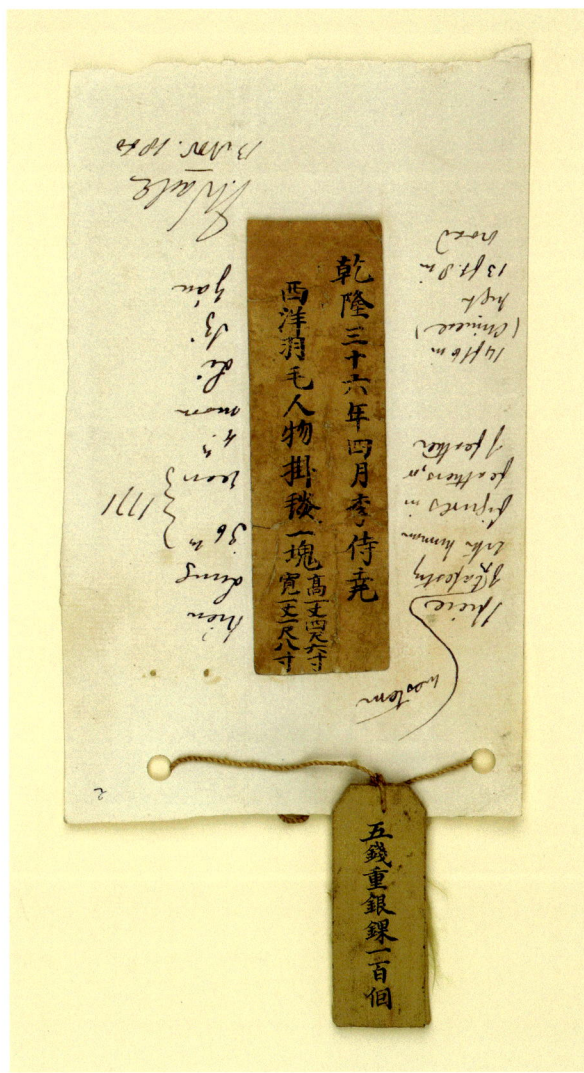

FIG. 81 Document attached to the tapestry *The Animals' Combat.* Ashmolean Museum, University of Oxford.

Encoding Global Aspirations

that if the Chinese did not purchase them, Rothe would plan to sell them to the government of Batavia.[102] This clearly referred to the Gobelins set of the *Grandes Indes* sold by Soufflot in December 1769, and it identified "Mr Le Chevalier Rothe" as the anonymous merchant mentioned in Soufflot's letter. The name Rothe appears several times in Bertin's notes and correspondence with Jesuit missionaries in Beijing, and Rothe himself actively helped Bertin transport Chinese objects to France through the French East India Company.[103] Bertin was certainly aware of the *Grandes Indes* transaction and perhaps had a strong influence on Rothe's decision. This "gamble" (as Soufflot called it), involving significant capital and complex logistics, continued Bertin's project to explore the commercial opportunities with China, yet it seems to have lacked the grander political and cultural ambitions embedded in the second *Tenture chinoise* sent earlier.

In selecting the *Grandes Indes*, with its pictorial representations of the New World, Rothe had carefully considered the propriety of the images and their appeal to the Chinese taste. Soufflot's letter of November 1769 reveals that, in addition to the discounted price, there was yet another reason for Rothe to choose this set: "There are almost no figures, which, he believes, will be less worrisome [for the Chinese], and there are Indian animals of all kinds, the presentation of which will astonish and please them."[104] Rothe's presumptions about Chinese taste probably came from Bertin's perceptions, which in turn were mediated by Ko and Yang's earlier report that representations of "animals, flowers, and landscapes" would be welcome in China.[105] Avoiding figures would prevent the potential miscomprehension of religious or allegorical themes, which were prevalent in French tapestries but unfamiliar to a Chinese audience. In addition, *galanterie* scenes portraying flirtatious, sensuous figures, which were fashionable in this period, could have been deemed improper in Chinese eyes. Ironically, the few Brazilian Indians depicted in the *Grandes Indes* are scantily clothed; in particular, the woman in *The Fishermen* bares her bosom in a full-frontal view (fig. 82). These seminudes fell in the very category of "indecent" figures in Chinese eyes, against which Ko and Yang had warned. In Chinese pictorial tradition, nudity and seminudity appeared almost exclusively in erotica. Rothe failed to see that such imagery would be extremely troublesome and would cause a great deal of cultural misinterpretation. A precedent had been set in 1670 when two printed cottons presented by the Portuguese embassy to the Qing court were rejected on the ground that they depicted nude human figures.[106]

According to Ko's letter to Bertin, after the *Grandes Indes* arrived in Canton, they did not encounter the same issue as the second *Tenture chinoise*.[107] A yellow Qing imperial label grouped with the tapestry *The Animals' Combat* from this set in the Ashmolean Museum offers the key to identifying the original circumstances in which the *Grandes Indes* was presented to the Qianlong emperor (see fig. 81). The label, in Chinese, reads: "On the fourth [lunar] month of the thirty-sixth year of the Qianlong reign [May 14–June 12, 1771], Li Shiyao [presented] a Western tapestry with feathers/human figures [*xiyáng yumao renwu guatan*], height: one *zhang* four *chi* and six *cun* [15 ft. 3⅝ in. (467 cm)], width: one *zhang* one *chi* and eight *cun* [12 ft. 5 in. (378 cm)]."[108] This label aligns well with a 1771 Qing Court record in the *Register of Provincial Tributary Gifts,* which indicates that "Li Shiyao, on the twenty-seventh day of the third [lunar] month, the thirty-sixth year of the Qianlong reign [May 11, 1771], [presented] four tapestries woven abroad [*yángzhi huatan*]" among other treasures during Qianlong's inspection tour in Shandong province. These tapestries were then entrusted to a Manchu bondservant to be taken back to the Imperial Household Department in Beijing.[109] Li Shiyao, whose name is mentioned in chapter 1, was then Governor General of Guangdong and Guangxi Provinces and renowned for his diligence and resourcefulness in gathering precious and rare objects to please the emperor. Over the course of his seventeen years as an official in Canton (1755–61, 1764–65, and 1767–77), Li presented gifts to Qianlong 107 times, including countless European goods purchased from foreign merchants in Canton.[110] Apparently, Li acquired the *Grandes Indes* from Rothe with the intention of offering the set to the emperor.

According to *The Veritable Records of Emperor Gaozong* [Qianlong] (*Gaozong Chun Huangdi shilu*), he returned to the Yuanming yuan after the inspection tour on the seventh day of the fourth lunar month (May 20, 1771). The yellow label accompanying the Ashmolean tapestry must have been written sometime after this date, when the tapestry was being reviewed or inventoried.[111] The yellow label is pasted upside down on a sheet with an English translation dated November 13, 1860, shortly after the looting of the Yuanming yuan. It came with the tapestry *The Animals' Combat* when the latter was acquired by the Ashmolean Museum in 1901 from the estate of Lieutenant General Henry Hope Crealocke (1831–1891), who reported

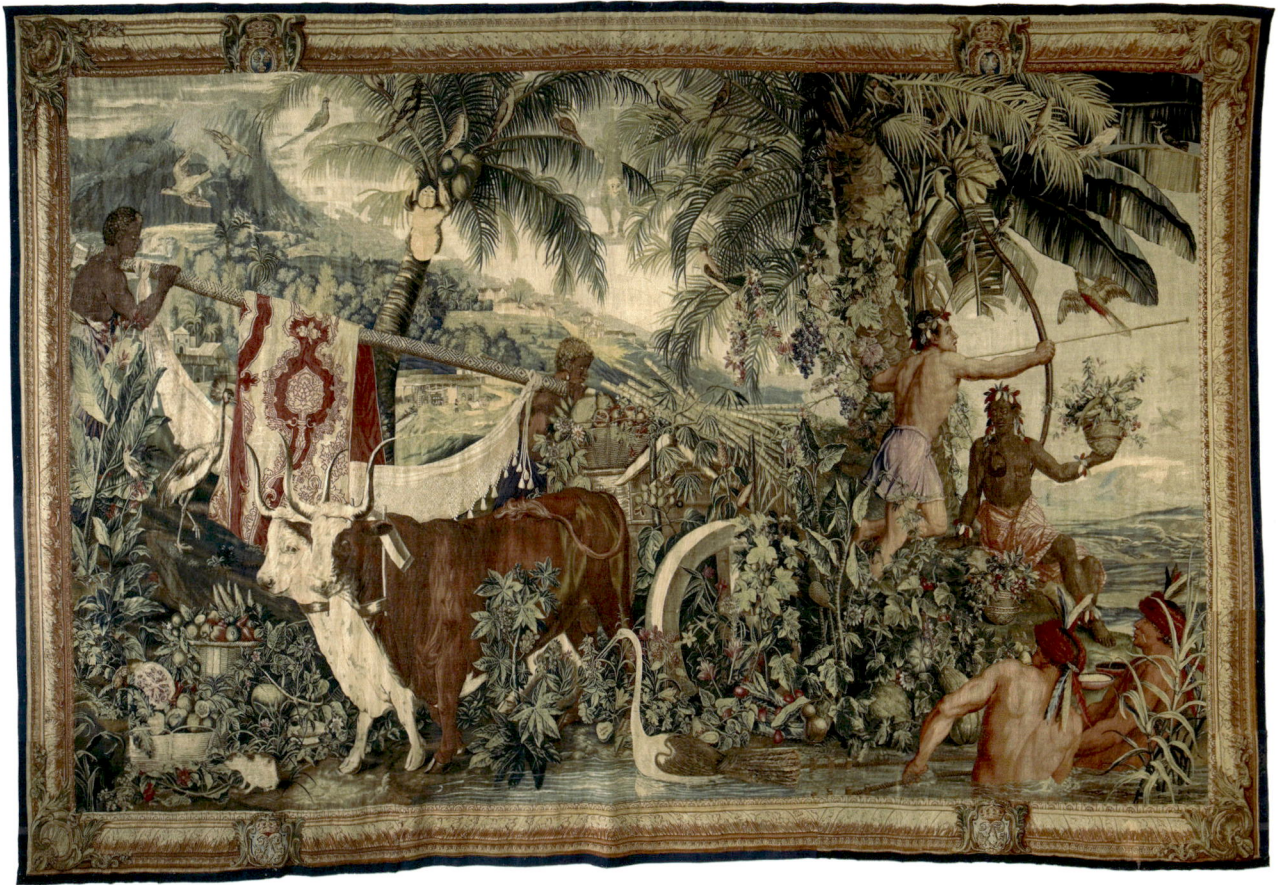

FIG. 82 *The Two Bulls* and *The Fishermen*, two pieces combined with an added border, from the second set of the series *Anciennes Grandes Indes* (*Tenture des Indes*), 1689–90. Made by the ateliers of Jean-Baptiste Mozin and Jean de la Croix, the Manufacture royale des Gobelins. Tapestry, wool and silk, 15 ft. 5 in. × 24 ft. 3⅜ in. (470 × 740 cm). Mobilier national, Paris (GMTT-190-001).

finding the tapestry in the Yuanming yuan in 1860.[112] The phrase on the Qing label describing the tapestry's content, "feathers/human figures," has ambiguous wording and grammar. It could be interpreted as figures dressed in feathered clothes or accessories; or, since "feather" could serve as a shorthand term for the painting genre of birds in Chinese tradition, the phrase could also indicate a picture with both humans and birds. Among the eight themes of the *Anciennes Grandes Indes*, either *The Fishermen* (see fig. 82) or *The Indian Hunter* (fig. 83) could fit the description, as they both represent birds and native inhabitants wearing feather headdresses. The indicated width in the Chinese label, equivalent to 12 ft. 4⅞ in. (378 cm), however, is closest to that of *The Animals' Combat* in its used condition at the time of its 1769 sale (12 ft. 5 in. [379 cm]).[113] Evidently, the gift recorder at the court created this confusion when four tapestries were presented together at the Qing court. Connecting these dots, we can conclude that four of the eight pieces from the fifth set of the *Grandes Indes* entered Qianlong's palace in 1771, and among the four, *The Animals' Combat* and either *The Fishermen* or *The Indian Hunter* were present. The subjects of the other two tapestries at the Qing court, as well as the whereabouts of the rest of the pieces from this set, remain unclear.

The Animals' Combat depicts a ferocious fight scene set on a riverbank overgrown with trees and flowering plants, among which a South American jaguar fiercely digs his claws and teeth into the back of a tapir, startling the birds in the background and overshadowing the small, agitated beasts in the foreground. By contrast, *The Fishermen* portrays a relatively serene image of native Brazilians under a large banana tree: a hunter is stretching his bow while two muscular fishermen in the river pull a seine. A buxom woman sitting in the center lifts a basket of plants signifying prosperity, a message echoed by the voluptuous landscape abundant with fruits and flowers. In *The Indian Hunter*, a similarly idyllic scene, a muscular indigenous man, seen from the back in three-quarter view, leans

Encoding Global Aspirations   95

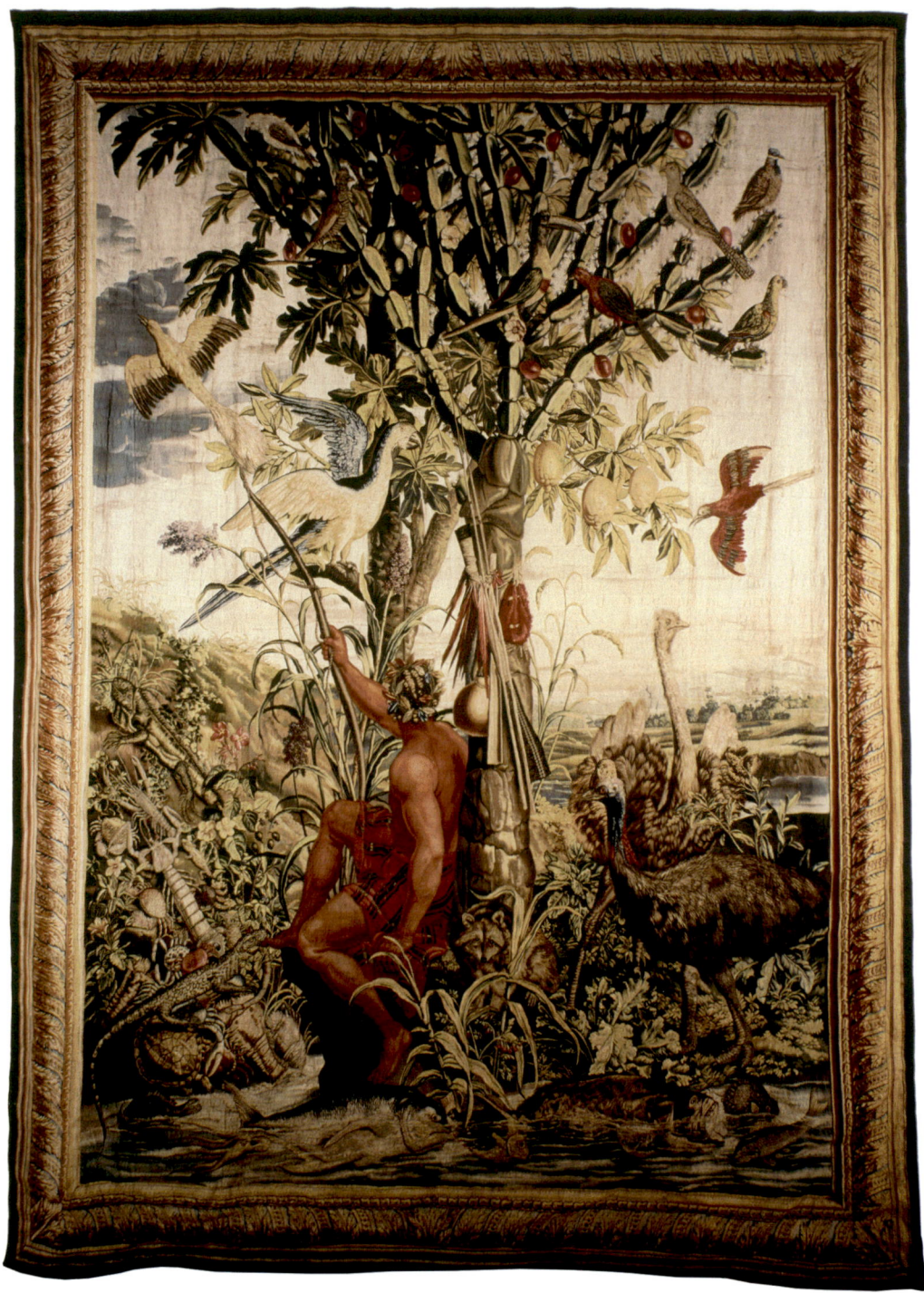

FIG. 83 *The Indian Hunter,* from the second set of the series *Anciennes Grandes Indes* (*Tenture des Indes*), 1689–90. Made by the atelier of Jean-Baptiste Mozin, the Manufacture royale des Gobelins. Tapestry, wool and silk, 15 ft. 1⅛ in. × 11 ft. 1¾ in. (460 × 340 cm). Mobilier national, Paris (GMTT-193-003).

against a luxuriant cactus tree among surrounding reptiles, fishes, and birds, including a cassowary and an ostrich, both of impressive size. These vivid representations of animals and people from afar evoke a sense of immediacy, as if observed on-site, but indeed they are idealized images of a fertile and untamed land, combining local subjects depicted firsthand on the spot and stereotypical exotic motifs. A visual feast of unfamiliar species, the tapestries place diverse animals, plants, and fishes in unlikely proximity and orchestrate their imaginary interactions.

Added to this pictorial program are other exotic animals. *The Striped Horse*, for example, features the great Indian rhinoceros, first made popular in a 1515 print by Albrecht Dürer (1471–1528), in harmonious cohabitation with an African zebra—a noble, heroic animal long anchored in European visual tradition (fig. 84).[114] Likewise,

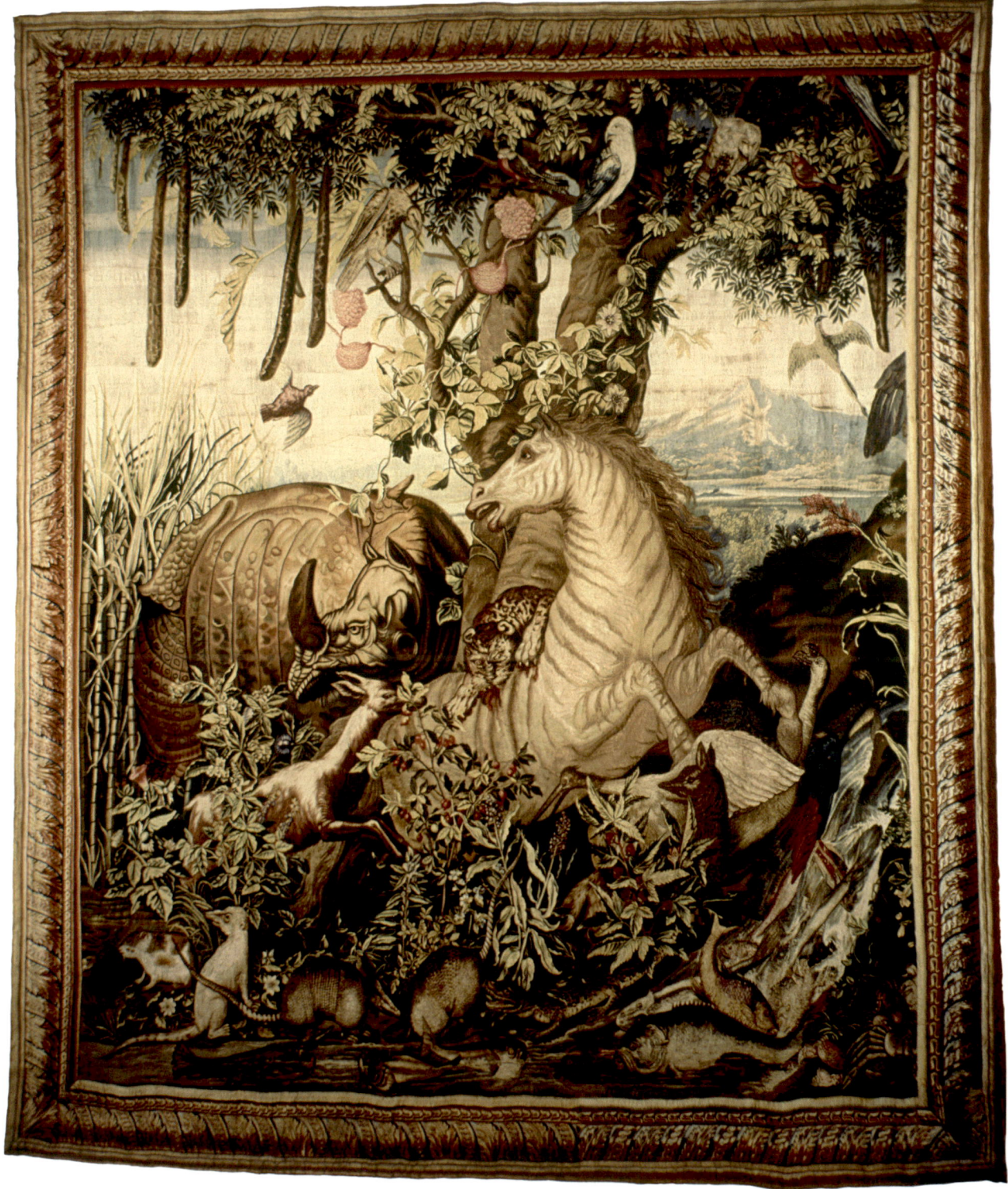

FIG. 84 *The Striped Horse*, from the second set of the series *Anciennes Grandes Indes* (*Tenture des Indes*), 1689. Made by the atelier of Jean de la Croix, the Manufacture royale des Gobelins. Tapestry, wool and silk, 15 ft. 6 ⅜ in. × 12 ft. 3 ⅝ in. (475 × 375 cm). Mobilier national, Paris (GMTT-193-001).

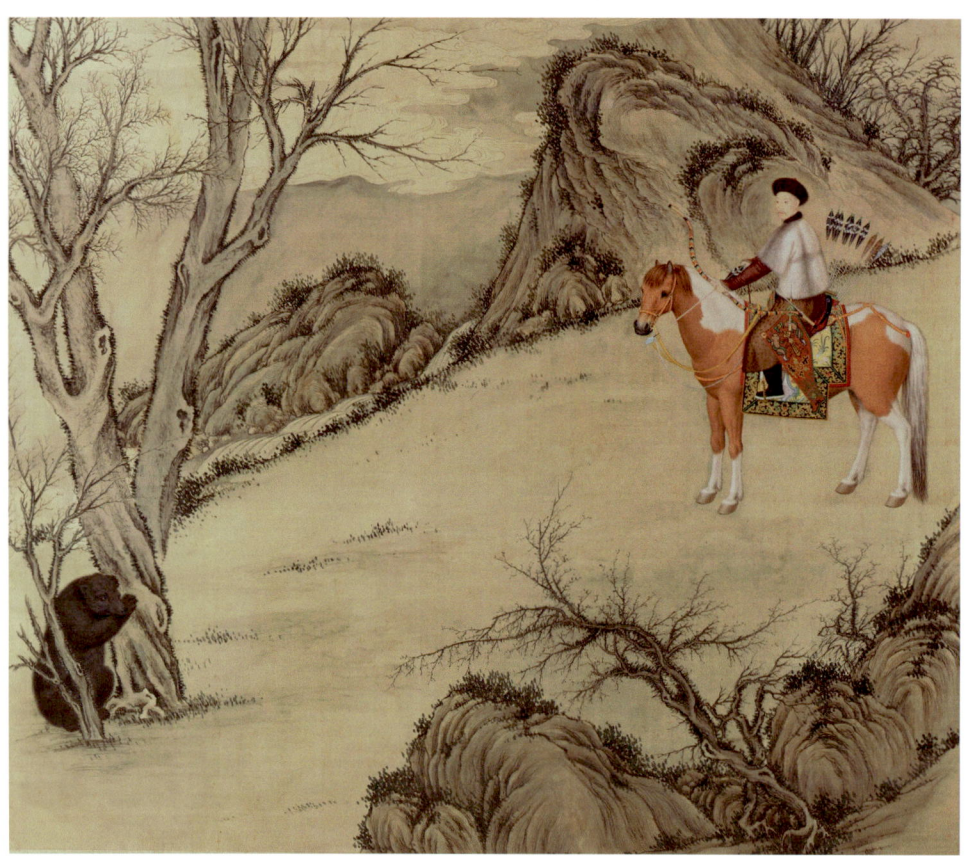

FIG. 85 Qing court artist(s), *The Qianlong Emperor Intimidating a Bear*, detail, mid-eighteenth century. Hanging scroll, ink and colors on silk, 8 ft. 6 in. × 5 ft. 7⅝ in. (259 × 171.6 cm). Palace Museum, Beijing (gu6510).

the cassowary in *The Indian Hunter*, a native of the island of Java, was an object of fascination at the court of the Holy Roman Emperor Rudolf II (r. 1576–1612) and later in Louis XIV's Royal Menagerie of Versailles.[115] The Marquis de Mondevergue, governor of the islands of Dauphine and Bourbon (now Madagascar and Réunion), purchased the bird from merchants sailing back from the Indies and presented it to Louis XIV in 1671.[116] The bird died in 1674, but Pieter Boel's depiction of it in profile was immortalized in the Gobelins tapestry series *The Months of Royal Residences: January* (woven between 1668 and 1713), and the same image later appeared in *The Indian Hunter* (see fig. 83). Grander than the Brazilian Indies, the robust world represented in the *Tenture des Indes* is at once an embodied encyclopedia of natural science and a poetic land redolent of legends and adventures. Its references to the collections in the Royal Menagerie point to a prominent link between imperial glory, the Enlightenment agenda, and rare, fanciful fauna from far-flung lands.

No record in the Qing imperial documents reveals Qianlong's response to the *Tenture des Indes*. The iconography of wild creatures and native peoples from the New World, however, would have resonated with the Manchu emperor's passion for hunting and his rising enthusiasm for encyclopedic projects to catalogue the animals, birds, aquatic creatures, plants, and ethnic peoples that constituted the universe as he understood it. As chapter 2 discussed, ritualized royal hunting served symbolically to demonstrate the martial power of the Manchu rulers. Among the numerous paintings that Qianlong commissioned to record his hunting events and idealize his martial prowess, his preferred composition features an intense moment when he, the undefeatable ruler, intimidates or kills a ferocious beast. The targeted animals in these representations, such as the bear frightened by Qianlong in one such painting, are often realistically depicted to enhance the credibility of these events (fig. 85). In accordance with Qing court paintings of hunting scenes but rendered even more vividly, the dangerous beasts in the *Tenture des Indes* would have inspired Qianlong to imagine himself as an omnipotent hunter that the scenes are in want of, thus enhancing his monarchical pleasure of conquest and subjugation.

The Kangxi emperor had already demonstrated a strong interest in zoological encyclopedia, as evidenced by two *Manuals of Sea Oddities* (*Haiguai tuji* [1688] and *Haicuo tu* [1698]) and an *Album of Pigeons* (*Gebo pu*), composed by artists at court. The former include multiple images of exotic marine creatures after scientific engravings in Conrad Gesner's (1516–1565) *Historiae animalium* (1558) and Jan Jonston's (1603–1675) *Historiae naturalis* (1649–50), which were then inventively colored by Qing court painters. These albums attest to Qing imperial knowledge of Western natural history.[117] The Qianlong emperor inherited this legacy and expanded the project of compiling zoological manuals to a grander level. In addition to the albums of imperial horses and dogs painted from life, from 1750 to 1761, he commissioned court artists to compile two massive series: the *Manual of Birds* (*Niaopu*) and the *Manual of Beasts* (*Shoupu*), comprising 360 and 180 images, respectively. These manuals combined empirical depictions of native species gathered from the vast Qing territories, illustrations of fantastic and mythical creatures drawn from ancient Chinese classics, and images of "foreign animals" adapted from European natural history illustrations.[118] For example, rhinoceroses were never present at the Qing court, but the *Manual of Beasts* includes an image of one adapted from Gesner's *Historiae animalium* after Dürer's famous print (fig. 86).[119] The rhinoceros animated in the tapestry *The Striped Horse* would have given Qianlong the impression that the fabled animal, static in his album, had come to life in his very own palace (see fig. 84).

Although it is unclear whether a cassowary existed in Qianlong's menagerie, the bird particularly fascinated the emperor, who had it depicted at least four times from 1774 onward. In that year Qianlong ordered an image of a cassowary as an addition (number 361) to the *Manual of Birds* (fig. 87).[120] In 1782 he commissioned a court painter, Yang Dazhang (fl. late eighteenth century) to paint a hanging scroll of two cassowaries. Both images are accompanied by Qianlong's explanatory inscription based largely on the cassowary entry in Claude Perrault's (1613–1688) *Memoires pour servir à l'histoire naturelle des animaux* (*Memoirs for a Natural History of Animals*; 1671–76). Lai Yu-chih has astutely observed that the objective, naturalistic representation of the cassowary in the *Manual of Birds* differed from traditional Chinese modes of depicting birds and was probably inspired by illustrations in the European natural histories by Jonston and Carolus Clusius (1526–1609), which were in the Jesuit library in Beitang.[121] In fact, the cassowary in the album bears a striking resemblance to the one in the lower right corner of *The Indian Hunter* in terms of its posture (in full profile with parted feet) and colors (fig. 88). Both have a light blue head transitioning into a bright blue neck with red on the back, a red wattle, and the same brownish gray color gradation of the feathers from the front of the body to the tail. It was this lifelike, colorful depiction of the bird in the tapestry—as opposed to the black-and-white engravings in European animal treatises—that probably provided a close visual

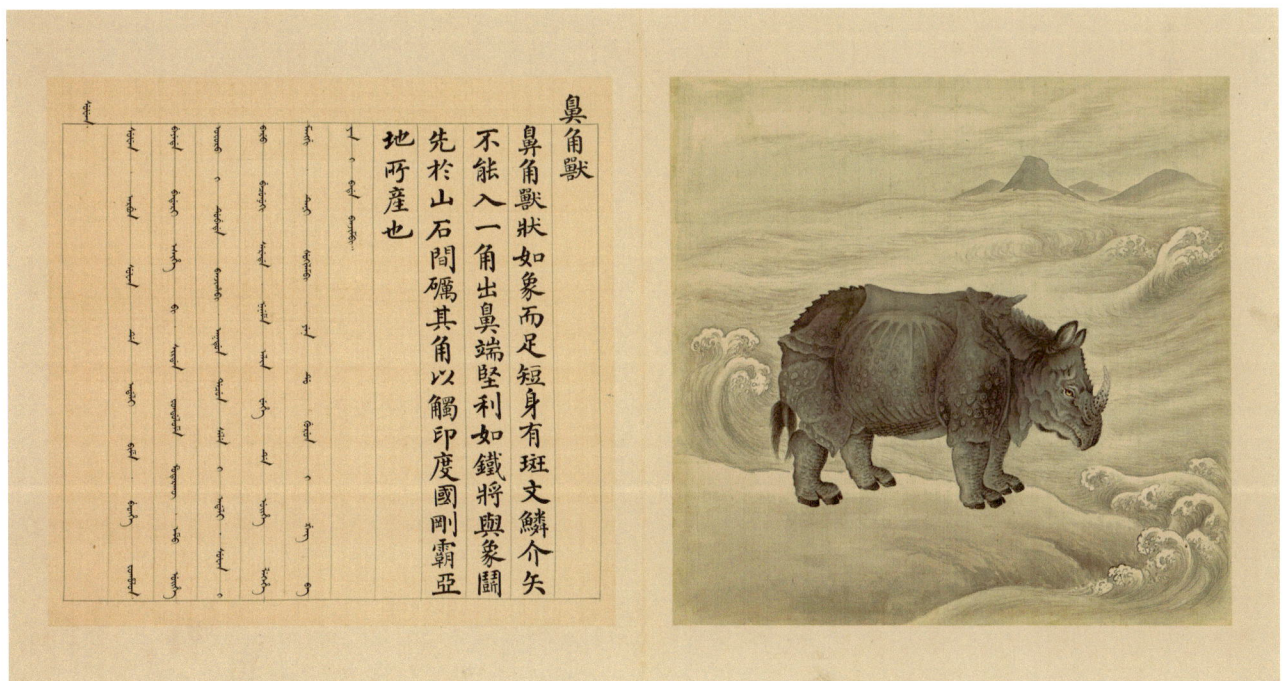

FIG. 86 Yu Sheng and Zhang Weibang, "Rhinoceros," in *Manual of Beasts* (*Shoupu*), 1761. Album leaf, ink and color on silk, each leaf 15⅞ × 16¾ in. (40.2 × 42.6 cm). Palace Museum, Beijing (gu6117).

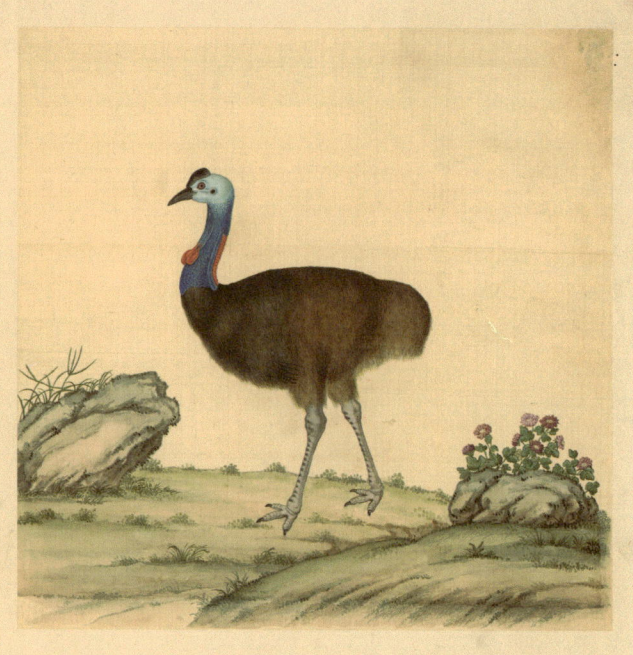
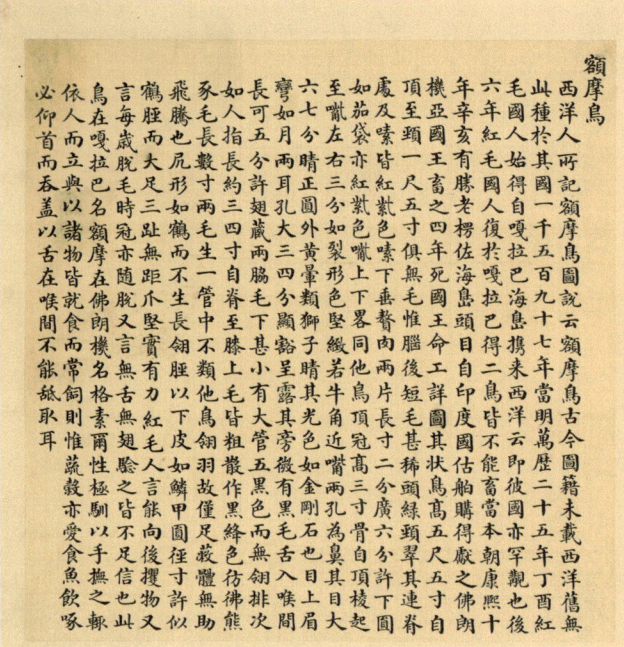

FIG. 87 Yu Sheng and Zhang Weibang, "Cassowary," in *Manual of Birds* (*Niaopu*), 1774. Album leaf, ink and colors on silk, each leaf 16 1/8 × 17 3/8 in. (41 × 44.1 cm). Palace Museum, Beijing (gu6118).

model for the Qing court's cassowary image. This origin helps explain why the Qing picture accurately renders the bird's head and neck in two shades of blue instead of following the inscription, which states, "The head is green, the neck jade green" (*tou lü jing cui*). Moreover, it is tempting to conjecture that Qianlong's sudden interest in producing cassowary images beginning in 1774 may have been sparked by the tapestry that arrived at the court in 1771. The woven cassowary in the landscape scene offered empirical, visual evidence of the same bird that Qianlong probably had encountered earlier in illustrated encyclopedias or seen in an isolated context in his menagerie.

As Lai Yu-chih argues, these albums of birds and beasts signaled the Qing Empire's connection to the global impulses in the early modern maritime age. Integrating European prototypes and visual styles to depict known and unknown animals, they constructed a "reality" in which the empire possessed all things within the universe. In Chinese dynastic history, the miraculous appearance of rare, exotic animals had long been regarded as an auspicious sign of the heavenly mandate of the ruler. By incorporating images of strange animals from ancient Chinese myths and foreign scientific sources into the imperial visual records, these Qing zoological manuals perpetuated the manifestations of auspicious animals and subsumed all species under an idealized imperial order to glorify the empire's legitimacy and far-reaching power.[122]

In light of the political significance of fauna imagery for the Qing Empire, the *Tenture des Indes* would no doubt have appealed to Qianlong. As large wall hangings with life-size representations that transformed a room into a fictional space, these pieces differed from albums intended for desktop viewing. Their monumental scale and highly realistic scenes of foreign beasts, fishes, and birds augmented the visual excitement, inviting the ruler to step into a fantastic world that he could view up close while heightening his imagined privilege of accessing and possessing a distant land. Furthermore, these image-bearing textiles had traveled far to enter Qianlong's court, as if the rare species they depicted, summoned by the heavenly order, had moved from remote corners of the world to the central kingdom and submitted to the emperor's divine power. The tapestries representing exotic creatures offered Qianlong tangible visual sources to expand his knowledge of and imaginings about global animals. Likewise, the depictions of foreign people in the *Tenture des Indes* reinforced the message that the Qing Empire "cherished men from afar" (*huairou yuanren*), a political gesture of the supreme ruler. The images of Brazilians also complemented another imperial pictorial project of grand

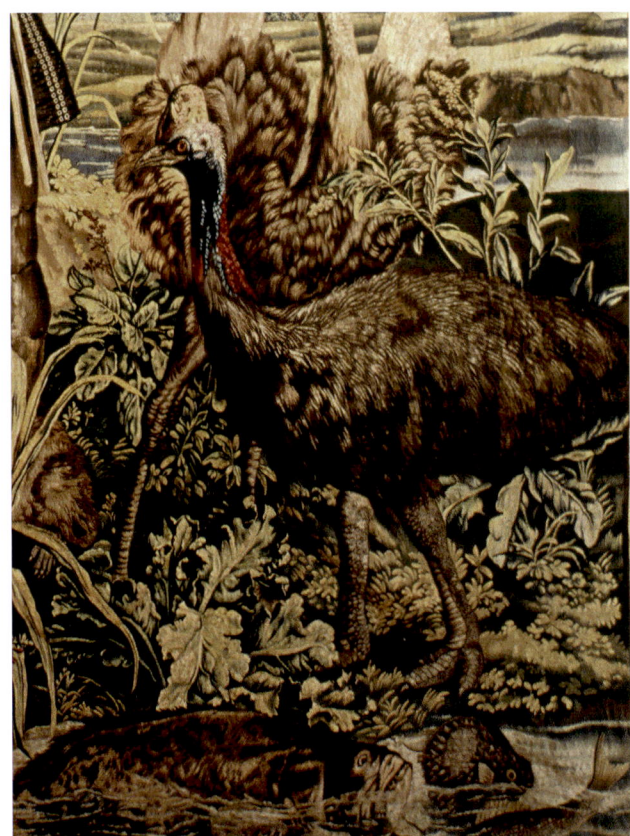

FIG. 88 Detail of fig. 83.

scale carried out around the same time as the manuals of birds and beasts—namely, the composition of the *Official Tribute* (*Zhigong tu*). The four scrolls of this series, comprising 301 images of paired men and women, represent people from thirty-seven foreign countries as well as 264 minority groups in the Qing Empire. Such visual records bore witness to the geographic and cultural boundaries of the Qing Empire's self-image.[123] Previously unknown to the Qing court and not represented in the Qing tribute scrolls, the Native Americans depicted in the *Tenture des Indes* enriched this imperial catalogue of people and allowed Qianlong, in his imagination, to further subsume distant lands into his universe. Additionally, the rich plant species on the tapestries, even more realistic and exotic than the florals in the Western silks examined in chapter 2, would have gratified Qianlong's growing enthusiasm for European botany.

From the perspective of the French merchant Rothe, the *Tenture des Indes* he transported to China was little more than commercial goods for testing the Chinese demand for luxury European objects. Through their acquisition and presentation to Qianlong by Governor Li from Canton, however, these tapestries came to serve as a powerful visual affirmation of Qing imperial superiority and its conceptual geography of the universe, becoming an integral part of an imperial pictorial program imbued with political significance. Governor Li was certainly aware of Qianlong's projects to compile manuals of birds, beasts, and people, as these missions were supervised by the central office of the Grand Council at the court and mobilized provincial bureaucratic networks for collecting and producing images.[124] An expert in flattering the emperor through rare and exceptional gifts, Governor Li carefully chose these tapestries as a thoughtful gesture to echo the imperial political agenda and to demonstrate his loyalty and servitude, while at the same time showcasing his resourcefulness to cull the best items from foreign traders and channeling them to the court. The French commodity was thus transformed into a coded, eulogistic object that conducted the dialogue between the provincial governor and the sovereign and strengthened the connections between a local bureaucracy and the central imperial power.

Although the surviving objects and documentation constitute only a portion of the total number of European tapestries sent to the Qing court, the three French suites discussed in this chapter nonetheless offer a window into some of the most important holdings in the Qing imperial collections as well as into the expectations and strategies of their European senders. In Europe, the two *Tentures chinoises* and the *Tenture des Indes* were already popular diplomatic gifts, embodying multiple dimensions of cross-cultural exchanges. For example, the *Tenture des Indes*—Dutch depictions of the New World presented to Louis XIV—was given to the Russian czar Peter the Great in the name of the French king when the former visited Paris in 1717 seeking support from France to prevent a war with Sweden. Peter the Great chose this cycle specifically during his visit to the Gobelins manufactory, a decision aligned with his agenda to Europeanize the Russian arts by closely following French models.[125] Sending these tapestries to China seemed a safe and natural choice, as the senders could count on the visual appeal and diplomatic potency these pictorial textiles had already demonstrated to initiate new conversations with an empire understood in France as powerful and civilized but also enigmatic.

It is notable that, to serve the mission of developing a liaison with China—whether political, cultural,

Encoding Global Aspirations

or commercial—all three sets shared the same theme of exoticism. The prevalence of exotic subjects in diplomatic and trade tapestries draws attention to the semiotic multivalence of such imagery in mediating early modern cross-cultural exchanges. First, tapestries representing cultural and visual "others" functioned to a degree like rare foreign objects and creatures, such as the famous great Indian rhinoceros, which moved from one court to another in a journey of honorary gift giving and regiving. Although the animal died in a shipwreck on its way to Pope Leo X (r. 1513–21), its image, famously captured by Dürer and made into objects of various media, increased and prolonged its global circulation and consumption.[126] Exoticism signified knowledge and mobility while conveying the sender's resourcefulness, cultivation, and cosmopolitanism. It glorified both sender and recipient, as the movement of these objects and images suggested a symbolic transmission of the cultural assets they embodied. Through its monumental form, costly materials, artistic associations, and refined craftsmanship, the tapestry medium further magnified such glory and privilege associated with exoticism.

In addition, the exotic scenes depicted in the *Tentures chinoises* and the *Tenture des Indes* appeared timeless, devoid of historical context and removed from contemporary events.[127] The opulent Chinese court, the vibrant Chinese market, the untamed nature of Brazil—all unfold in their own rhythms, disengaged from a European sense of history and time inherent in pieces representing mythical or biblical stories, political or military events, even fashionable *galanterie*. By referring to a remote place that was at once compelling and detached, exoticism offered a safe zone of flexible significations, circumventing the potentially unwanted political or cultural associations that allegorical, religious, or historical themes might have elicited. Meanwhile, the ambiguous cultural remoteness and hybridity of exotic images allowed them to be defamiliarized and domesticated at the same time in the different cultures in which they were experienced. The cultural distance carried by exoticism opened up numerous possibilities for self-projection and self-imagination both for senders and recipients. With their simultaneous references to the self and the other, exotic scenes were suited especially to negotiating cultural boundaries, enabling a dialogue, and functioning as an effective visual and material lingua franca in the diplomatic arena.

In her study of the *Tenture des Indes*, the art historian Carrie Anderson has shown how its various owners in Europe—Johan Maurits, Louis XIV, the Grand Master Perellos of Malta, and Peter the Great—viewed the imagery as an embodiment of individual political ambition.[128] Diplomatic relationships were mediated by the fluid messages evoked by the fanciful wildlife when these tapestries changed hands. In a similar vein, chinoiserie served as a transnational visual vocabulary across Europe, lending a shared typology from which each court or each powerful patron could generate individual meanings while forming a connection with others. For instance, Peter the Great embraced chinoiserie both to align the Russian Empire with Western European countries and as "a reflection of Russia's geographic and cultural position as intermediary between the East and the West."[129] The same semiotic malleability and versatility that characterized exotic imagery also hold true for the tapestries that traveled from Europe to China. In the case of the *Tenture des Indes*, whereas the French merchant capitalized on the rarity of the wildlife for the tapestries' commercial success, the Qing emperor would have registered the animal images as supplements to his imperial catalogues and viewed them as an affirmation of his central power in the universe. As for the second *Tenture chinoise*, when the imagined Chinese images were presented to the real Chinese sovereign, what served to communicate the sender's admiration for the recipient became a gateway, in the eyes of the latter, to the life and culture of the former. Distance was the key to engendering the shifting meanings of these tapestries when they traveled from France to China. For the European senders, the movement of these tapestries condensed the distance between the represented and the receiver, an act that demonstrated a respectful attitude and ambitious investment; from the perspective of the Qing recipient, the imagery and movement of these tapestries foregrounded a temporal and spatial distance, which fabricated another sense of exoticism, turning these pictorial textiles into an index of the curious life and culture of the senders' world.

The three cases discussed above vividly illustrate how the meanings of these tapestries were transformed as a result of their transcultural trajectories from Europe to China. Often in an unexpected turn from the senders' original intentions and anticipations, the tapestries that entered the Qing court acquired new sets of significance and value. Upon their arrival at the Qing palaces, they moved away from the diplomatic or commercial framework and became a constructive element in the artistic, cultural, and political systems of the Qing palaces.

European tapestries were for the most part displayed or stored in Qianlong's European Palaces in the Yuanming yuan. It seems that one major reason for not hanging them in other imperial residential buildings was their overly large dimensions. For example, an HJD entry from early 1788 records the failed attempts to install some "Western tapestries" (*xiyáng huatan*) in the islet palaces on Beihai and Nanhai, two lakes just outside the Forbidden City, as they were too large and "impossible to alter and fit."[130] In the case of European tapestries that could be altered, their borders were cut off and either repurposed as door curtains (*lianzi*) or saved for unspecified future uses.[131]

Qianlong's European Palaces functioned primarily as pleasure houses and repositories for the emperor's Western curios and machines, but he did not actually live there.[132] A letter from Benoist dated October 28, 1773, observes that, though no tapestries were to be found in Qianlong's bedchambers in other quarters in the Yuanming yuan, "the emperor has tapestries in several of his [European] Palaces where from time to time he takes strolls and reposes. These same palaces are also decorated with mirrors, paintings, clocks, light fixtures, and all kinds of other most precious ornaments that we have in Europe."[133] Father François Bourgeois (1723–1792) describes the Observatory of the Distant Ocean in a letter from 1786: "In the room that he had newly built for placing the tapestries of the manufactory of Gobelins [Beauvais], sent by the Court of France in 1767 [1766], there are magnificent trumeau mirrors everywhere. Note that this room, of a dimension of 70 [French] feet [74½ ft. (22.7 m)] in length, on a beautifully proportioned width, is so full of machines that one can hardly find a small path to pass through."[134] In this space, European tapestries joined other Western treasures possessed by the Qing emperor as trophies glorifying his empire. A poem about the observatory written by the Jiaqing emperor (r. 1796–1820) in 1802 clearly extols this building as a trophy house and sees its European-style decor and furnishings as encapsulating his father's "boundless benevolence that harmonizes the universe" and "the world's celebration of ascending peace and prosperity."[135]

Some Beauvais and Gobelins tapestries remained there until the siege of the Yuanming yuan in 1860. In his monograph *Expédition de Chine*, published in 1862 under the pseudonym Paul Varin, the French lieutenant colonel Charles Dupin (1784–1873) describes "a series of rooms decorated with Gobelins carpets [tapestries] with the arms of France" in the empty European Palaces, noting that the tapestries and paintings were "dilapidated, worn out, and felt long-time neglect."[136] Some of these tapestries were taken back to Europe and have since disappeared or remain unidentified or hidden, apart from one single piece—*The Animals' Combat*—now in a public collection. Many others were presumably destroyed in the fire set by the looting armies.

Although Qianlong admired French tapestries for their magnificent designs and superb workmanship, he did not integrate them into his day-to-day activities. As the next chapter will examine, his fascination with the European tapestry medium propelled the Qing imperial workshops to experiment with designing and weaving woolen tapestries after Western prototypes. These new productions in a hybrid style synthesized motifs, weaving methods, and materials from China and Europe while exploring new spatial concepts and visual modes. It was these pieces that Qianlong used to furnish his everyday living quarters and to fabricate visual narratives charged with political importance.

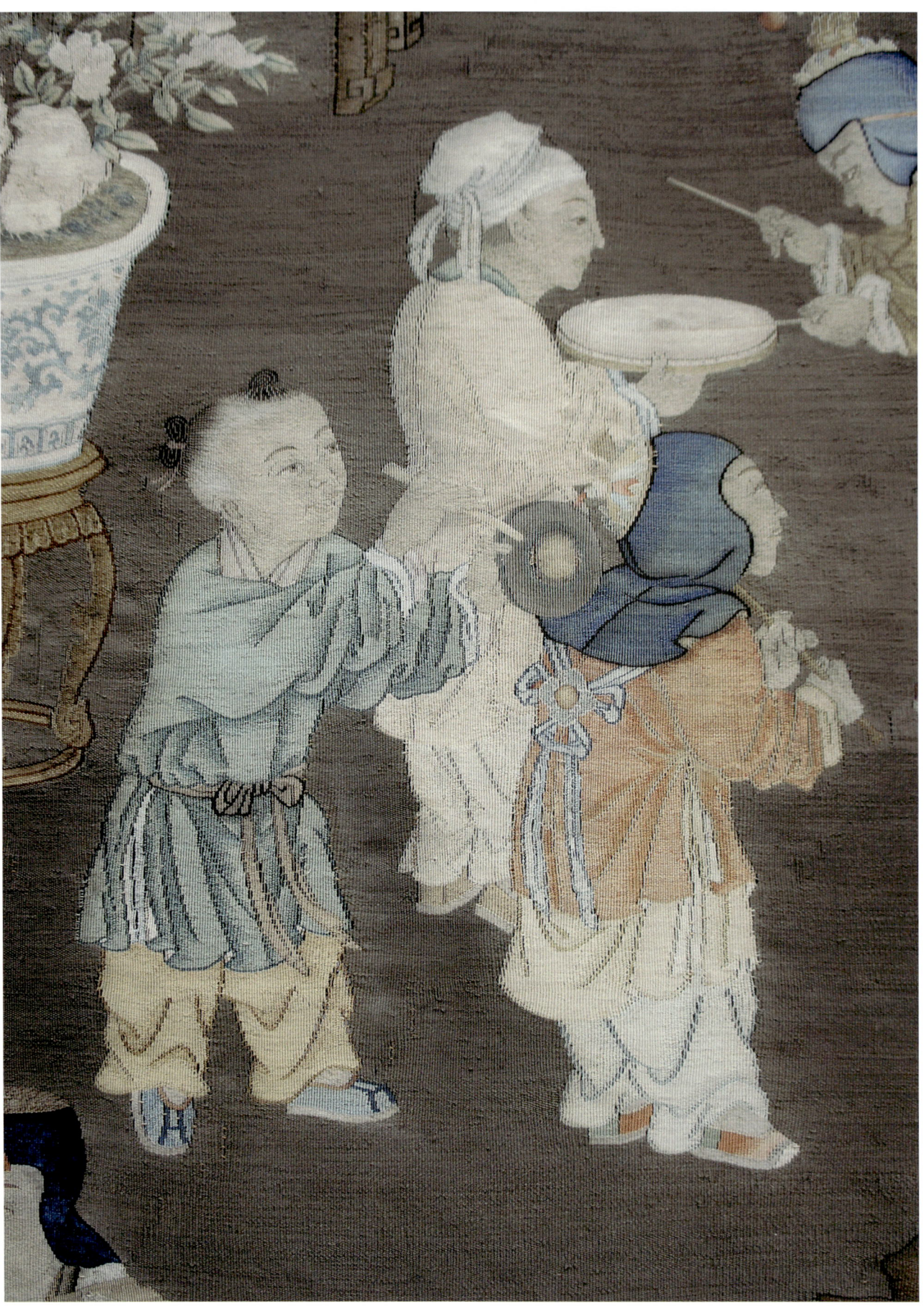

4 Staging Imperial Narratives
The Qing Western Tapestries

Qing imperial encounters with European tapestries gave rise to a new type of textile production at the imperial manufactories and an innovative mode for furnishing the palace interiors. From the 1760s through the 1770s, the Qianlong emperor sponsored a series of experimentations in designing Western-style woolen tapestries whose material forms, visual contents, and manners of display integrated European, Manchu, and Han Chinese elements. In Qing court documents, both original European tapestries and those made by the imperial manufactories in the Western style were categorized together as "Western woolen hangings" (*xiyáng guatan*) to distinguish them from Chinese-style pictorial hangings. Strictly controlled by Qianlong and reserved for private rooms with special importance, these new Western tapestries exclusively embodied Qing emperorship, offering him a potent visual and material form for constructing imperial narratives.

This chapter reconstructs the Qing imperial engagement with the European tapestry medium by exploring a series of imitative weavings and hybrid new designs. It focuses on case studies of two rare extant examples made by the Suzhou manufactory, which yield insights about the visual components subsumed into the "Western" tapestry designs and about Qianlong's inventive approaches to this site-specific pictorial medium. In these tapestries, appropriated European imagery and visual devices introduced fresh means to redeliver or reframe time-honored messages rooted in the Manchu-Chinese tradition, which nonetheless encoded pressing political aspirations. In particular, two features characteristic of this foreign textile medium—a spatial implication and a potential for the image to act on viewers—shaped Qianlong's perceptions of Western tapestries and inspired him to orchestrate a coordinated interplay between represented scene, architectural setting, and inhabitant of the room. The medium's architectonic tension and interactive visual potential enabled the emperor to stage his own physical presence in relation to the tapestry in space and offered him new ways to reenact fictional narratives charged with imperial significance.

A NEW PICTORIAL TEXTILE MEDIUM

Apart from differences in materials, themes, and visual styles, European tapestries were distinguished from Chinese hangings in their inherent architectonic dimension derived from the combined effect of size, imagery,

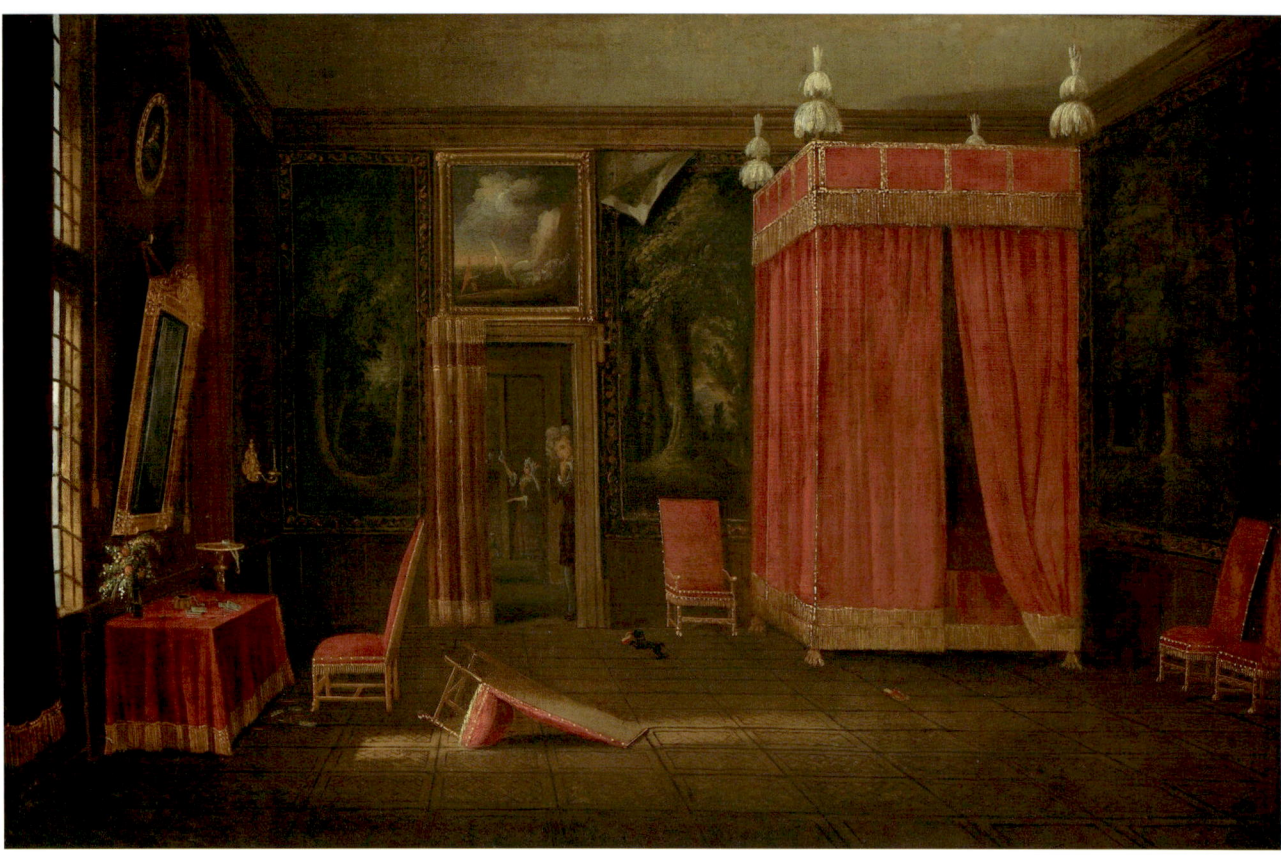

FIG. 89 French artist, *Scene in a Bedchamber*, c. 1690. Oil on canvas, 18 ¾ × 28 ⅜ in. (47.5 × 72 cm). Victoria and Albert Museum, London (P.25-1976).

and disposition in space. Although tapestries in Europe were movable and, at times, hung only for temporary occasions, in the seventeenth and eighteenth centuries, examples destined for domestic interiors were often designed and sized to fit specific rooms and interact with architectural elements such as wall joints, window frames, and wooden paneling. The depicted scenes thus superimposed another temporal and spatial layer onto the physical walls in a kind of malleable *mise en abyme* that the art historian Tristan Weddigen refers to as "textile space" or "textile microarchitecture."[1]

Early modern European representations of private and public interiors provide ample visual evidence of tapestries' architectonic tension as perceived and experienced during the period. In the anonymous French painting *Scene in a Bedchamber* (c. 1690), the borders of the verdure tapestries neatly align with the ceiling moldings and wall paneling, reasserting the architectural framework (fig. 89). Yet this structural order transferred onto the textiles quickly collapses when a corner of one tapestry that has detached from the wall threatens to undo both the illusion of the landscape and the room's structural stability. This removability set the tapestry medium apart from fixed

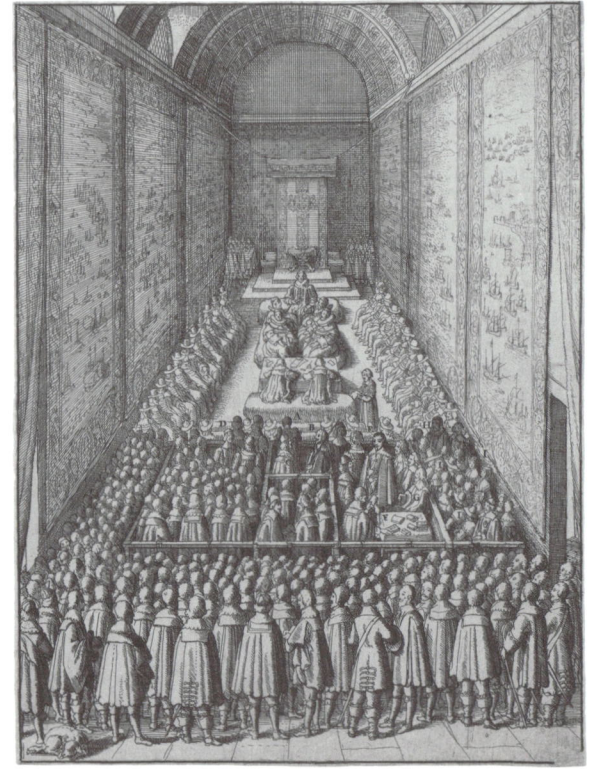

FIG. 90 Wenceslaus Hollar, *Trial of Archbishop Laud in the House of Lords*, 1644. Etching, 7 ¼ × 5 ⅜ in. (18.3 × 13.8 cm). British Museum, London (Q,6.20).

mural paintings, adding another layer of spatial complexity. Likewise, an engraving showing a formal, palatial setting—the interior of the House of Lords in the Palace of Westminster—offers a glimpse of a politically charged space shaped by the *Armada Tapestries* (commissioned in 1591 and lost to fire in 1834) of grand scale (fig. 90). The tapestries fully covered the walls below the cornices, and they could at once block out or be slightly lifted to reveal the doors. Meanwhile, thanks to their sizes coordinating with wall dimensions, tapestries could easily explore illusionistic designs to reconfigure an enclosed, structured interior into a fictional space. One notable example, the Gobelins suite *The Months of Royal Residences*, employs a consistent composition in ten of the twelve pieces: a view framed by a balustrade and columns from a veranda to a courtyard with a royal château in the distance (fig. 91). Each tapestry transforms the solid wall on which it hangs into an open vista.

Capable of mitigating architecture's solidity, softening its rigidity, and redefining its boundaries, European tapestries bestowed a room with rich visual and spatial dynamics, creating ambiguous interplays between illusion and reality. This was particularly true of large-scale tapestries containing life-size figures, which would have elicited an embodied and situated experience that shuffled between the actual material settings and the depicted spaces. In specific cases, art historians have shown how a tapestry's spatial property invited the beholders to take part in the woven scene and form a psychological relationship with the depicted figures.[2] This visual and conceptual dynamic involving imaginary and actual bodies, described as "intercorporeality" by Mimi Hellman in her analysis of the tapestries displayed at the Hôtel de Soubise, helped shape the owners' identities and contributed to a process of social formation.[3] Rather than constituting passive images relegated to confined zones on the wall, early modern European tapestries possessed the power to potentially act on inhabitants-viewers through spatially structured imagery, generating an embodied, interactive, and meaningful experience.

Traditional Chinese-style pictorial hangings, by contrast, did not evoke architectonic or intercorporeal implications as did their European counterparts. As kesi or embroidery, the Chinese pictorial textiles widely

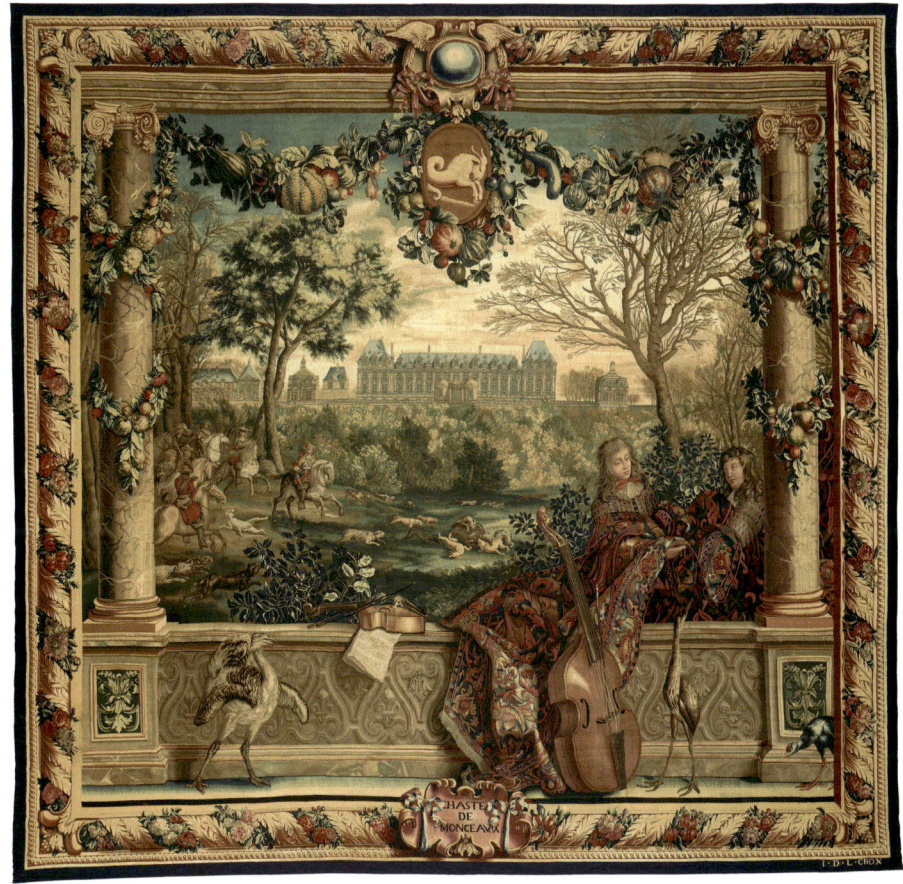

FIG. 91 *Château of Monceaux/Month of December*, from the series *The Months of Royal Residences* (*Les Maison royales*), before 1712. Made by the atelier of Jean de la Croix, Manufacture royale des Gobelins. Tapestry, wool and silk, 10 ft. 5 in. × 11 ft. 1⅛ in. (317.5 × 338 cm). J. Paul Getty Museum, Los Angeles (85.DD.309).

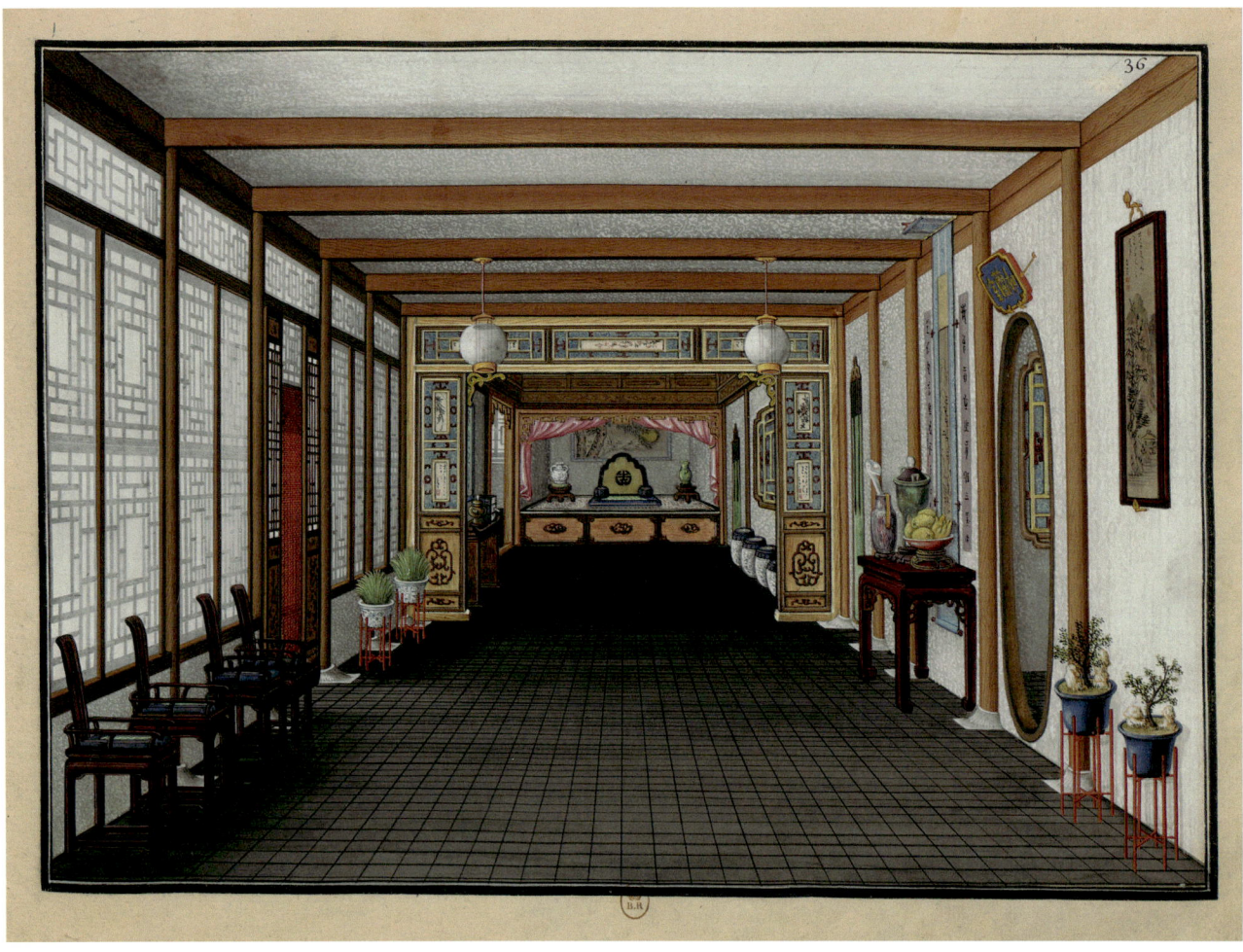

FIG. 92 Chinese artist(s), "Room for Ceremony and Audience in the House of Titled Princes" (*Salle de cérémonie & d'audience chez les princes titrés*), in the album *Essay on Chinese Architecture* (*Essai sur l'architecture chinoise*), part 2, pl. 36, c. 1773. Ink and color on paper, each page 13¾ × 17¾ in. (35 × 45 cm). Bibliothèque nationale de France, Paris, Réserve, OE-13(A)-PET FOL.

present in the Qing palace interiors often took the form of mounted hanging scrolls or framed panels. They were displayed and appreciated as freestanding, movable paintings that did not correspond to or subvert the architectural framework (see fig. 72). Qianlong-period depictions of palatial and princely interiors show how hanging scrolls or framed panels were typically displayed: they occupied only a small portion of the wall above a long table, fulfilling a decorative function similar to that of other objects scattered throughout the room (fig. 92). In contrast to the European examples described above, a kesi hanging, because of its scale and positioning, entailed a visual and psychological experience not necessarily mediated by the architectural space; nor would a work be purposefully created to conjure a liaison between the representation and the spectator. The advent of European tapestries at the Qing court introduced an entirely new spatial relationship between textile and viewer, which would have been quickly sensed by Qianlong and sparked his imagination. He took great pleasure in exploring this aspect when he embarked on the enterprise of making his own Western tapestries.

Qianlong's awareness of the architectonic nature of Western tapestries underlay all his experimentations in designing and displaying this new type of hanging. His initial effort, in 1761, to create equivalents to the Western tapestries at the Qing court was a commission for wall decorations for his European Palaces in the Yuanming yuan, and this project employed painting instead of weaving. In the spring of that year, Qianlong ordered Giuseppe Castiglione to oversee the task of painting hangings in imitation of Western tapestries for sixty-four walls in eighteen rooms of the recently completed Hall of Calm Sea (*Haiyan tang*), also called the Palace of the Fountain

(*Shuifa dian*) in Qing documents. The emperor's instructions specified that the Italian Jesuit artist should "paint on white flat woolen blankets [*bai tanzi*] made in Suzhou after the original Western tapestries" and that "if the Western tapestries currently hung there are not of the right size," he should "adjust the size when painting the copies."[4] These imitative pieces have not survived, and it is not clear whether Castiglione and his team simply copied the original European set(s) or developed new designs based on the European prototypes. The white Suzhou blankets, as seen in extant examples with painted Chinese floral patterns in the Palace Museum, have a plain weave structure.[5] It is noteworthy that the new hangings were conceived to cover all four walls in most of these rooms, and their measurements strictly corresponded to the dimensions of the walls. This way of masking the entire architectural surface with pictorial textiles was unprecedented in Manchu-Chinese furnishing conventions and was predicated directly on European aesthetics and practice. The choice of imitative painting, rather than actual weaving, may have been the quickest and most efficient way to produce such a large quantity of hangings in a limited period while closely mimicking the visual and material effects of European tapestries. Moreover, the artisans specializing in silk weaving and embroidery at the imperial textile manufactories may have not yet adapted to handling wool or developed enough skills to render images in the European pictorial mode. Soon after, as the HJD archives make clear, by 1769 at the latest, weavers at the Suzhou manufactory were fully capable of weaving figures "in the Western style of perspective with shading" (*xiyáng youyingzi xianfa*), which suggests that they quickly developed the skills and sensibility needed to render the Western visual style.[6]

Shortly after the French Society of Jesus presented Qianlong with the second *Tenture chinoise*, made in Beauvais and sent by Bertin, the period from 1768 through the 1770s saw Qianlong's surging interest in commissioning new woven versions of Western tapestries, which replaced the earlier method of painting copies. The Imperial Silk Manufactory in Suzhou was responsible for making these tapestries. The projects undertaken included altering European tapestries by adding or removing sections, closely copying European examples, and weaving new pieces based on cartoons designed by Qing court artists that synthesized European and Chinese elements.

In November 1768 the Imperial Workshops at court sent a European tapestry (*xiyáng huatan*) stored in the European Palaces to the director of the Suzhou manufactory along with Qianlong's order to have it enlarged by hiring local "makers of flat woolen textile" (*tanzi jiang*) to weave additional parts (*jiezhi*). The same order also stated that if the original tapestry could not be altered in that way, Suzhou should try to weave a new one in the required dimensions following the European example and use "the weaving method of the makers of flat woolen textiles."[7] Qianlong envisioned an experimental interpretation of foreign techniques and imagery using a local method for weaving woolen materials. No evidence gives clues to the nature of this weaving technique that Qianlong had in mind. Given that the Suzhou manufactory had long specialized in weaving silk tapestries, which essentially used the same technique of discontinuous weft weaving employed at European ateliers, the artisans there probably applied the familiar kesi methods to wool or other similar thick fibers on a larger loom.

Two Qing imperial woolen tapestries—one in the Palace Museum (fig. 93) and the other in the Cleveland Museum of Art (fig. 94)—clearly show that the artisans employed local materials and techniques to experiment with a foreign medium. They were woven in Suzhou in 1771 and 1776, respectively, and featured two versions of a design. The commissioning, iconography, and display of these two works will be examined in detail later in this chapter. A recent conservation project on the 1776 tapestry offers especially rich insights into the Suzhou workshop's choice of materials and weaving practice in fulfilling Qianlong's order for "woolen tapestries." In both versions, the designs were woven from bottom to top in the same manner as Chinese kesi so that the warps run in the same direction as the image; this contrasts with the predominant European weaving mode, in which the design is developed sideways and runs perpendicular to the warps' direction. Because of the Chinese warp-pattern orientation, the slits resulting from disconnected weft threads run in the vertical direction. While the slits serve as an effective means of image making to create outlines and color transitions, gravity has caused stress around these areas (fig. 95). To prevent the textile from splitting, many tiny stitches have been applied to join the slits during restorations. Seen from the unlined reverse side of the 1776 tapestry, there are, in contrast to typical French weaving, many long and floating loose threads. The fact that neither tapestry consists of strips stitched together indicates that an enormous loom was set up to accommodate the width of each tapestry.[8]

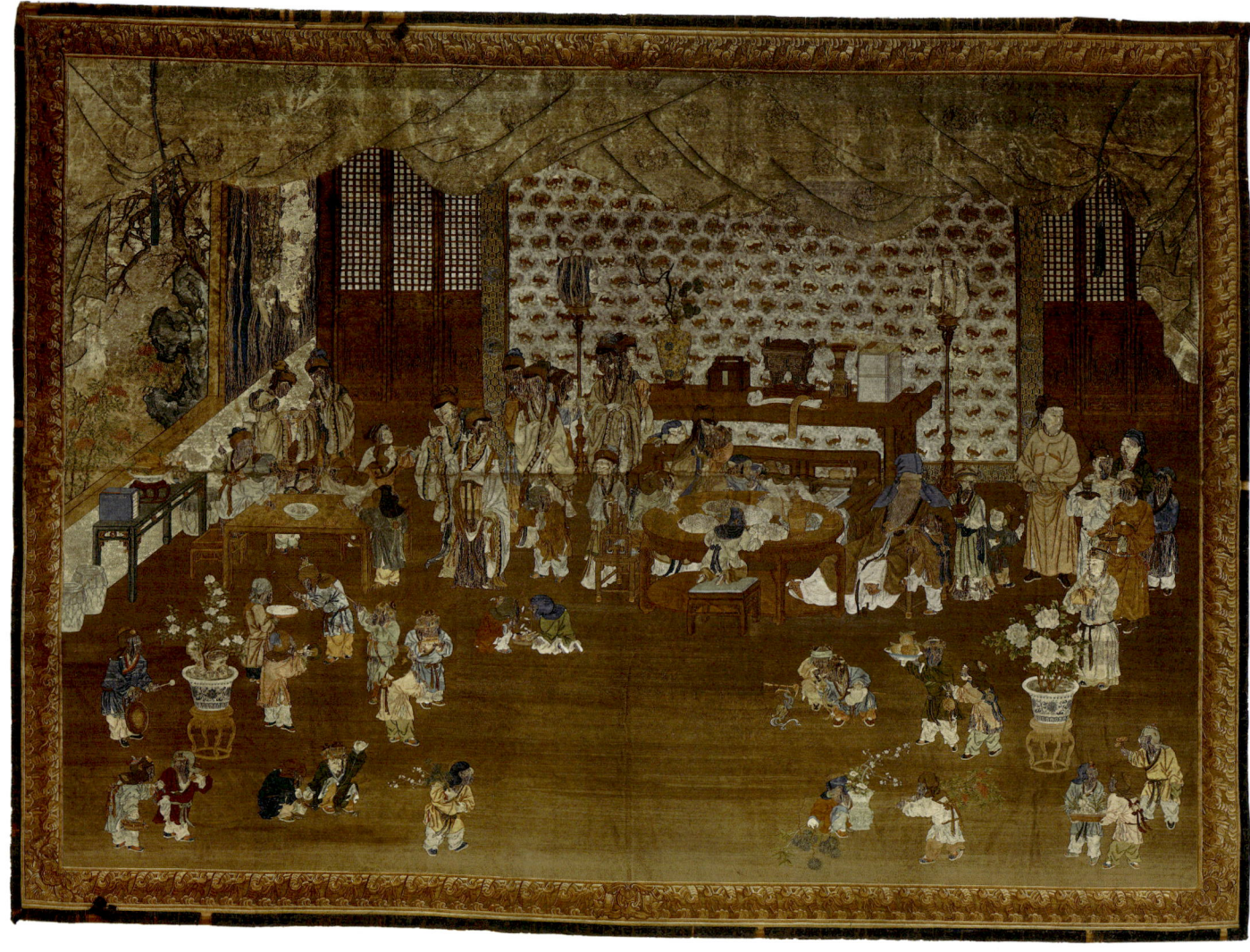

FIG. 93 *Family Gathering on New Year's Morning*, 1771. Made by the Qing Imperial Silk Manufactory in Suzhou. Tapestry, wool and silk, and silk embroidery for small details, 8 ft. 10½ in. × 12 ft. 1 in. (270.4 × 368 cm). Palace Museum, Beijing (gu212067).

Interestingly, the warp material of the 1776 tapestry has been identified as raw silk. Each warp thread is composed of multiple raw silk yarns twisted together to give some thickness and strength. The warps of the 1771 tapestry, visible through worn areas, have a similar appearance and texture and may well be made of the same fiber.[9] This choice of raw silk for the tapestry warp followed the tradition of Chinese kesi weaving. As tapestry is a weft-faced textile, warp threads are completely hidden beneath the weft threads on the surface. In the 1776 version, wool makes up the brown background and a large portion of the design, thus justifying the name and overall impression of a "woolen tapestry"; silk threads are generously used for depicting the figures' facial features and their clothes as well as for creating fine details of many motifs throughout. The result is an extremely refined and nuanced weaving. For example, in a detail of a young man's profile, his white sclera, black pupil, and light brown eyebrow, as well as the transition area where the hair roots merge into the face and the gray surface of his hat, are all rendered with fine silk threads whose shine and thinner texture form a subtle contrast to the thicker, matte, woolen part (see fig. 95). In another close-up of the border, which mimics a European gilded wooden frame, the weaver took great pains to reproduce the naturalistic style of the model by applying different shades of pale brown silk around darker wool threads. When viewed from a certain distance, the visual effect is that of light and

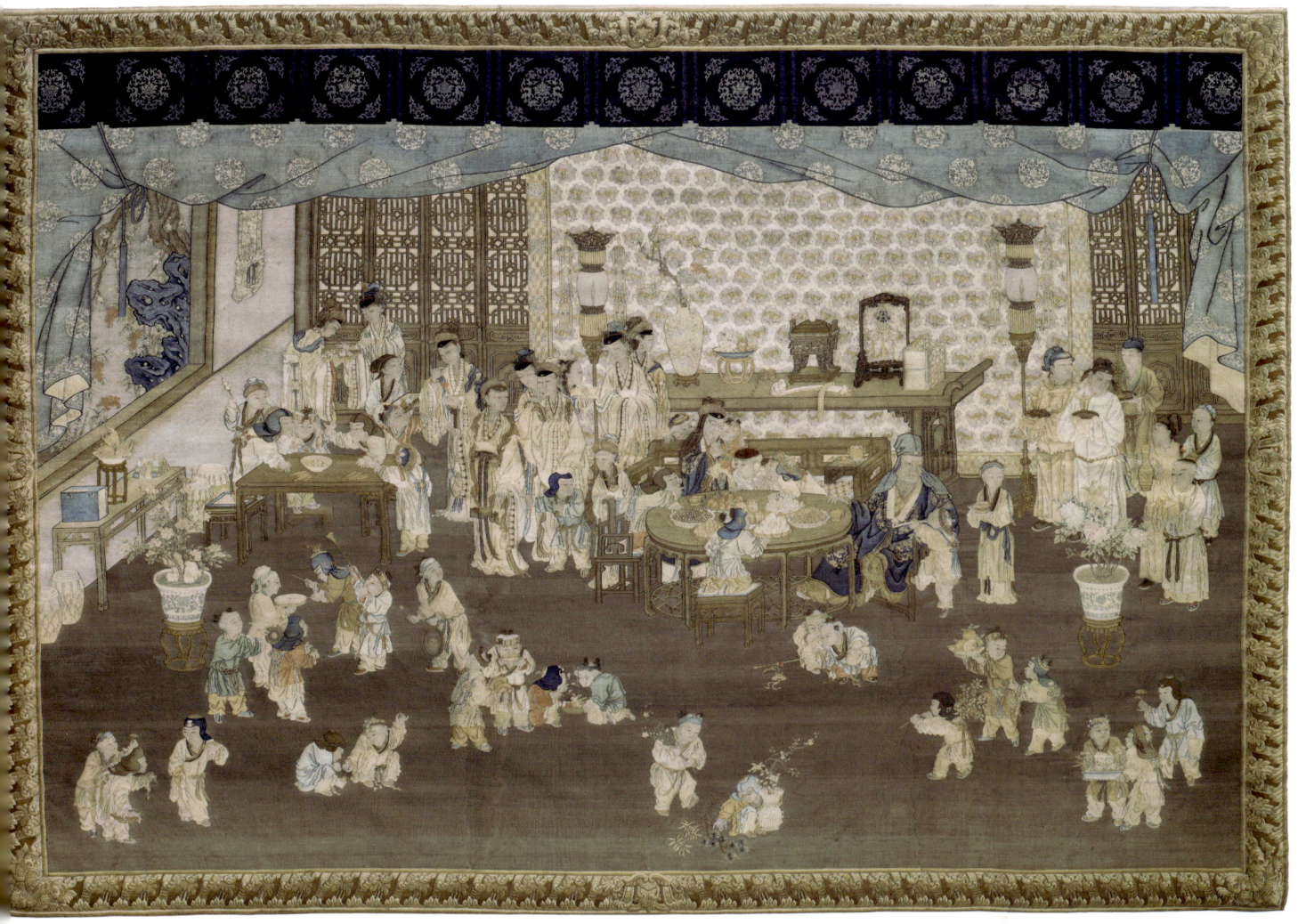

FIG. 94 *Family Gathering on New Year's Morning*, 1776. Made by the Qing Imperial Silk Manufactory in Suzhou. Tapestry, wool and silk, and silk embroidery for small details, 8 ft. 5½ in. × 12 ft. 4¾ in. (257.8 × 377.8 cm). Cleveland Museum of Art, bequest of John L. Severance (1942.825).

shadow (fig. 96). In a few areas in both the 1771 and 1776 versions, especially in the intricate patterns of the songjin textiles used as book boxes and screen borders, silk embroidery provides a solution for depicting the minute floral motifs (fig. 97). These close observations reveal that in the process of interpreting the foreign medium, Suzhou artisans drew largely from their own familiar tradition of silk tapestry weaving. The products demonstrate extraordinary skill and sensibilities in realizing the images as well as flexibility in finding solutions to new challenges.

The Qing court's projects of copying European tapestries often involved modifying the dimensions of the original designs to fit an intended space. For such commissions, the original tapestries, together with cartoons that adapted the designs to the new measurements, were dispatched to Suzhou. For example, a 1773 HJD entry records a project of weaving three tapestries for covering the windows of the Mountain Pavilion of Sweeping Breeze (*Yanxun shanguan*) in Rehe. To make the cartoons, the Imperial Workshops first prepared sheets that match the dimensions of the wall spaces; then the court artists drew scaled-down images after the European tapestries, a process involving removing some figures and foliage and adding new motifs; and finally, additional sheets representing the borders were attached to the central images. When the completed weavings were handed in by Suzhou, the European tapestries that were sent as models (*yàng*) were returned to the Yuanming yuan for storage.[10]

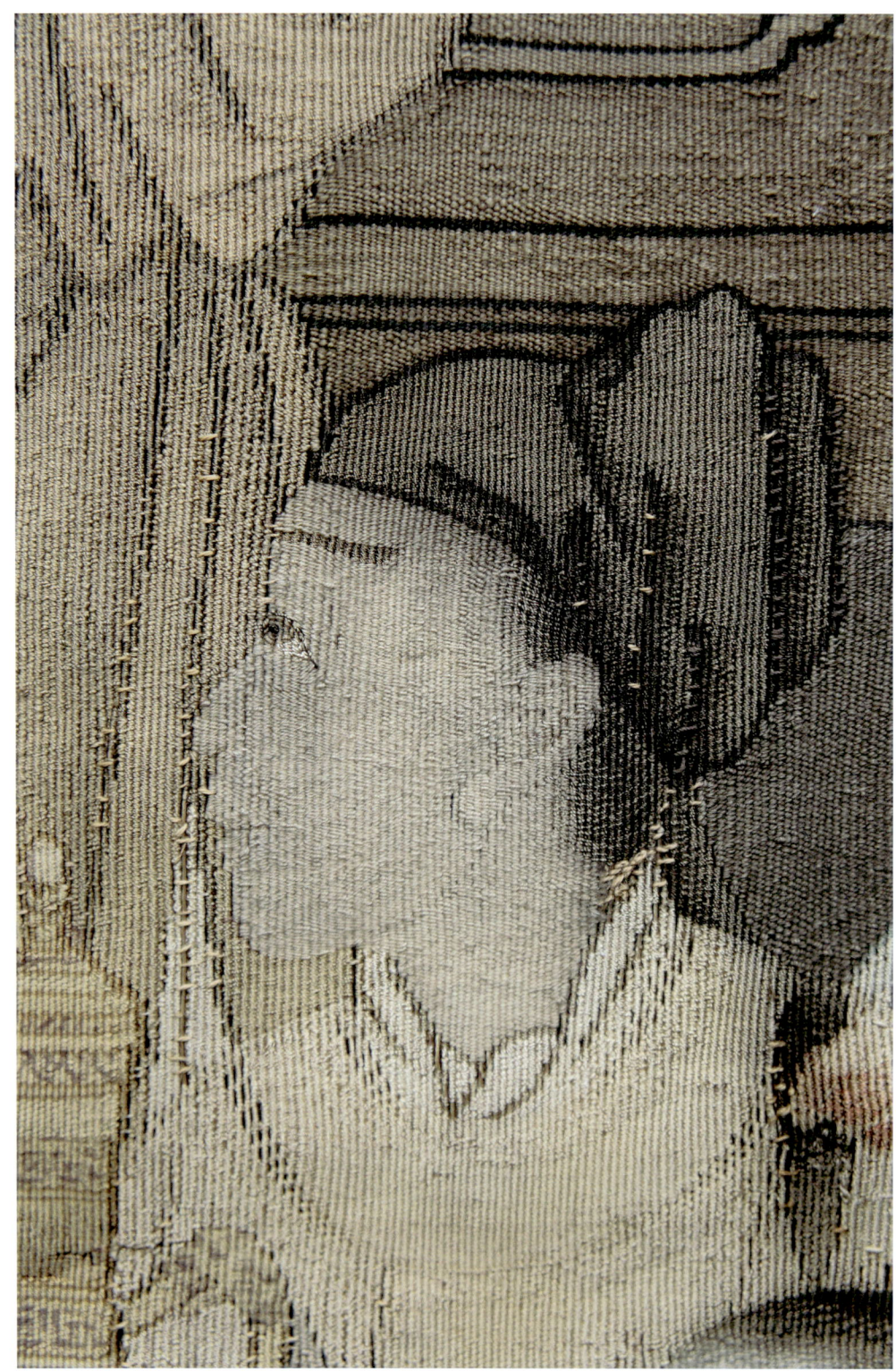

FIG. 95 Detail of fig. 94.

Photographs of four tapestries in the Qing imperial collections after the designs of the second *Tenture chinoise* offer a glance into the Qing court's imitative weaving (figs. 98A–D). Originally housed in the Rehe palaces, these tapestries were transferred to the Forbidden City in 1914 and remained there until around 1933, but currently they have not been located. Made sometime in the mid-1920s, the glass negatives show the reverse images of the actual tapestries that feature the four themes—*Chinese Hunt, Chinese Dance, Chinese Feast,* and *Chinese Fair*.[11] Although the dimensions of the tapestries are unknown, their individual proportions seen in the photographs differ significantly from the recorded dimensions of the French set sent by Bertin, which suggests that they were Qing court copies reproducing part of the original designs for a specific palace location with smaller wall spaces.[12] The Chinese weaving quite faithfully followed the French models and captured chiaroscuro well.

Besides modifying and reproducing existing European tapestries, the Imperial Workshops at court, under Qianlong's guidance, also created a number of new designs to be woven into Western wool tapestries in Suzhou. Qianlong frequently entrusted the German Jesuit missionary Ignatius Sichelbart (1708–1780) and the Chinese painter Wang Youxue (fl. 1727–?) to design the cartoons, and their works ranged from Western figures (*xiyáng renwu*) to floral patterns and decorative borders.[13] By 1768 Giuseppe Castiglione and Jean-Denis Attiret (1702–1768)—the two most talented Jesuit painters at the Qing court—had both died, and Sichelbart became the primary court artist responsible for paintings in the European style. Wang Youxue had studied under Castiglione and equally mastered the European painting techniques.

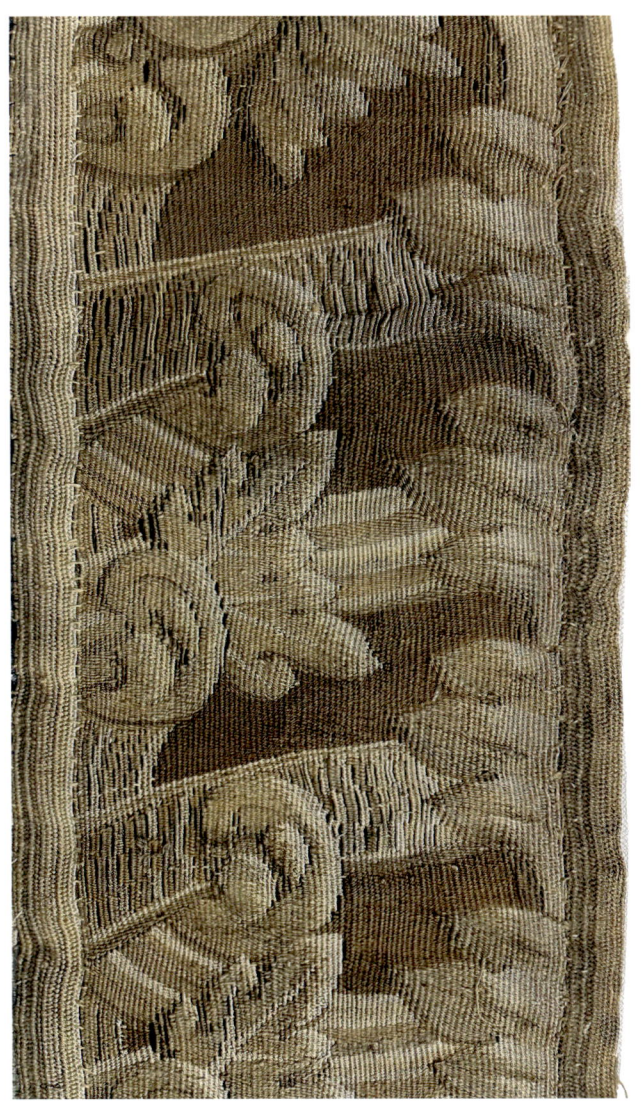

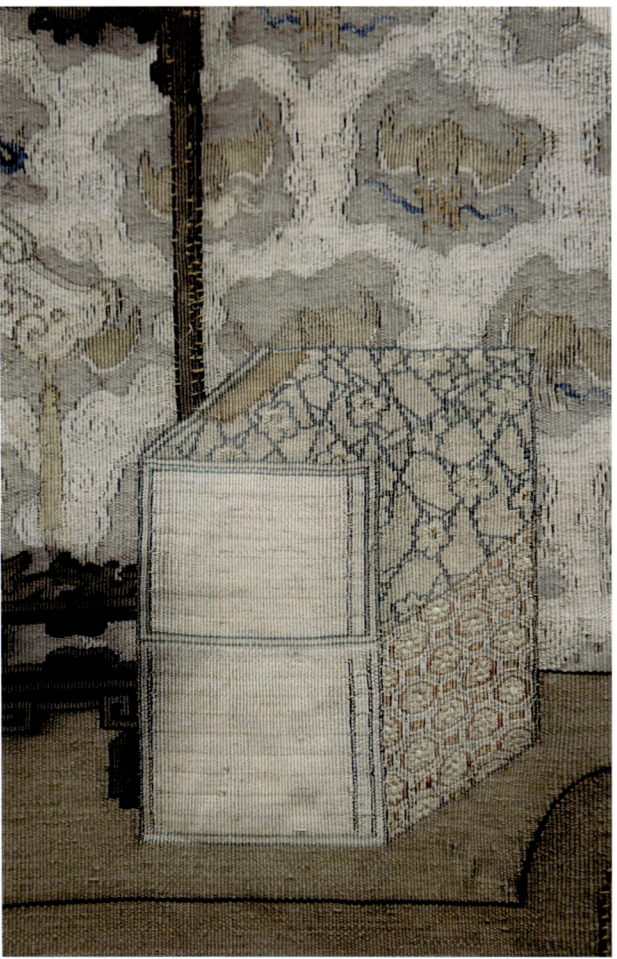

FIG. 96 (LEFT) Detail of fig. 94.

FIG. 97 (ABOVE) Detail of fig. 94.

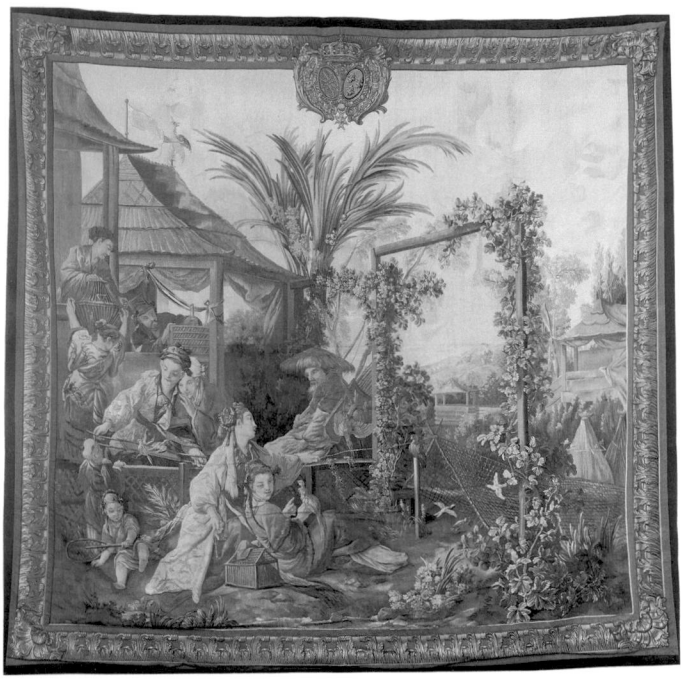

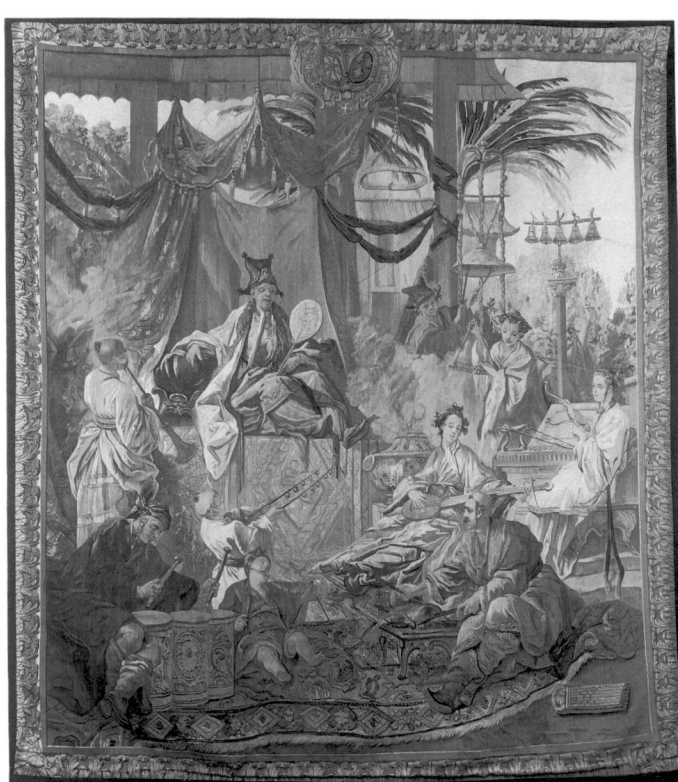

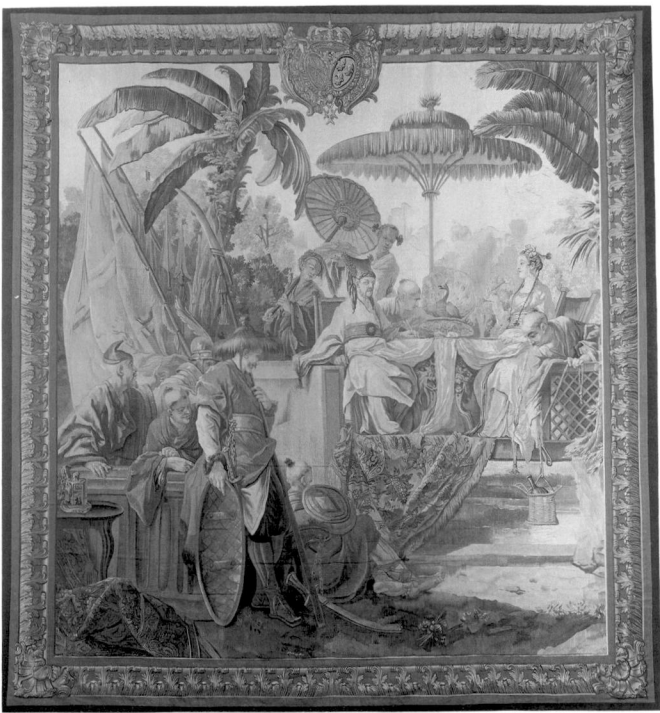

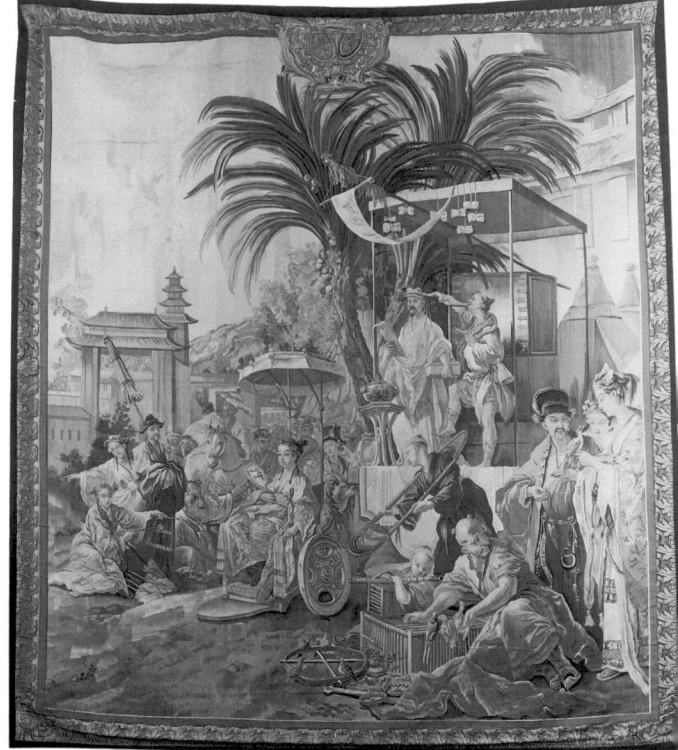

FIGS. 98A–D Photographs of four tapestries made in the Qing Imperial Silk Manufactory in Suzhou after the designs of the second *Tenture chinoise*. Scanned from glass negatives showing the tapestries in reverse. Tapestries, woven c. 1770s; glass negatives, mid-1920s. Palace Museum, Beijing.

98A (TOP LEFT) *Chinese Hunt*
98B (TOP RIGHT) *Chinese Dance*
98C (ABOVE LEFT) *Chinese Feast*
98D (ABOVE RIGHT) *Chinese Fair*

Compared to kesi and embroideries, Western tapestries constituted only a tiny fraction of Qing court pictorial hangings, but they played an exceptional and compelling role in furbishing the material environment, creating visual programs, and fabricating spaces in the palace interiors. All the Western tapestries made in the imperial workshops were specially commissioned and exclusively reserved for the Qianlong emperor himself, who enforced strict regulations regarding their production. His order of December 1768 stressed that the director of the Suzhou manufactory should not take any initiative to weave Western tapestries, nor should he produce these works regularly for the court like other textiles. Instead, the manufactory should conduct weaving only upon the emperor's request and when specific dimensions were provided. The same order also forbade Suzhou from undertaking commissions from anyone but the emperor.[14] Other types of imperial textiles were never subjected to such restrictions. The sovereign's sole access to and control of the new Western tapestry art form turned it into a medium directly linked with emperorship, which was constructed by three key aspects: material, location, and imagery.

First, wool held special ethnic significance for the Manchu rulers. In the Han Chinese textile tradition, which was centered in the south and dominated by silk, wool was not considered upscale or refined, but it had long been a staple and favored material of the non-Han regimes originating in the north and northwest of the Asian continent.[15] The Jurchen rulers of the Jin dynasty, for example, preferred felt tents furnished with woolen carpets and hangings, and the Mongol rulers of the Yuan dynasty used a variety of woolen textiles to furnish their palaces and yurts and set up weaving workshops for pile rugs and Uyghur-style rugs. Before relocating to central China in the mid-seventeenth century, the Manchus residing along China's northeast frontier led a lifestyle similar to that of the Mongols and the Jin Jurchens. The yurt was their major dwelling form. After the Manchu chieftain Nurhaci (1559–1626) established the capital in Shengjing (today's Shenyang) in 1625, he built a palace there that resembled a nomadic tent. Woolen textiles were used extensively to furnish the Manchu yurts and palaces.[16] Even after moving their capital to Beijing in 1644 and assimilating the culture and lifestyle of the Han Chinese, the Qing rulers retained many of the Manchu living habits. Despite the court's quick adoption of fine silks woven in the Jiangnan region for clothing and furnishings, woolen textiles still had a prominent presence in Qing palace interiors. During battles, hunting expeditions, and diplomatic events, the Qing emperors erected Mongol-style yurts as temporary lodgings and ceremonial spaces; these, too, were elaborately furnished with woolen textiles.[17]

The three types of wool fabrics used extensively at the Qing court all had Central Asian or European origins: pile rugs that were the specialty of the Uyghur regions, Mongolia, and Tibet; Dutch felts with printed designs; and European (mostly English and Dutch) plain wool cloth. Pile rugs bearing floral patterns or symbolic animal motifs varied in size and shape, ranging from large floor carpets placed under the throne to couch bed covers.[18] Dutch felts acquired through the port of Canton featured two-tone printed designs composed of sinuous, stylized floral patterns characteristic of Indian chintz for the European market. The Qing court regarded the products from Leiden, with their tight structure and precise printing, as of the highest quality.[19] These felts played versatile roles as floor coverings, upholsteries for daybeds, and wall linings for both palatial buildings and Mongolian yurts. The last type of woolen fabric, called *duoluo ni* or *duoluo rong* in Qing imperial documents, appeared frequently in the lists of diplomatic gifts presented by Holland, the Italian states, and England.[20] Although no extant objects in the Palace Museum carry a label with this name, some nineteenth-century documents suggest that it was plain-weave, monochrome broadcloth.[21] Qing imperial records show that *duoluo ni* or *duoluo rong* was lightweight, soft, and often made into canopies or hangings for imperial carriages.[22]

In addition to providing much-needed insulation during the cold winters in Beijing, wool textiles stood as a material symbol of the Manchu ethnic and cultural origin. As chapter 2 discussed, maintaining the Manchu heritage was central to the Qing rulers' ideology and imperial daily practice. Western woolen tapestries resonated with Manchu furnishing aesthetics while reinforcing their lifestyle principles. Among Qing imperial woolen textiles, tapestries were the only type that featured complex pictorial narratives. Their material texture, image repertoire, and display modes injected fresh aspects into this wool-centered ethnic tradition.

HJD records show that all new Western tapestries were conceived for specific walls in specific palace rooms.

Between 1768 and 1775, a period when Qianlong was particularly active in commissioning Western tapestries, he had these hangings displayed in all three locations of the imperial palaces: the Forbidden City, the Yuanming yuan (in the Chinese-style residential compounds rather than in the European Palaces), and the imperial Hunting Resort in Rehe. Remarkably, these new tapestries were never installed in grand halls for official audiences or state functions; instead, they furnished only informal but nonetheless highly important locations for the emperor's cultural activities, family life, and personal enjoyment. For example, the Palace of Peace and Longevity (*Ningshou gong*) in the Forbidden City was constructed as Qianlong's retirement quarters, as were the Tripitaka Hall (*Hanjing tang*) and the Purification Studio (*Chunhua xuan*) in the Garden of Eternal Spring (*Changchun yuan*) next to the Yuanming yuan. The private and exclusive nature of these tapestries is further revealed by the fact that inside these buildings, they appeared only in small chambers situated at the back or to the side, such as the "end room" (*shaojian*), "secondary room" (*cijian*), "warm chamber" (*nuange*), and "rear compound" (*houdian*). The warm chamber was normally a side room or a side complex in a palatial compound and could be heated. End rooms and warm chambers often functioned as the emperor's bedroom or study, and a rear compound usually contained a couch bed or platform bed for the emperor's relaxation and casual meetings. The locations for the new Western tapestries affirm that they were intimate furnishing textiles rather than propagandist pieces like many of their counterparts in Europe, where figural tapestries were often displayed in public or official spaces such as throne halls, reception rooms, and churches.

Qianlong's 1768 edict, mentioned earlier, expressed a strong concern for precise dimensions, which ensured that the commissioned tapestries perfectly coordinated with the intended spaces. These new works were inspired by the concept of embedded space characteristic of European tapestries, and their designs were conceived to enact an interplay with a room's architectural elements. In certain ways, the Qing tapestries assumed an even bolder role than their European equivalents in masking and dissolving structural elements: one of their primary functions was to cover up the windows on a north wall, thus completely blurring a threshold between interior and exterior. In Europe, a special type of narrow tapestry called *entre-fenêtres* filled the wall space in between two windows, but it did not block them. The nearest equivalent is perhaps the *portière*, hung in front of a door to prevent drafts, enhance aural privacy, and create an additional layer of ceremonial distinction, thereby marking degrees of access to prestigious spaces. The Qing court's practice of insulating the north window certainly fulfilled the practical need to ward off the wintry cold. As imperial documents show, completed tapestries usually arrived before winter began and were presumably removed during the warm seasons.[23] The scenes depicted in the textile would replace the bleak view outside the window with an imaginary vista, transcending not only space but also time.

To an extent, the Western tapestries find a spatial parallel in a unique genre of Qing imperial painting favored by Qianlong known as *tongjing hua*, "images of linked scenes," in the *tieluo* format—that is, painting to be pasted onto a wall. A tongjing hua usually extended over a full wall or occupied a structural juncture, such as a partition or staircase sidewall, and often incorporated the techniques of European *quadratura* and linear perspective.[24] Both the tapestries and the tongjing hua were removable pictorial images intended for secluded private chambers, and both generated self-contained, embodied visual experiences by connecting the viewers to the real architectural space and the pictures. The tongjing hua were restricted, however, by door openings and window frames; in contrast, the materiality of the tapestries permitted them to overlap with and conceal such structural components, thereby offering Qianlong new freedom to remake his private interiors into multilayered visual fields. Likewise, although the single-panel screen—a pictorial medium and architectonic feature long present in Chinese interiors—is similar to the Western tapestry in its capacity to blur spatial clarity and create meta-images, it was a flat and circumscribed surface articulated by a supporting framework and grounded on the floor (see figs. 124, 125).[25] Thus, the single-panel screen remained subordinate and dependent to the architectural space, whereas the autonomy of the tapestry allowed it to entirely transform an architectural structure.

The material form, size, and specific site of a tapestry worked together to animate its central images, whose subject matter, composition, pictorial style, and ornamental details played a major role in conveying meaningful messages and defining the attributes that the Qing emperor celebrated as "Western." Despite the fact that the Qing imperial archives contain scant information about the visual content of individual commissions, three rare extant pieces, two of which were introduced earlier, offer a valuable window into the Western themes and styles of Qing tapestries.

A WESTERN FAMILY BY THE RIVERSIDE: CHINOISERIE REIMAGINED

In June 1775 the Qianlong emperor ordered the French Jesuit missionary Louis Antoine de Poirot (1735–1813) to compose a picture of "Western figures in watercolor on silk" for a framed hanging. In particular, he instructed that the painting should "convey an atmosphere of a lively and joyful household" and "include both men, women, and children."[26] This commission was one of the many images representing generic Westerners that adorned the Qing palaces; their subjects ranged from coquettish maidens and amorous couples to blissful families. These pictures unfolded a poetic, eroticized, or auspicious scene of Western life without temporal or geographical specificities, and they synthesized motifs and narratives drawn from European images circulated to China, the repertoire of Chinese export arts, and European chinoiserie, in addition to traditional Chinese pleasure pictures. Western figures most frequently appeared in the types of objects that assimilated European techniques and styles, such as painted enamel, reversed glass painting, oil painting, and trompe l'oeil images pasted onto a wall. The visual styles and material forms of these works offered a doubled exotic pleasure for the Qing emperor to channel his private desires and wishes, while their themes and messages often anchored them in the Manchu-Chinese value system and pictorial tradition.

One intriguing example of this kind is an extant eighteenth-century woolen tapestry, probably made in the Suzhou manufactory, that represents a Western family in a landscape closely resembling the theme of Poirot's painting (fig. 99). It survives as a framed panel, but its large rectangular shape (77½ × 50¾ in. [197 × 129 cm]) suggests its original function as a hanging for a window or a niche wall. The HJD documents record similar window tapestries designed by missionary court painters. For instance, in April 1769 Qianlong ordered Sichelbart to draft cartoons depicting "Western figures" for three north windows in the Pavilion of Watching the Clouds (*Guanyun xie*), located in the Yuanming yuan, and he instructed the Suzhou manufactory to weave these pieces "after the color scheme of the [original] Western tapestries" (*zhao yángtan yanse*).[27] Long overlooked in the Palace Museum's furniture warehouse and lacking proper identification, the tapestry in question turns out to offer not only compelling evidence of the Qing court's exposure to the two Beauvais *Tenture chinoise* cycles, but also rich insights into the carefully negotiated visual layers subsumed under the Qing imperial concept of "Western."

Overall, the tapestry features a Europeanized composition and pictorial style. A family occupies the riverside in the foreground of the picture plane, while Western palatial structures and distant mountains are located on the opposite shore in the middle ground. A common arrangement in seventeenth- and eighteenth-century Dutch prints and European perspectival drawings, the scheme of a receding vista framed by sky-scraping trees had already been introduced to China by the mid-seventeenth century, as demonstrated by a woodblock illustration titled *Western Painting of Recessing Vista* (*Xiyáng yuanhua*) in the 1681 treatise *History of Lenses* (*Jingshi*), which was published by Sun Yunqiu (1628–1662), a Suzhou-based scholar (fig. 100).[28] In Chinese painting terminology, the word *yuan*, literally meaning "distance," refers to spatial recession in a landscape, thus clearly highlighting the Western way of rendering space in perspective, but the print itself was probably a composite of details drawn from various European sources. Although no textual evidence proves a direct link between Sun's print and the Qing court tapestry, their compositional similarity points to a visual language that was well established and understood as "Western" in style, one that had circulated for over a century in the network linking the cultural centers in south China and the court in Beijing.

Whereas the soaring trees are a decidedly Western framing device, one species represented in the tapestry—the banana tree—is a recurrent motif in Chinese painting and recalls the romanticized, mellow landscape of south China. Such an integrated Chinese/European pictorial dualism also manifests itself in multiple aspects of the tapestry's depiction of figures. On the riverbank, a husband and wife sit by a round table and enjoy drinks; surrounding them are adolescent girls and young boys absorbed in various activities. The master prominently occupies the center of the composition and appears considerably larger than the mistress, even though he is farther away from the viewer, which is consistent with Chinese cultural and visual norms. This disregard for the rules of perspective throws into relief the dominant role of the patriarchal

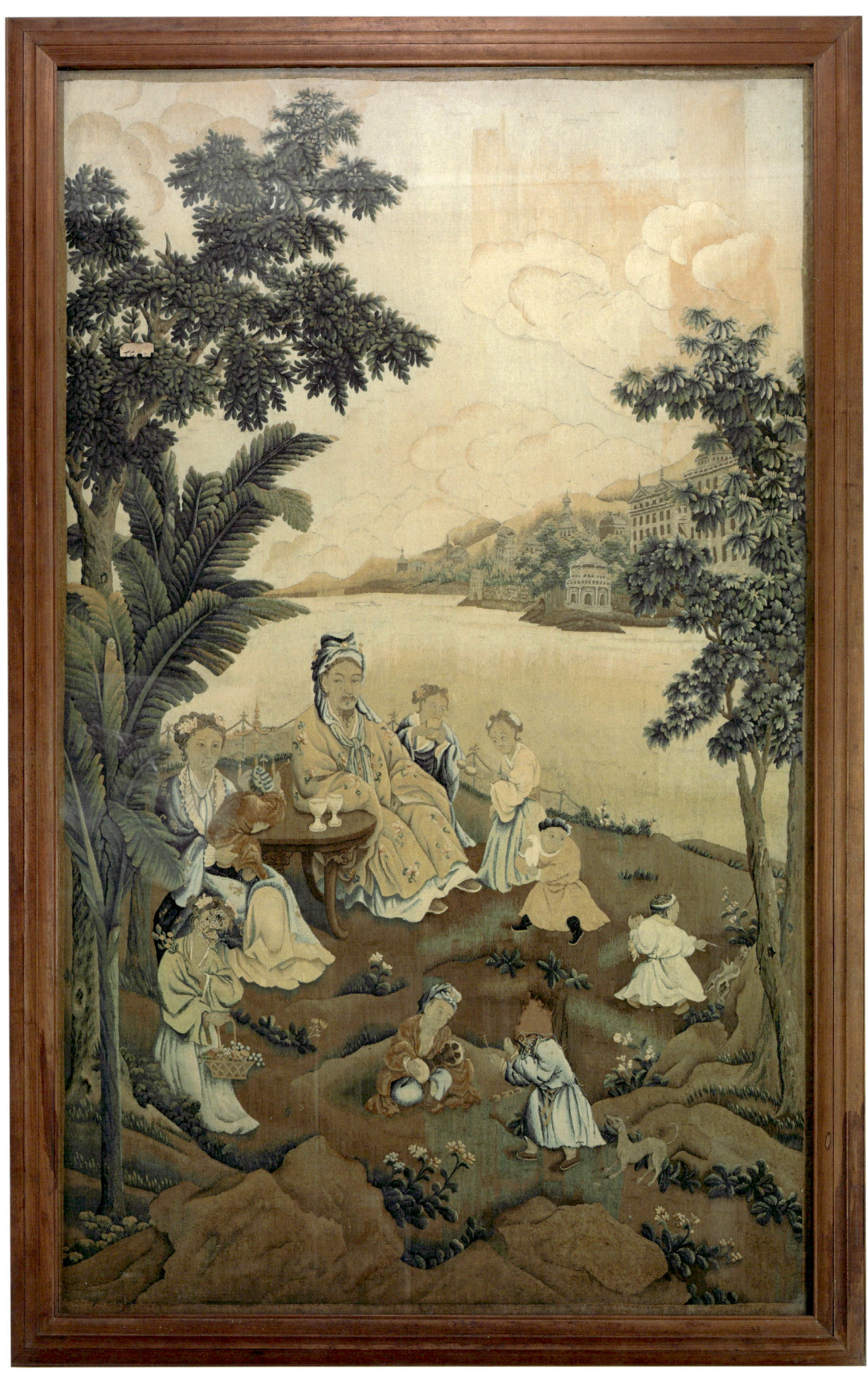

head of a household, long established in the Confucian ideological system. In the same vein, the female figures do not expose their feet, conforming to the Chinese ideals of proper feminine conduct and visual conventions. The lively boys are drawn from the Chinese picture genre of "children at play" (*yingxi*) and convey the auspicious message of a prosperous household. Various popular symbols for expressing good wishes are scattered throughout this image. For instance, the Chinese musical instrument *qìng* (an ensemble of chime stones), held by the toddler on the mother's lap, is a visual pun for celebration (*qìng*), following the well-developed Chinese trope of depicting homophone objects as auspicious signs.

Whereas the tapestry is replete with Chinese pictorial clichés grounded in widespread Confucian values, the figures themselves have a hybrid appearance that clearly signals them as Westerners. Their light-brown curly hair unmistakably suggests European personages, and the sartorial details, such as the floral pattern on the man's gown, the scalloped collar of the woman's outer robe, and the cravats worn by both, intentionally depict European textiles and dress style. Yet the unstructured look of their clothes is essentially Chinese and consistent with stereotypical Han Chinese–style costumes repeatedly depicted in late Ming and Qing paintings. This choice of familiar Chinese styles to render the intended Western dress exposes the different cultural visions and representational modes of the body in the two traditions. In the long heritage of Chinese art and philosophy, the body is a cultural ontology dispersed through metaphors rather than a concrete entity; thus, in representations, bodily proportions and contours often dissolve into a relatively flat and intangible form under voluminous clothing.[29] Even though European figural images showing a clearly defined body beneath a fitted, structured garment were not unfamiliar to the Qing court—they had been introduced through European portraits, prints, and vignettes on decorative objects—this mode did not find its way into Qing representations of Western people. For instance, in the imperial scroll *Official Tribute*, which depicts men and women in pairs from various Western countries, the European-style dress, especially the female garb, loses its native three-dimensional structure in favor of the Chinese-style soft drapes and folds.

It is not difficult to discern the iconographic affinities between the imagery of this tapestry and the chinoiserie scenes in the two French *Tenture chinoise* suites, discussed in the previous chapter. Indeed, visual details in the Qing tapestry convincingly suggest that inspiration came from the first *Tenture chinoise*, whose presence at the Qing court is not as clearly established by textual materials as that of the second set. The foremost clue is the theme of the tapestry. In the Chinese pictorial tradition, bucolic scenes of familial leisure in a natural setting are uncommon, as are depictions of a young husband and wife sitting next to each other drinking and relaxing. Normally, only an elderly couple in the role of grandparents would be portrayed together enjoying ceremonial events, with the exception of the erotic or semi-erotic genre, which would show a young man and his concubine side by side. A typical representation of a family—either real or imaginary—separates the husband and wife in different quarters, as

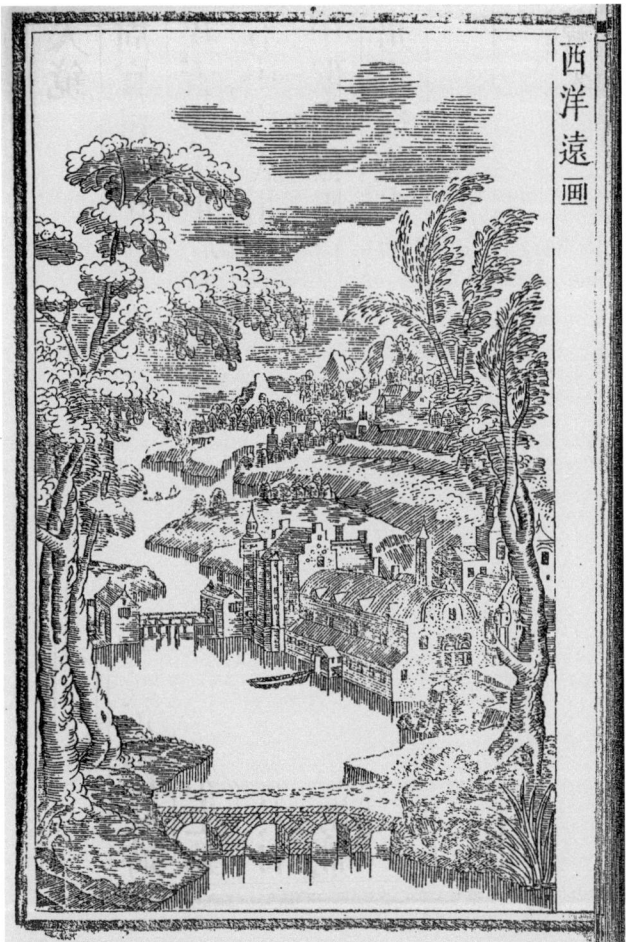

FIG. 99 (OPPOSITE) *A Western Family by the Riverside*, c. 1770s–80s. Made by the Qing Imperial Silk Manufactory in Suzhou. Tapestry, wool and silk, 77½ × 50¾ in. (197 × 129 cm). Palace Museum, Beijing (gu72661).

FIG. 100 (ABOVE) Sun Yunqiu, *Western Painting of Recessing Vista* (*Xiyáng yuánhuà*), in *History of Lenses* (*Jingshi*), 1681, 2:5v. Woodblock printed book, 8¼ × 5⅜ in. (21 × 13.5 cm). Shanghai Library.

Staging Imperial Narratives 119

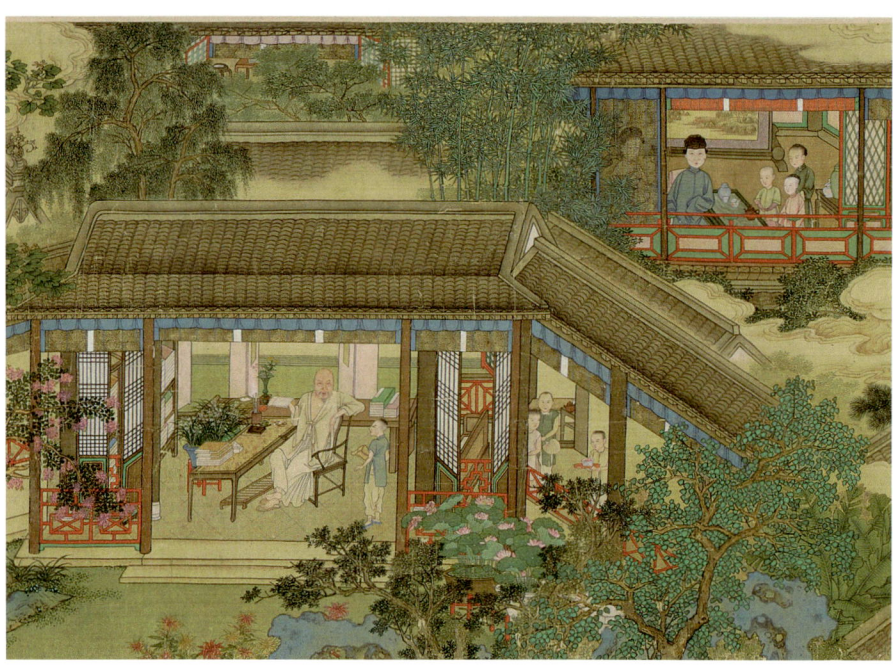

FIG. 101 Gu Jianlong, *Wang Shimin and His Family*, detail, seventeenth century. Handscroll, ink and colors on silk, 13⅞ × 47⅛ in. (35.2 × 119.7 cm). Minneapolis Institute of Art, gift of Ruth and Bruce Dayton (96.68.2).

exemplified by a family portrait of the scholar-painter Wang Shimin (1592–1680) by Gu Jianlong (1606–1688 or after). Wang, the master, occupies the front pavilion while his wife and consort stay in the rear, inner compound (fig. 101). This pictorial convention reflects Confucian ideals of ethical conduct that emphasize gender segregation and hierarchy.

By contrast, the depiction of a joyous couple relaxing outdoors, as seen in this tapestry of a Western family, betrays a European sensibility, and, as such, it paradoxically forms a common motif in European chinoiserie imagery. All the scenes in the first *Tenture chinoise* take place outdoors. The images are based in part on depictions by missionaries of the Manchu monarchs' outdoor activities in imperial gardens and resorts, and they to some degree follow a pictorial convention used in European tapestries to express allegorical and mythical themes, namely, placing figures in a fictive landscape.[30] The vignette depicted in the Qing tapestry may well have been inspired by *The Collation* from the first *Tenture chinoise*, which represents the "Chinese" emperor and empress partaking of refreshments outdoors by a round table: the emperor sits in the center with the empress by his side, and the two are surrounded by attendants and entertainers (fig. 102). It seems that the Qianlong emperor may not have understood the images in the *Tenture chinoise* as depictions of China and instead viewed them as an index of how Westerners behaved. Therefore, scenes in the French Chinese tapestries may have provided handy source images for the Qing court's imagination and depictions of Western life. There is another aspect in which the Qing tapestry appropriates the pictorial elements of the first *Tenture chinoise*. Like *The Emperor on a Journey* from this set (see fig. 76), the Qing tapestry depicts the riverbank in the foreground as an uneven field punctuated by small flowers and clusters of leafy plants. This rendering, divergent from the typical Chinese way of treating vegetation on the ground as abstract dots, serves to highlight a foreign landscape.

The chinoiserie figures in the two sets of French Chinese tapestries also provided models for the Western personages in the Qing tapestry. In particular, the hairstyles and accessories of the latter come directly from the second *Tenture chinoise*. In a striking anticipation of the code-switching later explored at the Qing court, the original Beauvais set has exchanged the black hair of the Chinese noblewomen in Boucher's original paintings for curly blond hair, in harmony with the taste and visual expectations of European noble patrons.[31] This modification indicates the wish of European viewers to project themselves into an exotic scene while retaining distinctive somatic and cultural markers from their home settings. In the Qing context, this wavy blond hair in turn stood out as a prominent feature of Westerners as depicted in all media, and it was duly adopted for all the foreign figures in the tapestry. In addition to the blond hair color, the women in the Qing piece have parted coiffures decorated with flowers, closely resembling those

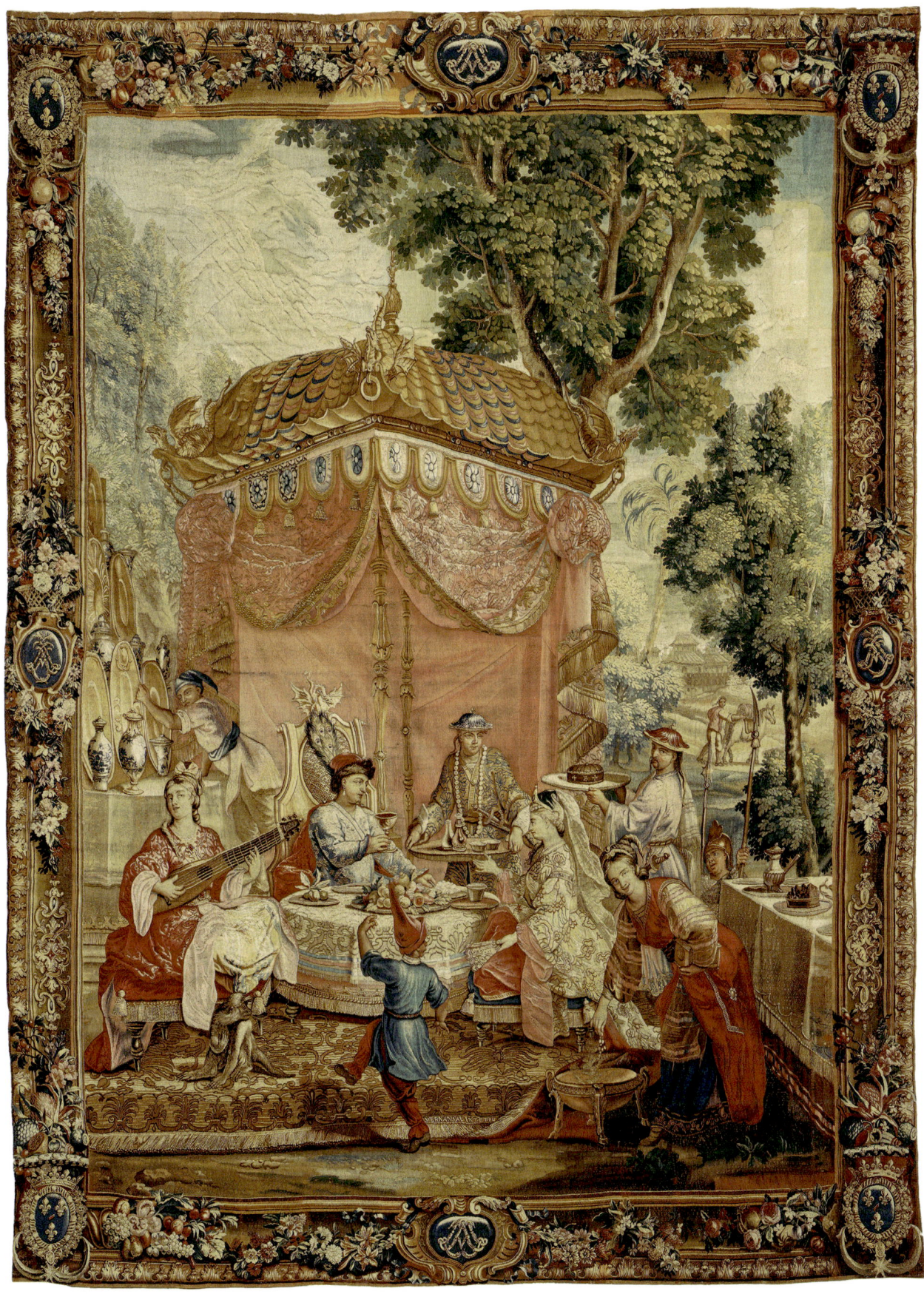

FIG. 102 *The Collation,* from the first *Tenture chinoise* series, c. 1697–1705. Made by the Manufacture royale de Beauvais. Tapestry, wool and silk, 13 ft. 10½ in. × 10 ft. 2 in. (422.9 × 309.9 cm). J. Paul Getty Museum, Los Angeles (83.DD.336).

of the noble ladies in the French tapestry *Chinese Toilette* (fig. 103; see also fig. 77). The long cravat loosely tied below the neck—an accessory worn by master and mistress alike in the Qing tapestry—is also taken from the second *Tenture chinoise*. An important accessory for men during the eighteenth century in the West, cravats were usually white. Elite men's formal attire often included ornate cravats featuring lace or flounces and tied in elaborate styles; a loosely knotted plain one frequently accompanied an informal robe worn indoors. Women sometimes sported a white cravat as a part of a riding habit or a casual indoor ensemble. In the 1770s and 1780s, Ottoman-inspired styles for women's fashion, such as "lévite" or "à la polonaise," were often accessorized with a cravat, which added to the exotic evocation (fig. 104). Interestingly, in the *Tenture chinoise*, noble "Chinese" ladies and maids wear loosely tied cravats in pink and gold but not white, and in the Qing tapestry, the color has changed to pale blue. If the French design exoticized a familiar European accessory with imaginary colors to accentuate "Chineseness," the Qing pieces appropriated this detail as a salient marker of a "Western" outfit. The Chinese design, too, reimagined the color at will.

This Qing tapestry unveils a window into the Qing court's approaches to Western imagery and style. Like many of the European chinoiserie works, the Western genre scene in this tapestry hovered between fantasy and a genuine curiosity about other people's lives and cultures. The resulting design manifested as a grand pastiche of fragmented details, quoting from a complex lexicon of images developed over a century of cross-cultural exchanges. Foreign sources were then filtered through Chinese pictorial norms and symbolism. While the Qing imperial patron sought visual pleasure in alien and exotic Western features, the ultimate satisfaction was granted by the fact that the Western scene fundamentally served to reinforce the auspicious messages of family harmony and multiple progeny—messages that were deeply rooted in Confucian values.

From the French Chinese hangings to the Qing Western tapestry, the transmission of images underwent a circular process in which the imaginary was reimagined, the exotic re-exoticized, and negotiated sources

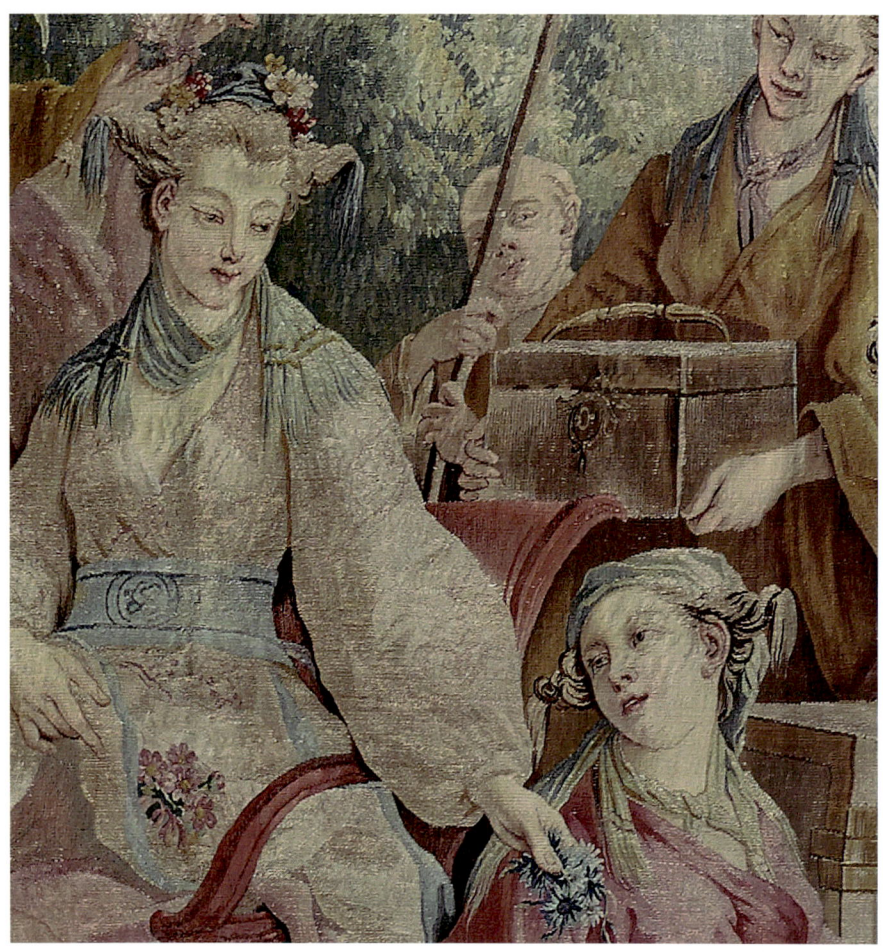

FIG. 103 Detail of fig. 77.

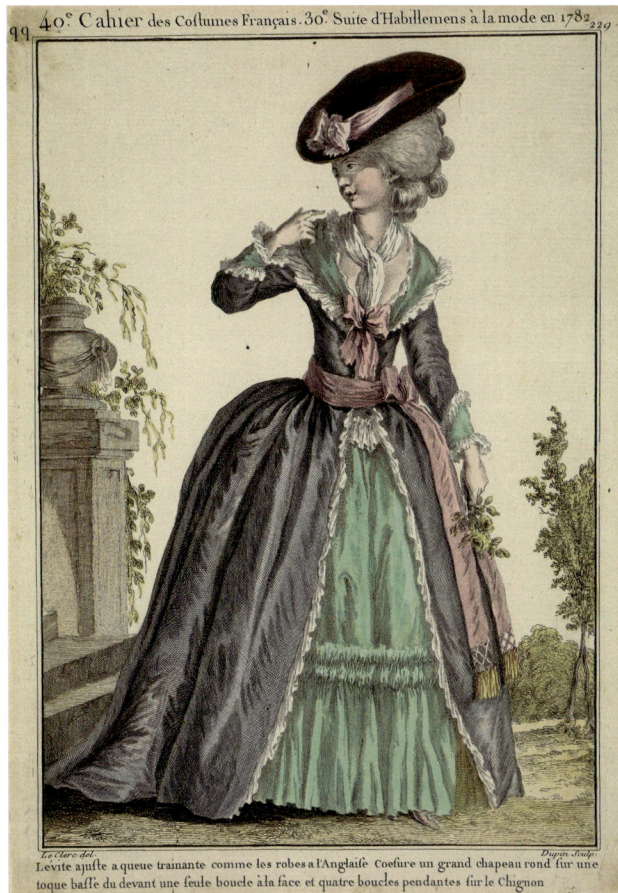

FIG. 104 Fashion plate illustrating a "lévite" dress and accessories, in *Gallerie des modes et des costumes français, 40e cahier des costumes français, 30e suite d'habillemens à la mode en 1782* (Paris: Esnauts et Rapilly, 1782). Hand-colored engraving on laid paper, 15¼ × 10 in. (38.7 × 25.4 cm). Museum of Fine Arts, Boston, the Elizabeth Day McCormick Collection (44.1537).

renegotiated. A synthesis of fantasies, European iconography, and various first- and secondhand materials about China, the French chinoiserie designs that in European eyes depicted a fanciful Chinese life underwent a dramatic turn in the Qing perceptions. For the latter, the same repertoire, lacking readily recognizable clues to indicate China, came to mediate the Qing vision of an equally exotic West and provided visual templates for the Qing court's representations of Western life and people. Parsing the layers and shifting meanings of the pictorial motifs in this trajectory sheds fresh light on the semiotic fluidity of the so-called chinoiserie repertoire. As a composite style encompassing visual and cultural elements that transcended geographic boundaries and was constantly reshaped by dynamic exchanges, chinoiserie indeed functioned as a global style of universal exoticism. In both France and Qing China, chinoiserie evoked something distant and foreign, accommodating respective designations of the "other" while being flexibly adjusted to harmonize with local visual conventions and cultural sensibilities. The circuitous exchanges of chinoiserie images and the capacious, often conflicting meanings that they accumulated in the process underscore their potential to be freely contextualized and repurposed. In early modern global exchanges, the perpetual yet unspecified exoticism embedded in the chinoiserie repertoire rendered the style as a liberating visual and cultural expression.

NEW YEAR CELEBRATION: ENACTING EMPERORSHIP

Among all the recorded Western tapestries that the Qianlong emperor commissioned, one design representing a New Year celebration scene held special visual attraction and symbolic significance for him. Through repeated orders, he fully explored its pictorial program and spatial implications to express personal yet deeply political messages related to emperorship and dynasty. Between 1769 and 1776, the HJD files recorded three weavings of this same design. The emperor ordered the first tapestry in November 1769, intending to hang it in front of the north window of the central bay (*mingdian*) in the rear compound (*houdian*) of the Hall of Mental Cultivation (*Yangxin dian*) in the Forbidden City. The Imperial Workshops executed a cartoon on paper measuring 5 *chi* 9 *cun* 2 *fen* high and 1 *zhang* 5 *cun* wide (6 ft. 2½ in. × 11 ft. [189.4 × 335 cm]) and sent it to the Suzhou manufactory for weaving. The finished piece reached the palace on January 11, 1771, and was installed as planned.[32] Three days later, Qianlong, apparently dissatisfied, demanded that a new version of the same design be woven in a larger size: "The height should be from the edge of the bed to the ceiling [beam]; the width should leave no blank space on the wall." The palace workshop then prepared an enlarged cartoon measuring 8 *chi* 4 *cun* 5 *fen* high and 1 *zhang* 1 *chi* 5 *cun* wide (8 ft. 10½ in. × 12 ft. 1 in. [270.4 × 368 cm]), which corresponded to the dimensions of the north window. The court document clearly labeled this tapestry as a "Western figured woolen hanging" (*xiyáng huatan*). Delivered on November 19, 1771, this new version replaced the first one, which was subsequently transferred to the Yuanming yuan for storage. This second weaving has survived in the Palace Museum (see fig. 93).[33] The emperor's predilection for this tapestry is evidenced by the record that on January 23, 1776, he commissioned yet another weaving for the north window of the east warm chamber in the Hall of

Staging Imperial Narratives   123

Delight in Longevity (*Leshou tang*) in his newly built retirement quarters, the Palace of Peace and Longevity. For this version, the court workshop provided an older cartoon of the tapestry currently hung in the Hall of the Mental Cultivation—the second weaving—and the emperor asked the Suzhou supervisor to modify the design as appropriate to suit the new dimensions; these were mistakenly written as "8 *chi* 4 *cun* high and 1 *zhang* 7 *chi* 9 *cun* wide" but indeed should have read "1 *zhang* 1 *chi* 9 *cun* wide" (8 ft. 9⅞ in. × 12 ft. 6 in. [268.8 × 380.8 cm]).[34] The completed piece arrived at the court on November 6, 1776. Its measurements correspond to those of a tapestry currently in the Cleveland Museum of Art that features the same iconography but in a slightly different composition (see fig. 94).[35]

The second weaving, when reimagined in situ, provides a particularly intriguing opportunity to probe Qianlong's ideas about the interplay among the tapestry's imagery, the architectural space, and the sovereign himself as the primary occupant of the room. Not only does a close analysis of this tapestry's design and the specific location and timing of its display offer further insights into the hybrid concept of "Western" in Qing court tapestries and arts in general; it also illuminates how Qianlong manipulated this foreign textile medium to fabricate an intercorporeal visual program through which he could act out a political narrative.

Qianlong played a pivotal role in planning the original design for this tapestry and gave meticulous instructions about its visual style in 1769: "The large borders should be ornamental bands in the Western style [*xiyáng shi huabian*]; the figures in the center should not be woven in the Western mode of perspective with shadows [*xiyáng youyingzi xianfa*] as in previous ones. The motif and style [*yàngshi*] should closely follow the cartoon provided and must not exude Western air [*xiyáng qì*]."[36] The previous tapestries that Qianlong noted could have been the imitative weavings of the second *Tenture chinoise* (see figs. 98A–D) or the Qing court's reproductions of other European pieces that rendered the figures with articulated chiaroscuro. The finished weaving, received in 1771, matched Qianlong's vision exactly: in the central field of the tapestry, the scene of a Chinese family gathering completely conforms to Chinese pictorial norms; there is no linear perspective or shading on the figures' faces, and a wide self-border in the style of a gilded rococo frame—a conventional design taken directly from eighteenth-century French tapestries—encloses the central image (see fig. 93).

Qì, or air, is an important concept in Chinese painting and calligraphy, referring to the cosmic energy, momentum, or rhythm of the brushwork and composition. Qianlong evoked it here in a more general sense to describe the overall visual impression. Interestingly, for a tapestry that was clearly labeled "Western," the emperor explicitly required it to show no "Western air." This paradox betrays Qianlong's perception of the "Western" style as both eclectic and selective. In the Qing imperial context, the "Western style" in pictorial representation was primarily understood as the modes of linear perspective and cast shadow, both introduced by Jesuit missionaries during the Kangxi period. Unlike linear perspective, which gained strong traction in Qing court arts, cast shadows on human faces did not appeal to Qianlong, who failed to read chiaroscuro as volume and modeling. As noted in a 1779 letter by Jean-Joseph-Marie Amiot (1718–1793), a French Jesuit who enjoyed a long career at the Qing court, the emperor disliked "shiny highlight painted in oil" and above all "the shadows, [for] when they were a bit strong, they appeared to him as stains."[37] John Barrow, English Secretary of the Admiralty from 1804 to 1845, who accompanied George Macartney's (1737–1806) embassy to China between 1792 and 1794, also records that, looking at a portrait of King George III (r. 1760–1820), Qianlong lamented the shading of the nose as an unfortunate defect, seeing the image as "soiled by the dirt upon the face."[38] This strong distaste led Qianlong to single out shadows on the figures' faces as a top concern in his instructions on the New Year tapestry. Except in human faces, Qianlong seems to have embraced a naturalistic style that employed shading. In weavings, he favored the striking three-dimensional effect achieved by using French silk in the points rentrés technique, which he also employed for his military trappings (see figs. 15, 16); in both the 1771 and 1776 versions of the New Year tapestry, the figures' clothes are subtly shaded along the folds (see chapter opener image).

As in the tapestry representing the Western family on the riverbank discussed earlier (see fig. 99), European elements in the New Year tapestry coexisted alongside Manchu-Chinese ones to produce a fresh, hybrid imagery, one that could merit the broad rubric of "Western" without treading on any visual or semiotic taboos. Rather than randomly collapsing into each other, culturally specific visual components were subject to careful scrutiny and strategically rearranged according to the overarching imperial aesthetics and logic.

The iconography of the New Year tapestry is extremely complex: it draws on time-honored pictorial conventions while alluding to an actual ritual event, and it strategically embeds in its program references to its intended location and the specific timing of its display. In the central field of the tapestry, a busy scene unfolds with over fifty family members in an interior hall structured by an expansive screen in the central background and a large window frame on the left opening onto an illusionary spring garden. At the center of the composition, two grandparents sit by a round table while sons, daughters-in-law, and adolescent girls diligently serve at their sides. Small, restless boys scattered across the open ground are immersed in individual activities such as arranging flowers, moving fruits, preparing fireworks, and playing musical instruments. The imagery is saturated with auspicious motifs symbolizing longevity, happiness, and prosperity, such as the *ruyi* scepter that a boy eagerly passes to the grandfather, the hundred red bats (a pun signaling "plentiful luck") on the screen, and the out-of-season peonies and lychees signifying affluence. The visual delight is enriched with acoustic and olfactory evocations created by the sonorous festival instruments and felicitous fragrant plants.

From fireworks to spring blossoms, numerous motifs in this tapestry indicate the New Year season, but two ritual objects in particular visualize the occasion of the New Year's Day celebration: a golden vessel and a candlestick, each held by an adult son on the right (fig. 105). The vessel, a miniature tripod, bears a two-character inscription: "*yonggu*," or "eternal stability," identifying it as the Golden Chalice of Eternal Stability (*jīn'ou yonggu bei*), a historical symbol dating back to the Liang dynasty (502–57) that alludes to a secure reign and an intact empire. Similarly, the candlestick, known as the Jade Candlestick of Long-Lasting Harmony (*yuzhu changtiao tai*), symbolizes a peaceful and harmonious reign, a metaphor drawn from the ancient canon the *Classic of Poetry* (*Shijing*; 11th–6th centuries BCE). Both the vessel and the candlestick depicted here closely resemble extant examples commissioned by Qianlong, affirming that the tapestry in fact portrayed actual objects (fig. 106). As a literary metaphor, this pair of motifs had long appeared in Qing imperial texts eulogizing the Manchu reign, but Qianlong fully literalized this ancient idiom by having concrete objects fashioned and formalizing their use in the ceremony called "Opening the Brush" (*kaibi*) or "Testing the Brush" (*shibi*), which was performed by the emperor alone on

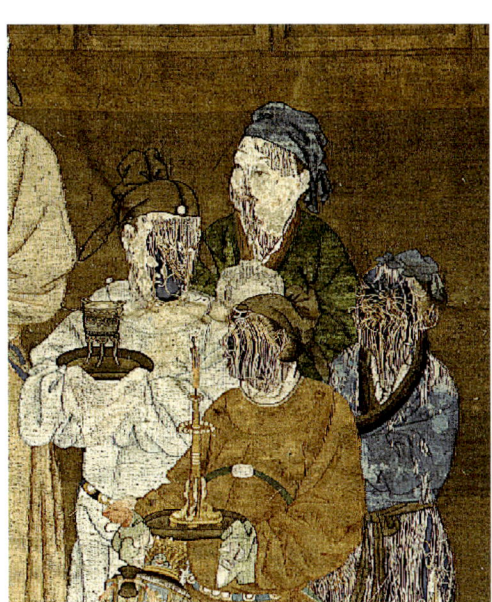

FIG. 105 Detail of fig. 93.

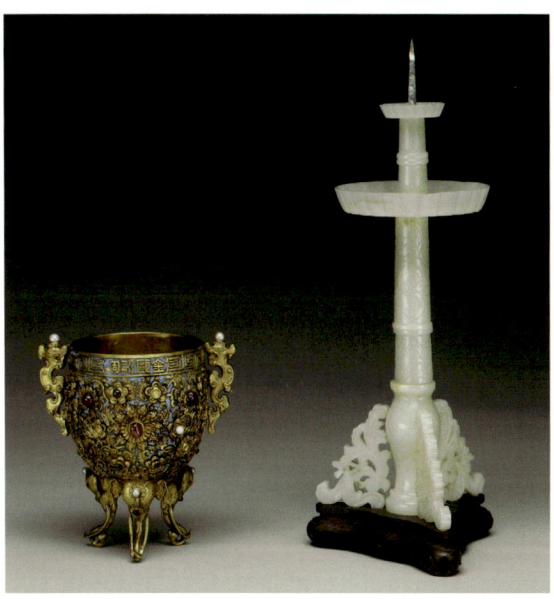

FIG. 106 (*Left*) Golden Chalice of Eternal Stability (*jīn'ou yonggu bei*), 1739. Made by the Qing Imperial Workshops. Gold, pearls, semiprecious stones, and kingfisher feathers, height 5½ in. (14 cm), depth 3⅜ in. (8.5 cm). National Palace Museum, Taipei (guza5490). (*Right*) Jade Candlestick of Long-Lasting Harmony (*yuzhu changtiao tai*), 1739. Made by the Qing Imperial Workshops. Jade, height 12 in. (30.6 cm), width 3¾ in. (9.5 cm). National Palace Museum, Taipei (guyu3208).

New Year's Day.[39] He purposefully incorporated these two motifs in the tapestry to create cross-references between the representation and the actual event, as the location for this hanging—the Hall of Mental Cultivation—shared the same architectural complex as that for the Opening the Brush ritual.

An 1807 writing by the Jiaqing emperor provides a thorough account of the procedure and purpose of this ceremony, illuminating the significance of these two ritual objects in terms of the time and location:

> My imperial grandfather [Yongzheng] initiated the ceremony Opening the Brush, and my imperial father [Qianlong] continued it. When I was officially established as the crown prince in 1795, [my imperial father] called me to the space known as *mingchuang* [Bright Window] in the front chamber of the east warm chamber in the Hall of Mental Cultivation. He instructed me on the ritual established in previous reigns and bestowed on me the imperial objects used in the Opening the Brush ceremony. I respectfully observe this protocol, careful not to neglect anything or make a mistake. Every year at the *zike* [11:00 P.M.–1:00 A.M., the first moment] on New Year's Day, I respectfully come to this place. On the table is a golden chalice filled with *tusu* medicinal wine and a jade candlestick [holding a candle], which I light with my own hand. I write with a brush, first in red ink and then in black ink. The top of the brush bears the inscription "Evergreen for Ten Thousand Years," and the brush is called "Brush of Ten Thousand Years." I write a few propitious phrases to pray for a year of smooth governing and for a harmonious reign. Afterward, I browse the calendar as a symbolic gesture of keeping time and being aware of seasonal changes.[40]

As the Son of Heaven, the emperor embodied the cosmological order and mediated between Heaven and Earth. Throughout the imperial dynasties in Chinese history, the power to control time and harmonize the agricultural seasons in the lunar calendar had been crucial in legitimating rulership, as by these means "the emperor could internalize the intrinsic movement of the universe" and "rule the world without using force."[41] As a ritual marking the beginning of another yearly cycle, Opening the Brush foregrounded the emperor's divine role in mandating time and ushering in a new spring—that is, reviving all creatures and putting everything back in order. The ritual paraphernalia, which were made of precious materials of gold and jade and embodied classical allusions, facilitated the emperor's performance of time renewal while materializing the mighty messages of state power and dynastic continuity. The archaic shape of the chalice recalled the ancient tripod, a vessel symbolic of the state, and the gesture of lighting the candle reenacted the idea of continuing the state's heritage.[42] Jiaqing's description in particular stressed the link between the chalice and candlestick (stand-in for the ephemeral candle) to the dynastic succession, as he inherited this ritual duty and these paraphernalia on the day he was made crown prince.

The Hall of Mental Cultivation, a secluded compound located just west of the central axis of the Forbidden City, was indeed an extremely important site that epitomized Qing emperorship. Strategically located and carefully protected, the hall functioned as a crucial nexus linking the outer and inner courts; the bureau of the Grand Council—the important privy council advising the emperor on policy making—was just outside its south gate (fig. 107). Since the Yongzheng period, this hall had served as the primary office and residence of the emperor. Qianlong in particular turned it into a multipurpose unit where he lived most of the time, received core and trusted ministers, reviewed state documents and issued edicts, practiced Tibetan Buddhism, stored and appreciated his most valued artworks, and wrote poetry.[43] The hall simultaneously embodied the sovereign's public state responsibilities, spiritual role, and private cultural pursuits, which were nonetheless politically charged. This architectural context, the ritual activities held there, and the visual programs inside it prescribed meanings to each other and together constructed emperorship.

The central building of the Hall of Mental Cultivation was divided into front and rear compounds, each consisting of a central bay flanked by a series of small, interlinked chambers (fig. 108).[44] The Bright Window—the space where Qianlong named Jiaqing as his heir and where the annual Opening the Brush ritual took place—was a small compartment located in the southwest corner of the east warm chamber in the front compound. Its name came from the illuminated paper for that window and evoked "sharp eyes and clever mind." Measuring only about 64½ sq. ft. (6 m²), it comprised a window on the south side, a door on the east, a solid wall on the west, and a partition on the north.[45] As the prime geographical direction in the Chinese cosmological system, south signified the

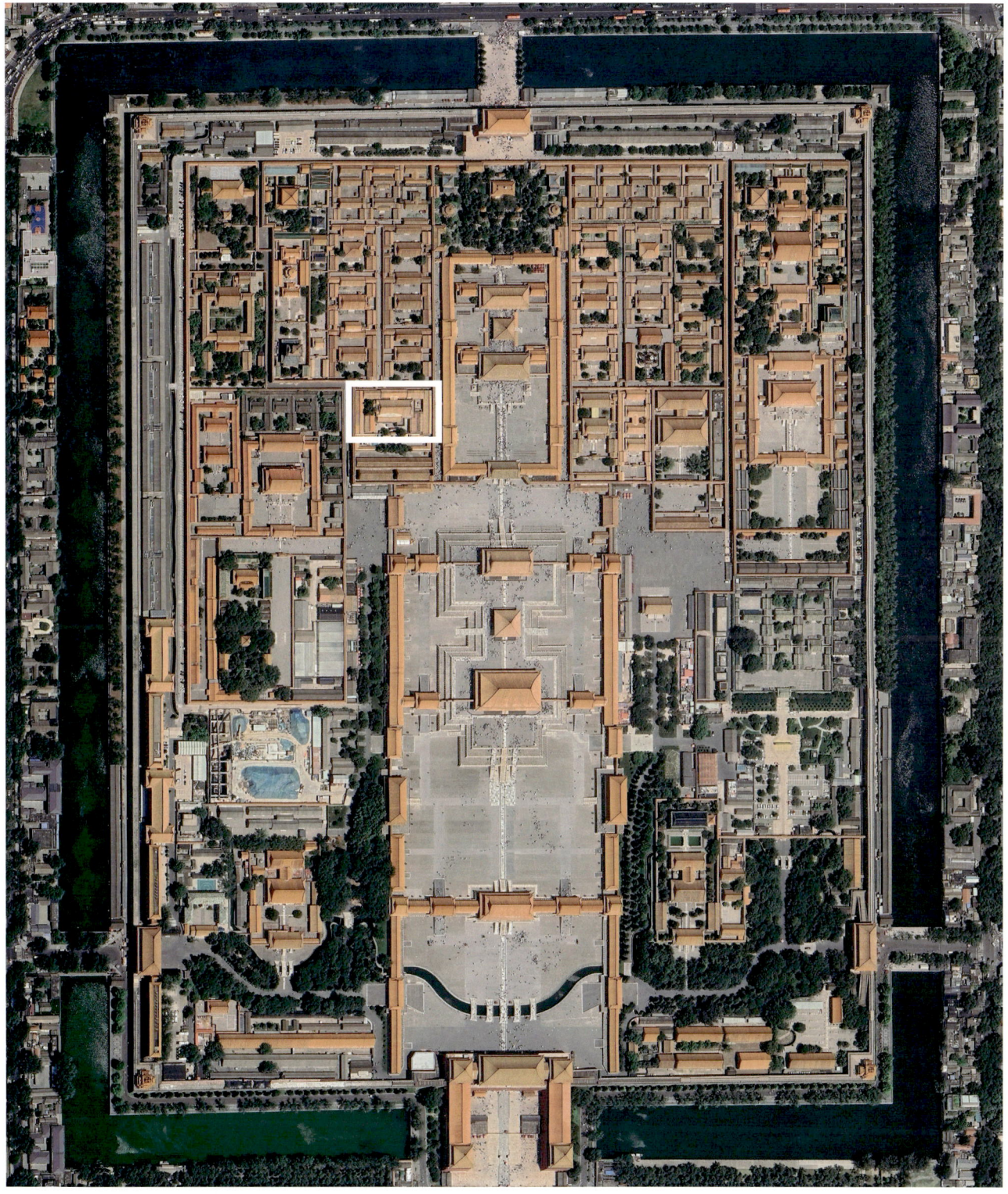

FIG. 107 The location of the Hall of Mental Cultivation inside the Forbidden City.

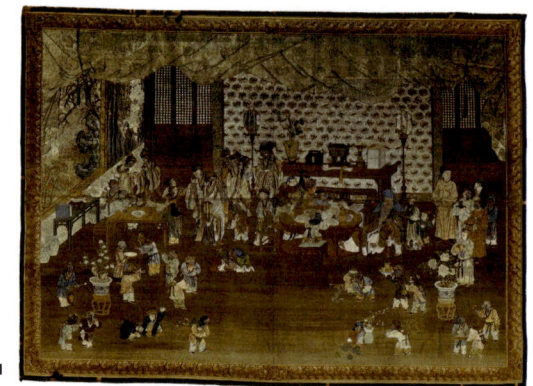

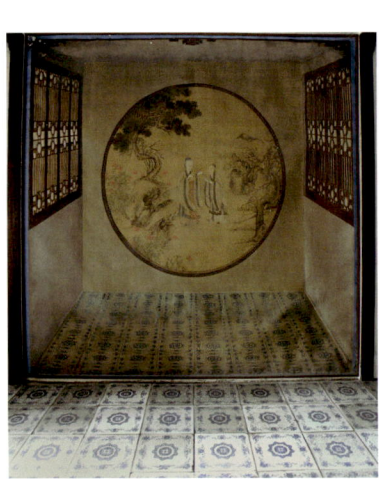

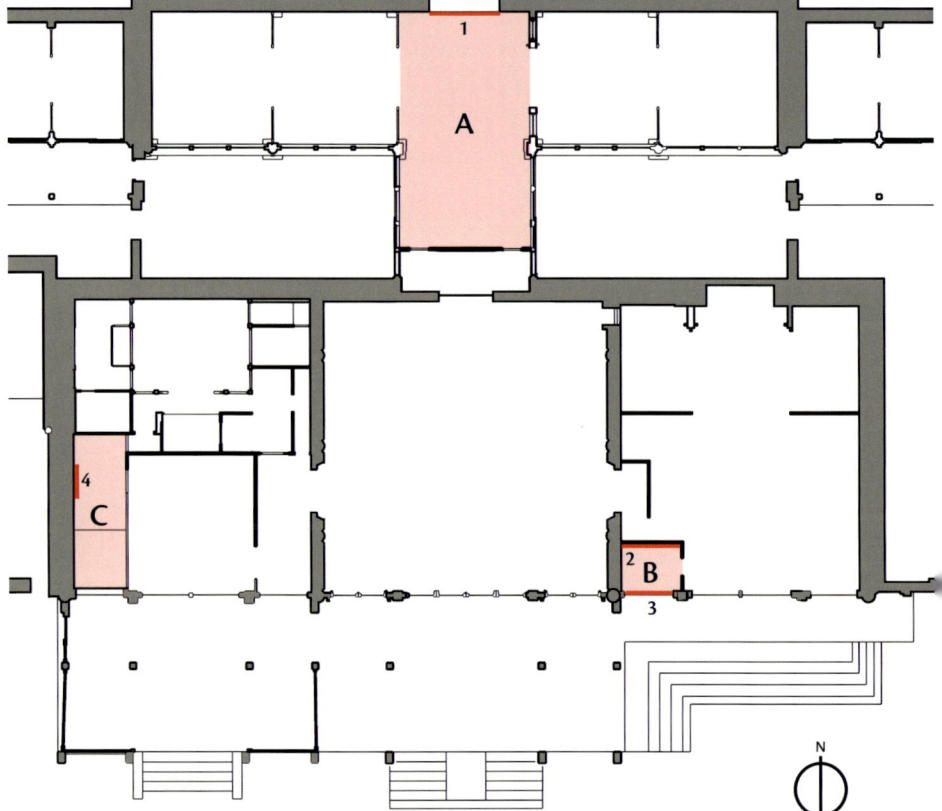

FIG. 108 Plan of the Hall of Mental Cultivation and the placement of the activity and artworks related to the theme of dynastic renewal in 1772. Diagram by Tao Jin.

    A Central bay of the north compound
        1 New Year tapestry, hung on the north window, 8 ft. 10½ in. × 12 ft. 1 in. (270.4 × 368 cm) (see fig. 93)
    B Bright Window (*mingchuang*)
        2 The tieluo painting *Ten Thousand Countries Coming to Pay Tribute* (c. 1761), pasted onto the north wall, 10 ft. 6¾ in. × 7 ft. 1 in. (322 × 216 cm) (see fig. 64 for detail)
        3 The ritual "Opening the Brush," performed by the emperor on New Year's Day by the south window (see fig. 106 for the ritual objects)
    C Hall of Three Rarities (*Sanxi tang*)
        4 The trompe l'oeil tieluo painting *Spring's Peaceful Message* (1765), pasted onto the west wall facing the door, 79⅛ × 81½ in. (201 × 207 cm)

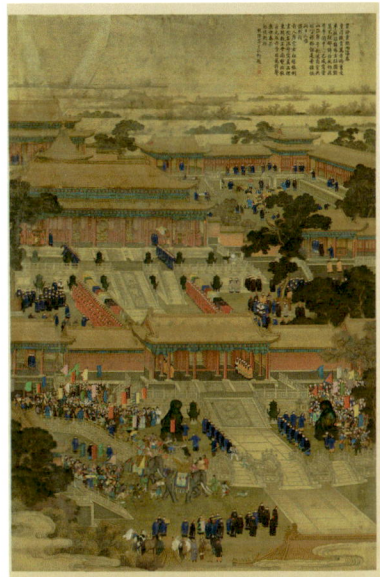

2

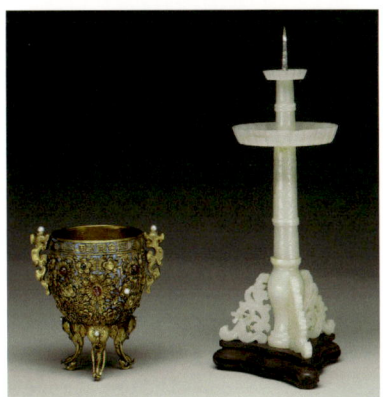

3

beginning of the season and thus perfectly resonated with the ritual marking the inception of a year. Two monumental paintings mounted in succession inside the Bright Window further amplified the political message of dynastic longevity and prosperity embodied by the intimate space. According to the HJD files, from some earlier date until the second lunar month of 1750, *New Year Celebration* (*Shousui tu*), a tieluo painting hung on the west wall above a couch bed. It depicted Qianlong in a stereotypical ancient Chinese costume surrounded by princes, two of whom hold the golden chalice and the jade candlestick (fig. 109). From 1766 through 1800, *Ten Thousand Countries Coming to Pay Tribute* (*Wanguo laichao tu*), a framed painting of an imaginary event taking place on New Year's Day, hung on the north wall (see B.2 in fig. 108; see also fig. 64).[46] As the Palace Museum curator Li Shi points out, in the narrow space of the Bright Window, the painting there could never be viewed in full; instead, it served to augment good wishes through a fictional representation.[47] Like *New Year Celebration,* the tieluo painting that once decorated the west wall, the New Year tapestry inserted the symbolic objects of the brush ritual into a crowded, lively family scene in an imaginary space suffused with auspicious signs. It transplanted these objects wielded by the emperor into the hands of his sons to perpetuate their visibility and to assert the imperial heritage.

From the back of the front compound, a short hallway led to the rear compound, a five-bay unit that served as the emperor's private quarters and bedroom. There on the north wall in the central bay hung the New Year tapestry, which captured the actual event that took place in an adjacent room but refabricated it as a fictional scene and space. By incorporating the New Year ritual objects as temporal indicators and symbolic motifs, the tapestry suspended this transient moment and prolonged its auspicious significance and political connotations. Given the similar iconography in both the tapestry and the painting *New Year Celebration* formerly mounted inside the Bright Window (see fig. 109), we may view the tapestry installed in 1771 as reviving the painted theme of the Opening the Brush ritual and relocating it to the north point of the central axis of the Hall of Mental Cultivation.

Remarkably, the same messages of spring's arrival and imperial succession were repeated a third time in the Hall of Mental Cultivation in the trompe l'oeil tieluo painting *Spring's Peaceful Message* (*Ping'an chunxin tu*), which was pasted onto a niche wall in the west warm chamber of the

Staging Imperial Narratives 129

front compound (see C.4 in fig. 108). In this image, created in 1765, two figures in generic Chinese scholars' robes but with the realistic visages of the Yongzheng and Qianlong emperors stand in a blooming spring garden. The former is handing a branch of plum blossom to the latter, a coded representation implying the transfer of the throne.[48] The location of this image—the west wall of Qianlong's private study, the Hall of Three Rarities (Sanxi tang)—symmetrically echoed the Bright Window compartment for the Opening the Brush ritual in the architectural plan.

Thus, in a compact triangle that centrally structured the Hall of Mental Cultivation, the same themes of dynastic renewal and continuity were reprised in three different forms: in the east as the actual but momentary activities of announcing the crown prince and performing the annual New Year's ritual; in the west as the trompe l'oeil painting of the two emperors welcoming spring; and in the north as the tapestry unfolding a family celebration. A distinctly Western dimension prominent in all the artworks helped construct the messages of the empire's prosperity and universal power. Whether thematic, technical, or stylistic, the Western elements included the motif of foreign tributes in the east wing, the linear perspective technique and the trompe-l'oeil genre in the west wing, and the European format and ornaments of the tapestry in the north hall. The tapestry played a crucial part in this complex, inter-referential visual program mapped onto the hall's architecture, in which the imperial fathers and sons, their costumed identities, and their imaginary, idealized selves collapsed into each other to form a rhythmic, perpetuated dynastic narrative. The tapestry, by incorporating both the real ritual and a fictional, costumed play, channeled the transition from the actual event to the coded trompe l'oeil painting, a passage literally articulated by the hanging's placement on the central north wall between the other two locations.

Both *Spring's Peaceful Message* and the New Year tapestry encapsulated a specific historical moment or event, but they eternalized it in a generic, timeless setting. Moreover, the figures' clothing—a type of stereotypical Han Chinese attire referred to in Qing court arts as "ancient dress" (guzhuang) or "Han dress" (hanzhuang)—facilitated a visual and cognitive transcendence beyond the limit of actual time. A style invented for pictorial imagery, this sartorial mode took shape in late Ming figure paintings with elements drawn from clothes of the Ming and previous dynasties, and it prevailed in the Qing period. In this system, adolescent and young men wear long, belted gowns with round necklines, whereas older men and scholarly figures are attired in robe-and-skirt combinations for casual occasions, or in calf-length overcoats with central openings for more formal scenes. Small boys sport short robes over trousers. Women wear either wide-sleeved jackets with decorative bands tucked inside two layered skirts, or long coats over this ensemble. Both outfits are often accessorized with ribbons and streamers.

In Qing court arts, the repertoire of Han Chinese dress appeared primarily in images illustrating ancient allegories and exemplary stories, generic beautiful women engaging in seasonal activities, or celestial figures embodying auspicious signs. This iconography enfolded a metaphorical, archaic time evoking universal virtues, a poetic, cosmological time devoid of historical specificity, and a transcendental, everlasting time. I postulate that for the Qing rulers, the invented "ancient dress" did not necessarily evoke an exotic Han Chinese culture vis-à-vis that of the Manchu, but more generally signified a temporal dimension beyond the measurable present time. The alternative names "ancient" and "Han" associated with this style also suggest the equation and interchangeability of the two concepts in Qing imperial perceptions. The sense of timelessness inherent in the generalized "Han Chinese style" relegated the Chinese culture and Han Chinese dynasties of the past to a realm outside the political temporality of the Manchu Empire. In reality, Qing rulers strictly forbade the Manchus from adopting Han Chinese dress so as not to corrupt their Manchu identity.[49] Yet in the pictorial domain, the imagined "Han Chinese dress," removed from any dynastic association or political threat, became a versatile visual language for expressing a sense of eternity.

For this reason, both Yongzheng and Qianlong took special delight in having themselves depicted in Han Chinese dress in fictional merrymaking scenes and festival celebrations—genres clearly distinguished from official imperial portraits and paintings commemorating political events, which realistically represent the emperors' court robes to articulate the historicity of his reign. Indeed, the represented Han Chinese costumes admitted the Manchu emperors into the same eternal world inhabited by ancient sages, celestial figures, and personifications of seasons. The universal and multiple temporalities connoted by the dress style enabled the Qing imperial patrons to freely enact historical, legendary, and poetic narratives.

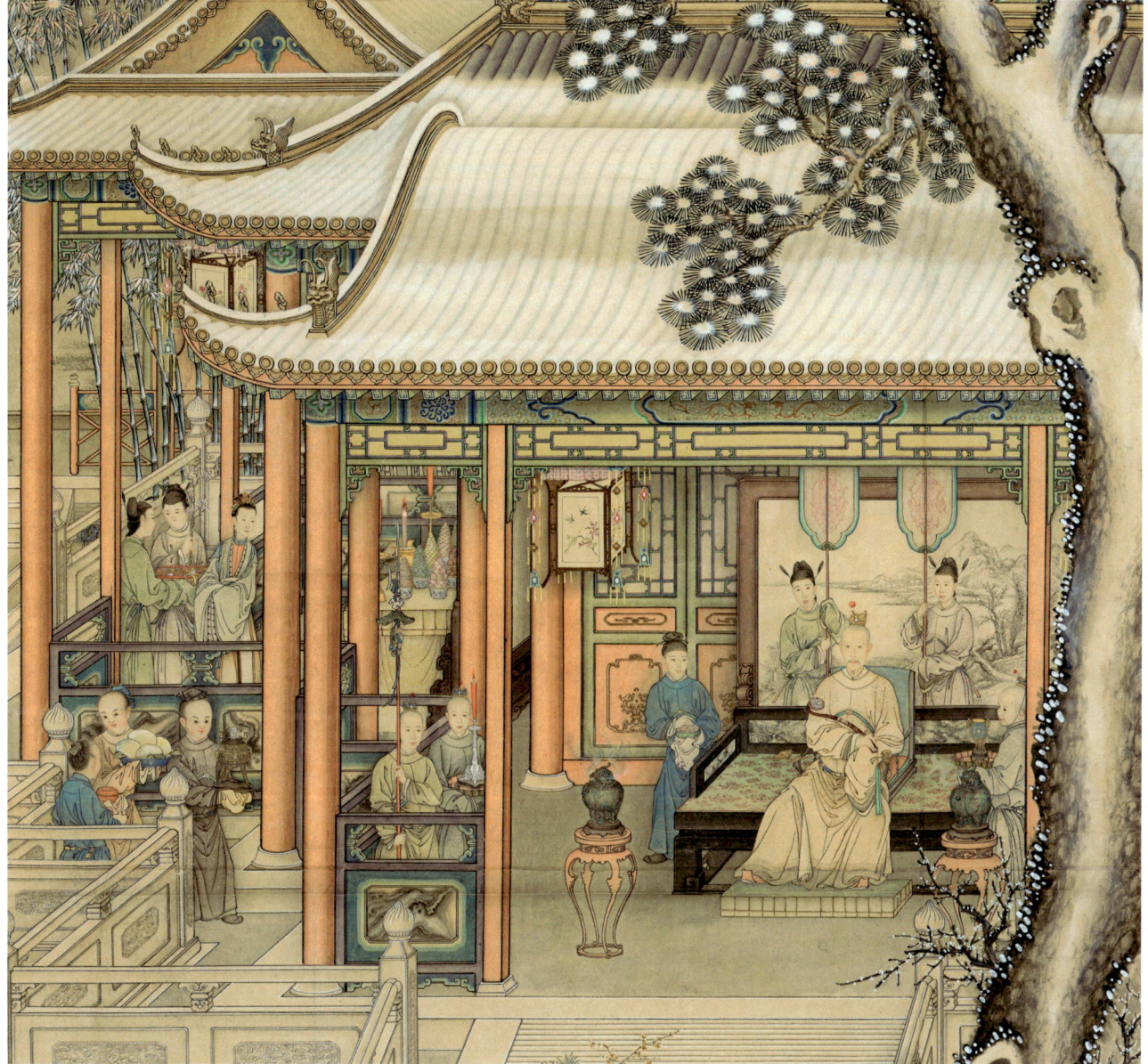

FIG. 109 Qing court artist(s), *New Year Celebration (Shousui tu)*, detail, c. 1740s. Affixed painting (tieluo), ink and colors on silk, 9 ft. 1⅝ in. × 6 ft. 9⅜ in. (278.5 × 206.7 cm). Palace Museum, Beijing (gu6477).

Therefore, the style was an ideal choice for this fictional and permanent New Year scene, even though the imperial family would actually wear hierarchical court gowns to celebrate this occasion.

The central image in the tapestry shows a strong affinity to a type of painting developed at the Qianlong court—the "New Year picture" (*suizhao tu*)—which depicts celebration scenes populated by generic figures or a mixture of real imperial family members and fictional ones, all dressed in ancient Chinese style. Usually large in scale, these paintings feature similar compositions consisting of an open pavilion in a courtyard set against a wintry landscape. Several of them portray the Qianlong emperor sitting inside the central pavilion and surrounded by young boys playing festival games, holding New Year's ritual paraphernalia, or handling objects that serve as visual puns for auspicious signs (see fig. 109). The visages of the emperor and several princes, and sometimes those of the consorts and attendants, are realistically painted, while other figures have generic faces. Their Chinese clothing enabled the celebration scene and family gathering to outlast a calendar moment and remain as

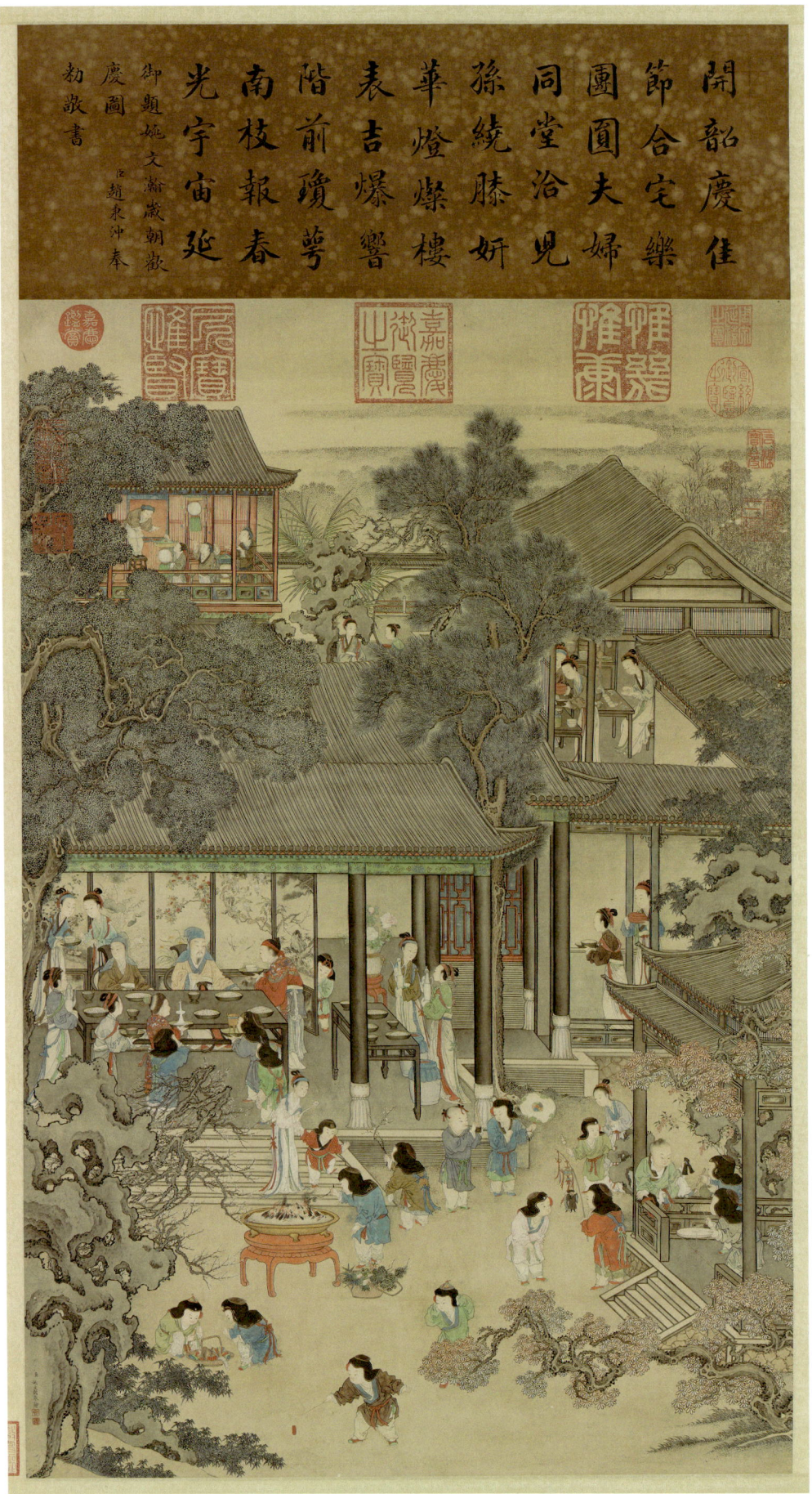

FIG. 110 Yao Wenhan, *New Year Celebration* (*Suizhao huanqing tu*), mid- to late eighteenth century. Hanging scroll, ink and colors on paper, 32½ × 21⅝ in. (82.4 × 55 cm). National Palace Museum, Taipei (guhua2874).

everlasting bliss. It is noteworthy that, in some of these paintings, deceased princes appear as part of the group.[50] The "ancient dress," which enabled the blurring of reality and the traversing of time, also allowed Qianlong to resurrect his lost sons and keep them forever by his side.

New Year pictures that did not incorporate imperial visages were also called "festival figure paintings" (*nianjie renwu hua*). The HJD files record a number of occasions when Qianlong commissioned both European missionaries and Chinese court artists to make such images.[51] A hanging scroll titled *New Year Celebration* (*Suizhao huanqing tu*), dated to the last third of the eighteenth century, by the court painter Yao Wenhan (fl. 1743–?), features imagery and figural styles that resemble those in the New Year tapestry. Some vignettes of the children in the tapestry seem to come from the same stock images (fig. 110).

Although the tapestry's political theme of dynastic continuity encoded in the motifs of a New Year celebration and a houseful of boys may seem a cliché in Qing court arts, it carried special significance in terms of the timing of the hanging's display. Qianlong planned to install the first version of the tapestry in the fall or winter of the thirty-fifth year of his reign (January 1770–February 1771). By Chinese reckoning, this was also the emperor's sixtieth birth year, an extremely important milestone in a person's life cycle, according to Chinese tradition.[52] When Qianlong commissioned the first version of the New Year tapestry and envisioned its display, it is very likely that he had this life event in mind. By this time, Qianlong had suffered through a succession of deaths—ten of his seventeen sons had died, as had his beloved empress, Xiaoxian (1712–1748)—and the choice of his heir had become an increasingly pressing issue.[53] For an elderly emperor at a critical age reflecting on his life and the future of the Qing Empire, the loss of so many sons and the difficulty of establishing a crown prince must have been devastating and distressing. In the Confucian value system, the most joyful thing for an elderly person was a household full of male descendants, and in the imperial context, the abundance of male offspring and their well-being ensured dynastic continuity and prosperity. Anxious about his heir and wishing to sustain a thriving imperial family, Qianlong undoubtedly found visual and psychological reassurance in the paintings, objects, and interior decorations that repeatedly featured joyous family scenes with boys at play, all represented in "eternal" Chinese costumes and thus untouched by the passage of time. Such images flourished especially in the period beginning around Qianlong's sixtieth birthday.[54] The New Year tapestry, which hung in the emperor's primary bedroom compound, was one of many projects in this focused image-making endeavor.

The iconography of this tapestry also anticipated the central theme of a grander pictorial and decorative program for Qianlong's retirement quarters, which he conceived sometime around his sixtieth year and ordered to be constructed right after his birthday celebration. When Qianlong became crown prince in 1735, he vowed that he would abdicate the throne in his sixtieth year of reign so as not to surpass the duration of his grandfather Kangxi's reign. At the age of sixty, during the same year he commissioned the New Year tapestry, Qianlong began to seriously consider his retirement plans.[55] The construction and decoration of this future residence—the Palace of Peace and Longevity, a garden complex on the northeast corner of the Forbidden City—took place between 1771 and 1779, though he never actually lived there after retiring in 1795.[56] This palace featured the theme of familial bliss throughout its decor, as exemplified by three full-wall trompe l'oeil paintings inside the Retreat for Cultivating Harmony (*Yanghe jingshe*) and the Pavilion of Jade Essence (*Yucui xuan*) (fig. 111).[57] It was no coincidence that Qianlong commissioned the third version of the New Year tapestry in 1776 for the Hall of Delight in Longevity in the retirement residence, which would serve as one more component in a large pictorial program repeating the same message across different rooms.

If the central image of the New Year tapestry fully embraced Chinese pictorial conventions and resonated with the Manchu emperor's dynastic concerns, the "Western-ness" of this "Western" tapestry resided in its framing devices, which were directly appropriated from European sources. As integrated parts of the overall woven design, the rococo-style border mimicking a gilded frame and the large curtain running along the top edge of the image did not simply add exotic ornaments to the hanging: they assumed multivalent roles to connect the tapestry's imagery, the space it occupied, and the viewer. First, the frame and the curtain operated as a self-conscious reflection on the unique materiality that distinguished the Western tapestry medium from hanging scrolls and trompe l'oeil wall paintings by alluding to the window concealed behind the artwork as well as to the malleability of textiles, which could be rolled and folded.

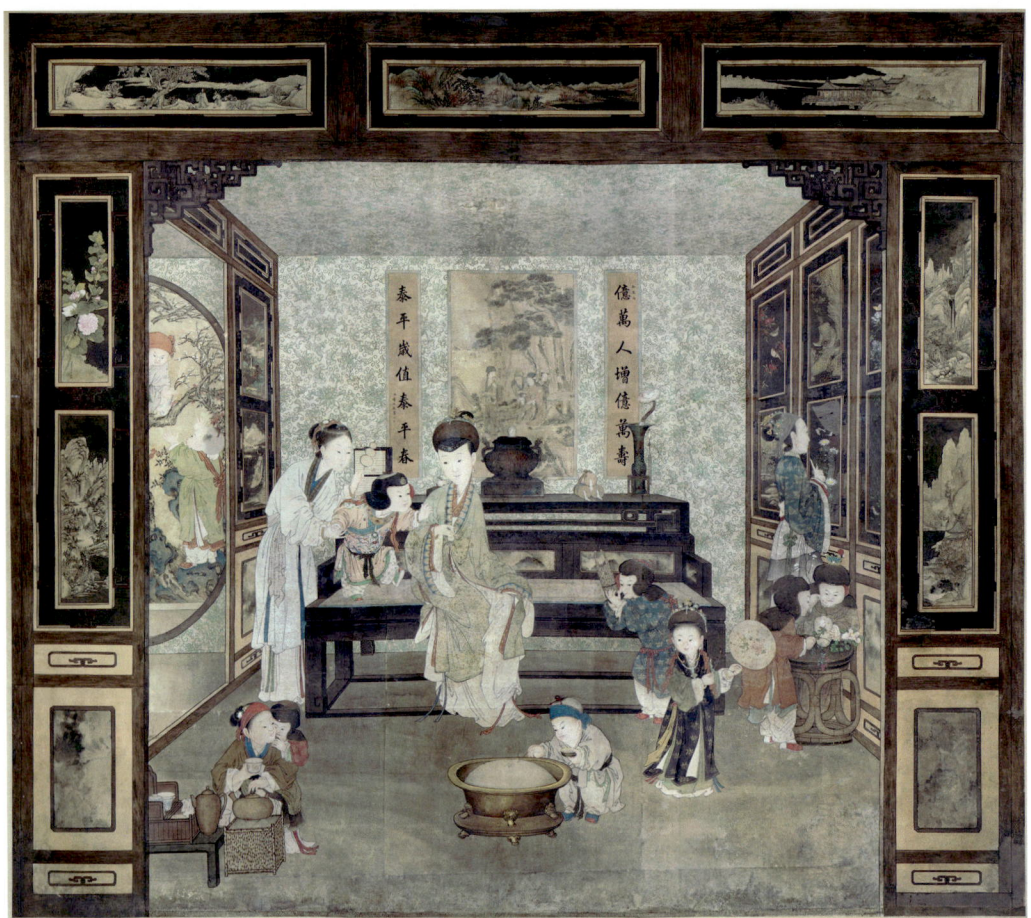

FIG. 111 Yao Wenhan, Wang Youxue, and others, *Women and Children in an Interior Hall*, 1775. Affixed painting (tieluo), ink and colors on silk, 10 ft. 4¾ in. × 12 ft. ¼ in. (317 × 366.5 cm). Palace Museum, Beijing (gu199017).

More importantly, as a dramatic threshold between the real and represented spaces, the frame and the curtain at once foregrounded a sense of boundary and complicated it. The two devices worked together to anchor the represented scene to the architectural space, drawing the inhabitant or spectator in the room into an interactive relationship with the central image while serving as theatrical visual apparatuses for the Qianlong emperor to reenact the tapestry's central theme.

The border of the New Year tapestry imitates a carved and gilded European frame with a convex profile in the rococo style, a common design in eighteenth-century French tapestries informed by actual painting frames.[58] Evidently, the second *Tenture chinoise* provided the primary model for the border design of the Qing tapestry. The four corners were intended to reproduce the rocaille-style shell motif featured in the Beauvais set (fig. 112), but it seems that neither the court artists who drew the cartoon nor the Suzhou weavers who produced the piece understood this rococo ornament. Both the 1771 and 1776 weavings render its structure and proportions rather awkwardly: the fan-shaped compartments are simplified and distorted, and the depth and volume are misinterpreted as incoherent decorative stripes (figs. 113, 114). The Qing pieces also replaced the original acanthus leaves running along the edges with abstract, convoluted rinceaux that only remotely resemble the French design (see fig. 96). A crestlike motif featuring a small palmette rising from a shell and flanked by striped bands sits at the center of the Qing versions' upper and lower borders—the places for a coat of art in French tapestries (fig. 115). Very different from the impaled arms of France and Navarre seen on the second *Tenture chinoise*, this Qing "crest" appears to be a modified version of the corner rocaille structure.

It is rather intriguing that Qianlong chose a border in a conspicuously foreign style to reframe time-honored Manchu-Chinese imagery. In early modern global exchanges, cross-cultural reframing often involved the aesthetic redefinition and cultural domestication of foreign objects. In Europe, for instance, ornate metal mounts in contemporary decorative styles were added to Chinese porcelain vases to highlight their preciousness and enhance their physical allure. In a similar way, European astronomical instruments in the Qing imperial

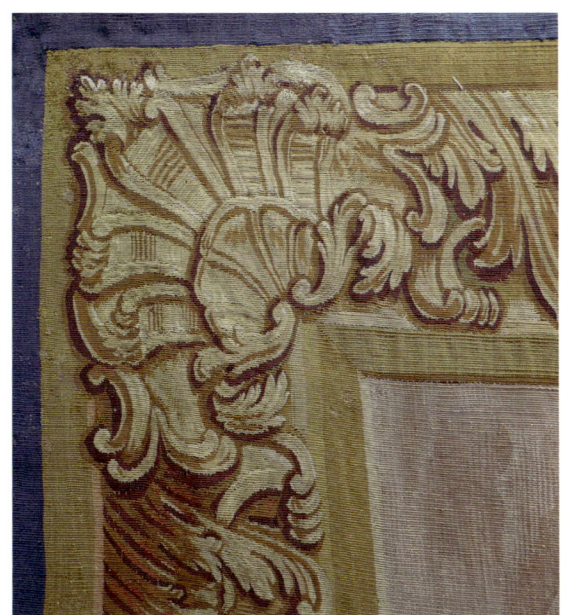

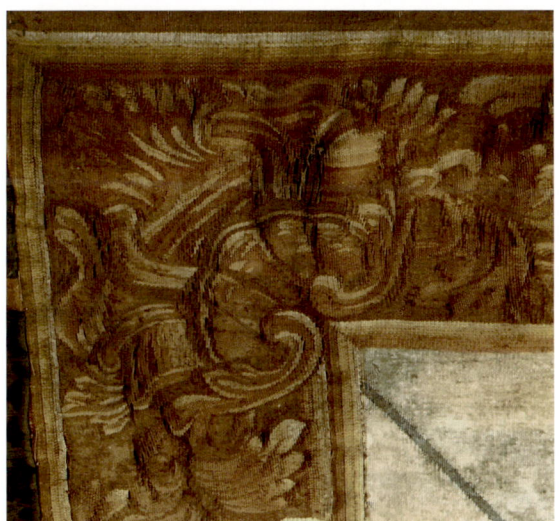

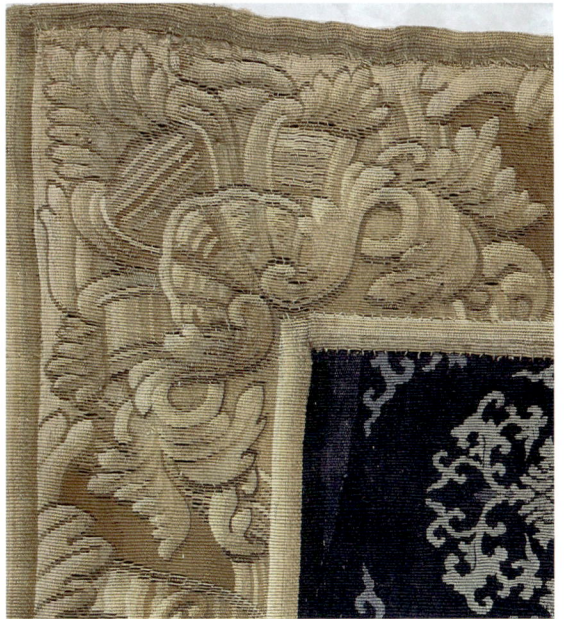

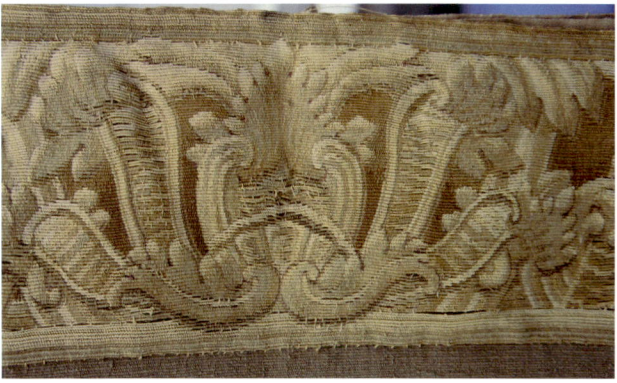

FIG. 115 Detail of fig. 94.

observatory were elevated with elaborately sculpted pedestals featuring Chinese cosmic symbols, especially dragons and clouds.[59] In contrast to this more typical pattern of transcultural reframing, in which foreign objects were admitted into a familiar aesthetic system or symbolic order through the native motifs that marked the boundary, Qianlong's choice passed as the very opposite act: here the rococo-style border served to defamiliarize the conventional pictorial idiom and to prescribe new ways of seeing and experiencing the image. The Western frame not only highlighted the foreignness of the novel tapestry medium, but also functioned as a new visual mechanism to deliver time-honored auspicious messages.

Although awkwardly rendered, the Western borders of the New Year tapestries would have been read by Qianlong as a trompe l'oeil Western painting frame rather than as generic decorative bands. Indeed, the emperor was familiar with the visual experience associated with framed images, which differed significantly from traditional Chinese-style silk and paper mountings characterized by a flat, soft, and flexibly sized surface field. While this mounting format continued to be used, the Qing court also placed pictorial panels within solid frames, an innovation that dovetailed with the imperial predilection for commissioning pictures executed in nonconventional

FIG. 112 (LEFT, TOP) *Chinese Fair*, from the second *Tenture chinoise* series, detail, c. 1758–60. Made by the Atelier André-Charlemagne Charron, the Manufacture royale de Beauvais. Tapestry, wool and silk, 11 ft. 9¾ in. × 20 ft. 10¾ in. (360 × 637 cm). Galerie Armand Deroyan et Maison Pierre-Yves Machault, Paris.

FIG. 113 (LEFT, CENTER) Detail of fig. 93.

FIG. 114 (LEFT, BOTTOM) Detail of fig. 94.

painting media, such as enameled copper, cloisonné, and precious stones. Made of plain or carved sandalwood, phoebe wood, or lacquered softwoods, these frames had a pronounced thickness and could thus demarcate the boundary of the image by forming a vivid material and visual contrast with it. Some of these frames featured Western-style ornaments. For example, in 1775, Qianlong ordered Sichelbart to paint "Western-style decorations" (*xiyáng shi huawen*) on a phoebe wood frame for a Western watercolor painted by Poirot.[60]

No surviving examples of original European gilded frames have surfaced from the collections in the two Palace Museums, but historical records show that seventeenth- and eighteenth-century European portraits were presented to the Qing emperors, including one of King Afonso VI of Portugal (r. 1656–83), a group of likenesses of Louis XIV and other French royals, and two unspecified portraits by the French painter Louis Vigée (1715–1767).[61] As important diplomatic gifts, these works would undoubtedly have come with elaborate frames in the fashion of the period. Bertin clearly noted that Vigée's portraits, included among his 1765 gifts for Qianlong, were sent "with glass and frames."[62] These paintings were probably small-scale, half-length portraits in pastel, like other works of Vigée, but full-length European likenesses also existed in the Qing palaces, as recorded by Paul Varin (Charles Dupin) in his 1862 memoir on his expedition in China. In Qianlong's European Palaces right before they were ransacked, the French lieutenant observed that the walls were decorated with "full-length portraits of beauties of the court of France, with their names at the bottom."[63] Presumably some of these paintings carried European frames that projected into space with their fanciful, three-dimensional gilded designs.

The ornate and lustrous gilded frames would have generated a new sensory experience unlike those associated with the muted Chinese silk mountings or solemn wooden frames that were ubiquitous at the Qing court. The woven borders of the two New Year tapestries, especially the 1776 version, capture this visual effect of unevenly reflected light. Closely following the French model, the Qing tapestries painstakingly represent how the light falls on the trompe l'oeil carved patterns, whose "high relief" showcases the contrast of bright and dark and the glistening "metal" surface. Threads in several shades ranging from dark gray to brown to light yellow are carefully manipulated to achieve the effect of highlights, shadows, and gradations of light (see figs. 96, 114, 115). As in the border of the second *Tenture chinoise*, the implied light in the Qing tapestries comes from the upper right, illuminating the outer edges of the top and right borders and the inner edges of the lower and left ones. In the French set, the direction of the light reflected by the woven frame is consistent with that cast on the figures in the central field, and the border seems a logical extension of the central pictorial field. By contrast, the central scene in the Qing tapestry indicates no precise light source; the frame's light effect hints at a hyperreal time and space detached from the scene it encloses. The trompe l'oeil frame of the tapestry projected its own space in between the framed content—a "special world" of representation—and the surrounding reality.

As the literature scholar and poet Susan Stewart puts it, the "special world" framed as an artistic representation both "envelops" and "does not envelop" its viewers. "The confrontation with and participation in the work of art

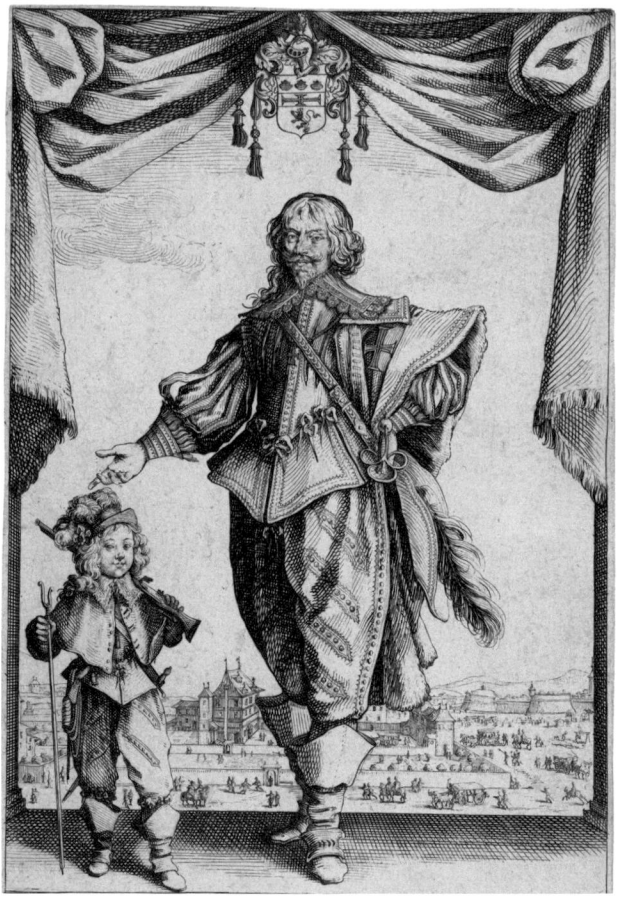

FIG. 116 Jacques Callot, *Portrait of Claude Deruet and His Son, Jean*, c. 1632. Etching and engraving, plate 11⅝ × 6¾ in. (29.5 × 17.1 cm). Metropolitan Museum of Art, New York, bequest of Grace M. Pugh, 1985 (1986.1180.343).

is as much a multiplication of realities as it is a transition between realities. . . . The frame is a communicative gesture, an invitation. . . . It is the scene of transformation."[64] In Qianlong's tapestry, the pronounced European frame oriented the boundary between multiple realities while itself being a projected reality, an illusionary surface. To step in and out of the frame was a two-way transformation between the worlds that unfolded in different temporal and spatial rhythms. When hung on the wall, the tapestry border not only framed the depicted scene; it simultaneously framed two layers of overlapping activities and narratives, turning the real world occupied by Qianlong that was encompassed within its limits into yet another vignette and spectacle.

The enormous overhead curtain suspended along the top edge of both tapestries below the border adds an additional layer of visual and spatial complexity. It does not belong to the interior scene but instead is situated on the same surface level as the frame. Like the frame, the curtain image as a boundary-making device rather than a mimetic representation was an appropriated European motif, and in that specific room, it, too, demarcated a transitional dividing line between the real and the fictional, while articulating an interface between the beholder and the image.

Stylized curtains in painted or sculpted form had long been a part of Chinese funerary and religious contexts, serving to delineate the afterlife or spiritual realms.[65] In Chinese pictorial art for secular and nonburial purposes, however, images of drapery did not have a significant presence until the eighteenth century, when a novel visual language of threshold drapery flourished, especially in Qing court arts. No longer depicted as a small detail attached to a building or a bed as in previous paintings, the curtain now gained prominence and autonomy in a picture's composition, directly confronting the viewer and possessing an expressive power. Jesuit painters serving at the Qing palaces probably introduced this new visual mode, which may have also been disseminated through European images circulated in the network uniting the port of Canton, the southern commercial centers of Suzhou and Yangzhou, and the Qing court. The European modes of depicting curtains—whether two panels symmetrically drawn, a single panel pulled to one side, or an overarching type looped and suspended above—graced Qing court paintings, decorative objects, and images incorporated into architectural spaces alike. This new motif engendered a fresh visual experience. The drapery encouraged an interaction between the viewer and the painted content; meanwhile, the confronting curtain induced a new theatrical sense, both in the presentation of and encounter with the image.

The motif of threshold drapery had a long tradition in European pictorial art, and since the Renaissance it had often served as a revelatory and glorifying device framing an icon, person, or scene. Symmetrically pulled curtains in religious paintings, famously rendered in Raphael's *Sistine Madonna* (c. 1513–14), have been variously interpreted as a symbolic instrument for revelation, an evocation of the divine, and an announcement of a vision.[66] By the seventeenth century, the use of such drapery for secular subjects as an honorary device was also widespread; a typical example can be seen in the circa 1632 print *Portrait of Claude Deruet and His Son, Jean* (fig. 116). This device, frequently present in European prints and undoubtedly familiar to Jesuit missionary painters, was adopted for the Qianlong emperor's informal portraits. In an oil painting representing him at a senior age sitting on a platform bed and writing, he is flanked by symmetrically drawn curtains (fig. 117). Given the life-size dimensions, perspective, and tieluo format of this portrait, it was probably an illusionistic image intended to fill a niche wall. As actual alcove beds in Qing imperial and royal residences were sometimes furnished with parted curtains, this honorary drapery in Qianlong's portrait doubled as a trompe l'oeil element (see fig. 92).

During the seventeenth and eighteenth centuries, European depictions of drapery became more dynamic and were used to frame portraits, religious themes, landscapes, event and history paintings, and genre images alike. A raised curtain arranged in an eye-catching shape and hung along the edge of the picture plane creates a deliberate visual ambiguity, as it appears disconnected from the main scene yet aligned with the external border, contributing to a dramatic sense of presentation, disclosure, or even voyeurism. Such images were among the European prints that reached the Qing court. One example is the engraved booklet *The Pleasures of the Enchanted Island* (*Les Plaisirs de l'isle enchantée*), which commemorated the 1664 performance under the same name at Versailles. It was part of the Cabinet du Roi prints that French Jesuits received from the Marquis de Louvois in 1685 and presented to Kangxi in 1688.[67] The frontispiece and the title vignette feature a curtain along the picture's

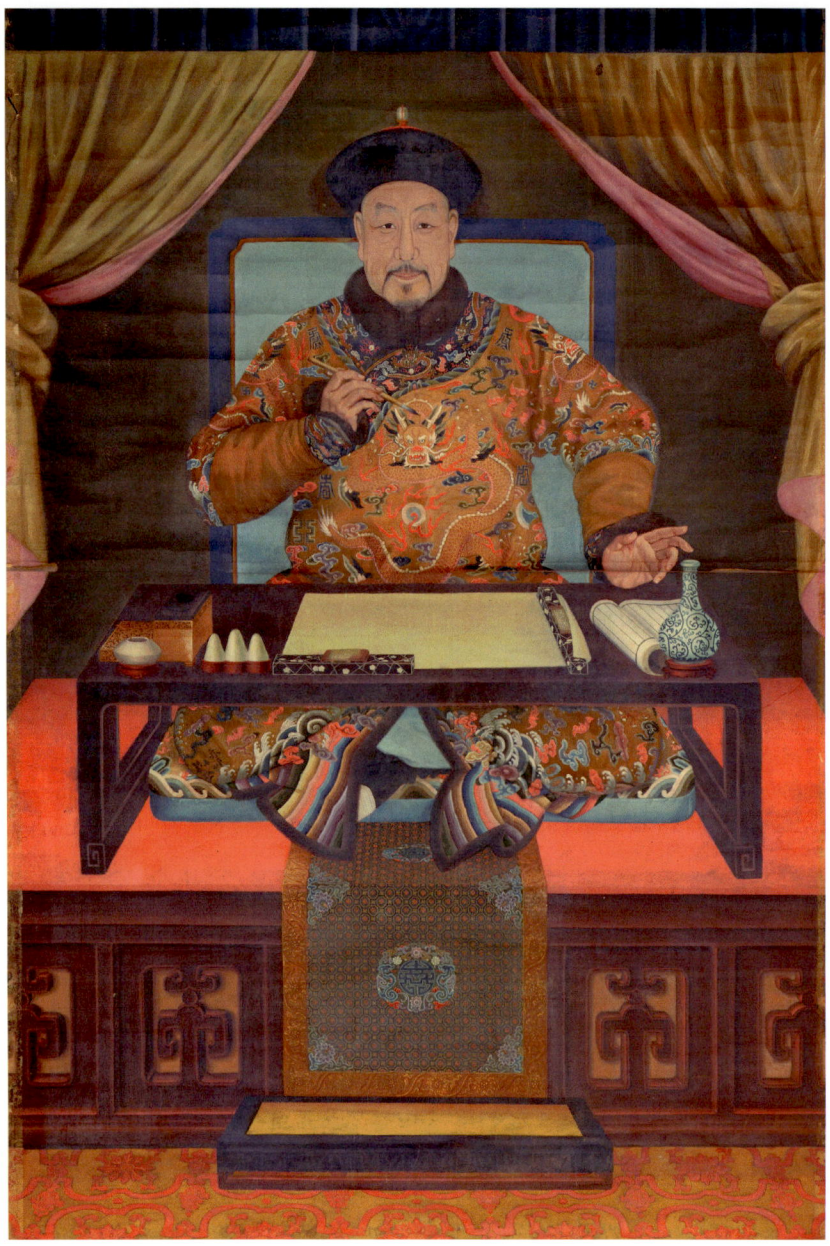

FIG. 117 Qing court artist(s), *The Qianlong Emperor Writing*, late eighteenth century. Affixed painting (tieluo), oil on paper, 80 ¾ × 53 ¼ in. (205 × 135.4 cm). Palace Museum, Beijing (gu6530).

upper edge, in a way quite similar to the one in Qianlong's 1776 New Year tapestry in its slim shape and parted arrangement (fig. 118). Gobelins and Beauvais tapestries also explored the design scheme of a unified frame-curtain arrangement, made possible because a tapestry's typical format included an integrated woven border. The frame-curtain can be seen in *The Meeting between Louis XIV and Philip IV on Pheasants Island* (*Entrevue de Louis XIV Roy de France et de Navarre et de Philippe IV, Roy d'Espagne dans l'isle des faisans*) from the Gobelins tapestry series *History of the King*, which was reproduced in an engraving in 1728 (fig. 119). Likewise, the piece *Don Quixote Undressed by the Duchess's Maids* (*Don Quichotte déshabillé par les demoiselles de la Duchesse*) from the Beauvais suite *Stories of Don Quixote* (*L'Histoire de Don Quichotte*) features a red curtain suspended below the gilded rococo frame (fig. 120). In the latter case, the curtain at once plays a rhetorical role and unveils a stage performance represented in the main field.

This European mode of depicting drapery as an expansive curtain drawn overhead introduced to Qing court arts a new sense of spectacle and theatricality. The term *theatricality* used here does not necessarily imply an actual performance, although in Europe this use of curtains was strongly associated with the stage, as exemplified in both the *Enchanted Island* engraving and the *Don Quixote* tapestry. In a broad sense, *theatricality* refers to an experience

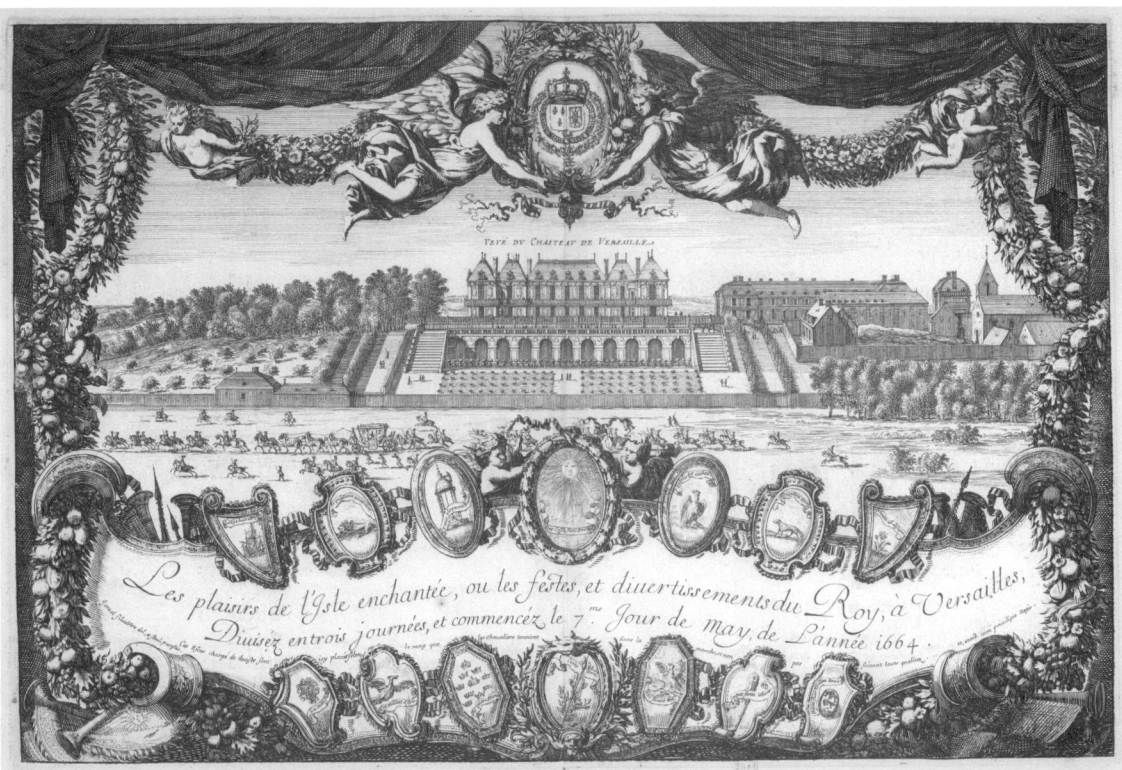

FIG. 118 Frontispiece to *The Pleasures of the Enchanted Island* (*Les Plaisirs de l'isle enchantée*), (Paris: Imprimerie royale, 1673). Engraved album. Bibliothèque nationale de France, Paris, Réserve, RES-V-498.

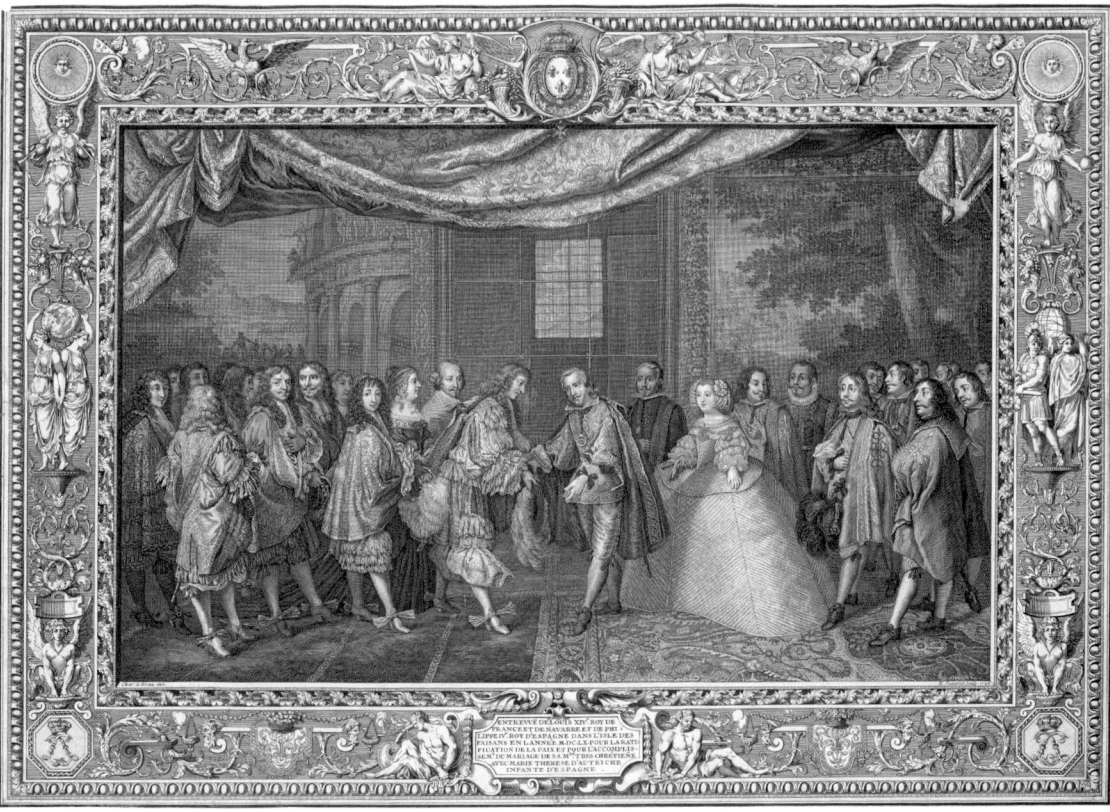

FIG. 119 *The Meeting between Louis XIV and Philip IV on Pheasants Island* (*Entrevue de Louis XIV Roy de France et de Navarre et de Philippe IV Roy d'Espagne dans l'isle des faisans en l'année M. DC. LX*), 1728. Engraving after the tapestry designed by Charles Le Brun. Bibliothèque nationale de France, Paris, Réserve, QB-201 (43)-FOL.

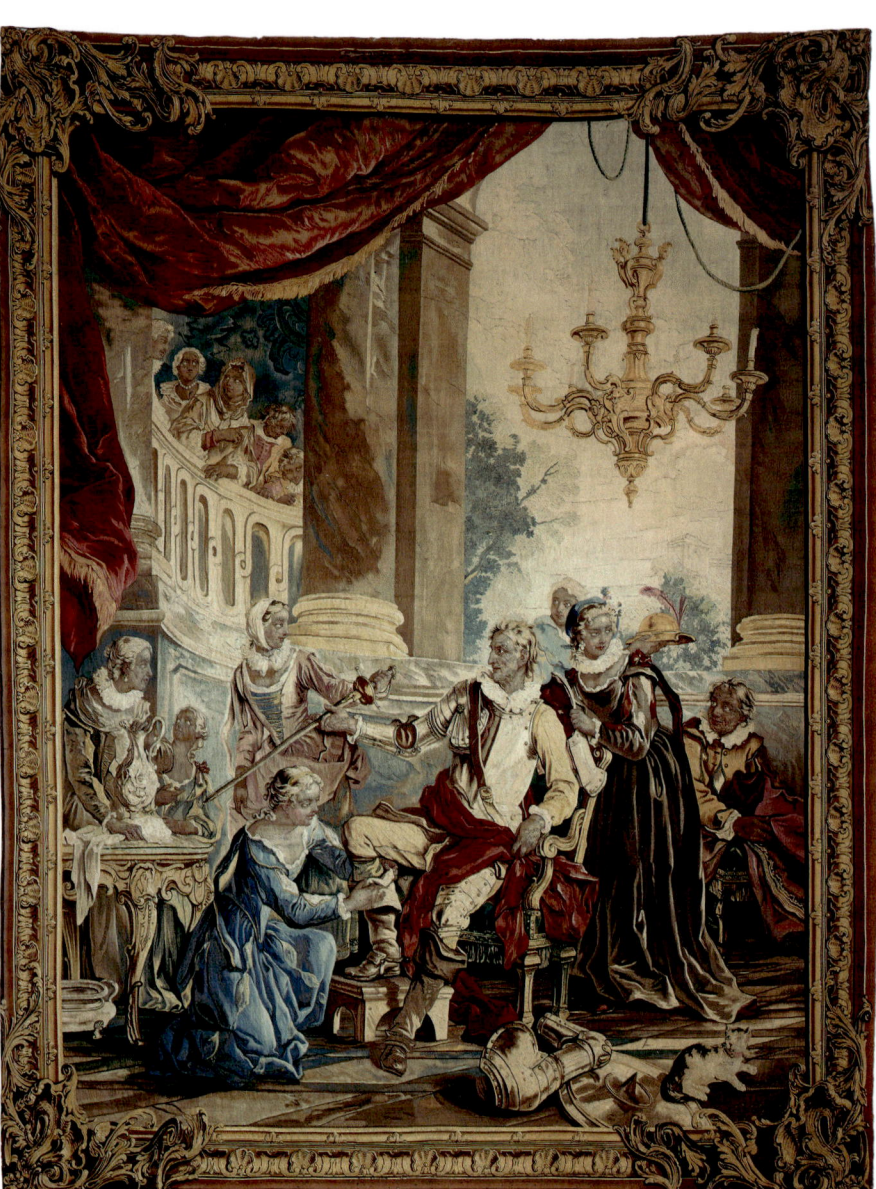

FIG. 120 *Don Quixote Undressed by the Duchess's Maids* (*Don Quichotte déshabillé par les demoiselles de la Duchesse*), from the series *L'Histoire de Don Quichotte*, eighteenth century. Made by the Manufacture royale de Beauvais. Tapestry, wool and silk, 11 ft. 9¾ in. × 9 ft. 2¼ in. (360 × 280 cm). Musée des Tapisseries, Aix-en-Provence.

or ambience evoked by stage-related elements that appear in a different context, as well as a dramatized moment of presentation or cognition. Since the fifteenth century, European theaters had deployed a front curtain to conceal and reveal the stage, and thus to demarcate the boundary between the real and the fictive. This function had become ubiquitous by the seventeenth century.[68] By contrast, late imperial Chinese theaters never employed a curtain at the front of the stage to signify the opening and closing of a play or transitions between the various acts. Instead, two small doors with or without curtains at the back of the stage, through which actors constantly entered and exited, mediated the perception of theatrical time and space.[69] During the eighteenth century, Qing imperial patrons were exposed to European-style representations of the front stage curtain and would have understood its theatrical implication as an alternative mode to Chinese theatricality. This new mode can be seen in a hybrid-style clock, made in Canton and presented to Qianlong, which combined a European mechanism and design with the auspicious Chinese motif of immortal monkeys offering longevity peaches for a birthday (fig. 121). A metal mount representing an overarching drapery along the upper edge and sides of the miniature theater frames the timed performance of the automata monkeys. To a degree, the curtains in the two versions of the New Year tapestries evoke a European-style front stage curtain.

The composition of a curtain draped above a domestic scene, similar to the one in the New Year tapestry, is widely seen in Canton export works dated to the mid- to

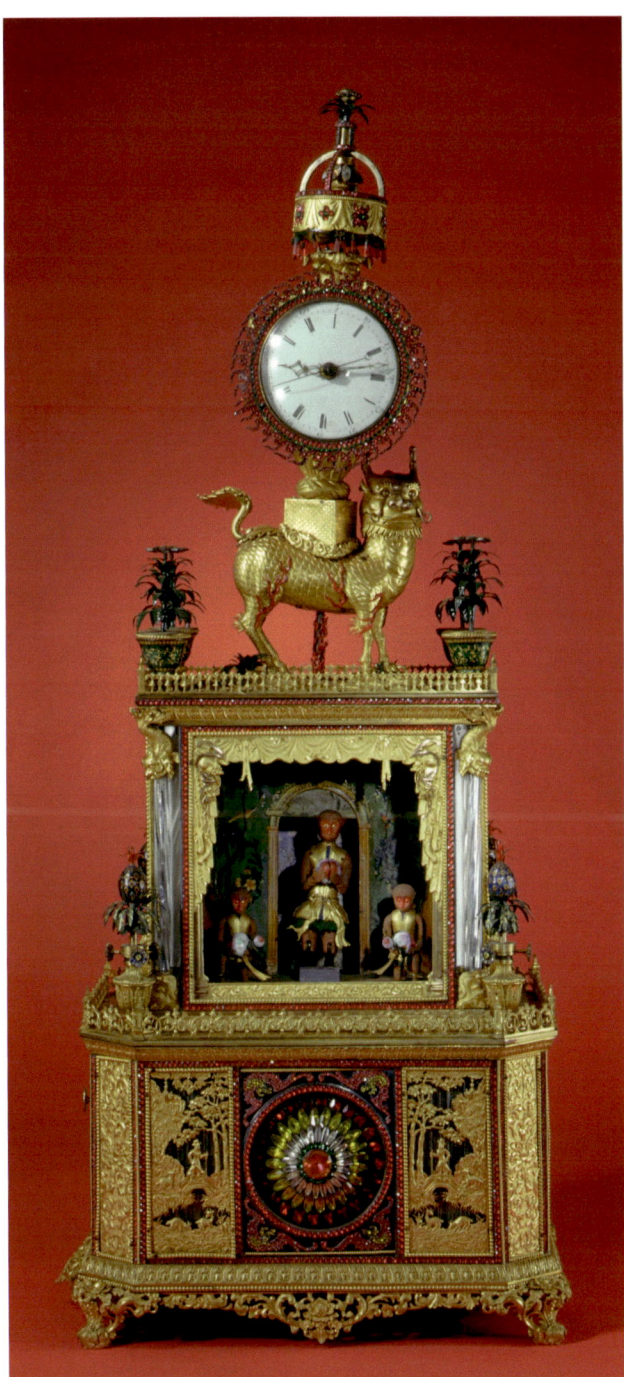

FIG. 121 Clock decorated with immortal monkeys presenting birthday peaches for longevity, mid- to late eighteenth century. Made in Canton for the Qing court. Gilt bronze, 43¼ × 15¾ × 16⅛ in. (110 × 40 × 41 cm). Palace Museum, Beijing (gu182712).

late eighteenth century, which suggests that both the court and Canton were informed by shared foreign sources. It is also possible that images and objects made in Canton helped disseminate the motif of the overhead curtain to the Qing court. Canton officials regularly presented local products in the Western style as gifts to the Qing emperors, and these objects often displayed a striking kinship with Chinese export works that assimilated European visual languages.[70] A multimedia export plaque made in Canton around 1770 and formerly in a Dutch collection bears a close resemblance to the 1771 version of the New Year tapestry in terms of the disposition and rendering of the curtain (fig. 122). In addition to the volumetric and rhythmic shape of the drapery, the plaque and tapestry share similar depictions of the small monochrome pattern on the fabric and the stylized, incised folds.

The European drapery motif circulated to Canton was taken up there as a design element for reframing Chinese domestic scenes in export paintings. The curtain imbued these images with the European sensibility of revelation and theatricality and at the same time heightened the exoticness of Chinese domestic life for European consumers, turning the viewing experience into an act of "unveiling" other people's culture. Mediating between China and Europe, the drapery redefined Chinese imagery through a European visual convention. When transplanted into Qing court arts, the same pictorial language of drapery reframed and redefined familiar Chinese imagery by prescribing a fresh viewing experience, while invigorating and reinforcing a time-honored narrative. It is not surprising that, despite its foreign-style disposition and shape, the curtain in the New Year tapestries is patterned with auspicious Chinese floral roundels, echoing the celebratory message of the central image. The 1776 version further incorporates a valance, the type commonly installed in Qing palace interiors. This contrast between form and content refracts the fundamental relationship between Western and Manchu-Chinese components in this Western tapestry design so favored by Qianlong.

As for the 1771 tapestry, it is only when we understand its central image and the Western framing devices as interactive elements in a unified program oriented toward a specific architectural setting can we comprehend Qianlong's thoughtful plan for this textile's design and display. Indeed, everything in the tapestry pointed to a conspicuous absence—the imperial body of the emperor himself. The HJD record clearly indicates that this

Staging Imperial Narratives   141

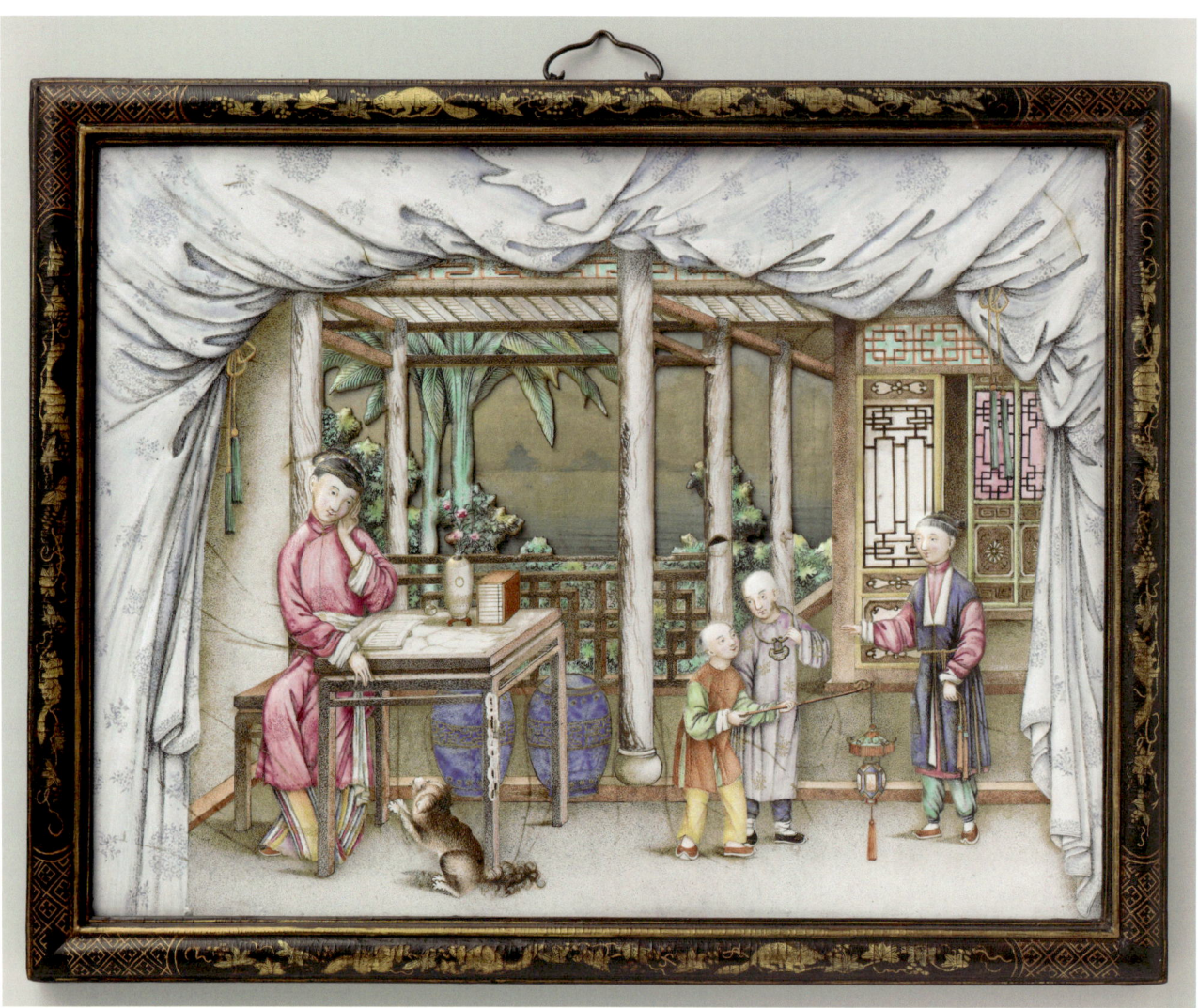

FIG. 122 Plaque depicting an interior with figures, c. 1770–75. Made in Canton for export. Image: enamel on copper, oil on paper; frame: wood with lacquer coating, 14 ⅝ × 19 ⅛ in. (37 × 48.5 cm). Rijksmuseum, Amsterdam (AK-NM-6620-C).

tapestry covered the entire blank space of the north wall above a bed in the rear central bay of the Hall of Mental Cultivation. This bed, as a 1778 HJD entry indicates, was a "throne bed" (*baozuo chuang*).[71] A typical throne bed in the Qing palaces consisted of a seat cushion, a back cushion, and two armrests—all of them movable—which were placed in the center of a platform bed (see fig. 92). Judging from the fixed architectural elements of this complex and a historical plan of this room dated to before the early 1870s renovation, we can infer that during the Qianlong period the tapestry fit in a space that was demarcated by two partition structures flanking the north window. The height of the tapestry corresponded exactly to the dimension between the top edge of the platform bed and the bottom of the ceiling beam.[72] The partitions helped create a meta space evoking a stage. When Qianlong sat on this throne right in front of the tapestry, his upper body would fit perfectly into the empty space deliberately left in the tapestry's central foreground (fig. 123). The emperor himself would thus complete the composition and literally become the focal point of the family scene.

The "gilded" frame and the drapery situated at the threshold between the represented scene and the actual room appeared to enclose the emperor as well, further integrating him into the auspicious space conjured in the tapestry. The curtain at once functioned as an honorary canopy to glorify him and heightened a theatrical sense of revealing his presence. Qianlong's central position, locked in by this visual program, was both physical and symbolic: by inserting his own body into the image, he threw into relief his role as the head of the imperial family. In Confucian doctrine, which the Manchu rulers adopted early on as part of their governing ideologies, the family stood as the primary social unit, and the harmony of the universe was grounded on the correct order in each of the five social relationships: sovereign and subject, husband and wife, parent and child, elder brother and younger brother, friend and friend. The state had its model in the family, and a monarch's ability to govern and ensure harmony in the universe fundamentally depended on his ability to manage a household.[73] Therefore, Qianlong's patriarchal dominance in a harmonious and prosperous family also suggested his status as the powerful father of the people, successfully ruling under the Mandate of Heaven. Intentionally designed to fuse Qianlong's physical body with the family scene, the tapestry facilitated a visual enactment of this message foregrounding his emperorship. The composition and placement of the tapestry also literally surrounded Qianlong with many young boys who were forever alive and energetic, thereby conjuring up a promising world of happiness far from the reality of deceased sons.

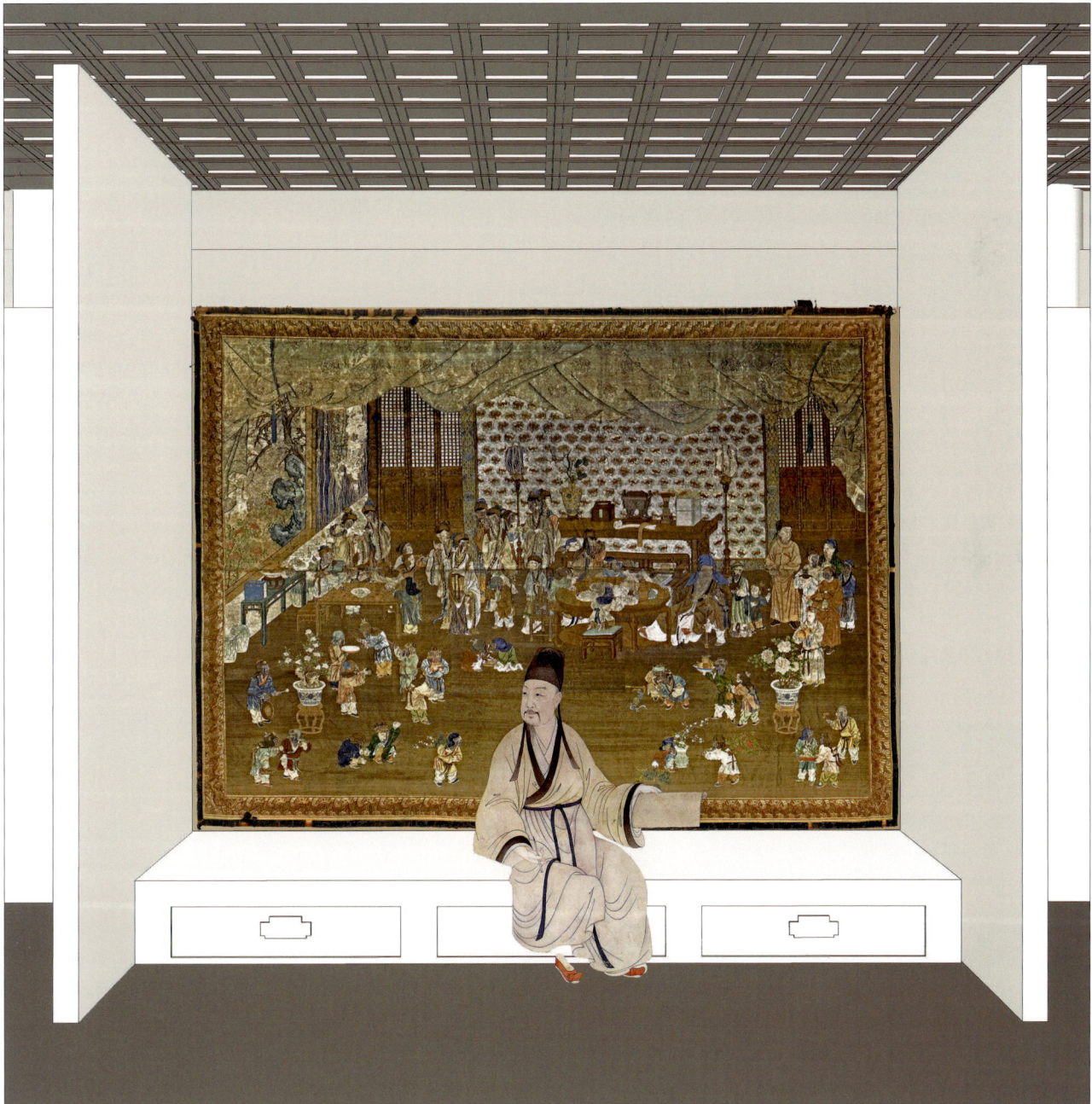

FIG. 123 The position of Qianlong's upper body in relation to the New Year tapestry when he sat on his throne bed. Architectural model by Tao Jin.

Staging Imperial Narratives 143

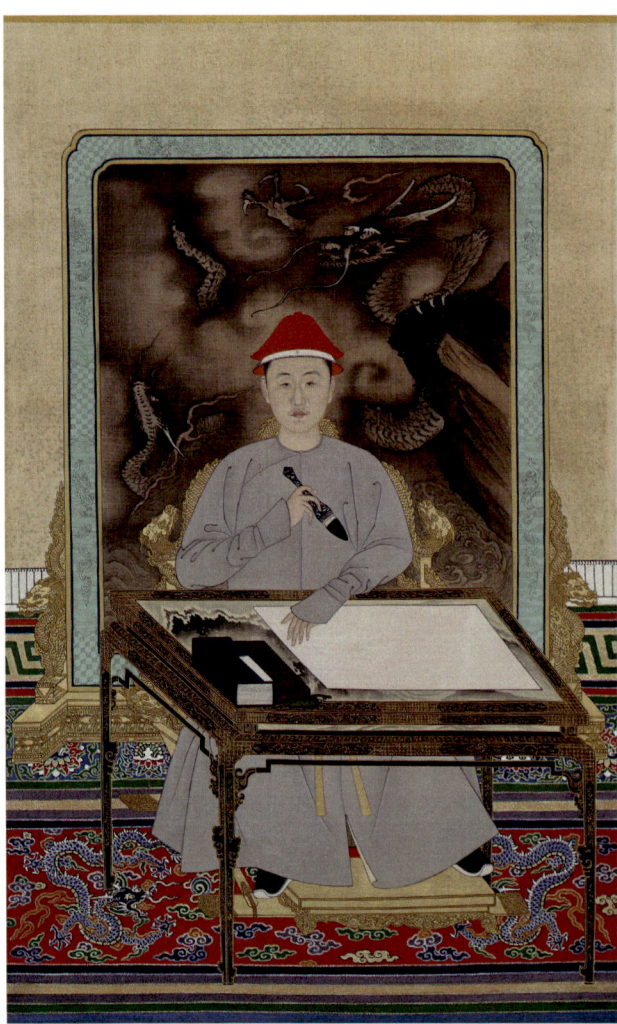

FIG. 124 Qing court artist(s), *The Kangxi Emperor Writing*, mid- to late seventeenth century. Hanging scroll, ink and colors on silk, image 19⅞ × 12½ in. (50.5 × 31.9 cm). Palace Museum, Beijing (gu6402).

The interplay between the emperor's body and a symbolically charged background image was a visual idiom already familiar to Qianlong. Typically, a freestanding screen would furnish the backdrop. The art historian Wu Hung has discussed the ways in which a painted screen placed behind a sitter had long been animated in Chinese art as an allusion to one's status and frame of mind.[74] Qing court images of the Manchu emperors clearly demonstrate a sensitivity in visualizing the ruler and his background screens as a unified whole. For example, in a portrait of the young Kangxi emperor writing in front of a dragon screen, where the emperor and dragon overlap, the latter dissolves into the clouds to make way for the former (fig. 124). As the imperial symbol, the forceful dragon seems to emerge from the emperor's body and manifest his divine identity. Qianlong was particularly fascinated by the visual play involving screens, most tellingly exemplified by the three versions of *One or Two?* (*Shiyi shi'er tu*)—paintings that represent the emperor sitting in front of an orthodox-style landscape screen and confronting his own bust portrait hung on it (fig. 125).[75] The frames of these screens, not unlike the tapestry's border, enclose both the painted image and the emperor in front of it, merging the two together. This interactive relationship between the screen and the sitter, however, was primarily an idealized vision or, rather, a representational idiom manifested only within an image. In reality, not a single screen from the Qing imperial collections shows a composition that accommodates the sitter's body. Only the 1771 New Year tapestry actually realized this ideal in its design. Thanks to its large format, which could transform an entire wall into an illusionary space, it was thus more effective than a standing screen in mapping this visual program onto the architectural space.

Unlike the Western silks examined in chapter 2 that were displayed during the Grand Military Review and the imperial hunt—occasions for demonstrating the Qing Empire's power—the New Year tapestry did not anticipate or require a specially designated audience in order for Qianlong to perform its theme; indeed, few people would have had access to this secluded room. As was the case with the *One or Two?* paintings and several other portraits of Qianlong in which his likeness was inserted into a costumed scene or a composition taken from an old master painting, the emperor engaged with the tapestry in a solitary performance and self-dialogue, and the process of embodying a particular narrative through visual metamorphosis sufficed to fulfill an imperial wish or insinuate a politic agenda.

In a feat of extraordinary imagination, Qianlong did not simply design the tapestry backdrop for his reenactment of the felicitous narrative related to emperorship; he also planned an echoing scene, or perhaps even a fictive audience, on the facing wall. In June 1771, during the same year when the first version of the tapestry was on display and the second one was being woven, Qianlong commissioned a new trompe l'oeil picture for the south wall opposite the New Year scene, for which Sichelbart helped correct the linear perspective.[76] Unfortunately, this painting has not survived, nor was its subject matter recorded. But in light of the theme of familial and dynastic prosperity that permeated this building, this image possibly adopted the same leitmotif and resembled the extant

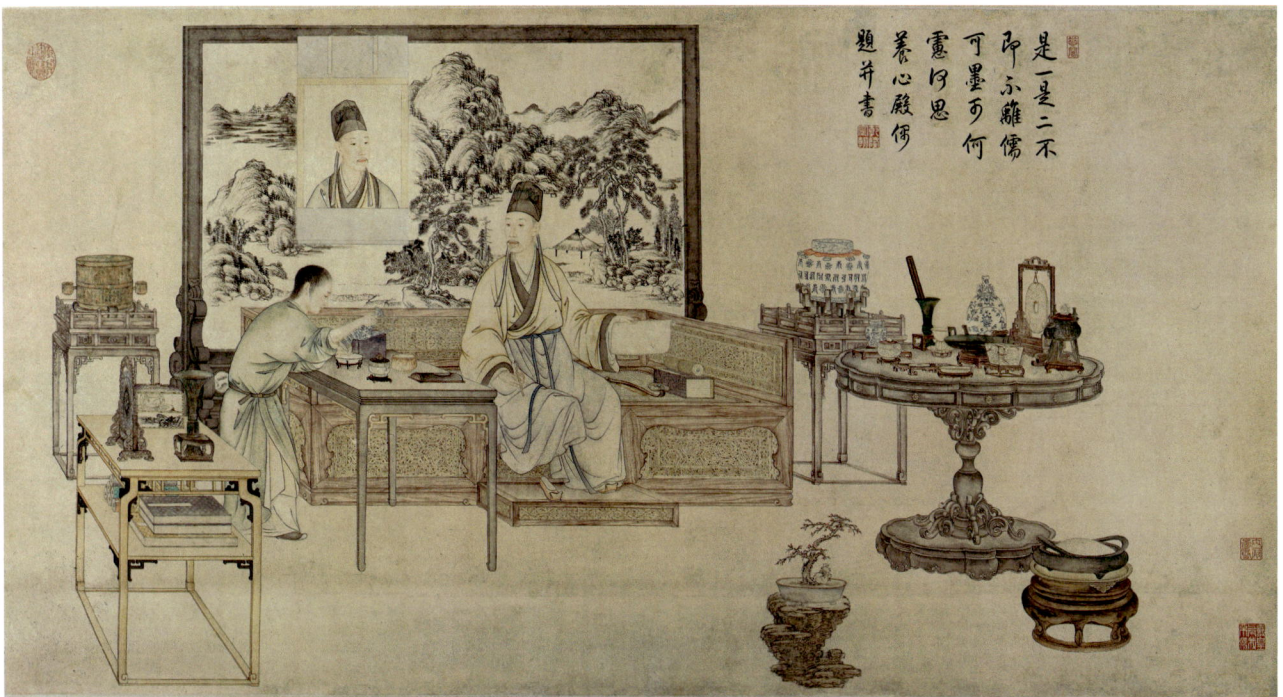

FIG. 125 Qing court artist(s), *One or Two? (Shiyi shi'er tu)*, version for the Hall of Mental Cultivation, mid-eighteenth century. Originally an affixed painting (*tieluo*), remounted as a hanging scroll, ink and colors on paper, 30⅛ × 58 in. (76.5 × 147.2 cm). Palace Museum, Beijing (gu6493).

examples of trompe l'oeil wall paintings in Qianlong's retirement quarter, which depict women and children in interior or outdoor settings (see fig. 111). Perhaps some painted figures were looking at the emperor, who gazed right back at them.

The tapestry thus partook in a full-room visual program that completely transformed the space of the central bay of the rear compound. More than mere interior decorations, the tapestry and the wall painting functioned at once as spectacles, viewing mechanisms, and conjured living images. They dematerialized the architectural boundaries and constructed a cross-referential, intercorporeal narrative that placed the emperor's imperial body at the very center, his physical presence coordinating and animating these two images and spatial systems to simultaneously stage a performance of his emperorship and create a viewership. Situated in an intermediary zone and hybrid in style, the drapery visually and symbolically mirrored the role of Qianlong, whose imperial presence and central domination connected the West and Qing China. This tapestry facilitated the enactment and manifestation of his emperorship on many levels.

The fact that this tapestry was deliberately conceived with site-specific visual cross-references and an intercorporeal narrative is further substantiated by the 1776 version, intended for the Hall of Delight in Longevity in the retirement palace (see fig. 94). This piece differs from the 1771 version in two significant ways: it replaces the Golden Chalice of Eternal Stability with two wine cups held by two sons, and it fills the empty space in the foreground previously reserved for Qianlong with two children. As these clues indicate, this tapestry moved away from the reference to the Opening the Brush ceremony; it probably simply functioned to transform a wall space without engaging with a sitter's body in front of it. With the tapestry disassociated from the site of the Hall of Mental Cultivation and the emperor's immediate physical presence, the meanings and visual effects of the New Year iconography and framing devices changed to accord with the new site and its new function.

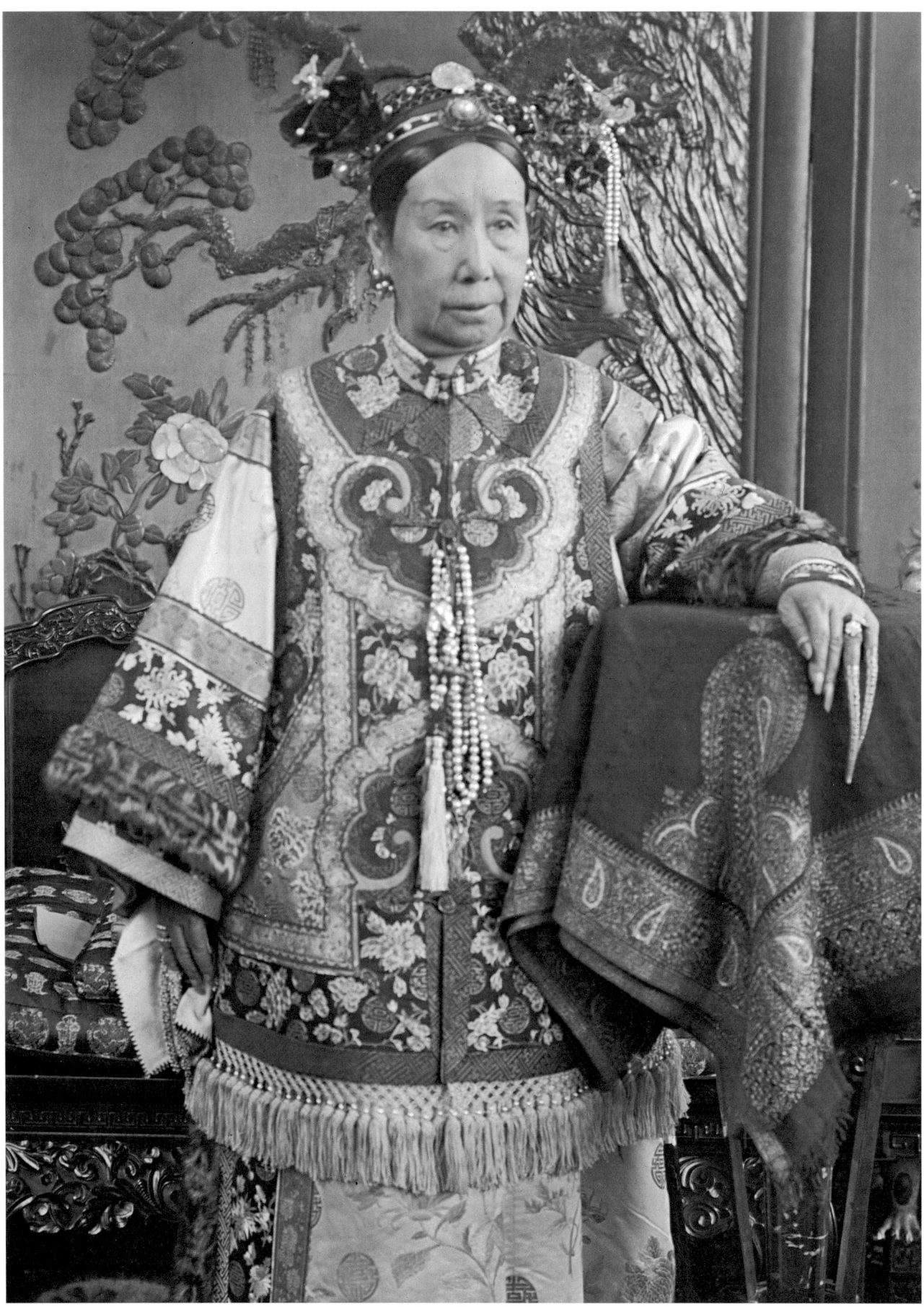

Conclusion

This book has reconnected a group of forgotten textiles that were once prominent at the eighteenth-century Qing court, remapping them in a transcultural framework and contextualizing key examples within Qing imperial political and religious programs. Originally sent as diplomatic gifts or commercial goods, the small number of European luxury silks and tapestries that reached the Qing palaces joined Chinese pieces inspired by their designs and techniques to form a distinct category of imperial textiles that were classified at the Qing court as "Western." As this book has shown, they constituted an unprecedented, innovative force in High Qing arts. By examining multiple key cases in which these textiles furnished new visual and material languages for conveying politically charged messages, this study illuminates how, in various settings, their foreign features enabled the construction of meanings crucial to maintaining Qing imperial rule.

In tracing the eastward movement of luxury textiles from Europe to the Qing Empire in the eighteenth century and uncovering their subsequent transformations and influences on the new culture, this book contributes a revisionist perspective to the current scholarship on early modern global textile history, which mainly views Europe as the consumer and China as the supplier in the network of trade. Although their numbers were small and their uses generally limited to the Qing court, these textiles exerted an exceptional historical significance both in Qing imperial arts and in Sino-European exchanges. They thus offer a unique window into multiple issues related to the early modern transcultural paradigm, among them the dynamic relationships between the global and the local, and the compatibility and adaptability of materials, imagery, and styles across cultures.

NETWORKS AND PLAYERS

The trajectories of the various textiles examined in this study crossed expansive geographic areas, including France, Italy, Portugal, Netherlands, England, Russia, and Siam; Canton, Suzhou, Rehe, and Tibet in the Qing Empire; and above all the Qing court in Beijing—the center at which multiple networks intersected. These entangled networks, both local and global, fueled by religious, commercial, diplomatic, political, or bureaucratic purposes, enabled the transfer and transformation of these textiles while shaping their meanings over these courses. The Jesuit missions in China served as the first conduit for transmitting objects, technologies, artistic styles, and knowledge between China and Europe. European missionaries were instrumental in facilitating the arrival of European tapestries at the Qing court and in advancing new designs for Qing imperial Western tapestries. Their artistic skills and knowledge of both European and Chinese court cultures contributed to the successful adaptation of this prestigious European textile medium into an equally powerful and expressive one that was fully integrated into the Qing palace environments and visual programs.

Two official trading systems permitted by the Qing government—the maritime trade with the European East India companies in the entrepôt of Canton and the overland commercial exchanges with Russia in the border city of Kyakhta—provided the second channel for the Qing court to acquire European textiles, in addition to the metal threads for weaving that were coveted by the Qianlong emperor. It is most likely that the luxury items that entered the court through these systems were special imperial orders rather than regular commodities imported for the mass market. The Russian trade in particular ensured the supply of a type of elaborate floral silk, which pleased Qianlong's taste and became a staple among the Western textiles that adorned Tibetan Buddhist spaces.

The third and most important channel for precious silks and tapestries to enter the Qing imperial domains was diplomatic contacts. European countries such as the Netherlands and Portugal periodically sent envoys to the Qing court and presented gifts that included not only their national products but also goods that had been outsourced, reexported, or regifted from their trading partners—in other words, objects already enmeshed in the network of cross-regional transactions. Once at the Qing court, such gifts were registered indistinguishably as "tribute" and bore witness to a world order that foregrounded the centrality and dominance of the Qing Empire. Another type of diplomatic liaison was unofficial, as when the French statesman Bertin sought to introduce French luxury goods to the Qing emperor and court elites through Jesuit priests in China, who acted as intermediaries. Although Bertin's idealistic vision of cultural and commercial exchanges ultimately went unfulfilled, his attempt nevertheless succeeded in stimulating the Qing imperial interest in French tapestries. Moreover, in an outcome never envisioned or desired by the French, this mission directly motivated the Qianlong emperor to produce his own versions of Western tapestries.

Within the Qing Empire, the court's procurement and production of Western textiles were supported by the well-implemented bureaucratic systems that linked the central government with regional administrations. As we have seen in the records of the Imperial Workshops, the court did not communicate with European merchants directly; rather, it was the supervisor of the Canton Customs Bureau who acted as agent and coordinated the special orders sent by the emperor. Likewise, when commissioning Western silks and tapestries, the court passed on the emperor's instructions to the directors of the Imperial Silk Manufactory in Suzhou, and its supervisor then oversaw the corresponding production. In addition, an internal tribute system enabled regional officials to demonstrate loyalty and resourcefulness through gift presentations to the emperor. Many rare and luxury objects entered the Qing court through this channel, including European silks and tapestries. Once selected for this purpose, the foreign commodities that arrived in China changed their course and became part of a new mechanism, one that operated to maintain the hierarchical relationship between the emperor and his subordinates.

The functions and new meanings of the Western silks at the Qing court were critical to another highly important network in the Qing Empire—namely, the political and cultural ties between the Manchu ruler and the leaders of Mongolia, Tibet, and the Uyghur region. This network was essential to maintaining the multiethnic and multicultural identity of the Qing Empire and to distinguish the Manchu regime from previous Han Chinese dynasties. In this context, Western silks served as a prominent material symbol to convey the values and traditions that Manchus and Inner Asian elites shared, such as hunting, military might, and the belief in Tibetan Buddhism. To an extent, we may conjecture that the distinctly non-Chinese patterns and material features of Western silks visually and conceptually resonated with these non-Han heritages, making them pertinent and evocative in Qing ritual displays and events.

The history of Western textiles at the Qing court reveals the growing interdependence of global and local networks. Yet as the individual cases presented in this book have shown, the transcultural exchanges that occurred through these networks were fraught with failed ambitions, unfulfilled commissions, conflicting perspectives, and misaligned expectations—all of which reflect the open-ended possibilities and resulting tensions in the increasingly connected early modern world. The transcultural framework invoked in this book was not a straightforward paradigm of direct dialogues, synchronized visions, and symmetrical exchanges between the various participants. Navigating such a complex, even unstable, terrain requires us to constantly shift the lens between the global and the local, dissecting and analyzing each turn of the objects' trajectories in order to flesh out a concrete transcultural history. A clear pattern of the global-local dynamics can be observed in our case of the Qing court's Western textiles: the Qing Empire played an active part in a globalized world connected primarily by flows of goods and knowledge, but this global order, as the Qing ruler perceived it, was fundamentally filtered through the imperial ideological system and conditioned by Qing local mechanisms. The material objects circulated in various networks ultimately served to celebrate the Qing Empire's power and heritages.

Untangling these threads requires us to identify and contextualize the key players who directed the movements, changes, and applications of global objects. In our case, the Qianlong emperor unquestionably played a central and dominant role in driving and orchestrating the Qing imperial projects related to Western textiles. Court documents recording the emperor's orders provide ample evidence of his personal taste and decisions. The extant objects themselves, when situated in specific contexts, reveal further clues about his perceptions of foreign media and styles as well as his political intentions for integrating them into Qing imperial programs—aspects that were rarely documented in writing. The textiles examined in this book also illuminate how each project involved multiple players in diverse roles, ranging from Jesuit missionaries, who often served as artists and mediators between China and Europe, European statesmen and ambassadors, officials at the Qing court and in regional administrations, to merchants and artisans whose names are largely absent from historical records.

In our stories, only a few Jesuits, envoys, and merchants traveled across the seas, and the movement of people seems less significant in the building of transcultural connections than the objects themselves, which linked widely dispersed people and transmitted knowledge and aesthetics. It is thus equally important to identify the limits circumscribing the actors involved in transactions and mediations between cultures, both to avoid misassigning agency and to recognize the true loci of creativity and adaptability. In the case of the Qing court's production of Western silks and tapestries, no evidence shows that European designers or weavers were ever present in China or engaged in any of the Qing imperial projects from afar. Nor were Jesuit priests at the Qing court known to have expertise in weaving techniques, as they did in other domains such as glassmaking, clock making, and enameling. Instead, it was local Chinese artisans in the imperial textile manufactories who interpreted and grasped foreign techniques and styles by studying the objects closely and drawing on the rich Chinese weaving traditions. Careful examinations of the visual and material characteristics of surviving textiles have revealed hitherto unknown details about the skills, sensibilities, and discernment that these artisans brought to bear in their experiments to create Western-style works.

MATERIAL AND IMAGERY

Reconstructing the story of global exchanges rests largely on identifying and parsing the local specificities—in iconography, material sensitivity, and modes of use—and it remains equally important to account for the factors that facilitated transcultural receptions. Certain material features and imagery were especially protean in the transcultural reception of Western silks and tapestries in China—namely, metal threads, wool, depictions of flowers and animals, and chinoiserie motifs. Each of these aspects was harmoniously adapted to the Qing imperial context to generate new meanings. These aspects also highlight shared aesthetic and intellectual grounds between the European and Qing courts, albeit remote or derived from unrelated traditions, which enabled the smooth assimilations of materials and images.

The lavish gold and silver threads used in European luxury silks had more dynamic textures and a more lustrous shine than traditional Chinese ones; they therefore stood out to the Qianlong emperor as the most appealing feature of the Western textiles. They offered fresh visual delight that gratified the Manchu taste for gold-suffused fabrics, an aesthetic peculiar to the non-Han regimes from northern China, whose long lineage included the Liao, Jin, and Yuan dynasties.[1] Meanwhile, the shine of metal threads in the textiles used for the Qianlong emperor's ritual regalia helped convey the image of a glorious ruler and a magnificent reign. Across early modern Europe, radiance and splendor achieved through gold and silver materials were also desirable among royals and nobles, for they symbolized wealth, glory, and virtue.[2] The Qing and European courts shared the predilection for brilliant textiles, which they both understood as a potent material language of power and prestige. Likewise, European tapestries, which were woven primarily with wool, suited the Manchu way of furnishing interiors, and their pictorial and spatial potentials as a stately textile medium introduced new image-making possibilities to the Manchu ethnic tradition and imperial agenda.

Among the decorative patterns and images in the Qing court's Western textiles, exotic flora and fauna especially captured the Qing imperial fascination, and they enriched the court-sponsored projects of cataloguing natural species within and beyond its territories. Like their European counterparts, the Qing rulers were swept up in the same global wave of interest in natural history, and they initiated projects to codify scientific knowledge in vast catalogues. Images of foreign plants and animals, a visual index to faraway lands within the reach of the Qing Empire, were central to the imperial imagination of the empire's prevailing, universal power.

The imagery and style later known in Europe as chinoiserie served as a versatile visual language that traversed the boundaries between far-flung places and mediated the mutual imagination between Europe and China. A global style par excellence, chinoiserie was created and developed through the networks of trade, Jesuit missions, and diplomatic embassies with the contributions of artists, voyagers, merchants, and consumers from both China and Europe. Its evocations of China as a place and an idea associated with civilization, refinement, and mystery made it a stylistic lingua franca connoting status and taste in European courts and aristocratic circles. The Qing court tapestry *A Western Family* studied in chapter 4 contributes yet another new dimension to these transcultural layers of chinoiserie by elucidating its appeal to the Qing emperor and its significations unrelated to "China." After the French tapestries bearing chinoiserie designs entered the Qing court as diplomatic gifts—intentionally chosen by Europeans to glorify the Qing emperor—these images embarked on an unanticipated new career as inspirations and models for Qing imperial representations of the West.

The imagery and styles surveyed here were primarily European in origin. Yet the Western tapestries produced by the Qing court tended to embrace a native iconography. Potent examples are the blissful family scenes with many children, a prevalent theme in Qing imperial arts that expressed auspicious wishes for the prosperity and longevity of the dynasty. Pictorial devices and details for depicting figures, such as clothing and hairstyles culled from European sources, were adapted to this paradigm. Western figures integrated into this time-honored Chinese idiom helped reiterate the primacy of family, a long-cherished Confucian value and the foundation of dynastic continuity. In this way, Western motifs played a role in the expression and reaffirmation of Qing imperial ideologies.

Collectively, the aspects examined in the book shed light on Qing imperial perceptions of the "Western" in the textile medium. This was not simply an abstract notion but consisted of specific material components, imagery, styles, and techniques. Hybrid in nature, these Western features were created through reorganizing and synthesizing a select range of European and Chinese elements into a new repertoire, which echoed deeply anchored visual traditions in the Qing Empire and at the same time foregrounded salient differences as fresh expressions.

LIMINALITY AND DISPLACEMENT

Culturally, physically, and symbolically, the Western textiles at the Qing court can be viewed as liminal objects that both delineated and blurred a boundary. First, they crossed the cultural and geographical borders between Europe and China, thus bringing the two textile traditions into direct contact. Second, in their physical placement, these textiles functioned primarily to create a threshold around the Qianlong emperor himself. Silks bedecked the horse the emperor rode and lined the screen behind him inside a Mongolian yurt, and tapestries formed a backdrop for the emperor's seat. In Qianlong's New Year tapestry, the most prominent Western components—the borders and the curtain—literally establish a threshold between the represented scene and the palace interior while also framing the emperor seated in front of the hanging. These devices mobilized the fictional and actual spaces into an intricate visual play. In their uses at the Qing court, Western textiles were conspicuous but carefully kept in an auxiliary position, helping the emperor at the center display and perform preconceived political messages.

It is not uncommon for transcultural elements to inhabit a peripheral or boundary space, a position that itself mirrors the act of mediation and translation between cultures. The more familiar mode involved annotating the presentations of foreign objects in a local key. The Qing court's Western textiles did just the opposite, however: they inserted starkly alien components to reframe and restage familiar native images and themes. The Western styles and motifs in these textiles conveyed no concrete, fixed meanings per se when transplanted from the European to the Qing court context. Rather, they introduced rhetorical visual layers to established, coherent narratives rooted in Chinese-Manchu traditions.

In this role, Qing imperial Western textiles enabled a state of displacement. Jonathan Hay has insightfully observed that the Qing court's Western styles, as "various forms of visual staging" "in a calculatedly exotic manner" were "not simply representational," but their more important function was to "enact an experience of self-displacement."[3] I would argue further that, as the cases in this book have shown, this visual theatricality stemmed from the tension between the familiar and the strange, aspects that coexisted in the hybrid Western style. By deliberately intervening in a habitual visual and cognitive mode, Western elements situated at the threshold ultimately directed attention to the more pivotal imagery at the center: the ideal ruler astride a horse, as in Qianlong's portrait, or the auspicious family in want of a patriarch in the New Year tapestry. The Western elements were carefully selected, circumscribed, and positioned, at the service of recomposing and redelivering Qing imperial narratives. This book has explored their constructive power derived from their threshold positioning and auxiliary status, which outlines an essential pattern of the Qing court's transcultural arts and material culture. Specifically, the unique material qualities of textiles—their malleability, combined with their embedded implications of the human body and architectural space—gained them immediate proximity to the emperor. In this privileged position, these textiles, more than any other type of Western object at the Qing court, offered the monarch greater possibilities to personally stage and play out his carefully conceived messages.

LEGACY AND NEW ITERATION

Despite the dynamic networks it activated and the broad horizons it touched on, the Qing imperial craze for Western silks and tapestries remained fundamentally an eighteenth-century phenomenon, inextricably linked to the personal interests and aspirations of the Qianlong emperor, who reigned at the summit of the Qing Empire's material wealth, political strength, and artistic creativity. During the nineteenth century, this enthusiasm and enterprise faded away. Documents kept by the Qing Imperial Workshops contain almost no entries on the production and display of Western textiles in that century. No Western tapestries dated to that period have been found in the imperial collections, and although a handful of eighteenth-century European designs continued to be woven in silk,

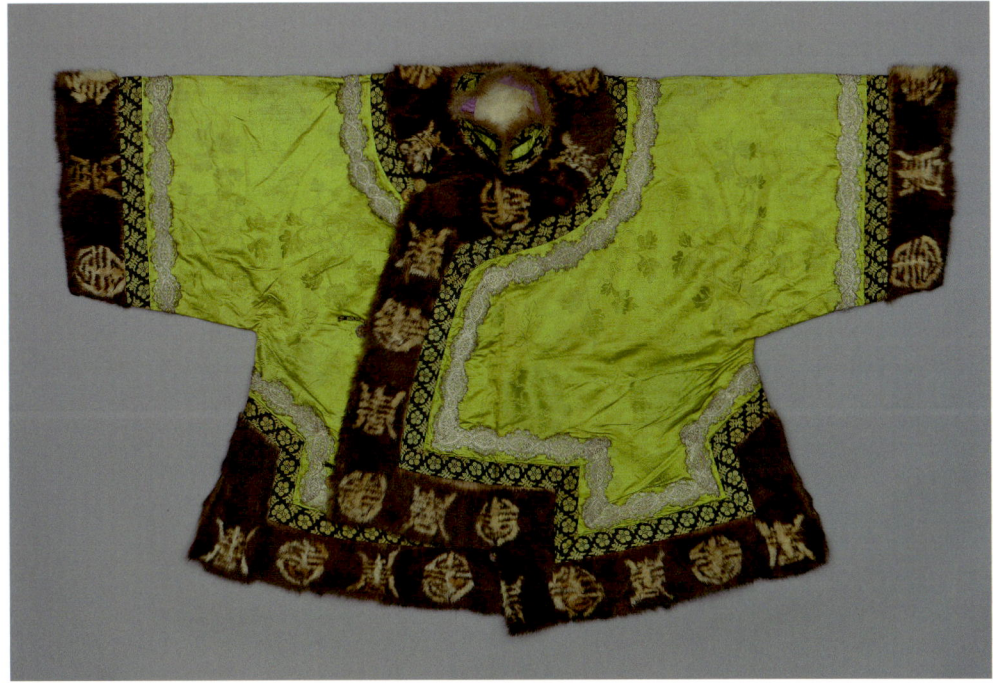

FIG. 126 Imperial woman's riding jacket (*magua*), 1875–1908. Silk damask, inlaid sable fur, ribbon with gold metal threads, and silver metallic lace, length 29 3/8 in. (74.5 cm). Palace Museum, Beijing (gu49938).

such as the English rococo botanical pattern (see figs. 48, 49) and the symmetrical, ogival structure carrying small flowers (see figs. 52, 53), the few nineteenth-century products in the Palace Museum appear derivative and less polished. Gone are the experimental weavings and the imaginative renditions of foreign repertoires—products that had been carefully crafted in the Qianlong period. We should therefore regard the Qing court's Western textiles as embodying the refined craftsmanship, opulent taste, creative spirit, and open cultural attitude of High Qing imperial arts.

A major reason for this decline is the dramatically shifting dynamics between the Qing Empire and the Western powers—the European nation-states, with the addition of the United States and Japan as the nineteenth century progressed—in terms of trade balance, political relationships, and military strength. By the 1830s, the cultural openness and mutual admiration that characterized the relationship between China and the West in the early modern period had been replaced by antagonism. The Opium Wars (1839–42 and 1856–60) forced open multiple treaty ports in China and ushered in a turbulent epoch of successive aggressions by Western imperialist powers. Although China in the nineteenth century exhibited great resilience in the face of these challenges as well as numerous domestic crises, the Qing dynasty could not withstand the tumult and came to an end in 1911.[4]

Global industrialization and expanded trade brought an influx of inexpensive Western goods to China during the second half of the nineteenth century, and new types of Western textiles, from woolen broadcloth to decorative trims, became increasingly available in the Qing Empire.[5] Two novel and popular categories associated with clothing found their way into the court. The first type

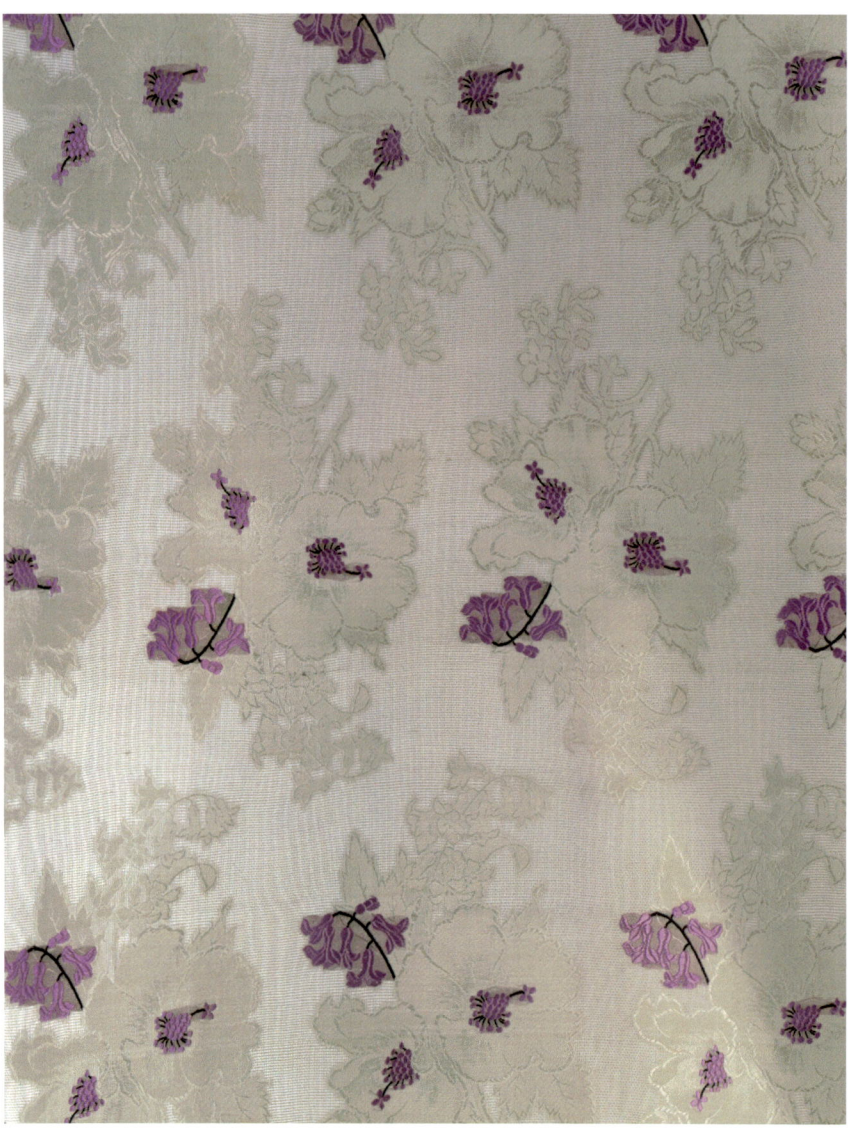

FIG. 127 Bolt of textile (detail), c. 1890–1910. Chinese, patterned silk gauze, 25 ft. 7⅛ in. × 22¼ in. (780 × 56.5 cm). Palace Museum, Beijing (gu21220).

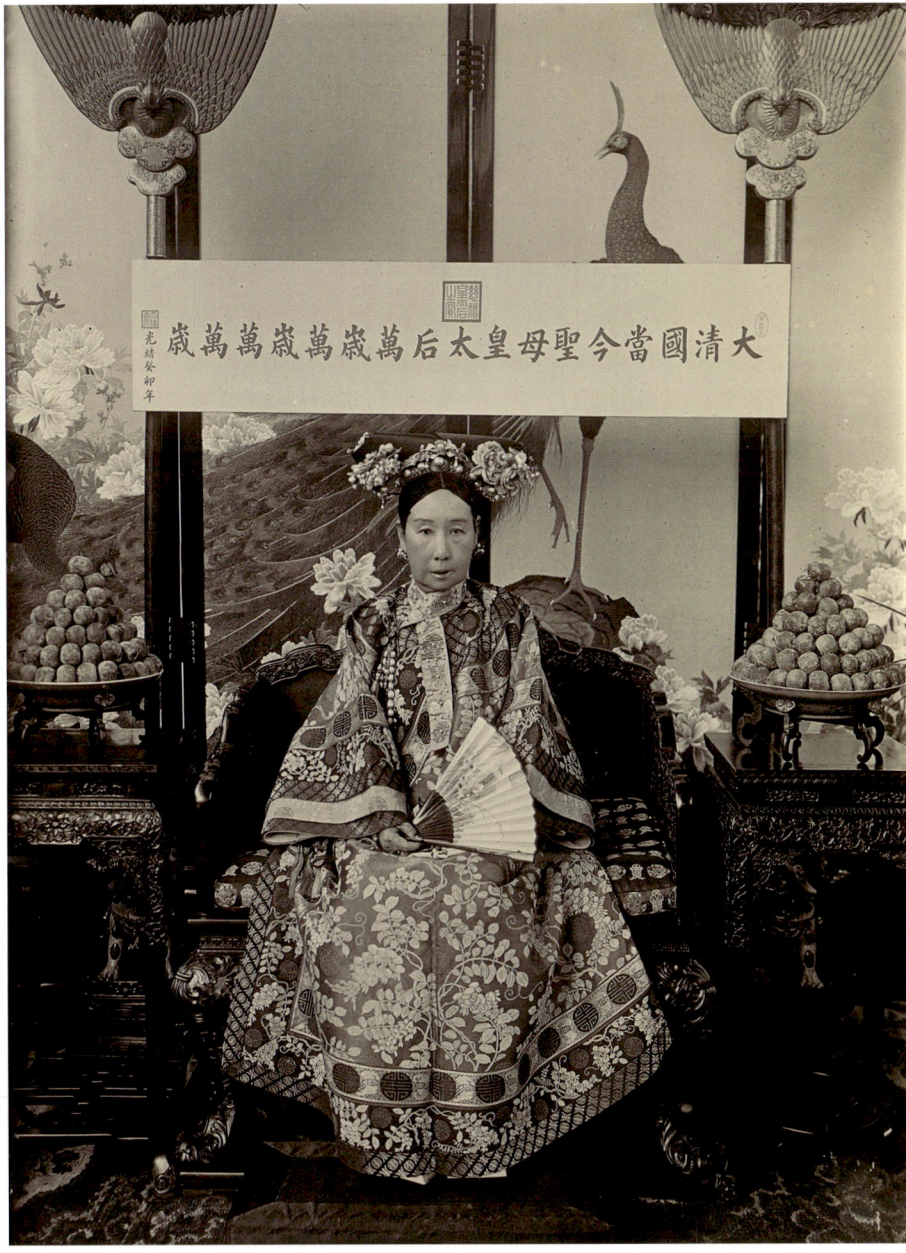

FIG. 128 Yu Xunling, *Her Imperial Majesty, the Empress Dowager of China*, 1903. Hand-colored gelatin silver print, 9 1/8 × 6 3/4 in. (23.1 × 17.2 cm). Museum of Fine Arts, Boston, gift of Sarah Buchan Jewell (1991.134).

comprised imported ready-made lace bands and ribbons used as embellishments for court ladies' informal garments. A bright green riding jacket dated to the Guangxu period (1875–1908), for example, sports a European silver lace trim (fig. 126). Indeed, ornate trimmings became popular among Han Chinese and Manchu women alike during this period.[6] The second type consisted of a variety of patterned gauze silks known as *taixi sha* (silk gauze of the Grand West), which featured the latest European-style floral patterns and were woven in China on newly developed mechanized looms (fig. 127). These products refracted new modes of commerce and manufacture bound to the economic encroachment of foreign investments and domestic industrialization. Unlike the Western figured silks and large woolen tapestries of the eighteenth century, which symbolized exclusivity and imperial privilege, these new mass-market products were fashionable items that shaped court taste from outside. The boundary that once defined the Manchu imperium and distinguished the members of the royal household from commoners had now become porous.

Nevertheless, the Qing monarch's legacy of employing prestigious foreign textiles in staged imperial images for political purposes did not disappear altogether. Toward the very end of the Qing dynasty, it found a renewed iteration in the photographic portraits of Empress Dowager Cixi (1835–1908), the de facto ruler of the empire during its last half century. Taken in 1903 and 1904 and intended as

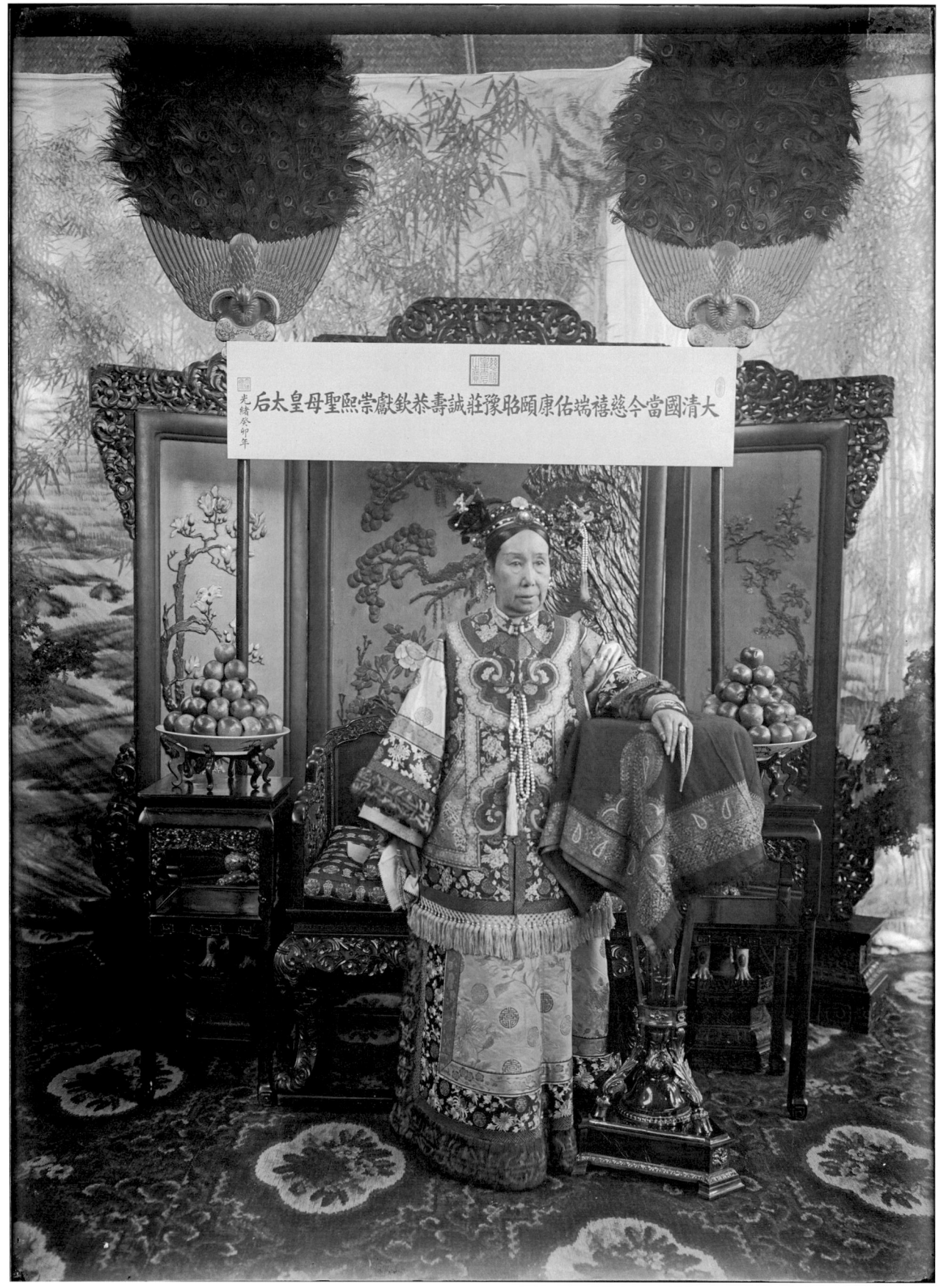

FIG. 129 Yu Xunling, *The Empress Dowager Cixi*, 1903. Gelatin silver print, 9½ × 7 in. (24.1 × 17.8 cm). National Museum of Asian Art Archives, Smithsonian Institution, Washington D.C. (FSA A.13 SC-GR-253).

formal gifts for foreign leaders, Cixi's photographs were the first images to break the deep-seated Chinese taboo against the public display and circulation of imperial visages. These photographs signaled the Qing rulers' belated embrace of international diplomatic practices and was an effort to align the weakened empire with powerful modern nations.[7] In many of these portraits, Cixi surrounded herself with foreign textiles, including a splendid Japanese silk screen embroidered with peacocks and peonies, made by the Takashimaya Company and most certainly a gift from the Meiji emperor of Japan in 1903; a machine-woven pile floral carpet imported from Europe; and an Indian or European paisley-patterned cashmere shawl draped over a stand (figs. 128, 129). The use of screens and carpets in these photographs drew on the visual tradition of formal imperial portraiture in the Ming and Qing dynasties, while the incorporation of Japanese and European works in the image resonated with Cixi's new foreign policies and domestic reforms that were based largely on Meiji models of modernization.[8] Moreover, the richly texturized and patterned interior created by the carpet and shawl simulated the settings in studio photographs of eminent sitters such as Queen Victoria (r. 1837–1901) of England and Empress Haruko (1849–1914) of Japan, whose state portraits were widely circulated in the late nineteenth century. As Qianlong had done with his 1758 equestrian portrait (see fig. 2), Cixi mobilized foreign textiles and iconography to convey Qing imperial magnificence—this time not to assert Qing superiority or her universal rulership, but to reinstate the empire as an equal player on the international stage and to represent herself as a modern matriarch.

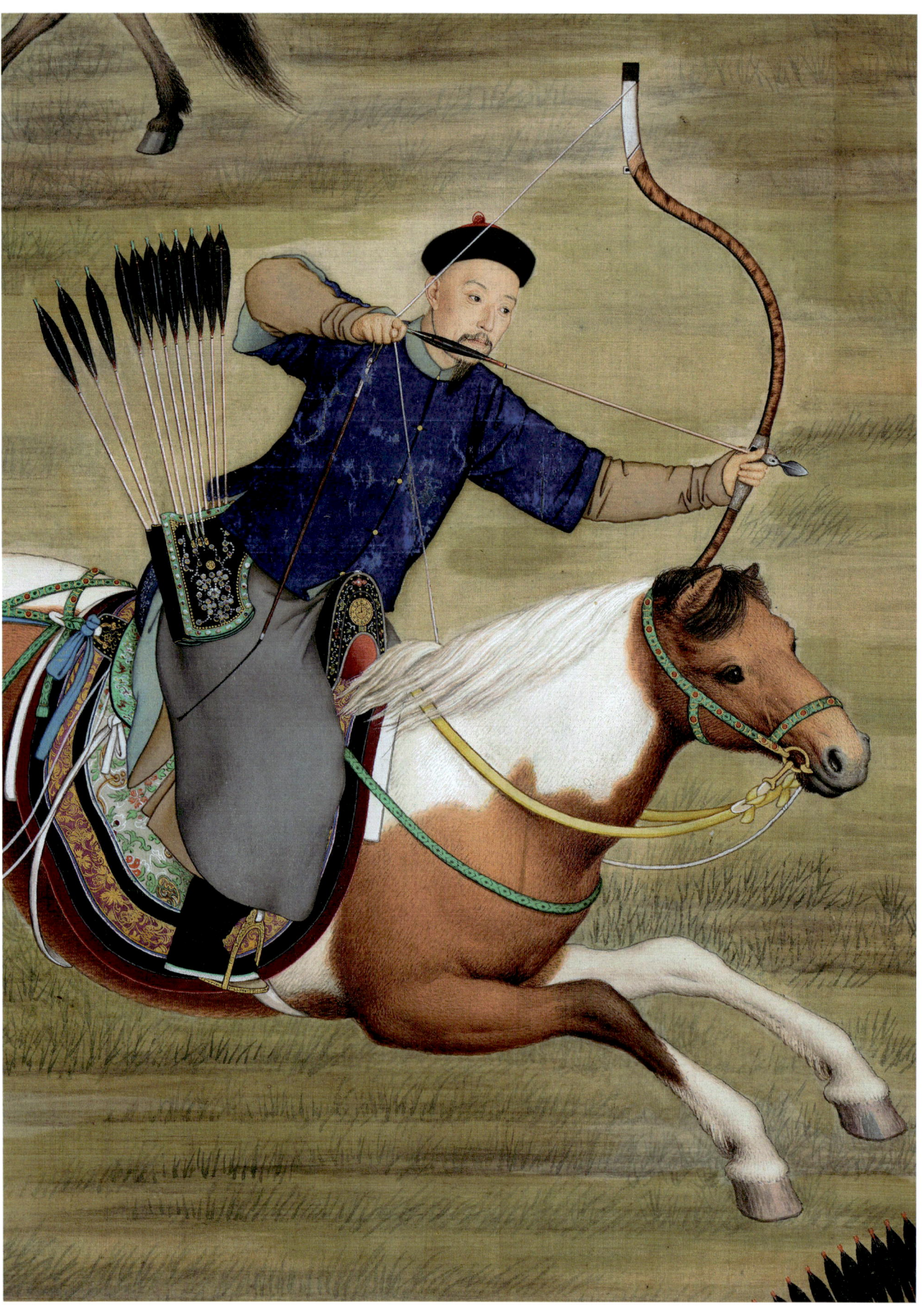

Textile Terminology and Measurement Systems

For standard textile terminology, this book primarily follows *Vocabulaire technique français* (2020 edition) and *Vocabulary of Technical Terms: English* (2021 edition), both issued by the Centre international d'étude des textiles anciens (CIETA), Lyon. Additional references are drawn from Dorothy K. Burnham, *Warp and Weft* (1980); Elena Phipps, *Looking at Textiles* (2011); and Sjoukje Colenbrander, *When Weaving Flourished* (2013), appendices. Translations and definitions of special Chinese terms are based on Dieter Kuhn with Zhao Feng, *Chinese Silks* (2012), glossary.

STANDARD TERMS

berclé The technique of alternating patterning weft floats of different colors to produce a hatching or shading effect. It can also refer to a similar technique used in tapestry weaving. This book uses the term only in the context of drawloom weaving. In drawloom weaving, the technique is also called *points rentrés*.

bind To fix a warp thread in place with a weft thread. A warp thread and a weft thread hold each other in place at a **binding point**, and the manner in which they interlace is called a **binding system** or **weave**. There are three basic binding systems from which all weaves are derived: tabby (or plain weave), twill, and satin.

brocade (v.) To form a pattern effect by introducing a supplementary weft into the ground weave. The movement of this supplementary weft is limited to the width required by the specific pattern it creates. A textile woven with this effect is described as "brocaded." CIETA does not recommend using "brocade" as a noun, as this usage tends to be vague and generalized, often referring to any textile with a woven pattern.

chenille A tufted fabric strip that can be used as thread for weaving. A chenille thread is created by first weaving a fabric (usually in plain weave) with spaced warp groups and then cutting it into strips along the length. Each strip has short tufts on both longitudinal edges resulting from the cut wefts. The strip can be used as a patterning weft thread and produces a furry texture resembling the short pile of cut velvet.

damask A self-patterned weave with one set of warps and one set of wefts in which the pattern is formed from two contrasting binding systems. The term also denotes the textile bearing such weave.

drawloom A hand loom for weaving figured textiles with intricate polychrome design. It is equipped with a special figure harness that controls some or all of the warp threads. In the most advanced types, used in both China (*hualou ji*) and France (*métier à la grande tire*) during the eighteenth century, a cord system is connected to the figure harness and controls the pattern.

Harness is a collective name for all the shafts in a drawloom. A **shaft** is a group of heddles fixed side by side so that they may be moved together at the same time. Each warp thread passes through a **heddle**, which separates the warp threads on the loom so that they may be raised or lowered to permit the passage of the weft threads.

The drawloom allows the weaver to coordinate two independently functioning systems to weave the design: the **ground harness** operates the warp threads that form the plain or simple ground weave, and it is controlled by the weaver using foot treadles; the **figure harness** controls the warp threads required to execute the pattern. The cord mechanism of the figure harness is activated by a thread puller (called the drawboy), who lifts selected warp threads in a particular sequence to allow the weaver to pass the weft threads.

figured (*façonné*) A term that describes textiles with repeating designs woven on complex looms with some patterning mechanism. Technically, the term designates weaves or textiles in which one or more of the warp sets are controlled by a figure harness.

float (n.) A portion of a warp thread or weft thread that is unbound for an extended area (passing over at least two threads between binding points).

gauze A type of weave in which the binding is achieved by the displacement of warp threads. It uses two kinds of warps: fixed warp threads and turning warp threads that cross the fixed ones. The term also denotes the textile formed by this weave. There are many variations, determined by the complexity of the movement of the turning warp threads.

ground The foundation fabric formed by the main weft and the main warp. The weave structure of this ground is called **ground weave**. Additional pattern, texture, and pile can be developed on the ground. Ground is to be distinguished from **background**, which refers to the visual backdrop for the motifs in a textile's design. A background may or may not be the actual ground.

lampas A complex figured textile in which a pattern, composed of weft floats bound by a binding warp, is added to a ground fabric formed by a main warp and a ground weft.

lancé A patterning effect created by a supplementary weft that passes across the entire width of the fabric to form a pattern or enrich the ground. The *lancé* wefts surface only on the front side of the textile where the design requires them; the rest float on the back of the textile and are bound at spaced-out binding points.

liseré A self-patterned effect created when parts of the ground weft threads are left unbound as floats.

loom width The complete width of a textile, including selvedges.

metal threads Threads composed partly or entirely of metal or metallic materials. Types of metal threads include *lame* (**lamella**), a narrow, flat strip of precious or base metal, or gilt or silvered leather, membrane, metal or paper; *filé*, a smooth metal thread composed of a lame wound around a core made from another material, typically silk; and *frisé*, a crinkled metal thread composed of a lame wound around a spiral silk core.

pattern repeat The smallest unit that contains all the characteristics of a pattern. This unit is mechanically repeated in a textile in the warp and weft directions. In some cases, one repeat can cross the entire width of the fabric. In a **straight repeat**, the pattern unit repeats side by side without variation. In a **point repeat** or **mirror repeat**, the straight unit alternates with its reverse on the vertical (warp) axis.

point paper (*mise-en-carte*) A pattern on graph paper that serves as a guide for setting up the loom. The term is generally applied only to patterns for a drawloom or a loom with a Jacquard mechanism. On the point paper, the curved lines of the initial design are translated into a steplike geometric system of vertical (warp) and horizontal (weft) lines.

points rentrés See berclé.

satin A basic weave structure consisting of one set of warps and one set of wefts. In a warp-faced satin, each warp thread passes over four or more adjacent weft shots and under the next one. The binding points are set over two or more warp threads on successive weft shots and are distributed in an unobtrusive manner to give a smooth appearance. Satin textiles, often made of silk, are particularly lustrous because the long floats reflect light.

selvedge The longitudinal edge of a textile, which is finished off when the weft threads loop around the first and last warp threads. The selvedge can consist of a narrow strip where the binding system, material, or color differs from the one employed in the rest of the fabric.

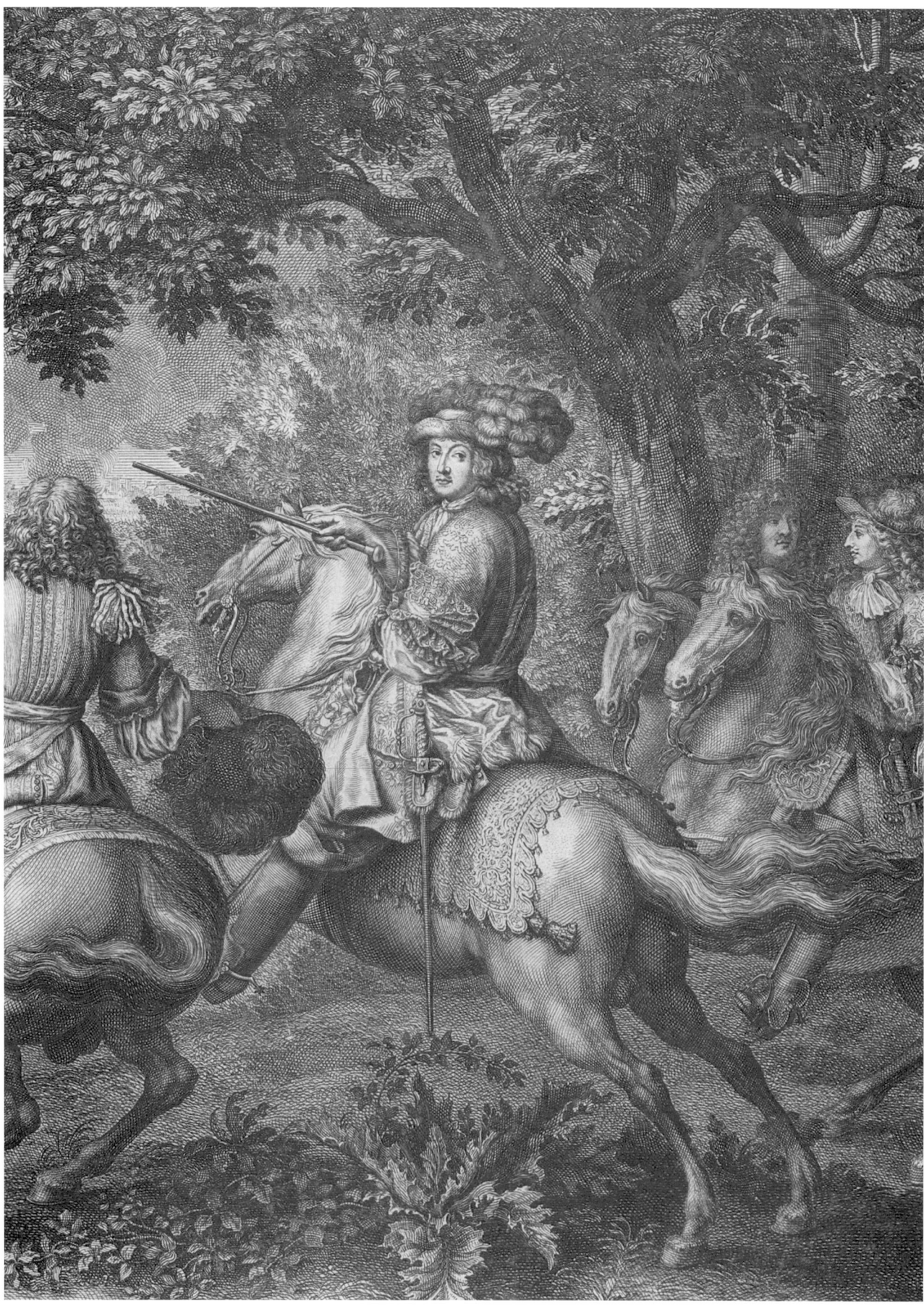

supplementary A term that describes warps or wefts (or both) that do not form the ground weave but instead are interwoven with the ground fabric to create patterns or textures.

tabby A basic weave structure composed of one set of warps and one set of wefts, interlacing in a system of over-one and under-one. Tabby is also called **plain weave**.

tapestry A term that refers to both an object and a weave structure. As an object, a tapestry is a large, pictorial wall hanging woven in the tapestry weave. The tapestry weave consists of one set of warps interlaced with one set of wefts made up of threads of different colors, each carried by its own shuttle. These weft threads are discontinuous and do not pass from selvedge to selvedge; that is, they are interwoven with warp threads only in the area required by the design. The binding system is usually tabby and weft-faced. Where the weft threads of two adjacent areas meet in the warp direction, they may be dovetailed, interlocked, or toothed. A **slit** is created where two weft threads are turned back around adjacent warp threads.

In Europe, two types of tapestry looms are used: the **high-warp loom** (*métier de haute lisse*), on which the warps are mounted in a vertical position; and the **low-warp loom** (*métier de basse lisse*), on which the warps are arranged horizontally. For both looms, weavers work from the back side of the tapestry. Tapestry weaving is guided by a **cartoon**, a full-scale painted model adapted from the initial design. In Europe, from the mid-seventeenth century onward, cartoons were rendered primarily in oil on canvas. For the high-warp loom, the cartoon is hung on the wall behind the weavers, who look through the warp threads at its reflection in a mirror placed in front of the tapestry. For the low-warp loom, the cartoon is cut into multiple strips of about 31½ in. (80 cm) wide, and individual strips are laid flat sequentially under the warp threads for the weavers' reference.

twill A basic weave structure consisting of one set of warps and one set of wefts, with a minimum of three warp threads and three weft shots forming a unit. The binding points are offset by one warp thread, always in the same direction, on successive weft shots, creating diagonal lines.

velvet A warp-pile weave in which the pile is produced by a set of supplementary pile warps that are raised in loops above the ground weave through the introduction of rods during the weaving. The loops may be left uncut or cut to form tufts.

warp The longitudinal threads of a textile. The term denotes both the individual threads and the set of all warp threads performing the same function. Placed on the loom first, the warps run perpendicular to the wefts.

warp-faced A term that describes the side of the textile on which the warp predominates.

weave (n.)/weave structure A system of interlacing warps and wefts on a loom. *See also* **bind**.

weft The transverse threads that interlace with the warp threads to create a textile. The wefts run perpendicular to the warps. In the weaving process, each weft thread is carried by a **shuttle**. One **shot** of the weft thread is a single pass of the shuttle through the open areas of the warp threads. A **continuous weft** passes across the entire width of the fabric. A **discontinuous weft** runs only in specific areas required by the design (as in tapestry weaving and brocading).

weft-faced A term that describes the side of the textile on which the weft predominates.

CHINESE TERMS

duan Silk with a satin weave. *See* **satin**.

hualou ji A drawloom equipped with a figure tower that contains the figure harness. *See* **drawloom**.

jin There is no single equivalent for this term in English. It is often mistranslated as "brocade." In the long history of Chinese silk weaving, *jin* has referred to a variety of polychrome silk textiles that fall into three technical categories: compound weaves (including warp-faced compound tabby, warp-faced compound twill, weft-faced compound tabby, and weft-faced compound twill), double weave, and lampas weave. In the **compound weave**, the warps or the wefts are divided into two or more sets, one of which appears on the face while the other or others appear on the reverse. The **double weave** is composed of two sets of warps and two sets of wefts, each interlacing with its respective set. The resulting textile has two layers formed simultaneously and a minimum of two color areas. All the eighteenth-century *jin* silks of Chinese and European origin discussed in this book feature a **lampas weave** (*see* **lampas**).

kesi A silk tapestry. *See* **tapestry**.

ling Twill damask, a type of twill weave distinctive to China. It is formed by two contrasting twill weaves, each in a warp-faced and weft-faced binding system. *See also* **twill**.

zhuanghua duan Silk fabric with brocaded patterns on a satin ground. The term is not always used in this strict sense in historical documents written by nonspecialists; it may therefore also refer to brocaded silks with a tabby, twill, or damask ground weave. *See also* **brocade**.

MEASUREMENT SYSTEMS AND CONVERSIONS OF THE EIGHTEENTH CENTURY

Ell was typically used for measuring textiles in England and France. For tapestries, the Gobelins manufactory used the French ell, while the Beauvais manufactory used the Flemish ell during the weaving process and the French ell for measuring finished pieces.

1 English ell = 45 in. (114.3 cm)

1 French ell (*aune de France* or *aune de Paris*) ≈ 46¾ in. (118.8 cm)

1 Flemish ell (*aune de Flandres*) ≈ 27⅜ in. (69.4 cm)

This measurement was that of the Brabant ell (*Brabantse el*), which was the standard measurement for textiles from 1725 onward.

For measuring architecture in France: 1 *pied de roi* ≈ 12¾ in. (32.5 cm).

In China, the system *caiyi chi* (measurements for tailoring) was used for measuring textiles.

1 cun ≈ 1⅜ in. (3.56 cm), 1 chi = 10 cun, and 1 zhang = 10 chi

At the Qing court, the system *yingzao chi* (measurements for architecture) was used for measuring tapestries, cartoons for the tapestries, and wall spaces for hanging tapestries.

1 cun ≈ 1¼ in. (3.2 cm), 1 chi = 10 cun, and 1 zhang = 10 chi

For measuring weight in China: 1 liang ≈ 1¼ oz. (37.3 g).

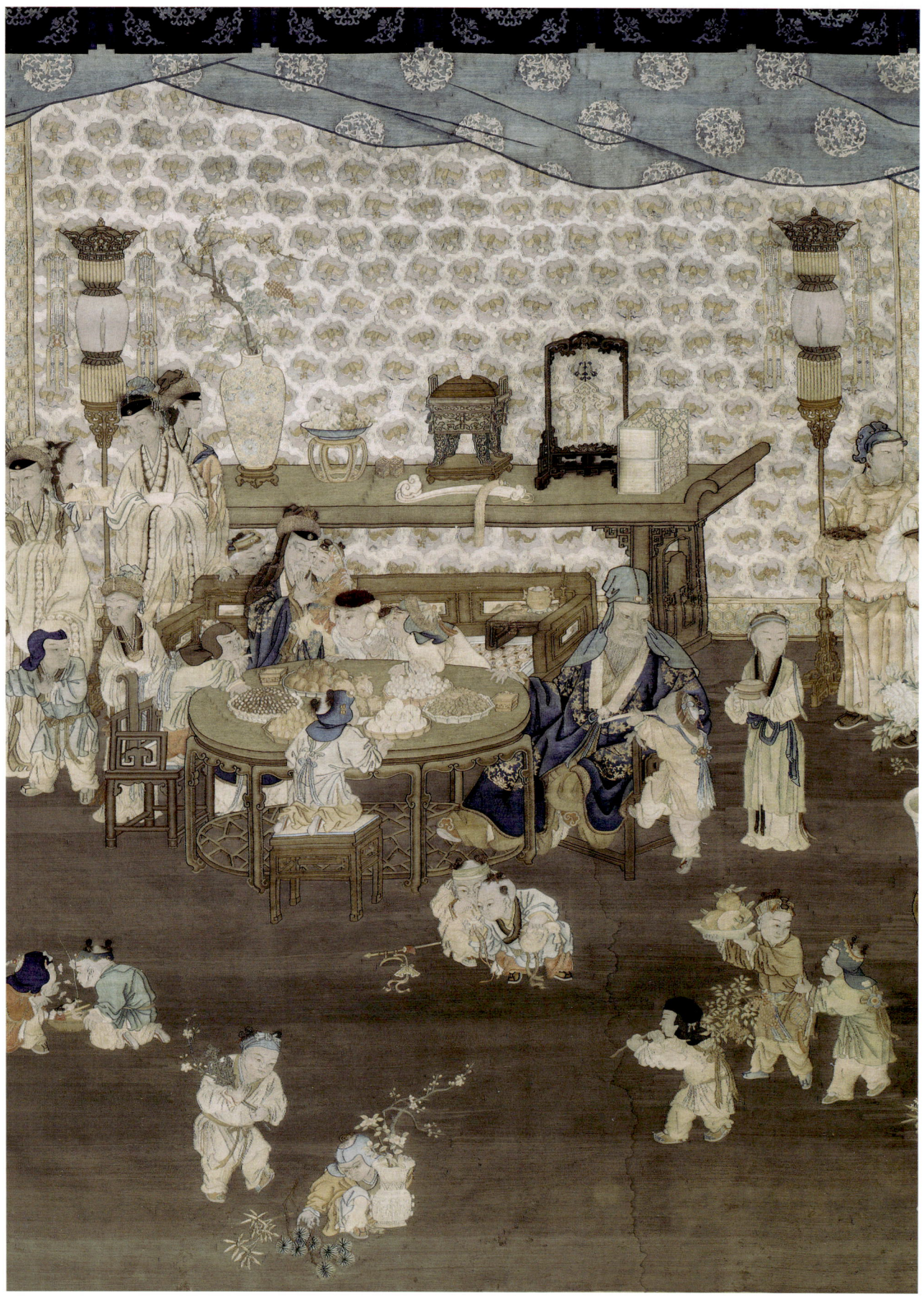

Chinese Glossary

baidi wucaihua yáng jinduan 白地五彩花洋錦緞
bai tanzi 白毯子
baoxiang hua 寶相花
baozuo chuang 寶座床
Beihai 北海
Beitang 北堂
biji 嗶嘰
caiji 彩罽
caiyi chi 裁衣尺
Changchun yuan 長春園
chaofu 朝服
chi 尺
Chunhua xuan 淳化軒
cijian 次間
Cixi 慈禧
cun 寸
dahong zhijin zhuanghua qilin bu luo 大紅織金妝花麒麟補羅
dahua yángjin 大花洋錦
dahuaduan 大花緞
Daoguang 道光
da xiyáng 大西洋
Da xiyáng guo 大西洋國
da xiyáng kuo songjin 大西洋闊宋錦
dayue 大閱
da zise jinduan 大紫色金緞
duan 緞
duoluo ni 哆囉呢
duoluo rong 哆囉絨
ehuang yinxian yángjin 鵝黃銀線洋錦

Eluosi duan 俄羅斯緞
fan 番
Fang Tiyu 方體浴
fen 分
Fengxian dian 奉先殿
Folangji 佛朗機
fotang 佛堂
fu 蝠
fu 福
Gao Heng 高恆
Gao Leisi 高纇思
Gao Shiqi 高士奇
Gaozong Chun Huangdi 高宗純皇帝
Gebo pu 鴿鵒譜
gongpin 貢品
gongwu 貢物
Gongzhong jindan 宮中進單
Guangxu 光緒
Guanyun xie 觀雲榭
Gu Jianlong 顧見龍
Guwu chenlie suo 古物陳列所
guzhuang 古裝
Haicuo tu 海錯圖
Haiguai tuji 海怪圖記
Haixi jihui 海西集卉
Haiyan tang 海晏堂
Hanjing tang 含經堂
hanzhuang 漢裝
Helan huaduan 荷蘭花緞
Helan tan 荷蘭毯

Helan wuse dahuaduan 荷蘭五色大花緞
hong jinhuaduan 紅金花緞
Hongli 弘曆
Hong Taiji 洪太極
hong yinduan 紅銀緞
houdian 後殿
hua 花
huaben 花本
Huafang zhai 畫舫齋
huairou yuanren 懷柔遠人
hua jinxian duan 花金線緞
hualou ji 花樓機
huangdi jinxian xifan huaniao jin 黃地金線西番花鳥錦
huanmen 歡門
huatan 花毯
hua yinduan 花銀緞
huazhan 花氈
Jiandu 監督
Jiangnan 江南
Jiangning 江寧
Jiaotai dian 交泰殿
jiaoyang Manzhou zhidao 教養滿洲之道
Jiaqing 嘉慶
Jichu daisi tu 雞雛待飼圖
jiezhi 接織
jifu 吉服
Jilei bian 雞肋編
Jile shijie 極樂世界
jin 錦

jīnbao di 金寶地

Jingsheng zhai 敬勝齋

Jingshi 鏡史

jīnhuaduan 金花緞

jīn'ou yonggu bei 金甌永固杯

jīnsi duan 金絲緞

jīnxian duan 金線緞

jīnyin huaduan 金銀花緞

jīnyinsi duan 金銀絲緞

Junji chu 軍機處

kaibi 開筆

kanchuang 檻窗

Kangxi 康熙

kesi 緙絲/剋絲/刻絲

kujīn 庫金

Kunyu tushuo 坤輿圖說

laiwen 來文

landi jīnxian xifan huaguo jin 藍地金線西番花果錦

Laozi 老子

Leshou tang 樂壽堂

liang 兩

Liangguang zongdu 兩廣總督

Lianghuai yanzheng 兩淮鹽政

lianzi 簾子

ling 綾

Li Shiyao 李侍堯

long 龍

magua 馬褂

mang 蟒

Menggu bao 蒙古包

ming 明

mingchuang 明窗

mingdian 明殿

minghuang 明黃

Minning 旻寧

mulan qiuxian 木蘭秋狝

mulan weichang 木蘭圍場

Nanhai 南海

Nanyuan 南苑

neiting yáng jīnxian 內庭洋金線

Neiwu fu 內務府

Nian Gengyao 年羹堯

nianjie renwu hua 年節人物畫

Niaopu 鳥譜

Ningshou gong 寧壽宮

nuange 暖閣

Nurhaci 努爾哈赤

pianjīn 片金

Ping'an chunxin tu 平安春信圖

qí 旗

qì 氣

Qianlong 乾隆

Qianlong Huangdi shetu tu 乾隆皇帝射兔圖

Qincan tu 親蠶圖

qìng 磬

qìng 慶

qing zhijīn chuanhuafeng songjin 青織金穿花鳳宋錦

Rehe 熱河

Rong Fei 容妃

ruyi 如意

sanfan zhiluan 三藩之亂

Sanxi tang 三希堂

Shandong yilu jingong chenshe qingdan 山東一路進貢陳設清單

Shangshu 尚書

shǎngyong 賞用

shàngyong haojin 上用好錦

shaojian 稍間

shaolu 哨鹿

Shaolu tu 哨鹿圖

Shen Fuzong 沈福宗

Shengjing 盛京

Shenyang 瀋陽

shibi 試筆

Shijing 詩經

shiqing 石青

shiqing jīnhuaduan 石青金花緞

shiqing yáng huaduan 石青洋花緞

Shiyi shi'er tu 是一是二圖

shou 壽

Shoupu 獸譜

Shousui tu 守歲圖

Shuifa dian 水法殿

Shunzhi 順治

Songjiang 松江

songjīn 宋錦

Song Yingxing 宋應星

Suizhao huanqing tu 歲朝歡慶圖

suizhao tu 歲朝圖

Sun Yunqiu 孫雲球

suomai Eluosi jīnhuaduan 所買哦囉嘶金花緞

Suzhou 蘇州

taixi sha 泰西紗

tan 毯/氈

Tang Ying 唐英

tanzi 氈子

tanzi jiang 毯子匠

tian'e rong 天鵝絨

Tiangong kaiwu 天工開物

Tianshui bingshan lu 天水冰山錄

tieluo 貼落

tongjing hua 通景畫

tou lü jing cui 頭綠頸翠

tuojian 橐鞬

tusu 屠蘇

Wang Shimin 王時敏

Wanguo laichao tu 萬國來朝圖

Wang Youxue 王幼學

Weihu huolu tu 威弧獲鹿圖

Wanshu yuan ciyan tu 萬樹園賜宴圖

wen 紋

wen 文

wuse maotan 五色毛毯

Wutai shan 五台山

Xian'e Changchun 仙萼長春

Xiaoxian 孝賢

Xiao xiyáng guo 小西洋國

Xie qiqu 諧奇趣

xifan 西番

Xinjiang 新疆

xinjian shuifa dian 新建水法殿

xiyáng 西洋

xiyáng da jīnduan 西洋大金緞

xiyáng fang 西洋房

xiyáng guatan 西洋掛毯

xiyáng huatan 西洋花毯

xiyáng jīn 西洋錦

xiyáng jīnduan 西洋金緞

xiyáng jīnhuaduan 西洋金花緞

xiyáng jīnhuajian 西洋金花箋

xiyáng jīnxian 西洋金線

xiyáng qì 西洋氣
xiyáng ren 西洋人
xiyáng renwu 西洋人物
xiyáng shi huabian 西洋式花邊
xiyáng shi huawen 西洋式花紋
xiyáng tan 西洋毯
xiyáng yinxian 西洋銀線
xiyáng youyingzi xianfa 西洋有影子線法
Xiyáng yuanhua 西洋遠畫
xiyáng yumao renwu guatan 西洋羽毛人物掛毯
yáng 洋
yàng 樣
Yang Dazhang 楊大章
Yang Dewang 楊德望
Yanghe jingshe 養和精舍
yáng huaduan 洋花緞
yángjin 洋錦
yáng jīnduan 洋金緞
yáng jǐnduan 洋錦緞
yángqi 洋漆
yàngshi 樣式
yàngshi Lei 樣式雷
Yang Tingzhang 楊廷章
Yangxin dian 養心殿
yángzhi huatan 洋織花毯
Yan Song 嚴嵩
Yanxun shanguan 延薰山館
Yao Wenhan 姚文瀚
Yi Lantai 伊蘭泰
yingxi 嬰戲
yingzao chi 營造尺
Yingzao fashi 營造法式
yinsi duan 銀絲緞
yinxian duan 銀線緞
Yi Qinwang 怡親王
yonggu 永固
Yonghe gong 雍和宮
Yongzheng 雍正
You Anning 尤安寧
You Bashi 尤拔士
yuan 遠
yuanjīn 圓金
Yuanming yuan 圓明園
yuanyàng 原樣

Yuanying guan 遠瀛觀
Yucui xuan 玉粹軒
yuebai 月白
Yue haiguan 粵海關
Yuhua ge 雨花閣
yunjǐn 雲錦
Yu Sheng 余省
Yu Xunling 裕勛齡
yuzhu changtiao tai 玉燭長調臺
Zaoban chu 造辦處
zhan 氈
zhang 丈
Zhang Weibang 張爲邦
zhantan 毡毯/氈氈
zhao yángtan yanse 照洋毯顏色
Zheng Zhao 鄭昭
zhicheng yuanshi hua 織成遠視畫
Zhigong tu 職貢圖
zhihua hongduan 織花紅緞
zhijīn duan 織金緞
zhijīn huaduan 織金花緞
zhi renwu huatan 織人物花毯
zhizao 織造
Zhuang Chuo 莊綽
zhuanghua duan 妝花緞
zhuangyan 莊嚴
zike 子刻
zise yáng huachou 紫色洋花紬
zongse xiyáng jǐn 宗[sic]色西洋錦
Zouxiao dang 奏銷檔

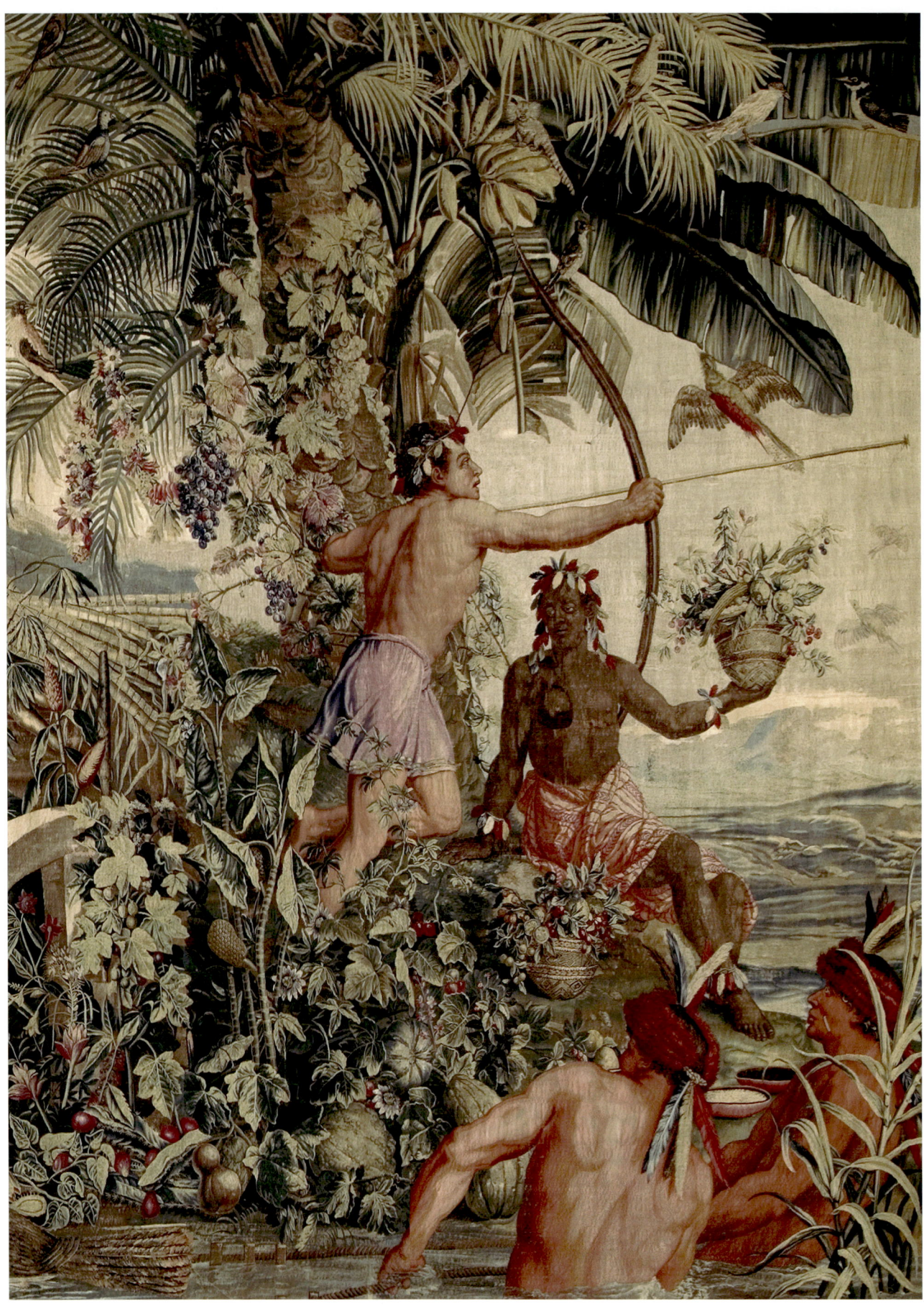

Abbreviations

AN: Archives nationales
BIF: Bibliothèque de l'Institut de France
BNF: Bibliothèque nationale de France
DQHD: *Qinding da Qing huidian shili*
HJD: *Neiwu fu zaoban chu gezuo chengzuo huoji qingdang*

Notes

Unless otherwise noted, all translations from Chinese and French are the author's.

INTRODUCTION

1. See Feng Ming-chu, *Qianlong Huangdi de wenhua daye*; and Ho Chuan-hsin, *Shiquan Qianlong*.
2. Crossley, "Rulerships of China," 1468.
3. For a review of the state of the field, see Wang, "Whither Art History?"
4. For studies of these equestrian portraits of Qianlong, see, e.g., Liu Lu, "*Congboxing shiyitu*," 23–25; and Pirazzoli-t'Serstevens, "Giuseppe Castiglione," 27.
5. Rado, "Encountering Magnificence"; and Rado, "Qing Court's Encounters with European Tapestries."
6. For recent publications exemplifying the global approach, see, e.g., Martin and Bleichmar, *Objects in Motion*; Cooke, *Global Objects*; and Bellion and Smentek, *Material Cultures*. For discussions specific to Sino-European exchanges, see, e.g., Wang, "Whither Art History?"; and Juneja and Grasskamp, *EurAsian Matters*.
7. Juneja and Grasskamp, *EurAsian Matters*, 7–8; and interview with Juneja, quoted in Gasparini, *Transcending Patterns*, 3.
8. See Thomas, "Yuanming Yuan/Versailles"; and Finlay, *Henri Bertin*, esp. 144–47.
9. Finlay, *Henri Bertin*, esp. chap. 4.
10. See also Wang, "Whither Art History?," 379–86.
11. Ibid., 381.
12. The group research project "Perspectives on Artistic and Cultural Exchanges between Europe and East Asia, 1600–1800" at Academia Sinica in Taipei (2011–14) and the Cluster of Excellence "Asia and Europe in a Global Context" at Heidelberg University have played a leading role in this wave of scholarship. For major collections of scholarship, see, e.g., Chu and Ding, *Qing Encounters*; and Juneja and Grasskamp, *EurAsian Matters*.
13. Recent publications include Finlay, "The Qianlong Emperor's Western Vistas"; Shih Ching-fei, *Riyue guanghua*; Kleutghen, *Imperial Illusions*; Musillo, *Shining Inheritance*; Curtis, *Glass Exchange*; and Pagani, *Eastern Magnificence*.
14. See Wang, "Whither Art History?," 381–82.
15. Ibid., 386.
16. Lai Yu-chih, "*Tuxiang diguo*"; Lai Yu-chih, "*Tuxiang, zhishi*"; and Lai Yu-chih, "*Qinggong dui Ouzhou ziranshi*."
17. A few examples published in previous exhibition catalogues have been wrongly identified as "Persian," "Indian," or made by the Qing Imperial Silk Manufactory in Jiangning. See Ho and Bronson, *Splendors of China's Forbidden City*, 107; Rawson and Rawski, *China: The Three Emperors*, 167; Huang Nengfu, *Zhongguo Nanjing yunjin*, 101, 104, 126, 134; and Gugong bowuyuan, *Ming Qing zhixiu*, 83, 117. The textile historian Zhao Feng was the first scholar to correctly point out the European origin of some of these pieces. See Zhao Feng, *Sichou yishu shi*, 195; and Zhao Feng, *Jincheng*, 315–19.
18. Peck et al., *Interwoven Globe*.
19. See, e.g., Jolly, *Taste for the Exotic*; and Peck et al., *Interwoven Globe*.
20. See, e.g., Bremer-David et al., *Woven Gold*; Knothe, *Manufacture des meubles*; and Anderson, "Material Mediators."
21. See Smentek, "Chinoiserie for the Qing"; Klatte, Prüssmann-Zemper, and Schmidt-Loske, *Exotismus und Globalisierung*, 100–107. For a discussion that extends to the Chinese context, see Rado, "Qing Court's Encounters with European Tapestries."

22. Zheng, *China on the Sea*, 210. In Qing documents, *xiyáng*, or *da xiyáng* (Great Western Ocean), referred to the region of Europe in a generic sense. As specific country names, *Da xiyáng guo* (Country of Great Western Ocean) meant Portugal, and *Xiao xiyáng guo* (Country of Petite Western Ocean) indicated Portuguese India. See Yang Jibo, "Ming Qing dang'an"; and the inscriptions on the Qing imperial scrolls *Official Tribute* (*Zhigong tu*), ca. 1748–80, the Palace Museum, Beijing, acc. no. gu6306.
23. For recent scholarship on chinoiserie focusing on European perspectives, see, e.g., Sloboda, *Chinoiserie*; and Johns, *China and the Church*.
24. See Hay, *Sensuous Surfaces*, 166; Kleutghen, "Chinese Occidenterie," 118; and Chu and Ding, *Qing Encounters*, 5.
25. On Western objects and style beyond the Qing court, see, e.g., Wang, "Whither Art History?," 386–92; Kleutghen, "Chinese Occidenterie"; Matteini, "Market for 'Western' Paintings." On the network linking Guangdong, Suzhou, Yangzhou and the court, see Yang Boda, *Qingdai Guangdong gongpin*; and Y. Wu, *Luxurious Networks*.
26. Grasskamp and Juneja, *EurAsian Matters*.
27. Although the geographical names of Asia, Europe, and America had already been introduced by the Flemish Jesuit missionary Ferdinand Verbiest (1623–1688) in his 1674 Chinese publication *Kunyu tushuo* (*An Illustrated Explanation of the World*) and its accompanying map, the Qing imperial vision and writings about the world rarely engaged with such concepts.
28. Juneja, "Global Art History."
29. Wang, "Whither Art History?," 382.
30. Rawski, "Re-envisioning the Qing," 829–50; Crossley, *Translucent Mirror*; and Elliott, *Manchu Way*.
31. Grasskamp and Juneja, *EurAsian Matters*, 7.
32. Sloboda, *Chinoiserie*, esp. chap. 1; Smentek, "Chinoiserie for the Qing."
33. See, e.g., Fan Jinmin, *Yi bei tianxia*; and Kuhn with Zhao Feng, *Chinese Silks*.
34. See, e.g., Chen, *Empire of Style*; Silberstein, *Fashionable Century*; and Gasparini, *Transcending Patterns*.
35. For recent art-historical reflections on materiality, see Yonan, "Toward a Fusion"; Rosler et al., "Notes from the Field."
36. See, e.g., Baxandall, *Painting and Experience*; Nelson, *Visuality Before and Beyond*; and Clunas, *Pictures and Visuality*.
37. Hellman, "Furniture, Sociability"; and Hellman, "Tapestries and Identities."

CHAPTER 1. FOREIGN SPLENDOR

1. On the Qing imperial silk manufactories, see Fan Jinmin, *Yi bei tianxia*, 167–240; Yan Yong, "Qingdai de guanying sizhi ye"; and Zhao Feng, *Zhongguo sichou tongshi*, 474–86.
2. Zhao Feng, *Zhongguo sichou tongshi*, 480, 484; and Yan Yong, "Qingdai de guanying sizhi ye," 84.
3. Zhao Feng, *Zhongguo sichou tongshi*, 485–86.
4. See "Textile Terminology and Measurement Systems."
5. See "Textile Terminology and Measurement Systems." An extensive definition of jin is given in Kuhn with Zhao Feng, *Chinese Silks*, 523.
6. Ibid., 527.
7. Ibid., 454.
8. Ibid., 372–75; and Fan Jinmin, *Yi bei tianxia*, 437–46.
9. The Taiping Rebellion (1850–64) ravaged the southern regions and severely damaged the imperial silk manufactories there, which recovered slowly after the 1870s. Most surviving artifacts from these bureaus date from after the late nineteenth century.
10. For detailed regulations on imperial dress, see Yunlu et al., *Huangchao liqi tushi*, vol. *Guanfu*. Despite the nearly identical forms of the dragon and the python, only the creature associated with the emperor, his mother, wife, and first-rank consort could be called a dragon.
11. Embroiderers and tapestry makers had more flexible techniques at their disposal for developing pictorial designs of landscapes and figures, and they drew on a wider range of sources, from paintings to popular prints. On vernacular embroideries in the late Qing period, see Silberstein, *Fashionable Century*. The advanced weaving technique for jin-lampas was also capable of rendering pictorial images, but it was rarely used for this purpose except for religious subjects. One example, the Buddhist icon image *Western Paradise* (*Jile shijie*) in the Palace Museum, Beijing (acc. no. gu73116), features extremely complex iconography in one single repeat of 9 ft. 6 in. × 5 ft. 9 in. (289 × 175 cm).
12. Zhao Feng, *Zhongguo sichou tongshi*, 423.
13. Hay, *Sensuous Surfaces*, 130.
14. On the changes in late Qing imperial portraiture in response to the international diplomatic climate, see Wang, "'Going Public.'"
15. The late Qing period, from the mid-1870s to 1911, saw another surge of Western designs in Qing imperial silks.
16. Zhao Feng, *Jincheng*, 311.
17. *Qinding da Qing huidian shili* (hereafter cited as DQHD), vol. 503: *Libu* 214/*chaogong* 2/*gongwu* 1, Shunzhi 13 (1656).
18. Poni, "Fashion as Flexible Production," 69.
19. L. Miller, "Making a Reputation," 190.
20. For a detailed description of the eighteenth-century French drawloom, see Colenbrander, *When Weaving Flourished*, 175–78. Also see "Textile Terminology and Measurement Systems."
21. On the English silk industry, see Rothstein, *Silk Designs of the Eighteenth Century*; and Schorta and Rothstein, *Seidengewebe des 18. Jahrhunderts*. On the Dutch silk industry, see Colenbrander, *When Weaving Flourished*.
22. Poni, "Fashion as Flexible Production," 42–45.
23. Rothstein, *Silk Designs of the Eighteenth Century*, 48.
24. Colenbrander, *When Weaving Flourished*, 107–16; on the import ban, see ibid., 110.
25. L. Miller, "Making a Reputation," 190–91; L. Miller, *Selling Silks*, 33–34.
26. Poni, "Fashion as Flexible Production," 48.
27. Joubert de l'Hiberderie, *Le dessinateur pour les étoffes d'or, d'argent et de soie* (1765), discussed in L. Miller, "Study of Designers," 1:174. On Joubert and this work, see L. Miller, "Representing Silk Design."
28. L. Miller, "From Design Studio to Marketplace," 237, 240; Poni, "Fashion as Flexible Production," 64.
29. L. Miller, "From Design Studio to Marketplace," 242, 249–50.
30. "Mémoire général sur la manufacture d'étoffes de soye, or et argent qui se fabriquent dans la ville de Lyon, écrit en janvier 1731," ff. 29–31, BNF, ms fr. 11855, discussed in L. Miller, "From Design Studio to Marketplace," 243–44.
31. Poni, "Fashion as Flexible Production."
32. Ibid., 41, 45.
33. Ibid., 38, 69.
34. L. Miller, "Making a Reputation," 193.
35. For an overview of the chronology of European silk design in the eighteenth century, see Rothstein, *Silk Designs of the Eighteenth Century*, 37–62.
36. Sargentson, *Merchants and Luxury Markets*, 108.
37. L. Miller, "Making a Reputation," 194–95.
38. See Arizzoli-Clémentel and Gastinel-Coural, *Soieries de Lyon*.
39. See the catalogue entries for two versions of this design at the Victoria & Albert Museum and the Metropolitan Museum of Art. https://collections.vam.ac.uk/item/O118377/the-partridges-panel-philippe-de-lasalle/ and https://www.metmuseum.org/art/collection/search/227482.
40. For examples of liturgical silks, see Picaud and Foisselon, *Sacrées soieries*.
41. Slomann, *Bizarre Designs in Silks*. For a recent study on bizarre silks, see

Ackermann and Otavská, *Seidengewebe des 18. Jahrhunderts I: bizarre Seiden*.

42. On the Japanese influence on bizarre silks, see S. Miller, "Disegni *bizarres*"; and S. Miller, "Europe Looks East."
43. From 1667 through the eighteenth century, the regulated French silk width for figured and plain fabrics was 11/24 French ell (*aune*), that is, 21¼ in. (54 cm). See Colenbrander, *When Weaving Flourished*, 139. See also "Measurement Systems and Conversions."
44. See Jolly and Otavská, *Seidengewebe des 18. Jahrhunderts III: Spitzenmuster*.
45. See Jolly and Otavská, *Seidengewebe des 18. Jahrhunderts II: Naturalismus*.
46. Rothstein, *Silk Designs of the Eighteenth Century*, 42; L. Miller, "Making a Reputation," 203, 209–10. On Jean Revel, see L. Miller, "Jean Revel: Silk Designer."
47. I am grateful to Deborah Metsger for identifying the species.
48. Rothstein, *Silk Designs of the Eighteenth Century*, 48.
49. For French examples, see Picaud and Foisselon, *Sacrées soieries*, cat. nos. 32, 37, 43, 44, 50.
50. Lekhovich, "Copies after Philippe de Lasalle's Silks," 91. On the Russian silk industry and its products, see Gordeeva, Efimova, and Kuznet͡sova, *Russkie uzornye tkani*, 59–115.
51. Lekhovich, "Copies after Philippe de Lasalle's Silks," 91.
52. Ibid., 95.
53. A special type of luxury silk called "gold treasure ground" (*jīnbǎo dì*), a subcategory of the "cloud brocade" (*yunjin*) woven in Nanjing, has the similar treatment of a gold lancé background and gold highlights. All the known "gold treasure ground" examples, however, are modern products. I speculate that the design and technical aspects of Russian gold silks, to which the Qing Imperial Silk Manufactories had access, may have lent inspiration to the "gold treasure ground." A full discussion is beyond the scope of this book.
54. HJD, Yongzheng 13 (1735), *Shouzhu wujian qingce: xinjin*, 6:777; HJD, Qianlong 24 (1759), *Xingqu wuliao qingce: shiyong*, 24:793.
55. DQHD, vol. 502: *Libu 213/chaogong 1/gongqi*.
56. DQHD, vol. 503: *Libu 214/chaogong 2/gongwu 1*, Kangxi 6 (1667); Kangxi 25 (1686).
57. DQHD, vol. 503: *Libu 214/chaogong 2/gongwu 1*, Yongzheng 5 (1727). The difference between "[figured] satin with gold threads" and "figured satin with gold" is not clear, and these terms are often used interchangeably in Qing imperial archives. The translations here closely follow the original wording.
58. DQHD, vol. 503: *Libu 214/chaogong 2/gongwu 1*, Kangxi 6 (1667) and Qianlong 17 (1752). On the Qing imperial painting recording the cows and horses presented by Holland in 1667, see Wang Ching-ling, "Tuxiang zhengshi," 88–99. For the 1752 Portuguese gifts, see Lacere, "Suite des nouvelles des missions," 526–27.
59. DQHD, vol. 503: *Libu 214/chaogong 2/gongwu 1*, Kangxi 59 (1720).
60. Martin, "Mirror Reflections."
61. Yulian Wu, *Luxurious Networks*, 64–70.
62. Liang Tingnan, *Yue haiguan zhi*, 625.
63. For selected lists of gifts presented by Canton officials, see Yang Boda, *Qingdai Guangdong gongpin*, 10–30.
64. Ibid., 15.
65. HJD, Qianlong 27/8/11 (1762), *Zalu*, 27:707.
66. HJD, Qianlong 28/10/10 (1763), *Jishi lu*, 28:29; the event recorded in this entry took place in Qianlong 26/4/15 (1761).
67. HJD, Qianlong 27/7/6 (1762), *Zalu dang*, 27:704.
68. Lai Hui-min, "Qianlong chao neiwu fu de pihuo maimai," 102–3.
69. Lai Hui-min, "Shijiu shiji Qiaketu maoyi," 7.
70. HJD, Qianlong 27/10/22 (1762), *Jishi lu*, 27:385.
71. Lai Hui-min, "Shijiu shiji Qiaketu maoyi," 9.
72. Clunas, *Superfluous Things*, 49–51.
73. *Tianshui bingshan lu*.
74. HJD, Yongzheng 1/1 (1723), *Kunei shouzhu dang*, 1:231.
75. HJD, Yongzheng 1 (1723), *Sanchu zhizao laijin dang*, 2:407–20.
76. On the use of these words for imperial furniture, see Wu Meifeng, *Sheng Qing jiaju xingzhi*, 339–41.
77. In the case of lacquer, *yángqi* (foreign lacquer) meant both *maki-e* lacquer imported from Japan and Qing court copies made in this style. See Chen Hui-hsia, "Yongzheng chao de yangqi." On its own, the term *yángjin* often meant a special type of silk satin woven with stylized small lotus patterns in gold threads. The word's etymology is not clear, but such silks had no association with Europe and were specifically used as mounting materials for Tibetan Buddhist icons (*thangkas*).
78. HJD, Qianlong 15/6/23 (1750), *Jishi lu*, 17:288.
79. HJD, Qianlong 16/7/7 (1751), *Jishi lu*, 18:388.
80. See Lai Hui-min, "Shijiu shiji Qiaketu maoyi," 7.
81. Yunlu et al., *Huangchao liqi tushi*, vol. *Wubei*.
82. Dai Jian, *Nanjing yunjin*, 56.
83. Ibid., 79–80.
84. Pauletti and Peri, *Oro filato*, 19.
85. Tomaso Garzoni, *La Piazza universale di tutte le professioni del mondo* (Venice, 1587), "Filatori da oro, & argento," discussed in Pauletti and Peri, *Oro filato*, 19.
86. See Diderot and d'Alembert, *Encyclopédie*, s.v. "Tireur d'or et d'argent."
87. HJD, Qianlong 13/11/5 (1748), *Suzhou*, 16:193. See also "Textile Terminology and Measurement Systems."
88. Other examples include a dragon robe in the Palace Museum, acc. no. gu42106, and one in the Huaihai Tang collection, Hong Kong. I am grateful to Sam Yu Tong for bringing the latter to my attention.
89. HJD, Qianlong 23/11/29 (1758), *Ruyi guan*, 23:496. The event recorded took place on Qianlong 24/2/6 (1759).
90. HJD, Qianlong 28/12/27 (1764), *Xingwen*, 28:117.

CHAPTER 2. "FOR HIS MAJESTY'S USE"

1. HJD, Yongzheng 2/12/1 (1725), *Pizuo*, 1:347.
2. HJD, Yongzheng 1–4 (1723–1726), *Sanchu zhizao laijin dang*, 2:407–20.
3. HJD, Yongzheng 2/11/19 (1725), *Jishi lu*, 1:355.
4. HJD, Yongzheng 1/4/21 (1723), *Jishi lu*, 1:163.
5. Pirazzoli-t'Serstevens, "Notes on European Decorative Arts," 8.
6. See, e.g., HJD, Yongzheng 3/9/20 and 3/10/18 (1725), *Biaozuo, huazuo*, 1:567–68, 570–72; Yang Boda, *Qingdai Guangdong gongpin*, 12, 42.
7. Pirazzoli-t'Serstevens, "Notes on European Decorative Arts," 12–14. See also Haemmerle, *Buntpapier*.
8. HJD, Qianlong 26/3/27 (1761), *Xingwen chu*, 26:653.
9. HJD, Qianlong 27/5/15 (1762), *Xingwen*, 27:340–41. The measurement system *caiyi chi* was used here. See "Measurement Systems and Conversions."
10. HJD, Qianlong 27/10/22 (1762), *Jishi lu*, 27:384–85.
11. Dai Jian, *Nanjing Yunjin*, 55–56.
12. Gao Shiqi, *Pengshan miji*, 269.
13. See the document in Biblioteca Apostolica Vaticana, Collezione Borgia, Cinese, 511 (6) and Latino, 565 121v., quoted in Curtis, *Glass Exchange*, 114; Shih Ching-fei, *Riyue guanghua*, 62.
14. See, e.g., HJD, Qianlong 25/4/24 (1760), *Suzhou*, 25:550–51.
15. Comprehensive and in-depth studies of Chinese silks for the export market are lacking. Notable publications include Lee-Whitman, "Silk Trade"; and Ferreira, "As alfaias bordadas sinoportuguesas."
16. For discussions on some of these silks, see, e.g., Jolly, "Soierie chinoise"; Rothstein, *Flowers, Blumen, Fleurs*, 20; and Rado, "Botanical Fantasy in Silks."
17. Rothstein, "Nine English Silks," 12, 15.

See also "Measurement Systems and Conversions."

18. The current skirt panel was part of a dress remade circa the 1870s. Other parts from the same dress are in the collections of Colonial Williamsburg, acc. no. 1992-85 A, B. The reuse of the textile demonstrates a continued appreciation for this precious silk long past its heyday of fashion. Alteration and refashioning were very common during the eighteenth and nineteenth centuries, even among the wealthiest elites. On this phenomenon, see, e.g., Baumgarten, *What Clothes Reveal,* chap. 6.
19. I am grateful to Deborah Metsger for identifying the species.
20. Browne, "Influence of Botanical Sources," 33; Anishanslin, *Portrait of a Woman,* 91–95.
21. See, e.g., Fan, *British Naturalists;* Bleichmar, *Visible Empire.*
22. Rothstein, "Silks for the American Market," 155; Anishanslin, *Portrait of a Woman,* 82.
23. Horace J. F. Jayne, former director of the University of Pennsylvanian Museum and a historian of East Asian art, acquired this piece in China in the early twentieth century, when Qing dynasty textiles were widely available at local antique markets. For some reason, this piece did not make its way abroad during the eighteenth century and remained in China. See Jolly, "Soierie chinoise," 79.
24. V&A, acc. no. T.740-1974. https://collections.vam.ac.uk/item/O140031/coat-unknown/.
25. Lee-Whitman, "Silk Trade," 21; Baumgarten, *What Clothes Reveal,* 84.
26. See, e.g., National Museum, Dublin, acc. no. NMIDT1908.566; National Museum of Scotland, Edinburgh, acc. no. A.1937.384; Röhsska Museum of Applied Art and Design, Gothenburg, Sweden, acc. no. RKM 206.42; Musée des Tissus, Lyon, acc. no. MT.30897. For discussions on some of these pieces, see, e.g., Kjellberg, "English 18th-Century Silks in Norway," 143; and Stavenow-Hidemark, "Silk Industry in Sweden," 164.
27. Wang Lianming, "Beijing Yesuhui Beitang huayuan," 217–21; Chiu, "Vegetal Travel," 98, 108n23, for the full list of species in French.
28. Chiu, "Vegetal Travel," 98.
29. On this album, see Ho Chuan-hsin, *Shenbi danqing,* 88–93.
30. On this album, see Chang Hsiang-wen, "Haixi jihui," 106–19.
31. Lai Yu-chih, "Overview of the Network."
32. For vessels decorated with such flowers, see Chang, "Haixi jihui," 117–18.
33. On this silk, see Jolly and Otavská, *Seidengewebe des 18. Jahrhunderts II,* 184–85; and Jolly, "Soierie chinoise."
34. Jolly and Otavská, *Seidengewebe des 18. Jahrhunderts II,* 186.
35. Wijayaratna, *Buddhist Monastic Life,* chap. 3.
36. See, e.g., HJD, Qianlong 16/12/28 (1752), *Muzuo,* 18:308–9; and Qianlong 46/1/5 (1781), *Jishi lu,* 44:539–41.
37. For a comparative history of Indian floral calicoes domesticated in England and North America, see Lemire, "Domesticating the Exotic."
38. See Peck et al., *Interwoven Globe,* cat. no. 62, "Buddhist Vestment (Kesa)," 217.
39. The other suit of armor is in the Metropolitan Museum of Art, acc. no. 30.76.31.
40. Elliott, *Manchu Way,* 276–77.
41. Ibid., 183.
42. Hou Chin-lang and Pirazzoli, *Mulan tu,* 9, 11.
43. *Gaozong Chun Huangdi shilu,* Qianlong 25/5/20 (1760) vol. 613; see also Elliott, *Manchu Way,* 186.
44. Hou and Pirazzoli, *Mulan tu,* 26.
45. Ibid., 82.
46. Ibid., 80–81.
47. Ibid., 83–84.
48. Elliott, *Manchu Way,* 184.
49. *Shizu Zhang Huangdi shilu,* Shuzhi 7/3/25 (1651), vol. 48.
50. For an overview, see Zhang Qiong, "Qingdai Huangdi dayue."
51. *Shengzu Ren Huangdi shilu,* Kangxi 24/11/18 (1685), vol. 123.
52. Elliott, *Emperor Qianlong,* 90–99.
53. *Gaozong Chun Huangdi shilu,* Qianlong 23/11/5 (1758), vol. 574. See also Liu Lu, "Congboxing shiyitu," 23–24.
54. Qianlong, "Qianlong ershisan nian."
55. Yunlu et al., *Huangchao liqi tushi,* vol. *Wubei.* On the production process of this regulation, see Lai Yu-chih, "'Tu' yu li."
56. HJD, Qianlong 4/10/11 (1739), *Pizuo,* 9:56.
57. HJD, Qianlong 20/4/10 (1755), *Pizuo,* 21:431.
58. Lin Chi-Lynn, "Qianlong de yidong gongdian," 43–45.
59. HJD, Qianlong 27/10/6 (1762), *Picai zuo,* 27:536.
60. See, e.g., HJD, Qianlong 8/12/4 (1743), *Pizuo,* 11:67.
61. *Gaozong Chun Huangdi shilu,* Qianlong 30/10/11 (1765), vol. 746; also see Zhang Qiong, "Qingdai Huangdi dayue," 95.
62. Yunlu et al., *Huangchao liqi tushi,* vol. *Wubei.*
63. Gugong bowuyuan, *Qinggong wubei,* 29.
64. HJD, Qianlong 10/10/7 (1745), *Anzuo,* 13:469.
65. See, e.g., HJD, Qianlong 27/10/6 (1762), *Picai zuo,* 27:536.
66. HJD, Qianlong 26/6/11 (1761), *Anjia zuo,* 26:111.
67. See Ho and Bronson, *Splendors of China's Forbidden City,* 182.
68. Lai Yu-chih, "Tuxiang diguo," 42–44.
69. See, e.g., the response of Korean envoys Yi Kiji (1690–1722) and Hong Daeyong (1731–1783) to the *quadratura* wall paintings in the Jesuit church Beitang in Beijing, quoted in Kleutghen, *Imperial Illusions,* 81–82; Gao, *Pengshan miji,* 269.
70. Hay, "Passage of the Other," 64.
71. Grabar, *Mediation of Ornament,* 226–27.
72. See Kleutghen, *Imperial Illusions,* esp. 4.
73. HJD, Qianlong 23/10/14 (1758), *Ruyi guan,* 23:480; also see Liu Lu, "Congboxing shiyitu," 23. The Grand Review was held on Qianlong 23/11/5 (December 5, 1758).
74. Rawski, *Last Emperors,* 252.
75. See Berger, *Empire of Emptiness;* and Luo Wenhua, *Longpao yu Jiasha.*
76. Rawski, *Last Emperors,* 244–51; and Crossley, *Translucent Mirror,* 223–62.
77. HJD, Qianlong 14/9/27 (1749), *Pizuo,* 17:169.
78. HJD, Qianlong 10/11/4 (1745), *Caizuo,* 13:460.
79. On the iconography and layout of the thangkas in this Buddhist hall, see, e.g., Wang Zilin, *Zijincheng yuanzhuang,* 2:362–401; and Luo Wenhua, "Jizu yu lifo."
80. HJD, Qianlong 31/12/3 (1767), *Picai zuo,* 30:293–94.
81. Ahmed, "Brocade for the Buddhists," 16–22.
82. For another eighteenth-century example made of silks of similar floral patterns, see Hillwood Estate, Museum and Gardens, acc. no. 44.7.
83. On the concept of *zhuangyan* in Buddhism, see Bai Huawen, "Jiang Zhuangyan"; and Teiser, "Ornamenting the Departed."
84. Teiser, "Ornamenting the Departed," 213–14.
85. Berger, *Empire of Emptiness,* 6, 11.

CHAPTER 3. ENCODING GLOBAL ASPIRATIONS

1. Tapestries can also be made in twill weave, as in Indian cashmere shawls, but the pictorial hangings discussed in this book are all in plain weave. See "Textile Terminology and Measurement Systems."
2. Wu Min, "Xinjiang jinnian chutu."
3. On the origin of the term *kesi,* see the passage in Zhuang Chuo (fl. 11th–12th century), *Jilei bian,* translated and discussed in Malagò, "*Kesi,* Chinese Literary Sources," 228.
4. Watt and Wardwell, *When Silk Was Gold,* chap. 2, esp. 57; Piao Wenying, "Introduction," 13–16.
5. Piao Wenying, *Kesi,* 46.
6. On Qianlong's project of collecting and displaying art, see Feng, *Qianlong Huangdi;* Ho, *Shiquan Qianlong;* and Chiang, *Emperor Qianlong's Hidden Treasures.*
7. Hay, "Kangxi Emperor's Brush-Traces," 311–12.
8. Li, "'Remediated Antiquarianism.'"
9. Some tapestries from the Germanic regions used linen for the warps, but

10. this remained a minor practice and was confined to relatively low-end works. See Cavallo, *Tapestries of Europe and Colonial Peru*, 1:47.
11. In 1665 Colbert also passed initiatives to provide state support to the Aubusson and Felletin workshops, which produced tapestries for the middle- and low-end markets. For recent publications on French tapestries, see Bertrand, "Tapestry Production at the Gobelins"; Bremer-David, "Manufacture Royale de Tapisseries de Beauvais"; Vittet, *Gobelins au siècle des Lumières;* and Bremer-David, *Woven Gold*.
12. See, e.g., Bertrand, "Louis XIV and Louis XV"; Knothe, "Tapestry as a Medium of Propaganda"; and Knothe, *Manufacture des meubles*.
13. The French titles are *Les Quatre éléments, Les Quatre saisons, L'Histoire d'Alexandre, L'Histoire du Roi,* and *Les Maison royales*.
14. Bertrand, "Louis XIV and Louis XV," 48.
15. Bertrand, "Tapestry Production at the Gobelins," 352–53.
16. Ibid., 354.
17. Bremer-David, "Manufacture Royale de Tapisseries de Beauvais," 413.
18. Campbell, "Tapestry," 194–95. Grand tapestries featuring biblical, historical, or hereditary themes, however, continued to hold propagandistic significance and were displayed in palace state rooms and churches.
19. Bremer-David, *French Tapestries and Textiles*, 67–68.
20. Coural, *Manufacture royale de Beauvais*, 43; Badin, *Manufacture de tapisseries de Beauvais*, 84–85.
21. Bertrand, "Tapestry Production at the Gobelins," 350; Weigert, *French Tapestry*, 123.
22. Cavallo, *Tapestries of Europe and Colonial Peru*, 1:18.
23. DQHD, vol. 503: *Libu* 214/*chaogong* 2/*gongwu* 1, Shunzhi 13 (1656), Kangxi 6 (1667), and Kangxi 8 (1669).
24. Vlam, "Sixteenth-Century European Tapestries"; Kajitani and Yoshida, *Gionmatsuri yamaboko kensōhin*, 21–23.
25. Huang Bolu, *Zhengjiao fengbao*, 2:121–22.
26. "Délivré aux R R. Pères Jésuites missionnaires allans à la Chine, suivant l'ordre de Monseigneur de Louvois. . . . Trois du livre des tapisseries des 4 elemèns et des 4 saisons. . . . Trois de chacune des trois tapisseries de *l'alliance des Suisses*, du *siège de Tournay*, et de *la défaite de Marsin*." Abbé de Varès, *Registre des Livres*.
27. On this project, see Duplessis, *Cabinet du roi;* and Grivel, "Cabinet du Roi."
28. See Liu Shi-yee, "Qianlong pingding Huijiang," 35.
29. Chou Kung-shin, "Faguo Luyi shisi shiqi," 257. See also Landry-Deron, "Mathématiciens envoyés en Chine."
30. See Félibien, *Tapisseries du Roy*.
31. Verhaeren, *Catalogue de la Bibliothèque du Pé-t'ang*, 183, entry 667. The Beitang library dissolved in the late 1950s, and some of its collections went to the National Library of China.
32. Félibien, *Quatre éléments;* and Félibien, *Quatre saisons*. See also Knothe, "Water," 363.
33. Meyer, *Histoire du Roy*, 128–129; Vittet, "King Visits the Gobelins," 375–77.
34. Knothe, "Water," 362–63.
35. Liu Shi-yee, "Qianlong pingding Huijiang."
36. DQHD, *Libu* 214/*chaogong* 2/*gongwu* 1, Yongzheng 5 (1727).
37. HJD, Qianlong 10/5/1 (1745), *Jishi lu*, 13:547.
38. HJD, Qianlong 14/2/2 (1749), *Zalu*, 17:705.
39. Benoist to Bertin, Pe King, October 12, 1766, in the compiled collection *Correspondance des RR. PP. jésuites missionnaires en Chine avec H. L. J.-B. Bertin* in the Bibliothèque de l'Institut de France (hereafter cited as BIF), transcribed in Cordier, "Correspondants de Bertin," 306.
40. Pirazzoli-t'Serstevens, "Pluridisciplinary Research," 4.
41. Finlay, "Qianlong Emperor's Western Vistas."
42. HJD, Qianlong 15/5/23 (1750), *Jishi lu*, 17:288.
43. See Henri Bertin to Aloys Ko and Étienne Yang, Versailles, January 27, 1769, in *Correspondance*, BIF, MS1521, f. 102v.
44. DQHD, vol. 503: *Libu* 214/*chaogong* 2/*gongwu* 1, Qianlong 17 (1752).
45. "Neuf pièces de tapisseries de Gobelins, . . . il [l'Empereur] les fit placer dans un nouveau palais qui dans ces dernières années a été bâti dans le goût Européen et que les Pères Jésuites qui en ont été les architectes appellent le petit Versailles." Lacere, "Suite des nouvelles des missions," 527.
46. See, e.g., DQHD, vol. 503: *Libu* 214/*chaogong* 2/*gongwu* 1, Yongzheng 7 (1729), Qianlong 14 (1749), and Qianlong 31 (1766).
47. List of tributary gifts from the Siamese king dated Qianlong 46/5/26 (1781), Grand Council (*Junji chu*) document no. 030433, reproduced in Feng, *Qianlong Huangdi*, 162–63.
48. The full titles of the two publications are *Het gezantschap der Neêrlandtsche Oost-Indische Compagnie aan den grooten Tartarischen Cham, den tegenwoordigen keizer van China; China monumentis, qua sacris qua profanis, nec non variis naturae & artis spectaculis, aliarumque rerum memorabilium argumentis illustrata*. For a discussion, see Reed, "A Perfume Is Best from Afar."
49. Belevitch-Stankevitch, *Goût chinois en France*, 10–48. For a recent publication on the French craze for China in the time of Louis XIV, see Rochebrune, *Chine à Versailles*. On the Siamese embassy to Versailles, see Martin, "Mirror Reflections."
50. Martin, "Mirror Reflections," 656.
51. The French titles are *L'Audience de l'empereur, L'Empereur en voyage, Les Astronomes, La Collation, La Récolte des ananas, Le Retour de la chasse, L'Embarquement de l'empereur, L'Embarquement de l'impératrice,* and *Le Thé de l'impératrice*. For studies of this set, see Standen, "The Story of the Emperor of China"; Jarry, *Chinoiseries*, 15–26; and Bremer-David, *French Tapestries*, 80–88.
52. Sotheby's London, *Catalogue of Tapestries*, November 20, 1964, 5 (lot 4). This tapestry was sold multiple times thereafter, including at Christie's London, April 12, 1984 (lot 3), and, most recently, Sotheby's London, December 7, 2000 (lot 74). On its auction history through 1995, see Bremer-David, *French Tapestries*, 95.
53. Hevia, *English Lessons*, 82–86.
54. Bremer-David, "Manufacture Royale de Tapisseries de Beauvais," 407.
55. For Ko's and Yang's full biographies, see Bernard-Maître, "Deux chinois"; and Finlay, *Henri Bertin*, 8–39.
56. Smentek, "Chinoiserie for the Qing"; Rado, "Qing Court's Encounters with European Tapestries," 121–24; Finlay, "Henri Bertin and Louis XV's Gifts."
57. The French titles are *Le Repas chinois, La Danse chinoise, La Pêche chinoise, La Foire chinoise, La Chasse chinoise,* and *La Toilette chinoise* (aka *Le Jardin chinois*). For discussions on this set, see Jarry, *Chinoiseries*, 26–32; Bertrand, "Seconde 'Tenture chinoise'"; and Adelson, *European Tapestry*, 322–42. For reproductions of Boucher's paintings for this set and the six tapestries, see Rimaud et al., *Une des provinces du rococo*, 186–201.
58. Bertrand, "Seconde 'Tenture chinoise,'" 173–76; Adelson, *European Tapestry*, 326.
59. Badin, *Manufacture de tapisseries de Beauvais*, 61, 84; Bertrand, "Seconde 'Tenture chinoise,'" 173, 176–77.
60. Archives nationales (hereafter cited as AN), O/1/2038. The width of each piece in this set is given in the same document in French ells (*aunes*): *Chinese Fair*, 5 aunes 10/16 ≈ 21 ft. 9¾ in. (6.64 m); *Chinese Feast*, 4 aunes 9/16½ ≈ 17 ft. 10⅝ in. (5.45 m); *Chinese Fishing*, 3 aunes 7/16½ ≈ 13 ft. 4³⁄₁₆ in. (4.07 m); *Chinese Hunt*, 3 aunes 9/16½ ≈ 13 ft. 10⅞ in. (4.24 m); *Chinese Toilette*, 3 aunes 2/16½ ≈ 12 ft. 2⅞ in. (3.73 m); *Chinese Dance*, 4 aunes 11/16½ ≈ 18 ft. 4½ in. (5.6 m). The

59. metric dimensions are given in Bertrand, "Seconde 'Tenture chinoise,'" 182n33. The height of this set is not indicated. Charissa Bremer-David suggested to me that it was probably the same as that of the set woven between 1758 and 1860 for the Crown, which is listed in the Beauvais weavers' register in Flemish ell (see B 168, f. 49) as 5 aunes 2/16 ≈ 11 ft. 8⅝ in. (3.57 m). See also "Measurement Systems and Conversions." On the Flemish ell, see Colenbrander, *When Weaving Flourished*, 218n270.

60. Bertrand, "La Seconde 'Tenture chinoise,'" 177.

61. Smentek, "Chinoiserie for the Qing," esp. 92–93, 104; Finlay, "Henri Bertin and Louis XV's Gifts," esp. 93, 108; Finlay, *Henri Bertin*, chap. 1, esp. 19–22.

62. Bertin to Ko and Yang, Versailles, December 31, 1766, in *Correspondance*, BIF, MS1521, f. 10r–10v. See also Finlay, *Henri Bertin*, 20–21.

63. See the document "Voyage et séjour par ordre du Roi de deux particuliers chinois, les sieurs Kô and Yang," 1–12, in *Correspondance*, BIF, MS1520, ff. 50r–55v.

64. For Ko and Yang's reports on these study tours, see "Remarques sur différentes manufactures," 1764, in *Correspondance*, BIF, MS1520, ff. 40–47. Their tours are described and their reports transcribed in Bernard-Maître, "Deux chinois," 161–80.

65. "On fait en Chine une espèce de tapisserie avec le poile de chameau. Elle ne mérite guères le nom de tapisserie. Ce ne sont que mille bigarrures sans beaucoup de goût ni de liaison, aussi les Chinois ne s'en servent-ils que comme d'une espèce de tapis de pieds. Deux ou trois tentures de tapisserie de ce pays ci dans le palais de l'Empereur luy feroient peutêtre plus de plaisir que tous les trônes magnifiques dont il orne sa cour. Il seroit surpris de l'éclat des couleurs et de la beauté du dessein. Les personnages et les fleurs sont préférables à toute autre représentation, mais il faut que les personnages soient décents, par ce que les Chinois sont sur cela extrêmement délicats." Ko and Yang, "Remarques," in *Correspondance*, BIF, MS1520, ff. 41r–41v.

66. "Les chinois seroient plus du goût et plus en état d'acheter ces tapis veloutés que les tapisseries de Gobelin. C'est pour quoy il seroit à souhaiter que l'Empereur de la Chine eût quelques unes des pièces qui représentent les animaux, les fleurs, et les paysages; la vüe de ces représentations vives et animées pourroit exciter l'envie des seigneurs de la cour d'en avoir de semblables." Ibid., f. 42v.

67. Ko was born in a modest Christian family in Beijing, and Yang came from the nearby countryside. See Bernard-Maître, "Deux chinois," 154.

68. "Voyage et séjour," 2, in *Correspondance*, BIF, MS1520, f. 50v.

69. Bernard-Maître, "Deux chinois," 184–85.

70. *Collection de manuscrits*, BNF, Fonds Bréquigny, 1:ff. 6–7. See also "Voyage et séjour," 11, in *Correspondance*, BIF, MS1520, f. 55r. For an annotated transcription of the gifts, see Finlay, "Henri Bertin and Louis XV's Gifts," 97–100.

71. Martin, "Special Embassies," 117.

72. Yang to Bertin, Canton, December 16, 1765, in *Correspondance*, BIF, MS1520, f. 150v.

73. Benoist to Bertin, Beijing, October 12, 1766, transcribed in Cordier, "Correspondants de Bertin," 295–312.

74. Benoist to Bertin, Beijing, September 10–November 10, 1767, transcribed in Cordier, "Correspondants de Bertin," 322.

75. *Gongzhong jindan*, Qianlong 31/11/9 (December 10, 1766), transcribed in Dong Jianzhong, "Chuanjiaoshi jingong," 96.

76. "L'empereur à la vüe des pièces si rares fut tellement enchanté qu'il s'éleva tout haut disant ces paroles: O les belles choses; il n'y en a pas de pareille dans mon empire. Ce fut comme un jour de fête à la Cour." Yang to Bertin, Canton, December 29, 1767, in *Correspondance*, BIF, MS1520, f. 167r.

77. "[Le grand Mandarin] il sortoit d'avec l'Empereur qu'il m'avoua avoir été saisi d'admiration en voyant les six pièces de tapisseries. Il me raconta comment Sa Majesté les ayant fait placer sous différents points de vüe et les ayant d'autant plus admirées qu'il examinoit avec plus d'attention la délicatesse de leur ouvrage." Benoist to Bertin, Beijing, September 10–November 10, 1767, transcribed in Cordier, "Correspondants de Bertin," 322.

78. "Ces tapisseries ont été comparées à celles qui avoient été présentées à l'empereur par l'ambassadeur de Portugal. La laideur de celle ci relèvent encore davantage la beauté de celles là." Yang to Bertin, Canton, December 29, 1767, in *Correspondance*, BIF, MS1520, ff. 168r–168v.

79. Bertin to Ko and Yang, Versailles, January 27, 1769, in *Correspondance*, BIF, MS1521, f. 99r.

80. Smentek, "Chinoiserie for the Qing," 104–5; and Finlay, "Henri Bertin and Louis XV's Gifts," 105.

81. Benoist's letter to Bertin stated the same and confirmed the latter's fear. Benoist to Bertin, Beijing, November 10, 1767, transcribed in Cordier, "Correspondants de Bertin," 323–24.

82. "Je compte bien aussi que les Missionnaires profiteront de cette occasion pour faire tourner à l'avantage de la nation françoise et de son commerce, le mérite de cet ouvrage, et pour lui procurer à cet égard la protection de l'Empereur et la faire surtout distinguer des autres nations Européennes." Bertin to Pierre Poivre, Versailles, December 31, 1766, in *Correspondance*, BIF, MS1521, ff. 88v–89r.

83. "J'ai lû avec une nouvelle satisfaction . . . qu'elles [les tapisseries] avoient fait sur l'esprit de sa majesté impériale tout l'effet que j'en avois espéré en luy donnant une haute idée de la perfection à laquelle les arts sont portés en France et à réveiller son attention en faveur d'une nation industrieuse et savante que les missionnaires depuis plus d'un siècle luy ont fait connoitre d'une manière avantageuse." Bertin to Ko and Yang, Versailles, January 27, 1769, in *Correspondance*, BIF, MS1521, ff. 98r–98v.

84. Although no record of its exact completion date has been found, a 1781 entry in the HJD refers to it as the "newly built palace of fountains" (*xinjian shuifa dian*); HJD, Qianlong 46/5/29 (1781), *Jishi lu*, 44:587.

85. *Plan d'une grande partie du parc d'Yuen-Ming-Yuen*, BNF, Estampes et photographie, HZ-444-Roul.

86. *L'Art pour tous*, July 15, 1861, 5; and August 31, 1861, 63. This piece was auctioned by Maison Braquenié on the rue Vivienne in Paris and acquired by Count Pozzo di Borgo; unfortunately, it was destroyed in a fire at his château in Montretout in 1871. Another piece from this set—*Chinese Toilette*—was taken from Yuanming yuan by the English colonel Greathed and exported to the United States in 1947. See Bertrand, "Seconde 'Tenture chinoise,'" 177.

87. See, e.g., HJD, Qianlong 33/10/22, *Xingwen fang*, 31:747.

88. The name of France was occasionally noted. For example, Qianlong mentioned "Folangji" (France) in his 1774 poem on the cassowary, cited in Lai Yu-chih, "Tuxiang, zhishi," 12.

89. "Est-ce que nos tapisseries de Beauvais et nos glaces qui ont si bien réussi n'ont pas donné désir à la cour et au souverain lui-même d'en avoir autres?" Bertin to Ko and Yang, Versailles, October 10, 1772, in *Correspondance*, BIF, MS1521, f. 150v.

90. For a copy of this collection, see Amiot, *Mémoires*, BNF, 4O2N-54. For a study of it and the Chinese materials that Ko, Yang, and French missionaries helped collect for Bertin, see Finlay, *Henri Bertin*.

91. For recent studies of the *Tenture des Indes*, see Klatte et al., *Exotismus und*

92. Anderson, "Material Mediators"; Anderson, "Old Indies."
93. Anderson, "Material Mediators," 76; and Bremer-David, "Striped Horse," 391–92.
94. The French titles are *L'Indien à cheval*, *Le Roi porté par deux maures*, *Le Chasseur indien*, *Le Cheval rayé*, *Les Pêcheurs*, *Le Combat des animaux*, *Les Deux taureaux*, and *Le Cheval isabelle* (aka *L'Éléphant*).
95. Fenaille, *État général des tapisseries*, 2:371–98; Whitehead and Boeseman, *Portrait of Dutch 17th Century Brazil*, 107–61. See also "Measurement Systems and Conversions."
96. Soufflot to Marigny, November 21, 1769, AN, O/1/1554, transcribed in Mondain-Monval, *Correspondance de Soufflot*, 242–44. "Nous avons aux Gobelins une ancienne *Tenture des Indes* d'autant plus passée qu'elle a été prêtée en plusieurs circonstances depuis environ 1720 qu'elle a été faite." Ibid., 242; for notes on the price, see 243.
97. The price proposed in the letter was 17,120 livres at 160 livres per square aune, and then the total was reduced to 16,000 (AN, O/1/1554); Mondain-Monval, *Correspondance de Soufflot*, 243. Thus, the price was calculated for a total of 107 square aunes, which corresponds to the new measurements given in the document "État des Tentures de haute et basse lisse de la Manufacture royale des Gobelins," AN, O/1/2043, transcribed in Fenaille, *État général des tapisseries*, 2:385. The measurements (taken on February 25, 1768) in this document, however, are wrongly calculated as 24 aunes 12/16 for the total width and 102 square aunes for the total area. The correct numbers, arrived at by adding up the measurements of the individual pieces, should be 26 aunes 12/16 for the total width and 107 square aunes for the total area.
98. Soufflot to Marigny, November 21, 1769, AN, O/1/1554, transcribed in Mondain-Monval, *Correspondance de Soufflot*, 243.
99. "L'acheteur est un négociant qui est tantôt à Paris, tantôt aux Indes et à la Chine. Il a su dans son dernier voyage que l'empereur de la Chine a été enchanté d'une tenture, probablement de Beauvais, que M. Bertin envoya il y a quelques années pour voir si ces ouvrages pourraient plaire à la Chine et procurer des échanges. . . . En conséquence notre négociant a fait une spéculation sur notre tenture. . . . Si sa spéculation réussit, il prendra peut-être successivement plusieurs tentures sans craindre comme à présent de trop risquer pour le prix." Ibid., 243–44.
100. For a summary of the eight weavings of the *Anciennes Indes*, see Whitehead and Boeseman, *Portrait of Dutch 17th Century Brazil*, 121; and Klatte et al., *Exotismus und Globalisierung*, 350–51. The first, second, and fourth sets were woven on low-warp looms, and the rest on high-warp looms.
101. Marigny to Soufflot, December 26, 1769, AN, O/1/1554, transcribed in Mondain-Monval, *Correspondance de Soufflot*, 244.
102. Ko to Bertin, Hou quang, September 8, 1771, in *Correspondance*, BIF, MS1520, ff. 205v–206r.
103. See *Correspondance*, BIF, MS1515, f. 12r, transcribed in Bernard [-Maître], "Catalogue des objets envoyés de Chine," 142, 144. Le Chevalier Rothe was Edmond Rothe, who and his brother François were active in French Canton trade. See Schopp, *Sino-French Trade*, 125. I am grateful to John Finlay and Kee Il Choi.
104. "Il n'y a presque point de figures, dont il croit qu'ils se soucient le moins, et qu'il y a des animaux des Indes de toute espèce dont la représentation pourra les étonner et leur plaire." Soufflot to Marigny, November 21, 1769, AN, O/1/1554, transcribed in Mondain-Monval, *Correspondance de Soufflot*, 244.
105. See the report in *Correspondance*, BIF, MS1520, f. 42v.
106. Wills, *Embassies and Illusions*, 118.
107. Ko to Bertin, Hou quang, September 8, 1771, in *Correspondance*, BIF, MS1520, f. 206r.
108. The measurement system *yingzao chi* was used here. See "Measurement Systems and Conversions."
109. The registers have a subtitle: "List of tributary gifts and displays along the Shandong inspection tour [*Shandong yilu jingong chenshe qingdan*], Qianlong 36/2/5 onward." *Gongzong jindan*, no. 53, First Historical Archives of China. I am grateful to Dong Jianzhong for sharing his transcription of this document.
110. Dong Jianzhong, "Li Shiyao jingong."
111. I am grateful to Dong Jianzhong for pointing out this fact.
112. On the back of the English note, Crealocke wrote, "Found in the palace of Yuanming Yuan . . . Oct-1861." The year 1861 was an error; it should be 1860. Also attached to this note is another yellow imperial tag reading, "100 silver ingots each weighing 5 *qian*." According to Dong Jianzhong, the presence of the tag is probably an accidental mix-up; it was not the price tag for the tapestry but rather the tag for another gift item consisting of small silver ingots.
113. This label is attributed to *Les Pêcheurs* in Klatte et al., *Exotismus und Globalisierung*, 102. The width of *Le Combat des animaux* as remeasured in 1768 in French aunes, however, was 3 aunes 3/16 ≈ 12 ft. 5 in. (379 cm), while that of *Les Pêcheurs* was 2 aunes 10/16 ≈ 10 ft. 3 in. (312 cm); see AN, O/1/2043, transcribed in Fenaille, *État général des tapisseries*, 2:385. *Le Combat* was repaired in 1861 and recently conserved by the Ashmolean Museum, and its current dimensions, 16 ft. × 12 ft. 8 in. (487.5 × 386 cm), differ from those recorded when it was presented to Qianlong in 1771, 15 ft. 4 in. × 12 ft. 5 in. (467 × 378 cm). It is not clear whether the new measurements include additional borders, and temperature and humidity conditions also cause textiles to change dimensions. The height 4 aunes (15 ft. 7 in. [475 cm]), used to calculate the price at the time of sale, was the standard height of the original weaving and did not reflect the actual condition.
114. Zebras, elephants, and rhinoceroses were not native to the Americas. See Bremer-David, "Cheval Rayé," 24–25.
115. Belozerskaya, "Menageries as Princely Necessities," 66–70.
116. Salmon, "Duke and the Cassowary," 72.
117. See Greenberg, "Yuancang *Haiguai tuji*," 38–51; and Greenberg, "Weird Science."
118. See Wang Lianming, "Qing Ai Qimeng"; Lai Yu-chih, "Tuxiang, zhishi"; and Lai Yu-chih, "Qinggong dui Ouzhou ziranshi." With later additions, the final image numbers for the *Manual of Birds* (*Niaopu*) and the *Manual of Beasts* (*Shoupu*) arrived at 361 and 183, respectively.
119. Lai Yu-chih, "Qinggong dui Ouzhou ziranshi," 36, 50; Lai Yu-chih, "Cong Dule dao Qinggong."
120. Lai Yu-chih, "Tuxiang, zhishi," 7–11. Lai suggests that the Qing court probably had a cassowary, but around 1776 it was no longer there; see ibid., 9, 16.
121. Ibid., 11–17, 28–31.
122. Ibid., 44–47; Lai Yu-chih, "Qinggong dui Ouzhou ziranshi," 50–51.
123. On these scrolls, see Lai Yu-chih, "Tuxiang diguo."
124. Lai Yu-chih, "Qinggong dui Ouzhou ziranshi," 11.
125. Anderson, "Material Mediators," 83–84.
126. Lai Yu-chih, "Cong Dule dao Qinggong"; Anderson, "Material Mediators," 77–78.
127. The tapestry *The King Carried by Two Moors* in the *Anciennes Indes* series depicts a Kongo Christian noble carried by his servants, which was based on the diplomatic visit of Kongo ambassadors to Dutch Brazil in 1642. European viewers did not necessarily know this historical reference and instead viewed the image as portraying a generic black king. See Fromont, *The Art of Conversion*, 153.
128. Anderson, "Material Mediators," 80–83.
129. Milam, "Betwixt and Between," 265.

130. HJD, Qianlong 52/12/7 (1788), *Dengcai zuo*, 50:365–66.
131. HJD, Qianlong 52/12/7 (1788), *Dengcai zuo*, 50:366; Qianlong 49/11/19 (1784), *Dengcai zuo*, 47:547; Qianlong 44/3/19 (1779), *Dengcai zuo*, 42:759.
132. Pirazzoli-t'Serstevens, "Pluridisciplinary Research," 5.
133. "L'Empereur a cependant des tapisseries dans plusieurs de ses Palais où il va de tems en tems se promener et se reposer. Ces même Palais sont aussi ornés de glaces, de peintures, de pendules, de lustres, et de toute sorte d'autres ornemens les plus précieux que nous ayions en Europe." *Lettres édifiantes et curieuses* (1776), 47.
134. "Dans la salle qu'il a fait nouvellement bâtir pour placer les Tapisseries de la manufacture des Gobelins, que la Cour de France lui a envoyées en 1767 [1766], il y a partout des trumeaux magnifiques. Observez que cette salle, d'une dimension de 70 pieds de long, sur une belle largeur proportionnée, est si remplie de machines, qu'à peine trouve-t-on au milieu un petit chemin pour passer." Quoted in Delatour, *Essais sur l'architecture des Chinois*, 165. See also "Measurement Systems and Conversions."
135. Jiaqing, "Ti Yuanying guan."
136. Varin, *Expédition de Chine*, 240–41.

CHAPTER 4. STAGING IMPERIAL NARRATIVES

1. Weddigen, "Materiality"; Weddigen, "Textile Spaces."
2. Weigert, "Chambres d'amour"; Hellman, "Tapestries and Identities."
3. Hellman, "Tapestries and Identities," esp. 83.
4. HJD, Qianlong 26/4/9 (1761), *Ruyi guan*, 26:691.
5. See Gugong bowuyuan, *Gugong cangtan*, 275.
6. HJD, Qianlong 34/10/29 (1769), *Xingwen fang*, 32:631–32.
7. HJD, Qianlong 33/10/22 (1768), *Xingwen fang*, 31:747.
8. The conservation was conducted by the Textile Conservation Lab at the Cathedral of St. John the Divine, New York, from 2022 to 2023. I am grateful to Marlene Eidelheit, Valerie Soll, and Margaret O'Neil for discussing the details with me. The 1776 tapestry has an interesting feature: whereas its bottom and top borders were woven in one continuous piece with the central image, the two side borders are separate pieces; these were sewn to the central design with one inch of overlay and skillfully joined to the top and bottom borders with invisible seams. This might have been done to accommodate a new measurement without modifying the loom setup.
9. Denyse Montegut performed the fiber identification for the 1776 piece. The worn areas of the 1771 version, especially around the faces, may be due to some corrosive dyestuff or colorant. The fiber of this piece has not been scientifically analyzed.
10. HJD, Qianlong 38/8/11 (1773). The cartoons were presented on Qianlong 38/10/23, and the finished tapestries were submitted on Qianlong 39/4/29 (1774), *Rehe suiwei*, 36:217–18.
11. In 1914 these tapestries became part of the collections of the newly founded Museum of Antiquities (*Guwu chenlie suo*) inside the Forbidden City. They were among the imperial treasures that were systematically moved to the south beginning in 1933 to avoid damage from the war. The four tapestries later entered the Nanjing Museum and have since remained there, but as of April 2024 they have not been located in storage. On the discovery of the four photographs and the trajectories of these tapestries, see Guo Fuxiang, "Luyi shiwu 'Zhongguo ticai' guatan." I am grateful to Pascal-François Bertrand for his comments on the reversed images and to Tingting Xu for her expertise in glass negatives.
12. For the dimensions of the French set, see chapter 3, note 59.
13. See, e.g., HJD, Qianlong 34/3/1 (1769), *Ruyi guan*, 32:492; and Qianlong 35/10/18 (1770), *Ruyi guan*, 33:638.
14. HJD, Qianlong 33/11/26 (1768), *Xingwen fang*, 31:751.
15. In wealthy Chinese households during the eighteenth century, imported Dutch and English woolen fabrics, such as broadcloth and camlet, were used for overcoats and raincoats but not for fine clothes. See Lai Hui-min, "Qian Jia shidai," 10–19.
16. Gugong bowuyuan, *Gugong cangtan*, 203; Elliott, *Emperor Qianlong*, 53.
17. Fu Chao, "Qinggong shenghuo zhong de pudian: Menggu ditan"; Lin Chi-Lynn, "Qianlong de yidong gongdian."
18. Gugong bowuyuan, *Gugong cangtan*, 23–24. Some of the finest pile rugs were woven in Beijing workshops sponsored by the court, where artisans recruited from the above-mentioned areas worked with woolen yarns supplied by the northwestern regions.
19. *Archives of the Grand Council Records* (*Junji chu dang*), 1756, microfilm, 41, First Historical Archives of China, cited in Fu Chao, "Qinggong shenghuo zhong de pudian: duoluo ni," 45.
20. For examples, see DQHD, vol. 503: *Libu 214/chaogong 2/gongwu 1*, Shunzhi 13 (1656), Kangxi 6 (1667), Kangxi 8 (1669), Kangxi 25 (1686), Yongzheng 5 (1727), Qianlong 17 (1752), and Qianlong 58 (1793). Wool serge (*biji*) and *duoluo ni/rong* were also staple items brought by English traders to the Canton port during the eighteenth century. For examples, see Zhongguo diyi lishi dang'an guan, *Ming Qing gongcang Zhongxi shangmao dang'an*, Kangxi 58/8/10 (1719), 1:157; and Qianlong 27/4/10 (1762), 3:1598.
21. Lai Hui-min, "Shijiu shiji Qiaketu maoyi," 27.
22. Fu Chao, "Qinggong shenghuo zhong de pudian: duoluo ni," 42–43.
23. See, e.g., HJD, Qianlong 34/10/29 (1769), *Xingwen fang*, 32:631–32; Qianlong 35/11/29 (1771), *Xingwen*, 33:535–36.
24. For studies of perspective paintings at the Qing court, see Kleutghen, *Imperial Illusions*; and Musillo, *Shining Inheritance*, chap. 8.
25. On screens in Chinese art, see Wu Hung, *Double Screen*; and W. Lin, "Screening the Chinese Interior."
26. HJD, Qianlong 39/5/28 (1775), *Jishi lu*, 37:483.
27. HJD, Qianlong 34/3/1 (1769), *Ruyi guan*, 32:492.
28. For discussions on this image, see Grasskamp, "EurAsian Layers," 370; and Wang, "Prints in Sino-European Artistic Interactions," 440. On the book *History of Lenses*, see Kile and Kleutghen, "Seeing through Pictures."
29. Hay, "Body Invisible," 51.
30. Bremer-David, "Collation," 436.
31. See Smentek, "Chinoiserie for the Qing," 100.
32. HJD, Qianlong 34/10/29 (1769), *Xingwen fang*, 32:631–32. The measurement system *yingzao chi* was used here. See "Measurement Systems and Conversions."
33. HJD, Qianlong 35/11/29 (1771), *Xingwen*, 33:535–36. The current dimensions of the Palace Museum tapestry, which I measured in June 2015, are 8 ft. 9 in. × 12 ft. 1 in. (267 × 368 cm), identifying it as the second weaving.
34. HJD, Qianlong 40/12/3 (1776), *Xingwen*, 38:668. According to research conducted by Guo Fuxiang, curator at the Palace Museum, the width recorded in the entry was much greater than that of the designated wall and therefore a mistake. The actual width of the wall between two columns, measuring 12 ft. 6 in. (380 cm), matches that of the Cleveland tapestry. See Guo Fuxiang, "Cong liangjian Qinggong cangpin," 99.
35. This tapestry was brought from China by Thomas J. Larkin of Bond Street, supposedly in the early twentieth century, but further details are unknown. It entered the Cleveland Museum in 1942 as a bequest

from John L. Severance. For an early note on this piece, see "Chinese Tapestry."
36. HJD, Qianlong 34/10/29 (1769), *Xingwen fang*, 32:631–32.
37. "Le luisant de l'huile ne plaisoit pas à sa majesté, les ombres surtout quand celles étoient un peu fortes lui paroissoient des taches." Jean-Joseph-Marie Amiot to Claude-François Attiret, Beijing, March 1, 1779, Getty Research Institute Library, 2013.M.13, f22.
38. Barrow, *Travels in China*, 325.
39. See Hou Yi-li, "Jin'ou yonggu."
40. Jiaqing, notes to his poem "Yuandan shibi."
41. Wu Hung, "Monumentality of Time," 113.
42. On tripods and monumentality, see Wu Hung, *Monumentality in Early Chinese Art*, 1–15.
43. Wang Zilin, *Ming Qing huanggong chenshe*, 82.
44. Ibid., 83–85.
45. On the meaning of the name, see Yu Minzhong et al., *Rixia jiuwen kao*, 243. On the changing configurations of the east warm chamber in the Hall of Mental Cultivation from the Kangxi to the Tongzhi periods, see Zhang Shuxian, "Tujie Qingdai Zijincheng"; and Li Shi, "Qianlong chao Yangxin dian," 76–77. The interior layout of the east warm chamber was modified several times during the nineteenth century, and a major reconfiguration took place around 1872, which resulted in a very different layout from that in the eighteenth century. See Zhang Shuxian, "Tujie Qingdai Zijincheng," 83.
46. Li Shi, "Qianlong chao Yangxin dian," 82–84, 88–89.
47. Ibid., 83, 91.
48. Wu Hung, "Emperor's Masquerade," 25–30; Wu Hung, *Double Screen*, 223–31. The 1765 image replaced an earlier, multimedia trompe l'oeil program featuring the same theme created in 1749. See Wu Hung, "Chongfan zuopin."
49. Wu Hung, *Double Screen*, 215.
50. Ch'en Pao-chen, "Cong sifu 'Suizhao Tu,'" 172–75.
51. See, for example, HJD, Qianlong 40/2/10 and 3/19 (1775), *Ruyi guan*, vol. 38, 13, 23.
52. In Chinese convention, a person is one year old at birth and grows a year older on each New Year's Day.
53. Ch'en Pao-chen, "Cong sifu 'Suizhao Tu,'" 175.
54. Some of these images are discussed in Kleutghen, *Imperial Illusions*, 103–42.
55. Wang Zilin, "Ningshou Gong huayuan," 17.
56. After abdicating the throne, Qianlong still lived in the Hall of Mental Cultivation and continued to oversee state affairs until his death in 1799.
57. Wang Zilin, *Zijincheng yuanzhuang*, 2:278–86; and Kleutghen, *Imperial Illusions*, 112–24.
58. Adelson, *European Tapestry*, 331.
59. Smentek, *Rococo Exotic*; Grasskamp, *Objects in Frames*, chaps. 1 and 2.
60. HJD, Qianlong 39/5/28 (1775), *Jishi lu*, 37:483.
61. For the portrait of King Afonso VI, see DQHD, *Libu* 214/*chaogong* 2/*gongwu* 1, Kangxi 9 (1670). The portraits of the French king and members of the royal family were among Louis XIV's gifts that French Jesuits presented to Kangxi in 1688. See Père Bouvet to Père de la Chaise, Beijing, November 30, 1699, in *Lettres édifiantes et curieuses* (1838–43), 3:21. For Vigée's portraits, see *Collection de manuscrits*, BNF, Fonds Bréquigny, 1:ff. 6–7.
62. "Avec glaces et bordures." *Collection de manuscrits*, BNF, Fonds Bréquigny, 1:ff. 6–7.
63. "Aux murs desquelles étaient suspendus des portraits en pied de beautés de la cour de France, avec leurs noms au bas." Varin, *Expédition de Chine*, 241.
64. Stewart, *Nonsense*, 23.
65. Shen, "Tombs at the Crossroads," 156–60; Schmid, "The Material Culture of Exegesis," 180–92.
66. Eberlein, "The Curtain in Raphael's Sistine *Madonna*."
67. See Abbé de Varès, *Registre des livres*. The register lists prints of the three festivals at Versailles, one of which was the 1664 performance of *Enchanted Island*.
68. Hénin, "Parrhasios and the Stage Curtain," 250.
69. Zeitlin, *Phantom Heroine*, 142–46.
70. For examples of such objects, see Yang Boda, *Qingdai Guangdong gongpin*.
71. HJD, Qianlong 43/4/5 (1778), *Dengcai zuo*, 41:694.
72. The north wall measures 10 ft. 6 in. (320 cm) high from the floor to the ceiling beam and 16 ft. 3⅝ in. (497 cm) wide between two columns, greater than the tapestry's width of 12 ft. ⅞ in. (368 cm). As seen on the historical plan made circa 1872, just before the renovation, the two partitions flanking the north window were clearly marked as multi-panel dividers featuring patterned woodwork designs (*kanchuang*). During the renovation, the north window was converted into part of the solid wall. I am grateful to Zhang Shuxian, curator at the Palace Museum, for showing me the historical plan prepared by the Lei family (*yàngshi Lei*), who were responsible for the Qing imperial architecture.
73. Kongzi, *Confucianism: The Analects*.
74. Wu Hung, *Double Screen*, 168–99.
75. For discussions on these paintings, see ibid., 231–36; and Kleutghen, "One or Two, Repictured."
76. This new painting replaced an earlier one, pasted onto the same wall, that was also executed with linear perspective. See HJD, Qianlong 36/5/9 (1771), *Biaozuo*, 34:733; and Qianlong 36/5/16 (1771), *Ruyi guan*, 34:485. The hallway was reconfigured during the nineteenth century.

CONCLUSION

1. On textiles from these periods, see Watt and Wardwell, *When Silk Was Gold*.
2. See, e.g., McCall, *Brilliant Bodies*, esp. chap. 1.
3. Hay, "Foreword," x.
4. For a recent reexamination of the arts and culture in nineteenth-century China, see Harrison-Hall and Lovell, *China's Hidden Century*.
5. See, e.g., Silberstein, "Fashioning the Foreign."
6. See Silberstein, *Fashionable Century*, 56–61. For examples of silk ribbons made in France featuring Chinese motifs for the late-Qing Chinese market, see Tennants Auctioneers, *Pattern Sale*, lots 2040–42.
7. See Wang, "'Going Public'"; Peng, *Artful Subversion*, chap. 1.
8. On this screen, see Rado, "Empress Dowager Cixi's Japanese Screen."

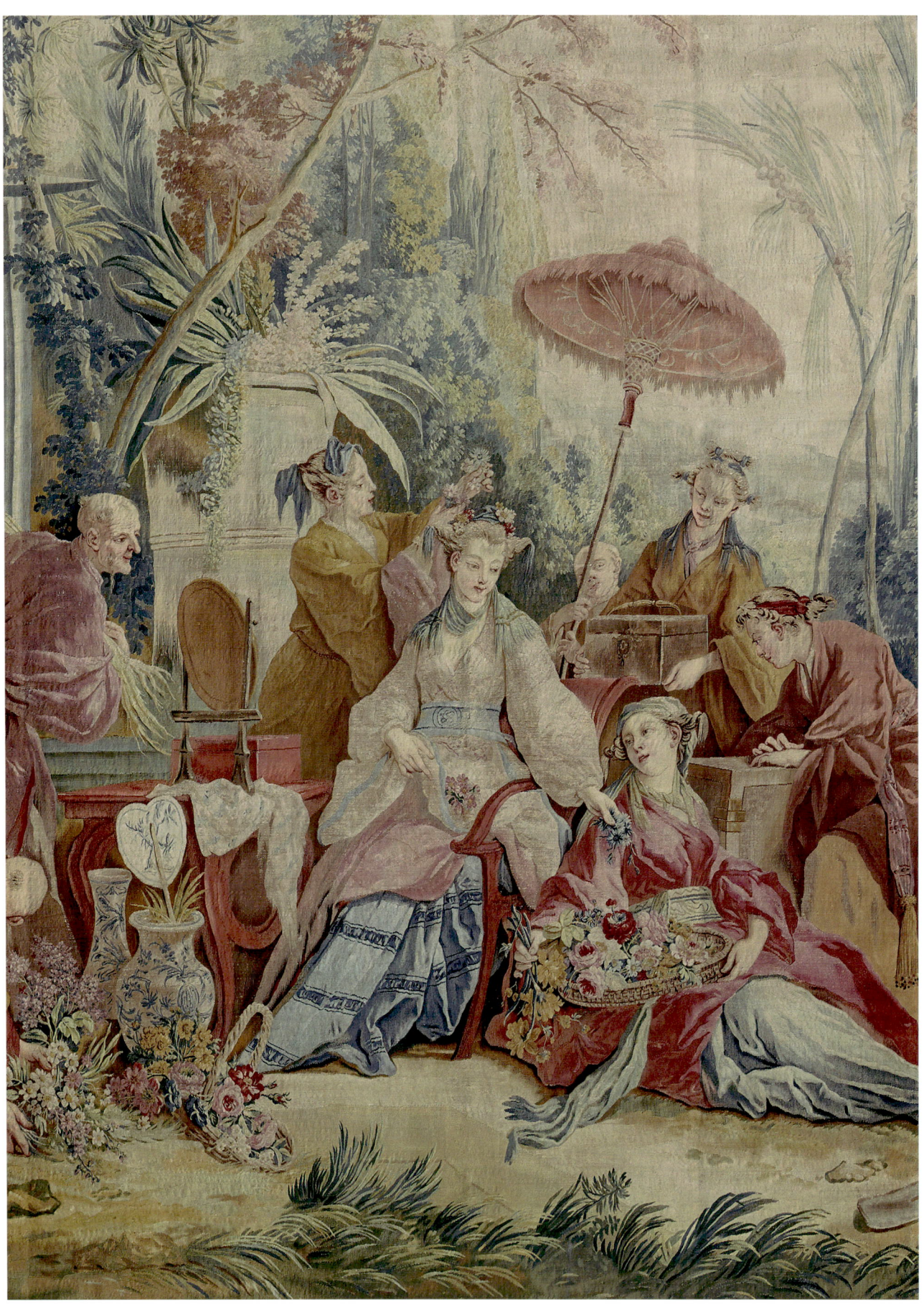

Bibliography

ARCHIVAL SOURCES

Abbé de Varès, *Registre des Livres de figures et Estampes qui ont été distribués suivant les ordres de Monseigneur le marquis de Louvois depuis l'inventaire fait avec M. l'abbé Varès au mois d'aoust 1684*. Bibliothèque nationale de France, Département des estampes réserves, Rés. YE. 144.

Amiot, Jean-Joseph-Marie, to Claude-François Attiret, Beijing, March 1, 1779. Getty Research Institute Library, 2013.M.13.

Archives nationales, sous-série O/1, Archives de la Maison du Roi sous l'Ancien Régime (XVIe–XVIIIe siècles). Files consulted: *Correspondance du contrôleur du département de Paris, Soufflot (copie)*, O/1/1554; and *Manufacture de Beauvais: correspondance, états de fabrication, etc.*, O/1/2038.

Collection de manuscrits constituée de la correspondance et des travaux historiques de L.-G. de Bréquigny. 165 vols. Bibliothèque nationale de France, Département des manuscrits, Fonds Bréquigny.

Correspondance des RR. PP. jésuites missionnaires en Chine avec H. L. J.-B. Bertin. 12 vols. Bibliothèque de l'Institut de France, MS1515–MS1526.

Neiwu fu zaoban chu gezuo chengzuo huoji qingdang 內務府造辦處各作承作活計清檔 [Archives of the Imperial Workshops under the Imperial Household Department]. Facsimile published as *Qinggong neiwu fu zaoban chu dang'an zonghui, Yongzheng–Qianlong* 清宮內務府造辦處檔案總匯, 雍正–乾隆 [Collected Files of the Imperial Workshops under the Imperial Household Department at the Qing Court, 1723–1795], compiled by Zhongguo diyi lishi dang'an guan 中國第一歷史檔案館 and Xianggang Zhongwen daxue wenwu guan 香港中文大學文物館. 55 vols. Beijing: Renmin chubanshe, 2005. Files from the following divisions are cited:
Anjia zuo 鞍甲作 [Workshop of saddles and armors]
Anzuo 鞍作 [Workshop of saddles]
Biaozuo 裱作 [Mounting workshop]
Biaozuo, huazuo 表 [sic] 做 畫作 [Mounting and painting workshop]
Caizuo 裁作 [Tailoring workshop]
Dengcai zuo 燈裁作 [Workshop of lantern making and tailoring]
Jishi lu 記事錄 [Memos]
Kunei shouzhu dang 庫內收貯檔 [Inventory of the imperial storage]
Muzuo 木作 [Wood workshop]
Picai zuo 皮裁作 [Leather and tailoring workshop]
Pizuo 皮作 [Leather and furnishing workshop]
Rehe suiwei 熱河隨圍 [During the Hunt in Rehe]
Ruyi guan 如意館 [Painting academy]
Sanchu zhizao laijin dang 三處織造來錦檔 [Records of the jin-lampas submitted by the three silk manufactories]
Shouzhu wujian qingce: xinjin 收貯物件清冊/新進 [Inventory of stored items: newly arrived]
Suzhou 蘇州 [The Imperial Silk Manufactory in Suzhou]
Xingqu wuliao qingce: shiyong 行取物料清冊/實用 [Inventory of items requested: actually used]
Xingwen 行文 [Orders]
Xingwen fang/Xingwen chu 行文房/ 行文處 [Bureau for issuing orders]
Zalu 雜錄/*Zalu dang* 雜錄檔 [Miscellaneous]

Plan d'une grande partie du parc d'Yuen-Ming-Yuen appelé par les Européens le Versailles de la Chine et des palais ou maisons de plaisance de l'Empereur Kien-Long contenues dans les XX planches gravées en taille douce à Péking que j'ai reçues en octobre 1787 de M. Bourgeois missionnaire français de la résidence de Péking. Bibliothèque nationale de France, Département des estampes et de la photographie, HZ-444-Roul.

Yunlu 允祿 et al., eds. *Huangchao liqi tushi* 皇朝禮器圖式 [The Illustrated Regulations for Ceremonial Paraphernalia of the Imperial Dynasty]. 18 vols. Beijing, 1751–72. Hand-painted edition, in the Palace Museum, Beijing, acc. no. gu6116. Volumes consulted: *Guanfu* 冠服 [Hats and Dress]; and *Wubei* 武備 [Armament].

Zhongguo diyi lishi dang'an guan 中國第一歷史檔案館, comp. *Ming Qing gongcang Zhongxi shangmao dang'an* 明清宮藏中西商貿檔案 [Trade Archives between China and the West at the Ming and Qing Courts]. 4 vols. Beijing: Zhongguo dang'an chubanshe, 2010.

Digital Archives

Diderot, Denis, and Jean-Baptiste le Rond d'Alembert. *Encyclopédie, ou Dictionnaire raisonné des sciences, des arts et des métiers, par une Société de Gens de lettres*, 1751–1772. University of Chicago, ARTFL Encyclopédie Project (Autumn 2022 edition), edited by Robert Morrissey and Glenn Roe. http://encyclopedie.uchicago.edu/.

Qinding da Qing huidian shili 欽定大清會典事例 [Collected Statutes of the Great Qing], 1758–1812. 920 vols. In the database *Hanji quanwen ziliaoku* 漢籍全文資料庫. Academia Sinica. http://hanchi.ihp.sinica.edu.tw.

Shizu Zhang Huangdi shilu 世祖章皇帝實錄 [The Veritable Records of the Emperor Shizu (Shunzhi)]; *Shengzu Ren Huangdi shilu* 聖祖仁皇帝實錄 [The Veritable Records of the Emperor Shengzu (Kangxi)];

and *Gaozong Chun Huangdi shilu* 高宗純皇帝實錄 [The Veritable Records of the Emperor Gaozong (Qianlong)]. In the database *Ming shilu, Chaoxian wangchao shilu, Qing shilu ziliaoku* 明實錄、朝鮮王朝實錄、清實錄資料庫. Academia Sinica. https://hanchi.ihp.sinica.edu.tw/mql/login.html.

PRIMARY SOURCES: CHINESE

GAO SHIQI 高士奇 (1645–1704). *Pengshan miji* 蓬山密記 [Secret Records of Pengshan]. Repr., Beijing: Xueyuan chubanshe, 2006.

HUANG BOLU 黃伯祿. *Zhengjiao fengbao* 正教奉褒 [Imperial Commendations on the Orthodox Teaching of Catholicism]. 2 vols. 1876. Repr., Shanghai: Cimu tang, 1904.

JIAQING 嘉慶. "Ti Yuanying guan" 題遠瀛觀 [On the Observatory of the Distant Ocean], 1802. In Jiaqing, *Yuzhishi chuji* 御製詩初集 [Collections of Imperial Poetry, 1st ser.]. In *Qingdai shiwenji huibian* 清代詩文集匯編 [Collectanea of Poetry and Prose Collections of the Qing Dynasty]. Repr., Shanghai: Shanghai guji chubanshe, 2010, 459:523–24.

———. "Yuandan shibi" 元旦試筆 [Testing the Brush on New Year's Day] and notes, 1807. In Jiaqing, *Yuzhishi erji* 御製詩二集 [Collections of Imperial Poetry, 2nd ser.]. In *Qingdai shiwenji huibian* 清代詩文集匯編 [Collectanea of Poetry and Prose Collections of the Qing Dynasty]. Repr., Shanghai: Shanghai guji chubanshe, 2010, 460:406.

LIANG TINGNAN 梁廷枏 ET AL., comps. *Yue haiguan zhi* 粵海關志 [Gazetteer of the Canton Customs Bureau]. 1835. Repr., Taipei: Ch'engwen chubanshe, 1968.

QIANLONG 乾隆. "Qianlong ershisan nian yuzhi zhongdong Nanyuan dayue jishi shi" 乾隆二十三年御製仲冬南苑大閱紀事詩 [Imperially Composed Poem on the Event of the Great Review at Nanyuan in the Second Month of Winter, the Twenty-Third Year of the Qianlong Reign]. In Qianlong, *Yuzhi shi erji* 御製詩二集 [Collections of Imperial Poetry, 2nd ser.]. In *Yingyin Wenyuange Siku Quanshu* 景印文淵閣四庫全書 [Facsimile of the Complete Library of the Four Treasuries, the Wenyuange Edition]. Repr., Taipei: Shangwu yinshu guan, 1987, 1304:499.

TIANSHUI BINGSHAN LU 天水冰山錄 [A Record of the Water of Heaven and the Iceberg], preface dated 1737, reprinted in *Congshu jicheng chubian* 叢書集成初編 [Compiled Collectanea, 1st ser.]. Repr., Shanghai: Shangwu yinshuguan, 1935–37.

YU MINZHONG 于敏中 ET AL. *Rixia jiuwen kao* 日下舊聞考 [Studies of Old Anecdotes Heard in the Precincts of the Throne]. 1785–87. Repr., Beijing: Beijing guji chubanshe, 2001.

PRIMARY SOURCES: ENGLISH AND FRENCH

AMIOT, JOSEPH ET AL., comps. *Mémoires concernant l'histoire, les sciences, les arts, les moeurs, les usages, &c. des Chinois par les missionnaires de Pekin*. 15 vols. Paris: Nyon, 1776–91. Bibliothèque nationale de France, 4O2N-54.

L'ART POUR TOUS: ENCYCLOPÉDIE DE L'ART INDUSTRIEL ET DÉCORATIF, no. 13 (July 15, 1861) and no. 16 (August 31, 1861).

BARROW, JOHN. *Travels in China: Containing Descriptions, Observations, and Comparisons, Made and Collected in the Course of a Short Residence at the Imperial Palace of Yuen-min-Yuen, and on a Subsequent Journey through the Country from Pekin to Canton*. London: A. Strahan, 1804.

CORDIER, HENRI. "Correspondants de Bertin, Secrétaire d'État au XVIIIe siècle." *T'oung Pao*, 2nd ser., 18, nos. 4–5 (October–December 1917): 295–379.

DELATOUR, LOUIS FRANÇOIS. *Essais sur l'architecture des Chinois, sur leurs jardins, leurs principes de médecine, et leurs moeurs et usages*. Paris: de Clousier, 1803.

DUPLESSIS, GEORGES. *Le Cabinet du roi: collection d'estampes commandées par Louis XIV*. Paris: Bachelin-Deflorenne, 1869.

FÉLIBIEN, ANDRÉ. *Les Quatre élémens peints par Mr Le Brun et mis en tapisseries pour Sa Majesté*. Paris: Chez Pierre le Petit, Imprimeur & Librairie Ordinaire du Roy, 1665.

———. *Les Quatre saisons peintes par Mr Le Brun et mises en tapisseries pour Sa Majesté*. Paris: Chez Pierre le Petit, Imprimeur & Librairie Ordinaire du Roy, 1667.

———. *Tapisseries du Roy, où sont représentez les quatre élémens et les quatre saisons avec les devises qui les accompagnent, et leur explication*. Paris: Chez Sebastien Mabre-Cramoisy, Imprimeur du Roy, 1679. Bibliothèque nationale de France, Département des estampes et de la photographie, AD-107-FOL.

FENAILLE, MAURICE. *État général des tapisseries de la Manufacture des Gobelins depuis son origine jusqu'à nos jours, 1600–1900*. 4 vols. Paris: Hachette, 1903–7.

LACERE, PIERRE-ANTOINE-ÉTIENNE. "Suite des nouvelles des missions, 1753." Archives des Missions Etrangères de Paris, *Procure de Macao*, 296: ff. 418–40. Transcribed in A. M. Martins do Vale, "A embaixada enviada pelo rei dom Jose I ao imperador Qianlong, em 1752, vista pelo procurador das missões estrangeiras de Paris em Macau." *Anais de História de Além-Mar* 5 (2004): 517–36.

LETTRES ÉDIFIANTES ET CURIEUSES: ÉCRITES DES MISSIONS ÉTRANGÈRES PAR QUELQUES MISSIONNAIRES DE LA COMPAGNIE DE JÉSUS, XXXIII RECEUIL. Paris: Chez Charles-Pierre Berton, 1776.

LETTRES ÉDIFIANTES ET CURIEUSES CONCERNANT L'ASIE, L'AFRIQUE ET L'AMÉRIQUE, AVEC QUELQUES RELATIONS NOUVELLES DES MISSIONS ET DES NOTES GÉOGRAPHIQUES ET HISTORIQUES. 4 vols. Paris: A. Desrez, 1838–43.

MONDAIN-MONVAL, JEAN. *Correspondance de Soufflot avec les directeurs des Bâtiments concernant la Manufacture des Gobelins (1756–1780)*. Paris: Librairie Alphonse Lemerre, 1918.

VARIN, PAUL. *Expédition de Chine*. Paris: Michel Lévy frères, 1862.

VERHAEREN, HUBERT GERMAIN. *Catalogue de la Bibliothèque du Pé-t'ang*. Paris: Société d'Édition les Belles Lettres, 1969. Originally Beijing: Imprimerie des Lazaristes, 1949.

SECONDARY SOURCES

ACKERMANN, HANS CHRISTOPH, AND VENDULKA OTAVSKÁ. *Seidengewebe des 18. Jahrhunderts. I: bizarre Seiden*. Riggisberg: Abegg-Stiftung, 2000.

ADELSON, CANDACE J. *European Tapestry in the Minneapolis Institute of Arts*. Minneapolis: Minneapolis Institute of Arts, 1994.

AHMED, MONISHA. "Brocade for the Buddhists: The Textile Trade between Benaras and Tibet." In *Textiles from India: The Global Trade*, edited by Rosemary Crill, 9–26. London: Seagull Books, 2006.

ANDERSON, CARRIE. "Material Mediators: Johan Maurits, Textiles, and the Art of Diplomatic Exchange." *Journal of Early Modern History* 20, no. 1 (2016): 63–85.

———. "The Old Indies at the French Court: Johan Maurits's Gift to Louis XIV." *Early Modern Low Countries* 3, no. 1 (2019): 32–59.

ANISHANSLIN, ZARA. *Portrait of a Woman in Silk: Hidden Histories of the British Atlantic World*. New Haven: Yale University Press, 2016.

ARIBAUD, CHRISTINE. *Soieries en sacristie: fastes liturgiques, XVIIe–XVIIIe siècles*. Paris: Somogy, 1998.

ARIZZOLI-CLÉMENTEL, PIERRE, AND CHANTAL GASTINEL-COURAL. *Soieries de Lyon: commandes royales au XVIIIe s. (1730–1800)*. Lyon: Musée Historique des Tissus, 1988.

BADIN, JULES. *La Manufacture de tapisseries de Beauvais depuis ses origines jusqu'à nos jours*. Paris: Société de propagation des livres d'art, 1909.

BAI HUAWEN 白化文. "Jiang Zhuangyan" 講莊嚴 [On Zhuangyan]. *Zhongguo dianji yu wenhua* 中國典籍與文化, no. 4 (1996): 105–10.

BAUMGARTEN, LINDA. *What Clothes Reveal: The Language of Clothing in*

Colonial and Federal America: The Colonial Williamsburg Collection. Williamsburg: Colonial Williamsburg Foundation, 2002.

BAXANDALL MICHAEL. *Painting and Experience in Fifteenth-Century Italy.* New York: Oxford University Press, 1972.

BELEVITCH-STANKEVITCH, HÉLÈNE. *Le Goût chinois en France au temps de Louis XIV.* 1910. Repr., Geneva: Slatkine Reprints, 1970.

BELLION, WENDY, AND KRISTEL SMENTEK, EDS. *Material Cultures of the Global Eighteenth Century: Art, Mobility, and Change.* New York: Bloomsbury, 2023.

BELOZERSKAYA, MARINA. "Menageries as Princely Necessities and Mirrors of Their Times." In *Oudry's Painted Menagerie: Portraits of Exotic Animals in Eighteenth-Century Europe,* edited by Mary Morton, 59–73. Los Angeles: J. Paul Getty Museum, 2007.

BERGER, PATRICIA. *Empire of Emptiness: Buddhist Art and Political Authority in Qing China.* Honolulu: University of Hawai'i Press, 2003.

BERNARD, HENRAI [HENRI BERNARD-MAÎTRE]. "Catalogue des objets envoyés de Chine par les missionnaires de 1765 à 1786." *Bulletin de l'Université l'Aurore* 震旦雜誌, 3rd ser., 9, nos. 33–34 (1948): 119–204.

BERNARD-MAÎTRE, HENRI. "Deux chinois du XVIIIe siècle à l'école des physiocrates français." *Bulletin de l'Université l'Aurore* 震旦雜誌, 3rd ser., 10, no. 38 (1949): 151–97.

BERTRAND, PASCAL-FRANÇOIS. "Louis XIV and Louis XV: Their Coronations and Their Tapestries, 1654 and 1722." In Charissa Bremer-David et al., *Woven Gold: Tapestries of Louis XIV,* 39–50. Los Angeles: J. Paul Getty Museum, 2015.

———. "La Seconde 'Tenture chinoise' tissée à Beauvais et Aubusson: relations entre Oudry, Boucher et Dumons." *Gazette des beaux-arts* 116, no. 1462 (November 1990): 173–84.

———. "Tapestry Production at the Gobelins during the Reign of Louis XIV, 1661–1715." In *Tapestry in the Baroque: Threads of Splendor,* edited by Thomas Campbell, 341–55. New York: Metropolitan Museum of Art, 2007.

BLEICHMAR, DANIELA. *Visible Empire: Botanical Expeditions and Visual Culture in the Hispanic Enlightenment.* Chicago: University of Chicago Press, 2012.

BREMER-DAVID, CHARISSA. "Le Cheval Rayé: A French Tapestry Portraying Dutch Brazil." *J. Paul Getty Museum Journal* 22 (1994): 21–29.

———. "The Collation." In *Tapestry in the Baroque: Threads of Splendor,* edited by Thomas Campbell, 434–39. New York: Metropolitan Museum of Art, 2007.

———. *French Tapestries and Textiles in the J. Paul Getty Museum.* Los Angeles: J. Paul Getty Museum, 1997.

———. "Manufacture Royale de Tapisseries de Beauvais, 1664–1715." In *Tapestry in the Baroque: Threads of Splendor,* edited by Thomas Campbell, 407–19. New York: Metropolitan Museum of Art, 2007.

———. "The Striped Horse." In *Tapestry in the Baroque: Threads of Splendor,* edited by Thomas Campbell, 390–97. New York: Metropolitan Museum of Art, 2007.

———, ET AL. *Woven Gold: Tapestries of Louis XIV.* Los Angeles: J. Paul Getty Museum, 2015.

BROWNE, CLARE. "The Influence of Botanical Sources on Early Eighteenth-Century English Silk Design." In *Seidengewebe des 18. Jahrhunderts: die Industrien in England und in Nordeuropa,* edited by Regula Schorta and Natalie Rothstein, 25–38. Riggisberg: Abegg-Stiftung, 2000.

BURNHAM, DOROTHY K. *Warp and Weft: A Textile Terminology.* Toronto: Royal Ontario Museum, 1980.

CAMPBELL, THOMAS. "Tapestry." In *5000 Years of Textiles,* edited by Jennifer Harris, 188–99. London: British Museum Press in association with the Whitworth Art Gallery and the Victoria and Albert Museum, 1993.

CAVALLO, ADOLPH. *Tapestries of Europe and Colonial Peru in the Museum of Fine Arts, Boston.* 2 vols. Boston: Museum of Fine Arts, 1967.

CHANG HSIANG-WEN 張湘雯. "Haixi jihui: Qinggong" 海西集卉：清宮院圍中的外洋植物 [Assorted Flowers from the West Ocean: Foreign Plants in the Qing Palaces]. *Gugong wenwu yuekan* 故宮文物月刊, no. 396 (March 2016): 106–19.

CHEN, BUYUN. *Empire of Style: Silk and Fashion in Tang China.* Seattle: University of Washington Press, 2019.

CHEN HUI-HSIA 陳慧霞. "Yongzheng chao de yangqi yu fang yangqi" 雍正朝的洋漆與仿洋漆 [On the Imperial Studio's Imitation of Japanese Lacquerware during the Yongzheng Reign]. *Gugong xueshu jikan* 故宮學術季刊 28, no. 1 (2001): 141–95.

CH'EN PAO-CHEN 陳葆真. "Cong sifu 'Suizhao Tu' de biaoxian wenti tandao Qianlong Huangdi de qinzi guanxi" 從四幅「歲朝圖」的表現問題談到乾隆皇帝的親子關係 [On the Father-Son Relationship between Qianlong and His Princes through the Representations of Four New Year's Paintings]. In Ch'en, *Qianlong Huangdi de jiating shenghuo yu neixin shijie* 乾隆皇帝的家庭生活與內心世界 [The Family Life and Inner World of Qianlong], 153–87. Taipei: Shitou chubanshe, 2014.

CHIANG, NICOLE T. C. *Emperor Qianlong's Hidden Treasures: Reconsidering the Collection of the Qing Imperial Household.* Hong Kong: Hong Kong University Press, 2019.

"A CHINESE TAPESTRY." *Burlington Magazine for Connoisseurs* 25, no. 163 (July 1914): 230–31.

CHIU, CHE-BING. "Vegetal Travel: Western European Plants in the Garden." In *Qing Encounters: Artistic Exchanges between China and the West,* edited by Petra ten-Doesschate Chu and Ding Ning, 95–110. Los Angeles: Getty Research Institute, 2015.

CHOU KUNG-SHIN 周功鑫. "Faguo Luyi shisi shiqi Zhongguo fengshang de xingqi yu fazhan" 法國路易十四時期中國風尚的興起與發展 [The Rise and Development of Chinoiserie in the Period of Louis XIV in France]. In *Kangxi dadi yu taiyangwang Luyi shisi tezhan: Zhong Fa yishu wenhua de jiaohui* 康熙大帝與太陽王路易十四特展: 中法藝術文化的交會 [Emperor Kangxi and the Sun King Louis XIV: Sino-Franco Encounters in Arts and Culture], 256–62. Taipei: National Palace Museum, 2011.

CHRISTIE'S LONDON. *Highly Important French Furniture and Tapestries.* April 12, 1984.

CHU, PETRA TEN-DOESSCHATE, AND DING NING, EDS. *Qing Encounters: Artistic Exchanges between China and the West.* Los Angeles: Getty Research Institute, 2015.

CLUNAS, CRAIG. *Pictures and Visuality in Early Modern China.* Princeton: Princeton University Press, 1997.

———. *Superfluous Things: Material Culture and Social Status in Early Modern China.* 1991. Repr., Honolulu: University of Hawai'i Press, 2004.

COLENBRANDER, SJOUKJE. *When Weaving Flourished: The Silk Industry in Amsterdam and Haarlem, 1585–1750,* translated by Peggy Birch. Amsterdam: Aronson, 2013.

COOKE, EDWARD. *Global Objects: Toward a Connected Art History.* Princeton: Princeton University Press, 2022.

COURAL, JEAN. *La Manufacture royale de Beauvais.* Paris: Édition de la Caisse nationale des monuments historiques, 1977.

CROSSLEY, PAMELA KYLE. "The Rulerships of China." *American Historical Review* 97, no. 5 (1992): 1468–83.

———. *A Translucent Mirror: History and Identity in Qing Imperial Ideology.* Berkeley: University of California Press, 1999.

CURTIS, EMILY B. *Glass Exchange between Europe and China, 1550–1800.* Burlington, Vt.: Ashgate, 2008.

DAI JIAN 戴健. *Nanjing Yunjin* 南京雲錦 [Cloud Brocades of Nanjing]. Suzhou: Suzhou daxue chubanshe, 2009.

DONG JIANZHONG 董建中. "Chuanjiaoshi jingong yu Qianlong Huangdi de xiyang pinwei" 傳教士進貢與乾隆皇帝的西洋品味 [Tributary Gifts Presented by Jesuit Missionaries and the Western Taste of the Qianlong Emperor]. *Qingshi yanjiu* 清史研究, no. 3 (2009): 95–106.

——. "Li Shiyao jingong jianlun" 李侍堯進貢簡論 [Brief Discussions on the Tributes from Li Shiyao]. *Qingshi yanjiu* 清史研究, no. 2 (2006): 111–16.

EBERLEIN, JOHANN KONRAD. "The Curtain in Raphael's Sistine *Madonna*." *Art Bulletin* 65, no. 1 (1983): 61–77.

ELLIOTT, MARK C. *Emperor Qianlong: Son of Heaven, Man of the World.* New York: Pearson Longman, 2009.

——. *The Manchu Way: The Eight Banners and Ethnic Identity in Late Imperial China.* Stanford: Stanford University Press, 2006.

FAN, FA-TI. *British Naturalists in Qing China: Science, Empire, and Cultural Encounter.* Cambridge: Harvard University Press, 2004.

FAN JINMIN 范金民. *Yi bei tianxia: Ming Qing Jiangnan sichoushi yan jiu* 衣被天下：明清江南絲綢史研究 [Clothing the Universe: Research on the Silk History in the Jiangnan Region during the Ming and Qing Dynasties]. Nanjing: Jiangsu renmin chubanshe, 2016.

FENG MING-CHU 馮明珠, ED. *Qianlong Huangdi de wenhua daye* 乾隆皇帝的文化大業 [Emperor Ch'ien-lung's Grand Cultural Enterprise]. Taipei: National Palace Museum, 2002.

FERREIRA, MARIA JOÃO PACHECO. "As alfaias bordadas sinoportuguesas (séculos XVI a XVII)." Ph.D. diss., Universidade Lusíada Editora, 2007.

FINLAY, JOHN. "Henri Bertin and Louis XV's Gifts to the Qianlong Emperor." *Extrême-Orient, Extrême-Occident* 43 (2019): 93–111.

——. *Henri Bertin and the Representation of China in Eighteenth-Century France.* New York: Routledge, 2020.

——. "The Qianlong Emperor's Western Vistas: Linear Perspective and Trompe l'Oeil Illusion in the European Palaces of the Yuanming yuan." *Bulletin de l'École française d'Extrême-Orient* 94 (2007): 159–93.

FROMONT, CÉCILE. *The Art of Conversion: Christian Visual Culture in the Kingdom of Kongo.* Chapel Hill: University of North Carolina Press, 2014.

FU CHAO 付超. "Qinggong shenghuo zhong de pudian: Duoluo ni yu yinhua zhan" 清宮生活中的鋪墊：哆囉呢與印花毡 [Covering at the Qing Court: *Duoluo ni* and Printed Felt]. *Shoucangjia* 收藏家, no. 3 (2014): 42–46.

——. "Qinggong shenghuo zhong de pudian: Menggu ditan yu menggubao zhaozhan" 清宮生活中的鋪墊：蒙古地毯與蒙古包罩毡 [Covering at the Qing Court: Mongolian Yurts and Tent Coverings]. *Shoucangjia* 收藏家, no. 5 (2014): 67–71.

GASPARINI, MARIACHIARA. *Transcending Patterns: Silk Road Cultural and Artistic Interactions through Central Asian Textile Images.* Honolulu: University of Hawai'i Press, 2019.

GORDEEVA, OL'GA, LUIZA EFIMOVA, AND MARINA KUZNETSOVA. *Russkie uzornye tkani XVII–načalo XX veka* [Russian Patterned Fabrics: XVII–Early XX Century]. Moscow: Gos. Istoričeskij Muzej, 2004.

GRABAR, OLEG. *The Mediation of Ornament.* Princeton: Princeton University Press, 1992.

GRASSKAMP, ANNA. "EurAsian Layers: Netherlandish Surfaces and Early Modern Chinese Artefacts." *Rijksmuseum Bulletin* 63, no. 4 (2015): 362–99.

——. *Objects in Frames: Displaying Foreign Collectibles in Early Modern China and Europe.* Berlin: Dietrich Reimer Verlag, 2019.

GREENBERG, DANIEL. "Weird Science: European Origins of the Fantastic Creatures in the Qing Court Painting, *The Manual of Sea Oddities*." In *The Zoomorphic Imagination in Chinese Art and Culture*, edited by Jerome Silbergeld and Eugene Wang, 379–400. Honolulu: University of Hawai'i Press, 2016.

——. "Yuancang *Haiguai tuji* chutan: Qinggong huazhong de xifang qihuan shengwu" 院藏《海怪圖記》初探–清宮畫中的西方奇幻生物 [A Brief Consideration of the National Palace Museum's *Manual of Sea Oddities*–Surprising Western Animals in Qing Court Painting]. *Gugong Wenwu Yuekan* 故宮文物月刊, no. 297 (December 2007): 38–51.

GRIVEL, MARIANNE. "Le Cabinet du Roi." *Revue de la Bibliothèque nationale*, no. 18 (1985): 36–57.

GUGONG BOWUYUAN 故宮博物院. *Gugong cangtan tudian* 故宮藏毯圖典 [Carpets, Tapestries, and Rugs in the Palace Museum]. Beijing: Zijincheng chubanshe, 2010.

——. *Ming Qing zhixiu* 明清織繡 [Textiles of the Ming and Qing Dynasties]. Hong Kong: Shangwu yinshuguan, 2005.

——. *Qinggong wubei* 清宮武備 [Armaments of the Qing Court]. Hong Kong: Shangwu yinshuguan, 2008.

GUO FUXIANG 郭福祥. "Cong liangjian Qinggong cangpin kan 17, 18 shiji Zhong Fa gongting jian de wenhua jiaoliu" 從兩件清宮藏品看17, 18 世紀中法宮廷的文化交流 [Examining Cultural Exchanges between the Chinese and French Courts in the Seventeenth and Eighteenth Centuries through Two Artifacts from the Qing Imperial Court]. *Wenbo xuekan* 文博學刊, no. 3 (2023): 88–103.

——. "Luyi shiwu 'Zhongguo ticai' guatan xunzong" 路易十五"中國題材"掛毯尋蹤 [Tracing the Trajectories of Louis XIV's "Tenture chinoise"]. *Gugong bowuyuan yuankan* 故宮博物院刊, no. 4 (2024): 53–65.

HAEMMERLE, ALBERT. *Buntpapier: Herkommen, Geschichte, Techniken, Beziehungen zur Kunst.* Munich: Callwey, 1977.

HARRISON-HALL, JESSICA, AND JULIA LOVELL, EDS. *China's Hidden Century: 1796–1912.* London: British Museum Press, 2023.

HAY, JOHN. "The Body Invisible in Chinese Art?" In *Body, Subject, and Power in China*, edited by Tani Barlow and Angela Zito, 42–77. Chicago: University of Chicago Press, 1994.

HAY, JONATHAN. "Foreword." In *Qing Encounters: Artistic Exchanges between China and the West*, edited by Petra ten-Doesschate Chu and Ding Ning, vii–xix. Los Angeles: Getty Research Institute, 2015.

——. "The Kangxi Emperor's Brush-Traces: Calligraphy, Writing, and the Art of Imperial Authority." In *Body and Face in Chinese Visual Culture*, edited by Wu Hung and Katherine R. Tsiang, 311–34. Cambridge: Harvard University Press, 2005.

——. "The Passage of the Other." In *Histories of Ornament: From Global to Local*, edited by Gülru Necipoğlu and Alina Payne, 62–69. Princeton: Princeton University Press, 2016.

——. *Sensuous Surfaces: The Decorative Object in Early Modern China.* Honolulu: University of Hawai'i Press, 2010.

HELLMAN, MIMI. "Furniture, Sociability, and the Work of Leisure in Eighteenth-Century France." *Eighteenth-Century Studies* 32, no. 4 (1999): 415–45.

——. "Tapestries and Identities at the Hôtel de Soubise: Figuration, Embodied Vision, and Intercorporeality." In *Body Narratives: Motion and Emotion in the French Enlightenment*, edited by Susanna Caviglia, 81–117. Turnhout, Belgium: Brepols, 2017.

HÉNIN, EMMANUELLE. "Parrhasios and the Stage Curtain: Theatre, Metapainting and the Idea of Representation in the Seventeenth Century." *Art History* 33, no. 2 (2010): 248–61.

HEVIA, JAMES L. *English Lessons: The Pedagogy of Imperialism in Nineteenth-Century China.* Durham, N.C.: Duke University Press, 2003.

HO CHUAN-HSIN 何傳馨, ED. *Shenbi danqing: Lang Shining lai Hua sanbainian tezhan* 神筆丹青：郎世寧來華三百年特展 [Portrayals from a Brush Divine: A Special Exhibition on the Tercentennial of Giuseppe Castiglione's Arrival in China]. Taipei: National Palace Museum, 2015.

———. *Shiquan Qianlong: Qing Gaozong de yishu pinwei* 十全乾隆：清高宗的藝術品位 [The All Complete Qianlong: The Aesthetic Tastes of the Qing Emperor Gaozong]. Taipei: National Palace Museum, 2013.

HO, CHUIMEI AND BENNET BRONSON. *Splendors of China's Forbidden City: The Glorious Reign of Emperor Qianlong*. London: Merrell, 2004.

HOU CHIN-LANG 侯錦郎 AND MICHÈLE PIRAZZOLI. *Mulan tu yu Qianlong qiuji dalie zhi yanjiu* 木蘭圖與乾隆秋季大獵之研究 [Studies on the Mulan Scrolls and the Autumn Hunt of Qianlong]. Taipei: National Palace Museum, 1982.

HOU YI-LI 侯怡利. "Jin'ou yonggu, yuzhu changtiao: Tan yuandan kaibi yuyongqi" 金甌永固，玉燭長調：談元旦開筆御用器 [The Golden Chalice of Eternal Stability and the Jade Candlestick of Long-Lasting Harmony: On Imperial Paraphernalia for the Ceremony of Opening the Brush on New Year's Day]. *Gugong wenwu yuekan* 故宮文物月刊, no. 346 (January 2012): 26–39.

HUANG NENGFU 黃能馥. *Zhongguo Nanjing yunjin* 中國南京雲錦 [Cloud Brocades of Nanjing, China]. Nanjing: Nanjing chubanshe, 2003.

JARRY, MADELEINE. *Chinoiseries: le rayonnement du goût chinois sur les arts décoratifs des XVIIe et XVIIIe siècles*. Fribourg: Office du Livre, 1981.

JOHNS, CHRISTOPHER. *China and the Church: Chinoiserie in Global Context*. Oakland: University of California Press, 2016.

JOLLY, ANNA. "Une Soierie chinoise d'après un dessin anglais du XVIIIe siècle." *CIETA Bulletin*, no. 80 (2003): 75–83.

———, ED. *A Taste for the Exotic: Foreign Influences on Early Eighteenth-Century Silk Designs*. Riggisberg: Abegg-Stiftung, 2007.

JOLLY, ANNA, AND VENDULKA OTAVSKÁ. *Seidengewebe des 18. Jahrhunderts II: Naturalismus*. Riggisberg: Abegg-Stiftung, 2002.

———. *Seidengewebe des 18. Jahrhunderts III: Spitzenmuster*. Riggisberg: Abegg-Stiftung, 2018.

JUNEJA, MONICA. "Global Art History and the 'Burden of Representation.'" In *Global Studies: Mapping Contemporary Art and Culture*, edited by Hans Belting et al., 274–97. Ostfildern, Germany: Hatje Cantz, 2011.

JUNEJA, MONICA, AND ANNA GRASSKAMP, EDS. *EurAsian Matters: China, Europe, and the Transcultural Object, 1600–1800*. Cham, Switzerland: Springer, 2018.

KAJITANI NOBUKO 梶谷宣子 AND YOSHIDA KŌJIRŌ 吉田孝次郎. *Gionmatsuri yamaboko kenshōhin chōsa hōkokusho: torai senshokuhin no bu* 祇園祭山鉾懸装品調査報告書：渡来染織品の部 [Study Report on the Paraphernalia Used in the Carriage Parade of the Gion Festival: Department of Imported Textiles]. Kyoto: Gionmatsuri Yamaboko Rengōka, 1992.

KILE, S. E., AND KRISTINA KLEUTGHEN. "Seeing through Pictures and Poetry: *A History of Lenses* (1681)." *Late Imperial China* 38, no. 1 (2017): 47–112.

KJELLBERG, ANNE. "English 18th-Century Silks in Norway." In *Seidengewebe des 18. Jahrhunderts: die Industrien in England und in Nordeuropa*, edited by Regula Schorta and Natalie Rothstein, 135–45. Riggisberg: Abegg-Stiftung, 2000.

KLATTE, GERLINDE, HELGA PRÜSSMANN-ZEMPER, AND KATHARINA SCHMIDT-LOSKE. *Exotismus und Globalisierung: Brasilien auf Wandteppichen: die Tenture des Indes*. Berlin: Deutscher Kunstverlag, 2016.

KLEUTGHEN, KRISTINA. "Chinese Occidenterie: The Diversity of 'Western' Objects in Eighteenth-Century China." *Eighteenth-Century Studies* 47, no. 2 (2014): 117–35.

———. *Imperial Illusions: Crossing Pictorial Boundaries in the Qing Palaces*. Seattle: University of Washington Press, 2014.

———. "One or Two, Repictured." *Archives of Asian Art* 62 (2012): 25–46.

KNOTHE, FLORIAN. *The Manufacture des meubles de la couronne aux Gobelins under Louis XIV: A Social, Political, and Cultural History*. Turnhout, Belgium: Brepols, 2016.

———. "Tapestry as a Medium of Propaganda at the Court of Louis XIV: Display and Audience." In *Tapestry in the Baroque: New Aspects of Production and Patronage*, edited by Thomas Campbell and Elizabeth Cleland, 342–59. New York: Metropolitan Museum of Art, 2010.

———. "Water." Catalogue entry no. 39 in *Tapestry in the Baroque: Threads of Splendor*, edited by Thomas Campbell, 362–63. New York: Metropolitan Museum of Art, 2007.

KONGZI 孔子 (CONFUCIUS, 551–479 BCE). *Confucianism: The Analects of Confucius*, translated by Arthur Waley. New York: History Book Club, 1992.

KUHN, DIETER, ED., with contribution of Zhao Feng. *Chinese Silks*. New Haven: Yale University Press, 2012.

LAI HUI-MIN 賴惠敏. "Qian Jia shidai Beijing de yanghuo yu qiren de richang shenghu" 乾嘉時代北京的洋貨與旗人日常生活 [Foreign Goods and the Bannermen Daily Life during the Qianlong and Jiaqing Periods]. In *Cong chengshi kan Zhongguo de xiandaixing* 從城市看中國的現代性 [The City and Chinese Modernity], edited by Wu Jens-hu 巫仁恕 et al., 1–35. Taipei: Academia Sinica, 2010.

———. "Qianlong chao neiwu fu de pihuo maimai yu Jingcheng shishang" 乾隆朝內務府的皮貨買賣與京城時尚 [Fur Trade by the Imperial Household Department and Fashion in Peking during the Reign of Emperor Ch'ien-lung]. *Gugong xueshu jikan* 故宮學術季刊 21, no. 1 (2003): 101–34.

———. "Shijiu shiji Qiaketu maoyi de Eluosi fangzhipin" 十九世紀恰克圖貿易的俄羅斯紡織品 [The Kyakhta Trade in Russian Textiles in the Nineteenth Century]. *Zhongyang yanjiuyuan jindaishi yanjiusuo jikan* 中央研究院近代史研究所集刊, no. 79 (March 2013): 1–46.

LAI YU-CHIH 賴毓芝. "Cong Dule dao Qinggong: Yi xiniu wei zhongxin de quanqiushi guancha" 從杜勒到清宮：以犀牛為中心的全球史觀察 [From Dürer to the Qing Court: A Global History Centering on the Rhinoceros]. *Gugong wenwu yuekan* 故宮文物月刊, no. 344 (November 2011): 68–81.

———. "Overview of the Network of European Botany in the Imperial Palace of Qing Dynasty via Giuseppe Castiglione's 'Time-Telling Plant from the West.'" *Academia Sinica Center for Digital Cultures E-Newsletter* no. 6 (June 10, 2015). https://newsletter.ascdc.sinica.edu.tw/news/Content.php?language=en&lid=779&nid=7120.

———. "Qinggong dui Ouzhou ziranshi tuxiang de zaizhi: Yi Qianlong chao *Shoupu* weili" 清宮對歐洲自然史圖像的再製：以乾隆朝《獸譜》為例 [Reproducing Renaissance Naturalist Images and Knowledge at the Qianlong Court: A Study of the Album on Beasts]. *Zhongyang yanjiuyuan jindaishi yanjiusuo jikan* 中央研究院近代史研究所集刊, no. 80 (June 2013): 1–75.

———. "Tuxiang diguo: Qianlong chao *Zhigongtu* de zhizuo yu didu chengxian" 圖像帝國：乾隆朝《職貢圖》的製作與帝都呈現 [Picturing Empire: Illustrations of "Official Tribute" at the Qianlong Court and the Making of the Imperial Capital]. *Zhongyang yanjiuyuan jindaishi yanjiusuo jikan* 中央研究院近代史研究所集刊, no. 75 (March 2012): 1–76.

———. "Tuxiang, zhishi yu diguo: Qinggong de shihuoji tuhui" 圖像，知識與帝國：清宮的食火雞圖繪 [Images, Knowledge, and Empire: Depicting Cassowaries in the Qing Court]. *Gugong xueshu jikan* 故宮學術季刊 29, no. 2 (2011): 1–75.

———. "'Tu' yu li: *Huangchao liqi tushi* de chengli jiqi yingxiang" 「圖」與禮：《皇朝禮器圖式》的成立及其影響 ["Illustrations" and the Rites: The Formation of *Illustrated Regulations for Ceremonial Paraphernalia of the Imperial Qing Dynasty* and Its Influence]. In *Gugong xueshu jikan* 故宮學術季刊 37, no. 2 (2020): 1–56.

LANDRY-DERON, ISABELLE. "Les Mathématiciens envoyés en Chine par Louis XIV en 1685." *Archive for History of Exact Sciences* 55, no. 5 (2001): 423–63.

LEE-WHITMAN, LEANNA. "The Silk Trade: Chinese Silks and the British East India Company." *Winterthur Portfolio* 17, no. 1 (1982): 21–41.

LEKHOVICH, TATIANA, WITH TECHNICAL RESEARCH BY LUDMILA GAVRILENKO AND VALENTINA SURKOVA. "Copies after Philippe de Lasalle's Silks by the Lazarev Manufactory Near Moscow: Problems of Attribution." In *Furnishing Textiles: Studies on Seventeenth- and Eighteenth-Century Interior Decoration*, 91–102. Riggisberg: Abegg-Stiftung, 2009.

LEMIRE, BEVERLY. "Domesticating the Exotic: Floral Culture and the East India Calico Trade with England, c. 1600–1800." *Textile: Cloth and Culture* 1, no. 1 (2003): 65–85.

LIN CHI-LYNN 林頎玲. "Qianlong de yidong gongdian: Qinggong zhi 'Menggu bao' yanjiu" 乾隆的移動宮殿–清宮製「蒙古包」研究 [Qianlong's Movable Palace: A Study on 'Mongolian Yurts' Made in the Qianlong Court]. Master's thesis, Taipei National University of the Arts, 2016.

LIN, WEI-CHENG. "Screening the Chinese Interior: Architectonic and Architecturesque." In *The Multivalent Screen: Materiality and Representation in East Asian Visual Culture*, edited by Foong Ping and Chelsea Foxwell, 73–100. Chicago: Art Media Resources, 2019.

LI SHI 李湜. "Qianlong chao Yangxin dian mingchuang tieluohua tanxi: Yi *Suizhao tu Wanguo laichao tu* wei zhongxin" 乾隆朝養心殿明窗貼落畫探析——以《歲朝圖》《萬國來朝圖》為中心 [An Analysis of *Tieluo* Paintings Pasted on the *Mingchuang* of the Hall of Mental Cultivation in the Qianlong Period: Focusing on the *New Year Ceremony* and *Ten Thousand Countries Coming to Pay Tribute*]. *Guggong bowuyuan yuankan* 故宮博物院院刊, no. 1 (2023): 76–91.

LI, YUHANG. "'Remediated Antiquarianism': A Case Study of Qianlong's Copy of Li Di's 'Two Chicks.'" Paper presented at the conference of the Association for Asian Studies, San Diego, March 21–24, 2013.

LIU LU 劉潞. "Congboxing shiyitu yu Qing Gaozong Dayuetu kaoxi" 《叢薄行詩意圖》與《清高宗大閱圖》考析 [On the Paintings *Illustration of the Poem Marching in the Woods* and *The Qianlong Emperor in Grand Review*]. *Gugong bowuyuan yuankan* 故宮博物院院刊, no. 4 (2000): 15–25.

LIU SHI-YEE 劉晞儀. "Qianlong pingding Huijiang tuxiang xilie: Fawang Luyi shisi zhangong bitan he banhua de qifa" 乾隆平定回疆圖像系列：法王路易十四戰功壁毯和版畫的啟發 [The Image Series of Qianlong Pacifying the Uyghur Frontier: Inspirations from the French King Louis XIV's Tapestries of the *History of the King* and His War Prints]. *Gugong bowuyuan yuankan* 故宮博物院院刊, no. 1 (2019): 31–58.

LUO WENHUA 羅文華. "Jizu yu lifo: Zijincheng Yangxindian yiqu de fotang yu Qingdi de xinyang" 祭祖與禮佛：紫禁城養心殿一區的佛堂與清帝的信仰 [Sacrifice to Ancestors and Worship to Buddha: The Buddhist Family Shrine in the Hall of Mental Cultivation of Forbidden City and the Qing Emperors' Religion]. *Gugong bowuyuan yuankan* 故宮博物院院刊, no. 1 (2022): 89–103.

———. *Longpao yu jiasha: Qinggong zangchuan fojiao wenhua kaocha* 龍袍與袈裟：清宮藏傳佛教文化考察 [Dragon Robe and Priest's Robe: Studies on Qing Court Culture of Tibetan Buddhism]. Beijing: Zijincheng chubanshe, 2005.

MALAGÒ, AMINA. "*Kesi*, Chinese Literary Sources in the Study of Silk Tapestry." *Annali di Ca' Foscari* 30, no. 3 (1991): 227–61.

MARTIN, MEREDITH. "Mirror Reflections: Louis XIV, Phra Narai, and the Material Culture of Kingship." *Art History* 38, no. 4 (2015): 652–67.

———. "Special Embassies and Overseas Visitors." In *Visitors to Versailles: From Louis XIV to the French Revolution*, edited by Daniëlle Kisluk-Grosheide and Bertrand Rondot, 108–21. New York: Metropolitan Museum of Arts, 2018.

MARTIN, MEREDITH, AND DANIELA BLEICHMAR, EDS. *Objects in Motion in the Early Modern World*, special issue of *Art History* 38, no. 4 (2015).

MATTEINI, MICHELE. "The Market for 'Western' Paintings in Eighteenth-Century East Asia." In *Eighteenth-Century Art Worlds: Global and Local Geographies of Art*, edited by Michael Yonan and Stacey Sloboda, 35–52. New York: Bloomsbury, 2019.

MCCALL, TIMOTHY. *Brilliant Bodies: Fashioning Courtly Men in Early Renaissance Italy*. University Park: Pennsylvania State University Press, 2022.

MEYER, DANIEL. *L'Histoire du Roy*. Paris: Édition de la Réunion des Musées Nationaux, 1980.

MILAM, JENNIFER. "Betwixt and Between: 'Chinese Taste' in Peter the Great's Russia." In *Qing Encounters: Artistic Exchanges between China and the West*, edited by Petra ten-Doesschate Chu and Ding Ning, 264–85. Los Angeles: Getty Research Institute, 2015.

MILLER, LESLEY E. "From Design Studio to Marketplace: Products, Agents, and Methods of Distribution in the Lyons Silk Manufactures, 1660–1789." In *Threads of Global Desire: Silk in the Pre-Modern World*, edited by Dagmar Schäfer, Giorgio Riello, and Luca Molà, 225–50. Woodbridge, U.K.: Boydell Press, 2018.

———. "Jean Revel: Silk Designer, Fine Artist, or Entrepreneur?" *Journal of Design History* 8, no. 2 (1995): 79–96.

———. "Making a Reputation from Innovation: Silk Designers in Lyon, 1660–1789." In *Fashioning the Early Modern: Dress, Textiles, and Innovation in Europe, 1500–1800*, edited by Evelyn Welch, 187–214. Oxford: Oxford University Press, 2017.

———. "Representing Silk Design: Nicolas Joubert de l'Hiberderie and le dessinateur pour les étoffes d'or, d'argent et de soie (Paris, 1765)." *Journal of Design History* 17, no. 1 (2004): 29–53.

———. *Selling Silks: A Merchant's Sample Book, 1764*. London: V&A Publishing, 2014.

———. "A Study of Designers in the Lyon Silk Industry, 1712–1787." 2 vols. Ph.D. diss., Brighton Polytechnic, 1988.

MILLER, SUSAN. "Disegni *bizarres* per tessuti di seta, 1680–1710." In *Seta: Potere e glamour: Tessuti e abiti dal Rinascimento al XX secolo*, edited by Roberta Orsi Landini, 83–109. Cinisello Balsamo: Silvana, 2006.

———. "Europe Looks East: Ceramics and Silk, 1680–1710." In *A Taste for the Exotic: Foreign Influences on Early Eighteenth-Century Silk Designs*, edited by Anna Jolly, 155–73. Riggisberg: Abegg-Stiftung, 2007.

MUSILLO, MARCO. *The Shining Inheritance: Italian Painters at the Qing Court, 1699–1812*. Los Angeles: Getty Research Institute, 2016.

NELSON, ROBERT S., ED. *Visuality Before and Beyond the Renaissance: Seeing as Others Saw*. Cambridge: Cambridge University Press, 2000.

PAGANI, CATHERINE. *Eastern Magnificence and European Ingenuity: Clocks of Late Imperial China*. Ann Arbor: University of Michigan Press, 2001.

PAULETTI, ALESSANDRA GEROMEL, AND PAOLO PERI. *Oro filato: I romanzo dei fili metallici preziosi dalle origini ad oggi*. Milan: Lurex, 1999.

PECK, AMELIA, ET AL. *Interwoven Globe: The Worldwide Textile Trade, 1500–1800*. New York: Metropolitan Museum of Art, 2013.

PENG, YING-CHEN. *Artful Subversion: Empress Dowager Cixi's Image Making*. New Haven: Yale University Press, 2022.

PHIPPS, ELENA. *Looking at Textiles: A Guide to Technical Terms*. Los Angeles: J. Paul Getty Museum, 2011.

PIAO WENYING 朴文英. "Introduction." In *Huacai ruoying: Zhongguo gudai kesi cixiu jingpinzhan* 華彩若英：中國古代緙絲刺繡精品展 [Splendid Colors: Masterpieces of Traditional Chinese Tapestries and Embroideries], 1–33. Shenyang, China: Liaoning Provincial Museum, 2009.

———. *Kesi* 緙絲. Suzhou: Suzhou daxue chubanshe, 2009.

PICAUD, GÉRARD, AND JEAN FOISSELON. *Sacrées soieries: étoffes précieuses à la Visitation.* Paris: Somogy, 2012.

PIRAZZOLI-T'SERSTEVENS, MICHÈLE. "Giuseppe Castiglione et le renouveau du portrait impérial au XVIIIe s." *Arts Asiatiques* 60 (2005): 22–30.

———. "Notes on European Decorative Arts at the Chinese Court during the Kangxi Reign: Importations, Copies and Adaptations." *National Palace Museum Bulletin* 45 (October 2012): 1–17.

———. "A Pluridisciplinary Research on Castiglione and the Emperor Ch'ien-lung's European Palaces, Part I." *National Palace Museum Bulletin* 24, no. 4 (1989): 1–12.

PONI, CARLO. "Fashion as Flexible Production: The Strategies of the Lyons Silk Merchants in the Eighteenth Century." In *World of Possibilities: Flexibility and Mass Production in Western Industrialization,* edited by Charles F. Sabel and Jonathan Zeitlin, 37–74. Cambridge: Cambridge University Press, 1997.

RADO, MEI MEI. "Botanical Fantasy in Silks: Transformations of a Rococo Floral Design from England to China." In *Material Cultures of the Global Eighteenth Century: Art, Mobility and Change,* edited by Wendy Bellion and Kristel Smentek, 81–105. New York: Bloomsbury Academic, 2023.

———. "The Empress Dowager Cixi's Japanese Screen and Late Qing Imperial Cosmopolitanism." *Burlington Magazine* 163, no. 1423 (October 2021): 886–97.

———. "Encountering Magnificence: European Silks at the Qing Court during the Eighteenth Century." In *Qing Encounters: Artistic Exchanges between China and the West,* edited by Petra ten-Doesschate Chu and Ding Ning, 58–75. Los Angeles: Getty Research Institute, 2015.

———. "Qing Court's Encounters with European Tapestries: The *Tenture Chinoise* and Beyond." In *Arachné: un regard critique sur l'histoire de la tapisserie,* edited by Pascal-François Bertrand and Audrey N. Maupas, 119–38. Rennes, France: Presses Universitaires de Rennes, 2017.

RAWSKI, EVELYN S. *The Last Emperors: A Social History of Qing Imperial Institutions.* Berkeley: University of California Press, 2009.

———. "Re-envisioning the Qing: The Significance of the Qing Period in Chinese History." *Journal of Asian Studies* 55, no. 4 (1996): 829–50.

RAWSON, JESSICA, AND EVELYN RAWSKI. *China: The Three Emperors, 1662–1795.* London: Royal Academy of Arts, 2005.

REED, MARCIA. "A Perfume Is Best from Afar: Publishing China for Europe." In *China on Paper: European and Chinese Works from the Late Sixteenth to the Early Nineteenth Century,* edited by Marcia Reed and Paola Demattè, 9–27. Los Angeles: Getty Research Institute, 2007.

REED, MARCIA, AND PAOLA DEMATTÈ, EDS. *China on Paper: European and Chinese Works from the Late Sixteenth to the Early Nineteenth Century.* Los Angeles: Getty Research Institute, 2007.

RIMAUD, YOHAN, ET AL. *Une des provinces du rococo: la Chine rêvée de François Boucher.* Besançon: Musée des Beaux-Arts et d'Archéologie, 2019.

ROCHEBRUNE, MARIE-LAURE DE, ED. *La Chine à Versailles: art et diplomatie au XVIIIe siècle.* Paris: Somogy, 2014.

ROSLER, MARTHA, ET AL. "Notes from the Field: Materiality." *Art Bulletin* 95, no. 1 (2013): 10–37.

ROTHSTEIN, NATALIE. *Flowers, Blumen, Fleurs: English 18th-Century Silks.* Riggisberg: Abegg Stiftung, 1998.

———. "Nine English Silks." *Bulletin of the Needle and Bobbin Club* 48, nos. 1–2 (1964): 4–35.

———. *Silk Designs of the Eighteenth Century in the Collection of the Victoria and Albert Museum, London.* Boston: Little, Brown, 1990.

———. "Silks for the American Market, Part II." *The Connoisseur,* no. 169 (1967): 150–56.

SALMON, XAVIER. "The Duke and the Cassowary." *FMR,* no. 126 (February/March 2004): 69–86.

SARGENTSON, CAROLYN. *Merchants and Luxury Markets: The Marchands Merciers of Eighteenth-Century Paris.* Malibu, Calif.: J. Paul Getty Museum, 1996.

SCHMID, NEIL. "The Material Culture of Exegesis and Liturgy and a Change in the Artistic Representations in Dunhuang Caves, ca. 700–1000." *Asia Major,* 3rd ser., 19, nos. 1–2 (2006): 171–210.

SCHOPP, SUSAN E. *Sino-French Trade at Canton, 1698–1842.* Hong Kong: Hong Kong University Press, 2021.

SCHORTA, REGULA, AND NATALIE ROTHSTEIN, EDS. *Seidengewebe des 18. Jahrhunderts: die Industrien in England und in Nordeuropa.* Riggisberg: Abegg-Stiftung, 2000.

SHEN, HSÜEH-MAN. "Tombs at the Crossroads of the Worlds of the Living and the Dead." In *Tenth-Century China and Beyond: Art and Visual Culture in a Multi-Centered Age,* edited by Wu Hung, 150–78. Chicago: Art Media Resources, 2012.

SHIH CHING-FEI 施靜菲. *Riyue guanghua: Qinggong hua falang* 日月光華：清宮畫琺瑯 [Radiant Luminance: The Painted Enamelware of the Qing Imperial Court]. Taipei: National Palace Museum, 2012.

SILBERSTEIN, RACHEL. *A Fashionable Century: Textile Artistry and Commerce in the Late Qing.* Seattle: University of Washington Press, 2020.

———. "Fashioning the Foreign: Using British Woolens in Nineteenth-Century China." In *Fashion, Identity, and Power in Modern Asia,* edited by Kyunghee Pyun and Aida Yuen Wong, 231–58. Cham, Switzerland: Palgrave Macmillan, 2018.

SLOBODA, STACEY. *Chinoiserie: Commerce and Critical Ornament in Eighteenth-Century Britain.* Manchester, U.K.: Manchester University Press, 2014.

SLOMANN, VILHELM. *Bizarre Designs in Silks: Trade and Traditions,* translated by Eve M. Wendt. Copenhagen: E. Munksgaard, 1953.

SMENTEK, KRISTEL. "Chinoiserie for the Qing: A French Gift of Tapestries to the Qianlong Emperor." *Journal of Early Modern History* 20, no. 1 (2016): 87–109.

———. *Rococo Exotic: French Mounted Porcelain and the Allure of the East.* New York: Frick Collection, 2007.

SOTHEBY'S LONDON. *Catalogue of Tapestries, Works of Art, Clocks, Ormolu, and Fine French Furniture.* November 20, 1964.

———. *Important Furniture, Painting and Works of Art.* December 7, 2000.

STANDEN, EDITH. "The Story of the Emperor of China: a Beauvais Tapestry Series." *Metropolitan Museum Journal* 11 (1976): 103–17.

STAVENOW-HIDEMARK, ELISABET. "The Silk Industry in Sweden in the 18th Century." In *Seidengewebe des 18. Jahrhunderts: die Industrien in England und in Nordeuropa,* edited by Regula Schorta and Natalie Rothstein, 163–72. Riggisberg: Abegg-Stiftung, 2000.

STEWART, SUSAN. *Nonsense: Aspects of Intertextuality in Folklore and Literature.* Baltimore: Johns Hopkins University Press, 1989.

TEISER, STEPHEN F. "Ornamenting the Departed: Notes on the Language of Chinese Buddhist Ritual Texts." *Asia Major,* 3rd ser., 22, no. 1 (2009): 201–37.

TENNANTS AUCTIONEERS. *The Pattern Sale: 100 Years of Textile Designs and Fabric Samples.* November 20, 2020.

THOMAS, GREG. "Yuanming Yuan/Versailles: Intercultural Interactions between Chinese and European Palace Cultures." *Art History* 32, no. 1 (2009): 115–43.

VITTET, JEAN. *Les Gobelins au siècle des Lumières: un âge d'or de la manufacture royale.* Paris: Swan Éditeur, 2014.

———. "The King Visits the Gobelins." In *Tapestry in the Baroque: Threads of Splendor,* edited by Thomas Campbell, 375–89. New York: Metropolitan Museum of Art, 2007.

VLAM, GRACE. "Sixteenth-Century European Tapestries in Tokugawa Japan." *Art Bulletin* 63, no. 3 (1981): 476–95.

VOCABULAIRE TECHNIQUE FRANÇAIS. Lyon: Centre International d'Étude des Textiles Anciens, 2020.

VOCABULARY OF TECHNICAL TERMS: ENGLISH. Lyon: Centre International d'Étude des Textiles Anciens, 2021.

WANG, CHENG-HUA. "'Going Public': Portraits of the Empress Dowager Cixi, circa 1904." *Nan Nü* 14, no. 1 (2012): 119–76.

———. "Prints in Sino-European Artistic Interactions of the Early Modern Period." In *Face to Face: The Transcendence of the Arts in China and Beyond: Historical Perspective,* edited by Rui Oliveira Lopes, 436–43. Lisbon: Artistic Studies Research Center and the Faculty of Fine Arts, University of Lisbon, 2014.

———. "Whither Art History? A Global Perspective on Eighteenth-Century Chinese Art and Visual Culture." *Art Bulletin* 96, no. 4 (2014): 379–94.

WANG CHING-LING 王靜靈. "*Tuxiang zhengshi: Helanguo ren yi niuma tu* suotan" 圖像證史：《賀蘭國人役牛馬圖》瑣談 [Image Proves the History: Some Thoughts on the Painting *Dutchmen Presenting Cows and Horses*]. *Gugong wenwu yuekan* 故宮文物月刊, no. 336 (March 2011): 88–99.

WANG LIANMING 王廉明. "Beijing Yesuhui Beitang huayuan zongkao: Qiyuan, gongneng, jiqi yinyu" 北京耶穌會北堂花園綜考：起源、功能及其隱喻 [Jesuit Beitang Garden Revisited: Origin, Function, and Political Imagery]. *Fu-Jen lishi xuebao* 輔仁歷史學報, no. 36 (2016): 197–244.

———. "Qing Ai Qimeng *Shijunquan tu* ce ji Qinggong quantu zongkao" 清艾啟蒙《十駿犬圖》冊及清宮犬圖綜考 [On Sichelbart's Album *Ten Noble Hounds* and Other Qing Court Images of Dogs]. *Zijincheng* 紫禁城, no. 2 (2017): 120–37.

WANG ZILIN 王子林. *Ming Qing huanggong chenshe* 明清皇宮陳設 [Interior Display of Ming and Qing Palaces]. Beijing: Zijincheng chubanshe, 2011.

———. "Ningshou Gong huayuan de yingjian yu yishu sixiang" 寧壽宮花園的營建與藝術思想 [The Construction History and Artistic Conception of the Qianlong Garden]. In *Qianlong Huangdi de mimi huayuan* 乾隆皇帝的秘密花園 [A Lofty Retreat from the Red Dust: The Secret Garden of Emperor Qianlong], 16–39. Beijing: Palace Museum, 2012.

———. *Zijincheng yuanzhuang yu yuanchuang* 紫禁城原狀與原創 [The Original Interior and Creativity of the Forbidden City]. 2 vols. Beijing: Zijincheng chubanshe, 2007.

WATT, JAMES C. Y., AND ANNE E. WARDWELL. *When Silk Was Gold: Central Asian and Chinese Textiles.* New York: Metropolitan Museum of Art in cooperation with the Cleveland Museum of Art, 1997.

WEDDIGEN, TRISTAN. "Materiality." *Art Bulletin* 95, no. 1 (2013): 34–37.

———. "Textile Spaces, Interior and Exterior." In *Display of Art in the Roman Palace, 1550–1750,* edited by Gail Feigenbaum and Francesco Freddolini, 162–65. Los Angeles: Getty Research Institute, 2014.

WEIGERT, LAURA. "Chambres d'amour: Tapestries of Love and the Texturing of Space." *Oxford Art Journal* 31, no. 3 (2008): 317–36.

WEIGERT, ROGER-ARMAND. *French Tapestry.* Newton, Mass.: C. T. Branford, 1962.

WHITEHEAD, PETER, AND M. BOESEMAN. *A Portrait of Dutch 17th Century Brazil: Animals, Plants, and People by the Artists of Johan Maurits of Nassau.* Amsterdam: North-Holland Pub. Co., 1989.

WIJAYARATNA, MÔHAN. *Buddhist Monastic Life: According to the Texts of the Theravāda Tradition.* New York: Cambridge University Press, 1990.

WILLS, JOHN E., JR. *Embassies and Illusions: Dutch and Portuguese Envoys to K'ang-hsi, 1666–1687.* Cambridge: Council on East Asian Studies, Harvard University, 1984.

WU HUNG 巫鴻. "Chongfan zuopin: *Ping'an chunxin tu* de chuangzuo ji qita" 重返作品：《平安春信圖》的創作及其他 [Return to Artwork: The Creation of *Spring's Peaceful Message* and Related Issues]. *Gugong bowuyuan yuankan* 故宮博物院院刊, no. 10 (2020): 250–62.

———. *The Double Screen: Medium and Representation in Chinese Painting.* Chicago: University of Chicago Press, 1996.

———. "Emperor's Masquerade: 'Costume Portraits' of Yongzheng and Qianlong." *Orientations* 26, no. 7 (1995): 25–41.

———. *Monumentality in Early Chinese Art and Architecture.* Stanford: Stanford University Press, 1995.

———. "Monumentality of Time: Giant Clocks, the Drum Tower, the Clock Tower." In *Monuments and Memory: Made and Unmade,* edited by Robert S. Nelson and Margaret Olin, 107–32. Chicago: University of Chicago Press, 2003.

WU MEIFENG 吳美鳳. *Sheng Qing jiaju xingzhi liubian yanjiu* 盛清家具行制流變研究 [Studies on the Stylistic Transformations of High Qing Furniture]. Beijing: Zijincheng chubanshe, 2007.

WU MIN 武敏. "Xinjiang jinnian chutu maozhipin yanjiu" 新疆近年出土毛織品研究 [Studies on Recently Excavated Woolen Textiles in the Xinjiang Region]. *Xiyu yanjiu* 西域研究, no. 1 (1994): 1–13.

WU, YULIAN. *Luxurious Networks: Salt Merchants, Status, and Statecraft in Eighteenth-Century China.* Stanford: Stanford University Press, 2017.

YANG BODA 楊伯達. *Qingdai Guangdong gongpin* 清代廣東貢品 [Official Gifts from Canton to the Qing Court]. Beijing: Palace Museum, 1987.

YANG JIBO 楊繼波. "Ming Qing dang'an wenxian zhong dui Putaoya de chengwei" 明清檔案文獻中對葡萄牙的稱謂 [The Names of Portugal in Ming and Qing Archives]. *Lishi dang'an* 歷史檔案, no. 4 (1999): 88–91.

YAN YONG 嚴勇. "Qingdai de guanying sizhi ye" 清代的官營絲織業 [Official Silk Industry of the Qing Dynasty]. *Gugong bowuyuan yuankan* 故宮博物院院刊, no. 6 (2003): 82–89.

YONAN, MICHAEL. "Toward a Fusion of Art History and Material Culture Studies." *West 86th: A Journal of Decorative Arts, Design History, and Material Culture* 18, no. 2 (2011): 232–48.

ZEITLIN, JUDITH. *The Phantom Heroine: Ghost and Gender in Seventeenth-Century Chinese Literature.* Honolulu: University of Hawai'i Press, 2007.

ZHANG QIONG 張瓊. "Qingdai Huangdi dayue yu dayue jiazhou guizhi" 清代皇帝大閱與大閱甲冑規制 [Qing Emperors' Grand Reviews and Regulations on Armor during the Grand Reviews]. *Gugong bowuyuan yuanlan* 故宮博物院院刊, no. 6 (2010): 89–103.

ZHANG SHUXIAN 張淑嫻. "Tujie Qingdai Zijincheng Yangxindian dongnuange de lishi bianqian" 圖解清代紫禁城養心殿東暖閣的歷史變遷 [Illustrated History of the Transformations of East Warm Chamber of the Hall of Mental Cultivation in the Forbidden City]. *Jianzhu shi* 建築史, no. 1 (2019): 73–86.

ZHAO FENG 趙豐. *Jincheng: Zhongguo sichou yu sichou zhilu* 錦程：中國絲綢與絲綢之路 [Brocade Journey: Chinese Silks and the Silk Road]. Hong Kong: City University of Hong Kong Press, 2012.

———, ED. *Sichou yishu shi* 絲綢藝術史 [History of Chinese Silk Art]. Beijing: Wenwu chubanshe, 2005.

———. *Zhongguo sichou tongshi* 中國絲綢通史 [History of Chinese Silks]. Suzhou: Suzhou daxue chubanshe, 2005.

ZHENG, YANGWEN. *China on the Sea: How the Maritime World Shaped Modern China.* Leiden: Brill, 2014.

Image Credits

© Palace Museum, Beijing (figs. 1, 2, 5, 7, 10A–B, 12–21, 30–33, 38–40, 43, 45, 48, 50, 52–54, 56–66, 68, 71, 72, 85–87, 93, 98A–D, 99, 105, 109, 111, 113, 117, 121, 124–127)
© Metropolitan Museum of Art (figs. 4, 28, 51, 116)
© National Palace Museum, Taipei (figs. 6, 41, 42, 44, 46, 106, 110)
© Victoria and Albert Museum (figs. 9, 11, 35, 89)
© State Historical Museum, Moscow (figs. 22, 23)
© Mei Mei Rado (figs. 24–27, 67, 69, 108, 123)
© British Library Board (fig. 29)
© Museum of Fine Arts, Boston (figs. 34, 104, 128)
© Philadelphia Museum of Art (fig. 36)
© Fashion Museum Bath/Bridgeman Images (fig. 37)
© Abegg-Stiftung, CH-3132 Riggisberg, 2001 (photo: Christoph von Viràg) (fig. 47)
© Nelson-Atkins Museum of Art (fig. 49)
© Minneapolis Institute of Art (figs. 55, 101)
© Lü Gang (fig. 70)
© Bibliothèque nationale de France (figs. 75, 92, 118, 119)
© Christie's (fig. 76)
© Galerie Armand Deroyan et Maison Pierre-Yves Machault (figs. 77, 103, 112)
© J. Paul Getty Museum and the Getty Research Institute (figs. 78, 91, 102)
© Ashmolean Museum, University of Oxford (figs. 80, 81)
© Mobilier national (figs. 82–84, 88)
© British Museum (fig. 90)
© Cleveland Museum of Art (figs. 94–97, 114, 115)
© Shanghai Library (fig. 100)
© 2021 CNES/Airbus, Maxar Technologies, Google Earth (fig. 107)
© Musée des Tapisseries, Aix-en-Provence/Jean Bernard 2023/Bridgeman Images (fig. 120)
© Rijksmuseum (fig. 122)
© National Museum of Asian Art Archives, Smithsonian Institution (fig. 129)

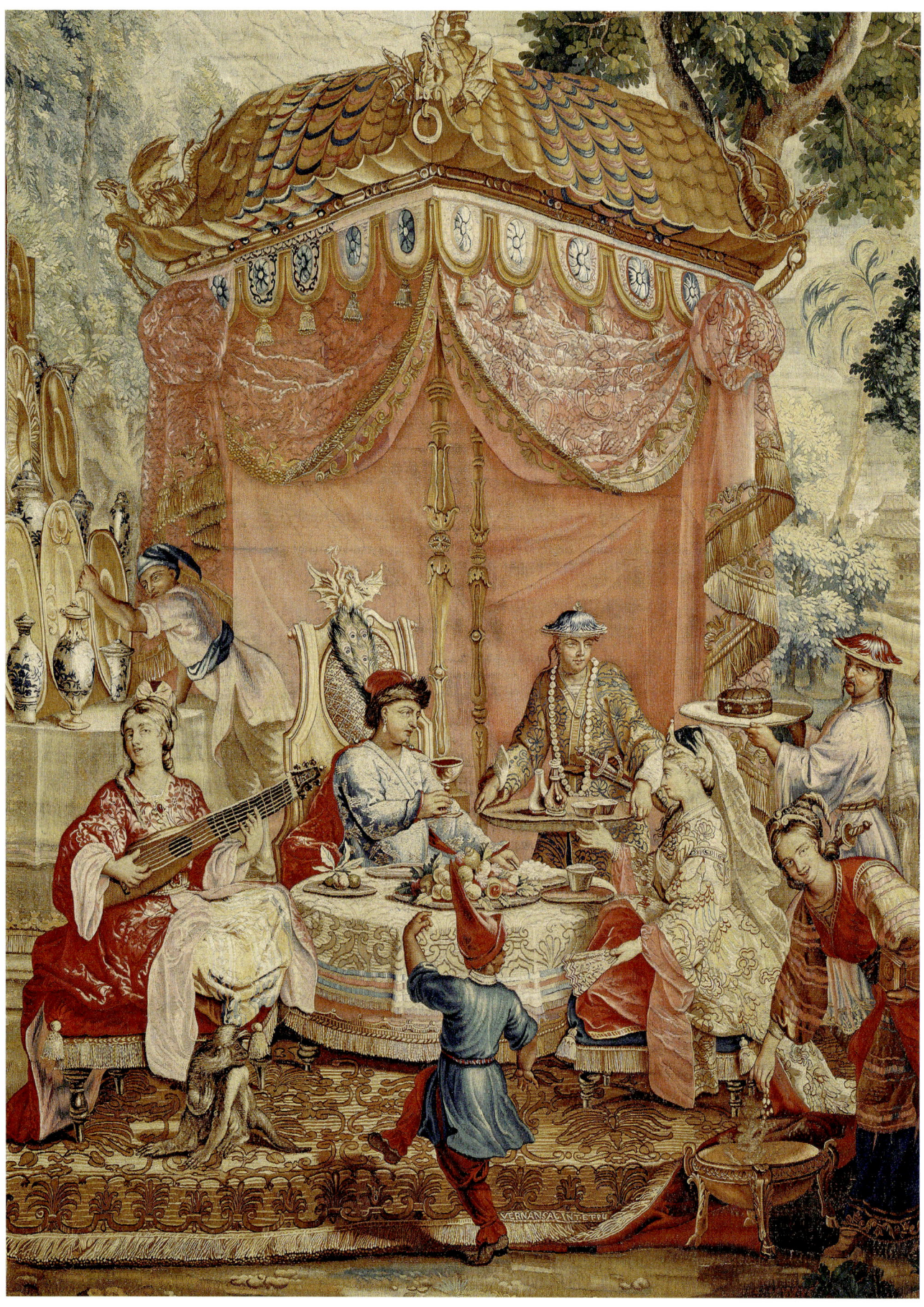

Index

Illustrations are indicated by page numbers in *italics*.

A

Afonso VI (Portuguese king), 81, 136
allegories: depiction in European tapestries, 83; depiction in Qing silk tapestries, 77; Han Chinese dress appearing in, 130
The Alliance with the Swiss, engraving of tapestry of, 81, *82*
Amiot, Jean-Joseph-Marie, 124
ancestor worship, 60
Anciennes Indes. See Tenture des Indes
Anderson, Carrie, 102
The Animals' Combat, Ashmolean Museum tapestry, 91–96, *92, 93*
archery sets, 62–71, *64–66*
Archives of the Imperial Workshops under the Imperial Household Department (*Huoji dang*, HJD), 12, 13. *See also* Qing Imperial Household Department
Armada Tapestries in English House of Lords, *106*, 107
L'Art pour tous (journal), 90
assimilated techniques and styles from Europe in Qing production, 1, 5, 149–50; Canton officials presenting local products made in Western style to Qing emperors, 141; depicting Western figures, 117; draperies and curtains in Qing-produced tapestries, 137–38; framing devices in Qing-produced tapestries, 110, 124, 133–37, *135*; receding vista framed by trees, 117. *See also* Western-style silks, Qing production of; Western-style tapestries, Qing production of
Attiret, Jean Denis, 113
Aubusson tapestry manufactory, 86, 171n10
Augsburg, brocade paper from, 40, *41*
auspicious symbols and motifs: in Chinese paintings, 119, 122, 131; in Qing imperial silks, 14–15, *15*, 18, 37; in Western-style tapestries produced by Suzhou, 119, 125, 141, 150
Autumn Hunt (*mulan qiuxian*), 59–61, 144

B

Baby Chicks Waiting to Be Nourished (*Jichu daisi tu*), 77
banana tree motif, 117
Barnier (French silk manufacturer), 20, 21
Barrow, John, 124
Beauvais tapestry manufactory: diplomatic gifts of tapestry suites from, 79; distinguished from Gobelins styles and themes, 79; establishment and role of, 78, 79; first and second *Tentures chinoises* woven by, 6, 9, 75, 84, 85–86, 109; foreign patrons ordering from, 79; frame-curtain arrangement, use of, 138, *140*; loom types used by, 79; nonspecialists attributing tapestries to Gobelins, 84, 89, 103; private interiors, tapestries for, 79. *See also Tenture chinoise* (first series); *Tenture chinoise* (second series)
Beijing: Catholic mission displaying French tapestries, 81; Qing rulers moving capital to, 115. *See also* Beitang Jesuit library; Forbidden City
Beitang Jesuit library (North Church, Beijing), 81, 83, 99, 170n69, 171n30
Belin de Fontenay, Jean-Baptiste, 84
Benoist, Michel, 83, 88, 89, 103
berclé. See points rentrés
Berger, Patricia: *Empire of Emptiness*, 73
Bertin, Henri-Léonard: ambition to gain Qing favor for France, 4, 86, 88, 89, 148; Jesuits' presentation of *Tenture chinoise* (second series) to Qianlong emperor on behalf of, 86, 88–89, 113, 148; *Mémoires concernant l'histoire, les sciences, les arts, les moeurs, les usages, & c. des Chinois, par les missionnaires de Pékin*, 91; Qianlong's reception of *Tenture chinoise* (second series), 91, 148; relying on Jesuit Chinese students to represent Qing imperial taste, 88; Rothe and, 93–94, 173n103; as Sinophile in eighteenth-century Europe, 4, 86, 91; *Tenture chinoise* (second series) chosen to impress Qianlong as gift, 89, 93; Vigée's framed portraits sent as gifts to Qianlong, 136

biblical scenes in European wool tapestries, 78, 81, 83, 171n17
bizarre silks, 21–23, *22–23*, 34, 42–43, *42–43*, 53, 63, *66*
Boel, Pieter, 98
Book of Documents (*Shangshu*), 14
borders of tapestries. *See* drapery; framing devices
botany. *See* plants
Boucher, François, 78, 79, 86, 89, 90, 120
Bourgeois, François, 89, 103
Bouvet, Joachim, 81
Brazil, depiction of, 79, 91, 93–96, 98, 100, 102. *See also Tenture des Indes*
Bremer-David, Charissa, 172n59
brocaded silk, 11, *12–13*, 15, 23, 27, 30, 32, 43, 45, 48, 71
Brokatpapier (brocade paper), 40
Bron et Ringuet (French silk manufacturer), 21
Buddhism: fabric fragments used as textiles for vestments and temple adornment, 53; lotus blossom, symbolism of, 73; transcendence and *zhuangyan* as visual aids for experiencing Buddha's sacred domain, 73; *Vinaya Piṭaka*, 53. *See also* Tibetan Buddhism

C

calligraphy and writing, 76–77, 124; *The Kangxi Emperor Writing*, 116, 144, *144*; *The Qianlong Emperor Writing*, 137, *138*
Callot, Jacques: *Portrait of Claude Deruet and His Son, Jean*, 136, *137*
Canton port and Customs Bureau: Canton officials presenting local products made in Western style to Qing emperors, 141; commissioning European merchants to fill orders from Qianlong emperor, 40, 83, 148; as official maritime trade center, 31–33, 148; Qianlong frustrated with slow or non-fulfillment of European silks, 33; Qianlong ordering to procure satins with gold and silver threads,

Canton port and Customs Bureau (*continued*) 33; Qing Imperial Workshop ordering "useful Western things" to be procured by, 34; silks among gifts presented to emperor by officials from, 32; silks woven in, 59; stationery paper decorated with European designs in gift registers of, 40; *Tenture chinoise* (second series), seizure upon arrival, 88

cassowary, *96*, 98, 99, *100–101*, 172n88, 173n120

Castiglione, Giuseppe, 50–51, 83; *Immortal Blossoms in an Everlasting Spring* (album), 51, *51–52*; *Imperial Banquet at the Garden of Ten Thousand Trees* (with Attiret and others), 62, *62*; as Jesuit painter at Qing court, 50, 113; *Portrait of the Qianlong Emperor* (1736), 16, *17*; *The Qianlong Emperor Hunting Hare* (scroll, in collaboration with other court artists), 66, *69*, *156*; *The Qianlong Emperor in the Grand Military Review* (1739), *x*, 1–2, 7; *The Qianlong Emperor in the Grand Military Review* (1758), 1–*2*, *3*, 7, 11, 66, 68–70, 155; Qianlong's commissioning painted blankets as Western tapestries for European Palaces, 108–9; *Troating for Deer*, 66, *70*

Catherine the Great (Russian empress), 21

Central Asian woolen tapestries' remnants, 75–76

chenille, 59, *60*, 63, *65*

chiaroscuro, 124

China illustrata (Kircher), 84

"Chinese brocade" manufactured in India, for Tibetan Buddhist temples, 72

Chinese painting: auspicious motifs and messages appearing in, 119, 122, 131; "children at play" genre, 119; Chinese/European pictorial dualism, 117; drapery and curtains appearing in Qing artwork, 137–38; male dominance in painting of family, 117–19; *qi* (air) in, 124; spatial recession in landscape painting, 117. *See also* trompe-l'oeil genre; *specific paintings by title or artist*

chinoiserie: cross-cultural exchange of, 7–8, 150; Dutch silks featuring designs of, 19; French tapestries with designs of, 5–6, 79; as global style of universal exoticism, 7, 123, 150; meaning of, 6; popular across European social classes, 6; for Qing court, source of Western motifs and styles, 7–8, 123; as transnational visual vocabulary, 7, 102; in Watteau compositions, 86; *A Western Family by the Riverside* and, *118*, 120. *See also Tenture chinoise* (first series); *Tenture chinoise* (second series)

church textiles: Catholic, 21, 27, 73; phelonion (Russian Orthodox priest's vestment), 28–30, *31*, 72; tapestry displays, 171n17

Cixi, Empress Dowager (1835–1908), *146*, 153–55, *153–54*

classical mythological scenes in European wool tapestries, 78, 81

Classic of Poetry (*Shijing*), 125

Clement XI (pope), 41

clock with drapery framing miniature theater of automata monkeys, 140, *141*

Clunas, Craig, 33

Clusius, Carolus, 99

Colbert, Jean-Baptiste, 18–19, 78, 171n10

colonial North America as market for Spitalfields silks, 46

Confucianism, 14, 69, 119, 120, 122, 133, 142–43, 150

corporeal and sensory engagement with textiles, 8–9, 11

costumes. *See* theatricality

Couplet, Philippe, 84

Courtois, Justin, 24

cravats, 122

Crealocke, Henry Hope, 94–95, 173n112

Crossley, Pamela, 1

cultural norms (Chinese): family as primary social unit, 142–43, 150; gender segregation, 120; harmony in universe and Qianlong as father of Chinese people, 143; male as head of household and dominant, 117–20; male descendants as greatest joy, 133; women shown with covered feet, 119. *See also* Confucianism

curtains depicted in artwork and tapestries. *See* drapery

D

damasks, 11, 19, 23, 32, 55, *151*

Daoguang emperor (r. 1820–50), 61

Daoism, 36

The Defeat of Marsin, engraving of tapestry of, 81, 82, *82*, *159*

deities, depiction in Qing silk tapestries, 77, *78*

Diderot, Denis and Jean-Baptiste le Rond d'Alembert: *Encyclopédie*, 18, *19*, 80

d'Incarville, Pierre-Noël Le Chéron, 50–51

diplomatic gifts from European countries, 2; diversity of, 32; European royal portraits gifted to Qing emperors as, 136; European silks as, 31–32, 147, 148; European woolen tapestries as, 5, 78, 79, 81–103, 147, 148; French tapestries chosen to glorify Qianlong emperor by incorporating chinoiserie, 150; recorded as "tributary objects" at Qing court, 31, 32, 81, 89, 90, 147, 148; Yongzheng emperor and, 32. *See also Tenture chinoise* (first series); *Tenture chinoise* (second series); *Tenture des Indes*; *specific countries*

diplomatic gifts to European countries: Kangxi sending to Europe items made in China by using European techniques, 41; Siam presenting to Louis XIV (French king), 32

displacement, 151

Don Quixote Undressed by the Duchess's Maids (Beauvais suite, *Stories of Don Quixote*), 138, *140*

dragon robes, 1, 12, *14*, 36, *37*, 169n88

drapery, 137–43; Chinese imperial theaters' using doors at back of stage instead of curtain at front, 140; European theaters' standard use of front curtain by seventeenth century, 140; export paintings for European consumers and, 141; in *Family Gathering on New Year's Morning*, 110, 133–34, 140, 141, 150; history of stylized curtains in Chinese funerary and religious contexts, 137; honorary canopy created by drapery in 1771 tapestry to glorify seated Qianlong, 142, *143*; hybrid-style clock made in Canton and presented to Qianlong with overarching drapery, 140, *141*; Jesuit painters using in informal portraits of Qianlong, 137, *138*; popularity of raised curtain in European art of seventeenth and eighteenth centuries, 137; Qing court's appropriation of European motif, 137–38; Renaissance painters using in religious and revelatory scenes, 137; secular use in European art, 137; symbolizing Qianlong's connecting West and Qing China, 145; trompe l'oeil aspect of parted curtains, 137; "unveiling" of different culture by European visual convention, 141

drawlooms: Chinese, *12*, *13*; European, 18–20, *19*; loom width determining manufacturing location, 45, 46, 48

Dumons, Jean-Joseph, 86

duoluo ni / *duoluo rong* (broadcloth-wool), 115, 174n20

Dupin, Charles (Paul Varin): *Expédition de Chine*, 103, 136

Dürer, Albrecht, 96, 99, 102

Dutch art's use of receding vista framed by trees, 117

Dutch East India Company (VOC), 31, 81, 84

Dutch silks/tapestries and trade. *See* Holland

E

East India companies, 148; British, 48; Dutch (VOC), 31, 81, 84; French, 83, 86, 88, 93–94

Eckhout, Albert, 93

Efendi, Mehmed, 88

Elliott, Mark, 60, 61

empress: duty and significance of Hall of Unified Peace (*Jiaotai dian*), 77; Xiaoxian's (Qianlong's empress), death of, 133. *See also* Cixi

enamelware, 5, 39, 41, 51, 67, 88, 117

Enderlin, Jacob, 40, *41*

end of Qing dynasty (1911), 21, 152

England: aristocratic purchase of *Tenture de Boucher* tapestries from Gobelins, 79; ban on Chinese silk imports in, 19, 48; bizarre silks and, 21; centers for high-quality silks, 19; Qing silks in, 48; rococo botanical design (c. 1742), *44*, 45–49, 51; woolen products from, 33. *See also* Spitalfields

erotica in Chinese pictorial tradition, 94, 117, 119

European ambassadors seeking favor. *See* diplomatic gifts from European countries

European Palaces. *See* Yuanming yuan

European silks in Qing imperial collections, 9, 11–37; adoption, adaptation, and manufacture of, 5; becoming timeless "Western"

188 Index

style, 37; bizarre silks, 21–23, *22–23*, 34, 42, 63; Canton trade as way to acquire, 33; change of European style away from lavish metal threads, effect of, 33; Chinese silks distinguished from, 34–35; as diplomatic gifts from European states, 31–32; European timelines for fashion unknown to Qing court, 30; fascination with, 18, 34–37; imprecise language to refer to European silks, 33–34, 63, 169n57; lace-patterned silks ("persiennes"), 23–24, *24*, 55, 59, 63, 65, 66, *66*; lancé weave (c. 1755–65), 27–30, *29*, 33, 36, 59, 169n53; liminality of, 150–51; liseré weave (c. 1755–65), 27–28, *28*, 30, 71; as luxury products, 9, 30; with metallic grounds and floral patterns, *2*, *3*; naturalistic style (1730s), 2, 16, 19, 24–27, *25–27*, 50, 51, 54, 59; nineteenth century's fading enthusiasm for, 151; Qianlong's portraits displaying, 8; Qing imperial perspective on, 31–37, 148; symbolism not underlying design principle for European as for Chinese silk, 30; as tribute from provincial Chinese officials, 31, 32–33; types of, 21–28

European tapestries in Qing imperial collections, 75–103; architectonic transformation of room by hanging large tapestries with life-size representations, 100, 105–7, 108–9, 116; compared to Chinese *kesi* tapestries, 107–8; compatible with Manchu way of furnishing, 150; as diplomatic gifts to Qing emperor, 5, 78, 79, 81–103, 147, 148, 150; embodied in global aspirations of both cultures, 75; *entre-fenêtres* and *portière* use of, 116; few surviving examples of, 84, 101; *L'Histoire du Roi* (The History of the King) album, 81–82, *82*; influence on architectonic design of Qing-produced tapestries, 108–9; initial inability to hang in older Qing palaces due to size, 103; intended to fit specific rooms and spaces, 106–7, *106*; interacting with inhabitants-viewers, 107; as large-scale wall hangings with life-size figures and animals, 77–78, 100, 103, 107; liminality of, 150–51; *mise en abyme* of, 106; new Qing palaces built to accommodate, 108–9; nineteenth century's fading enthusiasm for, 151; no European weavers present in China during seventeenth and eighteenth centuries, 81, 149; perception distinguishing from other types of interior textiles, 83; Qianlong's unfulfilled commission from Europe, 83; in Siamese tribute gifts to emperor, 5, 78, 79; as small percentage of Qing pictorial hangings, 115; *Tapisseries du Roy* (album) used by Louis XIV as propaganda program, 81–83; understood as pictorial images in woven form, 83; wool as chosen fabric for, 75, 77; wool tapestry weaving at zenith when first reaching Qing court, 77. See also *specific European countries*

exoticism: chinoiserie as global style of universal exoticism, 8, 123, 150; defamiliarization and negotiation of cultural boundaries, 102; European flowers in Tibetan Buddhist spaces and, 73; export paintings for European consumers and, 141; first and second *Tentures chinoises* and *Tenture des Indes* and, 75, 102; global interest in exotic flora and fauna, 21, 46, 49, 150; glorifying both sender and recipient, 102; Qianlong's interest in exotic flora and fauna, 7, 50–51, 148, 150; rare and exotic animals signifying heavenly mandate of Qing ruler, 100; tapestry medium as way to transmit, 102; women's styles of dress and, 122. See also bizarre silks; chinoiserie

F

Family Gathering on New Year's Morning: auspicious motifs in, 125, 141; Chinese *kesi* manner of weaving in, 109; Chinese-style dress of figures represented in, 133; Cleveland Museum of Art's tapestry (third version, 1776), *104*, 109–10, *111–13*, 124, 134, *135*, 136, 138, 141, 145, *162*; compared to French weaving techniques, 109; curtain along top edge, symbolism of, 133–34, 140, 141, 150; fine silk threads used for facial features in 1776 version, 110; framing devices mimicking European gilded wooden frames, 110, 124, 133–37, *135*, 150; in full-room visual program dematerializing architectural boundaries, 145; Golden Chalice of Eternal Stability (*jīn'ou yonggu bei*), 125, *125*, 145; Hall of Delight in Longevity as intended placement for 1776 version, 145; impression of "woolen tapestry," 110; Jade Candlestick of Long-Lasting Harmony (*yuzhu changtiao tai*), 125, *125*, 129; Palace Museum's tapestry (second version, 1771), 109–10, *110*, 123, *125*, *128*, 133, *135*, 141, *143*, 144–45; placement of trompe l'oeil painting across from first version, 144–45; Qianlong commissioning tapestry and due to unhappiness with first rendition, demanding a second, 123, 133; Qianlong commissioning third version for Hall of Delight in Longevity, 123–24, 133; Qianlong filling empty space in central foreground by sitting on throne, 141–43, *143*, 144, 145, 150, 151; Qing crest vs. French coat of arms in, 134–35, *135*; raw silk and wool used in 1776 version, 110; ritual objects associated with New Year's Day celebration, 125, *125*, 145; stock images of children same as in New Year pictures, 133; Suzhou artisan's reliance on traditional silk tapestry weaving skills and techniques, 109–11; time of hanging for first version in thirty-fifth year of Qianlong's reign, 133; "Western style" of, 124, 133–34

Fang Tiyu, 89

fan used to refer to non-Han ethnic groups and foreign countries, 34

fauna imagery, 98–100. See also zoology manuals and encyclopediae

Félibien, André, 81, 82

Felletin tapestry manufactory, 171n10

Flanders, weaving center of woolen tapestries, 5, 81

floral patterns in silks, *2*, *3*, *4*, 11, 13, 14–15, *15*, 20, 21, 149; interpretations of Western patterns, 55; lotus blossom, 55, 73; pineapple motif, 55, *55*; Qianlong emperor's preferences for, 37, 101; rose-patterned, 27–30, *29–31*, 71–72; Russian trade and, 148; smaller and more abstract patterns after mid-1760s in Europe, 30; Tibetan Buddhist spaces adorned with, 71–73, *72–73*. See also rococo style, botanical design

Forbidden City (Beijing), 127; eviction of last emperor from and end of Qing dynasty, 21; Hall of Delight in Longevity (*Leshou tang*), 123–24, 133, 145; Hall of Unified Peace (*Jiaotai dian*), 77, *77*; Palace of Peace and Longevity (*Ningshou gong*), 116, 124, 133; Pavilion of Jade Essence (*Yucui xuan*), 133; Pavilion of Raining Flowers (*Yuhua ge*), 71; Retreat for Cultivating Harmony (*Yanghe jingshe*), 133; Studio of Respect and Superiority (*Jingsheng zhai*), 71; Western-style tapestries in imperial palace in, 116. See also Hall of Mental Cultivation

foreign people, depiction in Qing court art, 100–101

The Four Elements: Gobelins tapestries, 79; engravings, 81

The Four Seasons: Gobelins tapestries, 79; engravings, 81

framing devices: European gilded vs. Chinese wooden frames, 136; European royal portraits gifted in frames to Qing emperors, 136; *Family Gathering on New Year's Morning* (two versions) mimicking European gilded wooden frames, 110, *111*, 124, 133–37, *135*, 150; French tapestries' border imitating carved and gilded rococo frame, 110, 124, 133, *134*; pronounced European frame as boundary between multiple realities, 137; Qianlong's reading of tapestry frame-like borders, *135*, 136; Qing court's use of solid frames for pictorial panels, 135–36; *Tenture chinoise* (second series), as primary model for Qing-produced tapestries, 79, 134, 136; trompe l'oeil frame of Qing-produced tapestries, *135*, 136–37; Western-style decorations on frame for Poirot watercolor, 136. See also drapery

France: alliance with Siam, 84; ban on Chinese silk imports in, 19; bizarre silks, 21, *22*; in competition with other countries for Chinese trade and power, 4, 86, 88, 89, 148; engravings of tapestries as diplomatic gifts to Qing courts, 81–82, *82*; floral designs on dress silks (mid-1750s), 27, *29*, 37; as leader in tapestry production, 5, 78; *points rentrés* technique from, 45; regulated silk width, 23, 169n43; silk industry, reputation of, 18, 19; silk probably made in, as diplomatic gifts from Dutch and Portuguese, 32; understanding of China, 101; unofficial diplomatic relationship with China,

France (continued)
86. See also Beauvais tapestry manufactory; French tapestries; Gobelins tapestry manufactory; Lyon's silk industry; specific kings and ministers

French East India Company (Compagnie française pour le commerce des Indes orientales), 83, 86, 88, 93–94, 173n103

French tapestries: aggrandizement of French king and, 79; border imitating carved and gilded rococo frame, 124, 133, 134; change in taste to smaller tapestries, 93; with chinoiserie designs, 5–6, 79, 150; Colbert's role in institutionalizing production, 78; as diplomatic gifts for foreign courts, 79; leadership in European manufacture, 5, 78; looms and working methods, 79, 80; peak of popularity of, 79; Qianlong's display in Observatory of the Distant Ocean (Yuanying guan), 103; for Qing emperors, 84–103, 150; shared characteristics with Qing imperial kesi, 81. See also Tenture chinoise (first series); Tenture chinoise (second series); Tenture des Indes

G

galanterie scenes, 94, 102
Gao Heng, 32–33
Gao Shiqi, 41–42
Garden of Perfect Brightness. See *Yuanming yuan*
Garden of Eternal Spring (*Changchun yuan*), 116; Purification Studio (*Chunhua xuan*), 116; Tripitaka Hall (*Hanjing tang*), 116
Garthwaite, Anna Maria, 27; rococo botanical design, 45–46, *45*, 59
gauze, 11, 12; *taixi sha* (silk gauze of the Grand West), *152*, 153
Genoa, Italy, 19
George III (English king), portrait of, 124
Gerbillon, Jean François, 81
Germany: centers for high-quality silks, 19; paper manufacture with embossed gold designs in, 40, *41*; tapestries from, 170n9
Gesner, Conrad: *Historiae animalium*, 99
Gion Festival (Kyoto) using fragments of Flemish tapestries, 81
glassware, 41, 67
global art history, 4–6; contributions of recent scholarship on Western styles in Qing imperial arts, 5; defining "global" and approaches, 4; as productive approach for studying textiles, 5–6. See also transcultural framework
global industrialization and trade of late nineteenth century, 152
Gobelins tapestry manufactory: engravings of tapestries as diplomatic gifts from Louis XIV, 79, 81–82, *82*; establishment and role of, 78–79; foreign patrons ordering from, 79; frame-curtain arrangement in tapestry design, 138, *139*; French crown offering foreign visitors tours of manufactories, 88; Ko's and Yang's education about, 88; loom types used by, 79; as maker of *Tenture des Indes*, 6, 9, 75, 84, 91, 93; training of designers, 20. See also *Months of Royal Residence*; *Tenture des Indes*; other specific tapestry sets by title

gold and silver threads: arrow and bow cases using, 63; bizarre silks, 21, *22*; European courts sharing predilection with Qing court for, 150; as general traits of Western silks at the Qing court, 9, 34, 63; in lace-patterned silks ("persiennes"), 23–24, *24*, 55, 59, 63; in naturalistic-style silks (1730s), 24–27, *25–27*, 69; in Russian floral silks, 27–28, *28*, *29*; Portuguese offering as gifts to Qing court, silk woven with, 32; as "useful Western things" Qianlong ordered through Canton Customs Bureau, 34; Qianlong's dragon robes woven with European gold and silver threads, 14, 36, *37*; prestige associated with European gold and silver threads, 40, 69, 149. See also metal threads

gold threads: alloys as European gold threads, 35; Dutch offering as tribute to Qing court, 31–32; *filé* (rounded thread with smooth silk core) and *frisé* (crinkled thread) used in Europe, 28–29, 35, *36–37*, 42, 43; flat vs. rounded gold threads in Chinese threads, 35, *35*; *lame* (flat gold strips) used in Europe, 35; Portuguese offering as gifts to Qing court, silks woven with, 32; Qianlong purchasing through Canton Customs Bureau, 33, 34; Qing imperial silks distinguished from Western ones, 34, 35; Western grand gold satin, 31. See also gold and silver threads

Grabar, Oleg: *The Mediation of Ornament*, 68
Grand Council (*Junji chu*), 33, 101, 126
Grande Fabrique (guild), 19
Grand Military Review (*dayue*), x, 1–2, *3*, 35, 59, 61–66, *64*, 69, 144
Grand Sacrifices, 12
Grant, Hope, 85
Grasskamp, Anna, 4, 7
Guangxu period (1875–1908), 153
Gu Jianlong: *Wang Shimin and His Family*, 120, *120*

H

Hall of Mental Cultivation (*Yangxin dian*): Bright Window (*mingchuang*), 126, 128–29, *129*, 130; Hall of Three Rarities (*Sanxi tang*), *128*, 130; integration of Western dimension into, 130; location of, 126, *127*; New Year Celebration (*Shousui tu*) tieluo painting, 129, 131, *131*; New Year celebration tapestry, Qianlong commissioning and placing in, 123, 124, 129–31, 141–42; Opening the Brush (*kaibi*) ritual, performance of, 126, *128*, 129, 130, 145; plans of, *72*, 126, *128*; Qianlong's primary residence, 126; significance of, 126; Spring's Peaceful Message (*Ping'an chunxin tu*) trompe l'oeil tieluo painting, *128*, 129–30; Ten Thousand Countries Coming to Pay Tribute painting (*Wanguo laichao tu*), 65–66, 68, *129*, 129–30; Western floral silks in the Buddhist hall in the west wing, 71–72, *72*. See also Family Gathering on New Year's Morning

Han Chinese: Han-style dress (*hanzhuang*) in Qing court iconography, 119, 130–33; in hierarchy with Manchus and Mongols, 61; ornate trimmings popular in women's dress, 153; Qianlong linking his reign to art and culture of, 76; Qing court distinguishing its Manchu regime from, 59, 70, 148; Qing rulers assimilating culture and lifestyle of, 7, 115; silk textile tradition dominant in, 115; Western-style tapestries produced by Qing, integrating European, Manchu, and Han Chinese elements, 105, 124, 130, 150, 151

Hangzhou (silk manufactory), 11–12; copying European silk patterns and threads, 40
Haruko (Japanese empress), 155
Hay, Jonathan, 16, 68, 77, 151
Hellman, Mimi, 8–9, 107
heraldic motifs in European wool tapestries, 78, 134–35, *135*
Het gezantschap der Neêrlandtsche Oost-Indische Compagnie (*The Embassy of the Dutch East India Company*) (Nieuhof), 84
Hevia, James, 85
high-warp looms for French tapestry weaving, 79, *80*, 93
The History of the King (Gobelins tapestry set), 79, 81, *82*, 138, *139*
HJD (*Huoji dang*). See Qing Imperial Household Department, for Zaoban chu
Holland: centers for high-quality silks, 19; diplomatic gifts from, 31–32, 148; Dutch tapestries/carpets gifted by Siamese king to Qing court, 84; Dutch felt with two-tone printed designs at the Qing court, 115; plain wool cloth (*duoluo ni* or *duoluo rong*) presented to Qing court as gifts from, 115; silks offered to Qing court as gifts from, 31
Hollar, Wenceslaus: *Trial of Archbishop Laud in the House of Lords*, 106, *107*
Hongli. See Qianlong emperor
Hong Taiji (1592–1643), 59
horsemanship, 59, 61
Hou Chin-lang, 60–61
Huang Bolu, 81
Huguenots, 19
hunting: Autumn Hunt, 59–61, 144; depictions on Qing scrolls, 66; Manchu rulers' ritualization of, 59–61, 98, 148; paintings of imperial hunt, 66–71, *67*, *69–70*, 156; as passion of Qianlong, 98; Qianlong depicted as intimidating or killing ferocious beasts, 98, *98*. See also archery sets

I

The Illustrated Regulations for Ceremonial Paraphernalia of the Imperial Dynasty (*Huangchao liqi tushi*), 62–63, *64*
imperial martial ceremonies, 9, 39. See also Grand Military Review; military rituals and regalia

Imperial Painting Academy: Qing dynasty, called *Ruyi guan*, 1, 13; Song dynasty, 50
Imperial Workshops (*Zaoban chu*). *See* Qing Imperial Household Department
India, "Chinese brocade" manufactured for Tibetan Buddhist temples, 72
Italian silk industry, 18; bizarre silks, 21; centers for high-quality silks, 19, 32; silk probably made in, as diplomatic gifts from Dutch and Portuguese, 32

J

Jans and Lefebvre ateliers, 93
Japan: bizarre silks and, 21; Cixi pictured with silk screen from, 155; nineteenth-century political and military strength vis-à-vis Qing Empire, 152; porcelain from, as diplomatic gifts from Siam to Louis XIV, 32; Portuguese and Dutch merchants presenting Flemish tapestries to shoguns, 81; Qing court imitations of lacquer ware from, 39; Qing imperial silk with floral pattern exported to, 55, *56*
Jayne, Horace J. R., 170n23
Jesuit missionaries: as astronomers in Qing court, 84; Cabinet du Roi prints received by and presented to Kangxi, 137; called *xiyáng ren* (Westerner), 6; foreign plants introduced to Qing gardens by, 50; French Jesuits winning Qianlong's favor, 91; glassware produced in Qing court workshops by, 41; as initial conduit for cross-cultural exchange with China, 147–48, 149; Kangxi and, 81; Ko and Yang as, 86, 88–89; Louis XIV's five "mathematicians of the king" traveling to China, 81; as painters in Qing court, 16, 50, 86, 113, 117, 120, 124, 133, 137, 149; possible influence in Qing's imperial use of Western floral silks, 72; presenting gifts to Qing court, 31, 81, 86, 88–89; Qing emperor consulting about functions and meanings of European objects, 83; receiving gifts in Beijing from Louis XIV, 81; specific areas of expertise of, 149; *Tenture chinoise* (second series), presented to Qianlong emperor by French Society of Jesus, 86, 88–89. *See also* Beitang Jesuit library, individual Jesuit missionaries at Qing court
Jiangning (silk manufactory), 11–12, *15*; copying European silk patterns and threads, 40. *See also* silk manufacturers
Jiaqing Emperor (r. 1796–1820), 103, 126
jin: mistranslation of, 13; polychrome designs on, 12; types of fabrics, 13. *See also jin-lampas*
Jin dynasty (1115–1234), 59, 115, 149
jin-lampas (lampas weave), 11, 13, 168n11; Chinese copies of European silks for emperor's exclusive use, 40, 153; European composition and weaving technique compared to Chinese, 23–24; French bizarre silk labeled as *xiyáng jin*, 34; furnishings in *Jingsheng zhai*, 71; furnishings of imperial yurt using, 62; in imperial storage, 34; replications of Western *jin-lampas* by imperial silk manufactories, 40–41; *songjīn* (Song dynasty-style), 16, *16*, 32, *33*; in tribute from Canton to Qing emperor, 32
João V (Portuguese king), 32, 41, 83
Jonston, Jan: *Historiae naturalis*, 99
José I (Portuguese king), 83–84
Joubert de l'Hiberderie, Antoine Nicolas, 19–20
Juneja, Monica, 4, 7
Jussieu, Bernard de, 50–51

K

Kangxi emperor (r. 1662–1722): Autumn Hunt established by, 60–61; ban on maritime trade lifted by, 31; Cabinet du Roi prints presented to, 137; calligraphy of, functioning as imperial presence, 77; choosing successor, 61; commissioning European objects through Canton Customs Bureau, 83; diplomatic gifts for Pope Clement XI and King João V from, 41; dragon screen as backdrop to image of emperor writing, 144, *144*; engravings of Gobelins tapestries among gifts from Louis XIV, 81, 137; European decorated paper given to, 40; French Jesuits and, 81; Grant Review, 61; Lama temples constructed by, 71; political significance ascribed to mastery of foreign techniques by, 41; recognizable in *The Story of the Emperor of China*, 84; reign of sixty years and Qianlong's vow to match, 133; Siam presenting Western tapestries as gifts to, 84; Sino-European exchanges and, 4; "Western style" using cast shadow and linear perspective introduced in period of, 124; zoological encyclopedia as interest of, 98
The Kangxi Emperor Writing, 116, 144, *144*
kesi. *See* silk tapestries
Kharachin Mongols, 60
Kircher, Athanasius: *China illustrata*, 84
Ko, Aloys (Gao Leisi, aka Louis Ko), 86–88, 91, 93–94
Korea, 31
Kyrgyz campaign, 62

L

lace, 27, 151, 153
lace-patterned silks ("persiennes"), 23–24, *24*, 55, 59, 63, 65, 66, *66*
Lacere, Pierre-Antoine-Étienne, 83–84
lacquer, 12, 18, 35, 39, 83, 169n77
Lai Yu-chih, 5, 65, 99, 100
lame (flat gold strips), 35
lampas weave. *See jin-lampas*
lancé technique, 13, 16, 24, 27–30, *29*, 36, 41, 42, 59, 169n53
Lasalle, Philippe de, 21, 28; *The Partridges*, *20*, 21
Lazarev Manufactory (Fryanovo, Russia), 28
Le Brun, Charles: engraving after tapestry *The Defeat of Marsin*, designed by, 81, 82, *82*; Gobelins designs and production overseen by, 78; *The Meeting between Louis XIV and Philip IV on Pheasants Island*, designed by, 138, *139*
legacy in nineteenth century: fading enthusiasm for Western silks and tapestries, 151; foreign textiles in China, 153–55
Leman, James: "bizarre" style, silk design, *22*, 23
Leo X (pope), 102
Liao dynasty (916–1125), 149
Liang dynasty (502–57), 125
liminality, 150–51
lingua franca: of chinoiserie, 150; of tapestries, 75
liseré technique, 27–28, *28*, 30, 71
Li Shi, 129
Li Shiyao, 32, 94, 101
looms: for French tapestry weaving, 79–81, *80*, 93; mechanized looms in late nineteenth century, 153; for silk tapestry weaving, 76, *76*; for Suzhou-made tapestries in Western style, 109. *See also* drawlooms
Louis XIV (French king, r. 1643–1715): French tapestries as aggrandizement of, 79; gifts dispatched to Jesuit missionaries in Beijing from, 81; King's Cabinet (publishing project), 81, 137; Maurits gifting paintings from Brazilian expedition to, 93; *The Meeting between Louis XIV and Philip IV on Pheasants Island*, 138, *139*; portrait gifted to Qing emperors, 136; Royal Menagerie of Versailles and, 98; Shen Fuzong's visit to Versailles, 84; Siam presenting diplomatic gifts of Chinese and Japanese porcelain and other treasures to, 32; sponsoring five "mathematicians of the king" traveling to China, 81; in tapestry *The Defeat of Marsin*, 82, *82*; *Tapisseries du Roy*'s role as propaganda for, 81–82, *82*; *Tenture des Indes*, as diplomatic gifts from, 101, 102. *See also* Colbert, Jean-Baptiste
Louis XV (French king, r. 1715–74): coronation of, 79; ordering *Tenture chinoise* (second series) multiple times for diplomatic gifts, 86
Louis XVI (French king, r. 1774–92), 79
Louvois, Marquis de, 79, 81, 137
Louvre Salon (1742), 86
low-warp looms for French tapestry weaving, 79, *80*
Lyon's silk industry, 18–28; bizarre silks, 21–23, *22–23*, 34, 63, *66*; as center of European silk weaving, 18–21, 30; copyright protection of designs, 21; customers of, 20; ecclesiastical textiles, 21, 27; floral and foliate motifs, *20*, 21; merchant manufacturers (*marchands fabricants*), 19–20; naturalistic style (1730s), 24, *25–26*; *points rentrés* (or *berclé*) technique, 27, *27*, 30; Qianlong's 1758 portrait with saddle blanket made of Lyonnais silk, 68–69, 150; royal court use of silks in ceremonies and furnishings, 21; shaping fashion system, 20; shifting design aesthetics, 21; silk designers (*dessinateurs*) and their training, 19–20

M

Macartney, George, 124

Manchu culture and identity: ancestral sacrifice and, 60–61; Autumn Hunt and, 60–61; Central Asian links and, 7, 61; clothing style, 59; gold-suffused fabric preferred in, 149; Grand Military Review and, 61; ornate trimmings popular among women, 153; Qing distinguishing from Han Chinese dynasties, 148; Qing reflecting cultural heritage of, 1, 7, 9, 39, 59, 76, 115, 117; similar lifestyle to that of Mongols and Jin Jurchens, 115; warrior tradition, 59–61; Western silks' use and, 39, 70–71; Western-style tapestries produced by Qing, integrating European, Manchu, and Han Chinese elements, 105, 124, 130, 150, 151; wool textiles and, 115. *See also specific Qing emperors*

Manual of Beasts (*Shoupu*), 5, 51, 99, *99*

Manual of Birds (*Niaopu*), 5, 51, 99, *100*

Manufacture royale de tapisserie de Beauvais. *See* Beauvais tapestry manufactory

Manufacture royale de tapisserie de Gobelins. *See* Gobelins tapestry manufactory

Marigny, Marquis de, 93

maritime trade: with European East India companies, 148; Kangxi emperor opening to Western trade (1686), 31; nineteenth century forcing Qing to open other ports, 152; Qianlong seeking to reestablish system for commissioning European objects through Canton, 83. *See also* Canton port and Customs Bureau; diplomatic gifts from European countries

martial arts. *See* military rituals and regalia

masculinity, 59, 70

mass-market textile products, 153

Maurits van Nassau-Siegen, Johan, 79, 93, 102

The Meeting between Louis XIV and Philip IV on Pheasants Island (Le Brun), 138, *139*

Meiji emperor of Japan, 155

Mémoires concernant l'histoire, les sciences, les arts, les moeurs, les usages, &c. des Chinois, par les missionnaires de Pékin (*Articles on the History, Science, Arts, Customs, Practices, etc. of the Chinese, by the Missionaries of Beijing*), 91

metal threads, 8–9, 11, 23, 30, *30*, 34–37; Chinese produced, 42; European courts sharing predilection with Qing court for, 150; European tapestries using in high-end productions, 77; *frisé* in Qing copies, 43, *43*; polychrome silks with Western threads, 2; Russia as source of, 148; sensory experiences of, 8; as source of fascination for Qianlong emperor, 18, 34–37, 149–50. *See also* gold and silver threads; gold threads; silver threads

Metropolitan Museum of Art (New York): "Interwoven Globe: The Worldwide Textile Trade, 1500–1800" (exhibition), 5

military rituals and regalia (Qing imperial): archery cases, 24, 63–66, *64–66*; Autumn Hunt and, 59–61, 144; dragons on armor, 36; emperor's yurt for imperial hunt and martial events, 62–63, *62*, 115, 150; hunting skills, 59–61; *The Illustrated Regulations for Ceremonial Paraphernalia of the Imperial Dynasty* (*Huangchao liqi tushi*), 62–63, *64*; metal threads in Qianlong emperor's regalia, 149; paintings of imperial hunt, 66–71, *67*, *69–70*, 144; riding and shooting, 61; saddle blankets, silk, 2, 24–27, *25–27*, 50, 62, 65–70, *67*, *69–70*, 150; Western house erected next to imperial yurt, 63; Western silks, use of, 39, 59–71, 148. *See also* archery sets; Grand Military Review

Miller, Lesley, 19, 20

Ming dynasty (1368–1644): drawlooms in, 13; Han-style dress (*hanzhuang*) used in figure paintings, 119, 130; lampas weave and, 13; motifs passed to Qing dynasty, 13; precise naming of objects, 33; *songjin* (Song dynasty-style) and, 16; velvet and, 18; weaving gold patterned silks in, 41; *xiyang*, meaning of, 6

modernization in nineteenth century, Cixi's portraiture in keeping with, 155

Mondevergue, Marquis de, 98

Mongols, 60–61, 148

Monnoyer, Jean-Baptiste, 84

The Months of Royal Residence (Gobelins tapestry suite), 79, 98, 107; *Chateau of Monceaux/Month of December*, *107*; *January*, 98

motifs. *See* patterning and motifs of Qing imperial silks

Mountain Pavilion of Sweeping Breeze (*Yanxun shanguan*, Rehe), 111

Mount Wutai temples, 72

N

Nanjing, gold treasure ground silk woven in, 169n53. *See also* Jiangning

naturalistic style: in paintings, 66, 69; in silks, 2, 16, 19, 24–27, *25–27*, 50, 51, 54, 59; in tapestries, 124

Netherlands. *See* Holland

New Qing History, 7

New Year celebration: pictorial conventions, 125; as significant scene for Qianlong emperor, 123. *See also Family Gathering on New Year's Morning*; Hall of Mental Cultivation; "New Year picture"; Opening the Brush (*kaibi*) ritual

"New Year picture" (*suizhao tu*): "ancient dress" (*guzhuang*) or Han-style dress (*hanzhuang*) in, 130–33; auspicious symbols in, 131; composition of open courtyard in wintry landscape, 131; "festive figure paintings" (*nianjie renwu hua*) without imperial visages, 133; mixture of real imperial family members with fictional or deceased ones, 131–33; *New Year Celebration* (*Shousui tu*) tieluo painting, 131, *131*; *New Year Celebration* (*Suizhao huanqing tu*) scroll (Yao Wenhan), *132*, 133; Qianlong commissioning both European missionaries and Chinese court artists to make, 133; Qianlong depicted with deceased sons in, 133

Nian Gengyao, 40

Nieuhof, Johan: *Het gezantschap der Neêrlandtsche Oost-Indische Compagnie* (*The Embassy of the Dutch East India Company*), 84

nineteenth-century China, foreign textiles in, 153–55

Nordic countries: royal patrons of Beauvais tapestries, 79; as markets for English silks or reexported Qing imperial silks, 48. *See also* Sweden

Northern Song dynasty (960–1127), 16

Nurhaci (Manchu chieftain), 115

O

Official Tribute (Qing imperial tribute scrolls), 5, 101, 119, 168n22

One or Two? (*Shiyi shi'er tu*), 116, 144, *145*

Opening the Brush (*kaibi*) or Testing the Brush (*shibi*) ritual: iconography of *Family Gathering on New Year's Morning* (tapestry, 1771) referencing to, 125–26; imperial performance of, 126, *128–29*, 129, 130, 145; Jianqing emperor's account of, 126; spatial relations to paintings and tapestry in the Hall of Mental Cultivation, *128–29*, 129, 130

Opium Wars (1839–42, 1856–60), 85, 152

Orientalism, 4

Ottoman-inspired styles, 19, 21, 122

Oudry, Jean-Baptiste, 86

P

Painters of the King (France, *peintres du roi*), 20

The Partridges (Lasalle), *20*, 21

patterning and motifs of Qing imperial silks, 13–18; auspicious symbols, 14–15, *15*, 18, 37; cosmological and hierarchical symbols, 14, 16, 18; dragons, 14, *14*, 16, *17*, 18, 36, *37*, 168n10; floral, butterfly, and animal symbols, 14–15, *15*; geometric shapes, 16, *16*, 18; human figures rarely shown, 15; imperial symbols (including twelve symbols), 13–14, *14*, 18, 37; Ming patterns inherited, 13; pythons, 14, 168n10; rose patterns, 27–30, *29–31*, 71–72; *shou* character, 15; *songjin* (Song dynasty-style), 16, *16*, 32

Pedrini, Teodorico, 40

Perellos of Malta (Grand Master), 102

Pernon (French silk manufacturer), 21

Perrault, Claude: *Memoires pour servir à l'histoire naturelle des animaux* (*Memoirs for a Natural History of Animals*), 99

Peter the Great (Russian czar), 101, 102

Pirazzoli-t'Serstevens, Michèle, 40, 60–61

plants: global interest in exotic flora and fauna, 46, 49, 150; imported to British Empire, 46; as motifs in European wool tapestries, 78, 101; Qianlong's interest in European plants, 7, 50–51, 101, 148, 150

Pleasure Boat Studio (Nanyuan), 69

The Pleasures of the Enchanted Island (*Les Plaisirs de l'isle enchantée*, engraved album), 137–38, *139*
point paper (*mise-en-carte*), 19–20, *19*, 47
points rentrés (or *berclé*) technique, 27, *27*, 30, 45, 46, 49, 54, 69, 124
Poirot, Louis Antoine de, 117, 136
political changes from eighteenth to nineteenth century, 152
political message: Gobelins tapestries as, 78–79, 91; Kangxi emperor and mastery of foreign techniques, 41; Qianlong legitimating his rulership by engaging with Han art and culture, 76–77; Qianlong's design for *Family Gathering on New Year's Morning* and his emperorship of harmony and prosperity, 142–43, *143*; Qianlong's intentions to integrate foreign styles and media into, 105, 124, 149–51; Qianlong's portraits and, 144; Qing-produced Western-style silks and, 41–42; silk tapestries of Qianlong's calligraphy and text as his proxies, 76–77; *Tenture chinoise* (first series), as diplomatic gift, 85; *Tenture chinoise* (second series), intentions behind choice of sending to Qianlong, 86, 88–89, 113, 148; textiles' foreign features enabling, 147. *See also* diplomatic gifts from European countries; tribute system (Qing)
polychrome figured silks: as Chinese specialty, 6; Dutch offering as gifts to Qing court, 31–32. *See also* brocaded silk; *jin-lampas*
polychrome woolen textiles (*wuse maotan*), 81
Poni, Carlo, 20, 21
porcelains, 18, 20, 51, 54, 86, 88, 134
Portugal: diplomatic gifts from, 31, 32, 81, 83–84, 85, 148; France competing against in presenting tapestries to Qing emperor, 89; nude figures on printed cottons presented to Qing court by, 94; velvet as trade good from, 18
Post, Frans, 93
Potala Palace (Lhasa), 72
Prussia, woolen products from, 33

Q

qi (air) in Chinese painting and calligraphy, 124
Qianlong emperor (r. 1736–95): archery set used by, 65–66; calligraphy of, as representations of imperial body and face in textual form, 77; celebrating sixtieth birthday, 133; central role in driving and orchestrating Qing imperial projects related to Western textiles, 109, 115, 117, 123–24, 129–31, 133, 141–42, 148, 149; deaths of sons and, 133, 143; depicted as Bodhisattva of Great Wisdom, 71; depicted in Han Chinese dress in fictional celebratory scenes, 130–31; dynastic continuity as concern of, 133; East Turkestan Campaign, 83; equestrian pose of, 1, 7, 151, 155; European tapestries as interest of, 75, 81, 83, 84; exotic animals and birds of interest to, 7, 50–51, 99–100, 148, 149, 150; French tapestries not integrated into daily activities of, 103; instructions on designs and manufacture of imperial silks, 12, 77; innovative approaches to Western tapestry medium, 105, 116, 150–51; Kangxi choosing as his successor, 61; Lama temples constructed by, 71; Manchu ancestry of, 1, 76; as multicultural ruler, 7, 101, 148; personal taste reflected in commissioning orders, 37, 101, 122, 124, 149, 151; poem by (Imperially Composed Poem on the Event of the Great Review at Nanyuan), 62; portraits of, *x*, 1–2, *3*, 7, 8, 11, 16, *17*, 66, *67*, 69, *69–70*, 71, *98*, 130, 137, *138*, 151, 155; rococo botanical pattern and, 50; satins with gold and with silver threads purchased by, 33, 34; silk tapestries at zenith in reign of, 76, 77; territorial consciousness of, 7, 42, 100–102, 150; Tibetan Buddhism, practice of, 71; vow of retirement to match his grandfather Kangxi's sixty-year reign, 133; Xiaoxian's (empress), death of, 133
The Qianlong Emperor Hunting Hare (*Qianlong Huangdi shetu tu*) (scroll), 66, *69*, 156
The Qianlong Emperor Intimidating a Bear, 98, *98*
The Qianlong Emperor Writing, 137, *138*
Qing court theater costumes, 12, 27, 48–49, *50*, 59, *60*, 63
Qing Imperial Household Department (*Neiwu fu*), 11–12, 39–41; Imperial Workshops (*Zaoban chu*), 11, 34, 36, 37, 111, 113, 123, 148; *Registers Attached to Financial Reports* (*Zouxiao dang*), 33
Qing imperial identity: affirmation through ancestral rituals and sacrifices during Autumn Hunt, 60; bright yellow (*minghuang*) as restrictive imperial color, 49; diversity of Qing subjects and, 7, 101, 148; High Qing imperial arts and, 152; images of imperial body and visage forbidden from public display, 77, 155; *jin-lampas* (lampas weave) for emperor's exclusive use, 39, 40, 153; linked to visual experience, 8, 67–68; "luminous" radiance of gold and silver threads associated with wise and benevolent ruler, 69; motifs exclusive to emperor, 14; symbols on clothes and furnishings and in all spaces regularly occupied by emperor, 18; Tibetan Buddhism and, 71; Western woolen tapestries and exclusivity, 9, 16, 105, 115, 153. *See also* Manchu culture and identity
Qing imperial power: as center of universe, 7, 31, 32, 42, 71; demonstrated through mastering of foreign techniques, 39, 41–42; extent of, 1, 7, 42, 100, 150; Kyrgyz's and Kazakh's allegiance to, 62; material objects circulated through Qing imperial ideological system serving to aggrandize, 149; reinforcing through Autumn Hunt, 59, 61, 144; reinforcing through Grand Review, 1, 59, 61–62; superiority to foreign states, 42, 61; "tributary objects" from foreign countries and, 31, 32, 51, 65–66, 89–90, 148; Western silks signifying, 69–71, 144; Zunghar, conquest of (1755) and, 61–62. *See also* military rituals and regalia; tribute system (Qing)
Qing production of European-style silks. *See* Western-style silks, Qing production of
Qing production of European-style tapestries. *See* Western-style tapestries, Qing production of

R

Raphael, 78; *Sistine Madonna*, 137
A Record of the Water of Heaven and the Iceberg (*Tianshui bingshan lu*), 33
Records of the Jin-Lampas Submitted by the Three Silk Manufactories (*Sanchu zhizao laijin dang*), 39–40
Register of Provincial Tributary Gifts (*Gongzhong jindan*), 88–89, 94
Rehe: Lama temples in, 71; location for imperial hunt, 60; Mountain Pavilion of Sweeping Breeze (*Yanxun shanguan*), 111; Qing copies of *Tenture chinoise* (second series) originally in palaces in, 113, *114*; Western tapestries displayed in palaces in, 116
Reims Cathedral's display of Gobelins tapestries for Louis XV's coronation, 79
Revel, Jean, 24
reversed glass painting, 117
Revolt of the Three Feudatories (1673–81), 61
rhinoceros, depiction of, 95, 99, *99*, 102
Rhodes, Geoffrey, 85
rococo botanical design in silk (c. 1742), 44–55; both English and Qing examples sharing similar weave structure, 45; Chinese gold filé threads in Palace Museum version, 48, *49*; Chinese produced version for export, 46–48; Chinese version as man's fancy-dress coat in Victoria and Albert Museum, 47–48; Chinese version as woman's dress in Fashion Museum, Bath, 47, *47*; Chinese version in Philadelphia Museum of Art, 46–47, *46*; cross-cultural circulation and metamorphoses of, 45–46, 53–54; culturally specific tastes reflected in, 45; as dress textiles, 47–48, *47*; English version in Museum of Fine Arts, Boston, *44*, 45–46, 170n18; European garments using either Spitalfields or Chinese export works, 48; exotic nature of design, 49; extant versions of, 45; Garthwaite design, 45–46, *45*, 170n18; ground weave differences between English and Chinese versions, 49; loom width and manufacturing location, 45, 46; nineteenth-century China continuing to use, 152; Nordic countries as markets for English silks or reexported Chinese silks, 48; Palace Museum versions of, 48–49, *48–49*, 54, *54*; *points rentrés* technique and, 45, 46, 49; Qianlong's fascination with, 50; shades used to match palette restrictions of Qing court, 49; theater costume for female role using, 48–49, *50*; version in Nelson-Atkins Museum of Art, 54, *55*; versions in Abegg-Stiftung (Switzerland) from Tibet, 53, *53*
rococo style: acanthus leaves, 45, 134; drapery with rococo frame in Beauvais suite *Stories*

rococo style (*continued*)
of Don Quixote, 138; Qing court artists and Suzhou weavers reproducing rocaille-style shell motif, 134; tapestries' self-borders imitating frames in, 110, 124, 133–35; *Tenture chinoise* (second series) and, 79, 90, 134; as Western and exotic elements adapted in Qing-produced tapestries, 90, 134–35

Rölpé Dorjé, 71

Rong Fei (consort of Qianlong), 65

"Room for Ceremony and Audience in the House of Titled Princes" (from *Essay on Chinese Architecture*), 108, *108*, 142

Rothe, Mr Le Chevalier, 93–94, 101, 173n103

Rubens, Peter Paul, 78

Rudolf II (Holy Roman emperor), 98

Russia: chinoiserie and, 102; ecclesiastical silk vestments, 28–30, *31*; French influence on silk designs from, 28, 37, 71; gold silks as inspiration for Chinese gold treasure ground, 169n53; gold threads as trade goods from, 34, 148; Moscow as center for high-quality silks, 28, 30; Nordic countries importing Chinese silks through, 48; prototype informing silk designs and techniques at Qing court, 59; Qing court ordering Suzhou copies of silks from, 40–41; Qing imperial trade records with, 33; rose-patterned silks, manufacture of (1760s–90s), 27–28, *29–30*, 71–72, 148; silks of Russian type in Tibetan Buddhist spaces in Qing palaces, 71–72; silk trade with Qing court opened by treaties (1689 & 1727), 33, 148; silk weaving in Moscow, 19; woolen textiles traded from, some possibly manufactured outside of Russia, 33

Ryukyu, 31

S

saddle blankets (silk) (1730s), 2, 24–27, *25–27*, 50, 62, 65–70, *67*, *69–70*, 150

Said, Edward, 4

Saint-Gobain mirror manufactory, 88

satin ground, 11, 12, 13, 21, 27, 32, 33

Savonnerie carpets, 88

Scene in a Bedchamber (French artist), 106, *106*

screens as backdrop in artwork, 144–45; Kangxi emperor seated in front of dragon screen, 144, *144*; Qianlong's appearance in front of screen and his image hung on screen (*One or Two?*), 144, *145*; Qianlong's fascination with visual play of screens, 144

selvedge-to-selvedge lancé technique, 41

Sèvres porcelains, 88

Shanghai. *See* Songjiang

Shen Fuzong, 84

Shunzhi emperor (r. 1643–61), 61, 84

Siam: Dutch tapestries/carpets presented to Qianlong emperor by, 84; emissaries carrying package in silk wrapping cloth, depiction of, 65–66, *68*, *129*; engravings of French tapestries as diplomatic gifts to, 82; French alliance with, 84; Louis XIV receiving diplomatic gifts from, 32, 84; Qing court receiving diplomatic gifts of European silks from, 31, 32; Qing court receiving diplomatic gifts of European tapestries from, 84; Saint-Gobain mirror manufactory tour by Siamese ambassadors, 88

Sichelbart, Ignatius, 113, 117, 136, 144

The Siege of Tournai, engraving of tapestry of, 81, 82

silk manufactories (Qing imperial), 11–18; categories of silk patterns, 13–16; drawlooms, *12*, *13*; emperor's control of designs and quality, 12; European gold and silver threads allocated to, 40; flat gold vs. rounded gold in Chinese threads, 35, *35*; organizations and specialties of the three manufactories, 1–12; patterning techniques, 13; as purveyors of non-textile products for imperial court, 12; regular and commission orders for imperial court, 12, 13, 36; regular supplies to imperial court, 12, 13, 34; silk as predominant material for imperial clothing and display, 11–12; *songjin*, 6, *16*, 32; woven Buddhist icon *Western Paradise (Jile shiji)*, 168n11. *See also* Hangzhou; Jiangning; patterning and motifs of Qing imperial silks; silk tapestries; Suzhou; Western-style silks, Qing production of; Western-style tapestries, Qing production of

silk patterns and motifs. *See* patterning and motifs of Qing imperial silks

silk tapestries (*kesi*), 12; compared to European tapestries, 81, 83, 107–9; copying famous paintings and calligraphies in, 76; decorative role of, 108; distinctive slit effect of weave, 76, 109; in Hall of Unified Peace (*Jiaotai dian*), 77, *77*; loom for weaving, 76, *76*; looms compared to European, 79; materials and techniques for, 76, 109; methods applied to Qing court's Western tapestries, 109; as mounted hanging scrolls, *78*; Qianlong's cultural lineage and image established through, 76–77; in Southern Song dynasty, 76; Suzhou and Songjiang as centers of, 12, 76; zenith in Qianlong era, 76

silk trade, 2; ban on Chinese silk imports in France and England, 19, 48; Chinese silks exported to Europe, 2, 45, 46, 48, 49; eastward as well as westward trade in silks, 11, 147; eighteenth century between China and Europe, 18, 32–34; problem of term "Chinese export silks," 43, 55–56, 59; types of European silks regularly imported to China, 32, 33. *See also* rococo style, botanical design

silver threads: prestige of European silks with silver threads at Qing court, 35; Qianlong purchasing through Canton Customs Bureau, 33, 34; rarely used in regular Qing imperial silks, 34–35. *See also* gold and silver threads

Slomann, Vilhelm, 21

social norms. *See* Confucianism; cultural norms

Song dynasty (960–1279), "flowers and birds" genre in painting of, 50

Songjiang, as center for silk tapestry weaving, 76

Song Yingxing: *The Exploitation of the Works of Nature (Taingong kaiwu)*, *12*, *13*

Son of Heaven, 1, 14, 77, 126

Soufflot, Jacques-Germain, 93–94

Sousa e Meneses, Alexandre Metelo de, 32

Southern Song dynasty (1127–1279), 76, 77

Spain: botanic exotica from abroad, fascination with, 46; centers for high-quality silks, 19

Spitalfields (east London), 19, 22, 27, 44, 46, 48

stationery paper from Europe, 40, *41*

Stewart, Susan, 136

The Story of Alexander (engraving of Gobelins tapestry), 79

The Story of the Emperor of China. *See Tenture chinoise* (first series)

Sturgis family's English version of rococo botanical design, *44*, 46, 170n18

Summer Palaces. *See* Yuanming yuan

Sun Yunqiu: *Western Painting of Recessing Vista (Xiyáng yuanhua)*, 117–19, *119*

Suzhou (silk manufactory), 11–12, 105; best qualified to weave Western-style silks, 40; bizarre silks probably produced by, 42, *42*; as center for silk tapestry weaving, 76; mastery of tapestry weaving in European visual style, 109–13; production system, 12; products and specialties, 12, 16, 36; Qianlong directing Castiglione to paint on white blankets from, 109; Qianlong forbidding provision of Western-style tapestries to anyone but emperor, 115; Qing imperial commissions for special dragon robes made in, *14*, *36*, *37*; Qing imperial commissions for Western silks woven in, 40–43, *42*, *43*, 59, 148; silk tapestries (*kesi*) woven in, 12, 76, 77, 78. *See also* Western-style silks, Qing production of; Western-style tapestries, Qing production of; *specific tapestries by titles*

Sweden, 48, 79, 101

T

tabby ground (plain weave ground), 11, 32, 45, 46, 48, 63, 157, 160

Takashimaya Company, 155

Taking a Stag with a Mighty Bow, 65, *67*

Taksin (Zheng Zhao, Siamese king r. 1767–82), 84

Tang Ying, 34

tapestries. *See* Western-style tapestries, Qing production of; European tapestries in Qing imperial collections; woolen tapestries

Tapisseries du Roy, 81, 82, *82*

Temple of Offering for the Ancestors (*Fengxian dian*), 60

Ten Thousand Countries Coming to Pay Tribute. *See* Hall of Mental Cultivation

Tenture chinoise (The Story of the Emperor of China) (Beauvais, first series, 1688–1731), 75, 79, 84–86; *The Collation*, 120, *121*, *186*; *The Emperor*

on a Journey, 84–85, *85*, 120; exotic scenes in, 102; influence on Qing court designs for Western tapestries, 117, 119, 120; message that expressed Europe's admiration of China, 85; nine themes of, 84; outdoor scenes in, 120; Portuguese embassy as likely sender of series, 85; Qianlong's understanding of, 120; remnant from looting of Yuanming yuan, 84–85

Tenture chinoise (Beauvais, second series, 1743–75), 75, 79, 86–91; Bertin sending via Ko and Yang to Qianlong, 86, 88–89, 113, 148; Bertin's goals of promoting direct communication and commerce with China and unfulfillment, 88–91, 148; best documented of European tapestries that entered China, 86; border design as primary model for Qing-produced tapestries, 79, 134; Boucher paintings as basis for, 79, 89, 90, 120; *Chinese Fair*, 86, 90, *91*, 135; *Chinese Toilette* (aka *Chinese Garden*), 86, *87*, 122, *122*, 176; classified as tributary objects at Qing court, 89, 90; collapsing distance between France and China through their travel, 101–2; design sources, 86; as diplomatic gifts, 86; exotic scenes in, 102; imaginary scenes of Chinese daily life, 86; influence on Qianlong's favor for French Jesuits and Bertin's Chinese collections, 91; influence on Qing court designs for Western tapestries, 117, 119, 120, 122, 134–35; price, 86; problematic status upon entering China, 88–89; Qianlong building Observatory of the Distant Ocean (*Yuanying guan*) to house, 89; Qianlong's reactions to, 89; seizure upon arrival in Canton, 88; Suzhou making copies of four from series, 113, *114*

Tenture de Boucher (Gobelins), 79

Tenture des Indes (Gobelins, *Anciennes Indes*), 75, 79, 84, 91–102; *The Animals' Combat*, 74, 91, *92*, 93–95, *93*, 103; Brazilian subjects of, 79, 91, 93–96, 98, 100, 102; brought to China as commercial goods, 91; Chinese reaction to seminudes in, 94; eight paintings gifted to Louis XIV by Maurits from Brazilian expedition, 93; exotic animals and scenes depicted in, 98–100, 102; *The Fishermen*, 93, 94–95, *95*, *166*; foreign people depicted in, 100–101; height of five sets called *Grandes Indes*, 93; height of three sets called *Petites Indes*, 93; *The Indian Hunter*, 93, 95, *96*, 99, *101*; influence on depiction of cassowary in *Manual of Birds*, 100; *The King Carried by Two Moors*, 93, 173n127; in line with Qianlong's interests, 100; no record of Qianlong's response to, 98; as objects to strengthen connections between provincial bureaucracy and emperor, 101; presentation to Qianlong emperor by Li Shiyao, 94; Rothe's role in purchasing and transporting series to China, 93–94; sale of old and faded set from Gobelins, and price, 93–94; *The Striped Horse*, 93, 96, *97*, 99; *The Two Bulls*, 93, *95*; woven eight times (1687–1730) as *Old Indies*, 93

territorial consciousness of Qianlong, 7, 42, 100–102, 150

theatricality: central positioning of ideal ruler or auspicious family, 151; Chinese vs. European theaters, in perceptions of time and space, 140; frame and curtain serving role for, 134, 137–38, 141, 142; hybrid Western style creating visual theatricality, 151; Qing court theater costumes, 12, 27, 48–49, *50*, 59, *60*, 63; silks with rococo botanical pattern used in theatrical costumes, 48–49, *50*; textiles allowing emperor to personally stage and play out his message, 105, 142, 151; use of term, 138–40. *See also* drapery

Three Gods, 77, *78*, 108

throne bed, *108*, 142, *143*, 150

Tibet, 53–54, 61, 69–70, 72, 148

Tibetan Buddhism: attributes of Qing imperial Buddhist art, 73; Hall of Mental Cultivation and, 126; imperial gifts of Western silks to Tibetan monasteries, 53, 72; Manchus and Inner Asian elites sharing belief in, 148; Qing imperial patronage of, 71; Qing emperor's gifts to spiritual leaders of, 40; Texts in Tibetan scripts in Qianlong's ceremonial helmet, 1; Tibetan Buddhist icon (*thangka*), 71, 168n11, 169n77, 170n79; Western silks adorning Buddhist spaces in Qing palaces, 9, 39, 53, 71–73, *72–73*, 148; Western-style silks used today in Tibettan Buddhist temples, 72, 73. *See also* Buddhism

tieluo format (painting to be pasted onto wall), 3, 62, 116, 128–29, 131, 134, 137, 138

tongjing hua (images of linked scenes), 116

transcultural framework, 4–6, 134–35, 102–3, 147–51. *See also* chinoiserie; exoticism; global art history

Treatise on Architectural Methods (*Yingzao fashi*), 16

tribute system (Qing): gifts from European countries as "tributary objects," 31, 32, 51, 81, 88, 89–90, 148; from neighboring tribute states (Korea, Vietnam, Siam, Ryukyu), 31, 32, 65–66, *68*, 84; from regional and government officials, 6, 32–33, 94, 141, 148; *Tenture chinoise* (second series), classified as tributary pieces, 89, 90. *See also* diplomatic gifts from European countries

trompe-l'oeil: paintings, 67, 69, 117, *128*, 129–30, 133, *134*, 137, 144–45, 175n48; tapestry's use of border frame and drapery, 135–36

twill, 12, 32, 45

U

United States, 152

Uyghur, 65, 70, 115, 148. *See also* Zunghar, conquest of (1755)

V

van der Meulen, Adam Frans, 82

Varanasi, India (formerly Benares), 72

Varin, Paul. *See* Dupin, Charles

velvet, 18, 19, 32, 54, *55*, 63

Venice, 19

Verbiest, Ferdinand, 168n27 (Intro)

The Veritable Records of Emperor Gaozong [Qianlong] (*Gaozong Chun Huangdi shilu*), 94

The Veritable Records of the Emperor Shengzu [Kangxi] (*Shengzu Ren Huangdi shilu*), 61

Vernansal, Guy-Louis, 84

Versailles. *See* Louis XIV

Victoria (English queen), 155

Vietnam, 31

Vigée, Louis, 88, 136

W

Wang, Cheng-hua, 5

Wang Shimin, 120

Wang Youxue, 113. *See also* Yao Wenhan

Watteau, Antoine, 86

Weddigen, Tristan, 106

wen (pattern) and *wen* (civility), link between, 16

Western. *See xiyáng* (Western), concept of

A Western Family by the Riverside, ii, 117–22, *118*; auspicious symbols in, 119; bucolic depiction of young husband and wife as anomaly in Chinese pictorial tradition, 119; circuitous exchanges of chinoiserie images and conflicting meanings related to, 123; Confucian social norms observed in, 119; cravats depicted in, 122; European landscape style in composition of, 119; European sensibility in, 120; hair color and, 120–21; hybrid of Western and Chinese clothes in, 119; iconographic affinities with two *Tenture chinoise* series, 119, 120–22; representational mode of body in keeping with Chinese norms, 119; revealing Qing approach to Western imagery and style, 122, 150

Western imperialism of nineteenth century, 152

Western Painting of Recessing Vista (*Xiyáng yuanhua*) (Sun Yunqiu), 117–19, *119*

Western-style silks, Qing production of, 9, 39–73, 148; "awkwardness" of, 55–56; bizarre silks, 42–43, *42–43*, 63; Chinese local artisans mastering foreign techniques and styles, 149; Chinese silk with floral pattern made into Japanese kesa, 55, *56*; classified as "Chinese export" works, 55–56; classified as "Western/foreign" silks, 59; copying designs from Western stationery paper, 40; copying Russian silk sample, 40–41; cross-cultural circulation of styles, 55–56; imperial gifts of Western silks, 54; lace-patterned silks, 55, *56*; liberties taken by Chinese weavers in, 41, 43; loom width of Chinese vs. English manufacture, 45, 46, 48; morning glories design, 56, *57–58*, 59; no European designers or weavers present in China during seventeenth and eighteenth centuries, 149; political message of, 41–42; Qing court not distinguishing between European originals and Qing copies, 39; standardized designs for Qing Western silks, 56, 59;

Index 195

Western-style silks (*continued*)
superiority of Qing imitations to originals, 41; theater costumes and, 59; uneven quality at different manufacturing locations, 59; weave structure and designs informed by Russian floral silk, 59; Yongzheng emperor first commissioning copies, 39–40. *See also* rococo style, botanical design

Western-style tapestries, Qing production of, 105–45, 148; architectonic nature of Western tapestries as feature of, 108–9, 116; auspicious motifs in, 119, 125, 141, 150; categorized as "Western woolen hangings," 105; Chinese local artisans mastering foreign techniques and styles, 149; displacement and, 151; European figures and sensibility in, 120, 122, 124, 133–34, 150; exclusively reserved for Qianlong emperor, 115, 153; four tapestries from Rehe palaces and later moved to Forbidden City (*Chinese Hunt, Chinese Dance, Chinese Feast,* and *Chinese Fair*), 113, *114*, 171–72n59; integration of European, Manchu, and Han Chinese elements, 105, 124, 130, 150, 151; as intimate furnishing textiles and not for official audiences, 116; modification of models to dimensions of intended space, 111, 116; naturalistic style and, 124; new designs woven by Suzhou into Western wool tapestries, 113; as new pictorial textile medium, 108–17, 150; no European weavers present in China during seventeenth and eighteenth centuries, 81, 149; Qianlong commissioning painted designs to be woven as Western tapestries, 117, 123, 124, 134; Qianlong commissioning painted blankets equivalent to Western tapestries, 108–9; Qianlong commissioning woven versions of European tapestries, 109, 115, 117, 123, 148; secluded private chambers transformed by hanging to cover architectural features, 116, 117; similarities to *kesi* weaving techniques, 109; visual content and themes, 117–45, 150; as window coverings, 111, 116. *See also* drapery; *Family Gathering on New Year's Morning*; framing devices; screens as backdrop in artwork; *A Western Family by the Riverside*

Women and Children in an Interior Hall (Yao Wenhan, Wang Youxue, and others), 133, *134*, 144–45

women's styles of dress, 122, *123*; cultural norms and, 119; riding jacket with lace trim, *151*, 153

woolen tapestries, 81–102; appearance in Qing court, 76, 77, 81; popularity and refinement in Europe, 75, 77; rarity in China, 75–76; significance of wool for Manchu rulers, 115. *See also* European tapestries in Qing imperial collections; Western-style tapestries, Qing production of

wool fabrics, types of, 115; Dutch felts, 115; European (English or Dutch) plain wool cloth (*duoluo ni* or *duoluo rang*), 115, 174n20; pile rugs, 115

wrapper for *Empress Supervising the Rites of Sericulture* (*Qincan tu*), 16, *16*

writing. *See* calligraphy and writing

Wu Hung, 144

X

Xiaoxian, Qianlong's empress (1712–1748), 133

xiyáng (Western), concept of, 2, 6–8; hybrid concept in Qing court tapestries and arts, 124, 150; imprecise use of term for European silks at Qing court, 33–34, 43; Ming dynasty use of term, 6; other terns used by art historians to refer to Western-style objects at Qing court versus, 6; Qing dynasty use of term, 6, 117, 124, 147, 168n22; strategic use of style to serve Qing imperial ideologies, 6

Y

Yan Song, 33

Yang Dazhang, 99

Yang, Étienne (Yang Dewang), 86–89, 91, 94

Yang Tingzhang, 89

yángjin, meaning of, 169n77

Yao Wenhan: *New Year Celebration* (*Suizhao huanqing tu*), *132*, 133

Yao Wenhan, Wang Youxue, and others: *Women and Children in an Interior Hall*, 133, *134*, 144–45

Yi Lantai: *Front Side of the Observatory of the Distant Ocean*, *90*

Yi Qinwang (Prince Yi, 1686–1730), 39–40

Yonghe Monastery (Bejing), 72, *73*

Yongtai (eunuch), 83

Yongzheng emperor (r. 1723–35): commissioning copies of Western silks, 39–40; depicted in Han Chinese dress in fictional celebratory scenes, 130; diplomatic gift from Portugal to, 32, 83; Hall of Mental Cultivation and, 126; hunting and, 60; Lama temples constructed by, 71; Qing woven Western silks given to Nian Gengyao, 40; Sino-European exchanges and, 4; in *Spring's Peaceful Message* (*Ping an chunxin tu*) trompe l'oeil tieluo painting, 130

You Anning, 40

You Bashi, 40

Yuan dynasty (1279–1368), 13, 115, 149

Yuanming yuan: European furnishings and other trophy possessions in, 103; European Palaces, 50, 83, 89, *90*, 103, 108–9, 136; Hall of Calm Sea (*Haiyan tang*) or Palace of the Fountain (*Shuifa dian*), 108–9; hybrid style of architecture and garden, 83; looting by French and English armies (1860), 84–85, 89, 94–95, 103, 136; Observatory of the Distant Ocean (*Yuanying guan*), 89, *90*, 103; Palace of Harmonious Delight (*Xie qiqu*), 83; Pavilion of Watching the Clouds (*Guanyun xie*), 117; storage of European tapestries used as models by Suzhou, 111, 123; *Tenture des Indes* looted from, 91

yurts: Manchu, 115; Mongolian (*Menggu bao*), 62–63, *62*, 115

Yu Sheng: *Assorted Flowers from the West Ocean*, 51, *52*

Yu Sheng and Zhang Weibang, 5, 51; "Cassowary" (*Manual of Birds*), 99–100, *100*; "Rhinoceros" (*Manual of Beasts*), 99, *99*

Yu Xunling: *The Empress Dowager Cixi*, *154*, 155; *Her Imperial Majesty, the Empress Dowager of China*, 153, 155

Z

zebras, 96, *97*

Zhang Weibang. *See* Yu Sheng

Zhao Feng, 167n17

Zheng Zhao (Siamese king Taksin, r. 1767–82), 84

zhuanghua duan (silk featuring brocaded patterns), 13–14. *See also* brocaded silk

zoology manuals and encyclopediae, 98–100; *Album of Pigeons* (*Gebo pu*), 98; Kangxi emperor's interest in, 98; *Manual of Beasts* (*Shoupu*), 5, 51, 99, *99*; *Manual of Birds* (*Niaopu*), 5, 51, 99–100, *100*; *Manuals of Sea Oddities* (*Haiguai tuji* and *Haicuo tu*), 98–99; Qianlong emperor's interest in, 99

Zunghar, conquest of (1755), 61–62